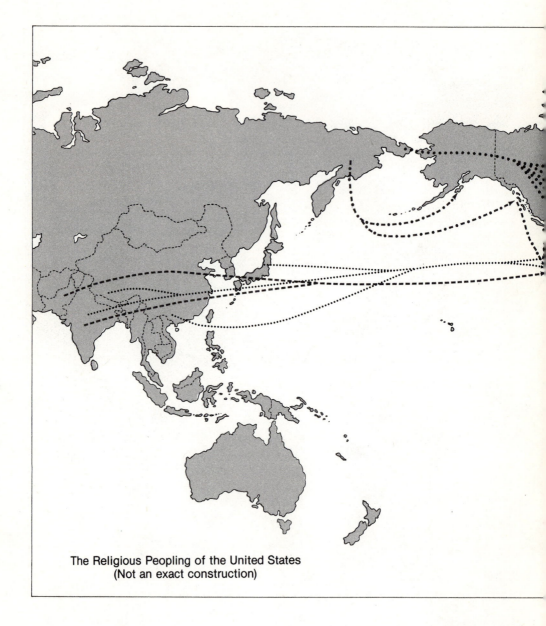

The Religious Peopling of the United States
(Not an exact construction)

•••••• American Indians

.—.—. Jews

——— Roman Catholics

------- Protestants

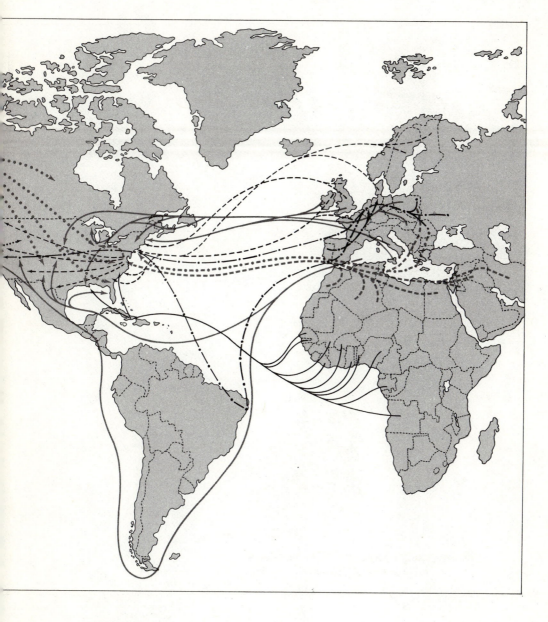

———————— Afro-Americans

–·–·–·–· Nearer Easterners (Eastern Orthodox)

– – – – – Middle Easterners (Muslim)

·············· Farther Easterners (Buddhist & Hindu)

The Wadsworth Series in Religious Studies
Robert S. Michaelsen, Series Editor

AMERICA: RELIGIONS AND RELIGION
Catherine L. Albanese

WAYS TO THE CENTER:
AN INTRODUCTION TO WORLD RELIGIONS
Denise L. and John T. Carmody

AMERICAN BUDDHISM
Charles S. Prebish

EXPLORING RELIGION
Roger Schmidt

AMERICA
RELIGIONS AND RELIGION

Catherine L. Albanese
Wright State University

Wadsworth Publishing Company
Belmont, California
A Division of Wadsworth, Inc.

Religion Editor: Sheryl Fullerton
Production Editor: Donna Oberholtzer
Designer: Janet Wood
Copy Editor: Catherine Lavin

Printed in the United States of America
1 2 3 4 5 6 7 8 9 10—85 84 83 82 81

Library of Congress Cataloging in Publication Data

Albanese, Catherine L
    America, religions and religion.

    Includes bibliographies and index.
    1. United States—Religion. I. Title.
BL2530.U6A43   291'.0973   80-21031
ISBN 0-534-00928-X

To the memory of my grandfather,
Frank S. Spiziri (1878–1958),
one among the many

———————————————————————————

CONTENTS

FOREWORD

This book is unique: within one volume the author has brought together informed and informative treatments of the most significant of the multiple and diverse religious groups and traditions in America and insightful discussions of those religious elements which bind together diverse people of this nation. The result is twofold: (1) an accurate (and readable) single volume overview of a lively and significant subject, and (2) a landmark among such surveys.

Those who set out to deal authoritatively and coherently with the subject of religion (and religions) in America must, if they are to succeed, master both detail and synthesis. In the course of such efforts over more than a century, treatment of detail has both widened and deepened while the synthetic framework has changed markedly. Most early treatments deal primarily with the major Christian denominations, groups which had evolved almost entirely out of the context of Christendom in Europe. Subsequently some attention was also given to Judaism, then to such indigenous groups as Mormonism and Christian Science, then to groups and emphases with Oriental or Asian roots, and, more recently, to Afro-American religion. Dr. Albanese goes a few steps further by including systematic treatment of Native American traditions and the distinctive religion of one region of the United States.

Organizing assumptions in the treatment of religion (and religions) in America have ranged from stress on the providential coincidence of the Protestant Reformation with the discovery and early settlement of America to stress on the uniqueness of the American religious scene due to the separation of church and state and the resultant importance of "voluntaryism" in the American religious experience. Some have fixed upon a sociological approach which tends to see religion in America as shaped primarily by economic and other environmental factors. Dr. Albanese's approach is informed by a view which understands that religion encompasses all of life—both the ordinary and the extraordinary, and both the detail of a particular religious denomination and the generality of unifying and cohesive assumptions and beliefs in our pluralistic society. This approach draws from the methods and resources of the history, sociology, and anthropology of religion and ably applies these specifically to the American scene.

University of California, Santa Barbara   Robert S. Michaelsen

PREFACE

Americans during their formative years were a people in movement through space. . . . This is the mighty saga of the outward acts, told and retold until it has overshadowed and suppressed the equally vital, but more somber, story of the inner experience. Americans have so presented to view and celebrated the external and material side of their pilgrims' progress that they have tended to conceal even from themselves the inner, spiritual pilgrimage, with its more subtle dimensions and profound depths.
—Sidney E. Mead, The Lively Experiment, pp. 7–8

So wrote Sidney Mead almost three decades ago as he explored the space, time, and religion of the American people. There was a "one story" to be celebrated, an epic tale of triumph written, as Mead said, "with cosmic quill." Yet in the midst of the heroic narrative, inner experience remained unexplored, even by the doers of the mighty deeds.

Mead knew then, and we know now, that not all of these Americans were alike. Over and over again, we have grown familiar with clichés about the fact and experience of pluralism in the United States. To be plural means to be more than one, to be many. To be a pluralistic land means to be one country made up of many peoples and many religious faiths. Yet when we look at America's history books—and more to the point here, America's religious history books—we find that they generally tell only one story, incorporating the separate stories of many peoples into a single story line arranged chronologically. The one story is the "mighty saga of the outward acts," as Mead so clearly saw. For if you tell the one story of America, perforce, it will center on the history-makers, the Anglo-Saxon and Protestant majority who dominated the continent and its culture into our own times. To keep the story line going, you will focus on exemplary deeds and overall achievements while treading lightly, if at all, on the deeper, more hidden realities of spirituality.

There is surely a point to such single-line storytelling, for it conveys the idea of a common culture shared by all Americans. At its best, it binds many diverse peoples into one political community, one nation. It does so by picking up the threads of their separate stories and showing how the many encounter and assimilate with the dominant group, always to form part of the one continuous narrative. However, to face up to the implications of pluralism means to recognize that it is problematic to recite, even if artfully and inclusively, one story *before* exploring the realities of the many stories. Like it

xix

or not, to do so suppresses the distinctive identities of the many peoples who count themselves part of the American venture. True, some accounting of their presence can be and, in contemporary versions, usually is expressed through the single story plot. Still, the inner and spiritual stories of these diverse peoples are swept away into the march of mainstream American history. Telling merely one story, without first telling many stories, is possible only at a considerable cost—that of losing touch with the richness and texture of American pluralism.

This book arises from a conviction that the cost is too high. Standing within the pluralistic experiment, the book tells, first, not one, but many stories. Only thereafter does it search for the tentative oneness amidst the manyness of the United States. Moreover, it seeks to tell a different kind of story by viewing religious history as a complex recital that leads inevitably to the inner reaches of the human spirit and imagination. In other words, the text deals with two kinds of events.

First are the simple, clear-cut, and short-term events with which any history usually deals. Where useful and available, dates will be noted and leaders named; new organizations and popular configurations will be recorded and outer achievements marked. Second, and more important for the history of religions, are the inner and spiritual events that find outer expression in religious settings. Unlike the names and dates of a more politically oriented history, these spiritual events are not neat, tidy, and easily comprehended in conventional historical summaries. Most of the time, they unfold gradually, over centuries. To borrow—and modify—an idea from the French historian Fernand Braudel, they are events of "long duration." Such long-term events do not have sharp and precise edges, like a gilt frame around a battle painting of the Civil War. Long-term events are grasped as emerging out of the experience of a people, vocalized and expressed through sacred story and ritual, everyday behavior, and sometimes institutions. Hence, this book takes the time to follow the pathways from outer expression to inner experience. It assumes that the inner stories are immensely significant in American religious history.

In keeping with the goal of relating the religious stories of the many and the one, the text is concerned with popular religion, the religion of the people. It tries to explore each religious world from the point of view of its entire community. For that reason, issues of more concern to leaders than to other participants—governance and politics, for example—are downplayed, although they are not wholly ignored. For the same reason, considering the many stories before the single story has added significance. Although ordinary people are aware of pluralism, they usually do not choose to confront it head on. Rather, they live in their own separate centers of religious meaning constructed from an inherited past and a necessary present.

However, the book also recognizes that people *do* live out their inner and religious histories within the larger society—in an ultimately public space that involves other groups of people. Therefore, a general sociological framework forms a kind of horizon for the text. Although problems exist with any typology of religious groups, the framework of this book is based on conventional understandings of churches, denominations, sects, and cults (defined in the Introduction and thereafter). More important, the book implicitly works from ideas derived from the sociology of knowledge. When, for example, Americans are called strangers in the land, the background of the social setting for their experience is never very far away in the text. The social reasons why Americans know what they know are seen as important to the religious question. Finally, in the formulation of its basic theme the book has profited from anthropological insights concerning the importance of boundaries. As social spaces where two peoples or two realities meet, boundaries assume monumental importance in America. They are discussed further in the Introduction, and, in this context, so is the understanding of religion which governs the text.

As background for this discussion, it is assumed that definitions of religion may be divided into three types: substantive, functional, and formal. *Substantive* definitions of religion focus on the inner core, essence, or nature of religion and define it by this thing-in-itself. They tend to emphasize a relationship with a higher being or beings (God or the Gods) and to be favored by theologians and philosophers. *Functional* definitions of religion emphasize the effects of religion in actual life. They stress the systems of meaning-making the religion provides and how it helps people deal with the ills, insecurities, and catastrophes of living. Functional definitions are favored by scholars in the social sciences. Lastly, *formal* definitions of religion look for typically religious forms gleaned from the comparative study of religions and find the presence of religion where such forms can be identified. Religious forms include sacred stories, rituals, moral codes, and communities; and formal definitions of religion tend to be favored by historians of religions. Since this book is not a theoretical work, in the strict sense it does not define religion. But it does *describe* religion working from the discipline of the history of religions, and so its understanding of religion is formal. Because the book is also open to sociological and anthropological categories, its understanding is to some extent also functional.

The order of chapters in Part One is mostly historical, as the Introduction explains. The first five chapters introduce the early cast of characters—Native Americans, Jews (who arrived with Christopher Columbus), Catholics, Protestants (to be treated again in Part Two), and Afro-Americans—more or less in the order of their appearance. The following three chapters trace new religious developments in the chronological order in which they became significant. The final chapter in Part One, on regional religion, focuses on a religious culture of long duration—that of Southern Appalachia. A major function of the chapter is to introduce the concept of regional religion as a fruitful way to study a religious people. Many other regions could have been selected for such a study, but Southern Appalachia was chosen as the sole example in order to explore one region in depth.

Moreover, other case studies are included in many of the chapters. The criterion for their selection has tended to be intrinsic religious interest more than the numerical size of the group. Indeed, if the text were to operate on the numerical principle in Part One, most of the material would be about Protestants, with a section on Catholics and a brief mention of Afro-Americans, Jews, and other groups close in size. However, from the viewpoint of an interest in religious forms and meanings, counting people is not the best approach to the study of religion in America. More than that, such an approach may be exceedingly deceptive since, of necessity, it favors those religions whose members build strong, enduring organizations that keep conventional written records. Many religions in nineteenth- and twentieth-century America were structurally too diffuse for such endeavors and, besides, were ideologically alienated from this whole approach to religious reality. Yet their presence in our culture may be far greater than we would at first suspect. Later in the book we will see that this is true for metaphysical traditions like New Thought and for Eastern imports like yoga.

In contrast to Part One, Part Two examines the "one story" of religion in America and therefore uses a more topical approach. The one story has three aspects, and a religious logic suggests that the sequence move from the most clearly recognizable and familiar face of religion to its less well-known manifestations. Within the chapters, the narrative runs from past to present when that is possible. However, overriding such movement in short-term events is the abiding presence of the long-term event that is the one religion of America. From the beginning, the basic structure of that religion was, in rough form, present. So the text traces the elements of structure, form, and content according to methods that will disclose the inner and spiritual meaning of America. A concluding chapter, which deals with the one religion and the many religions of America, works historically within a thematic framework. It surveys the relationships among the many and the one as, again, a long-term event.

Footnotes are avoided throughout the book in order not to burden the beginning student. At the end of each chapter, however, is a short and highly selective bibliography that serves two purposes. First, it suggests sources to the student for further and more extensive discussion of material in the preceding chapter. Second, it indicates, in a general but not exhaustive way, sources which the text itself reflects. As a rule, new terms are explained when used initially, avoiding the necessity for a glossary. Biblical quotations are from the Revised Standard Version unless otherwise noted in parentheses. Any reference to God or the Gods in the text is capitalized because the book acknowledges the truth of all of the Gods in the power that they hold and deliver in people's lives. The past tense is employed as much as possible throughout the text as well. This does not necessarily imply that religious beliefs and practices discussed have fallen into disuse but rather that they are events of long duration begun, in most cases, before our time.

In its goal of bringing to readers a faithful report of the many religious people in America, the book has profited from the insights of many individuals. If writing this work has taught me anything, it has brought home how much scholarship is a community affair. Charles H. Long introduced me to the distinction between ordinary and extraordinary religion on which subsequent chapters rest. Martin E. Marty influenced me with his own wide interest in questions of pluralism. Numerous friends and colleagues knowledgeable in specific traditions read and criticized, with painstaking care, earlier drafts of sections of the text. For their advice and encouragement in doing so, I thank Jonathan M. Butler, Theodore Chamberlain, Jay P. Dolan, Robert S. Ellwood, Jr., Eric L. Friedland, Sam D. Gill, Philip Gleason, Stephen Gottschalk, Richard A. Humphrey, Charles H. Long, Alfonso Ortiz, Sharon Welch Patton, Albert J. Raboteau, Frank E. Reynolds, Ernest R. Sandeen, Jan Shipps, Jane S. Weeks, Rose Wendel, and Ronald M. White. In addition, I owe other debts to the scholars who read the entire text and made helpful suggestions for its improvement. For these good offices, I thank Martin E. Marty, Robert S. Michaelsen, Frank E. Reynolds, Ernest R. Sandeen, Sandra S. Sizer, J. Benton White, and Peter W. Williams. I thank, too, Sidney E. Mead, who granted me permission to quote from *The Lively Experiment* and ably criticized this preface. Needless to say, while all of these people have enlightened and assisted me, I alone am responsible for any remaining errors and omissions, and I am also responsible for the interpretation the text reflects.

Further, the Liberal Arts College of Wright State University has been tremendously supportive, allowing me to rearrange and lighten my teaching schedule in order to have the spring quarter of 1979 free for research and writing, and extending a research grant to me to aid in manuscript preparation. That assistance brought me Virginia Blakelock, whose helpfulness extended far beyond the excellence of her typing. Patricia A. Schwab and Veda D. Horton in the Religion Department also assisted generously with the typing. David L. Barr, my colleague in the department, proved an invaluable consultant on points concerning biblical matters, and all of my colleagues cheered and supported me. Dean Eugene B. Cantelupe and his office assumed the financial burden for my seemingly endless photocopying requests; Margaret Roach of the university library prepared the index; and Stephen Haas and others also at the library rendered many services.

Finally, to my parents, Louis and Theresa Albanese, who were my earliest teachers, I owe debts still larger. It was they who gave me my first understanding of the vitality of a community of one people against the backdrop of pluralism. And that is also why I have chosen to dedicate this book to an ancestor whom I remember dearly and whose memory I cherish.

INTRODUCTION

The Elephant in the Dark

There is a story that both Buddhists and some Muslims claim as their own and like to use as a teaching device. It is a story about an elephant and about a group of blind men who had never before encountered one. Each of them felt the mysterious beast, took note of the sensations, and later in conversation described the experience. Some who had felt the head of the animal claimed that an elephant was just like a pot. Others who had felt the elephant's ear claimed that it was like a harvest basket used to separate grain. Still others had touched the elephant's tusk, and they announced that an elephant was part of a plow, while, finally, another group who had patted the trunk thought an elephant was a plow, whole and complete. The moral of the story, of course, goes beyond elephants to the secrets of the universe and of life. Each individual tries to fathom these secrets from a place of personal darkness. Each describes the portion experienced, and none can speak about the whole. The lesson is to accept the fact of human limitation with humility and the fact of cosmic complexity with awe. Nobody ever will know the whole story because the vastness that surrounds us far exceeds our senses or our ability to understand.

What does all of this have to do with American religious history? Quite a bit. In our study, in some sense we will be like the blind folk trying to feel the elephant. First of all, there will be so much elephant to feel: there will be so many American religions to explore. Each American Indian tribe in the land before the Europeans came had its own form of religion. In turn, each later immigrant group brought to the new country religious commitments from the Old World. Europeans brought Judaism, Roman Catholicism, and many forms of Protestantism. Africans brought Islam and the remembered beliefs and practices of many tribal religions. Orientals, by the late nineteenth and early twentieth centuries, contributed forms of Buddhism, Hinduism, and other Eastern religions. Meanwhile, conditions in America favored the growth of new religions, native to this continent, thus adding to the picture of religious diversity.

Secondly, we will be feeling our religious elephant in the dark. We will be in the dark because even as we try to study American religious history, there is an

1

ongoing debate among scholars about what we mean by religion in the first place. While this uncertainty about the meaning of religion may seem surprising and even shocking, it is a more ordinary experience in scholarship than we might suspect. In fact, in our own everyday lives we have probably known similar uncertainty, although not perhaps about religion. We have all at one time or another stared into a landscape or into the distance of a city street. As we stood or sat, thinking of nothing in particular, just looking at the scene, we may have noticed after a while that the finely chiseled outlines of separate objects seemed to disappear. We may have experienced an optical effect in which the borders which separated one thing from another were not so solid anymore. The world, which five minutes ago was fixed and stable, had dissolved its firm boundaries, and one reality mixed itself with the next to our great confusion.

In the same way, staring long and hard at what we call religion tends to dissolve its firm boundaries. Scholars have become less certain about what gets counted as religion, and so our study of American religious history must reflect the ambiguity. In other words, our task will be in some ways like trying to see an elephant in the dark. Initially, we will need to understand what we mean by religion. If we are to make progress in our study, that understanding will have to be one which can yield results in helping us to see American religious history. After we settle—for our purposes—the question of religion, for most of the book we will need to look at the United States of America, studying the main examples of religion that we find there.

Both of these tasks—trying to understand what religion means and trying to understand specific religious systems—are the work of a field of study called the history of religions. This text, therefore, is a study of religion in America from the perspective of the history of religions. We will be asking two questions in the following pages. In the first, we will want to know what is *religious* about American religious history. In the second, we will seek to discover what is *American* about American religious history. We begin with the task of trying to understand, in a general sense, what we mean by religion.

DEFINING RELIGION

From the viewpoint of common sense, every one of us knows what religion is. Surely, it is one of those obvious realities that we have either grown up practicing or observing others practice. It is just there—a fact as unavoidable in the social landscape as a mountain or a tree would be in a natural setting. Everyone knows what religion is—that is, until one tries to define it. It is in the act of defining that religion seems to slip away.

We might want to limit it to a relationship that humans consider themselves to have had with God or the Gods, but someone could point out that the oldest Buddhists did not believe in any God, while another person might ask if atheists were religious. We might want to call religion a way of living, an ethical system such as Confucius taught, but somebody could counter that all people had some way of living or other and that meant all of them had a religion. We might say religion had to do with a quality of experience, a powerful feeling that people

2

have had when they have confronted something totally "other." Yet a few in our group would be sure to suggest that the most powerful experience that they could remember at a religious service on many a Saturday or Sunday morning was being lost in a daydream. We might become very brave and venture that religion was the thing in life a person was most ultimately concerned about, but one sarcastic member of our group would be sure to ask if that meant race horses and the lottery as well as less material realities.

Why is it that so common a feature of human life proves so baffling? What is it about religion that eludes our grasp? Is the inability to define, like the optical illusion, simply because we are staring too long into the religious landscape? Or are there other problems as well, intrinsic to the nature of religion? A definition, says *Webster's Third New International Dictionary*, is an "act of determining or settling." It is "the action or the power of making definite and clear or of bringing into sharp relief." Definition, in fact, comes from the Latin word *finis*, which means an end or limit—a boundary. A definition tells us where some reality ends; it separates the world into what is and what is not that reality. So a definition certainly works to end optical illusions, firming up the object in its landscape rather than dissolving it.

But there are special reasons why religion eludes definition that move beyond the general problem of staring at it too long. Religion cannot be defined very easily because it thrives both within and outside of boundaries. It crosses and crisscrosses the boundaries that definitions want to set up because, paradoxically, it, too, concerns boundaries. The boundaries of religion, however, are different from the logical boundaries of good definitions. In the end, religion is a feature that encompasses *all* of human life, and therefore it is difficult and, indeed, impossible to define it.

Rather than continuing to try to square the religious circle, it might be more fruitful to think not of defining religion but, instead, of trying to describe it. To describe something is to say what it generally looks like and how it usually works. It is not to say what its innermost realities are, and it is not to say definitely what separates these realities from every other object in the world. Still, describing a thing can tell us much about what it is. Looking at the past and present appearances of religion can tell us what clusters or sets of functions and forms go along with it. Learning to recognize these functions and forms helps us to know when we are looking at religion. Hence, in what follows, we will not so much try to define religion as to describe it.

Religion and Boundaries

What we know about various kinds of religions suggests that they arose in the context of dealing with boundaries. For many peoples, physical boundaries that marked the limits of the territory of one or another group were highly charged with emotional significance. They divided land that was safe and secure, the source of nurture and sustenance, from land that was alien and unfriendly, the home of hostile spirits and strange or warring tribes. So it was that any exchanges conducted across these boundaries were stressful occasions, and so it was that people strengthened themselves for these exchanges through the use of ritual. In the formula of word and act, people at a dangerous place on the physical landscape could call on special help and assistance; they could ease their encounter with whatever was alien to themselves.

This special assistance came from the mysterious and fearful unknown, from forces that transcended, or went beyond, ordinary life. In other words, alien land and people were countered by a second form of "otherness," more powerful than the first. By enlisting the help of this second "otherness," the first was overcome, and life could go on as intended. These "other" forces that saved a difficult situation by their power were called religious. And the rituals through which they were contacted were religious rituals.

But territorial boundaries were only one kind of border with which people dealt. There were also the limits of their own bodies, the boundaries of skin and tissue which separated each person in a group from every other person. Crossing the boundary of one's body could not be avoided: it happened every day in the simple acts of eating and drinking, of defecating, or of enjoying sexual intercourse. It occurred even when words passed from one person out into the air to the next, and rituals like prayer before a solemn speech or meeting grew up around these exchanges of language. In many cultures, prayer also accompanied the taking of food and drink. Similarly, the products of human bodies at their boundaries—hair, spittle, nail parings, feces—were invested with a power that made them dangerous or helpful, depending on the circumstances and the talents of the user. Thus, in a number of cultures, people feared that an enemy who found strands of their hair or their nail parings could bring evil upon their persons. Hair and nail parings, along with the other "boundary" products of the body, possessed a mysterious energy that made them focuses for ritual. Religious specialists learned to use them in magical ceremonies, and people stood in awe of these products of their own bodies.

Finally, there were the temporal boundaries in the life cycle that any person passed through. In events such as birth, puberty, marriage, and death, a person crossed the border between one form of life, which was known and secure, and a new kind of life, which was perhaps somewhat fearful. These were crisis events, and so there were rites that would ease the passage across the boundaries from one stage in the life cycle to another. In our own society, we are familiar with ceremonies of baptism for infants and with Bar/Bat Mitzvahs and confirmation rites at adolescence. Marriage brings us its solemnity as even in the simplest of ceremonies two people exchange their commitment to each other for life. At death, both wakes and funerals form the usual rites of passing.

In general, throughout the history of human societies, the concern for boundaries was apparent. Borders continued to be places invested with religious awe—the imposing birdlike garudas at the entrances of Hindu temples or the equally ferocious gargoyles at the outside corners of medieval Christian cathedrals. These signs and boundary markers like them warned all comers that they were crossing a frontier into a sacred precinct. They effectively divided one world from another. In a striking example from the United States, many Roman Catholics in the Upper Midwest placed on their lawns statues of the Virgin Mary, which performed a similar function. Anyone who has seen the vast sameness of the prairie and has imagined its unending wildness for Europeans before the creation of their towns can understand why a Virgin would be wanted on the lawn—defining the sacred space of the family and separating it from the far reaches of unnamed territory.

Even in the realm of language, religious or theological discourse has always tried to speak about the unspeakable. It has been "limit" language, language that pushed to the edge of human knowledge and tried to talk about what went beyond. Death, judgment, heaven, hell, these were the last things in Christian theology. They were also passes across the boundary of the world we know, attempts to make sense of mysterious realities from a different world. When religious people used such language, they were trying to describe a landscape they had only seen, as Paul said, "in a mirror dimly" (I Cor. 13:12). They were trying to name through language signs and symbols features of a country they had not seen with bodily eyes.

It should be clear by now that we are part of a long tradition of mixing boundary questions with religious questions. Thus, our religion concerns the way we locate ourselves in space through the arrangement of sacred rites and holy places as boundary markers. It concerns, too, the way we locate ourselves in time through origin stories or theological traditions that also express boundaries. But location is always social. It concerns our place among other human beings, and it means staking out a claim on the landscape of identity.

This internal landscape provides a new territory in which boundaries become important. So an especially fascinating modern version of the religion/boundary theme is the quest for identity. As social beings who turn within, people act out the same concerns about boundaries that they do in external space. By searching for identity and finding it, individuals metaphorically establish inner boundaries, discover through testing who they are not, and begin to affirm who they are. In the process, each individual finds that these personal boundaries overlap with those of other people and groups, so that there can be a free process of exchange. In other words, a person locates others who occupy the same inner territory and, because of the shared internal space, feels at one with them and their concerns. This is the meaning of identification with others.

Religion throughout the ages has tried to answer the continuing human question, Who am I? More particularly, religious writers of our century have made much of the issue of identity, since the intense pluralism of the modern world has given people many choices about the boundaries of the inner space they will occupy. In more traditional societies, most people grew up in a culture that took the inner world for granted, with ancient and prescribed rules for living. But in a mobile society, as in our postindustrial era, this picture of fixed inner space rapidly disappears. The presence of many possibilities for finding a land of one's own means that many decisions have to be made, some of them for alternatives not traditionally religious. Many interior regions must be denied, and others must be affirmed. Hence, in our era, identity has become a problem in a way that it was not during much of the past.

Two Kinds of Religion

The preoccupation with boundaries that comes with the search for identity points to an important fact. People are concerned not just about how to

5

cross boundaries but also about how to live well within them. Finding one's identity means finding the inner space and social space within which it is possible to thrive and grow. And so, if religion is about boundaries, it is not just about crossing them but, as in the question of identity, about respecting them, too. Therefore, learning to live well within boundaries and learning how to cross them safely gives rise to two kinds of religion. The first kind is *ordinary religion*—the religion that is more or less synonymous with culture. Ordinary religion shows people how to live well within boundaries. The second is *extraordinary religion*—the religion that helps people to transcend, or move beyond, their everyday culture and concerns. Extraordinary religion grows at the frontiers of life as we know it and seeks to cross over into another country and another form of life. In the West, extraordinary religion helps us to contact God. Let us look briefly at each of these two kinds of religion.

Ordinary religion, we might say with the scholar Joachim Wach, is the trunk of the tree of culture. In the most general sense, ordinary religion is the source of distinguishable cultural forms and the background out of which the norms arise that guide us in our everyday lives. Yet ordinary religion is obstinate to precise definition. The reason is that it is the taken-for-granted reality that we all assume, the statements and actions that make up our picture of the way the world is and is not, the things we do not have to think about or would not dream of arguing over because they are so obvious. Ordinary religion puts its premium on the things which are deeply present and unconsciously revered here within the borders of everyday culture. So this kind of religion can reveal itself in intuitive statements and vague sayings about the meaning of life: "Whatever will be, will be"; "It is better to give than to receive"; "Every cloud has its silver lining"; and the like. This kind of religion is better at being implicit than explicit.

In a more specific sense, ordinary religion can reveal itself in the many customs and folkways that are part of a culture: expected ways of greeting people; wedding etiquette concerning clothes, manners, and obligations; habits of diet; and holiday behavior, to mention a few. Each of these, if examined, can tell worlds about the main values of a society. Each is a concrete expression of the way in which people are accustomed to think and act. As such, each is a boundary marker that helps people to locate themselves and make sense of the everyday world. For example, a bridal gown suggests the traditional values of the importance of marriage and family for a young woman. The distinctiveness of wedding attire speaks for how significant such values still are in America, for how strongly the bride—and the culture—uses the institution of marriage to mark social space.

In other words, ordinary religion is at home with the way things are. It functions as the (mostly unexamined) religion of a community as community. Because it is about living well within the boundaries, it values the social distinctions that define life in the community and respects the social roles that people play. It honors the ranks that they hold and the general institutions of government, education, family, and recreation to which they assent.

Extraordinary religion, on the other hand, involves an encounter with some form of "otherness," whether natural or supernatural. It is specific and particular, easily recognizable as religion, and possible to separate from the rest of culture. Indeed, if ordinary religion is diffused throughout culture, extraordinary religion is condensed—present in clear and strongly identified religious forms that stand out from their background. Extraordinary religion encourages a special language that also distinguishes it from the rest of culture, and its sense of going beyond the boundaries often finds expression in universal statements, intended to apply to all peoples. The special (theological) language of extraordinary religion maps a landscape that living people have not clearly seen. It gives people names for the unknown and then provides access to the world beyond. It assures people that the "other" world does touch this one but is never merely the same as it. In Christianity, for example, God, grace, and salvation all describe realities beyond the material world. These terms chart the unknown and suggest how it beckons people away from their more ordinary concerns. Moreover, extraordinary religion often encourages religious activity not only on the part of the community as a whole but also on the part of separate individuals who tune themselves with particular intensity to the message delivered to the community. Mystics and prophets, who have seen visions and experienced special mental states, are its heroes and heroines.

Yet we call this religion extraordinary not because it is hard to find or to express but because it concerns itself with what is extraordinary in our day-to-day existence. That is, it deals with how to negotiate boundaries and still return to the ordinary world. Extraordinary religion may involve ecstasy, but it may also involve a simple and uneventful Sunday morning church service. The point is that people in some symbolic way voice their concern with crossing boundaries to the "other" side. Such concern is what makes the religion extraordinary, and as we shall see, such concern is what makes it very visible, very easy to find.

As we move through the religious landscape of the United States, we will find that here, as elsewhere, ordinary and extraordinary religion are often difficult to separate. In fact, in traditional societies the two were often very closely blended, and people used the same or similar symbols to express both everyday and transcendent concerns. For instance, in Judaism the most repeated ritual of extraordinary religion was the Sabbath meal, a weekly family observance which joined a formal framework of prayer and blessings to ordinary conversation and enjoyment around the dinner table.

One sign of modernity in the West has been the increasing separation of extraordinary from ordinary religion. And as we will notice, Protestantism, more than any other religious movement, tried to bring a clear distinction between the two. However, even with this Protestant goal and even with the overall Protestant character of the United States, there were numerous examples of the fusion of ordinary and extraordinary religion. Sometimes, as in the Jewish example of the Sabbath meal, people tried to make the extraordinary world easy and familiar by setting it in the midst of ordinary reality. At other times, people became so involved in the extraordinary claims of the "other" world that they drew everything possible along with them. For example, in the cult movements of the later twentieth century, many people were making a radical break with their former lives to embrace a total commitment to extraordinary concerns.

7

Components of a Religious System

Both ordinary and extraordinary religion exist as religious systems; that is to say, they are composed of parts related to other parts, which together add up to one whole. For convenience, we can think of these parts as the four Cs: creed, code, cultus, and community. These four terms, taken together, express the collection of related symbols that make up a religious system. Each of these, therefore, is present in both ordinary and extraordinary religion.

First of all, religion is expressed in *creeds*, or explanations about the meaning of human life in the universe. Such creeds may take various forms from highly developed theologies and sacred origin myths to informal oral traditions and unconscious affirmations that surface in casual conversation. Secondly, religion is expressed in *codes*, which are rules that govern everyday behavior. These may take the form of the great moral and ethical systems of antiquity, but they may also be the customs which have become acceptable in a society, the ethos in which people live. Thirdly, religion is expressed in *cultuses*, which are *rituals* to act out the insights and understandings that are expressed in creeds and codes. Not to be confused with small and intense religious groups known as cults, ritual cultuses, with their formal and repeated character, underline and reinforce the meanings evoked by creeds and codes.

Finally, religion is expressed in *communities*, groups of people either formally or informally bound together by the creed, code, and cultus they share. In ordinary religion, such communities tend to be ethnic or cultural (Indians, blacks, Polish people), informally knitting together people who share a common land, history, and language. In extraordinary religion, such communities, especially in the West, have tended to be formal institutions (Catholicism, Methodism, Adventism), designated in terms of their social organization as churches, denominations, sects, and cults.

In the chapters that follow, we will have more to say about each of these forms of extraordinary religious community. For now, let it be clear that the names we use are descriptive terms to reflect the level and kind of organization in the different groups. Churches (which in our sense include non-Christian groups) are the most broadly inclusive, and denominations are more or less inclusive. Meanwhile, sects and finally cults, at the other end of the spectrum, are the most exclusive and so have the fewest members. Similarly, churches are the most accommodating to the rest of the culture and the least demanding of their members, while cults deliberately try to cut themselves off from the rest of society and make the most radical demands on members. Churches are most at home in settings in which there is a national religion; and therefore, properly speaking, Old-World churches have become denominations—voluntary communities of believers—in the United States. Here separation of church and state has meant that there could be no official national religion.

We learn from the components of a religious system that religious beliefs—ideas—are only one part of a religion. Code, cultus, and even community all refer to concrete ways in which religion is acted out. More than a form of belief, religion is a matter of practice. Body and emotions play as large a role in a living religion as philosophical concepts. Perhaps, in fact, they play a larger role. Of course, there are connections between all parts of a religious system. Religious practice in code, cultus, and community organization expresses the ideas of the religious creed. Similarly, the religious creed provides an intellectual rationale for why people act in the religious ways that they do. Mind and body are both necessary to human religious life.

A Short Description of Religion

So far in our discussion, we have noticed that the history of religions has been a history of how to deal with boundaries. We have seen that in ordinary religion people learned how to live well within the boundaries of their world and that in extraordinary religion they learned to cross them to reach the "other" world. We have found that in both of these kinds of religion, people have followed a systematic path in expressing their religion through creeds, codes, cultuses, and communities.

It is time now to sum up what we have learned in a short descriptive statement (some might call it a "working definition") to guide us as we explore religious history in America. Religion here can be understood as a *a system of symbols (creed, code, cultus) by means of which people (a community) orient themselves in the world with reference to both ordinary and extraordinary meanings and values.* Orientation means taking note of where the boundaries are and placing oneself in relation to them. This may mean either carefully within the boundaries or out on the frontier or sometimes a little of each. The point is that the process goes on continually wherever people are. From this perspective, while many people live without Gods, nobody lives without a religion. Moreover, many people absorb seemingly contradictory elements and live comfortably in more than one religious system.

Describing religion in this way will be helpful to us later because it gives priority in understanding religion to concrete human experience and expression. It does not tell us what the substance or core of religion is, but it tells us how religion functions (to deal with boundaries), and it tells us what forms (creed, code, cultus, community) it takes. Describing religion in this way also avoids making religious ideas the most important part of religion. As we will see in our study of the United States, for many people religion was not so much thought about as acted out. By contrast, the problem with many attempts to define religion has been that, in one way or another, they have fallen into the trap of making the specific content of people's ideas essential to the meaning of religion. That is, definitions of religion have traditionally ended by assuming that religion *had* to be about the Gods, the transcendent world, or a sacred realm. Then people could feel and do as they were inspired with reference to this intellectual object of religion. Body and emotions were always second to the intellectual contents of the mind—contents expressed in a special language that was recognizably religious.

FINDING RELIGION IN AMERICA

We have been pursuing at some length the question of the meaning of religion, but thus far we have paid little attention to the theme that will be uppermost as our study progresses. We have not begun to speak yet about the

United States. The silence, in fact, has been deliberate because we will be trying to look at not simply the external features of church or sect in the United States but the meaning of religion there. In short, we will be looking for what is *religious* about American religion, and in order to do that it helps to know what we mean by religion. Now it is time to discuss more carefully the scope of our project in seeking to understand religion *in America*.

The phrase "in America" is here used as a shorthand for the political boundaries of the United States and all that happens within them. It is true that the phrase "in America" may have arisen in the beginning to reflect the cultural imperialism of the United States—as if our neighbors to the north and south did not exist. In this study, however, we use the expressions "Americans" and "in America" to refer to the people and territory of the United States simply for convenience. Moreover, we should recognize that the story of religion in the United States cannot be told fully until it becomes part of the larger story of religion on the North American continent. At the same time, the limitations of space in our text will force us to stick to the borders of the continental United States. We will cross the boundaries to deal with extraordinary religion, but with some regret we will not cross them to deal with Canada or Mexico.

Many Religions and One Religion

American religious history, as the text sees it, is the paradoxical story of the manyness of religions and the oneness of religion in the United States. The *manyness of religions* means religious pluralism. It refers to the distinct religions of the many peoples who have come to call the United States their homeland. Conversely, the *oneness of religion* means the religious unity among Americans. It refers to the dominant and public cluster of organizations, ideas, and moral values which, historically and geographically, have characterized this country. We begin, therefore, with a short discussion of religious manyness and oneness in America. In so doing, we hope to gain at least some kind of overall glimpse of the religious "elephant" with which we began.

Religious manyness, or pluralism, is so much at the center of our story that did it not smack of irreverence we might expand our elephant tale to describe America as a religious "zoo," a menagerie of many religious animals of sometimes altogether different species. Each of these "species" was a form of extraordinary religion. But each also included generous portions of ordinary religion, stemming from the ethnic cultural roots of the extraordinary religion, usually in a foreign land. Thus, the religions of manyness have repeatedly introduced novelty into the existing situation, and they have done so both historically and geographically.

Historically, as each new native or immigrant group affirmed its religious independence on American soil, it brought an added element. People had to take account of a new religious group and make room for it. Moreover, other Americans had to find a way to include it in the script and operating procedures that governed religious liberty. Geographically, as different areas of the United States became the home of diverse peoples, a particular group might give the life and style of the area a regional flavor that was, in fact, a religious flavor from the group. Thus, the Amish left an indelible impression on the life of Lancaster County, Pennsylvania, as the Hopi Indians did on northeastern Arizona, and Chinese immigrants on parts of San Francisco.

Further, each people that became part of the United States, whether native or immigrant, changed through time. More important, each people changed by, in, and through its relationships with the public mainstream that gave America its religious oneness. So we need to take account of the interaction of the many (other) centers with the one (public) center in which the many were shaped by the one. We will see, too, as our study progresses, that the one was shaped by the many and, also, that the many were shaped by their mutual condition of "otherness" and their exchanges with one another. If every religion was about boundaries, the story of religion in the United States was doubly so. Perhaps this was the reason why European observers in the nineteenth century reported that America seemed more religious than any other nation they had known. And again, this might be the reason why many of the groups were so strongly impressed by the geographical reality of the land. Working out a relationship to the land became in symbolic fashion a way of working out a relationship with the one public center and with other peoples among the many. Working out a relationship with the land was a way for a religion to discover its American identity.

Meanwhile, the religion of oneness represented the continuing theme in both time and space, the collapse of boundaries (again) between peoples to transform them all into partisans of the center. Although the Roman Catholic tradition had been strong in both the West and Southwest, historically, this religion of oneness has been mostly Protestant, Anglo-Saxon, and white. It has, however, picked up many fellow travelers along the way, especially among the Northern European immigrants. New realities and new events have made their impressions on it, but it has nonetheless maintained a clear and lasting identity.

This religion of oneness inherits the concerns of extraordinary religion from its Protestant heritage. But it is, above all, the ordinary religion of American culture that comes to us through the media, the public-school system, government communications, and commercial networks. In both its ordinary and extraordinary forms, it is the religion of a kind of "ruling" elite among Americans—those who through their past history, education, and leadership roles control the main carriers of our culture. This ruling elite, whether it has intended to or not, has shaped the mainstream of American culture.

To cite but one example, for several centuries the influence of the ruling elite dominated the textbooks of our land. Far and away the earliest and most striking attempts at public education had been made in seventeenth-century New England. There the plans for each new town were required to include plans for its schoolhouse. As each small schoolhouse in New England came into existence, it needed books, and so texts were supplied, at first from overseas and then from native authors. These texts included affirmations of the theological beliefs of Puritans regarding Adam's sin and the grace of God (extraordinary religion). More significant in the long run, they also included observations about human behavior and success as, for instance, in classics like Aesop's Fables (ordinary religion). It was natural that when other communities sought to establish schools, they looked to New England for books or at least for models of how to write them. Then in the nineteenth century, when the common-school movement spread across America demanding free public schools for all, again there was a search for adequate texts. And again the models came from New England. Thus, it is not surprising that millions of American school children learned far more about Puritanism in New England than, say, the Moravian or Cherokee Indian religions in Georgia.

Historically, sheer numbers *were* on the side of the religion of oneness. Many, especially among the early immigrants to the nation, embodied the values that it taught. Therefore, from another point of view the religion of oneness is not so much the religion of a ruling elite as that of a democratic elite. It contains the assumptions, understandings, and moral judgments that made their greatest mark on the early American community because they were shared by the largest single group of people. It reflects, in short, the public face of America. At the same time, geographically, the religion of oneness means the ways of looking at religion and the styles of religious behavior that are generally present throughout the country. Even in places where the religion of oneness is now relatively unimportant, at least it commands the public media. In other words, even though Catholics and Indians predominate in the Southwest and even though blacks make up the majority in some inner cities, that picture is not clearly reflected in the dominant image that religion in America presents.

More about Boundaries

Like the meaning of religion itself, the meaning of religion in America is linked to the question of boundaries. Earlier in our discussion of boundaries, we spoke of the issue of identity as a problem of setting up and respecting inner boundaries. This internal process, however, has external and social results; that is, we tend to act out our inner struggles and decisions. We like to give them flesh by creating concrete social expressions of them in the world. The existence of many religions and one religion in America is an example of this process. Hence, whether religion is ordinary or extraordinary, as we have already seen, it is expressed in communities.

From this perspective, the many religions and one religion of America are engaged in a dispute concerning boundaries. The many religions, each of them distinct, want to draw clear boundaries between themselves and others. Indeed, the clearer the boundaries, the tighter and more cohesive the religious group becomes—a fact that we noticed in our brief treatment of the differences among religious groups ranging from churches to cults. Meanwhile, the one religion of America seeks unity by including everyone within its religious landscape and drawing one great boundary around the whole. In its quest for unity, it aims to swallow up the diversity that separate boundaries help to guarantee.

The difference between these boundaries, disputed by the many religions and the one religion, and that "other" boundary, which extraordinary religion crosses, is profound. The boundaries of the many religions and the one religion are *social:* they concern problems about the relationships among people in ordinary life. On the other hand, the boundaries of extraordinary religion go beyond social arrangements: they present people with a chance to cross over into a sacred and otherworldly domain. Thus, the quarrel over boundaries between the many religions and the one religion helps us especially to understand what is *American* about American religion. By contrast, the crossing of worldly boundaries in extraordinary religion emphasizes what is *religious* about American religion. To put the matter another way, the dispute between the many religions and the one religion concerning boundaries takes place mostly within the boundaries of ordinary religion.

The Manyness of Religions in America

The text that follows is divided into two parts. In Part One, which is the longer section, we take up in some detail the manyness of religions in America. Our approach is topical and at the same time historical. Thus, we begin with the religions of Native Americans, the people who originally dwelled in the land. As we will see, the manyness of these first religions prefigured the religious and ethnic pluralism that would later characterize the United States. After our account of American Indian religions, we introduce the major European religions that came to the New World. Beginning with the Jews who took ship with Christopher Columbus, we continue with the Roman Catholics who, with the Spanish and French, maintained an early presence in the land. Then we turn to the Protestants, who arrived as English colonists and thereafter dominated the political and religious history of the country. In the Old World, from a social point of view both Jews and Roman Catholics had been organized in churches, religious communities which included everyone born within a given ethnic group or territory. By contrast, Protestants, although at first they followed the territorial idea of churches, later introduced the beginnings of personal choice in religion. From them the denominations arose, more selective and voluntary than churches, but still broad and inclusive in a total cultural setting.

With the religions of Native Americans and Europeans introduced, the text turns next to the religious life of Afro-Americans. Present from the early seventeenth century, these people brought with them the heritage of their African tribal religions and also of Islam. In the New World, much of the heritage was lost, but much still remained, blending with the American experience and Protestant Christianity to form an authentic religion of blackness. Now the text moves on to consider the effects of the new environment on religious creativity. The sects and communes of nineteenth-century new religions absorbed the tensions of religious pluralism and transformed them into religious gold— original religious solutions to the problems that plagued people in a world that seemed to grow less friendly. In the occult and metaphysical traditions, which are treated next, we see people face the growing unfriendliness of America by turning not to sectarian communities where ethnic bonds could be cultivated but instead to other homesteads in their minds. By turning within, people sought a fixed and sure abode as America continually changed and daily became less understandable.

Then, by the end of the nineteenth century, Eastern peoples began to immigrate to America in greater numbers, bringing their native religions with them. At the same time, some non-Oriental Americans who had been seeking inner homesteads were attracted to the inwardness of these Eastern religions. We take up the story of both groups in a discussion of Eastern religions in America, a discussion that brings us to the sixties and the seventies when the manyness of cult movements was giving a new religious revival to Americans. Finally, the last chapter in this section explores the meaning of regional religion by focusing on one case in which it has thrived. In the religion of the Southern Appalachian mountain people, we see an instance of how land and people blended to produce a distinct religious ethos that expressed a separate identity and spirituality.

The Oneness of Religion in America

If the picture that emerges from Part One is largely that of many unconnected religious groups, that is part of the thrust of the story. In some sense, American religious history is like the short, crisp notes of musical staccato, a variety of sounds, almost touching each other but not necessarily blending—at least not at the beginning. But played against the staccato, there is another melody that has woven itself through American religious history. This is the melody of the religion of oneness, and in Part Two we listen to its major themes.

First of all, we hear the theme of the Protestant mainstream, that public voice with which religion in America sounded. We learn its characteristics, all of which seem to blend one into the other with ease and harmony. We learn, for instance, how separation of church and state produced a situation in which every religious society was a voluntary organization, leading in turn to a need for religious activism to guarantee membership in a setting of religious competition. We learn, too, about how a concern for moral rules to govern such activity led to increasing moralism in the mainstream religion of the United States, of how intellectual difficulties in religious thought were avoided in order to appeal to the greatest audience of active people, of how revivalism emerged to capture religious feeling that was preferred to religious thought.

Secondly, we hear the theme of civil religion, the religion of the nation-state, in which the idea of America itself became a center for religious worship. We listen to the early Puritans who gave us the beginnings of civil religion in their communities where church and state were fused into one. We hear, too, the drumbeat of the American Revolution which joined the old Puritan notion of the New Israel to the God of the Declaration of Independence, ruling by natural law and granting natural rights to all. We follow the drumbeat down through the years of the nineteenth and twentieth centuries into our own era, listening to presidential speeches and foreign-policy decisions that confirmed the religion of nationalism. We hear it at Fourth-of-July celebrations and at times of national crisis when patriotic voices grew strong.

Finally, the speeches and songs of the civil religion persuade us to listen for still a third theme—the larger cultural religion of the United States. Civil religion in one way was a form of this religion, but it had also been deliberately manufactured by legislators and government leaders. In the less self-conscious forms of cultural religion, people themselves created an ordinary religion to express the specifically American ways in which they found meaning in life. So we learn how nature and the land have become religiously significant for many Americans, while others have turned to technology and the machine as sources of direction and value. We hear religious celebrations in the shouts from baseball and football stadiums, and we find a religious dimension to the evening news. We listen to the voices, too, of American heroes from Davy Crockett to Elvis Presley for the clues they give to the ordinary cultural religion of Americans. Then we listen for the rhythms of the annual calendar with its cycle of feasts from Halloween to Labor Day, each of them telling us something about the religion of oneness in America.

As we listen, we begin to see. Although there is darkness, we can begin to trace the dimensions of the American religious elephant. The manyness and the oneness are interconnected, each affecting the other and both together writing the pages of American religious history. In the concluding chapter, we examine some of the relationships between manyness and oneness—relationships in which the one influenced the many, the many made changes in the one, and the many also transformed their ways of life in the presence of one another.

IN OVERVIEW

We have been thinking about American religious history from the perspective of a discipline called the history of religions. Part of the ongoing work of that discipline is to understand what makes something religious. Although it has proved extremely difficult for scholars to tell us completely, we have seen that the question of boundaries is important to answering the question of religion. The boundaries are both external and internal; they are also both social boundaries between different peoples and spiritual boundaries between this world and one thought to go beyond it. The last two kinds of boundaries (social and spiritual) correspond roughly to two kinds of religion. The first of these, ordinary religion (concerned with social boundaries), is what we normally refer to as culture. The second, extraordinary religion (concerned with spiritual boundaries), tries to reach beyond culture to encounter an "other" dimension to life, such as God or the Gods. Both ordinary and extraordinary religion express themselves as religious systems. As such, both contain creeds (belief systems), codes (norms for behavior), and cultuses (ritual actions), which combine to give a community a language for naming and expressing various meanings and values in life.

When we apply these understandings to the United States, we find that things are complicated by the importance of the social boundaries in this country. Mostly related to ordinary religion, these social boundaries establish a "one" religion that has been historically dominant from the point of view of numbers, government, various supporting institutions, and social prestige. The social boundaries also indicate the presence of many religions, the expressions of the various peoples who live within the United States. In the chapters that follow, we deal with the many religions in Part One and the one religion in Part Two. Then in a conclusion, we explore the complex series of relationships between one and many.

Telling the story of American religions and religion in this way *is* aiming for a good deal. And we have to admit at the outset that we will only partially succeed. Sometimes, factual records will be lacking, and more times the elusive inner records of people's experiences will defy recovery. Sometimes, the subtleties and intricacies of response and reaction in the pluralistic situation will all but prevent a refined analysis (further elephants? further darkness?). But the "messiness" of the materials is not an excuse for refusing to try to understand them, and it is in this spirit that we need to go forward. We begin at the beginning, therefore, with the religions of Native Americans.

SUGGESTIONS FOR FURTHER READING: DEFINING RELIGION IN AMERICA

Comstock, W. Richard. *The Study of Religions and Primitive Religion.* New York: Harper & Row, 1972.

Eliade, Mircea. *The Sacred and the Profane.* New York: Harcourt, Brace & World, Harvest Books, 1959.

Evans-Pritchard, E. E. *Theories of Primitive Religion.* Oxford: Clarendon Press, 1965.

Marty, Martin E. *A Nation of Behavers.* Chicago: University of Chicago Press, 1976.

Mead, Sidney E. *The Lively Experiment: The Shaping of Christianity in America.* New York: Harper & Row, 1963.

Niebuhr, H. Richard. *The Social Sources of Denominationalism* (1929). New York: New American Library, Meridian Books, 1975.

Streng, Frederick J. *Understanding Religious Life.* 2d ed. Belmont, CA: Dickenson Publishing, 1976.

Troeltsch, Ernst. *The Social Teaching of the Christian Churches.* 1911. 2 vols. Translated by Olive Wyon. Reprint. Chicago: University of Chicago Press, 1976.

Van Gennep, Arnold. *The Rites of Passage* (1909). Translated by Monika B. Vizedom and Gabrielle L. Caffee. Chicago: University of Chicago Press, 1960.

Wach, Joachim. *Sociology of Religion* (1944). Chicago: University of Chicago Press, Phoenix Books, 1962.

PART ONE

The Manyness of Religions in America

CHAPTER 1

Original Manyness:
Native American Traditions

At one time or another, each of us has seen an old photograph of a tired Indian warrior idling his horse or of an ancient Indian woman, wrinkles lining her face, looking dimly into the sunset. The message was clear enough: Indians had come to the end of their trail. They were a vanishing race, and while there were still remnants and survivals of their cultures around, it was up to scholars to collect them and up to ordinary folk to appreciate them with dutiful nostalgia. Yet if we are to take seriously the record of events in the second half of the twentieth century, the message was wrong. Native Americans, along with many other ethnic minorities in America, enjoy a new vigor as they demonstrate that their cultures have endured and grown in the face of the dominant Euro-American mainstream. In fact, in law courts and public marches, Indians have signaled militancy, while they have begun to reclaim the relics of their ancestors which whites have displayed on museum shelves.

Central to this manifestation of Native American cultural health have been Native American religions. Articulate representatives of Indian people, such as Vine Deloria, Jr., in his *God Is Red,* have seen the ancient beliefs and rituals as a strong foundation for contemporary political endeavors. While we may argue that politicized religions are changed religions, the point is that the religions have shown themselves as the source of Native American identity and vitality. Any study of American Indian experience must begin and end in religion. It must learn to trace the sacred circles the Indians themselves followed.

The resiliency of these Native American religious traditions in the midst of the political battles of the twentieth century is already a clue to something we will meet again and again. For Indians, ordinary religion—the cultural religion within boundaries—and extraordinary religion—the clear attempt to reach beyond them—were fused. Indian nations such as the Oglala Sioux had no word for religion in their native language because they had not separated the ordinary details of living from the mysterious forces which surrounded them. They saw their beliefs and activities as part of the same whole.

19

NATIVE AMERICAN DIVERSITY

If the picture of the tired warrior at the end of the trail is wrong, however, it is wrong not just because it speaks of the death of Indian cultures. It is also wrong because it suggests that there is any one Indian to represent all Indians or any one Native American tradition to represent them all. Native American culture, in the singular, or Native American religion, in the singular, or discussion of "the American Indian," again in the singular, is mostly a convenient fiction when we need to contrast Native Americans with Euro-Americans. In reality, about 550 different Indian societies and distinct languages have been identified in North America. Even three decades ago, about 150 Native American languages were still being used north of the Rio Grande, while today various Indian sectors of the population are increasing at a rate faster than the white, helping to reinforce Native American diversity.

Indian languages have been divided into five major groups which, in themselves, suggest the diversity of Indian cultures. To the east were Algonkian speakers, among them the tribes that first encountered the English on the shores of Massachusetts Bay and Virginia. Still others who spoke Algonkian dwelled in the eastern part of the Midwest and in a far western pocket. Running like a wedge between the eastern and midwestern Algonkian speakers were the Six Nations of the Iroquois, who spoke varieties of Hokan-Sioux, the language group of vast areas in the southeastern United States, the central prairies, and portions of southern California as well. In parts of the Southwest and the West, Uto-Aztecan, which had affinities to cultures further south, was spoken, while also in the Southwest and parts of the Northwest, Athabascan was the language family for many of the tribes. Meanwhile, Penutian speakers dwelled in the Northwest, and, if we include Alaska, we introduce a sixth language family, that of the Eskimo-Aleut, which flourished in broad coastal belts alongside the Athabascan spoken further inland.

Just as languages and geographical areas expressed the diversity of the Indians, so did cultural characteristics. Some Native Americans were hunter-gatherers, others were agriculturalists, and still others fared with various combinations of the two. Some societies were highly organized, while others were loosely knit. Some seemed to absorb elements from the cultures of their neighbors, but others remained more isolated. Some gave prominence to women in kinship organization and in actual responsibilities. Others were, as anthropologists say, patrilineal (taking their rights from the man's side of the family) and patrilocal (living after marriage in the man's household or village/band). Basketry, pottery, and weaving flourished among many groups, but in still others if they existed, they were not too important. Shelters were erected in various styles and sizes and materials. Some groups were warlike, and others fought only with great reluctance, regarding the slaughter of another human being as a form of pollution.

In such a picture of manyness, it seems fair to ask if there were as many Native American religions as there were Native American languages and cultures. The question, of course, already betrays a Euro-American way of seeing and organizing things, and its answer is present in the fusion of the ordinary and the extraordinary we have mentioned in Native American cultures. For Native Americans, culture was tradition was religion; so there were as many American Indian religions as there were separate peoples and societies. As a matter of fact, one of the strongest points of cultural collision between Indians and whites was in their understandings of religion. Indians thought that every *people* had its sacred stories and rituals on which their world was based. Euro-American Christians argued that their religion was the universal truth for all. Even though in mission practice they spread the values of European culture along with Christianity, in theory, at least, they thought Christianity transcended culture. Indians, in other words, would hardly ride a country circuit to win converts whom they could not adopt wholesale into their tribes. On the other hand, Euro-Americans saw converting the "heathen" as one of the reasons they should settle the New World.

COMMON CHARACTERISTICS IN RELIGION

Although there was an ethnic profusion of American Indian religions, however, it is possible to talk about common characteristics which run through most, if not all, of them. Looking at these common characteristics is most helpful when we want to see Native American religions as a related series which can be contrasted with Euro-American religions. Because so much of our later discussion will deal with Euro-American religions, we need to look at these mutual elements in Indian religions. We need to have some sense of the differences among them and some sense of how history has changed the past, too, but let us begin by noticing what traditional Native American religions have had in common.

In general, Native American religions possessed a strong sense of continuity with the things they held sacred. Both in space and in time, Native Americans saw the holy and mysterious aspects of the world as very closely related to their daily existence. In space, whereas Euro-Americans conceived a three-level universe with God, human beings, and nature inhabiting different realms, Native Americans looked upon a world to which they were bound by ties of kinship. There were the Grandfathers who were Thunder Beings; there was Grandmother Spider; and there was the Corn Mother. There were animals who took on human form such as Coyote the Trickster or sacred birds or sacred buffalo. There were gifted human beings such as shamans—holy people who, as sacred healers, mystics, and magicians incorporated into one, could fly like birds and talk to the animals. Among the Plains Indians, even ordinary people could speak to guardian animal spirits in special vision quests. The world, in short, was a huge extended family network, with the Indians existing as younger and humbler brothers and sisters among their more venerable relations.

In time, too, the Indians saw powerful ties of continuity that bound them to the sacred events which had occurred before the dawn of history. These events, shrouded as they were in mystery, were the acts of creation which had caused the world and the Indian peoples to be. For Native Americans, they were the enduring models on which life in the years that followed was to be based. There was no break between these models and the happenings that made up the ordinary history of a tribe. History, indeed, was not secular but sacred; and it had begun in the origin myth, or sacred story, of the people. Thus, when N. Scott Momaday, a twentieth-century Kiowa Indian, tried to explain what his people meant to him, he did so in a narrative (*The Way to Rainy Mountain*, 1969) which combined the Kiowa myth of origins with historical traditions concerning the tribe and then with recollected stories of his immediate ancestors and his personal appropriation of all three sets of traditions. When Edmund Nequatewa, a twentieth-century Hopi, attempted to describe Hopi "truth" for outsiders (*Truth of a Hopi*, 1936), he began with Birdmen in the underworld where the Hopi originated and included the founding of the village of Hotevilla—in a quarrel among Hopis about sending their children to United States government schools. Myth and history were collapsed because, just as Indian space existed as one whole, so, too, did Indian time.

In such a world in which metaphors of kinship abounded and myth was as real as clashes with the government of the United States, the material world was, above all, holy. While Euro-Americans tended to separate material from spiritual realities and in their religions exalt the spiritual, Native Americans expressed in many ways their sense of the sacredness of matter. The distinction between a natural and a supernatural realm, an easy shorthand for describing Euro-American religions, was forced and strained when applied to the religions of Native Americans. They saw power at work, awesomely and mysteriously, in every portion of nature. It was personal power, and the forces of the universe could be named as relatives. But it was never or hardly ever abstract power which in its real form was separate from nature. The sacred beings were forms of animal and plant life which, in a pact long ago, had pledged their bodies as food for Indian peoples. Thus, Pacific Coast Indians had to be careful in taking the flesh from the salmon, for the skeleton, when placed in the river waters, would receive new flesh as the sacred beings reproduced themselves. Other Native Americans evolved elaborate rules of courtesy for hunting or planting, apologizing to the spirits of the life forms they took, offering first "fruits" to these spirits, and being careful to use every portion of the sacred body they had killed. Because nature—the material world—was sacred, Indians mostly tended to be natural ecologists in an age before the Euro-American concept was born.

If the outer world which surrounded Native American peoples was sacred, so, too, was the inner one. Dreams revealed holy, hidden things which often would not be known in other ways. The Iroquois had their dream-guessing rite in which individuals presented themselves to the tribal council so that personal dreams and their meanings could be discerned. On the Plains, leaders of the hunt were men who had prayed for months and had significant dreams. For the Mohave in the West, the warrior who would take scalps must first have had the "good dream for taking scalps," the sign of religious power for the undertaking. Sometimes in dreams the free soul traveled to far distant places to learn important lessons, and other times dreams brought visions from guardian spirits.

This inner world which dreams disclosed was intimately related to the one outside. Bridging the space between inner and outer, an Indian person should have a name which indicated his or her kinship with nature and at the same time told something of inner essence. For many Native Americans, names were changed as significant deeds and happenings etched new marks in the story of their character. So there could be Black Hawk, or Afraid of Horses, White Rabbit, or Moves from Your Sight Little Red Star. The colors were significant here, for each of the four directions had its color which brought with it certain qualities as gifts of the direction. Thus, the red of the north might be the color of wisdom, while the white of the south might give innocence and trust. The black of the west might bring deep thought and introspection, and the yellow of the east might be the sign for inner light.

Changing a name, however, was only one form of a process that Native Americans saw all around them. Transformation was almost in European terms a "law," and Indian lore was filled with accounts of animal/human changes, as we have seen. Trickster figures such as Hare or Raven or Coyote were shapeshifters who could assume any form they chose in the midst of their adventures. They were beings of creative power who had helped to put the present world in order. At the same time, they seemed to embody a principle of disorder which continually disturbed the regular workings of society.

Thus, the "hero" of the Winnebago Trickster cycle violated the first rule of a warrior: that he must keep himself away from women, who possessed an alien power capable of interfering with the warrior's power. Trickster, in other words, could change from world maker to world breaker and back again. He could also shift from the sly, cunning creature who could outwit Bear or Coyote to the fool who fought himself because his right arm and left arm did not know they belonged to each other and who burned his own anus to punish it for not standing proper guard while he slept. He was male, yet he became female, married a chief's son, and bore him three little boys. Most of the time, as a male, he carried his penis around in a box with him and did not quite know how to treat it. Yet when Chipmunk managed to gnaw most of it up, Trickster used the pieces to make potatoes, artichokes, ground-beans, and rice for the people.

Trickster, in short, was the epitome of existence without boundaries, thrown open in every direction to become what inspiration and circumstance decreed. He posed the major issue for Native American religions directly. Continuity and discontinuity, identity and transformation were statements about boundaries and frontiers. Indians seemed to be saying that the lines which bound them in the sacred circles of their communities were all-important, and yet at the same time, they were admitting how fragile and, indeed, fictive these lines were. Transformations indicated that the world was really one substance, and their Trickster figures continually reminded them of this truth.

Native Americans highlighted the importance of transformation in their ceremonies. Many societies had sacred clowns who were at once funny and terrible beings. They could do foolish things, such as dressing themselves backwards and acting in the same backward and upside-down manner. They could embarrass others by sexual joking or mimicking, and they could tease mercilessly. Yet they were very serious figures, such as the Sioux clown, or *heyoka*, who had assumed his calling because of visionary power from a Thunder Being. Sometimes clowns brought punishment and retribution to the people, like the Fool Dancers of the Kwakiutl, who threw stones, or the False Faces of the Iroquois, who sprayed hot cinders. Indeed, clowns were to ritual what Tricksters were to myth cycles, and by turning the standing order inside out, they pointed to the permeability of boundaries and the necessity, sometimes, of destroying them. Creative disorder, they seemed to be saying, could and would regenerate the order on which religion and society depended.

Often, in ceremonies, masked dancers carried transformation further still as they impersonated different Gods and guardian spirits and sometimes, in the ecstasies of the dance, became the figure they impersonated. In the Pueblo villages of the Southwest, according to tradition, the Kachina dancers came from the mountains to perform on ritual occasions during the year. Meanwhile, in hunter societies, shamans could transform illness into material objects which could be sucked or drawn out of their patients. Special dreams were transformed into ceremonies by being acted out, among the Plains people, in ritual dramas. Myth became history, and history was changed into myth. All in all, it was the deceptiveness of appearances which Native American religions proclaimed. This ordinary world touched another; in fact, it was another. Sacredness, the transformations told, was never very far away. It was all around.

Living in such a world, Native Americans conceived their religious task as the process of tuning themselves to a harmony with nature which surrounded them. Harmony with the natural (and sacred) world conferred power in the hunt, on the field, in war, or in government. Power came from the solemn recitation of origin myths which brought Indian peoples into harmony with their beginnings. It came from the sacred objects and forces that manifested themselves in ritual—in the sweat lodge, in a sun dance, or in a sacred game of ball—and led to harmony with the universe.

In these ceremonies and even in more mundane tasks such as constructing a dwelling, Indians were preoccupied with the directional points. They lived out the importance of orientation toward boundaries in a particularly graphic way. Four—for the four directions—was a privileged number that appeared again and again in myth and legend as well as in ceremony. The number five was privileged as well, for it added the center to the four corners. So, too, was seven, since to the four directions of the horizontal plane, seven added a vertical dimension. There was the zenith, or highest point, the nadir, or lowest depth, and the center where the Indian person stood. Understood in this way, religion became a centering process in which the Native American learned to maintain harmony by living equidistant from all the boundaries. Life blossomed not on the edges of society, as transformation had hinted, but in the middle.

Standing in the middle with the six directions at equal points around him or her, the Native American described a great circle. It was like the circle of the world itself, or the circles traced by natural vegetation; like the circle which figured so frequently in ceremonies and also in the construction of dwelling places. Circles were sacred for Indians because they reflected and imitated nature. To be in harmony meant to live as part of the great circle, or the medicine wheel, of the world. Thus, in their religions, Native American peoples were living out their own versions of the ancient world view of correspondence. Their societies were small-scale replicas of the larger reality which surrounded them. It was up to them to be the manifest expression of the powers which were nature's secrets. At the same time, by looking at the picture as painted on the larger canvas, the canvas of nature, they could better comprehend life's meaning and appropriate work. Because they were made of the same stuff as the natural and sacred world, the boundaries were always permeable and could be easily crossed. Yet because the natural and sacred world was one of centers and circumferences and directions, Indian peoples could plant themselves securely in the middle place, in the ordinary world where they did not venture toward the frontiers.

Euro-Americans, on the other hand, tended to see the world in more divided ways. The sacred world of divine power was separated from the profane one of ordinary existence. God had caused the world to be, and his law governed its movements: in that sense, he could be said to dwell within it. Yet he also far transcended it, and meanwhile his human creatures had increased the separation between God and the world by the fall in the garden of Eden. Sin had entered the world, and it had affected not just human beings but all of nature. For Euro-Americans, the world had become, as we have said, a three-level affair. God tried to control human beings, and human beings tried to control nature. If there was rebellion in both cases, it only emphasized the fact that the seamless garment of one creation had been, in the Euro-American view, pulled apart. That there were important values attached to the divisions of creation and creator we will see when we begin to consider Euro-American religions in more detail.

For now, however, our task is to understand what we can about Native American religious traditions. For the most part, we have been discussing them in terms of what they had in common, and beyond indicating the vast array of tribal societies and languages, we have paid very little attention to their differences. It is, of course, difficult to touch on the differences in a study such as this, but in order to give some sense of the range that has existed in American Indian religions we will briefly take up the religions of two distinct Indian societies, the Oglala Sioux and the Hopi. The first is a hunter-gatherer society of the Plains, and the second is an agricultural Pueblo culture from the Southwest. By looking at what religion means in each of these traditions, we will gain some sense of the real differences that made American Indian religions separate and distinctive traditions.

THE OGLALA SIOUX

At the present time, the Oglala Sioux, who suffered at the hands of the United States military in the Wounded Knee Massacre of 1890, are perhaps the best-known single group of American Indian people. They were one of the thirty-one or so Indian nations who in the nineteenth century roamed the prairies of North America between the Mississippi River and the Rocky Mountains, setting up temporary camps and moving them as the seasons changed and they pursued the buffalo. More specifically, the Oglala Sioux belonged to the Teton division of the Seven Fireplaces of the great Sioux family. They dwelled in the western portion of Sioux territory and, along with other tribes of the Teton Sioux, spoke Lakota.

Like the other Tetons, too, the Oglala had originated in what is now the state of Minnesota and had come onto the Plains where in about 1750 they obtained horses, an event which changed their fortunes and led to their wealth and fame as buffalo hunters. With horses they no longer had to travel and hunt on foot, carrying their belongings on their backs or with their dog travoys. Ironically, the horses had come from whites—from the Spanish of the Southwest from whom they had strayed or been stolen or traded. Thus, the beginning and end of the flowering of Sioux culture were linked to Euro-Americans. But in this heyday of their fortunes, the religion which the Oglala lived reflected the centrality of the buffalo and taught the lessons of a sacred world in terms of the values of Native American hunters. Like American Indian religions in general, it blended the ordinary and extraordinary worlds together.

The origin myth of the Oglala, like that of many another Indian people, concerns their emergence from the earth—in this case through the intrigues of a Trickster figure, Inktomi the Spider. Through a wolf, Inktomi wooed the people with food and clothing until Tokahe and three strong companions came to the upper world to investigate its virtues for themselves. Here, Inktomi plied them with more gifts and promised them youth, so that they returned to the people in the world below with glowing tales of what they had experienced. Although the old chief and an old woman warned of cold wind and the need for hunting in the upper realm, Tokahe led out six families. The results were not so fortunate as they had hoped, and the children cried for food while Inktomi laughed. Yet all was not lost, for they met Old Man and Old Woman, who taught them to hunt, clothe themselves, and make tipis. Oglala life had begun: Tokahe and the six families were, in fact, the first people in the world.

This is but one of a cycle of myths which explained the origins of things in intricate detail. In the beginning, there had been Skan who gave movement to all, but it was Inktomi the Trickster who performed the real work of transformation which made of the Oglala a people on the earth instead of under it. In other words, there was the vanishing God, Skan, and then a culture hero, Inktomi, who provided the creative impetus for the present world. Such a pattern was frequent among Native American myths of origin, but what is important here is that this sacred story told the mystery of *Oglala* beginnings. It was about a particular people, not about the world in general. Like all myths, the story this one told is a true one, explaining the meaning of existence in the world as the Oglala knew it. We are a people of the earth, they were saying, and although creation was a kind of trick that was played on us (we did not really know what it meant to be born; we did not really have any choice), still we have learned to feed and clothe and shelter ourselves. Our life goes on.

The origins of life, however, not only concerned physical existence. There were origins, too, for the rituals which acted out the meaning of being Oglala Sioux. So the mythology explained the gift of the sacred pipe to the people when once two of the men were approached by a beautiful woman in white buckskin with a bundle on her back. Later she entered the Oglala Sioux camp, came to the lodge, and with ritual attention to the directions, presented the sacred pipe to the chief. "With this sacred pipe," she said, "you will walk upon the Earth; for the Earth is your Grandmother and Mother and She is sacred." Ever after, the pipe figured in the solemn rituals of the Oglala—the sign of their bond to one another and to the earth, their common source. The pipe, in fact, accompanied the gift of ritual. For likewise, the mysterious woman offered the people a round stone containing seven inscribed circles, each of the circles representing a rite which they would receive. After she had taught them the first of these rites—a ceremony for keeping the spirits of the dead—she walked away, turned into a red and brown buffalo calf, rolled over, and became a white buffalo calf, and then a black one.

White Buffalo Calf Woman, as she was called, had given the Oglala a ceremonial repertoire, with the sacred pipe at its center, for the expression of all their religious needs. Thus, in the first rite of ghost keeping, the Oglala were able to deal more easily with death. The soul or spirit of a deceased person could be kept for a period of time ranging from six months to two or more years. A kept "ghost," instead of starting immediately on the ghost road to its fate, would remain close to relatives. Keeping the ghost in this way was believed to enable it, through the proper rites, to be sure of returning to its beginnings. At the same time, ghost keeping served as a reminder to others of the fact of death. Elaborate ceremonies surrounded the making and keeping of a ghost bundle including a lock of hair from the dead person. Members of the family observed all kinds of ritual taboos, and a special dwelling was built for the bundle. When the day arrived on which the spirit was at last released, the ceremonies were equally elaborate.

The other rituals of the Oglala included the sweat lodge ceremony, the vision quest, the sun dance, the "making of relatives," the girl's puberty ritual, and a sacred ball game. Each of them was characterized by minute prescriptions for word and gesture, hinging always on the use of the directional points. Each ritual, in other words, located the Oglala in a world of meaning by a centering process with regard to space. As religious people, they paid attention to the directions because in ordering themselves properly in relationship to the cardinal points, they created the harmony which was the essence of their way. In the sweat lodge ritual, for instance, there were rules which governed the construction of the lodge, the use of space within it, the roles which the persons who participated played. The leader had to move sunwise as he entered the lodge; the heated stones placed at the bottom of the special hole were four in number for the four directions; the two stones placed on top represented zenith and nadir; the very top stone of all signified Spotted Eagle. There were thus seven stones (again, a sacred number), and prayers had to be offered over them before more stones could be added to give the necessary heat for the ritual purification. Later, after the door had been sealed, the ritual went forward with attention to the four directions as various gestures and actions were performed.

The vision quest, or *hanbleceya* ("crying for a vision"), gave men—and sometimes women—in the community the opportunity to use the power of ritual in a situation which was distinctly tailored to individual character. The ritual in its central part was performed alone on a solitary and sacred hill away from the camp, usually for the first time in adolescence. It was meant to enable the person who undertook the quest to gain power through a vision in which guardian spirits revealed their relationship to the seeker and bestowed on him the knowledge/ power he desired. The ritual was conducted under the guidance of a holy man and involved the smoking of a sacred pipe, preliminary purifications in the sweat lodge, fasting, and prayer. Once the seeker reached the sacred hill, there was the same attention to directions we have previously seen: four saplings formed poles at the four directions, and the seeker traced a cross by returning to the center from each of the four.

Because the heart of the ritual occurred alone over a period of one to four days and because it yielded knowledge and power fitted to the needs of the particular seeker, the vision quest has often been cited as a sign of the "individualistic" nature of the religion of hunters. Yet to speak of the "individualism" of Oglala Sioux religion or its vision quest is a bit misleading. The vision quest, despite the loneliness of the seeker's encounter with the sacred, began and ended in community. The holy man who guided the quest was the representative of the spiritual wisdom of the Oglala Sioux as a people. The purification in the sweat lodge was never solitary but always the collected work of those who supported the questing individual—usually his relatives and the holy man. And when at last the vision had been granted and the seeker had heard the Thunder Beings, or the animals and birds had spoken, he had to return, relate his experience in the presence of the others, and listen as the guiding holy man interpreted its meaning. In short, the vision became "flesh" when it had been ratified by the community through its authorized representatives. If there was a place for the individual in Oglala Sioux religion, it was a place which was very carefully circumscribed. The gift of the seven rites was a gift to all the people.

The communal character of Oglala religion was especially evident in the sun dance. The only ritual which occurred at a special time of year, the sun dance was held in the early summer after the buffalo "harvest." Often it was an intertribal affair involving a huge encampment in which many people came together. The ritual extended over four days, and each day had its proper ritual tasks, its formal and necessary ceremonies. A lodge was constructed, a cottonwood tree selected and trimmed according to prescription to form the sacred pole at the center, and the pole painted and decorated with symbolic offerings, among them reminders of the buffalo. In a dance which followed, warriors in their finest attire circled the pole, running to each of the directions to flatten the ground and symbolically "killing" the images of a man and a buffalo at the pole. But the culmination was the actual dance around the pole which gave the lengthy rite its name. Performed either gazing at the sun from morning until night or with skewers digging into the flesh of the dancers, attached by thongs to the pole, the dancers were literally bound to the sacred center. Under their leader they danced themselves into an ecstasy of sacrifice until they fell exhausted or the flesh was pulled from their bodies and they were released. They had fasted for the duration of the dance and demonstrated in this hunting version of a first-fruits festival that, in return for the gift of life in the buffalo, they would give themselves in the flesh.

The remaining rituals of the Oglala did not stint in their prescriptions for careful and symbolically elaborate ceremonial behavior. The "making of relatives" was designed to unite two people to each other in a bond considered closer than that between relatives, committing them to dying for each other, if necessary. The puberty ritual for girls, the buffalo ceremony, at first menstruation placed young women in the care of the sacred buffalo and secured for them a relationship with White Buffalo Calf Woman. At their menstrual periods thereafter, women lived temporarily alone, a practice common among Native Americans, who believed that women possessed a power which, if it came into contact with that of the hunter-warriors, could damage it. The religious power of women figured in the seventh rite of the Oglala as well. In a rite which perhaps symbolized the game of life, a young girl threw out a ball to people standing at the four directions. The ball stood for knowledge and the people struggling to catch it were struggling, said the Oglala, to free themselves from ignorance.

The ball used in the seventh rite, like so many of the symbolic objects which were part of the rituals, was *wakan* or holy. *Wakan* was a quality possessed by the elements such as thunder and lightning, by the animals or plants, sometimes by human beings, and sometimes even by objects. *Wakan* was that dimension of reality which caused transformation. It was the mysterious and awesome force which surrounded the Oglala in the world the sacred buffalo had given, and *wakan* in its culminating aspect was *Wakantanka*, a power which has been equated with the God of Christianity and Judaism. Yet it is difficult to translate into Euro-American terms the nuances of *wakan* and *Wakantanka*. Both might be said to be more adjectival—more qualifying—than substantive— fixed entities or things. *Wakantanka* perhaps meant something like "holy, sacred," and yet *Wakantanka* meant sixteen different godly beings who collectively were *Wakantanka*. The difficulty in understanding or conceiving *Wakantanka* rests ultimately with the different models of relationship to the sacred which characterize Indians and Euro-Americans. Indians tend to see sacredness as a quality suffusing all things and to personify the Gods ambiguously so that at the same time they both are and are not separate from nature. Euro-Americans tend toward more precision—and separation—in their concept of the supernatural.

It should be evident, however, that if any being was a *wakan* being among the Oglala, it was the buffalo. Myth and ritual together demonstrated how central the sacred buffalo was. Oglala religion, as Oglala life, centered around the being from which/whom they drew all of their sustenance—economic, in the buffalo hunt and the many uses for buffalo meat, hide, and even teeth thereafter; economic, true, but even more, spiritual. It was the buffalo who gave the Oglala a center and an identity. If they were people of the earth, they were people of the earth because they were people of the buffalo.

The people of the buffalo traveled a long path from 1700 to the twentieth century. Despite the advances of an alien Euro-American culture which threatened to take away their lands and livelihood, the Oglala proved stubborn in the maintenance of their identity. No longer depending for their survival on the leadership of a hunter-warrior, twentieth-century Oglala survive as a people because of their religion. In the canon of sacred story, in the abiding presence of the buffalo through the sacred pipe and the seven rites which were its gift, the people of the buffalo have come to know themselves as one among the many peoples of the United States.

THE HOPI

Although we have been all too brief in our discussion of the religion of the Oglala, we must move now to a consideration of a much different group of Native Americans. We do this to gain some sense of the diversity that existed in the religions of Native Americans, similar as they were in overall understandings and ethics. The Hopi are a people who are numbered among the Pueblo or "village" Indians of the American Southwest, so named because they dwelled together in adobe and stone apartment villages. River or eastern Pueblo peoples, the Tanoans and the Keresans, settled along the Rio Grande in what is now the state of New Mexico, but to the west in the desert was the country of the Zuni (New Mexico) and the Hopi (Arizona). Life in the desert proved to be to the advantage of cultural continuity, for, with greater isolation from Spanish, Mexican, and Anglo-American conquerors than their eastern cousins, the Hopi maintained an identity and ritual life largely untouched by Christianity.

Hopi origins are veiled in mystery. Over two thousand years ago, their ancestors came into the Southwest. Groups of hunter-gatherers who learned to farm, the Basketmakers, as they have also been called, dug pits in the floors of caves to store their food and eventually began to live in pit houses in the caves or out in the open. From about A.D. 900 to 1300, their culture reached its heights in the era of the cliff dwellings, carved into the sides of the mountains at places which were easy to defend, and the apartment terraces, villages which are still characteristic of the Pueblo peoples. Old Oraibi, the ancient ceremonial village of the Hopi, dates back to this time, having been built mostly after 1300, with beginnings, though, as early as 1150.

Thus, the Hopi have had ancient agricultural traditions behind them. While they were also hunters and gatherers in the past, particularly when their crops had failed, hunting and gathering gradually declined. The Hopi continued to be farmers, growing crops of corn, beans, and squash as staples. Tilling the soil was a man's job in this society, but social organization revolved around women, since the communities were organized in matrilineal clans. The Hopi villages spoke Shoshonean, which belonged to the Uto-Aztecan language family, and some of their beliefs and customs reflected the influence of Mezo-American Indian cultures. But they also inherited a variety of hunter-gatherer values, such as awe of the dead, and of practices, such as reliance on healers. Their villages were ceremonial centers in which the terrace apartments were grouped around the plazas, the sites of outdoor dances and formalities, and the kivas, the sacred pit houses where the various clans conducted rituals from which women were excluded.

Curiously, although women had been debarred from participation in kiva rites, the origin myths of the Hopi told of the primacy of feminine sacred symbolism. The Hopi had emerged from the dark womb of Mother Earth, their most sacred stories told them, and the kiva itself, essentially a large hole dug in the earth, was a forceful reminder. Each Hopi village had its own slightly different version of the origins of things, but there was general agreement on the major motifs. In one version from Oraibi, two Hard Being women (deities of hard objects such as shells, corals, turquoise, and beads) caused dry land to appear and then created birds, animals, a woman, and a man.

In another sacred story that related subsequent events, the people enjoyed a good life in the world below, until evil entered into the hearts of the chiefs and the people, sexuality ran rampant, and hatred and quarreling grew apace. In their plight the chiefs tried to find an escape, and they fashioned a Pawaokaya bird, singing over him to give him life. Meanwhile, the chiefs planted a pine tree and a reed beside it to reach the hole into the upper world. The bird flew in circles around the two "ladders," found the opening but found nothing else, and returned exhausted. So the chiefs made a hummingbird and then a hawk who, in turn, repeated the search and also came back unsuccessful and exhausted. Finally, the chiefs created Motsni, who flew through to the upper world, found the site of present-day Oraibi, and also encountered, sitting there alone, Masauwuu or Skeleton. When he heard Motsni's tale, Skeleton explained that he was living in poverty but the people were welcome to join him. So they came, emerging from their plant ladders to the world above. Later, aided by Spider Woman, they fashioned a symbol that turned into the moon and another that became the sun. The people had begun to make their way, and given the gift of corn, small though it was, the Hopi had also been given an identity. After a series of migrations, the clans arrived at their villages, and life, as the Hopi knew it, had begun.

As if to corroborate the myth, on a rock to the south of Old Oraibi the symbol of the emergence is said to be carved. It is an abstract symbol representing the womb of Mother Earth by means of a maze intersected at its opening with a cross line. The line is the umbilical cord which connects the Hopi to the womb of the Earth Mother and at the same time the way through which they came out into the world. Meanwhile, in each sacred kiva of the Hopi was a *sipapu*, the opening to the world below. Most of the time covered by a stone, at the end of the year it was opened at the initiation ceremonies so that the dead could leave the womb of Earth to participate.

With a superb blend of folk memory and folk philosophy, the origin myth of the Hopi fused tradition with interpretation. Emergence from earth had been, in a way, historical truth for the Hopi, since their ancestors had dwelled in the pit houses that were replicated in the kivas. Similarly, matrilineal organization must have existed for a long time, for in the beginning the Hard Being women (deities) had created a woman first and then a man, a model for customs in Hopi society by which women owned their houses and household goods and, in a sense, their children, who derived their clan kinship from their mothers. Finally, Skeleton and the small gift of corn suggested the precariousness of life in the desert growing subsistence crops. Yet, as with the Oglala, the truth of the Hopi myth did not depend on historical recollection. Once again, it was the statement of identity which made the myth true, for in telling who they were, the Hopi were also telling what meaning and significance attached to their lives. Like the Oglala, although in the particularity of their own sacred story, the Hopi were saying that they were people of the earth.

The Hopi were like the Oglala in being people of the earth, but they were people of the earth who were farmers, not hunters. Nowhere was this more clearly demonstrated than in the cycle of rituals which formed a kind of liturgical year in the Hopi villages. While the Sioux possessed only one calendric ritual in the sun dance, for the Hopi every rite depended on the cycle of the seasons. Harmony with nature, in their case, was expressed in harmony with its changing seasons: transformation, so central for all Native Americans, meant following the movements of nature through cyclic time. And as the motivating force behind the calendar of rites lay the ever-present need for water to make the crops grow in this dry, sparse desert region. Once again, as for the Oglala so for the Hopi, religion and everyday economic need were not strangers. Just as the buffalo was central for the Sioux, water was primary for the Hopi. In both cases, ordinary religion and extraordinary religion had been fused. Rituals were the vehicles for maintaining the boundaries so that life could be lived within the safe fences of economic and social organization. Rituals were also the way to cross over the farthest frontiers and experience the awesome power of the sacred.

In general, the rites of the Hopi year possessed certain common features. In a pattern which showed the fragmentation of the clan system and yet managed to effect some degree of reconciliation, each of the ceremonies was conducted by one or more hereditary chiefs and clans. At its most basic level, therefore, it might be more appropriate to talk about the religions of the Hopi than the religion of the Hopi; each clan had its specific area of religious responsibility and so its particular religious truth and action to teach. One might say that everybody got the chance to "do their thing" during the Hopi liturgical year. All of the liturgies, or ritual works, aimed at the production of rain, as we have mentioned, for fertility and growth. All of the liturgies utilized as well similar ritual techniques: the offering of prayer sticks called *pahos*, the building of an altar of sacred objects, the sprinkling of corn as medicine to lead to the transformations of nature which the people desired, the recitation of the Emergence myth, the verbal forms of prayer, attention to the four directions, and the use of song and dance. Finally, the rituals usually followed a similar time pattern with eight days of preparation and then eight days of secret rites culminating in a public dance on the ninth day. With a full calendar of annual ceremonies, the Hopi were spending roughly one-third to one-half of the year in ritual concerns. Liturgy was, in short, at the center of their lives.

The major division in the ceremonial year was between the Kachina rituals from December through July and the non-Kachina ones from August through November. In order to understand the significance of the Kachinas during their portion of the ceremonial year, we need to digress here for some discussion of these beings. Actually, Kachinas might refer to three different realities in Hopi society. They were, first of all, spiritual beings. Inner and invisible forms, they gave a spiritual dimension to outer and physical existence. They were not Gods in the Euro-American sense but were honored spirits—of the dead, of minerals, plants, and animals, even of the planets. They were intermediaries from the sacred world who, during the second half of the year, dwelled in the San Francisco peaks on the outer edge of Hopi country (the border, once more) and visited the Hopi villages during the first half when the Kachina rituals were held. Well over 250 in number (some say as many as 600 are known), the Kachinas were never worshiped but rather looked upon as friends and endowed with a variety of human qualities. New ones were continually appearing as old ones were forgotten so that the catalogue of Kachina spirits was fluid and variable. So, too, were their personalities, ranging from benevolent, kindly spirits to others who inspired fear by their whippings in punishment of offenders in Hopi society.

Such physical contact with spiritual beings suggested the second meaning of Kachinas for the Hopi. Kachinas also referred to the male dancers who during the Kachina ceremonies impersonated both male and female Kachinas. Wearing distinctive masks which represented particular Kachinas and conferred sacred power, often inheriting the right to identify with these spirit persons, the dancers ideally danced themselves into an ecstasy in which they lost all sense of personal identity and *became* the Kachinas they impersonated. Kachina dancers, in other words, achieved the transformation which Native Americans experienced all around them, crossing the frontier which divided ordinary reality from the sacred.

In its third and final usage, Kachinas referred to the elaborate and exquisitely carved dolls which the Kachina dancers gave to Hopi children during the ceremonies to teach them about the Kachina beings. Made in traditional and highly stylized patterns from cottonwood root, the Kachina dolls were not exactly toys in the modern American sense, but neither were they sacred objects believed to contain power. Rather, they were perhaps "show" objects which would grace the Hopi home, reminding all and especially the children of the Kachinas the dolls represented. Beings, dancers, and dolls, all the Kachinas pointed to the mysterious and extraordinary reality which lay behind the ordinary world of the Hopi. The grotesqueness of carved masks and dolls suggested a world beyond this one, vibrant as the masks and dolls with color and imbued like the spirits of the San Francisco peaks with a power which was "other."

We return here to a consideration of the ritual calendar of the Hopi, divided as it was into Kachina and non-Kachina ceremonies. By now it should be evident that Kachina ceremonies were those visited by the Kachina beings as they were impersonated by Hopi dancers. The Hopi understood that the dual calendar was necessary because, in the world below this one, life corresponded to arrangements in Hopi society. Thus, whatever rituals occurred during the first part of the year above were replicated during the second half in the world below. The Kachinas had to be elsewhere in the summer and fall: this was why they could not dance in the village plazas with the Hopi.

The Kachina rituals included the Soyal before the winter solstice when the sun ceased its journey southward, the Powamu, or bean dance, in February, and the Niman, or home dance, in July. In the culminating rituals of Soyal, a cornhusk, which symbolized fertility, was brought to every person in the village so that all might breathe upon it, sending thus a message to the spirit beings. After a ceremony in which sexual intercourse was simulated ritually by the male corn collector to encourage a corresponding fertility in nature, seed corn was gathered from the villagers and blessed. Later in a sacred kiva dance, Muyingwa, who embodied vegetation, leaped and danced. Prayer sticks were distributed to every house so that their presence throughout the year would provide a continuing plea to the spirit beings for the fertility the Hopi desired.

In the February Powamu, preparations had included a secret planting of beans in the kivas, where, kept warm and moist, the beans began to grow. Kachinas then appeared to take the bean plants through the village as gifts to the people, promises of the abundance to come. Early in spring came the ceremony to honor the Great Serpent Palulukong who conferred fertility on crops and also on people. In a dramatic sequence, his voice was heard in the midst of the ritual, and within the kiva puppets with huge serpent heads made from corn represented him and knocked over rows of corn plants to represent the future harvest. Niman, at summer solstice, marked the time when the Kachinas left the Hopi villages. By now, the first corn had come, and the Kachinas danced as a group for the Hopi as the people expressed their gratitude.

The disappearance of the Kachinas, of course, did not signal the disappearance of ritual. In August, Flute and Snake-Antelope ceremonies were held in alternate years with the hope that they would bring some final rain, supplying new dirt for the Hopi to plant their corn a second time. Executed like all the Hopi rites by the clan or clans that had given their liturgy to the pueblo, the Flute ceremony featured strange and haunting music, elaborate symbolic adornment to represent the Hopi universe, and a procession to the sacred Flute Spring to procure water to be offered in prayers for rain. Meanwhile, the Snake and Antelope societies performed a ritual dance with snakes and then released the snakes into the desert to carry the Hopi prayers for rain. The Hopi were bringing back the Snake people, once driven in anger from one of their villages: as in the Flute ceremony, they were seeking a reconciliation with nature so that nature, restored to harmony, would give nourishment and life.

Later, in September and October, three ceremonies were performed by the women's societies. Since women were seen as passive beings who received the male seed and carried it to term, their prominence in ceremonies at this time was especially important. They should be open and ready to receive the seed so that human society would grow and blossom. So, too, the earth should begin to be ready, for soon it would be planting time again when, as the great womb of nature, the earth would nourish the beginnings of life.

Finally, in November, came the Wuwuchim, the last of the non-Kachina ceremonies but actually the first liturgy among the three major winter ceremonies. Wuwuchim was the great initiation ritual of the Hopi when the *sipapu* was kept open so that the spirits of the dead could take part. Its symbolism of death and rebirth was everywhere apparent with the presence of a new fire, the closing of roads to the four directions (signifying the death which must precede rebirth), a night of ritual washing of hair, and the recitation of the Hopi myth of Emergence. The candidates for initiation, young Hopi males ready to become "men," remained in the kiva enveloped in their blankets, as they heard the sacred story of origins and experienced in themselves, it was hoped, the mysteries of spiritual death and rebirth. Harmony with nature meant that just as the cycle of the seasons brought death and rebirth to the natural world, so, too, the Hopi should conform their lives to the seasonal rhythms by undergoing an inner form of dying and being reborn.

It should be clear that with their attention to the planting cycle, their masked Kachinas, and the content of their religious concerns, the Hopi had a religion which was significantly different from that of the Oglala. This was the case not only for the Hopi but also for the numerous other Indian societies that flourished in what is now the United States. In many instances, it was true, people who were more closely related in culture had similar religious systems. The point, however, is still that each was a distinct entity, not the same as the others. Each had its sacred stories of origin, its ceremonial cycle, its identity as "the people," cherished by the sacred powers and in turn cherishing them. Each people saw themselves in microcosm as the collected children of nature.

In the case of the Hopi, erosions in the liturgical life of the villages began to occur. At the same time, witchcraft grew with the spread of anxiety. Beliefs in witchcraft and sorcery had, indeed, been of long duration: the myth of the Emergence, in its complete form, had spoken of the presence of sorcery both in the world below and the world above. But as time passed, witches and sorcerers seemed to mutiply everywhere, and fear and dissension struck at the heart of Hopi society. While the Hopi demonstrated into the twentieth century the persistence of their rituals, the strength of their religious bond could dilute, but not destroy, the acids of modernity. Like the religion of the Oglala, the religion of the Hopi had sought to preserve and protect the ordinary even as it conducted them into the mysteries of the extraordinary world. Still, the decline of the Hopi liturgical cycle and the increase of witchcraft beliefs and practices suggested the action of history on Native American religions. With the new resurgence of Native American religious traditions, however, decline is hardly the last word to be spoken.

CHANGE IN NATIVE AMERICAN TRADITIONS

While all we can do is touch upon the subject here, it is important to note this evidence that, for the Hopi and for all Native Americans, religion does not stand still while the world changes around it. Like the Hopi who struggled to maintain their traditional ways, other Native Americans continued, with greater or less success, to hold to their ancient myth-ritual religions. However, some responded in more directly confronting ways to the new cultural forces which they encountered. In general, these responses were threefold. Native Americans, first of all, kept up the practices of their traditional religions but added to them a syncretistic blend of elements derived from Christianity. Secondly, Native Americans expressed their anguish and yet millennial hopes (for the end of this world and the birth of a new one) in the face of the Euro-American advance; they did so by taking up a variety of new religions beginning in the second half of the nineteenth century. Thirdly, Native Americans were converted to various denominational forms of Christianity.

Syncretism (the mixing and harmonizing of elements from different religions) occurred in those regions that had been missionized by Spanish Roman Catholic priests; that is, in the Southwest and California. In the Rio Grande Pueblos of New Mexico, for example, after the initial period of encounter from 1540, there was little or no contact with Catholic priests in the late eighteenth century and through most of the nineteenth. Thus, the Pueblos for a period of about 150 years were free to modify the new rituals which Roman Catholicism had brought so that they might serve Native American ends. The result was liturgical calendars in the various pueblos which for the most part were based on traditional Native American beliefs and practices, but added to them was an amalgam of Catholic ceremonies which seemed to satisfy Pueblo needs. There was little interest in Jesus or the Virgin, in heaven and hell, or in the Christian understanding of God. Yet a saint's day became an occasion for festivity, and Holy Week and Christmas, while not historical commemorations of events in the life of Jesus, were times for prayer. Similarly, All Souls' Day provided an opportunity to honor departed ancestors with gifts.

Perhaps the most prominent example of a new and millennial religion was the ghost dance which swept the Plains in the late nineteenth century. When the old religions seemed to fail as the whites pushed the Indians out of their lands, new religious prophets arose to proclaim rites and ceremonies that would bring the power to end the white ascendancy and restore the Indians to the harmony with the earth and themselves that they remembered. Among these new religious prophets was a Paiute Indian from Nevada named Jack Wilson or Wovoka. He claimed to have died twice and to have seen God. Thereafter, he began to predict that the earth and whites would be destroyed by flood, but the Indians should perform the ceremony of their ancient round dance so that the flood would wash under them and they would survive. Then the earth would spring to life with the abundance of new creation, and in the fresh, green land which succeeded the arid Nevada terrain the Indians would be reunited with their deceased ancestors and dwell together in plenty.

The ghost dance, as it was called, spread rapidly among other Native American peoples as delegations from various tribes came to learn the ceremony. It had perhaps its most tragic repercussions among the Oglala Sioux, who reshaped the dance to their own ritual sense and life needs. They began to wear ghost shirts as they danced—long white garments decorated with red-colored symbols and eagle feathers which they believed were bulletproof. This conviction contributed to the debacle at Wounded Knee as the Oglala, wearing their ghost shirts, thought they could not be harmed by the bullets of the United States Seventh Cavalry. Other new religions among American Indians did not end so badly. For example, the nineteenth-century Seneca religion led by the prophet Handsome Lake (d. 1815) resulted in the enduring organization of *Gaiwiio*, the Old Way of Handsome Lake. In the twentieth century the peyote cult has flourished as the Native American Church.

Denominational Christianity had sprung up in various forms with the first presence of Euro-American Christians. Every European people which settled in the New World had as a conscious objective the conversion of the "heathen" to Christianity. The Spanish and French brought their priests, and the English sent Protestant missionaries. So there were "praying Indians" in colonial New England towns such as Natick, Massachusetts, while later (1769) in California Franciscan missionaries created segregated mission communities of Christian Indians. Throughout the nineteenth century, with the development of the reservation system the knowledge of Christianity was introduced to the Indians. Today it would be difficult to find a reservation without the presence of one or several Christian churches. However, as we have already noted, in recent times the traditional religions have enjoyed a new prestige as vehicles for maintaining Native American identity and encouraging political action. The "Longest Walk" of 1978, for instance, was a political march across the continent to Washington, D.C., to demand Indian rights. Yet leaders of the march spoke of their pilgrimage as a spiritual one which had renewed their religious energies and restored them to contact with their ancient traditions.

IN OVERVIEW

The ancient traditions of Native Americans were diverse, as we have seen, but they held many things in common. Their sense of continuity with the sacred world was expressed in beliefs regarding kinship with nature and in myths that reflected no break between the events of creation and the ordinary history of the people. For American Indians, the outer, material world was holy in itself, and so, too, was the inner world of dreams. Moving between the different worlds meant existence without firm boundaries. Hence, transformations occurred frequently, and holy beings were shapeshifters, able to assume new form or change the world around them. In all of this, living in harmony with nature was the great religious requirement, for the human world should correspond with the model nature provided.

Among the Oglala Sioux of the North American Plains and the Hopi of the Southwest, different versions of Native American religion gave ordinary and extraordinary meaning to existence. Thus, like Indian societies in general, both collapsed ordinary and extraordinary religion into one. At the same time, the Oglala, a hunter-gatherer society, and the Hopi, an agricultural people, are case studies in Native American diversity. Their respective traditions show us how American Indian religion really means American Indian religions. Still further, American Indian religions multiplied with the coming of Europeans. Sometimes there was a syncretism in which elements from European Christianity were grafted onto the Native American growth. At other times, new and millennial religions sprang up, while in still different cases Native Americans became converts to various Christian denominations.

The story of American Indian religions is a microcosm of the religious encounters which would confront each of the immigrant peoples to America. All would come with the ways of their ancestors; all would intend to preserve them. Yet each people was one among many "nations" present in the New World, and the presence of other ways led to changes in earlier religions. Syncretistic religion or new religion or conversion were not confined to Native Americans, but were widespread.

If other tribes and peoples shared the Indian experience, the "tribes" of Israel—the Jews—were a special case in point. Like Native Americans, for centuries they had been sojourners more than settlers, and also like Native Americans, they sought to preserve their historic destiny even as they emulated their Protestant neighbors.

SUGGESTIONS FOR FURTHER READING: AMERICAN INDIAN RELIGIONS

Beck, Peggy V., and Walters, A. L. *The Sacred: Ways of Knowledge, Sources of Life.* Tsaile, AZ: Navajo Community College, 1977.

Brown, Joseph Epes. *The Sacred Pipe.* Baltimore: Penguin Books, 1971.

Deloria, Vine, Jr. *God Is Red.* New York: Grosset & Dunlap, 1973.

Hultkrantz, Åke. *The Religions of the American Indians* (1967). Translated by Monica Setterwall. Berkeley: University of California Press, 1979.

Momaday, N. Scott. *The Way to Rainy Mountain.* New York: Ballantine Books, 1970.

Neihardt, John G. *Black Elk Speaks.* Lincoln: University of Nebraska Press, 1961.

Nequatewa, Edmund. *Truth of a Hopi.* 1936. Reprint. Flagstaff, AZ: Northland Press, 1967.

Powers, William K. *Oglala Religion.* Lincoln: University of Nebraska Press, 1977.

Tedlock, Dennis, and Tedlock, Barbara, eds. *Teachings from the American Earth: Indian Religion and Philosophy.* New York: Liveright, 1975.

Underhill, Ruth M. *Red Man's Religion.* Chicago: University of Chicago Press, 1965.

Voth, H. R. *The Traditions of the Hopi.* 1905. Reprint. Millwood, NY: Kraus Reprint, 1973.

CHAPTER 2

Israel in a Promised Land:
Jewish Religion and Peoplehood

In 1492 when Christopher Columbus touched land in the New World, among his crew were some Marranos, Spanish Jews who in fear of the Inquisition had converted to Christianity but secretly continued to practice Judaism. Their presence on board ship was one of those accidents of history that, in retrospect, seem especially fitting. Ancient Israel had, in its time, begun a religious revolution that became the source not only of later Judaism but of Christianity as well. So it was appropriate that the descendants of ancient Israel should be among the first Europeans to see the Americas.

The late fifteenth century had given some European Jews pressing reasons to venture across the Atlantic. In 1492, the same year that Columbus sailed, they were expelled as a people from Spain, and in 1497 the same fate befell them in Portugal. Thus, Jews sought refuge in whatever lands seemed likely to welcome or, at least, tolerate them. While many fled the Mediterranean basin to Palestine, and notably to Italy and Turkey, others turned to liberal Holland, where they flourished as the largest Spanish-Portuguese Jewish community in exile. After the Dutch won their political independence in the 1590s, they began to establish a far-flung colonial empire. Jews participated in the new Dutch success, and when in 1630 the Dutch moved into eastern Brazil, the Jews, with some Marranos already there, were partly responsible. So began a prospering Jewish settlement in the New World—only to be cut short suddenly in 1654 when the Portuguese reconquered their territory in Brazil. Once again, the Jews fled, some to Dutch colonies in the Caribbean, some back to Amsterdam in Holland, and some to New Amsterdam, a young Dutch colony in North America.

Peter Stuyvesant, the Dutch governor of this colony on the Hudson River, was not pleased. He was overruled, however, by the Dutch of old Amsterdam who, as proprietors of the Dutch West India Company which had Jewish shareholders, urged that the Jews be permitted to stay. Thus, within ten years, Jewish people were not only engaging in trade and commerce but also buying property, bearing arms, and joining the militia in defense of the colony. Yet the Dutch future in New Amsterdam was limited, and in 1664 the colony fell to the British. It had become New York, and a little over a century later it would be one of the thirteen British colonies which formed the fledgling United States. The Jews had become one among the many who would help to shape American religious history.

Moreover, from the beginning of their history in the New World, the Jews had repeated an age-old pattern of wandering. Moving from place to place through European history, there was no land that without reservation they could call home. Indeed, their history of wandering was more ancient still. One of the oldest verses in the Bible reads, "A wandering Aramean was my father" (Deut. 26:5); and although the origins of the Hebrew people are shrouded in mystery, we know that their earliest representatives were nomads. As we will see, this nomadic sense was not only an external condition but also became internalized to shape Jewish religious experience and expression throughout history. Wandering Arameans, like the Native Americans the Jews were often forced to wander by the misfortunes of history. Like the Native Americans, too, they dwelled in small, homogeneous communities in which religion and peoplehood were inextricably blended. Indeed, some Americans told tales of a kinship between Jews and Indians. As early as the seventeenth century, stories circulated in the United States describing Native Americans as remnants of the lost tribes of Israel. Somewhere, a chord had been struck, and Americans in symbolic ways pointed to a likeness between Indian and Jewish peoples.

Yet, as we will notice, there were many ways in which the Jews were unlike Indians and more like other Europeans who immigrated to the New World. The story of their arrival in America is an epic that bears striking resemblances to the history of other ethnic groups, and we turn now to a brief sketch of the Jewish entry into this new promised land, America.

THE JEWISH IMMIGRATIONS

We have seen already that the oldest Jewish immigrants had come from Brazil to New Amsterdam, which became New York. These Jews were Sephardim, and their religious culture and ritual practice followed the Babylonian tradition of Jewish law and liturgy. Evolved in the sixth century A.D. in Persian rabbinic academies, this Babylonian tradition has been consciously so designated to recall the ancient legacy of the Jews. Further, as the Sephardic Jews inherited the tradition, it had been influenced by the period of Muslim domination of Spain. Distinctive in their law and liturgy, the Sephardim also spoke a distinctive Jewish dialect called Ladino, a blend of medieval Spanish with Hebrew, Arabic, and other elements; and their liturgical music was known for its rich, melodious chants.

The Sephardic Jews of New York were at first a very small community. They were mainly tradespeople, lacked a rabbi and synagogue, and frequently intermarried with the local population. By 1692, however, they had established the first synagogue in North America; and although they were never expressly granted the right to worship publicly, they literally took it, and no one in British New York objected. Meanwhile, other Sephardic Jews had settled in Newport, Rhode Island, where they acquired a burial ground in 1677 and less than a century later (1763) built the magnificent Touro synagogue. Gradually, the Sephardim, along with a small number of Northern European Jews who had arrived by this time, established small congregations in eastern seacoast cities from Boston to Charleston, South Carolina.

After 1820 a new and much larger wave of Jewish immigration swept into America. The newcomers were Ashkenazim, Jews of German origin who followed a combined Babylonian and Palestinian tradition in law and ritual practice, using a Northern European rubric in their religious services. When these German Jews came, there were only about 5,000 Jews in the United States out of a total population of some 13 million. Within the next half century though, between 200,000 and 400,000 Jews from Central Europe entered the country, and the sheer size of their presence transformed Jewish life in the New World. Sephardic ascendancy faded, although the Sephardim continued as a kind of Jewish aristocracy throughout the nineteenth century. Meanwhile, the Germans brought with them not only Ashkenazic customs and practices but also a movement toward the reform of Judaism.

In order to understand the budding Reform movement the immigrants brought with them from Germany, we need to understand what happened to European Judaism as a result of the eighteenth-century intellectual movement known as the Enlightenment. With its emphasis on human reason and the law of nature, the Enlightenment had thrived in the heady spirit of liberty, equality, and brotherhood which the revolutions in the United States and France had unleashed. As a result the Jews found that, as the eighteenth century became the nineteenth, various European countries began to invite them out of their ghettoes—the segregated communities in which they had been forced to live. Now, they were told, they could experience the full enjoyment of civil rights. This Emancipation, as it was called, slowly eroded the close-knit Jewish communities of the past, as more and more Jews became middle-class citizens of their respective countries.

In this context, many Jews became more and more concerned about "passing" in Gentile society. They did not wish to attract attention to themselves by strange habits and antiquated customs. Thus, a new emphasis on decorum began to affect the way some Jews conducted their synagogue services. The long, drawn-out chanting, the absence of a sermon, the alien Hebrew language, the prayer shawls that covered members of the congregation, all these seemed old-fashioned and outmoded to a self-conscious and recently emancipated Jewry. This primary emphasis on practice, on what a Jew should *do* to be religious, was in keeping with the oldest traditions of Judaism, as we shall see later in more detail. But proper practice was linked to proper thought. The Jewish Reform movement of Germany began to question the authority of the rabbinic tradition as established in the Talmud, the huge compilation which embraces elaboration or amplification of Jewish law. Reform Jews also repudiated the ancient expectation of a personal Messiah who would lead the Jews back to Palestine, hoping instead for the messianic age, an era of justice, compassion, and peace for the world. Jewish people had no country, they declared, except the land in which they were born, bred, and exercised rights as citizens.

In the United States, the Reform movement grew among the German immigrants, fueled by their desire to "pass" in the adopted land. With the promise of a civic and social status more secure than their position in Germany ever had been, the Jews strived to blend unobtrusively with their Protestant and American neighbors. In the twin lights of modernity and the American flag, much that had seemed acceptable in the old country came under new scrutiny—and was changed. When Isaac M. Wise (1819–1900) arrived in 1846, he quickly became the leader of the Reform party, and by midcentury, Reform had become the most prominent Jewish movement in the national life.

The majority of the new immigrants were modest peddlers and shopkeepers who engaged in retail trade. They spoke their own dialect called Judaeo-German; and in spite of the presence among them of some rabbis attracted to America from Europe, they produced no learned class. Instead of restricting themselves to the eastern seacoast as the earliest immigrants had done, these Ashkenazim spread out across the country, so that soon cities like Cincinnati and San Francisco could boast a flourishing Jewish community. Despite their liberalism, most Reform rabbis strongly disapproved when immigrants intermarried with other Americans and lost their ties to the Jewish community. In the dominant spirit of the Reform movement, however, most were eager to embrace American culture.

The German immigration was outnumbered, however, by a third and tidal wave of Jewish immigration, more than 1.7 million strong. The newcomers arrived, beginning in about 1880 and continuing until 1914, when the outbreak of the First World War and, a decade later, the enactment into law of immigration quotas (the National Origins Act) effectively ended massive Jewish immigration. This third influx of Jewish people was far different in character from the other two. These Jews were Eastern Europeans, from countries like Russia, Rumania, Poland, and Austria. Here they had endured hardship and persecution, living in the *shtetls*, towns and communities within a designated area where Jews were permitted to dwell. No tempting bait of suffrage and civil rights had been held out to these folk, and their mental world, formed through years of alienation, did not include the desire of their German and Sephardic cousins to mingle freely with Protestants and mainstream Americans. They came to the New World in order to be free to be themselves, and in the beginning they did not think that being themselves should mean becoming like other Americans. They were poor and mostly illiterate in English, and they settled in huge numbers in major cities such as New York and Chicago, becoming part of a vast army of workers in factories or struggling along as artisans and small shopkeepers. It was these people who were to form the backbone of the deliberate and self-conscious Orthodox Judaism which in America became the strictest Jewish "denomination."

Clearly, the new immigrants were an embarrassment to the thriving American Jewish community already in the United States. Beyond that, the transition from the traditional Judaism of the *shtetl* to the suave, Americanized version promoted by Reform-minded rabbis seemed impossible to imagine, let alone perform. Still, despite the poverty and social awkwardness of the immigrants, the bond of Jewishness meant that the older American Jewish community could not look away. There was a warmth and inner meaning to the old ways that the immigrants brought, and the attraction of tradition, the responsibility of relationship, and among some, a growing disenchantment with Reform, encouraged the growth of yet a third form of Judaism. Out of this mix Conservative Judaism was born.

The story after the Eastern European influx is one of growth and material prosperity, of education and involvement in the social and political life of America. It is also a story of a continuing search for the meaning of Jewishness in the American context, and it is one to which we will return later. For now, however, we need to take up the question of what Jewishness and Judaism mean in themselves. Our question is in some sense artificial, for as wanderers, Jews had dwelled in many lands and had absorbed into their traditions many foreign and Gentile customs. Still, we need to take a general look at the structure of Jewish experience and expression before we relate it further to the sojourn in an American Zion.

JEWISHNESS AND PEOPLEHOOD

Being Jewish had always meant being a people as well as serving God. The two notions were really one notion in the minds of the Jews of history, and that understanding was articulated from biblical times in ancient Israel's confidence that God had bound himself to the nation in a covenant. In this irrevocable agreement, he had promised to be the God of Israel even as Israel pledged to be his people, so that religious blessings and benefits came to the community as a particular historical group. Thus, the origins of Jewry were tied to an ethnic and religious identity that were fused, and to state the matter in the terms of the text, ordinary and extraordinary coalesced in traditional Jewish experience. It was only post-Enlightenment modernity that tried to bring about a separation, dividing Jewishness, an ethnic and cultural reality, from Judaism, a religion. As children of that Enlightenment, let us pursue the distinction briefly.

Jews were a people, first of all, because they viewed themselves as the inheritors of a common history. Their oldest remembrances, recorded in the Hebrew Bible, told of their descent from Abraham, their sojourn in Egypt and exodus under the leadership of Moses and the power of God, their acceptance of the gift of the Law at Sinai, and their eventual entry into Canaan, the land God had promised them. Other recollections dwelled on their exile in Babylon and their return to Jerusalem where they raised up the Temple that had been destroyed by foreign troops. Still later, the rabbinic tradition would record the destruction of the Temple for a second time in A.D. 70. With the devastation of the homeland, the folk memory would continue to recall the stories of the faithful who remained in Palestine and of the remnants who scattered throughout the Roman Empire, making their way to parts of Europe, the Middle East, and Northern Africa.

Jews were a people, secondly, because their common history had been one of mutual suffering. From earliest times, because their land lay on the great routes that joined the Tigris-Euphrates valley of Mesopotamia to the valley of the Nile in Egypt, the ancestors of the Jews had borne years of war and insecurity. Later, when they no longer had a land to call their own, they still perpetuated the memory of Israel. Their strict monotheism and refusal to give up their distinctive customs and practices in the host countries where they settled led to persecution. As Christianity broke away from Judaism, its early scriptures reflected its struggle to be free of the synagogue, and anti-Semitism was spread by accusations that the Jews had killed Jesus. In this climate, the history of medieval Jewry was one of segregation, exclusion, and sporadic attempts at extinction. Pogroms tried to wipe out Jewish communities at intermittent intervals; and ultimately, as we have already seen in Spain and Portugal, a number of governments ordered mass expulsions of the Jews.

Moreover, the Enlightenment was hardly an unalloyed blessing. Jews found their old and segregated communities no longer legally and socially recognized. Instead, they possessed a set of civil rights which in most cases, they discovered, did not confer social equality and even, practically speaking, legal equity. The ultimate horror occurred in "enlightened" Germany under Adolf Hitler (1889–1945): it is the event we call the Holocaust, and it meant the destruction of 6 million Jewish people for no other reason than the fact that they were Jewish.

Jews were a people, finally, because their history and their suffering were indissolubly bound to their sense of having been chosen by God for special tasks. From the beginning, when they had expressed this relationship with God in terms of a covenant, they had seen themselves as different. The covenant marked them off from other nations: it drew boundaries that identified a people united in their commitment to the Law of God. At the same time, it separated them from the rest of the world. Moreover, Israel's God was not like other Gods. He demanded an exclusive allegiance and, by the time of the classical prophets in the eighth century B.C., he proclaimed himself the only God for all the nations. When Christianity and later Islam drew from Jewish roots the heritage of monotheism, the Jewish sense of chosenness could only be reinforced. Jews were the people to whom God had disclosed his true nature: he had told them his name, and they would never be the same because of that. In one sense, Jewish suffering came because, as the prophets had warned, the Jews had transgressed the Law, failing to fulfill the special tasks God required of them. Yet in a second sense, why Jews should suffer in being the keepers of the Law and revelation of God was a divine mystery. Their faithfulness came in enduring, in respecting the mighty secrets of God and proving themselves loyal whatever befell.

Hence, Jewishness was born in the dynamic tension among a common history, mutual suffering, and a sense of being chosen. Did the being chosen lead necessarily to the history of suffering? Did the suffering bring about the idea of being chosen as a way to give meaning to the inexplicable? And did the sense of chosenness itself excite the enmity of others so that persecution grew apace? Had the Jews, in choosing to maintain their identity as a separate people, chosen as well their history as an oppressed people? We will never know the answers to these questions because they are circular in nature. But they do point up sharply the relationship between Jewishness and questions of boundary.

Eternally "other," Jews have always been people on the boundary, living their lives in two worlds, with a foot, so to speak, in each. As a marginal people, the Jews have experienced the strain of separateness, but they have also experienced its stimulation. Throughout history, they have been remarkable for their creativity, in our own times advancing knowledge in the sciences and sensitivity in the arts. Likewise, throughout history they have been in a near-ideal position to render criticism to a host culture and society. In every land where they settled, Jews knew enough to understand, but they also preserved a set of values that prevented them from being blinded by cultural routine. They could penetrate the level of cultural assumptions to find new models for understanding or acting, and the results of this incisive blend of creativity and criticism have given our world such intellectual giants as Sigmund Freud, Karl Marx, and Albert Einstein.

From a religious point of view, Jewish existence on the boundary leads us back to the blend of ordinary and extraordinary that characterizes Judaism. If the two kinds of religious experience were fused for the Jews, it was because their history had taught them the advantages of living at the place where two realities met and mingled. We turn now to a closer scrutiny of what Judaism, the revealed religion, traditionally represented.

JUDAISM AND REVEALED RELIGION

In our discussion of Native American traditions, we saw that Indians in their emphasis on harmony with nature lived out the ancient world view of correspondence. For Indian societies, the human community was a microcosm, a small-scale reflection of the macrocosm of nature all around. Religion meant adjusting any disruptions of the cosmic rhythms in the human sphere, restoring wholeness through the power of myth and ritual. The earliest recollections of the Jewish people, present in the Hebrew Bible, suggest that they viewed the world in similar terms, seeing, for example, a close relationship between the fertility of land and crops and the reproductive fruitfulness of women and men. But something happened to the religious consciousness of Israel, and that something was tied up with the cultural revolution that gave us the Judaeo-Christian tradition. Gradually, Israel shifted its expression of the reality of the macrocosm by replacing metaphors of space with metaphors of time. In other words, instead of continuing to speak of the space of nature, people began to dwell on the time of history.

This shift was reflected in the transformation of the religious festivals that the Jews celebrated. Although in their earliest forms the festivals were probably seasonal rites following the agricultural cycle of planting and harvest, they came to be historicized. As an example, Passover seemed originally a ritual event to mark the release of the earth from the grip of winter, the sowing of seed, and the renewal of clan and kinship ties. But as time passed, new interpretations were added, and the Jews came to see Passover as a historical feast to relive the exodus from Egypt and the birth of the Jewish nation: the Jews had passed over from slavery to freedom, even as the Angel of Death had slain the Egyptians but passed over the firstborn among the infant sons of Israel. So this feast—and the other feasts that followed a similar pattern—made a historical occurrence the plan and model for Jewish existence. The macrocosm lay no longer in cosmic space but in time.

Along with this shift from space to time came a sense of a greater separation between the divine and the human than the old model of correspondence had expressed. Briefly, Israel came to see that God had *caused* the world—but not out of his own "body." There was a gap between the sacred and the profane worlds, a gap reflected in the story in Genesis of the fall of Adam and Eve from paradise. Therefore, with this world view of causality, it was necessary that things be done either by God or the Jewish people to insure that, though separate and distinguishable from God, the world would still experience his power. Nature had been demoted, so to speak, and instead of continuing to identify with it, the Jews saw themselves as creatures made in the image and likeness of God and, indeed, given by God the right and the duty of controlling and subduing nature.

In its full expression, this world view differed radically from the older notion of correspondence, present as well in Native American societies. When Christianity, the child of later Judaism, broke away from its parent stock, it took with it the heritage of causality, and so we have in rough outline the patterns that would lead to cultural collision between Indians and Europeans in the New World. If Jews were in some ways like Indians, they were also in very significant respects different from them.

To return to the Jewish religious understanding, however, we need to see that for the Jews the community of Israel—without God—would be in the same plight as nature. Thus, steps had to be taken either by God or by the people to establish some relationship, to turn the gap between divine and human into a bridge between them. God had done just this in his revelation, and he had bound Israel to himself with the covenant. The Jews could respond to God and tighten the bond by their faithful observance of the Law. In this simple and incisive appreciation of the nature of things, Judaism, the religion, found its identity.

The sense of a relationship with God expressed in the covenant also started Israel on a path that led to the pure monotheism of the eighth-century prophets. From the time of the Abraham tradition in the third millennium, the ancestors of the Jewish people had begun to express their devotion to a single clan or tribal deity. In the late second millennium, the Moses tradition only underlined how exclusive should be Israel's adherence to one God. But the religion of Moses was henotheism more than monotheism, for while it emphasized worship of one God it still understood that other nations worshiped different deities. It was only when the prophets began to interpret the history of Israel in light of the covenant that they came to see the God of Israel as the universal God of all the nations, a realization that contained the essence of monotheism. Briefly, when the armies of foreign nations marched against Israel, the prophets saw these events as God's punishment for his people's unfaithfulness to the covenant. This meant that nations such as Persia and Assyria were controlled by the divine hand and belonged, in effect, to the same God as the God of Israel. It was only a short leap to the understanding that no other God existed and the God of Israel was the God of all.

Similarly, the sense of a relationship with God expressed in the covenant led Israel to the discovery of history that lay behind the world view of causality. By pledging his commitment to the Jewish people, God had entered history, establishing a pattern in which, at each new crisis, he would intervene in human affairs. And if the Almighty troubled himself with the course of human events, then acting and doing must be important. The God who acted led in a logical trajectory to a people who acted. As the notion of the covenant had already implied, *how* people acted became a significant question.

It was in this context that the Jewish people developed their great traditions which were gathered in the Law. Implicit in God's first covenant with Abraham, the Law became explicit in the first five books of the Hebrew Bible, called the Torah. Here, the rules for living, prescriptions for both ceremonial and moral righteousness, were recorded for future generations. To be a Jew, then as now, meant to accept the burden of the Law. Indeed, it was not what people *believed* that made them Jewish, but what they *did*, for the Jews had discovered that actions spoke louder than words.

To sum up, Judaism as a religion grew out of the covenant between God and Israel. The covenant healed the widening rift between the divine and the human that had been expressed in the world view of causality. It disclosed for Israel the significance of time as a new kind of "space" in which God acted. Because God acted, it led to the realization that action and human history were important, and hence it led to the development both of a Law to guide action and of a prophetic tradition to recall people to the pure practice of the demands of God's Law.

JEWISH ORTHODOXY AND THE CONSECRATION OF TIME

With this short survey of Jewishness and Judaism as background, let us return to our discussion of the Jewish immigrants who entered the United States. Like other Europeans among the many, they shared basic insights and beliefs which characterized the Judaeo-Christian tradition. But Jewish immigrants differed from many of their fellow Europeans or Euro-Americans in the emphasis they placed on the doing of the Torah. While Christians in America tended to be activists, as we shall see in Part Two, their theological tradition still stressed the importance of right or correct belief. On the other hand, in Judaism, there was no theological tradition in the Christian sense but rather a rabbinic tradition of interpretation of the Torah. Thus, Judaism in America meant a series of concrete acts which led to the consecration of time.

For the early immigrants who followed the uncontested Orthodoxy of the past—and later for observant Reform and Conservative Jews as well—the consecration of time meant two kinds of things. First of all, it meant ritual action in a regular communal cycle of feasts and historical commemorations and in an individual life cycle marked for each person by significant times of passage from one stage of maturation to the next. The consecration of time meant, secondly and equally, consistent dedication in moral action. For later immigrants, as we have already seen to some extent, the rise of the three great "denominations" of Judaism was largely the result of arguments in the American Jewish community about *how* time should be consecrated and what role traditional ritual should play.

The Ceremonial Cycle

Perhaps the single, most compelling symbol of the Jewish consecration of time among the early immigrants was the Sabbath. The creation myth of the biblical book of Genesis had led, step by step, to its climactic account of how on the seventh day God rested (Gen. 2:2), thus establishing the seventh-day Sabbath as a holy day. Yet the holiness of the Sabbath did not require a temple or church to give it honor. Since the sixth century B.C., when the Jews had been exiled in Babylon, they had learned to live without the animal sacrifices of the Temple in Jerusalem. Sometime in that era, the beginnings of the later synagogue had developed. A special place in which the Torah could be read and studied, the synagogue had its chief presider in a religious teacher and leader called a rabbi. But even though the scrolls of the Torah were kept in an honored place in the synagogue, the heart of Judaism lay in the home. Perhaps it took the earliest Jews nearly forty years to establish their first synagogue in North America because, as long as they had their homes and families, they had the essentials of Judaism in their midst.

As a high point of the traditional Sabbath was—and is—a ritual meal eaten after sundown on Friday evening to inaugurate the feast. Previously, the house had been cleaned, a white cloth laid on the table, and the best dishes and utensils spread. The choicest foods were prepared and twisted loaves of Sabbath bread (called *hallah*) placed under an embroidered napkin. The mistress of the house then lit the Sabbath candles (at least two) and spoke the blessing: "Blessed art Thou, O Lord our God, King of the Universe, Who hast hallowed us by Thy commandments and commanded us to kindle the Sabbath lamp." At the beginning of the meal, the head of the household (the father) read or chanted a scriptural text, pronounced the *Kiddush*, or sanctification, and blessing the bread, began to break it and distribute it to members of his family. The dinner that followed was far from solemn, for the festival was one which should lighten human hearts and bring them joy.

At sundown on Saturday evening, the Sabbath closed with another home-centered ritual to mark the end of its light. In the *havdalah*, or separating, the head of the household took a special candle made of two plaited pieces of wax and, reciting a prayer to thank God for the separation of the sacred from the profane which the Sabbath symbolized, extinguished it in a full glass of wine. In between, the Sabbath was traditionally honored by a strict separation from work and everyday activity. No travel was allowed, no business could be transacted, no money exchanged, writing accomplished, or other chores performed. At the same time, the Sabbath called its people to leisure and recreation through visiting family and friends, going on strolls, and the like. But above all, it called them to mental and spiritual re-creation through the reading and study of Torah. This is why on Saturday morning it became customary to hold a synagogue service.

With its symbolism of separation to mark the Sabbath off from the rest of time, it is clear that as consecrated time the Sabbath was the time of extraordinary religion. Its roots lay in the revelation of the transcendent God of Israel who had created human beings out of nothing. As a memorial to the God who acted in history, it brought transcendence into time, establishing there a religious monument which was to time what a cathedral was to space. And yet, because in the Jewish scheme of things religion and peoplehood were one, the Sabbath was extraordinary time made ordinary. In fact, in the Sabbath meal with its blend of ritual formality and unstudied family conversation, we can see, encapsulated, the Jewish fusion of ordinary and extraordinary religion. The people of God were still *people*, and because it was their religion that had made them a people, because it was their God who had made a covenant with them, transcendent reality had entered the ordinary world.

If the Sabbath made time holy at weekly intervals, it was joined by a cycle of seasonal feasts that made time holy on an annual basis. Judaism observed these feasts according to a lunar calendar of 353 or 354 days, with an extra month added every fourth year to bring the reckoning into line with the solar calendar that determined planting and harvest seasons. Three major observances, originally attached to the agricultural cycle, provided the foundation for the yearly liturgy. These were Passover (*Pesach*), at the beginning of the planting season, which had been historicized to recall the exodus from Egypt; Weeks (also called *Shavuot* or Pentecost), at the end of the barley harvest, which commemorated the giving of the Law (Torah) to Moses on Mount Sinai; and Booths (also called *Sukkot* or Tabernacles), at the end of all agricultural work for the year and just before the beginning of winter rains, which commemorated the wandering of the Jews in the desert before they entered Canaan.

Both agriculture and history shared a chronology in which Passover came first, logically followed by Weeks and then Booths. From the religious point of view, however, it was really the autumn season of Booths that marked the beginning of the Jewish year. Booths looked toward the future, for the wilderness wandering of the Jews had been the final preliminary to their entry into the promised land. Thus, the feast was prospective: it told of the inauguration of new things, and it was fitting that *Rosh Hashanah*, the Jewish New Year, should occur just before the feast of Booths. Indeed, so named because the Jews had constructed and lived temporarily in huts, or booths, to remind them of their desert sojourn, Booths was the third stage in a long and solemn festival season. The New Year, *Rosh Hashanah*, came first. Ten days later, it was followed by the Day of Atonement, *Yom Kippur*, in which Jews fasted, did penance, and confessed their sinfulness before God. Finally, four days later came the week-long Booths with its theme of new hope and confidence for the future.

Perhaps the most solemn moments of the Jewish liturgical year occurred on the Days of Awe, *Rosh Hashanah* and *Yom Kippur*, when the shofar, a special trumpet made of a ram's horn, was blown. Both the New Year and the Day of Atonement were days of religious remembrance in which both God and humans recollected their past and gathered the fruits of such remembrance to shape the future. God recalled the deeds of his people, while the people remembered their creation and covenant with God, their chosenness as his Israel, their successes and failures in faithfulness. The shofar blew to remind Israel of its calling, like a thread piercing time to bind year after year into the bundle of the covenant. Hence, while the Jews did not kneel at any other time of year, on *Rosh Hashanah* and *Yom Kippur* a significant part of the synagogue services was the ritual prostration, usually performed by the rabbi and the cantor in the name of the congregation, to acknowledge God's lordship over the earth as creator.

Finally, like all the solemnities of the Jewish year, the New Year and the Day of Atonement were not simply remembrances in the ordinary way in which we use that term. They were recollections which made the past present again. That is, they destroyed the work of time to bring pious Jews in touch with the religious acts they recalled. They re-created past time so that its power could be tapped for life in the present and the future. Again, the blast of the shofar brought this reality home. With its extraordinary sound, unheard at any other time of year, it broke through profane time to bring Jews into the presence of sacred and timeless truth.

Similarly, it was significant that at the other "beginning" of Jewish festivals, at the springtime Passover, the solemn ritual meal which a Jewish family shared carried the same message. The meal, called a *seder*, was a remembrance of the meal the ancestors had eaten on the night they fled from Egypt. In this historicized version of the ancient Palestinian harvest festival, the Jews ate unleavened bread (*matzah*) because they had no time to wait for the bread to rise, bitter herbs to remind them of the bitterness of their journey, and a mix of chopped nuts, apples, raisins, and cinnamon, like the mortar they had placed between bricks when they were slaves in Egypt. Parsley dipped in salted water, a roasted egg, the shank bone of a lamb, and four ceremonial cups of wine, all had symbolic meaning, and all were meant to re-create, as vividly as possible, the night of the exodus event. At the heart of the ritual was a recitation of the myth, or sacred story, of the flight from Egypt. To introduce the telling, the youngest boy in the family asked a question which, like the horn of the shofar, cut through time to make the past present again. "Why *is* this night different from all other nights?" the boy queried. His father answered in kind: this *is* the night we fled the Egyptians—and went on to tell the sacred tale. Time and its work had been undone; the family and its guests had been transported to the moment of the exodus; they could recapture its power anew as they continued their ordinary lives.

Beyond these celebrations we have discussed, there were a number of other feasts and fasts linking the parts of the year to one another, making the entire year holy, and, as we have said, rendering the extraordinary an ordinary event. Most important among these minor commemorations were *Purim* and *Hanukkah*. *Purim* was based on an account contained in the biblical book of Esther. Read formally from a scroll, or *megillah*, on the evening and the morning of this winter feast, the story told how Esther and Mordecai triumphed over Haman of Persia on the very day on which he planned to exterminate the Jews. Once again, it brought sacred and extraordinary events into everyday reality by making *Purim* a time of carnival. Among Ashkenazic Jews in Europe, children had dressed in masquerade costumes, often representing figures from Jewish history, and had gone door to door begging. The custom came to the New World with the immigrants, and *Purim* carnivals continued to be popular, especially among the young.

Hanukkah, called the Feast of Lights or Dedication, was actually not biblical. It still became one of the most popular of Jewish festivals. Occurring at the time of winter solstice, it recalled not the natural return of the sun in lengthened daylight hours but instead the rekindling of the great candelabrum in the Temple of Jerusalem by Judas Maccabeus and his followers (165 B.C.). The Syrian-Greek monarch, Antiochus IV, who held Jerusalem under his sway, had tried to make the Temple into a shrine to the Greek deity Zeus. Judas with his brothers and other followers stormed the hill of the Temple, drove out the Greek troops, purified the sanctuary of Greek pollution, and restored the traditional services. The eight-day festival that according to tradition the Maccabees then inaugurated was perpetuated in Jewish homes by the lighting each evening for eight days of the *menorah,* or candelabrum. On the first evening, only one candle was lit, on the second, two, on the third, three, continuing until the eighth night when all of the candles had been kindled. It was a festival of remembrance, and it celebrated the Jewish right to be different. The deed of the Maccabees had proclaimed that because the Jews lived in the middle of a Greek culture, they did not also have to be Greek. They could keep their religion and peoplehood and live these out in freedom.

Just as the Jewish year had its cycle, so, too, did the life of an individual, and the key events in a Jew's lifetime were marked by ritual and solemnity. From the first, a Jew should be a son or daughter of the Law, and so it had been a custom to carry the scroll of the Torah to the very door of the lying-in chamber where mother and infant were resting. If the child were a boy, he was circumcised on the eighth day, so that, now formally admitted to the community of kinship, he would bear in his flesh a sign of the covenant between God and Israel. At thirteen, the same boy would become Bar Mitzvah, a "son of the commandment." In effect, he had become an adult from the religious point of view and demonstrated his maturity by reading from the scroll of the Torah in the synagogue. In America, among many Conservative and Reform congregations, his sister might become Bat Mitzvah, a "daughter of the commandment," as well.

At marriage, ritual impressed both bride and groom with the importance of the human duty they were to undertake. As they stood together under the bridal canopy of white silk or satin, the marriage contract was read to them, the Seven Blessings were pronounced, the pair drank from the cup of betrothal, and then the glass was smashed to recall the destruction of the ancient Temple. Meanwhile, death, with its austere and simple rituals, returned Jews to the earth from which they had come. Family and community would not forget, however. After the prescribed mourning period, there would be yearly commemorations of the dead when, on the anniversary of passing, the *kaddish,* or prayer of praise, would be recited by the surviving kin. In addition to these individual services, there would be an annual collective remembrance, the *Yizkor* service. Especially popular in the United States, the *"Yizkor* days" recalled for Eastern European Jews not only their dead but also their traditional ways, often for the most part laid aside in the rush of business and, as we shall see, in the process of becoming American.

Thus, ritual interpreted the meaning of natural growth and change at the highpoints in the life cycle of each individual Jew. But ritual also impressed the devout with the meaning of their Jewishness in everyday life. The dietary laws prescribed just what foods should be eaten and how they should be consumed. Animals were divided into the clean and unclean, and only those which had a cloven hoof and chewed the cud could be consumed. Most specifically, in terms of American dietary habits, pork was forbidden. In the case of seafood, any aquatic creatures had to possess fins and scales, hence eliminating shellfish from Jewish cuisine. Finally, meat and milk dishes could not be mixed together, and at least several hours must expire before an observant Jew could consume milk if that person had already eaten meat.

The origins of these practices are lost in history, and speculation on the development of these customs has produced a host of intriguing explanations. In the post-Enlightenment American context, however, they quickly became a badge of Jewishness, separating out this one group among the many and affirming their distinctiveness for themselves and for others. Coming from a biblical past in which God had in an extraordinary manner acted in history, the dietary laws recalled in everyday, ordinary time the extraordinary mission of Israel. They were one more example of how in the Jewish understanding, just as ethnicity and religion went together, so, too, did life within the boundaries of this world and life that transcended them.

The Moral Law

We have seen that the consecration of time meant fulfillment of the ceremonial requirements of the Torah. But also and equally, it meant to live the life of moral righteousness which the Law demanded. There were two tablets to the Law that God had given to Moses on Sinai. The second, and longer, promulgated the ethic by which Jews should live in their *human* relationships. If God was the God of justice and mercy, his people should emulate him in their regard for one another. The myriad ceremonial prescriptions of the Law were to bring home the meaning of the *shema* (Deut. 6:4-9, Deut. 11:13-21, and Num. 15:37-41), the solemn summary of the covenant—of the unity of God and the duty of loving and serving him—recited morning and evening by the pious Jew. Love for the creator led inevitably to love for the fellow creature, and Judaism as a religion evidenced collective concern for the widow, the orphan, and all those in need.

Still more, the commandments of the Law went beyond external behavior to the inner spirit that motivated it. A person could sin, even without acting, if he or she looked with envy on the life of another. Through the prophet Ezekiel, God had promised the Jews to change their hearts of stone for hearts of flesh (Ezek. 11:20), and through Jeremiah, he had announced that he would write his Law deep within the hearts of his people (Jer. 31:33). Thus, the covenant began and ended *within*, and right behavior without a right heart was not sufficient. Reversing the equation, a right heart *always* led out into the world where deeds were done. With their stern preaching of social justice and compassion toward all, the message of the prophets refined the meaning of the covenant and announced a universal ethical message that could apply to every people.

The Moral Law in America

As Jews responded to their new situation in America, it was the ethical prescriptions of the Law that assumed added importance. For the midnineteenth-century Reformers, the ethical teachings of the prophets became more and more central. They held that the husk of outmoded ritual practices should fall away to reveal the true essence of Judaism. Thus, Isaac M. Wise thought that Jewish chosenness meant a divine mission to spread throughout the world the prophetic call for justice and mercy. Indeed, he thought, there was a special congruity between Judaism and America, for with its ideal of democracy, the United States offered the perfect stage for the ethical action and idealism the ancient Jewish prophets had demanded.

Later, Kaufmann Kohler (1843–1926), his successor as president of Cincinnati's Hebrew Union College, took Wise's ideas to still more radical conclusions. Divine revelation, he argued, occurred in the natural historical process. Hence, the revelation of Judaism was natural and historical. Its essence lay in its ethics, and its true aim was to bring in the messianic age by the salvation of human beings in history. In 1885 a conference of Reform rabbis called by Kohler met in Pittsburgh to adopt the widely influential Pittsburgh Platform. This statement of Reform principles, while rejecting the vast body of Mosaic and rabbinic law, held to the moral law taught in the Torah and expressed a commitment on that basis to the struggle for equality between rich and poor. The mission of Israel, as Kohler and other Reformers saw it, was the moral redemption of society.

In their transformation of the meaning of Judaism in America, the Reformers received assistance from an unexpected source. This assistance was indirect and unintentional, but it added to the prophetic emphasis of Reform Judaism, showing that the true essence of Judaism was the quest for righteousness in social relationships. The assistance came from one segment of the Eastern European immigration after the 1880s. While many of these Jews retained as nearly as they could their Orthodox customs and practices, others substituted social radicalism for Jewish ceremonialism. This had happened for some, in the old countries, when they had responded to anti-Semitic harassment by abandoning the religion that made them objectionable. In America, however, there was a new motive for rejecting Orthodoxy. It betokened foreignness, and hence, especially the second generation found ways to reject it. Jewish socialism led many to the Socialist party and to the formation of socialist labor unions and newspapers. Meanwhile, as Jews became more affluent, they became leaders in social welfare programs. Doing the Law had been secularized, but the old zeal for righteousness and justice remained.

We can see in Jewish socialism and philanthropy the influence of American experience on traditional Jewish life. It is time now to pursue the American saga of Israel with greater insistence. It was true that acculturation had been a fact of all Jewish history since the Jews had scattered throughout the lands of Europe, North Africa, and the Middle East. Moreover, Jewish ritual had continually incorporated pagan and Christian elements, transforming them to Jewish purposes. If this had been true in the past, it seemed even more the case in America. Briefly, the story of the American Israel is a story of increasing separation between Jewishness, the culture, and Judaism, the religion. It is the story of the rise of three great denominations—Reform, Conservatism, and Orthodoxy—and a number of related religious movements.

AMERICAN JEWISH DENOMINATIONALISM

Our discussion has already touched at major points on Reform Judaism. What we have not noticed thus far, however, is that the Reform movement was in the forefront of the effort to turn away from the old model of religioethnic unity to the new one of Judaism as a religion. The Pittsburgh Platform had declared that its subscribers were no longer a nation but instead a religious community. The Reformers proceeded to implement their religious community with zeal. By 1889 they had organized in the Central Conference of American Rabbis, and by 1894 they published the *Union Prayer Book* as a new order of synagogue service. Under the new liturgy, the synagogue came more and more to resemble a Protestant church of the period. The service was almost entirely in English and conducted mostly by the rabbi, in contrast to the older Jewish pattern of full congregational participation. Prayer shawls disappeared, as did segregated seating for women, while at the same time organs and mixed choirs of men and women were initiated. So far did Reform Jews go in some congregations that they adopted a Sunday Sabbath, more in keeping with the practices of their Christian neighbors. At the same time, the annual liturgical cycle was less faithfully kept and other traditional rituals laid aside.

Still, even the Reform movement at some level cherished the ideal of Israel as a people. Amid this new religion of rationalism and progress, there was a loyalty to the age-old custom of circumcision and the ban on intermarriage with non-Jews, indicating the hidden presence among these "liberated" Jews of a reverence and regard for Israel's religioethnic identity. However, it was the Conservative movement that self-consciously came forward to preserve the Jewish sense of peoplehood—even, it seemed for some, at the expense of religion. In order to understand Conservatism, we must return to the first rumblings of dismay at the path Reform Judaism was charting. Throughout the midyears of the nineteenth century, there had been moderates who, while they recognized the need to blend American with Jewish elements, nevertheless saw in tradition a source of nourishment and life. Reform leaders were a vocal minority, but they hardly represented all of the Jewish presence in America. The increasing discontent with their leadership came to a head in 1883, when the first graduating class from Hebrew Union College received rabbinical ordination. At the festive dinner to honor the occasion, two rabbis rose from their places and left the room in horror: the Jewish caterer had served shrimp, one of the forbidden foods, for the opening course.

The "shrimp incident," as it came to be called, became a dramatic symbol and catalyst for the movement that began to grow rapidly thereafter. When the Pittsburgh Platform was adopted two years later by Reform rabbis, it only served to provide an added spur. Meanwhile, the great wave of Eastern European immigration had begun, and as we have already noted, immigrant needs also supplied fuel for the Conservative movement. Sabato Morais (1823–1897), the rabbi of a Sephardic synagogue in Philadelphia, emerged as the leader of the Conservatives, and his efforts along with those of others led to the establishment of the Jewish Theological Seminary in New York as an institution to train Conservative rabbis. The association that was formed in 1885 in connection with the seminary introduced its constitution by speaking of fidelity to Mosaic Law, the traditions of the ancestors, and a love for the Hebrew language—all three to become, more and more, badges of ethnic identity.

The seminary had fallen on hard times by 1897 when Morais died, but in the early twentieth century it was revived with the explicit intention of serving the Eastern European Jews. Solomon Schechter (1847–1915) was brought from England to serve as its president. A Rumanian by birth and a distinguished scholar, he attracted an illustrious faculty to the seminary. More than that, he articulated far more clearly than earlier leaders the ethnic emphasis that was to become the identifying mark of Conservatism. In his notion of the "catholic Israel," he expressed his faith that by a kind of mystical inner unity Jews would find the middle way between the full demands of the Law and the requirements of modernity. Consensus would arise from the *people*, and that consensus would bind them to their ancestral heritage.

In 1918 Mordecai Kaplan (b. 1881) of the Jewish Theological Seminary began a synagogue center movement. Throughout the twenties and thereafter, Jewish centers were popular institutions, adding to the traditional synagogue and its services a host of nonreligious activities. The Jewish center should be a place where all Jews, whether religious or not, could feel at home: Jews, after all, were a people. Meanwhile, Kaplan continued to ponder the relationship between religion and Jewish cultural identity until in 1934 he published *Judaism as a Civilization*, where he argued that Judaism was a religious civilization rather than a religion. He sought the reestablishment of Jewish community life in America by uniting all Jews, whether Conservative, Reform, Orthodox—or "non-religious." The following year he founded Reconstructionism, a movement which, as an offshoot of Conservatism, spread his ideas about the importance of traditional ceremonies and rituals not as expressions of supernatural religion but as distinctive signs of Jewishness. Reconstructionism remained small—with only eight congregations in the country by 1970—but it voiced important concerns that were shared by Conservative Jews.

Conservatism found support for its attachment to Jewish ethnic identity in Zionism as well. This movement for the reestablishment of a Jewish nation-state began in its modern form in the late nineteenth century with Theodor Herzl (1860–1904) and his World Zionist Congress. The idea of a return to Israel was attractive to American Jews of Conservative and also, to some extent, Orthodox persuasion. On the other hand, Reform Jews at first strongly opposed Zionism because of their insistence that Judaism meant a religion and not a national group. It was not until 1935 that they moved to a position of official neutrality. Meanwhile, small Hasidic sects, the descendants of an eighteenth-century Eastern European mystical movement, also expressed their vehement opposition to Zionism. For them, the secular ideal of establishing a Jewish nation-state violated the religious hope for the Messiah who, according to tradition, would lead the Jews back to the land of Israel.

With the Holocaust of Nazi Germany (1939-1945), however, Reform and Hasidic Jews were both compelled to rethink their positions. As the news of German atrocities and the full horror of what had happened reached America, Jews of all persuasions were profoundly shaken. The very foundations of their covenant with God seemed to be called into question. Whatever religious answers they groped toward, Jewish people became convinced that they themselves must take an active role in shaping their future. They could no longer trust the nations of the world and the Western heritage of the "Enlightenment." Nor could they any longer wait for God. Thus, when the modern state of Israel finally came into existence in 1948, it received enthusiastic endorsement and support from American Jewry and has continued to do so. By the last quarter of the twentieth century, to be Jewish more than ever meant to be part of a people. In Israel the people saw their ancestral and their newly reborn spiritual home.

If Reform stressed Judaism, the revealed prophetic religion, while Conservatism promoted Jewishness, the ethnocultural reality, then Orthodoxy perhaps represented the Jewish attempt to maintain the unity of the past. Orthodoxy became a self-conscious movement as first, Reform and then, Conservative Jewry carved out more "progressive" postures for themselves. It was Orthodoxy with its Eastern European faithful that tried, as nearly as it could, to retain the religious observances of the past, to hold on to all 613 commands of the Law—or as much of that as possible. In the terms that we have been using, we might say that Reform Judaism, by its emphasis on organized religion as a separate function, tried to make of Judaism an extraordinary (if restrained and Americanized) religion. Meanwhile, Conservatism fostered ordinary religion as it encouraged Jewishness among observant and nonobservant alike, and Orthodoxy, in trying to keep both religion and peoplehood intact, fought to continue the Jewish amalgamation of both. Still, the lines were not nearly so clear. Conservatism often seemed to share the basic assumption of Orthodoxy that peoplehood and religion were one. And Reform, by the last quarter of the twentieth century—perhaps influenced by a wave of ethnic pride that swept the United States—had rejected many of the extreme formulations of its past. More and more, cantors chanted portions of the service in Reform synagogues in Hebrew and, especially among the young, a new devotionalism was springing up.

The denominational divisions within the Jewish community were a good example of how the American experience had been internalized. We will have more to say in Part Two about the denominationalism that became characteristic of a nation in which church and state were separate. For now, though, we need to look at more of the ways in which Jews were like other Americans of European descent and as time passed became even more like them.

AMERICAN JUDAISM AND CONTEMPORARY LIFE

First of all, Jews were already like other Americans, and with their heritage of adaptability in many different host cultures, as a group they were able to rise quickly to middle-class status. They shared with Americans of Calvinist inclination a religion that stressed law and deed. Thus, the "Protestant ethic" did not seem foreign to the newcomers, and they were as ready as their once-Calvinist neighbors to exhibit industry, perseverance, thrift, and prudence. The Jewish tradition of study of the Torah led to a commitment to the values of study and education in the secular realm, so that many Jews rose quickly to professional status. At the same time, their closely knit families and mutual-assistance patterns provided security and encouragement in the new environment.

Secondly, Jews changed in America to become more like other Americans. Nurtured by the new milk and honey of religious liberty, Judaism in theory should have grown from strength to strength. Yet, often overlooked, religious liberty in America meant freedom *from* religion as well as freedom of religion. In the Old World of Jewish ghetto and *shtetl*, such choice had not been possible. Thus, it was the voluntary nature of religious commitment in the new land that led, ironically, to the mass defections from Judaism characteristic of the late nineteenth and the twentieth centuries. For those who remained within the pale of Jewish religion, denominationalism, as we have seen, became an expression of American pluralism. Furthermore, denominationalism pointed to the fact that in America, unlike in the small and self-contained Jewish communities of Europe, no one authority spoke for the Jewish people. While in the Old World the rabbi had given uncontested direction to the *local* community over which he presided, in the *continental* United States various efforts at Jewish ecclesiastical unity met with only moderate success.

Indeed, so diverse had Judaism become that, by the late 1970s, Reform rabbinical candidates at Hebrew Union College were being drawn to the new position called "polydoxy," as articulated by Alvin Reines, one of their professors. In this understanding different religious outlooks and practices were regarded as legitimate so long as they helped a person to affirm his or her Jewishness. While some Jews regarded polydoxy as secular and relativistic, others saw it as a meaningful expression of their Jewishness. So there was no one normative version of Judaism in the American context, and as one Jewish scholar, Joseph L. Blau, has said, it is necessary to talk about the Judaisms in the United States. All starting points were equally valid for religious people in the new land: this was the glory and anguish of living among the many.

Meanwhile, by the 1960s, roughly half of the Jewish population identified in some form with Conservative Judaism (although they may not have been actual members of a synagogue). Reform Judaism appealed to about another quarter, followed by Orthodoxy, which counted a fifth or less of all American Jews in its ranks. Still, because Orthodox congregations tended to be small and dedicated, almost half of all Jewish synagogues belonged to the traditional branch of Judaism. Among all Jews, more people were attending synagogues and reading the Bible, yet fewer could say that their beliefs in God or revelation in the Bible were firm. Belief in life after death, underplayed in much of Jewish history, had declined, and more Jews than ever admitted that they never or infrequently prayed. Furthermore, as some strived for greater homogeneity, blending more completely than ever with the general American population, others found new spiritual energy in the mystical tradition that had always persisted as an undercurrent in Judaism. Hasidic Judaism, with its emphasis on the divine spark in every person and its cultivation of intense prayerfulness and devotion to the Torah, appealed to many. Jewish people, although a minority of probably less than 5 percent of the total population, comprised the largest Jewish population in the world—in the seventies over twice that of the modern nation of Israel. They had become many in the land of manyness, and in doing so they had become American.

IN OVERVIEW

To summarize, the story of American Jewry is the story of both a people and a religion. In three waves of immigration, the Jewish people brought to this country a religious identity forged by common history, mutual suffering, and a sense of chosenness. The revealed religion that was fundamental to this religious identity stressed history more than nature and organized its cultus around a recollection of God's acts in relationship to the community of Israel. Bound to God by a covenant, Israel consecrated time through regular remembrance and through ethical action, both the ways that observant Jews fulfilled the requirements of the Law, or Torah.

In America differences over how the commandments of the Torah should be observed resulted in the formation of three major Jewish "denominations." Reform Jews, who tended to separate Judaism as a religion from Jewishness as ethnic identity, were the most liberal. They loosened social boundaries as they encountered the pluralism of America. Orthodox Jews, by contrast, drew the boundaries tightly and tried to preserve as much as possible of European Jewish culture, blending religion and peoplehood together. Conservative Jews, who occupied the middle position, also blended religion and peoplehood together but strived to find a path to fulfillment of the Torah which was more practical in light of modern lifestyles. At present Jewishness as the bond of peoplehood has become more important throughout American Judaism. In this development, we see a recent expression of the ancient Jewish heritage, which linked extraordinary religion to the ordinary religion of daily living.

Jews lived in the tension between revealed religion and peoplehood, between extraordinary and ordinary religion, and between manyness and oneness. If they had found a promised land in the New World even as they looked to Zion of old, another group of Americans also lived between two Zions. Roman Catholics came over the sea to reap the promises of America. At the same time, they, too, kept one eye elsewhere—on the domes of St. Peter's in Rome.

SUGGESTIONS FOR FURTHER READING: JUDAISM

Blau, Joseph L. *Judaism in America: From Curiosity to Third Faith.* Chicago: University of Chicago Press, 1976.

Cahan, Abraham. *The Rise of David Levinsky.* New York: Harper & Row, 1966.

Gaster, Theodor H. *Customs and Folkways of Jewish Life.* New York: William Sloane Associates Publishers, 1955.

————. *Festivals of the Jewish Year.* New York: William Sloane Associates Publishers, 1953.

Glazer, Nathan. *American Judaism.* The Chicago History of American Civilization. Chicago: University of Chicago Press, 1957.

Heschel, Abraham J. *The Sabbath: Its Meaning for Modern Man.* New York: Farrar, Straus, and Young, 1951.

Neusner, Jacob. *American Judaism: Adventure in Modernity.* Englewood Cliffs, NJ: Prentice-Hall, 1972.

————. *The Way of Torah: An Introduction to Judaism.* Belmont, CA: Dickenson Publishing, 1970.

Roth, Cecil. *A History of the Jews: From Earliest Times through the Six Day War.* Rev. ed. New York: Schocken Books, 1970.

Trepp, Leo. *Judaism: Development and Life.* 2d ed. Belmont, CA: Dickenson Publishing, 1974.

CHAPTER 3

Bread and Mortar:
The Presence of Roman Catholicism

When the ships of Christopher Columbus brought the first Marranos to the Americas, they sailed under the flag of Catholic Spain. So it was that Roman Catholics were among the first Europeans to set foot in the New World. Supported by the wealth and power of the Spanish throne, Roman Catholic missionaries determined to convert the natives of the new lands to Christianity, even as they ministered to the soldiers and other colonials who established the territorial claims of New Spain.

SPANISH MISSIONS

As early as 1513, Juan Ponce de Leon made his way into the Florida peninsula. Although no priest accompanied him on the voyage of discovery, eight years later he was back, this time with priests to establish missions among the Indians. Understandably, the Indians were hostile to the presence of the foreigners and drove them off. Then, by 1526 two Dominican priests traveling with the party of Vasquez de Ayllon were part of their attempted settlement along the Chesapeake. The settlement failed, as did a series of Spanish ventures in Florida in the following years. Still, by 1565 St. Augustine had been founded, and by 1595 missionary work had begun in earnest. Just over a half century later, the Spanish could boast of nearly forty missions with 26,000 Indians who had heard and approved the Christian message.

Meanwhile, north of the Gulf of Mexico in the American Southwest, Spanish Catholic missionaries had already begun to work. Francisco Vasquez de Coronado had seen New Mexico in 1540, and three friars from his entourage remained. When Spain officially took control of New Mexico in 1598, the Franciscans began a ministry there. These missions flourished until the 1630s when they began a slow decline, ending about a half century later in a rebellion by the Native Americans in the area. By 1694, though, the missionaries were back, for Don Diego de Vargas had reconquered the territory: in 1750 they were counting twenty-two missions and 17,500 Indian converts. Similarly, in southern Arizona the Jesuit Eusebio Francisco Kino (1645–1711) founded San Xavier del Bac in 1700 and, with his fabled journeys that led to the establishment of other missions, claimed to have baptized 30,000 Indians.

In California the Franciscan Junipero Serra (1713–1784) would equal the successes of Kino. Beginning with a mission at San Diego in 1769, Serra was able to plant a line of mission establishments on the main road up and down the California coast. Along an immense stretch of territory, at least 600 miles in length, the California mission system at its peak included twenty-one stations where over 21,000 Indians were engaged not only in saving their souls according to Catholic wisdom but also in farming, raising livestock, weaving, and related occupations. Still further, the California Franciscans reported that they had baptized thousands more. But by 1821 Mexico had declared its independence from Spain, and thirteen years later the missions were secularized and Indian converts melted away.

Outnumbered by the Indians, the Roman Catholic missionaries from Spain brought their Native American converts a kind of shotgun Christianity, assisted by soldiers in garrisons never far away. But they were also sincerely convinced of the divine command to bring the Christian message to the Indians. Without the chastened perspective of a later age which would introduce a new regard for the religions of Native Americans, they thought that they were snatching the Indians from the arms of Satan—and bringing them civilization as well. For these missionaries, Roman Catholicism represented the one true religion, while European customs and manners epitomized civilization.

FRENCH MISSIONS

The story of the Roman Catholic efforts of New France was not dissimilar, although the French perhaps encountered even more open hostility on the part of Indian peoples than did the Spanish. The French had begun their involvement in the New World with regular visits by shipping vessels to the Newfoundland coast in the sixteenth century. By the next century, they had become interested in colonization, and a French Protestant community, the Huguenots, made plans to establish an outpost in Nova Scotia. While these Protestant settlers could have their own ministers to aid them spiritually, the French government decided that Catholic priests should also go along to convert the Indians. Thus, French Franciscan missionaries entered the New World, later to be joined by Jesuit priests in Quebec.

Here, after 1625, the Jesuits strived to master Indian languages, and later they set up mission stations for the Huron Indians. But the Hurons responded only in token numbers, and this fact combined with attacks by the Iroquois Indians on the Hurons led to the failure of the missions. There were Jesuit martyrs in the process, among them the well-remembered Jean de Brébeuf (1593–1649). Yet ironically, for political reasons the Iroquois subsequently found it necessary to conciliate the French, and by 1668 the Jesuits had taken advantage of the opportunity and opened missions in upper New York.

Work among the Iroquois lasted only about two decades until the English swept into the area, but as early as the 1630s the Jesuits had also been preaching in the Illinois country to various Ottawa peoples. Here, throughout the seventeenth century they had mission stations. St. Ignace, the largest of these, was founded in northern Michigan in 1670, while La Pointe Mission, established in 1665 in northwestern Wisconsin, later acquired fame as the place from which the Jesuit Jacques Marquette (1637–1675) had set out to explore the Mississippi River with Louis Joliet. In the interim, French colonies began to encircle the missions, and there was intermarriage with the Indians and a continuing Roman Catholic influence. Meanwhile, after 1680 in what is now the state of Maine, the Jesuits followed the earlier effort by Capuchin priests and worked in missions to the Abenaki Indians.

The voyage down the Mississippi had given the French confidence to enter new territory, and where French trappers and settlers went, the missionaries followed. By the end of the century, priests were working with the Natchez people in the South, and several years later (1703) they had formed a parish in what is now Mobile, Alabama. Meanwhile, with a mission near New Orleans, the Jesuits were preaching to the Arkansas, Yazoo, Choctaw, and Alibamon tribes. New Orleans itself became a settled French colony, and Roman Catholicism grew apace among the Europeans. Further north, a group of transplanted Acadians settled. They were French people from Nova Scotia who had refused to accept British rule there after 1755, and they brought with them to Louisiana their Roman Catholic religion and customs to be handed down to their descendants as part of Creole culture.

ENGLISH COLONIES

By contrast to both the Spanish and French patterns, Roman Catholicism entered the English territories, not through missions to Native Americans, but through the settlement of English Catholics. When George Calvert, the first Lord Baltimore (1580–1632), acknowledged his Roman Catholicism in England, he resigned as Privy Councillor to King James I. Still, he did not completely lose favor with the English crown, and later King Charles I decided to grant him a charter to found a colony north of Virginia. Although George Calvert did not live to carry out his plans, his son, Cecil, received the sealed charter in his stead.

Cecil never came to Maryland himself, but his brother, Leonard Calvert (1606–1647), arrived in 1634 as the first governor of the colony. Religious liberty was guaranteed to all by a legal enactment in 1639 and a decade later by the Act of Toleration. Catholics were a minority in the population, though, and when the Puritans gained governmental power, they repealed the Act of Toleration (1654) and outlawed Roman Catholicism. Although Lord Baltimore later regained power, by 1688 and the Glorious Revolution in England, the Catholic defeat was complete. Ironically, in the colony initially established by a Catholic, Roman

Catholics began to pay taxes (1692) in support of the Church of England, and from 1718 until the outbreak of the American Revolution, they were refused voting rights.

In New England, after a brief period of toleration in Rhode Island until 1664, Catholics also led a troubled existence. It was only the American Revolution that enabled them to worship freely, and by 1785 there were perhaps about 600 Catholics in the New England area. Similarly, beginning in 1691, New York applied religious tests to exclude Catholics from public office. Earlier, there had been a Catholic governor, Thomas Dongan (1683), but the era of toleration had been short-lived. It was Pennsylvania, however, that provided the best conditions, after Maryland, for Catholic settlement. Germans and some Irish came, the Jesuits worked among them, and by 1770, there were probably about 3,000 adult Catholics in Pennsylvania, while Maryland had some 10,000.

Small as the English Catholic presence was in America when compared to the missionary efforts of Spain and France, it was from the English colonies that the constitutional structure emerged within which Roman Catholicism would later flourish. Land that had been claimed by New Spain and New France, in the nineteenth century, would become part of the United States, and with this territory would come an assortment of Roman Catholic communities. Still more, from overseas hundreds of thousands of Catholic immigrants would come pouring into the country. But before we pursue the Roman Catholic saga in the United States, we need to understand something of the religion that commanded the loyalty of these Americans.

ROMAN CATHOLIC RELIGION

If the religion of Native Americans had been a consecration of space and the religion of the Jews had been an equal consecration of time, for Roman Catholics both space and time could be vehicles for the sacred. From the perspective of space, Catholicism expressed its religious sense in its fundamental sacramentalism. From the perspective of time, it articulated sacred realities through its annual liturgical cycle. Meanwhile, both the dimensions of space and time were combined in a series of popular devotions that flourished alongside the liturgy.

The Consecration of Space: Sacramentalism

Let us begin with Roman Catholic sacramentalism. A sacrament in any religion is a sacred sign—a person, a place, an object, an action, that is regarded as holy. More than that, a sacrament is a place where the divine or transcendent world breaks into the human one. It is, in other words, a boundary phenomenon, and as the bridge between two worlds, a sacrament in some mysterious way really contains the sacred power that it stands for. In a sacrament, therefore, ordinary and extraordinary reality are present, the one revealing the other even as it disguises it in ordinariness. Coming out of an understanding of the world related to the idea of correspondence, Catholic sacramentalism taught that the material world was so closely analogous to the spiritual realm that it could both enclose and disclose the transcendent. Heaven was bound to earth by a series of links in a chain, and, for example, even the lowly earthworm was in some measure a reflection of the transcendent world. Matter for Catholics was sacred; the natural world, good and holy.

Catholicism had developed its sacramental sense through the early and middle centuries of Christian history, combining a Jewish legacy with Greek philosophy and the remnants of Graeco-Roman popular religion in the Mediterranean lands where Christianity spread. By medieval times, popular Christian belief held to seven sacraments, and these seven became the most concrete expression of a pervasive Catholic sacramentalism. For both medieval people and later Roman Catholics, the seven sacraments were baptism, confirmation, penance, eucharist, holy orders, matrimony, and extreme unction. Five of them formed a series of sacred actions that assisted people as they passed, again, across a boundary from one stage in life to the next. The remaining two, penance and the eucharist, nourished them, meanwhile, in the regular course of their lives.

Baptism (now termed the rite of initiation) in the name of the Father, the Son, and the Holy Spirit constituted an infant or an adult convert a member of the communion of saints, the Christian community of all those now on the earth and those who had passed in faith from this world to the next. By obliterating the original sin that these Christians believed was passed down from Adam and Eve, baptism purified humans and through divine grace transformed them into children of God. Significantly, baptism accomplished these results through the symbolic use of water. Just as water washed away the effects of natural pollution, so the sacrament should cleanse the effects of spiritual stain so that humans could be fit for intimacy with God.

By the same token, confirmation used chrism, or holy oils, to anoint a Christian as a sign of his or her spiritual maturation and adulthood. Just as royal and military leaders had, for centuries, been anointed as they undertook their tasks, so adults in the communion of saints should be given an effective sign of their status. The bishop who administered the sacrament gave a physical blow to the candidate in the old and traditional form of the rite—a further sign that, as an adult in the church, the confirmed (strengthened) Christian should be prepared to witness to the faith even to the point of suffering for it. Similarly, holy orders used chrism to anoint ordinary men in a series of steps to the full powers of the Catholic priesthood. Matrimony—at present simply called marriage—used the spoken words of a man and a woman in a pledge of mutual faith and love to make them husband and wife, sometimes sealing their covenant with an exchange of rings. Extreme unction—in recent times called the sacrament of the sick—once again used chrismatic oils to anoint a person in serious illness. The sacrament signed him or her with the strength to regain physical health or to complete successfully the final journey of a Christian lifetime.

Before the last end, however, there were penance and the eucharist for nurture along the way. Penance—now known as the rite of reconciliation—demanded the confession of sins and a true act of sorrow spoken by the penitent to a priest. Through the power of God given to him in his ordination, the priest then forgave the repentant sinner in the name of the Christian Trinity: the sinner was reconciled to God and the people of God in the church. In the eucharist, Jesus Christ, the Son of God, became physically and spiritually present to become the food of Christian believers.

Thus, all of the sacraments used material elements and human actions as vehicles through which sacred power became present. But it was the eucharist that of all the sacraments was the center of Roman Catholic life and most clearly expressed its sacramental understanding of the world. The eucharist, which literally means "thanksgiving," was a ritual action to recall both the Last Supper Jesus had eaten with his disciples and the death he had endured on the cross as a sacrifice for human sin. More commonly known as the Mass, the eucharist had existed from early Christian times, but throughout the Middle Ages it gradually assumed the form in which European Catholics brought it to the New World. At the heart of the ritual were the elements of bread and wine which, through a series of sacred words and actions on the part of a priest, were changed, Catholics believed, into the body and blood of Jesus Christ. Present on the altar, Jesus was offered to his Father in atonement, an unbloody sacrifice that yet repeated the sacrifice of Calvary. Meanwhile, the priest who offered the Mass acted not in his own name but in the name of Jesus. Thus, in the Mass it was Jesus who was really offering himself to his Father. Like the bread and wine, the priest was a sacramental sign, a vehicle through which the power of Jesus could act. And as in Jewish ritual, the power of the sacred action cut through time to make people present not at a mere commemoration but at the actual event on Calvary.

While the Mass was a sacrifice, it was also a sacred meal, at once a memorial to the last meal Jesus had eaten with his followers and a foretaste of the heavenly banquet. So it was that the bread and wine, now become the body and blood of Jesus, were consumed at the Mass by the priest, and the bread by other devout communicants. For the sacred action to come full circle, the sacramental signs of bread and wine must be used as they were in ordinary life. They must nourish human beings, and through that nourishment they would give spiritual grace, the gift and power of God. Again, the sacrament cut through time, so that the memorial to the Last Supper and the foretaste of paradise were not simply signaled but made real in the lives of participants.

Sacramentalism did not end with the seven sacraments. Rather, it was a pervasive means of understanding the whole mystery of the church, human life, and even the natural world. In the Catholic scheme of things, the church ideally should be as broad as the human race. In practice, it included all those born into a territory, a people, a culture. Unlike a sect or denomination which drew boundary lines between its membership and the world at large, the church sought to include all, saints and sinners too. For Catholicism, the church was the sign of God's presence in the world: it was one, holy, universal (catholic), and apostolic, and from the sacramental perspective the sign of God really *was* God present among humans.

Similarly, the pope of Rome was the sign of the church, representing the whole of its reality to God and, at the same time, acting as the conduit through whom God communicated with human beings. Hence, the pope was the vicar, or representative, of Jesus Christ, and his solemn and official teachings were popularly regarded as infallible. (They were so declared by a church council only in 1870.) The Roman papacy, with its traditions and trappings, stood equal to the Bible as a source of spiritual authority. Like a new Israel, Rome was the specific human location where the God of all the universe had chosen to communicate with human beings. This was why the church was *Roman* Catholic.

Finally, at the apex of this structure was Jesus, the great sign and sacrament of God, revealed both in the scripture and in the continuing tradition of the church. In taking human flesh, Jesus had spoken the clearest word of all about the goodness of the natural world and the sacredness of matter. If God had bothered to become human in Jesus, then humanness—existence in *this* world—had its worth and value. The church only exalted that value by revealing its spiritual proportions, and in its wholeness Roman Catholicism had a thisworldly as well as otherworldly orientation. Indeed, the church was most properly understood as the Mystical Body of Christ. Likewise, monks and nuns, as members of religious orders that vowed poverty, chastity, and obedience, were material signs of Jesus in the world and of his kingdom to come. True, they were doing as all people would in paradise, neither marrying nor giving in marriage (Matt. 22:30). Yet they shared and affirmed simple joys of living: they ate and drank and worked for and in the church. Hence, they were witnesses to the messianic age which, although hidden, was already breaking upon the world.

Alongside this major sacramental scheme, Catholicism recognized a humbler sacramentalism of the material world. Any natural object could become a sacramental, a place where humans could meet and encounter the grace of God. Thus, a priest could bless water to make it holy and confer a blessing, too, on a sacred painting or statue. People could wear commemorative medals dedicated to Jesus, his mother, Mary, or one of the saints. They could light candles in darkened shrines as signs of their prayerful remembrance of a loved one, receive ashes on Ash Wednesday to remind them that they would one day return to the dust, cherish rosary beads in a pocket or purse as talismans of the Virgin Mary's protection, acquire and venerate relics of the saints.

The Consecration of Time: The Liturgical Cycle

Just as sacramentalism expressed the Catholic consecration of space, the liturgical cycle expressed its consecration of time. Structured very much like the Jewish annual cycle of feasts and fasts, the Catholic year began with the Advent season, which occurred during the month of December. At this time, the church awaited anew the coming of Jesus Christ. Then on Christmas day Roman Catholics commemorated his historical birth into the world as well as his spiritual birth in human hearts. The joyous season which followed was punctuated with feasts that recalled events in the gospels: the remembrance of the "holy innocents," infants slain by Herod in his angry search for Jesus; the Epiphany in which the Magi, or wise men, paid homage at the crib of Jesus in Bethlehem; the baptism of Jesus by John the Baptist at the Jordan River. Then, as the year lay in the last grip of winter, Catholics kept a forty-day period of prayer and fasting called Lent. It recalled the forty days that Jesus had spent in the desert before beginning his public ministry, and it culminated in the observances of Holy Week to commemorate the passion, death, and resurrection of Jesus.

Beginning on the Sunday before Easter, known as Palm Sunday, Catholics relived the triumphal entry of Jesus into Jerusalem before his passion and death. They received blessed palms and formed in procession around the church, singing "Hosanna to the Son of David" (Matt. 21:9), as had the Jews of old. In the early part of the week, scriptural texts read at each daily Mass recalled Jesus's words and deeds during the last days preceding his arrest. Then, on Maundy or Holy Thursday (believed to be originally the same day as the Jewish Passover), Catholics commemorated in a special way the Last Supper and the institution of the eucharist. This was the day on which the holy oils to be used during the coming year were blessed, and this was also the day on which the priest who celebrated Mass washed the feet of ordinary folk, a re-creation of the action in which Jesus had washed the feet of his disciples at the Last Supper (John 13:4–5). Joy and sadness mingled in the celebration: Jesus was giving to all the ages the lasting gift of himself under the elements of bread and wine; yet Jesus was also about to go to his death for the sins of humankind. He was the paschal Lamb to be sacrificed so that his people could pass over from slavery in sin to freedom in grace.

Good Friday was the only day of the year on which Roman Catholics, properly speaking, could not be present at a Mass. There was a service which resembled the eucharistic action of the Mass, but unlike any other day the priest did not consecrate bread and wine, changing them into the body and blood of Jesus. Instead, there was a communion service using the reserved sacrament, kept on a side altar after the Holy Thursday celebration. Since Good Friday was the day on which Jesus had died, it was fitting that Catholics should be bereft of his presence. The sense of sorrow and loss pervaded the scriptural texts of the liturgy, everything serving to underline the significance of what had occurred.

But the most sacred day of the church year was Easter, and the liturgy used every means available to make the point. A long vigil service the previous evening ended with a Mass at midnight to honor the resurrection of Jesus. The vigil had been filled with the sacramental symbolism of new birth and new life: the lighting of a new fire from flint; the blessing of a huge new Easter candle, representing Jesus, which would stand in the sanctuary during the Easter season; the blessing of baptismal water for the succeeding year; the solemn repetition by the congregation of baptismal vows. In the Mass that followed, the scriptural texts were sprinkled with alleluias: Christ had risen and was still with his people.

Then, forty days after Easter, Catholics celebrated the ascension of Jesus into heaven, where, they believed, he sat at his Father's right hand, reigning with him in the kingdom. Ten days later, just as the Jews recalled the giving of the Torah (*Shavuot*, Pentecost), Catholics kept the feast of Pentecost. For them, however, it was a commemoration of the coming of the Holy Spirit upon the apostles. Tongues of fire had descended on them as they waited in an upper room, the fire transforming them into men with courage and zeal to spread the message of the gospel, the tongues enabling others to understand them, although they could not speak the language of the apostles.

The remainder of the liturgical year was a long series of Sundays after Pentecost, spread through the summer and autumn months, during which successive aspects of the life and teachings of Jesus were considered. Interspersed throughout this period, as through other parts of the year, were major feasts commemorating Jesus, Mary, or the saints. Almost no day in the Roman Catholic year was without its special liturgy, with scriptural texts read at the Mass to bring its lesson home. If a so-called ferial (or "free") day did occur, the priest used scriptural texts from the Mass of the preceding Sunday, always performing the eucharistic action to consecrate bread and wine.

As in the Jewish calendar, the feasts of the Catholic year were historicized rituals, remembering the events which formed the fundamental story of Christian beginnings or the men and women who were its flesh-and-blood heroes. Still, as in the Jewish liturgy, underneath the symbolism of history lay the symbolism of nature and the material world. Roman Catholics awaited the birth of Christ, the light of the world, as the year lay dying on the last days before winter solstice. Jesus was born during the week of the solstice, like the first ray of the sun which, ancient religions taught, had conquered the winter darkness at that time. Lent brought a season of fasting during the last lingering days of winter, while Easter came on the Sunday following the first full moon after the vernal (spring) equinox. It was the feast of new life, held when new life was bursting forth from nature. Appropriately, Catholic folk customs in many lands had included Easter eggs, natural symbols of fertility and birth.

Paraliturgical Devotions

In addition to the official liturgy, keeping its sacred time were a multitude of paraliturgical devotions (literally, devotions alongside the liturgy). These combined sacramental space and consecrated time. Each Catholic country had its own special favorite among them; and in America, therefore, popular devotionalism flourished with importations from many lands. These devotions were special and personal ways to worship Jesus, venerate Mary, or honor the saints.

Among special devotions to Jesus, the cultus of the Sacred Heart was perhaps the most widespread among American Catholics. Originating in France with the religious experiences of the nun Margaret Mary Alacoque, who in 1675 claimed a number of times to have seen Jesus, the devotion stressed the infinite love and suffering of Christ. Its iconography included the portrayal of the bleeding and pierced heart of the savior surrounded with a crown of thorns, often fashioned as a badge which a person could pin to inner or outer clothing. By the middle of the nineteenth century, an official feast honored the Sacred Heart during the church year, and meanwhile devout Catholics tried to attend Mass and receive communion during nine successive months on the first Friday of each. They believed the promise of Jesus to Margaret Mary Alacoque: if they kept the nine first Fridays, they would not die in a state of serious personal sin, and their salvation would be assured.

Other devotions to Jesus included special worship of the reserved sacrament at a time called Forty Hours, to commemorate the time Jesus spent in the tomb before his resurrection. In a period of that length, the communion bread, a small circular wafer, was exposed to public view in a special sacred vessel. There was also Benediction of the Blessed Sacrament when, in a brief ceremony, the priest raised the sacrament in the same vessel to bless the assembled congregation, making the sign of the cross over them with it. Additionally, there were fourteen Stations of the Cross, usually representations in raised relief along the walls of the church. "Making the Stations" meant following Jesus in prayerful solicitude along the road to Calvary. Still other Catholics had special devotion to the Infant of Prague (Czechoslovakia), a doll-like statue of the infant, dressed in bejeweled satin with a crown on his head, a representation of the kingship of Jesus even in the child.

Devotion to Mary was even more widespread than paraliturgical devotion to Jesus. In the rosary, Catholics had a chain of beads on which, while repeating prayers to the Father and to Mary, they recalled the mysteries of her life as an inspiration for their own. In use since late medieval times, the rosary also had a feast to honor it on October 7. Other Catholics expressed their devotion to Mary by wearing the scapular, two pieces of brown wool cloth worn over the shoulders as a symbolic undergarment. No one, Catholics believed, could die unrepentant or unprepared while he or she wore the scapular. Beyond these devotions, Catholics venerated Mary under various titles, many of them deriving from the place names of locations in which she was said to have appeared to ordinary or saintly folk. Various Marian shrines were erected to honor these apparitions, and these were often the sites of popular pilgrimages. Some of the titles of Mary made their way into the liturgical calendar, and there were, for example, feasts honoring Our Lady of Lourdes (a nineteenth-century French apparition); Our Lady of Good Counsel (a miraculous picture in an Italian church), Our Lady of Guadalupe (especially popular in the Southwest, the apparition of Mary to a poor Indian near Mexico City).

Meanwhile, the saints were not neglected, and various cultuses honored them, each having its special following among the Catholic populace. Thus, St. Jude was the patron of hopeless cases, and St. Rita was the saint of the impossible. St. Blaise helped in the case of sore throats, and a special blessing for the throat could be had on his feast day. St. Agnes was patroness of sexual purity, and in the nineteenth century St. Thomas Aquinas became patron of Catholic schools. Each nationality among the Catholics had its favored saints, and, indeed, each locality in the old countries had had its special cultuses. One of the results of the American experience was that St. Stanislas (the Pole) and St. Rocco (the Italian) both received their due among American Roman Catholics.

Other paraliturgical activities were organized by means of special parish groups. Often the men of a parish could belong to the Holy Name Society, committed to the avoidance of blasphemy and profanity. Women could join the Sodality of the Blessed Virgin Mary, dedicated to promoting womanly chastity in and out of marriage as well as to encouraging the catalogue of other virtues Mary was said to embody. One organization was dedicated to the teaching of Christian doctrine, while other groups sewed altar vestments for the liturgy or expressed their devotion to a particular saint through a formal organization.

Hence, to be a Roman Catholic was to be surrounded with sacrament and liturgy from cradle to grave. No day was without its reminders of the invisible world, and each day was a tapestry in which ordinary and extraordinary were interwoven. The natural world was not a barrier to the supernatural realm: rather, properly regarded, it led a person into it.

Ethics and Morality

It is not surprising, therefore, that Catholic attitudes toward ethics and morality included the same basic regard for the natural world that sacramentalism and the liturgical cycle embodied. Formulated most clearly by Thomas Aquinas in the thirteenth century, the Roman Catholic ethic grew out of a respect for natural law. This was the law implicit in the growth and development of any creature—plant, animal, or human. Moral action was action in accordance with this law of nature. Immoral action was unnatural action. Thus, human beings throughout the world abhorred the killing of one of their own kind: it was a natural law written in human hearts that murder was wrong. Similarly, right-thinking people respected the property of others, and stealing also violated the law of nature. It was in matters of sexuality, though, that the implications of natural-law teaching led Catholics down a path very different from that to be taken by many of their Protestant neighbors. The sexual act was naturally open to the reproduction of the human species; whatever interfered with that natural openness violated the divine and natural purpose of sexuality. From this perspective, artificial birth control was wrong and sinful. In the later twentieth century, when abortion became an issue, it was still more reprehensible from the point of view of natural-law teaching. Abortion, as traditional Catholics saw it, was murder.

Natural law, however, had been clarified and strengthened by revealed law. Catholics, just as their Jewish and Protestant neighbors, looked to the Ten Commandments that Moses received on Sinai as the source for norms of behavior. They looked as well, with Protestants, to the new law taught by Jesus in the Christian gospels. But much more clearly than Protestants, they had elaborated a scale of offenses against the law. After original sin had been forgiven in the sacrament of baptism, humans were still capable of committing actual sins of greater or lesser magnitude. There was, first of all, mortal sin, a serious offense that, if unforgiven, could condemn a person to damnation for all eternity. And secondly, there was venial sin, which though less serious still weakened a person's resistance to more serious forms of evil and dulled his or her spiritual keenness. Both kinds of sin could be forgiven, if a person were truly sorry, through the sacrament of penance to which we have already alluded.

Even so, sin left its remains after the reception of the sacrament. Once having fallen, it was always easy to fall again. Beyond that, the remains of sin meant that after death a person would have to undergo a period of suffering and purification before he or she were fit to enter heaven. In order to lessen that time in purgatory, a Catholic might obtain an indulgence through pious acts or prayers specifically recommended by the church for that purpose. There was no tension for a Catholic here: the pope, as the sign of Christ, who was the sign of God, set an indulgence on an act or prayer. Heaven obeyed, because the pope meant the presence of God in the world. The Holy Spirit was with the church, and the

Catholic who trusted would not be led astray. In the sixteenth century, indulgences had been the tinder that began the fire of the Protestant Reformation, but in the Catholic scheme of things they played an uncontroversial, if humble, part.

For all this emphasis on an exacting, personal account of sin and grace, Roman Catholicism, like Judaism, was the religion of a community, who collectively were the people of God. Hence, the ethic of Roman Catholicism was also and ultimately a social ethic. It dealt with the waging of war and the keeping of peace, with the problem of poverty and the distribution of goods, with the relationship between the city of God and the city of this world in the secular state. In medieval times, Catholicism had existed as Christendom, a public and cultural reality that included both church and state. In the modern era, it still sought to adjudicate the proper roles of church and state, more sensitive perhaps than many to the implications of church-state separation in America. Salvation, in short, came to a holy community, and individuals must find their place in this communal scheme of things. Nineteenth-century and later popes were particularly strong in pointing to what this meant in terms of capital and labor in an industrialized society, but the message of community and social concern was part of the traditional heritage of Roman Catholicism.

THE AMERICAN SAGA OF CATHOLICISM

Keeping in mind this traditional heritage, we turn now to the American saga of Catholicism. We need to explore the direction of the changes which the American experience brought, changes which, as we will see, came from both within and without the church. Briefly, these changes were brought about by the ethnicity of the American Catholic church and by its pluralistic setting. Ethnicity refers to the *internal* condition of being many national churches in one church; pluralism, to the *external* condition of being one church among many denominations. Together, the two conditions were aspects of one problem—that of how Roman Catholics should respond to their new American situation. And together, the two conditions generated a tension which in microcosm reflected the larger tension between oneness and manyness characteristic of American society.

Ethnicity

Ethnicity became an important coefficient in the American Catholic experience as the country expanded into new territory and at the same time waves of immigrants poured in. Each national group had evolved its own creative mix of ordinary and extraordinary religion when in its traditional setting it combined folk custom and ethos with general Roman Catholic teaching. Organizationally, there would be problems as worshipers from different European nations tried to share communion plate and pew. Still more, there would be conflict about whose way of being Catholic was right. Both Roman Catholics and other American observers wanted to see a single church that could be easily understood and explained. This meant that some one or other of the ethnic groups within the church was likely to impart its flavor to the whole. As we will see, this is exactly what happened with Irish ascendancy over American Roman Catholicism.

We have already observed that the earliest Catholics in the lands that later became the United States were Spanish, French, Native American, and English. Moreover, in colonial times Pennsylvania's Catholics had been mostly German, whereas New England had been the home of a small number of Irish Catholics. From the beginning, there was friction among these different nationalities in the church. Different cultures and customs frequently led to different points of view and different practical stands on a series of issues—so that ethnic differences became a part of larger misunderstandings. Thus, in Louisiana French and Spanish Catholics had been hostile toward one another until the Louisiana Purchase of 1803 aroused them to join ranks against the common Anglo-American enemy. By the early nineteenth century, too, newly appointed French bishops were experiencing conflict with the Irish. Still earlier, in the late eighteenth century Germans had expressed their hostility toward an Anglo-Catholic leadership by the formation of a separate Holy Trinity church in Philadelphia (1787).

But the most serious ethnic struggles occurred in the second half of the nineteenth century when Irish immigrants became the backbone of American Catholicism and other groups fought to maintain their identity as nationalities within the church. Mostly poor cotters caught in the potato famine of Ireland, in the 1840s and thereafter the Irish arrived in huge numbers, bereft of resources and forced to settle in eastern urban slums. Although their knowledge of the English language helped them to adjust, their lack of literacy and working skills combined with their poverty to hamper them. Because their clergy had helped them in the old country during the potato famine and because, also, their clergy had enough education to become cultural brokers in the new and alien setting, the Irish remained loyal to their religious leaders. It was true that, just as in Ireland, many were attached to the church by little more than baptism. Still, the many who were practicing Catholics marked their religious observance with a style that was their own. Their Catholicism tended toward legalism and literal observance of church law, at the same time emphasizing personal morality and individualistic piety. Often antiintellectual, it encouraged their sons and daughters to serve the church as priests and nuns.

Thus, it was Irish Catholics who, by the sheer power of their numbers—almost 1 million by 1850—and by their willingness to enter ecclesiastical service, came to dominate the hierarchy of the American church. Moreover, when the Catholic leadership called for the development of a separate parochial school system, it was Irish nuns who for the most part staffed it, enabling them to pass on to generations of Roman Catholic school children their interpretation of Catholicism. Irish brick and mortar built the church, and in the middle of the twentieth century, it was still the Irish who gave American Catholicism its public face. Indeed, the Irish were to Catholicism what mainstream Protestantism would be to other religious orientations in America—the one among the many.

Of considerable significance among the Catholic many with whom the Irish dealt were the Germans. Present, as we have seen, from colonial times, their numbers increased through immigration after the War of 1812, their ranks steadily expanding until 1855. Indeed, by 1850 there were over 500,000 Germans in the United States. Generally more affluent and better educated than either the Irish or other Catholic groups, many of them left their eastern ports of entry and headed for the Midwest. Here their settlements spread out in the cities and farmland that described a triangle between Cincinnati, St. Louis, and Milwaukee. They were deeply attached to their language and traditions, wanting them to be used in their churches and schools. Hence, they demanded parishes organized on the basis of nationality rather than territory. With their love of music, relaxed observance of the Sabbath, and opposition to the temperance movement, their Catholicism possessed its own folk flavor, often at odds, especially, with the attitudes of the Irish.

From 1855 German Catholics had organized themselves into the Central Verein, a strong and vital organization that continued into the twentieth century. Then in 1871 Peter Paul Cahensly (1838–1923), a businessman in Nassau (Germany), organized the St. Raphaelsverein as a society to aid German immigrants to the New World. By 1891 the society presented a petition to the pope, claiming that immigrants were being lost to Catholicism in huge numbers because they lacked priests and institutions of their own nationality to minister to them. The American church should be multilingual and multinational if it was to succeed. "Cahenslyism," as it came to be called, exaggerated the defections from the American church and brought German European support to the struggle between the Germans and the Irish. Although the movement finally failed in its most ambitious goals, it was a strong indicator of the continuing conflict within American Catholicism.

In the last third of the nineteenth century, however, the immigrant tensions that had begun in an earlier age were complicated by the arrival of new groups. The "new immigration" from 1880 until the First World War brought a steady flow of Southern and Eastern European Catholics into the American church. Well over 3 million Italians had arrived by 1920 and, among a variety of Eastern European national groups, nearly as many Poles. Yet for various reasons neither ethnic group seriously altered the public face of American Roman Catholicism.

The Italians came mostly from southern Italy and Sicily, poor and illiterate for the most part, and, like the Irish before them, settling in eastern seacoast cities. For the Italians, perhaps more than for most other immigrant groups, religion and culture were interfused, indistinguishable realities that always returned to their source and center in the extended family. This preference for familial over ecclesiastical identification had only been magnified by the recent history of church-state relations in Italy. The pope had been the temporal ruler of the northern Italian Papal States until 1870, and so Italian Catholics had come to extend to the official church the same kind of distrust they felt toward political government. As they immigrated to America, these Italian Catholics were benignly anticlerical and unwilling to lend the church either their children, as priests and nuns, or their money, to supply the mortar for new shrines and schools. With their own spirit of relaxed adherence to official rules and regulations, they did not accept the legalism of the Irish.

By contrast, the Poles were intensely devoted to the institutional church. Coming from peasant backgrounds, many who immigrated to America eventually became farmers, but numbers of them settled in cities like Chicago, Milwaukee, Detroit, and Cleveland. For centuries, the Polish people had joined their nationalism to their religion, and so in America, like the Germans, they sought to maintain a distinct national ethos, preserving their language in churches and schools. To some extent, the pattern of conflict was repeated: there were struggles between clergy and laity in different parishes over financial matters, and by the early twentieth century, there was a movement for equal representation with other national groups in the American hierarchy. Indeed, tensions with a non-Polish hierarchy resulted in the formation in Scranton, Pennsylvania, of the separate Polish National Catholic Church in 1904.

Still, most Polish Catholics chose to remain within the Roman Catholic communion. And since history was by this time on the side of continued Irish hegemony, the real aim of Polish Catholics was survival more than dominance. Their success could be measured by the fact that as late as 1950 there were still 800 Polish parishes in the United States. Beyond this, they contributed to the American church a series of new devotions, such as that to the Black Madonna (the Virgin) of Czestochowa, and they gave to the church their sons and daughters in Polish Catholic religious communities.

More recently in the twentieth century, the huge circle of immigration seemed almost to be completed. Through the arrival by 1970 of some 9 million Spanish-speaking people of Mexican, Puerto Rican, and Cuban origins, Spanish Catholicism, the earliest European Christianity in America, reappeared in a new form. About 95 percent of this great influx had a Catholic heritage, but these people were also the least church oriented of any immigrant group. A swelling Mexican presence had begun in the early twentieth century, spilling over the borders into Texas, California, and the Southwest. Later, by midcentury, Puerto Ricans were entering New York City in heavy concentrations, while the Cuban revolution of 1959 brought Cubans in massive numbers to the Miami area. These Latin Catholics were anticlerical, and, in the United States as in their homelands, many turned from their nominal Catholicism to an intense and active Pentecostalism. Still, their liturgies were distinctive in their Latin warmth and music; and in their absorption of Catholicism, like the Italians, they displayed an overlapping between ordinary and extraordinary religion. In their closely knit subcultures, the principles of sacramentalism and community were neither theoretical nor theological constructs but lived realities. Indeed, sacramentalism was so radical that it left very little need for a separate church at all, and the community was so natural that it did not need to be blessed by viewing it as the Mystical Body of Christ. Organized religion, in short, had become culture, as the extraordinary elements in Catholicism merged into ordinariness. So the composition of "public Catholicism" went largely unaltered, not affected one way or another by Latins who felt no need to get involved in the official church.

Meanwhile, by the last third of the twentieth century, some Roman Catholics whose roots lay in earlier European immigrations were celebrating what the Slovak-American Catholic Michael Novak has called the "rise of the unmeltable ethnic." They were glorying in a nostalgic recollection of their past. Being part of the silent majority of the American middle class had proved for them, as it had for other groups, colorless and vapid. At the same time, ethnic organization among blacks, Indians, and Chicanos urged them toward greater visibility. Manyness, we might say, was interacting with other forms of manyness, so that there was a new regard for ethnicity in the American Catholic church. Although the Irish continued to predominate, the age of the monolith simply had not come.

Pluralism and Americanization in Historical Perspective

It is time now to consider the second major factor that affected the course of Roman Catholicism in the United States — its pluralistic setting. This *external* condition meant that, both for outsiders and insiders, no matter what its theoretical claims to universality, the Catholic church in America was a minority. For outsiders, the Catholic presence was a sometime threatening quantity, and so Protestant fears generated a series of nativist and protectionist movements. For insiders, emulation of the American and Protestant mainstream led to a series of attempts by some to "de-Romanize" the church, while others more conservatively sought a retreat into separateness. For these people, the preservation of their ethnic heritages became a way of avoiding the mainstream. Hence, as we have noticed, pluralism and ethnicity were, indeed, related issues.

We will take up the question of nativism in more detail in the Conclusion. Here, however, it is important to note that nativism was a continuing fact of Catholic life throughout much of the nineteenth century and into the twentieth. By 1830 an anti-Catholic weekly called *The Protestant* was established to counter Roman corruption, and the crusade against Catholicism had begun.

In 1834, in an often-cited incident, a mob set fire to the Ursuline convent in Charlestown, Massachusetts, while in Philadelphia a decade later at least two churches were burned. Meanwhile, a series of associations were formed in order to combat the dangers that many Americans perceived in Catholicism. In 1842 there was the American Protestant Association, and in 1854, the Know-Nothing party. Later, in 1887 the American Protective Association was formed for similar reasons, and then in the 1920s the revived Ku Klux Klan took up cudgels against the Catholic church. Fueled by fears inspired by the "otherness" of the assorted "papist" immigrants, these organizations expressed sentiments that were shared by many who did not belong to them. They were monuments to the stresses and strains which Protestant America was experiencing as it strived to come to terms with the massive immigration.

For some Catholic insiders, nativist harassment was met by a strong desire for retreat and segregation. Hostile toward Anglo-America, many working-class immigrants of German and Polish origins joined the majority of the Irish and their clergy in a strong conservative stance. Led among the hierarchy by Michael A. Corrigan (1839-1902), the archbishop of New York, and Bernard

McQuaid (1823–1909), the bishop of Rochester, in the late nineteenth century they worked to isolate the church from the onslaughts of a Protestant culture. They were especially fearful of the public schools where, they thought, a kind of common-denominator Protestantism was being promulgated. It was in this atmosphere of caution and reserve that the Catholic school system was born, with the demand by the Third Plenary Council of Baltimore (1884) that every parish establish its own parochial school.

For other Catholic insiders, however, mainstream American culture had its alluring face. Even at the beginning of the early national period, some lay Catholics, in the absence of a prohibition by Bishop John Carroll (1735–1815), had taken a strong hand in parish affairs. Like congregational Protestants, they were often close to calling and replacing their own pastors, sometimes even becoming schismatic by doing so. Trusteeism, as it was called, took advantage of the fact that the civil law had been written to accommodate both church-state separation and Protestant church polity, conferring corporate ownership of church property on the lay trustees of a congregation. Heightened sometimes by struggles between various national groups within the church, trusteeism was a recurring problem for bishops for some sixty years. Trustees hailed their democratic rights, and the old hierarchical and sacramental model was challenged by the new order. Eventually, property rights were vested in the bishop of each diocese as a corporation sole but not before there had been much disruption of traditional patterns.

The democratic trustees were succeeded in the latter part of the nineteenth century by democratic bishops, who formed a liberal camp in opposition to the conservatives we have already discussed. Led by James Cardinal Gibbons (1834–1921) of Baltimore and even more aggressively by Archbishop John Ireland (1838–1918) of St. Paul, a number of these bishops sought to open Catholic ghettoes outward toward American culture. They wanted to end every kind of Catholic isolation and to "Americanize" the church. Catholics, they thought, should wholeheartedly embrace the American style and the American way of doing things.

Thus, Gibbons actively intervened in 1887 to prevent Rome from condemning the Knights of Labor, an early labor organization supported by Irish Catholics. With the strong endorsement of Gibbons and Ireland, Bishop John Lancaster Spalding (1840–1916) of Peoria crusaded for the foundation of a Catholic university where graduate theological study could go on. His success was apparent in 1889 when the Catholic University of America opened its doors in the nation's capital. Meanwhile, Ireland remained dubious concerning the value of a separate parochial school system and repeatedly urged the American church to live in its own age and its own setting. For Ireland, the Roman Catholic church in America should become an *American* Catholic church. As Ireland and other liberals saw it, the official separation between church and state in the United States was not just a practical arrangement under which Roman Catholicism had managed to thrive. Rather, it was an ideal situation and one which American Roman Catholics should enthusiastically support.

But the liberals did not continue their efforts toward the Americanization of the church with impunity. Matters came to a head in 1899 when Pope Leo XIII published an encyclical letter, *Testem Benevolentiae*, which condemned a number of opinions collectively labeled "Americanism." A key example of this Americanism for the pope was the willingness to regard natural virtues more highly than supernatural ones. Here, natural virtues meant active and thisworldly gifts that were congenial to the Protestant American style. Supernatural virtues meant those which were more "passive" and otherworldly in character, like the traditional humility and obedience that were associated with Catholic saints. A second instance of Americanism was the willingness to adapt to the theories and methods of modern popular culture, bringing a relaxation of the ancient rigor of the church. A third instance was a tendency toward individualism in religion, although traditional Catholicism had stressed the role of the church in salvation.

Americanism has often been called the "phantom heresy," because as soon as the encyclical letter was published American bishops unanimously asserted their freedom from the errors named therein. They were not Americanists, the suspected liberal bishops said, nor did they know any Americanists. Pope Leo XIII had effectively put an end to the Americanization of the Catholic church—at least for the time being.

Meanwhile, on the popular level, the second half of the nineteenth century brought to the fore an institution imported from Europe which at the same time fit closely with American Protestant spirituality. The Catholic mission movement gave to the church its own brand of revivalism, helping to stop defections and to excite the piety of ordinary working-class folk. Held in a parish, usually for one to two weeks every four or five years, a mission featured traveling preachers whose sermons were designed to stir up fear of eternal punishment, sorrow for sin, and recommitment to Roman Catholicism. Like Protestant revivals, missions used mass evangelistic techniques to reach their audiences, the preachers planting a mission cross, preaching with an empty casket to dramatize a point, or tolling a sinner's bell at evening.

Each mission aimed in the context of Catholic sacramentalism at individual conversion or rededication. For the Catholic who came to listen, the sermon should lead inevitably to the confessional where sins were heard and forgiven. It was a fact that after the Catholic Counter-Reformation of the sixteenth century, Catholic piety had entered an evangelical and individualistic era. Still, it seemed a fair assessment that the presence of American Protestantism in a general way supported the pattern of Catholic revivalism. Traveling preachers, the use of self-conscious techniques, an emphasis on conversion and stern morality, the preference for emotion over intellect, a pervading individualism—all of these the mission movement shared with Protestant revivalism.

Pluralism and Americanization: The Later Twentieth Century

In the twentieth century, it remained for Rome itself to unleash the forces that would stimulate a new era of Americanization for the church. The Second Vatican Council (1962–1965)—a meeting in Rome of all the bishops of the church with the pope at their head—did not so much *cause* the changes as catalyze them by discarding older forms and admitting new ones. Already, in the fifties, American Catholics had begun to come of age. They were reaching social and economic equality with their Protestant neighbors, and so they were more and more thinking and acting like members of the mainstream. When Vatican II used the work of the American Jesuit priest John Courtney Murray (1904–1967) in its official Declaration on Religious Freedom, it was offering a resounding endorsement of the American way. Although they were no longer alive to savor the fact, the nineteenth-century liberals, the Americanists who thought that church-state separation was an ideal and not just a necessity, had come into their own. The American Catholic experience with religious pluralism, with the manyness of free and individual choices, had shaped the message of the world church.

Just as significantly, in the wake of Vatican II American Catholicism registered changes in the area of worship and in the area of morality. The fruits of a long and scholarly liturgical movement were reaped when the council paved the way for Mass texts in the language of each nation instead of the traditional Latin. Many accretions to the Mass which had grown up over the years were cut away, while scriptural sermons and congregational singing were stressed. Although the justification for these changes was that they conformed the liturgy more closely to the pattern of the early church, in fact the changes underlined the verbal content of the service at the expense of the symbolic. In so doing, the changes did not destroy sacramentalism, but they did modify it. The reformed liturgy came closer to the model of Protestant spirituality, a model which we will regard more closely in the next chapter.

At the same time, sociological study suggested that Sunday Mass attendance—always high because failure to attend was considered a serious sin—had declined in the United States. Likewise, the rich paraliturgical devotionalism of the past was challenged and eroded by the reforms. Once again, Catholics were coming closer in their religious practices and attitudes to their Protestant and American neighbors.

In the 1960s and 1970s as well, a charismatic movement swept the church. In some measure it was a twentieth-century successor to the old nineteenth-century mission revivalism. Yet it went further. Attracting a well-educated middle class which included many clergy, it preferred experience to theology and actively cultivated ecumenical relationships with American Pentecostals. The movement stressed the Pentecostal baptism of the Holy Spirit which brought a person gifts of prophecy, exorcism, healing, and speaking in tongues. Charismatic religious rhetoric was often borrowed from Pentecostals, and so, too, were characteristic gestures such as the raising of hands at prayer and the laying on of hands for healing. Charismatics often met in private homes during evening hours to conduct their prayer sessions, but they did begin to organize, establishing a Center for Communication and Service in 1969 and sponsoring a Conference on Charismatic Renewal in Rome in 1975. While the bishops sometimes regarded them nervously because of fear of heresy, they needed the zeal of charismatic Catholics at a time when the American church had grown lax.

If there was laxity—or a different spirit abroad in the church—it was nowhere more evident than in the area of morality and ethics. Overall, individualism in morality grew at the expense of regard for community. This was evident in a looser sexual ethic, which sociological surveys discovered especially among young Roman Catholics. There was more willingness to condone sexual expression outside of marriage, more support for artificial birth control and even abortion. Once again, the data suggested that Catholics resembled their Protestant neighbors more closely in the area of sexual morality than they ever had previously. Implicit in the change was a move from the old sense of absolutes based on natural and revealed law given to a community to a new appreciation of the situational and the relative. Catholics were moving to an ethic based on history, and the move led them closer to Protestant America.

Meanwhile, individualism was apparent as more and more priests and nuns sought dispensations from their vows to return to the secular world. Other priests and nuns in the democratic and collegial spirit fostered by Vatican II demanded greater responsibility in the government of their institutions, while some priests also demanded the right to marry. Similarly, the laity, with church encouragement voicing concern for the management of their parishes, formed councils to assist their priests. While the parishes did not return to nineteenth-century trusteeism, the American democratic model was not difficult to find.

Finally, morality grew more Protestant and American in a proliferation of radical and prophetic stances. A prophet in the history of religions was a figure who by the power of words criticized the existing state of things, striving to purify it of present corruption and restore it in its fundamental truth. Such a figure stood outside the religious situation in its contemporary form, compelled by the clearer vision of what ought to be. With this message of correction and criticism, a prophet was profoundly different in character from a priest, whose role was to uphold the standing order by repeating the rituals that, sacramentally, gave strength for present need. Every religion has had something of the prophet and something of the priest in its history, but at the same time it was certain forms of Protestantism which most strongly cherished the figure of the prophet and Catholicism, by contrast, which most clearly appreciated the vital and positive role of the priest. As we will see in the next chapter and in Chapter 10, American Protestantism with its Puritan roots had often preached a prophetic morality. On the other hand, Catholicism in its traditional form had usually preferred the holiness of priestly action.

By the 1960s and 1970s, however, some American Catholics willingly took up prophetic roles. So, for example, the Berrigan brothers, Daniel (b. 1921) and Philip (b. 1923), Roman Catholic priests, led their followers in anguished protest against the Vietnam War, willing even to go to jail for their message. The Berrigans spoke and marched, raided draft headquarters, poured animal blood on records, and inspired dozens of others to behavior in kind. The Berrigans and their supporters were radicals of the left, but Roman Catholic prophets were also radicals of the right. In the seventies, the Pro-Life movement, strongly subscribed by Catholics, led a militant antiabortion campaign that escalated from impassioned speeches and enlarged pictures of the human fetus to marches, protests, and even sometimes physical harassment of the clinics where abortions were performed and of the women who chose to undergo them. Indeed, the antiabortionists resembled the Prohibitionists of an earlier era in the fierceness of their stand and the aggressiveness with which they pushed it forward. Theirs was a religious zeal against what they sincerely saw as the perpetration of murder. But the style of that zeal had more to do with the context of Protestant America than with anything in recent Roman Catholic history.

The last third of the twentieth century saw a Catholicism which had changed remarkably from its small beginnings in America. By 1975, 27 percent of the population expressed their religious preference as Roman Catholicism, but statistical surveys indicated a decline in devotional practice for many of them. Less than half of American Catholics questioned in 1973 thought that the pope was the vicar of Christ, and fewer than a third of them considered him infallible. The reiteration by Pope Paul VI of the church's traditional stand against artificial birth control (1968) alienated many, and the refusal of the church to sanction remarriage after divorce disaffected still others. Catholic growth, which had flourished with the years of open immigration, had slowed; thousands of priests and nuns had returned to ordinary life, and new recruits fallen off drastically; other Catholics had left their ancestral faith. The language of crisis dominated the horizon of Catholic thinking.

In one sense, the bread-and-mortar church was still there: the Irish constituted 15 percent of the Catholic population, 30 percent of its clergy, and half its hierarchy; and within the larger church there were still, if unofficially, the ethnic enclaves of national churches. A huge network of Catholic schools and colleges had scarcely folded up and disappeared. The radical moralists of left and right had gained Catholicism nationwide notice in the media, while the sacraments, still seven in number, gave solace to millions.

Yet the sacramentalism which had shaped the Catholic understanding of religion and human life had begun to crumble. Paraliturgical devotions seemed to melt away after Vatican II, and Catholics seemed to melt away from the churches, too, with the introduction of the new English liturgy. The sexual revolution and a revised sexual ethic signaled a profoundly different moral sense from the past. The refusal to accept the authority of the pope and bishops meant that they were no longer regarded in the same traditional sense as sacramental signs of Christ. The old order of things, in which ordinary and extraordinary mingled in sacramental unity, was yielding to a new pattern. Ordinary and extraordinary now were more separated and compartmentalized. Like Reform Jews and like mainstream Protestants, as we will see, Roman Catholics by discarding some of their sacramentalism were making clearer distinctions between the two. It was true that American Roman Catholics had made a complex move away from a medieval and toward a modern world view and that this move was shared by many in world Catholicism. But the move was especially complicated by its context "in America." Roman Catholicism was giving way to *American* Catholicism and, if you will, to Protestant-American Catholicism.

IN OVERVIEW

From the time of Christopher Columbus, Roman Catholicism had been present in the new land. Early Spanish and then French missionaries brought their first taste of Christianity to American Indians, while with the arrival of English Catholic colonists in the seventeenth century, Catholicism entered the

English seaboard colonies. The religion that was shared by all of these Catholics found holiness in both nature and history. Through its sacramental vision, Roman Catholicism saw the material world as both the symbol and reality of divine things. This understanding crystallized in the seven sacraments of the Roman Catholic cultus, but it was visible throughout the Catholic system. At the apex of the system was Jesus Christ, whose presence Catholics celebrated in an annual liturgical cycle commemorating events in the gospel accounts of his life, death, and resurrection. Meanwhile, in a moral system that had developed over the years, Catholics lived their commitment to nature and historical revelation, adhering to natural law, scripture, and church tradition. Like Native Americans and Jews, in both cultus and code they tended to blend extraordinary with ordinary religion.

With this heritage behind it, the Catholic church in the United States faced changes brought by its internal ethnicity and the external pluralism of American culture. Spanish, French, Native American, and English Catholics were joined, as time passed, by German and Irish Catholics and later by Southern and Eastern Europeans and by Hispanic peoples. These groups often strived to maintain the separate boundaries of their ethnic identity, and there were sometimes collisions among them. In this situation of internal manyness with its attendant tensions, the Irish by the midnineteenth century came to dominate and continued to do so in the twentieth century. In turn, the pluralism of American culture led to profound changes which swung the Catholic church more and more away from its "Roman" axis. Extraordinary and ordinary religion grew more separate, as Catholic boundaries opened out toward America. By the late twentieth century, catalyzed through the actions of Vatican Council II, the Roman Catholic church in America had become an American Catholic church which looked increasingly like the churches of mainstream Protestants.

Who were the people who had so influenced the religions of Catholic and Jewish immigrants? What kind of religion had drawn the many more and more toward it, leading them with its cultural hegemony and oneness? It is time now to look at the mainstream Protestantism of America—a Protestantism which in the late twentieth century, like Catholicism, regarded itself with anxiety and worried about its spiritual malaise and sense of crisis.

SUGGESTIONS FOR FURTHER READING:
ROMAN CATHOLICISM

Abbott, Walter M., ed. *The Documents of Vatican II.* New York: Association Press, 1966.

Cross, Robert D. *The Emergence of Liberal Catholicism in America.* Cambridge, MA: Harvard University Press, 1958.

Dolan, Jay P. *Catholic Revivalism: The American Experience, 1830–1900.* Notre Dame, IN: University of Notre Dame Press, 1978.

———. *The Immigrant Church.* Baltimore: Johns Hopkins University Press, 1975.

Ellis, John Tracy. *American Catholicism.* Rev. ed. Chicago: University of Chicago Press, 1969.

Greeley, Andrew M. *The American Catholic: A Social Portrait.* New York: Basic Books, 1977.

McAvoy, Thomas T. *A History of the Catholic Church in the United States.* Notre Dame, IN: University of Notre Dame Press, 1969.

McKenzie, John. *The Roman Catholic Church.* Garden City, NY: Doubleday, Anchor Books, 1971.

Underhill, Evelyn. *Worship.* 1937. Reprint. Westport, CN: Hyperion Press, 1979.

CHAPTER 4

Word from the Beginning:
The Churches of Mainstream Protestantism

Probably every school child in America has heard the tale of how the Pilgrims with their Indian friends celebrated the first Thanksgiving, a harvest festival to thank God that they had survived in the New World for the year. Similarly, almost every child has heard the Virginia narrative of how Captain John Smith was saved from certain death at the hands of the Indians by Pocahontas, the daughter of the chief Powhatan, and of how some years later she became a Christian and married John Rolfe.

In light of later American history, these are curious vignettes. They are both tales of ethnoreligious communion between English Protestants and Indians. The subsequent story of relations between these peoples was not so sunny. There were wars between them; conversion attempts by the English went forward with extreme tardiness and few missionaries; "empty land" became the characteristic English justification for moving further into the wilderness that was the Indians' home.

Yet there is a poetic justice about these early tales. If communion is based on common elements between different peoples, then the two groups did have something in common. For both, manyness was a social condition in the midst of which they lived and a feature of their mental landscape. Indians, as we have seen, dwelled in nations that in themselves possessed ethnoreligious unity but were surrounded by other, separate Indian nations. English Protestants had left a land in which religious nonconformity meant that they had cultural ties with many of their compatriots but religious differences. Further, just as the many Indian nations disclosed a basic core of oneness—similarities in world view, ethos, and structure of religious ritual—so the many Protestant groups in America betrayed a tendency toward religious oneness. In one sense, Protestants came to be the most diverse religious people in America, counting themselves as members of well over two hundred different denominational groups. In another sense, though, they were the most unified group in America, and their common ideal was so persuasive that it became the religious vision of all Americans. We will pursue much of this latter theme in Part Two, but for now we need to look at the unity of mainstream Protestantism in itself. We will look at it first as an inherited religious vision and then as an *American* religious vision.

THE RELIGION OF THE REFORMATION

Protestantism was born in sixteenth-century Europe with the idea of reformation at the center of its religious sense. In the preaching of the two great Reformers, Martin Luther (1483–1546) and John Calvin (1509–1564), prophetic protest was lodged against the priestly religion of medieval sacramentalism. The Reformers saw the many layers of symbolic and ritual expression that had grown up around Christianity not as links in a chain to heaven but as obstacles to true communion with God. They wanted to call the church back to its original purity. They wanted to harangue it until, in penitence, it discarded religious practices which for the Reformers simply got in the way, substituting the material for the spiritual, the human for the divine.

In the terms of our text, the Reformers wanted to do two things. First of all, they wanted to bring about a clear division between extraordinary religion (the way to reach God) and ordinary religion (material human culture). Secondly, they wanted to purge Christianity of elements of the world view of correspondence that had crept in, returning to a purer version of the world view of causality. In other words, they wanted to emphasize the great gap between the divine order of things and the natural human world. Without God's help through the grace of Jesus Christ, humans were powerless when their salvation was in question. They were sinners who on their own could not do anything to win the grace of God. And just as God must perform a decisive act to save them, so they must live out their loyalty to him by decisive action in the world. Curiously, although Protestantism separated the world from God, it also led its followers out of their churches and onto the public stage of history.

Thus, prophetic protest was the original message of Protestantism. As the inspired messenger of God, the prophet who recalled people to their true mission and destiny was its great religious figure. And the word which the prophet spoke made Protestantism the religion of the Word. Formed seemingly without matter—of breath or wind—the Word was Spirit. So the realm of the spiritual became the means by which Protestantism could conduct criticism. Prophetic protest was the principle on which the other, more concrete principles of the Reformation were built.

First among these principles was that of scripture alone. The Word was not any word at all but a specific Word present in the Bible: it was Jesus and the law which the religion of Jesus enjoined. In the beginning, the gospel of John had announced, there was the Word (John 1:1). Protestantism never forgot the scripture as it rebuked the medieval church for its adherence to tradition and the Roman papacy. Sacramentalism had led away from the truth of the Word from the beginning; it was a corruption of the scriptural message of salvation.

The second principle which the Protestant Reformers preached was that of justification through faith. As they saw it, this was intimately bound up with the idea of scripture alone, for justification by faith was the content of the biblical message, the core meaning taught in scripture. Here, justification was a legal term used to connote salvation, and faith meant the trust that human beings felt for God in Jesus. That is to say, faith was not as in the medieval Catholic church a collection of doctrinal truths to be accepted. Instead, it was a response to a divine and infinitely trustworthy person. Faith put the emotional experience of an individual at the center of religion, an emphasis that later Protestantism in America would develop even further. Taken as a complete statement, justification by faith announced that there was nothing that humans could do on their own to gain salvation. It implied the Reformed doctrine of total depravity, or corruption, and the huge abyss which in the causal view of things separated the human from the divine.

A third principle on which the Reformation was built was the priesthood of all believers. Here, too, the Reformation departed from the medieval church. The older church, with its sacramental understanding of the role of the priest, saw him as a ritual leader who represented the community before God. In this scheme of things, the community—as one collective reality—offered a common act of worship to heaven. Now, with the priesthood of all, Protestants brought individualism into the communal consciousness of the church. If each person was a priest, then each as an individual was offering worship to God. Worship in a group brought the fellowship of common *worshipers* but not, in the older Catholic sense, of one common act of worship.

The fellowship of common worshipers led to the fourth great principle of the Reformation, which was the church. The Reformers saw the need for a social expression of Christianity, and for them the church was the communion of saints. The place where those who had received saving faith were gathered, the church was also the place where the Word was rightly preached and the sacraments (baptism and the eucharist) were rightly administered. *Preaching* the Word had a new centrality in this definition of the Reformers, and, significantly, administering the sacraments came second to the sermon. While in medieval Catholicism, a sermon might or might not be preached at a eucharistic service, for the Reformers the most important bread to be broken was the bread of the Word. Further, the idea of the communion of saints, while long a part of Christian teaching, still stopped short of the more cohesive metaphor of the Body of Christ. Protestants together, unlike Catholics, were not one sacrament in the sight of God. Their fellowship was a gathering of the many.

Hence, the basic principles of the Reformation brought a subtle individualism to Christianity. In the context of sixteenth-century Europe, this budding individualism reflected trends that had already been present in the private spiritual quests of monks and nuns. It also agreed with other trends that were present in the philosophy being taught in the universities of the time. Most importantly, it spoke to the individualism which was growing with a new middle class. Being neither rich nor poor, the middle class felt the challenge of having enough to be able to struggle for more but not having enough to rest content. Thus, their place in the middle of society fostered personal striving and, hence, individualism. In Protestantism the middle class had a religion that fit its vision of the world and its spiritual needs.

Beyond this, the basic principles of the Reformation brought a new emphasis on the content of preaching and with it a new theological consciousness. Individuals needed to hear the Word in order to receive the message of faith and salvation. Once they heard it, they needed to ascertain what it really meant. So the history of Protestantism in Europe and in early America was a history of theological questioning and refinement. In contrast to Catholicism, which mostly remained attached to the theology of the sixteenth century until Vatican II, Protestantism spawned vigorous theological debate. Once the center of religion was no longer the matter of the sacramental order, it became the spirit of comprehension of the Word.

Finally, the basic principles of the Reformation led to a new call for moral action in the world. As in the Old Testament, the Word of God did not call humans to be idle but instead to witness to their beliefs by their deeds. Protestantism, as we have already noted, led out of the churches and into the world. This meant that, while the two-edged sword of the Word separated extraordinary from ordinary religion, it also cut away distraction, so that there could be a reunification of the two. Protestants, as well as others, experienced an overlapping of boundaries between the extraordinary and ordinary realms. If the churches led people back to the world, then extraordinary religion marched them straight into the midst of the ordinary. But different from medieval Catholicism, the overlapping of the boundaries between the two did not come through the natural world that supplied the raw material for ritual action in the sacraments. The overlapping of boundaries came, instead, through the medium of history; that is, through the men and women who, inspired by right preaching of the Word, now went forth to do deeds of Christian witness in the world.

In the Lutheran Reformation of Germany, which spread also to the Scandinavian countries, the Protestant movement proceeded cautiously, holding to the sacramental past even as it preached the Word. Luther, when compared to Calvin and other continental Reformers, was both a liturgical and theological conservative. Thus, for Luther and his followers the eucharist was the Word which had become visible. The Mass with some changes continued for about two hundred years; and in Sweden a rich attention to liturgical detail clothed the new intent of the worship service in some of the trappings of medieval Catholicism. There were clear signs of the new order though. Congregational singing indicated the importance of the laity and their personal response to the liturgical action. New church architecture often placed the pulpit in such a position that it vied with the altar for dominance in the sanctuary space. The Bible was read in the language of the people instead of in Latin, and gradually the eucharist became an occasional, rather than a weekly, celebration. Still, Luther and early Lutherans believed that Jesus was present in the sacrament, and in their attachment to the person of Jesus, they continued a medieval emphasis on the divine humanity. There was warmth more than austerity in the Lutheran reforms and, with the preaching of trust in the compassion of Jesus, a devotionalism centered on human feelings of closeness to God.

But the Lutheran Reformation did not go far enough for Calvin and for many others. Calvin had arrived at his Protestant insights independently of Luther, and his emphasis was, as it developed, somewhat different. Overwhelmed by a sense of the majesty and otherness of God more than the humanity of Jesus, his plan for worship matched the nature of his vision. A Calvinist church in its austerity proclaimed that God was totally unlike anything natural or human. With the table of the Ten Commandments the only ornament on the wall, the asceticism of the building directed God's people to the contemplation of his law. Everything in the liturgy turned on the Word, and the architecture of bareness was itself a sacramental symbol of the gospel message. As new buildings came into existence, the pulpit stood central in the sanctuary and proclaimed that preaching was the essence of the service. In order to worship, a clear mind rather than stimulation of the senses was required. Thus, hymns, prayers, scriptural lessons, and the sermon all strived to cultivate that clarity of vision Calvin sought. Communion, in which the presence of Jesus was acknowledged, was at first prescribed monthly and then four times yearly. Above all, for Calvin the presence of Jesus was revealed in the Bible, which was God's law book. Understanding it would lead Christians elected for salvation out into the world, where they could witness to Jesus by their lives.

In the Reformed free city of Geneva (now in Switzerland), Calvin was able to see the Word made flesh. By a series of political steps taken with the consent, though sometimes reluctant, of the city fathers, he transformed the government into a theocracy, a state ruled by God or his representatives in the church. Hence, far more than Luther, Calvin joined the religious and the political realms, making it possible to view religion as moral action in the public sphere. The impulse of the Calvinist Reformation collapsed extraordinary religion inward toward the ordinary center of things. Moreover, it encouraged a sense of the chosenness of those whom God had elected for salvation. The sense of chosenness, with a conviction of righteousness not far behind, was hardly complete, at least in Calvin's time. The elect were hidden in the church and the city, and there were no signs to determine clearly who they were. It was part of God's mystery that the saints should have their identity veiled, even from themselves. The reason for the theocratic constitution of the city of Geneva was to create a social climate in which the saints could flourish, but Calvin never thought of Geneva as a city in which *only* the saved resided.

With his religion of law and his stern doctrine of the predestination of saints and sinners, Calvin had begun a spiritual system which led, increasingly, to what the sociologist of religion Max Weber has called innerworldly asceticism. Calvin had initiated the earliest stage of the "Protestant ethic," a moral system that seemed to thrive on the evidence of its own success. Briefly, as saints became anxious about the question of their salvation, they looked to their behavior to seek assurance. One of the signs of saving faith was, after all, a righteous and reformed pattern of living. Gradually though, the saints in practice began to attach more weight to this pattern than to their faith, to put the cart of good deeds before the horse of grace, so to speak. It was not too much of a shift to begin to see external righteousness, good works, as a guarantee of salvation—and a guarantee which could be strengthened by more and more good action. Thus, ironically, an ethic of works and work came to flourish at the center of the religion which had taught justification by faith. In America the Protestant ethic would help to tame a continent to Euro-American ways and imprint its character on the public face of the nation. Moreover, it would assist in the assimilation of religious and ethnic groups, such as the Jews, who shared a commitment to the value of law and the ethic of thrift, industry, and hard work—the "Protestant ethic."

Unlike Catholicism, which was a very old religion, Calvinism, born in the sixteenth century, was very young. Its structure would be transported to the New World as the major religious influence on the English colonies there. And because it was young, it would continue to grow in America, changing—like Catholicism—in terms of the needs of the new situation, but also changing because it was natural for a young (and successful) religion to grow rapidly.

THE REFORMATION IN OLD ENGLAND

Before Calvinism migrated to America, however, it traveled across the English Channel. Here the Reformation had moved from the king, through the ranks of government, and thence to ordinary folk. The Reformation was an act of state accomplished by King Henry VIII (1509–1547), after the pope refused him a divorce sought on the grounds that his wife had not given him a male heir. The result of the laws passed by Parliament under Henry was the Church of England, and the form of religion that emerged was Anglicanism. Under Queen Elizabeth I (1533–1603), it assumed its shape as the way of comprehension, in which various tendencies in belief were absorbed or comprehended in one church. For Anglicanism, theological diversity was acceptable, provided that there was uniformity in ritual. The *Book of Common Prayer* established the rubrics for that uniformity, and so long as men and women gathered around the same altar table, in effect, they might hold Lutheran, Calvinist, or even Anglo-Catholic opinions as they chose.

Hence, the Anglican church under Elizabeth and afterward sought to find a middle way between Catholicism and Protestantism. Renouncing the papacy and many medieval devotions, open to various Protestant interpretations and practices, it still retained much of the flavor of an older sacramentalism. In this context, there was a growing body of English opinion that Elizabeth's reforms had not gone far enough. Those who shared this view came to be called Puritans because they sought to purify the church, and their movement flourished in England for a century, encompassing a number of different strands and tendencies. Among the Puritans were Separatists, who thought that the only route to purity was complete separation from the Church of England, and non-Separatists, who thought that the church could be cleansed from within. Moreover, among the non-Separatists, by the 1640s there were some who thought that each congregation should govern itself in complete independence from every other (Congregationalists or Independents) and others who thought that individual congregations should be related to larger bodies called presbyteries and synods (Presbyterians). Finally, left-wing Separatist groups, important among them Baptists and Quakers, also arose.

Despite these differences, there was much that every Puritan group shared. For all of them, purifying the church meant purging it of the Roman holdovers from the past and adhering more strongly to Calvinism. Like the nineteenth-century Reform Jews of Germany and the United States, Puritans sought a greater decorum in worship, and they identified it with the austere and simple liturgies of John Calvin. More than Reform Jews, though, they developed the theological rationale that accompanied their ritual reforms. Moreover, as the movement grew, it came to incorporate elements from the left wing of the continental Reformation, more radical than Calvin had been. Puritans began to think of their churches as "gathered" or free—voluntary associations of individuals who had professed their faith with understanding, subscribed to a church covenant or compact, and demonstrated their intent by the upright moral character of their lives. In contrast, both Calvin and Luther had seen churches as territorial, including all of the inhabitants of a place.

However, as in the Calvinist churches of Europe, preaching for the Puritans became the central act of public worship. As new "meetinghouses" displaced older churches, architecture told its story with bare walls and dominant pulpit. As in continental Calvinism, worship was meant for the ear and the mind, not for the eye. Gone were the ornamental vessels and vestments, the incense and candlesticks, all the accouterments of a high-church liturgy, which Anglicanism preferred. Instead, there was the simple rhythm of psalm, scriptural lesson, and prayer, interrupted by the major event of the sermon. Communion occurred only infrequently, and when it was held it was understood as a sign of faith and love for one another. Sometimes, in order to stress that communion was a meal and in imitation of the simple setting of the Last Supper, Puritans sat around a table. Their leaders broke bread from common loaves and then passed the loaves to the rest of the people who broke off their share as well.

Yet in the services there was a new experiential emphasis which went beyond the churches of continental Calvinism. Worship, the Puritans thought, should be spontaneous, the expression of a personal relationship with God. Thus, early Congregationalists encouraged extempore preaching and often accompanied it by heartfelt groans from members of the congregation. Early Baptists (Puritans opposed to infant baptism) thought hymns were artificial and would not allow them in their churches. In emphasizing adult baptism, they stressed that it was the surrender of a believer to God, an act of decisive choice on his or her part and not, as in the medieval understanding, a sacramental mystery. While this early spontaneity of Puritan worship would later decline, its experiential quality would have important corollaries, as we shall see, when the Puritans immigrated to America.

Beyond this, in the spirit of the Calvinism they had appropriated, the Puritans stimulated a new consecration of time, an austere dedication which expressed their adherence to the world view of causality and their commitment to moral action in history. From the time of their rise under Elizabeth, the Puritans had preached against the holy days, some 165 of them, which interrupted the daily work schedule for religious festivals. These observances sanctioned "idleness," which invited onslaughts from the devil. Celebrated by Elizabethans with physical activity, sports, and play going, they distracted from true religion rather than encouraged it. Salvation came to those who expressed their loyalty to God in the work ethic that his law demanded. Thrift, sobriety, industry, and prudence—all were to be cultivated instead of the moral looseness and flabbiness which the holy-day calendar engendered.

In place of this old liturgical calendar—even in place of its great central feasts such as Christmas and Easter—the Puritans stressed the Sabbath. Kept on Sunday in honor of the resurrection of Jesus, it lasted, in the ancient Jewish fashion, from sunset to sunset. On this day, for the Puritans all work should cease so that humans could spend their time attending to divine things. Meanwhile, they should strenuously avoid the frivolous recreation, the sporting and gaming and play going, that Anglicanism had permitted. Such recreation only served to distract men and women from service to God, and it sometimes led them into more serious forms of dissipation and vice.

Puritan Sabbatarianism gained support even among those in the mainstream of the Church of England. And in America, as we will discuss, it supplied the model for the Sabbath observance throughout the English colonies. In effect, the Puritans in their Sabbath campaign had surgically separated extraordinary religion from ordinary religion. The festival cycle, which had knit natural and supernatural concerns together in an intertwining sequence, was abrogated, while the abolition of all forms of worldly recreation on the Sabbath stressed the separation between human and divine things. Meanwhile, the time taken from the frequent holy days of the older order was freed for the pursuit of work, a pursuit which supported the new demands that industrialization and the factory system would make on ordinary people. If the Word of the Reformation led out into the world, its Puritan translation was accompanied by some unforeseen twists. Henceforth, at least in the public organization of society, sacred and secular would begin to occupy separate compartments.

THE REFORMATION IN THE ENGLISH COLONIES

In America this separation of the sacred and the secular realms continued and intensified. But the story of European Protestantism in the English colonies is a story of its Americanization. There were strong ties to the past, and the heritage of the Reformation was never lost for the early Protestant settlers. Still, the experience of the new land shaped the older Protestantism in profound ways. It is to the American transformation of Protestantism that we now turn.

The earliest immigrants to the English colonies on the Atlantic coast of North America were Anglicans and Puritans, both with pronounced Calvinist leanings. Moreover, the Puritan movement gradually assumed organizational structure as Congregationalist, Presbyterian, and Baptist churches, all three denominations of the so-called "old dissent" of England. So there was a considerable pattern of religious unity in Protestant America from the first, and that pattern of unity would continue to characterize mainstream Protestantism. The unity, of course, was a unity in diversity, and denominationalism became the framework for American Protestantism.

Unlike a church, which included all of the people born in a given territory, a denomination was a voluntary organization. Thus, by definition it was not universal but particular. It was a group of people called, or "denominated," out of the larger communion of saints; that is, it was only a branch of the church, not the whole of it. Still, the reasons for belonging to one denomination rather than another were serious and important. The Word did not cut empty air, and often it separated church bodies into two, or three, or more.

The sources for denominationalism lay in the Puritan movement of England which we have been discussing, but in America because of circumstances denominationalism assumed far wider dimensions than it ever had in England. American necessities, in short, compelled a move away from the old model of a state church (the Church of England) and toward a free-church model. Religious liberty gradually spread until, with the United States Constitution, it became the law of the land. Every church, no matter what its theological claims, became in America a denomination, a voluntary society of gathered members, separate yet not separated from every other Christian church. Moreover, while denominations were not the same as all-inclusive churches, they were also very different from sects and cults, as we will see in later chapters. They affirmed the world and even in their more critical moods never withdrew totally from it; they accepted the Christian tradition as transmitted by the Reformation and did not claim a new revelation.

From the first, there were boundary difficulties involved in this concept of a denomination. To be separate, yet not separated, from the larger church meant to live in a tension midway between two different understandings. The boundaries between a denomination and a church were easily traversed and easily blurred. Thus, Protestantism with its denominational accommodations was always open to amorphousness, always in danger of merging its manyness into a kind of religion-in-general. On the other hand, because the borders dividing one group from the next were relatively weak, there could be a good deal of mutual cooperation between denominations as they sought to make America a Christian nation.

In overview, then, the early denominations brought to America a common Puritan-Anglican past, and they combined it with a common task of settlement in the new land. In this process, they gradually turned more and more away from the Word as theology and toward the Word as experience and action. Evangelical piety brought a new emphasis on the emotional dimension of religion, even as it continued the separation between the ordinary and extraordinary orders. Meanwhile, the laity, who acted decisively in the world, imprinted their character on the structure of American Protestantism.

Anglican Virginia

The Virginia colony, dating from 1607, had been the earliest English settlement in the New World. Here Anglicanism and the *Book of Common Prayer* were the prescribed order, but there were also Calvinist leanings in the Anglican establishment. Puritanism was part of its mood, though unofficially. Like the New England colonies which followed, Virginia was founded to counter the Roman Catholic presence of Spain and France in the New World; it was meant to establish an outpost of the true religion of Protestant Christianity in the American wilderness. Thus, although the fact is often overlooked, the colony of Virginia had a religious as well as a financial motive for its beginnings.

Moreover, the Puritan observance of the Sabbath was as demanding in Virginia, for a time, as it would be in New England. Under Sir Thomas Gates in 1610 and Sir Thomas Dale the following year, the law required attendance at divine service and threatened death for a third offense of nonattendance. It compelled people to be present at Sunday afternoon catechism and forbade gaming, intemperance, or other violations of the Sabbath peace. Even weekdays were occasions for religious services, which everyone had to attend twice daily, with an extra sermon on Wednesdays. For almost a decade, this regime was the law, and even thereafter the Sabbath in Virginia was largely Puritan in its style.

But despite this public piety, there were other problems, among them disease and Indian wars. So in 1624 the London Company—the private commercial organization which established the colony—made it over to the English crown. As a royal colony, Virginia continued to be Anglican, although with modifications. The parish system of old England did not work in the vast expanses of Virginia territory, while ministers were few and often lacking in Christian zeal. A vestry system, in which the congregation controlled clerical positions by making annual reappointments, further weakened the effectiveness of the clergy. By the time plans were being made to send a bishop to the Virginia church, the Civil War in England prevented it, and meanwhile, missionary efforts among the Indians were not very successful. Thus, the failure of Anglicanism to build a strong establishment created a kind of vacuum into which more Calvinist forms of Protestantism could later move. The weakness of the Church of England in Virginia—and the other southern colonies as well—helped to determine the future of mainstream Protestantism.

Puritan New England

In New England the Separatist Pilgrims—no longer part of the Church of England—touched land at Plymouth Rock in 1620. They had come from Holland, where they had fled when their church in England had come under more and more harassment by the government for its nonconformity. A decade later a group of non-Separatists—still officially in the English church—landed at Salem and then founded Boston, beginning the Massachusetts Bay colony. The Pilgrims, by landing outside the jurisdiction of Virginia, and the Massachusetts Bay Puritans, by taking their charter to America with them, both managed to carve out virtually independent republics for themselves in the early years. Here they could create their vision of a religious society which would rival Calvin's Geneva. They would be a light to the nations, a city on a hill, a New Israel in the wilderness.

Before too long, there were other colonies in New England, as members of the Massachusetts Bay colony, for one reason or another, struck off on their own. And in all of the colonies, the dream of the New Israel brought with it clear transformations of the Puritanism of old England. There was little possibility of a parish system without the bishops and organizational structure of Anglicanism. Instead, the congregational system of independent churches flourished under a strong clerical leadership. The sense of isolation from the corruptions of the Old World and of immersion in the untainted vigor of the new fostered an increasing sense of chosenness and righteousness. Combined with the ideal of a New Israel or New Geneva, the mix led to a form of church-state alliance, which, as we will see in Part Two, provided the beginnings of a later unofficial civil religion in the United States.

Puritanism expressed its sense of chosenness by increased attention to the doctrine of the covenant, which had been part of its English heritage. This pact, or agreement, between God and his people was modeled on the covenant between God and Israel of old. It made the Puritans, as members of one community of the elect, God's own people. If they fulfilled their part in the covenant through lives of virtue and righteousness, then God would surely be faithful to them. On the other hand, if plague or witchcraft, Indian wars or conservative Anglicans, should trouble their settlements, these were signs that something was amiss in the Christian commitment of the people.

The idea of the covenant became a practical arrangement in the civil government, which was also established on a covenantal basis, and in the congregational churches, each of which had covenants of association for members. In a further transformation, belonging to the church covenant became more difficult in Massachusetts Bay than it ever had been among the Puritans of England. By about 1636 Puritans began to require a new experiential test for church membership. No longer was it sufficient to confess the Christian faith through intellectual understanding and assent. Now an emotional conviction of one's sinfulness and a felt sense of saving faith were required. Thus, no matter how upright the character, no matter how loyal the covenant faith, unless there was a conversion experience, there could be no membership in the church. While the Puritans could never be absolutely certain that all members of the church were visible saints—people who were assured of salvation—they had decidedly limited their margin for error. When an individual thought that he or she had felt saving faith, that person went before the elders of the church or sometimes the congregation itself. The personal experience was heard and, if acceptable, ratified by community agreement. Like an Oglala Sioux warrior returning from his vision quest, the stamp of the community was necessary to authenticate the private encounter with spiritual forces. In New England the Reformation meant individual seeking, but it also meant community affiliation.

Quaker Pennsylvania

In Pennsylvania English settlement came through a religious group which had arisen out of the left wing of the Puritan movement. The Society of Friends had taken the individualism, already part of English Puritanism, and carried it to radical conclusions. When in 1681 the Quaker William Penn received the charter to a vast expanse of land in the New World, he had the means to inaugurate his "holy experiment." Subject to persecution both in old and New England, the Quakers came to Pennsylvania where they could follow out their conviction that there was something of the divine in every human being. They taught a mysticism of inner light which meant that there was no need for church, creed, or priesthood. In worship they sat quietly together, hoping to sense the presence of God, and when they did, they spoke as the Spirit prompted them. The communion of saints, for them, was a community in contemplation, sharing the fruits of that contemplation with one another. Meanwhile, the bare walls of the meetinghouse spoke their radical protest against Anglican ornateness and aided each Quaker in an attempt to move beyond the distractions of the material world and penetrate into the mystery of the divine.

The Quaker vision brought with it legal toleration for any person who believed in God. Thus, like early Rhode Island with its Baptist origins, Pennsylvania became a haven for various religious groups, and a wide and genuine pluralism flourished there. The Quakers mostly controlled affairs, and there were tensions occasioned by the diversity of peoples who settled in the colony. Still, Pennsylvania, more than Massachusetts Bay, seemed a model for the democratic venture of the later United States. In Massachusetts Bay the church was established by law, and only full church members (those who had experienced the requisite conversion and were accepted into the congregation) could vote and hold civil office. In Pennsylvania there was religious freedom even for Roman Catholics and Jews. The church had been dissolved into individual conscience, and the primacy of conscience led inevitably to the law of toleration. Even though in 1705 the English government forced some limitations on this liberal policy, Quaker toleration continued in its broad outlines throughout the eighteenth century.

The Later Colonial Period

With the Quakers setting a model for toleration into the eighteenth century, Pennsylvania became the mecca for a new wave of immigrants. Scotch, Scotch-Irish (Scotch who had earlier immigrated to Ireland), and German peoples entered the colony and helped to shape it. The Scotch and Scotch-Irish were Presbyterians, who settled in the Philadelphia area and also moved west and south into the Anglican colonies. The Germans, many of whom were Lutherans, swelled the population as well, with two-thirds of them settling in Pennsylvania.

Life in the new country, though, was hardly conducive to the growth of organized religion. Indeed, from the middle of the seventeenth century, the Puritans of Massachusetts Bay had seen the membership rolls of their churches shrink ominously when their adult children were unable to testify to experiences of conversion as required for church membership. Many of this new generation believed firmly in Christian truth and led lives of upright morality. All that was missing was the emotional encounter with saving faith. Hence, in 1662 the Puritans in a church synod accepted a compromise. The Halfway Covenant, as it came to be called, provided that infant grandchildren of the saints should be baptized and thus made "halfway" members of the church. Children of the saints, though without an experience of saving faith, would likewise be considered halfway members, provided that they met all other requirements. Since voting rights in the colony depended on membership in the church, this move had civic consequences in preserving at least some breadth to the political base of Massachusetts Bay. But more important here, some Puritans read the necessity for the measure as a sign of religious "declension," or decline.

Whether or not they were right, we do know that church membership throughout the colonies was very low. In fact, at the time of the American Revolution, it was probably less than 10 percent. Earlier in the eighteenth century, an intense religious movement had swept the colonies. Known as the

Great Awakening, it began in New Jersey in 1726 when Theodore J. Frelinghuysen (1691–1748?), a Dutch Reformed pastor, stirred his several congregations by his preaching. Soon the neighboring Presbyterians, led by Gilbert Tennent (1703–1764), experienced similar religious excitement. In New England the preaching of Jonathan Edwards (1703–1758) at Northampton in 1736 sparked a like response; and the people groaned, sobbed, and sometimes fell before God's power, as it manifested itself in the Word. By 1740 George Whitefield (1714–1770), a renowned preacher from England, was traveling through the colonies and fanning the electric sparks of revival into fire. Whitefield brought a communications revolution with him, for in his attempts with John Wesley to reach the factory workers of England, he had turned to open-air preaching. Crowds would gather and swell, held by the magnetic oratory of the speaker. Freed from the constraints of a formal sanctuary, they could more spontaneously express the personal feelings that awareness of their sins and God's mercy engendered. Moreover, the fact that the minister who preached was an itinerant, a traveler who moved from place to place, seemed to excite the crowds, too. There was a freshness about the Word when it fell from the lips of a stranger, and the newness brought religious excitement in its train.

Thus, from one end of the colonies to the other, the Great Awakening brought a red thread of evangelical pietism to bind the different Protestant churches together. Part of its effect was to shift some membership patterns so that nominal Anglicans and Congregationalists became Baptists and Presbyterians. More important, however, it created in Protestant religion a common style that was nationally identifiable. Experiential religion—evangelicalism—had swept the Protestant mainstream and would continue to characterize it. Further, the common style was expressed mostly in a cluster of churches, which contained most of the Protestant church members of the era. By the end of the colonial period, Congregationalists and Presbyterians accounted for 40 percent of all churches, while Baptists and Anglicans numbered 15 percent each of the total. Meanwhile, Congregationalists, Presbyterians, and Baptists (with modifications) all subscribed to the Westminster Confession, the English Calvinist statement of faith formulated by 1647.

CONTINUED GROWTH AND CHANGE IN AMERICAN PROTESTANTISM

Despite the promise of the Awakening, church membership did not increase through the latter part of the eighteenth century and, in fact, probably declined. The reasons were various. It was true that statistics were misleading, since many more heard the Word preached in the churches than counted themselves church members. Still, deism had been brought into the colonies by English soldiers during the French and Indian War (1755-1763) and by French soldiers during the American Revolution (1775-1783). An outgrowth of the European intellectual movement known as the Enlightenment, deism taught a general religion of God as creator revealed through the book of nature. It subscribed to moral standards of good and evil and a system of rewards and punishments in an afterlife. But it nowhere admitted the necessity of Jesus, the Bible, or the Christian church.

A second reason for low church membership was the disruption occasioned in different churches by the Revolutionary War. With men and even pastors enlisting and with the countryside turned into a battlefield, church life could hardly be unaffected. Still more, Anglicanism and the infant Methodist movement had close ties to the mother country and after the war had to undergo reorganization. By 1784 the Methodists had an independent American organization, followed in 1789 by the Protestant Episcopal church, reconstituted out of what had once been Anglicanism.

A third reason for low church membership was the continuance of circumstances that had been present from the seventeenth century. America from the European point of view was a new land and a wild land. Institutions and attitudes that were taken for granted in the Old World had to fight to make their way in the new. On the frontier, a church was far less necessary than a house, and a Bible far less practical than a hunting rifle or an ax. Yet this situation, discouraging though it seemed, did lead some churches to move still closer together. Thus, the Congregationalists and the Presbyterians by the end of the war regarded themselves almost as a single church, dividing territory amicably between them and, by their Plan of Union in 1801, cooperating in home missionary efforts on the frontier. Beyond this, in the early nineteenth century Protestant voluntary societies, formed without official church ties, distributed Bibles and tracts and furthered the moral reform of society. For them as for most of the Protestants of this period, the leading problems that American Christianity had to face were "infidelity" and "barbarism."

The Methodist Era

By 1790 the new United States had entered a time of rapid growth and development. In that year the population was some 4 million, with one out of every twenty people living west of the Appalachian Mountains. By the time of the Civil War (1861-1865), there were over 30 million people in the country, and about half of them had left the eastern seaboard for the new settlements further west. Church membership, meanwhile, increased ten times from 1800 to 1850, and while in 1800 only one out of every fifteen persons was Protestant, by 1850 one out of seven belonged to a Protestant church. Overwhelmingly, the era was a time of Methodist growth and expansion.

Indeed, Methodists numbered well over 1 million by 1850. They were far and away the largest American Protestant congregation, the Baptists trailing them by some 500,000. When we consider that the Methodist church had just been organized in 1784, this is an impressive record of growth. And if we look more closely, we can see that the Methodists achieved their success for at least two reasons. First of all, their religious message fit the climate and mood of Americans in the nineteenth century. Secondly, their organization was well adapted to new conditions on the frontier and also to the more settled areas in the East.

Even in colonial times, there had been an erosion of Calvinist belief among Protestants. In New England, for example, the character of preaching gradually changed so that themes like the sovereignty of God and the predestination of the elect and the damned gave way before sermons concerned with morality and, by the end of the eighteenth century, the availability of salvation for all. People who were continually feeling their success in building up a new country found it hard to believe that they could not also do something to win their salvation, and the new style of preaching suited their new situation. Churches such as the Universalists (1779) and the Unitarians (1825) were born out of this new spirit. Like these congregations, the Methodists—with their teachings of free will, the possibility of human perfection, and the universal availability of salvation—were telling Americans what they already knew and, also, most wanted to hear.

Methodist spirituality and worship were equally attractive. The founder of Methodism, John Wesley (1703–1791), had been a loyal member of the Church of England and for years had seen his movement as part of that church. The hymns that he used in his services were highly sacramental in their understanding of the eucharistic presence, and he had urged Methodists to frequent communion. But in America these high-church tendencies disappeared, and greater stress was placed on the Bible and preaching. Communion became infrequent and, perhaps in its place, love feasts became popular. Unlike the banquet of the Lord's Supper in which the bread of communion was broken and shared, love feasts were banquets of the Word. Members came together to share experiences of the power of God and the compassion of Jesus, which they had felt in their lives. Love feasts were testimonials in which ordinary people witnessed to the character of their Christian faith and so encouraged one another.

The very name, Methodist, suggests the importance of organization in the new Methodist societies. Methodists were people who should live by a rule, or method, and John Wesley's remarkable efforts to structure his movement were part of his legacy to the American church. At the head of the church was a superintendent, or bishop, under whom the church was divided into districts. Each district had its presiding elder and in turn was carved into circuits, huge areas over which a traveling preacher could ride to visit Methodists in far-flung territory. Meanwhile, in each circuit there were local units called classes, visited at intervals by the circuit riders, but conducting worship largely on their own. They met weekly to encourage and strengthen one another, prayed, studied scripture, and offered testimony. When they could find one, they turned to the services of a lay exhorter, who would preach the Word and hearten them in their efforts.

The nineteenth century, therefore, has been called the Methodist era because it was the period in which Methodism became the predominant form of American Protestantism. But Methodism gave its name to the period, too, because it was a generic name for the religious style that swept Protestantism. Briefly, there was a shift from the older Puritan form of evangelicalism to a new, more popular version. As we have seen, American Puritanism had included a strong experiential vein in its insistence on the importance of conversion. But the American Puritans, like their English coreligionists, were also theological sophisticates who delighted in the well-thought and well-turned sermon. Seven years after their landing in the New World, the Puritans of Massachusetts Bay had founded Harvard College (1636) for the education of a learned ministry. They continued to be exercised over theological questions throughout the eighteenth century, and new schools such as Yale (1701) and Andover (1808) were founded because of theological differences. There was in this pattern something of the spirit of John Calvin with his sense of the Word and its fundamental appeal to the intellect. In the nineteenth century, however, Protestant Christians moved more and more away from the intellectual Word, preferring instead a total immersion in the emotional and experiential Word. There was theological decline and general antiintellectualism, while sentimental pietism and religious individualism prevailed.

The great symbol for the era became the frontier camp meeting, where revival preachers, sometimes five or six of them at one time, sought to stir the hearts of ordinary folk to conversion. We will have more to say about this aspect of American Protestantism in Part Two, but here it is important to note how closely the conversion model fit the teaching of Methodism. Like the earlier Puritans, John Wesley had been convinced that true religion did not consist in mere intellectual assent to Christianity but rather in a felt experience of holiness. Revivalism benefited many American denominations, but it benefited the Methodists most of all; conversely, revivalism spread a "Methodist" style of religion among many Protestant groups.

Important among these were the Baptists and the "Christians," a new American denomination which was organized after 1832 as the Disciples of Christ. Baptist farmer-preachers, though not so mobile as Methodist circuit riders, spread the revivals in the South and West, bringing to their task a curious blend of attachment to the older Calvinistic theology and disdain for seminary education. Meanwhile, the "Christians" flourished in the valley of the Ohio.

As early as the post-Revolutionary era, there had been a movement to return to authentic New Testament practice and to abolish the creeds and confessions that separated Protestants into sects and denominations. By 1804 Barton W. Stone (1772–1844), a Kentucky Presbyterian, was expressing similar sentiments and demanding that he and fellow believers be called by only the name of "Christian." Five years later in southwestern Pennsylvania, Thomas Campbell (1763–1854) and Alexander Campbell (1788–1866), his son, preached the message of return to the pure Christianity of New Testament times. The two movements amalgamated, and the Disciples were born. Significantly, Stone had been associated with the revivalism of the frontier, and the understanding of the Bible that the movement expressed was distinctly "Methodist." Stone and his coreligionists, in fact, had been forced out of association with the Presbyterians by a heresy trial.

This last was an apt expression of the fact that, even in the Methodist era, denominationalism was a continuing feature of Protestant life. We will see in another chapter that sectarianism also prospered at this time in many nineteenth-century new religions. Here, though, we must note briefly the sources of new denominations in mainstream Protestantism. One such source was growing dissension between the Presbyterians and Congregationalists who earlier had created a model for close cooperation. A major factor in the interdenominational difficulties was friction within Presbyterian ranks between so-called Old School adherents, who were strict Calvinists, and New School folk, who were modified Calvinists. The trial of Lyman Beecher (1775–1863), like Barton Stone's heresy trial, was indicative of the new developments. Beecher, though a famous revivalist and president of Lane Theological Seminary in Cincinnati, faced charges of being only moderate and lukewarm in his Calvinism. A man who had freely moved from the Congregational to the Presbyterian organization, Beecher now found himself in danger of being read out of the church because of its internal struggles. Although the charges against him were withdrawn, a year after his trial, in 1837, the Old School party expelled the New Schoolers from the church, and there were two Presbyterian churches where there had been one.

Even as doctrinal difficulties were causing splits in older denominations such as the Presbyterians, immigration from overseas was bringing many members of European national churches to America. Representatives of groups like the German and Swedish Lutherans and the Dutch and German Reformed had been present since colonial times. But now older national churches were receiving new members from abroad, while new national churches were sending their members to America, too. As in Roman Catholicism, extraordinary religion in each national church was blended with ethnic and ordinary religion, so that no one such church was the same as any other. However, unlike Catholic churches which managed to keep a nominal unity through their papal and hierarchical constitution, these national churches in America became denominations.

Later, slavery and the Civil War became a source of friction for older, mainline churches, and so denominations dissociated into northern and southern factions. Baptists, Methodists, Presbyterians, Lutherans, and Episcopalians all divided into separate churches either before or during the war. Moreover, while there had been independent black congregations since the late eighteenth century, black denominational growth received a major boost after the Civil War, a subject we will discuss in more detail in the next chapter. In sum, the Methodist era with its evangelical pietism did not mean the end of Protestant differences. The Word still compelled men and women to take doctrine seriously, while social forces occasioned yet other problems and processes of separation.

Into the Twentieth Century

The post–Civil-War era brought the Gilded Age, so-called because, beneath the glittering surface of society, there was a sense of spiritual malaise. Then, after more than a decade of expectancy, America entered the twentieth century, enjoying a continued wave of prosperity until the outbreak of the First World War in 1914 and more than a decade later the Great Depression. During this period, Protestantism either affirmed American culture, withdrew from it as much as possible, or tried to transform it.

In so doing, Protestantism, as the religion of the Word, formulated new theological statements to guide action in the world. But there was a characteristic American quality to these statements, which distinguished them from the older form of theologizing. We remember that the Word, in whatever form, impelled men and women to moral action. However, in the American version, the Word itself took on a pragmatic quality so that it seemed transparent to the problems and needs of the time. Thus, liberalism and reaction, wealth and poverty, evolution and science, all became the content of the theological message. The new Word began not with the gospel but with the situation of the world. Meanwhile, the experiential dimension of Protestantism followed the path charted by the theological Word. Either it identified so closely with American culture that ordinary religion absorbed the extraordinary. Or, in leaving the world, it discovered again the need for extraordinary religion. Or finally, by seeking to change the world, Protestantism sought a rhythmic alternation between ordinary and extraordinary forms of religion, with the ordinary still in the lead.

In the first place, Protestantism affirmed culture through the content of its popular preaching. The clerical hero of the age was Henry Ward Beecher (1813–1887), the son of Lyman Beecher, who, for a forty-year period from 1847 to 1887, held the pulpit at the Plymouth Church in Brooklyn. His sermons drew crowds numbering in the thousands, and the sermons were also widely distributed in pamphlet form. Beecher had moved far to the left of even the modified Calvinism of his father, and his New Theology was evangelical liberalism, centering emotionally on an individual relationship with Jesus and leading confidently toward an acceptance of the world. It was the humanity of Jesus that inspired the emotional sermons of Beecher, and he saw the humanness of Jesus as a sign of natural human possibility. Things as they were, were good, and an experiential encounter with the sentimental warmth of Beecher's Word should lead a person to see that. Thus, the church and the world became related aspects of one religiocultural whole. Prophetic protest died in the birth of a new culture religion; extraordinary religion was nearly extinguished in ordinariness. Still, there was a biting edge to Beecher's Word, for it led him to speak out on a range of issues from slavery and women's rights to immigration and municipal corruption.

In the Gospel of Wealth, however, the biting edge seemed wholly lost. The preaching of Russell H. Conwell (1843–1925) was a good example of this direction in popular Protestantism. For Conwell and for others who agreed, poverty was sinful, and it was the duty of every good Christian to get rich. His sermon "Acres of Diamonds" was initially delivered in 1861 and repeated some 6,000 times after that, urging on his hearers that there were acres of diamonds in their own backyards, if only they took the trouble to dig them out. Conwell's preaching—and the Gospel of Wealth—was Christian baptism for the burgeoning capitalism of the era. In the age of early millionaires and corporate robber barons, Conwell and his breed signaled that the church was on the side of the world, especially when it was powerful and rich. Yet there was an innocence about Conwell's Word with its supreme confidence, its euphoria, about human nature. The sky was the limit, he was saying, and humans could achieve anything they genuinely chose.

More intellectual in its articulation of the need to accept the world was Protestant Liberalism, a response to new cultural developments including science and Charles Darwin's theory of evolution (1859). There was continuity between some proponents of the New Theology, like Henry Ward Beecher, and these Liberals, but New Theology spoke more to ordinary folk, and Liberalism, to an elite. The task, as Liberalism, or in its more extreme form, Modernism, saw it, was to reconcile the Christian gospel to the modern world. Here, modernity became the norm by which the Word was measured, and in any conflict, the gospel must be restructured according to the insights that science and general cultural development had provided. Old biblical tales, such as that of Adam and Eve in Eden, had to be reinterpreted in light of the new knowledge. At the same time, "higher criticism" of the Bible grew. So-called to distinguish it from the lower criticism, which sought to find the exact text of any passage, higher criticism raised historical issues and challenged old theories of authorship, dating, and contextual meaning of the biblical documents.

More generally, the Liberals were preaching a revolutionary reversal of old Calvinist thought. While Calvin had been overwhelmed by the transcendence of God—his distance from the human world—the Liberals taught immanence, the presence of God in the midst of the world. While Calvin taught human depravity and the inability of any human act to gain salvation, the Liberals abolished original sin and taught natural goodness. They shared a basic optimism about creating heaven not merely in the next world but in this one through concerted human effort. While Calvin had seen Jesus as God's Word clothed in human flesh, the Liberals saw him as a kind of elder brother, first among the many, who disclosed to humans all that they could know of God. Jesus had the value of God for Liberals, but whether or not he *was* God, as traditional Protestantism had thought, was never said. Finally, while Calvin's Word honed the intellect to doctrinal and spiritual precision, the Word of the Liberals urged them to inner emotional experience. Evangelical pietism, with its emphasis on heartfelt feeling, continued in a new and more sophisticated form in Liberal teaching. Thus, the intellectual difficulties of the scientific age were short-circuited by the religion of the heart.

Liberal acceptance of the world was countered head on by the second response of Protestants to their changing world, that of partially withdrawing from it and rejecting it. Fundamentalism grew strong in the same climate which fostered Liberalism, and the Fundamentalist-Liberal controversy became the key to Protestantism in the late nineteenth and early twentieth centuries. Fundamentalism, like Liberalism, grew out of earlier movements. First of all, there was the millennialism which had expected the final coming of Jesus and the end of the world. This had flourished in a number of midcentury Protestant groups, some of whom we will discuss in our chapter on nineteenth-century new religions. Fundamentalism drew from millennial sources, but it added a second feature—a commitment to rationalistic study and interpretation of the Bible, which had enjoyed prestige at Princeton Theological Seminary (New Jersey) from early in the century.

In a series of Bible conferences held at Niagara, Ontario (Canada), beginning in 1868, a group of conservative evangelicals hammered out a response, both millennial and rational, to the challenges of science and modernity. Later, with a series of twelve volumes published between 1910 and

1915 and widely distributed, the movement grew. Called *The Fundamentals*, these volumes taught the inerrancy of the scriptures, the divinity and virgin birth of Jesus, his death on the cross in substitution for the sins of all human beings, and his bodily resurrection and imminent second coming. In this context, the millennialism of the Fundamentalists refuted the assumption of continual human betterment, which was the message of the age of progress. Instead, it taught that the world was swiftly worsening and that only the power of Jesus in his second coming could save the elect. It added to the experiential Christianity of the Liberals and traditional evangelicals a hardheaded dogmatism which argued closely from the biblical text. Understanding the Bible with a new, and sometimes strained, literalism, it dissolved the difficulties which science and the modern world presented in a triumphant Word of God.

With a shifting cultural climate, Fundamentalism dropped from prominence after 1925, but it enjoyed a resurgence in the sixties and seventies, when conservatism again gripped America. People were frightened and confused by the country during these years: the Vietnam War, the Watergate scandal, financial uncertainty and shrinking energy resources, the sexual revolution and the strains placed on families by the new demands of women for equality—all evoked a mood of retreat to old certainties. The Liberals, with their loose doctrinal standards and their pleas for social involvement, did not provide the spiritual goods that many Protestants wanted—a sense of religious security, the assurance of salvation. So, although sometimes Liberals did not like to admit it, Fundamentalism was authentically mainstream, a new twist to older forms of Protestantism and a movement embraced by millions in the Protestant tradition.

The same was true, though not from the beginning, for a second movement of partial world rejection within Protestantism during this era. The Holiness-Pentecostal movement had major roots in the Methodist doctrine of Christian perfection taught by John Wesley and in the Calvinist Keswick theology of sanctification (named for an English town in which annual religious conferences were held from 1875). For the founder of Methodism, there were two distinct operations of grace to be experienced: justification, which came at the time of conversion, and sanctification, which was the spiritual event that brought perfection with freedom from sin. Such perfection, or "holiness," had attracted many to Methodism earlier in the nineteenth century. At the same time, the revivals of Charles G. Finney (1792–1875) had spread an alternate form of perfectionism which stressed, instead of sinlessness, a state of trust and dedication that, through the Holy Spirit, could empower Christians to work for social reform. This Finneyite version of Christian perfection helped to create a climate in which Keswick views were readily accepted. They were inspired by the dispensationalist teachings of John Nelson Darby (1800–1882), to be discussed in Chapter 10, which also influenced the Fundamentalists. Keswick "holiness" argued that sanctification occurred gradually throughout the course of a person's life and that in a distinct work of grace the Holy Spirit empowered an individual for Christian existence. Following Darby's conviction that the present dispensation (age) would give way before a new era of the Holy Spirit, Keswick-oriented Christians saw in the Holiness movement the first stirrings of the mighty events associated with the second coming of Jesus at the end of time.

In the last third of the century, as many Methodist churches grew more formal and restrained in worship, a Holiness revival began to flourish. After a Holiness camp meeting at Vineland, New Jersey, in 1867, the National Camp Meeting Association for the Promotion of Holiness came into existence. Other Holiness organizations followed, and for a while Holiness remained within the Methodist church, just as earlier Methodism had remained within Anglicanism. But as time passed, one wing of the Holiness movement (the Keswick) had no connection to Methodism, and there were other problems created by the increasingly middle-class status of Methodism. Finally, the unavoidable tensions came to a head. By 1893 and thereafter, various Holiness associations either seceded or were expelled from the Methodist church, and Holiness began an independent history.

The more traditional of the Holiness people formed congregations such as the Church of the Nazarene. Meanwhile, a more radical element, profoundly moved by a rediscovered form of religious experience, attracted new followers and became known as Pentecostalists. These emerging Pentecostals had taken their cue from the New Testament writings of Paul and from the account of the descent of the Holy Spirit upon the apostles at Pentecost (Acts 2:1–20). They sought to receive the second baptism of the Spirit with speaking in tongues and the additional scriptural gifts of prayer, prophecy, and healing. In the late nineteenth century, there had been reports of tongues speaking at some Holiness meetings. But the seeds of the great Pentecostal revival were planted in Topeka, Kansas, at the turn of the century, after Charles F. Parham (1873–1937) founded Bethel Bible College. In an atmosphere of intense community, students searched the scripture under Parham's direction until, beginning with the century on 1 January 1901, Agnes Ozman, one of the Bethel students, had a full experience of speaking in tongues.

When Parham opened a Bible school in Houston, Texas, in 1905, William J. Seymour (d. 1923), a black Baptist Holiness preacher, came into contact with him and carried the message of the baptism of the Spirit with speaking in tongues to Los Angeles. There, from 1906 the fabled Azusa Street revival held strong until 1909, without doubt the longest continual revival in American history. In a rented hall that had once been an African Methodist Episcopal church and later a stable and a warehouse, Seymour made space for his people, who prayed for the gifts of Pentecost. At first only about a dozen came, but the San Francisco earthquake shocked California and encouraged religious interest. Then, although news of the meetings had initially been spread by word of mouth, the *Los Angeles Daily Times* began to cover them as curiosities, and the publicity brought out the crowds. Interracial and multiethnic, the followers of the revival were truly cosmopolitan, the first sign of the international scope the movement was to assume. Ethiopians and Chinese, Indians and Mexicans, various European nationalities, Jews, and, of course, American blacks prayed and felt the Spirit together, dwelling in expectation that the second coming of Jesus would be soon.

In this atmosphere of miracle and millennial faith, the Pentecostal movement was launched, interracial in its early organization. In groups like the

Assemblies of God, Pentecostalism grew not only in the United States but also throughout the world. By 1970 it could count over 8 million adherents, at least 1.5 million of them in America.

By turning inward for an experience of holiness and for the ecstasy of the Spirit with gifts of tongues and healing, the Holiness-Pentecostal movement paralleled Fundamentalism in its rejection of a Protestant culture religion. There were further connections between the two in that the Holiness-Pentecostal movement took the scripture as literally as the Fundamentalists. Moreover, both had sharply divided the extraordinary from the ordinary world in the doctrine or the experience of transcendence. The Word again spoke out against the world, yet, different from traditional Protestantism, its message led not to the public arena where history was made but to private quests for God. There was a distinctively modern and American note about this expression of the Protestant tradition, and as we will discuss in later chapters, some of these insights were shared by others who did not count themselves Protestant.

If one body of Protestants after the Civil War began to affirm culture more strenuously and a second group partially withdrew from it, a third movement within Protestantism strived to transform culture. This Social Gospel movement had had predecessors in earlier nineteenth-century Protestant movements to reform society through various crusades, such as those against alcohol and slavery, a subject we will discuss in more detail in Part Two. Moreover, the Social Gospel grew largely out of evangelical Liberalism, although from the first it was less content with social conditions in post–Civil-War America than the more world-affirming Liberals had been. As business flourished and economic power became more and more concentrated in the few, many were paid very little for their work and led lives of poverty and squalor in urban slums. The Social Gospel movement saw the true task of Christians as a job of rescue of the poor and renewal of the political, economic, and social order. The kingdom of God, it thought, must come on earth; a millennium must be inaugurated through human effort.

Under Washington Gladden (1836–1918), a Congregationalist minister from Columbus, Ohio, the movement began to receive notice in the 1880s. Later, Walter Rauschenbusch (1861–1918) provided a theological foundation for the Social Gospel in the early twentieth century with several influential works. Rauschenbusch had labored as a young minister in the Hell's Kitchen district of New York City, and after he returned to his seminary in Rochester as a professor, he never forgot what he had seen. Religion for Rauschenbusch, as for so many other Protestants before him, led out of the churches and into the world. Now, though, there was a distinct economic group which was to feel the impact of the gospel, and that gospel should strive to change not only individuals but the social structures which thwarted them. Salvation came in the collective reconstitution of society; a personal relationship with Jesus was not enough.

Thus, the Social Gospel was like Liberalism in stressing the ordinary dimensions of religion. But it went beyond Liberalism in bringing the force of Christian revelation to the task of changing the character of ordinary society. In other words, there was an element of the transcendent, or the extraordinary, in the Social Gospel message, and so the old spirit of prophetic criticism, the

Protestant principle, revived in the movement in a new way. Still, prophetic criticism was directed to the world, not the church, and ordinary religion was strong in the Social Gospel venture. It sought to order conditions in the here and now as the means to establishing contact with God. It strived for the material betterment of human society so that the kingdom of God became the transformation of the present.

The Later Twentieth Century

The Social Gospel would be a continuing legacy to mainstream Protestantism as the twentieth century continued. Its popularity waxed and waned with the climate of the times, but it never completely disappeared. Other turn-of-the-century movements continued, too. The Liberal-Fundamentalist split seemed a permanent feature of the Protestant landscape, while, as we have already noted, both Fundamentalist and Holiness-Pentecostal groups increased in importance. Sometimes Liberals, Fundamentalists, and Holiness-Pentecostals were organized in separate congregations. But more and more, in the later twentieth century, there were divisions *within* denominations, so that some within the same church might be Liberal and others Fundamentalist in inclination. Some might prefer traditional patterns of worship, while others in the denomination sought charismatic gifts. Even within their own denominations, the new Fundamentalists and Holiness-Pentecostals included people more affluent than many of their predecessors, and there were other differences as well. Moreover, a number of conservative and evangelical churches tried to mediate between the Liberal and Fundamentalist positions, while, outside the Calvinist tradition, Lutheranism grew in membership and importance.

In the midst of their continuing denominational manyness, mainstream Protestant groups faced a series of common problems. First of all, the increased urbanization of American culture caught many Protestants off guard and ill prepared. Protestantism had been a rural religion, and now it had to face an America whose future lay with the cities. Secondly, the increased secularization of American culture was equally frightening. The growth of the electronic media—radio, television, and film—had powerfully affected the image of society that was projected into people's lives, while a highly mobile lifestyle, its ever-quickening pace, and the increasing breakdown of families played havoc with old religious values. Ordinary religion was flattening the transcendent dimension, so that extraordinary religion had little place in the public organization of society. Third, the increased pluralism—the manyness—of American culture led many Protestants to an acknowledgment that theirs was a "post-Protestant America," and the path toward the future seemed shrouded and, at times, chaotic. Finally, denominationalism bred a series of boundary problems, and a sense of shapelessness seemed to grip the mainstream. Old-line denominations looked more and more alike, while religion-in-general made it seem as if anyone not a Jew or Catholic in American society must, by definition, be a Protestant.

There were various attempts at resolving the problems, some of them more and some of them less successful. Thus, churches tried to speak to urban dwellers by making worship only one facet of their mission. Protestant churches, expanding on social patterns developed during earlier rural days, held classes and picnics, conducted sporting events, and hosted church suppers to reach out to a larger public. Meanwhile, the secularism of American culture was challenged by the movement called theological realism, or neo-orthodoxy. Originating in Europe, there and in the United States it tried to bring an end to the uncritical optimism of the age of progress. Influenced by the thought of the (American) Niebuhr brothers, Reinhold (1892–1970) and H. Richard (1894–1962), Protestants sought again the prophetic Word that had inspired their ancestors. With the Niebuhrs, they saw that there was evil in the present constitution of society, and they thought that the mystery of evil could never be completely eradicated by human effort. The Word must stand in judgment over every human endeavor.

Both the problem of secularism and the increasing pluralism of American life probably had something to do with the emergence within Protestantism of the ecumenical movement, which worked for the ultimate reunification of separated churches. The movement had begun as early as 1910, when a world missionary conference was held in Edinburgh, Scotland, and by 1948, the World Council of Churches had come into being. Then in 1950 the National Council of Churches of Christ followed. The movement had a distinctly Liberal flavor, even as it committed itself to binding up old wounds and to seeking first the charity of Christ. Ecumenism was also fostered by a number of denominational mergers, such as that in which the Congregational Christian church joined with the Evangelical and Reformed church in 1957 to become the United Church of Christ, and another in 1968 when the United Methodist church was formed by the Methodists and the Evangelical United Brethren.

Yet, if ecumenism promised Protestants a united front against secularism and the pluralism of post-Protestant America, it also added to a loss of identity. The old ideal of gathered churches seemed lost in the amorphousness of expansion. At the same time, in suburbia, local community churches had compounded the problem by aiming to serve all Protestants in a given area, whatever their denomination. Thus, if a denomination was only part of the larger communion of saints, it was very difficult to tell where a person should stand to be counted, and there was a continuing sense of malaise in some Protestant circles.

On the other hand, conservative and Fundamentalist Protestants had more clearly demarcated their boundaries through their demands for doctrinal clarity, and by the sixties they were the fastest growing Protestant bodies. By 1970 Baptists accounted for an impressive 19 percent of the church-going population in America, with over half of them concentrated in conservative/Fundamentalist Southern Baptist congregations. They were trailed at a considerable distance by the Methodists, who accounted for 10 percent. Third in line were the Lutherans, who now included 6 percent of all churchgoers, followed by the Disciples of Christ (3.7 percent), the Presbyterians (3.1 percent), and the Episcopalians (2.3 percent). In a Gallup poll conducted in 1976, nearly half of all Protestants questioned (48 percent) claimed to have had a "born again" experience, while 42 percent considered the Bible the inspired Word of God and 58 percent said that they had witnessed to Jesus Christ. Clearly, in conservative Protestantism, the descendants of the Reformation had found the Word of the scripture still vital.

Just as vital, evangelical pietism was the continuing hallmark of American Protestantism. Direct experience, rather than theoretical knowledge, was the ideal of Protestant Americans with their heritage of frontier practicality.

For the conservatives, the relationship between extraordinary and ordinary religion had been handled by separating the two so that crossing the borders to touch God was an important, if segmented, aspect of living. For those of more liberal persuasion, even the extraordinary had become ordinary, and a sense of the sacred was hard to find in the midst of the action in the world the Liberals enjoined. In fact, with a sense that something was amiss, Liberals sometimes tried to counter the prevailing trend with self-conscious ritual celebrations in the midst of their political activism. Clearly, both conservative and liberal solutions to the relationship were implicit in the Reformation. Even in the sixteenth century, the Word had spoken of an individual communion with God. Even in the sixteenth century, it had emptied the monasteries and urged men and women to lives of upright moral witness in the world. Yet both solutions had brought to the Reformation a religious sense shaped by *American* history and culture. The solutions were Protestant, but they were also and very much American.

Even more, the relationship between ordinary and extraordinary religion in mainstream Protestantism was compounded by the social problem of oneness and manyness in the American context. To state the matter baldly, in a survey in 1975, a majority of 61 percent of all Americans expressed a Protestant religious preference. With such statistics on its side, it was clear that the public face of religion in America was Protestant. In effect, Protestantism was the extraordinary religion of the national oneness. Changed by the many in a variety of ways, it still maintained its hegemony because it had merged with American culture. In so doing, Protestantism had become truly an empire, a condition of its—and America's—existence that we will take up again in Part Two. And in so doing, the Word from the beginning seemed in grave danger of becoming the word from the Potomac.

IN OVERVIEW

The Protestantism that had begun in the Reformation had come a long way in the New World of the United States. The sixteenth-century Reformers had preached a religion of prophetic protest with scripture alone, justification by faith, the priesthood of all believers, and a fellowship of common worshipers as its expression. The teachings of the Reformation brought into being a series of churches in which a subtle individualism combined with a new interest in the preaching of the Word and a call for moral action in the world. As Protestant church buildings became simpler and more austere and pulpits more prominent in their sanctuaries, they expressed a cultus and a code that led out of the church and into public life. Paradoxically, the spirit of Protestantism separated extraordinary from ordinary religion in its emphasis on the gap between God and the material world. But it brought them together in a way in its insistence on a thisworldly ethic.

In England the spirit of Protestantism was reflected in the Church of England and in the many strands of the religious movement called Puritanism. With its Calvinistic leanings, Puritanism fostered a spirit of still greater reform and promoted the settlement of English colonies in the New World. Here New England and (in the loose sense) Virginia were both settled by Puritans, and so was Quaker Pennsylvania. Gradually, other Protestant peoples, the Scotch-Irish, the Germans, and the Dutch among them, became part of colonial society. After the Revolution and a period of very low church membership, the Protestant churches rebounded with the Methodists and, after them, the Baptists becoming the largest denominations. In this atmosphere of growth and change, denominationalism meant the rise of new religious communities while revivalism attracted converts to many denominations.

The post–Civil-War period and the early twentieth century brought challenges from a rapidly changing American society to the Protestant churches. In general, Protestants either affirmed culture, as in Liberalism; they partially withdrew from it, as in Fundamentalism and the Holiness-Pentecostal movement; or they tried to transform it, as in Social Gospel activities. By the late twentieth century, Fundamentalist and conservative evangelical churches were enjoying revived strength, the neo-orthodox theological movement had made its mark, and the ecumenical movement continued. But in the terms of our discussion, boundary difficulties were plaguing Protestantism. Liberal-conservative tensions could be understood as boundary problems, with the central issue whether the success of Protestantism had changed it too much into the ordinary religion of present-day American culture.

Some Protestants, however, had never been happy with either the ordinary character of mainstream Protestantism or the ordinary character of American culture. A nation within the Protestant nation, they also spilled over its borders, remembering their separate past and wondering if they would also have a separate future. These Americans had African rather than European roots, and, like the Indians before them and the Jews of Euro-American origin, their religion and nationhood were closely blended. Black Americans, like others among the many, had their own religious center.

SUGGESTIONS FOR FURTHER READING:
MAINSTREAM PROTESTANTISM

Anderson, Robert M. *Vision of the Disinherited: The Making of American Pentecostalism.* New York: Oxford University Press, 1979.

Bainton, Roland H. *The Reformation of the Sixteenth Century.* Boston: Beacon Press, 1952.

Brauer, Jerald C. *Protestantism in America: A Narrative History.* Rev. ed. Philadelphia: Westminster Press, 1965.

Brown, Robert McAfee. *The Spirit of Protestantism.* New York: Oxford University Press, 1965.

Hudson, Winthrop S. *American Protestantism.* Chicago: University of Chicago Press, 1961.

Marty, Martin E. *Righteous Empire: The Protestant Experience in America.* New York: The Dial Press, 1970.

———. *Protestantism.* Garden City, NY: Doubleday, Image Books, 1974.

Morgan, Edmund S. *Visible Saints: The History of a Puritan Idea.* New York: New York University Press, 1963.

Sandeen, Ernest R. *The Roots of Fundamentalism: British and American Millenarianism, 1800–1930.* Chicago: University of Chicago Press, 1970.

Weber, Max. *The Protestant Ethic and the Spirit of Capitalism.* 1920. Translated by Talcott Parsons. 2d ed. New York: Charles Scribner's Sons, 1958.

White, Ronald C., Jr., and Hopkins, C. Howard. *The Social Gospel: Religion and Reform in Changing America.* Philadelphia: Temple University Press, 1976.

CHAPTER 5

Black Center:
Afro-American Religion and Nationhood

Toward the end of August in the year 1619, a Dutch ship slipped into harbor at Jamestown, Virginia. On board were at least twenty "Negars," who were sold as indentured servants to the Virginia colony. So began the African presence in the land that became the United States—an ironic and twisted beginning in which, in the land of volunteers, the interrupted lives of nonvolunteers were redirected into channels of oppression. Over the next several decades, there was a continual slow trickle of human cargo into Virginia to labor on the tobacco plantations. By 1649 there were about 300 slaves out of a population of 15,000. After 1660 there was a statute law on the books concerning slavery, and by the end of the seventeenth century, other Africans were pouring into Virginia and the neighboring Maryland colony.

To the north, as early as 1638 Captain William Peirce brought blacks as slaves from the Providence Island colony to Massachusetts Bay. Shippers and traders across the Atlantic, the Puritans freely engaged in the sale of human flesh and reaped their profits. Thus, the colonies almost without thought started down the road to the bondage of Africans that would bring 427,000 or more blacks to their land. Although this was a small fraction of the nearly 10 million blacks who came to various parts of the New World, by 1865 through natural increase there were about 4 million Afro-Americans in the United States alone. The importation of African slaves from abroad had been outlawed in 1808 and, while there was some smuggling, declined thereafter. Still, at the beginning of the nineteenth century, there were about 1 million blacks in the country, representing some 20 percent of the population. In short, one person in five was black, and Afro-Americans had become a significant group. Whether Euro-Americans liked it or not, blacks would have much to do with the future shape of the American experience as religion and as culture.

By and large, these Africans who came as slaves to America had originated from tribal peoples in West Africa and the Congo-Angola region. They included Mandinke, Yoruba, Ibo, Bakongo, Ewe, Fon, and other nations, some of them followers of Islam and many of them practitioners of traditional native African religions. In order to understand the religious world the slaves would fashion for themselves in America, we need to look at these traditional West African religions which had nurtured them.

WEST AFRICAN RELIGIONS

There, in a situation which was roughly analogous to that of Native American cultures, West African religions were rich and diverse, with each people possessing its treasured myths of origins, its Gods, its ritual and magical practices. Yet underneath the diversity, as in the case of Native Americans, there was a common fund of meaning and value. Hence, although we will need to simplify a great deal in order to do so, it is possible briefly to sketch the "religion" beneath the religions.

Generally, the sacred world of West Africans was one of continuity between different aspects of life. It was based in a strong sense of community, in which individuals understood themselves as part of a people, and no person could live in isolation, either materially or spiritually. Without a sense of original or actual sin in the Judaeo-Christian sense, the West Africans considered wrongdoing as an offense against one or another among the people, and upon this ground of mutual regard, their cultures flourished. Similarly, if West Africans were bound to one another by ties of kinship and nationhood in the present, they were tied as closely to the past. The ancestors were a reality never forgotten, and time could not dissolve the relationship with them. Like a continuous thread, memory linked the living to their dead, and ritual reinforced the memory. Burial ceremonies were elaborate affairs with a full liturgy of prescribed customs from the preparation of the body to continued periods of mourning at set intervals after death. Ancestors still lived in the land beyond, and they took an interest in their descendants on earth. They might grant fertility and health, or they might punish neglectful kin. As guardians of law and custom, they mediated between the Gods and ordinary folk, sometimes becoming Gods themselves as ancestors of entire clan or kinship groups.

The transformation of some of the ancestors into Gods suggested that continuity extended to the divine world. There was no sharp break between heaven and earth in the West African scheme of things, but, rather, sacred and profane shaded off into one another. All of life possessed its power, its spiritual energy, which could be tapped and used for good or for ill. At the same time, religion sought to sanctify life, renewing it through contact with the Gods. So the Gods were distinguished because their power was extraordinary. Among them, there was the high God who had created all things, an ultimate fact of life upon which all else depended. Once this high God had started up the world, however, generally he did not interfere with the ordinary conduct of events. Unlike the Judaeo-Christian God, the tribal high God from West Africa was usually regarded as nonintervening, and West Africans did not often pay homage in a regular way, instead calling on God from time to time but not making him the object of a cultus. God for West Africans was just *there*, a simple and unavoidable fact of life.

However, he did not change history, and no West African would have expected him to prevent slavery.

But there were other Gods beside the high God, and it was these whom West Africans regularly contacted through their rituals. Intermediary Gods might once have been ancestors, as we have already seen, or they might have arisen independently. Associated with natural forces or beings like thunder, rain, or animals, these Gods directed the world in its course and brought good and evil to human beings. Meanwhile, various animal Trickster figures also blurred the boundary between the sacred and the profane. Beings who could upset and disturb the governing order, the African Tricksters functioned much like their American Indian counterparts. As hares, spiders, or other small and insignificant creatures, the Tricksters worked their chaos, confounded the proud and wise, and introduced the possibility of a new order into the ordinary flow of events.

Both Gods and Tricksters were remembered in a rich store of sacred stories. The mythologies of the various holy beings in the West African universe explained the origins and interrelationships between Gods and the world. Sometimes, too, the myths mingled with recollections of the past history of a particular people. Past and present—more than the future—were the important moments, and memory was consecrated by rituals performed to contact the Gods. There could be animal sacrifice, in which gifts of life were offered in honor of them, or divination, in which various techniques were used to discern their will and intentions. Or there could be music and dance in which communion with the Gods might be realized. With the rhythm of drums to set the pace, persons who wanted to contact the Gods danced out their desires until, by a divine reversal, a God would "mount" the dancer and begin to dance him or her. Possession by a God meant the full integration of self with the divine. God transformed the private consciousness of a devoted follower so that the boundary between this world and the next had been penetrated.

At the same time, the ordinary world also had its way to obtain power. Magic of various kinds thrived in the West African world and was used to heal illness or to work harm on an enemy, to bring fertility to nature and to women, or to assure the success of a venture in love or war. The cosmos of the West Africans was one in which the extraordinary world shone through the ordinary and a sacred and imaginative quality colored everyday events. In other words, religious expression became part of the ordinary business of living. Thus, followers of one or another God would often wear special colors and eat designated foods that were identified with the God. They usually turned in worship to a God who had been honored by their parents, and they saw all the intermediary Gods not simply as otherworldly beings but as practical intruders who could lend assistance in humble and ordinary concerns.

NEW LAND, NEW RELIGION

With the sudden reversal of their fortunes, many West Africans found themselves uprooted from their land and systematically deprived of their kin, their culture, and their Gods. The slave trade was a business, and it depended for its success on transforming human beings into marketable commodities. During the period of middle passage between African ports and New World destinations, blacks were deliberately isolated from those who came from their tribe or spoke their language. Without the support of kin, friends, speech, or religion, an African would be unlikely to plot a revolt. He or she would be forced to become a docile piece of property, depending for sheer survival on what little the captors provided. In the holds of ships many Africans died, and those who managed to hold on became slaves under a law code which deprived them of basic human rights. Unlike slavery in West Africa, where captives from enemy tribes were treated as dependents who could inherit property and contract marriage, the blacks who came to the English colonies in America enjoyed none of these prerogatives.

Yet legal fiction could never add up to truth. The slaves were people and not objects. More than that, they were *a* people who, although they had often been warring enemies in Africa, had also been very much alike. They shared a basic view of the world and the relationship of the Gods to the human condition. They spoke for the most part dialects—although not easily translatable into one another—of perhaps two major languages. So there was much that blacks could mutually affirm as they began to take up the remnants of their lives in the New World. Their fundamental ways of looking at religion and at life had been and would remain similar. Their common experience of servitude and degradation would give them another and different set of bonds to share.

Afro-American religion was born in the hearts of these Africans and their children in succeeding generations. It was built on bits and pieces of a common African past, reconstructed to provide strength and solace in the new situation. It was built, too, on the experiences that the slaves had endured in America, mixing their sense of involuntary presence into the cement of religion. And finally, it was built with materials that came to the slaves from the religion of their masters. Afro-American religion was constructed in part from the Judaeo-Christian tradition. Together, these three sources—the West African background, the condition of slavery in the present, the language of European Christianity—provided the elements for a new religion to fit the conditions of a distinct people in a new land.

From West Africa blacks kept many customs and practices which had become habitual. But more than externals, West Africans kept their internal way of ordering reality and looking at the world. Thus, most fundamentally, they continued to see life in terms of a blend of ordinary and extraordinary worlds, bringing together the sacred and the profane and giving meaning to the humdrum pursuit of ordinary tasks. The old African Tricksters continued to be present in a new set of tales the slaves told about figures like Brer Rabbit. Small and insignificant, like the hare of old Africa, he outsmarted the great and powerful, showing that his cunning was a match for any animal's strength. It was true that Brer Rabbit and his animal friends gave blacks a way to express their hostilities and to celebrate the triumph of the weak (like slaves) over the strong (like masters). But it was also true that the new animal tales contained the same religious understanding as the West African tales—that chaos was the source of creativity and that by upsetting the standing order with his antics, Brer Rabbit was restoring the situation, making the tired world vigorous again.

Similarly, the old African Tricksters were present in the religious art of conjure that flourished among the slaves. Here, under the guidance of a root doctor, who resembled in many ways a West African priest-healer, spells were cast and healing work went on. Conjure brought extraordinary power to bear on the ordinary details of life. Its magic would kill or cure, work love or create havoc. Using herbs and other natural substances (and sometimes manufactured goods, especially if belonging to the intended subject), root work, as it was called, often made use of a conjure bag. A source of power like the medicine bundle of a Native American, the conjure bag was intended for some one person, and it produced its effect when that person knowingly or unknowingly touched it. In their attachment to conjure Afro-Americans were expressing their belief that no part of life was without meaning and no situation merely an accident. Like the New England Puritans, they saw life in the hands of sacred forces. Nothing just "happened"; everything had its spiritual cause and cure. Disease, for example, was the work of an indwelling evil spirit or of the spell cast by an enemy's malice. With an extraordinary cause, illness could only be healed by an extraordinary means. Physicians, for Afro-Americans, had to be religious specialists.

Conjure was often also called hoodoo, and by this name it revealed its connections with the religion of voodoo, which grew especially among blacks in New Orleans. By 1850 voodoo was at its height in this city, and its influence was spreading in Louisiana and parts of the South. Based on *vodun*, a Dahomean (West African) religion that flourished in new form in Saint-Domingue (Haiti) and other parts of the French West Indies, voodoo had been present in French Louisiana from its early days when blacks had come from the Indies. But after the Haitian Revolution of 1804, numbers of new blacks from the West Indies entered New Orleans, many of them with French masters fleeing from the victorious Negro regime. The influx of these black people succeeded in making New Orleans the capital of voodoo in the United States.

As a system of worship, voodoo made use of drums and dance, song and possession. With priests and, more often, priestesses presiding over its ceremonies, it provided a ritual context in which the old West African ideal of personal transformation under the power of the God could be realized. Accounts of the voodoo cultus, as they were reported in the public newspapers of the day, were often exotic. They described a ritual in which, through the presence of a snake representing the God, the priestess made contact with sacred power. She then began to deliver inspired messages, and the ordinary folk in turn became transported, God-possessed as well. In the rich cultural mix reflected in the ceremonies, there were elements derived from Roman Catholic worship, as had also been the case in the West Indies. Thus, as an example, altars, candles, and prayers to the Virgin Mary were often part of the voodoo ceremony. But as in the West Indian setting, Catholic elements were used to express West African or Afro-American religious insights.

Root work, or hoodoo, had been the practical magical and healing art associated with voodoo. In places which voodoo never reached in its complete form and in times after voodoo had declined, root work continued, becoming part of the ordinary religion of southern, and even northern, blacks. Yet with or without such externals, African ways of seeing the world and interacting with it persisted. When Afro-Americans turned to Christianity, they brought to it, often without taking notice, the centuries of their prior heritage. We will look for traces of that heritage as we take up the question of black Christianity. And as we do so, we will notice the ways in which the experience of slavery became part of Afro-American religion, too.

BLACK CHRISTIANITY

Most of the slaves who turned to Christianity embraced Protestantism, and our account will chiefly concern them. Yet, in Louisiana, where the voodoo cult was centered, and in Maryland, some blacks became Roman Catholics. Significantly, both of these regions had been settled by Europeans of Catholic background, Louisiana by French, and Maryland by English Catholics. Although the formality of Roman Catholic ritual did not offer the opportunities for ecstasy that had been part of West African religion, the sacramental character of Catholicism, with its use of material elements in ritual settings, was attractive. So, too, were the many Catholic saints, who acted as intermediaries with God the Father in something of the same way as the Gods of West Africa had tapped the power of the high Creator God. Hence, Catholicism enjoyed a modest presence among both slaves and free blacks. That presence continued after the Civil War and into the twentieth century, so that by 1975 there were well over 900,000 black Roman Catholics. Still, this was but a small fraction of the total black population.

By contrast, the major theme in the story of black religion is the story of how it accepted American Protestantism and changed it to express its own past history and present turmoil. And in the process of doing so, in the midst of the bondage of slavery, Afro-Americans gave birth to a sense of inner freedom and dignity and grew in the conviction of separate peoplehood. Their conviction carried them through their time of trial and continued to support them through the new troubles that emancipation brought. Their sense of inner freedom and dignity enabled them to affirm life and take delight in it, though life was still lived in slavery. Like their West African kin left behind, Afro-American Protestants looked to a religion of joy in the present, even when the present involved suffering.

The early history of black contact with Christianity in the English colonies had not been so promising. Many slaveholders did not want to expose blacks to Christian influence, fearing that baptism might imply that as equal children of God through faith blacks ought not to be held as slaves. Some argued that blacks had no souls to be saved, while others remembered the common-law tradition of England by which baptism made a slave free. Indeed, by 1706 six colonial legislatures had laws on their books denying that baptism conferred freedom on a slave.

Meanwhile, Afro-Americans seemed hardly more excited about embracing Christianity. The first adult baptism of a black slave had occurred in New England in 1641, but on the whole, American blacks were indifferent to Anglican Christianity. Moreover, when after 1701 the Society for the Propagation of the Gospel in Foreign Parts (S.P.G.) sent English missionaries to America to convert the slaves, their methods proved unsuccessful. The S.P.G. had a literary model of religion and favored religious nurture in a carefully tended household of faith. Like people of the Word, members of the society wanted to begin catechetical schools, teaching blacks to read the Bible and the *Book of Common Prayer* and to understand Christian doctrine. This process was too lengthy to be practical. It encountered linguistic and cultural difficulties among the slaves and reluctance as well among their masters, who feared that education might make blacks less docile. It suffered, finally, from the scarcity of missionaries to carry out the program.

Gradually, though, the picture started to change. The churches began to mount a campaign to convince slaveholders that the conversion of the slaves to Christianity would not alter their earthly situation. Even more, they argued, Christianity with its teachings of humility and obedience would provide a means of social control for recalcitrant blacks. Christianity, in short, would make for better slaves, a more secure life, and an improved economy. Warming to this kind of persuasion, slaveholders began to open their farms and plantations to Christian missionaries. In turn, the missionaries came from new sources. Succeeding the Anglicans of the early eighteenth century were, by the end of the century and the beginning of the next, an army of Baptist and Methodist preachers. Unburdened by the literary model of conversion, these missionaries could work quickly and dramatically to gather a Christian community. Blacks took to the kind of Christianity they announced with far more enthusiasm than they had brought to Anglicanism, and by 1760 the conversion of blacks to Christianity had become a noticeable event.

In overview, there were two kinds of Christianity in the southern world. First of all, there was the official Christianity promoted under the auspices of wary masters for slave consumption. Through special plantation missions designed for the purpose, slaves were brought into the church. Yet at their height these missions were never large-scale endeavors, and they hardly reached all the slaves, at least half of whom worked on farms with fewer than twenty laborers. Thus, as late as 1840 the majority of rural slaves had not become members of the church. But in addition to the Christianity that was under white control, there was a second and more attractive form which blacks directed for themselves. It is to this black Christianity that we now turn.

The Invisible Institution

Thriving in the midst of the white-dominated Christianity of the masters, black Christianity has often been called the "invisible institution"—a church or churches without membership rolls and ordained pastors, without official meeting places and approved ceremonies. It had begun under the eyes of the masters when they sometimes permitted their slaves to hold separate services in a local church or chapel. But after about 1830 to 1835, slave revolts in South Carolina, led by Denmark Vesey (1822), and in Virginia, led by Nat Turner (1831), frightened the owner class. Both revolts had grown up in intensely religious circumstances. They had been spawned by prophetic and apocalyptic ideals in which the slaves believed they were instruments of divine justice, bringing radical change through catastrophe. So laws were passed to prohibit religious services by slaves without white supervision. The invisible institution became the religion of a double blackness, carried on in the shadows and under cover of the night, always in danger of interruption and punishment so severe that it might even mean the death of a slave. Yet the invisible institution made the slaves, more intensely, a community: it brought blacks together as a people, a nation within the nation. Like so many others who were pouring into America from abroad during these years, blacks were coming to understand themselves as one among the many.

Centering on the life of prayer and worship, the invisible institution created sacred space and sacred time in which members of the slave community could express their religious ideas and sentiments. On some plantations, blacks could go to the praise house, a special chapel constructed for their needs, where regular services, prayer sessions, witnessings, and the like could be held. But most of the time and especially after 1831, blacks were not so fortunate. Instead, they held meetings in the woods at evening, or secret sessions in the cabin of one of the slaves, or even spontaneous hymn sings around a fire after a hard day's work. Wherever they made these places, they were "hush harbors," where black people could speak their religion into precarious reality. Here prayer would be raised only in whispers and song only in the quietest tones. Lookouts would be stationed to give warning of strangers, and often a huge pot or kettle would be overturned on the ground because the slaves believed it would help to contain the sound. If the power of the Spirit forced someone to begin to shout, he or she could be sure that the others would quickly subdue the excitement and silence the dangerous sound.

Just as blacks found sacred space in the hush harbors, they found sacred time in the rhythm of the gathered worship of the community, in the rituals that marked significant moments during the course of each individual's lifetime, and in the privileged happenings called conversions, which also came to individuals. For the community, sacred time was created through the words of the preacher and the melodies of the spirituals which knit those present together into one body and one spirit.

In the sermon of the preacher, blacks evolved a sacred art form which even today enriches the lives of many in the rural South and other parts of the country where it has spread. The sermon was said to be "spiritual," to distinguish it from the more learned style of preaching, in which the words were delivered from a prepared manuscript. Since black preachers were largely uneducated, their calling was "in the Spirit," and it was prompted by that Spirit that they could preach at all. So by the early nineteenth century, they were turning necessity into virtue, glorying in the freedom which the situation lent them.

In their understanding, the preacher should be possessed by the Spirit, and hence a spiritual sermon, if it were properly inspired, should break into a chanted and finally a sung sermon. The preacher might begin by quoting a text from scripture, but as the Spirit worked, the text fanned out quickly into a context, and in a ringing rhythm of associations the preacher began to chant at a swifter and swifter pace. Like the lines of an unrhymed poem, his chant came, with a rough and breathy sound at the end of each line to mark the rhythm. Meanwhile, the congregation did their part, giving the Spirit to the preacher by their spirit, interrupting him with shouts and humming themselves into a rhythmic communal ecstasy. Together, preacher and people would make one another glad until finally they broke into song.

A successful sermon was one in which the dull, dead prose of everyday life had been transcended in this communal affirmation of the presence of the Spirit, who was a giver of poetry and song. And in the rhythmic pulse which announced his coming, there were echoes of the rhythmic drums of West Africa and the songs which, in other ages and an ocean away, had brought the Gods.

Alongside of the rhythm of the chanted sermon, there was the rhythm of the spirituals. With words and thematic content based on the Bible, the spirituals were haunting melodies which had developed over the years, probably through a blending of West African and Protestant musical forms. They were above all *communal* songs in which intense experiences of the presence of God and unity with one another were created. Their fullest expression came in the meetings of prayer or praise at which the preacher chanted and individuals opened up with witness to the power of Jesus in their lives. At the same time, they could be sung anywhere, bringing to the everyday world the presence of that other reality of the sacred which rendered even slavery bearable.

When performed at intentional prayer meetings, spirituals were songs in motion. They were accompanied by hand clapping and head tossing, by cries and moans, and by a form of sacred dancing called the ring shout. In this liturgy, largely brought by the slaves from West Africa, a leader would line out the verses of the song, while a group of others, called shouters, moved around in a circle. Singers who stood outside the circle made by the shouters would give out the chorus, at the same time tapping their feet and clapping their hands in support of the circle of shouters. With a shuffling step, this inner circle moved quickly to the beat set by the singers and shouted the sounds of religious devotion that gave the ring shout its name. Sometimes, the shout would go on all night until the dawn brought release from the grip of the Spirit.

Always, the spirituals brought spontaneity and flexibility, so that they could express the moods of various members of the group and draw them into the setting of community. Often someone particularly depressed by a master's cruelty or the loss of a loved one could be heartened by these songs, in which words could be invented to suit the situation by adding new verses to existing choruses. Often, too, the same words and choruses could carry double meanings, so that even as the slaves sang of spiritual freedom in the other world, they also expressed their yearning for physical freedom from the shackles of slavery. "Didn't my Lord deliver Daniel, and why not every man?" asked one spiritual. "Go down Moses . . . Tell old Pharaoh/To let my people go," sang another—so clear in its allusions to the slave situation that it was reportedly censored. Sometimes even, the spirituals could provide a code language by means of which plots could be solidified to escape on the underground railroad to the North or to Canada. "I am bound for the land of Canaan" might be a signal announcing a slave's intentions to break away to a new life outside the South.

Chanted sermons and spirituals based black people in a community of prayer from which they drew their sustenance. That same community was also sensitive to the cycle of each member's lifetime and gave honor and assistance at those important times when an individual most needed them. Thus, especially for a slave who was Baptist, the ritual of baptism was a memorable event when, wearing a white robe, the new church member went down to a stream or pond to be fully immersed in the water. Preacher and people were at hand, the preacher to do the immersing and the people to support the project with their spirituals and their shouts. Likewise, if two persons should marry, the community was there to provide a public witness and to set the seal of their approval on the contract. In a world in which marriage was a doubtful proposition, often broken by the sale of one of the partners by a callous owner, the solemnizing of marriage in the context of the community provided support. It affirmed the dignity and integrity of the partners who, despite the situation, freely chose one another. The ceremony was usually simple enough: most often, the couple jumped over a broomstick either together or in sequence. Sometimes, too, a preacher would preside, and the ceremony would be more formal. In either case, the necessary act of public witness had been accomplished. Afro-Americans had created their own ritual to express the essential, and the couple could begin their life together secure in the blessing of God and their people.

Then at death, permission granted, there would be a solemn ceremony. Often held at night, so that work during the day would not be interrupted, the funeral procession surrounded by the darkness suggested again the black center out of which Afro-Americans lived. People might carry pine knots as torches as they moved together to the burial site, singing spirituals along the way. At the grave, the preacher would offer some prayers, and a simple post would mark the location. Then as they left, in a custom brought from Africa, the company would leave old belongings and broken earthen pots at the burial place, suggestive of the spirit which had broken with its earthly way of living. Usually there would be a sermon some time later—separated from the funeral by an interval ranging from days to months. Here the dead person—and sometimes a number of people who had died in a given period—would be memorialized. Thus, as in Africa, death did not mean forgetfulness but the cultivation of remembrance. The ancestors lived on in the minds and hearts—and words—of the members of the community.

Behind these events by which the community honored its members lay the prior experience of individual conversion, which brought each person into Christianity. In this process, Afro-Americans thought of God as a "time-God," who would act according to his own divine rhythms; and hence, waiting on God was built into their religious culture. Conversion, when it came, was initiated by the divine hand—never the result of human effort or worthiness. Many of the accounts of conversion from among the slaves stressed the action of an arbitrary God, who resembled a kind of Great Owner, acting according to caprice rather than logic.

Often of a highly visionary quality, these accounts would begin with a person's experience of "getting awfully heavy." Here conviction of sin was the burden that the convert bore, and that conviction was reinforced by visions in which a little man conducted a tour of hell and the infernal regions where sin would be punished. The experience was as oppressive in the extraordinary sphere as slavery was in the ordinary. Crying for mercy and feeling the hopelessness of the situation, the convert would be rescued then by the mercy of God. A vision of the Almighty on his throne or of the heavenly regions filled with angelic choruses might accompany this experience. Often, the colors of white and gold predominated in these visionary landscapes, along with the intense green of a country that seemed a plantation paradise. Jesus might be white with golden hair; his outstretched hand might be at once white and gleaming. His message, though, transcended the visual language in which it was cast: it was a message of relief and salvation. The convert was surrounded by the grace of God which overcame all obstacles. Mercy and salvation were assured, and shouting with the joy of it, the new convert would rush to tell the rest about the experience.

Thus, the involuntary condition of slavery had been at the same time affirmed and overcome. God had been manifestly the Master; he controlled the slave-convert by his will and acted in his own time; he was white or dressed in white; and he presided over a heaven which resembled a giant plantation. Yet, precisely by imaging God in these terms, a slave-convert had at hand the means to relativize the human condition of bondage. The earthly fiction of slavery was decisively modified in the face of the divine ownership. God had a prior claim which destroyed the absoluteness of any plantation owner's bill of sale.

Conversion was the focus of religion in the invisible institution. Like other aspects of Afro-American Christianity, it employed Protestant language to express what was an authentically black understanding, weaving together the West African past and the present condition of slavery. In other words, Protestant themes were *interpreted* through the twin lenses of Africa and of slavery.

In their ideas and experiences of God as one who transformed a person even physically, without changing the social or historical situation, blacks expressed their ties to Africa. Their freedom, as in Africa, was a kind of magical flight, a gift of visionary transcendence, which radically altered the meaning of events. In their experience of patience and expectation as they waited on a willful God, Afro-Americans internalized their outer condition of slavery. They wove together Protestant and plantation themes by their choice of metaphors of Israel and the exodus from Egypt. Just as the biblical nation of the Hebrews had been slaves in ancient Egypt, so the slaves led lives of bondage in the American Egypt. But just as Israel had been led to freedom by the power of God and the staff of Moses, so, too, they would one day be free by the power of Jesus, who was their fellow sufferer, and at the time of the Civil War, by the hand of Abraham Lincoln. In a world in which ordinary and extraordinary were one continuous reality, this was no incongruity. Rather, every experience and every situation served to express the black center of Afro-American religion.

THE BLACK CHURCH IN FREEDOM

The center began to be visible when the invisible institution left the shadows and became an official black church. Actually, this had started to happen among free blacks in the North by the end of the eighteenth century, although it would be nearly a century later before in both the North and South the church would be autonomous. While not all black religion was contained in the black church, from the first the church organization provided a vehicle for religious and even political expression among Afro-Americans. If blacks were a nation, then their church was a *polis*, an independent city in which they governed themselves and planned their interactions with other peoples. It was no surprise, therefore, that in the twentieth century, the leadership for the black civil-rights movement came largely from the church.

As early as 1787, Richard Allen (1760–1831) and Absalom Jones (1746–1818) had founded the Free African Society in Philadelphia, after they were nearly dragged from their knees praying when they had mistaken the places that they were to occupy in a Philadelphia Methodist church. The insistence on segregated seating for blacks showed the limits of Methodist toleration, and the Free African Society provided a community of support for blacks of different religious persuasions until in 1793 Jones organized the Church of St. Thomas (Episcopal) and Allen and the majority formed the Bethel Church (Methodist). By 1816 the movement which Allen had begun took on a more formal character when a number of churches came together as the African Methodist Episcopal Church. Meanwhile, in New York Peter Williams, Sr. (1760?–1834?), left a white Methodist church at the head of a group of blacks and founded, in 1801, the Zion Church. By 1821 it, too, was organizing as a national church, the African Methodist Episcopal Church Zion.

In the South, before the decade of 1830 brought heightened fears of black autonomy, Baptist congregations had been particularly open to black independence and control. Because of the nature of Baptist polity, or church government, separate black churches had enjoyed a measure of freedom, and black committees within white churches had presided over the spiritual lives of church members who were black. Still, even after the enforcement of restrictions, some black churches managed to survive. Thus, the Baptist Sunbury Association of Georgia in 1845 was composed of seven black churches which among them had four ordained preachers who were black. Earlier, in 1821 the black Gillfield Baptist Church in Petersburg, Virginia, could boast of a membership of 441 people, making it the largest church in the Portsmouth Association, to which it belonged. There were separate black Baptist churches throughout the South and as far as Kentucky and Louisiana in the West. Sometimes they succeeded in wielding considerable authority despite the efforts of white associations to limit or even disband them.

It was after the Civil War, however, that the black church in both the North and the South came into its own. Both the African Methodist Episcopal Church and the African Methodist Episcopal Church Zion sent missionaries to the South, where they worked with great success among the newly freed blacks. At the same time, a series of independent black church organizations incorporated themselves, separating legally from the mainstream Protestant churches. In the space of two decades, the Colored Primitive Baptists (1866), the African Union First Colored Methodist Protestant Church (1866), the Second Cumberland Presbyterian Church (1869), the Reformed Zion Union Apostolic Church (1869), the Christian Methodist Episcopal Church (1870), the National Baptist Convention, U.S.A. (1880), the Reformed Methodist Union Episcopal Church (1885), and the Independent African Methodist Episcopal Church (1885), all came into existence. Meanwhile, thousands of other blacks continued as congregations organized under the white Baptist and Methodist denominational bodies. Overwhelmingly, whether they established independent churches or remained within the white organizations, blacks were Baptists or Methodists. It was through these churches that they had fashioned their own Afro-American religious expression through the years of the invisible institution, and their loyalty to these churches continued in the decades following emancipation and on through the twentieth century.

There were problems and tensions in this age of the multiplication of Afro-American churches and church members. Some in the more traditional black churches, like Jewish immigrants and some white Protestants, made an issue of decorum. With middle-class aspirations and values, they were often former house slaves (or their descendants), who had worked close to their masters in a two-class system of plantation slavery. In the new situation, they were offended by the spirituals, for example, that were cherished by so many. They were outraged, too, by a looser sexual ethic which prevailed among numbers of free blacks and wanted instead a firm commitment to Victorian morality. Others, who remained in the lower-class majority, were mostly former field slaves or their children. On the plantations, they had lived without close contacts with whites. Now they felt alienated by the "airs" of the would-be middle class, perhaps recalling the manners of house slaves during the pre–Civil-War era. More than that, they sought a church where they could feel at home in a confusing and often hostile world. Like many white Protestants from a similar socioeconomic background, they wanted a religion of the Word—but a Word that could be felt and expressed intensely as well as heard and done.

Yet, despite the difficulties, the black churches succeeded in reaching their members and in providing for them an institutional focus in the uncertain days after emancipation. They became schools in responsibility and community leadership, and their graduates, as we have already implied, continued to serve the black community in many capacities. As the nineteenth century drew to a close, at least one-third of all American blacks were church members, with numbers reaching to some 3 million. A century before, only 4 or 5 percent of the black population had been within the church. The record of growth, as these figures indicate, was staggering. Furthermore, the black churches involved themselves in educational endeavors, supporting universities and seminaries for the training of Afro-Americans. They helped to organize benevolent societies for the mutual aid of struggling people. In addition to these "sickness and burial" societies, they cooperated in the formation of black fraternal organizations, such as the Knights of Liberty and the Grand United Order of True Reformers. In short, they surrounded the members of their congregations with spiritual and material assistance, providing them refuge and support as they encountered a world in which they were learning the ambiguities of legal freedom.

BLACK RELIGION IN THE TWENTIETH CENTURY

With the twentieth century came changes for the black community which were as consequential as nineteenth-century emancipation. There was, first of all, a huge migration from southern farms to cities in both the North and the

South. Secondly, there was a growing chorus of nationalistic hopes and aspirations, searching for ways to make black freedom a complete reality. Thus, whereas 75 percent of all Afro-Americans lived in the rural South before 1900, by the last third of the twentieth century, three-quarters of them were city dwellers, and half of all blacks lived in northern cities. Meanwhile, Afro-American peoplehood was expressed in a series of movements from the back-to-Africa strategy of Marcus Garvey to a new intellectual trend called black theology.

The migration to the North and to industrial cities had considerable implications for black churches. There was a sense of rootlessness and alienation as blacks contended with strange and hostile urban forces. Sociological divisions became more pronounced, and upper, middle, and lower classes more clearly defined. Along with these sharper divisions, preferences in church organization and style of worship only increased in distinctiveness. Like Jews and like Catholics, Afro-Americans who were upwardly mobile felt the pull of mainstream Protestantism. To be American meant in some sense to become more and more like the one center of gravity which it provided, and so some joined white denominations. At the same time, independent African Methodist and Baptist churches flourished, offering to the black middle classes a sense of religiocultural identity even as they conformed to the decorum of mainline Protestant churches. Meanwhile, the new Holiness and Pentecostal movements attracted some, and a series of cults in northern cities drew others. It was these religious bodies which seemed to reach out most clearly to those overwhelmed by overt discrimination and the impersonality of city life. Overall though, Baptists and Methodists continued to predominate, as they had in the nineteenth century. Roughly, nearly two-thirds of Afro-American church members counted themselves Baptists, and almost a quarter identified with Methodism.

The Holiness-Pentecostal Movement

The rise of the Holiness churches had come toward the close of the nineteenth century, as we recall from the last chapter. Afro-Americans were prominent in their formation and growth, and we noted their crucial role in the beginnings of Pentecostalism after the turn of the century with the Azusa Street revival. Among blacks, it was poor people in the cities who mainly formed Holiness and Pentecostal churches. Here, in small communal settings they could express a religious sense that was close to the black religion of slave times. With their stress on the felt presence of the Spirit, the Holiness-Pentecostal churches appealed to the Afro-American longing for transcendence through ecstasy. They cultivated the inspired preaching that was familiar. They brought along the heritage of the spirituals in a new development called gospel music, which combined themes from the spirituals with blues and jazz, likewise incorporating drums and tambourines into the performance of sacred music. Further, they encouraged the work of healing as a religious exercise—something familiar to blacks from the long tradition of root work and conjure. At the same time, these churches taught perfection—holiness—and so demanded from their followers a disciplined and sanctified life. In this way, they provided a structure to guide people as they tried to order their lives in the midst of urban chaos.

Finally, there was something distinctly new about black Holiness-Pentecostalism. Although friendly to whites, many of the Holiness-Pentecostal churches thought of Jesus as a black man, and as they did so, they articulated a new regard for blackness in itself. It was from its humble beginnings in these churches of the people that blackness as a religious and ethnic symbol would begin the process of transforming Afro-American religion.

Organizationally, the spiritual independence of these churches was expressed in a multiplicity of denominations that proliferated seemingly everywhere. Often their names were a striking reminder of the intensity of religion they fostered. Thus, South Carolina had its Fire-Baptized Holiness Church of God of the Americas (1922), Arkansas its Church of the Living God, the Pillar and Ground of Truth (1925), and Cincinnati its Latter House of the Lord for All People and the Church on the Mountain, Apostolic Faith (1936). Probably the largest of the churches was the Church of God in Christ, originating as a Holiness church in a cotton-gin house in Lexington, Mississippi, and later incorporated in Memphis, Tennessee (1897). Reorganized in 1907 as a Pentecostal church, it spread not only in the United States but also throughout the world, with over 2 million members by 1964. Its founder, Charles H. Mason (1857–1963), had moved from Holiness to Pentecostalism and in the process become a legend in his time, with many white Pentecostalists seeking ordination at his hands. By 1970 the church that he had established boasted 425,500 members distributed in 4,500 churches in the United States alone. This was almost half of the total membership in the black Holiness-Pentecostal movement, which probably numbered some 1 million faithful in its ranks.

The Coming of the Cults

If pluralism and independence were hallmarks of the Holiness-Pentecostal churches, they were even more characteristic of the new urban cults, thousands of which mushroomed in storefronts and local residences. Many of them were influenced by forms of voodoo and Spiritualism (discussed in a later chapter), but there were also strong connections between these cults and the churches. Pentecostalism had seen in the experience of speaking in tongues a charism, or gift of the Holy Spirit. Such a gift made a person *charismatic*—filled with the Spirit. An individual so inspired often obeyed the Spirit's promptings, left an original church, and with an inner sense of great authority, began a separate religious movement. Likewise, the Spirit often impelled the inspired man or woman to discover a new revelation which, adding to the leader's authority, was a major departure from the Christian tradition.

Thus, with a charismatic leader and a new revelation, the religious body which grew up, though relatively small, was clearly distinguished from the religion of the past. Moreover, it encouraged in its adherents an experiential realization of the message of the leader, so that the old quest for ecstasy was fulfilled anew within the cult. Different from a denomination, a cult did not see itself as part of a larger church. Different, too, from a sect (as we will see in the next chapter), a cult initiated more radical departures from the Christian tradition. But like a sect, a cult did enforce the boundaries that marked its members off from the rest of society. By so doing, it strengthened their sense of identity and peoplehood, providing an antidote for the bewildering facelessness of city life. It offered an intense religious community and a completely supportive cultural system through which members could find a fusion of extraordinary and ordinary religion for every need.

A good example of a charismatic leader and his successful cult is Father Divine (1876?–1965) and his Peace Mission Movement. The origins and early life of the Reverend M. J. Divine (Father Divine) are mysterious and obscure. Perhaps, as one informant claimed in the thirties, he had been born as George Baker, but Father Divine himself denied it. Whatever his early years were like, he must have been a traveling preacher for some time when, according to reports, he appeared in Americus, Georgia, in 1912 and Valdosta, Georgia, in 1914. Here the future Father Divine taught a blend of mysticism and practicality in which, if a person were truly identified with the Spirit of God, health and plenty would result. Most probably, he drew this insight partially from the perfectionism of Holiness religion and partially from the mind-cure teachings which, as we will discuss in a later chapter, were part of New Thought. Yet Father Divine made the insight his own, and it became the basis of a lifetime of religious leadership.

Before the end of the decade Divine had left Georgia and appeared in New York. He had become convinced of the presence of God within each person and at the same time continued to reflect on the connections between spiritual wholeness and a life with sufficient food and shelter and a modicum of human dignity. Grounded in this mystical yet pragmatic spirituality, he started a religious community and moved to an eight-room house in Sayville, Long Island, in 1919. So began a long era during which Father Divine presided over a community of devoted followers whose lives were transformed by their relationship with him. His hospitality and generosity became legendary, as members of the Peace Mission sat around a banquet table containing everything they might possibly desire to eat. If the Father, who was also Messiah, were present, there ought to be a messianic banquet; and Father Divine did not deny the conclusion of many who followed him that he was God. Yet his implied claim flowed naturally from the ecstasy of Holiness religion in which, in the enthusiasm of worship, a person could be seized and taken over by God, becoming one with God and, therefore, God in his or her own person. Further, according to some, Father Divine claimed that he would not die and also believed that, if a follower were genuinely devout, he or she, too, would neither grow sick nor die. If the report was true, it is not hard to see why. Sickness and death were signs of spiritual malfunction, and the Spirit-filled person, as a man or woman of power, ordinarily should not experience them.

Preaching the doctrine of peace on earth, offering food and shelter at a nominal price, and helping blacks to find employment, often by encouraging the creation of cooperative businesses, Father Divine opened his doors to white followers as well. There could be no discrimination within the walls of his mansions, and while there was strict segregation by sex, integration by race was as strict. When in 1946 Father Divine married Edna Rose Ritchings, a golden-haired Canadian woman, he set an example of black-white unity. Indeed, after his death in 1965, it was Mother Divine who continued the movement from its headquarters in Philadelphia where it had been relocated since 1941.

Meanwhile, in keeping with both Holiness and New Thought emphases, drugs, tobacco, and alcohol were banned, and a disciplined lifestyle was enjoined among the members. In their midst there were two kinds of followers, it was true: an inner group, who surrendered all their possessions to the movement, and an outer circle, who followed less radically. Still, for both groups the Father Divine Peace Mission Movement was an all-encompassing religion. As Afro-American religion had always done, it saw the ordinary and extraordinary as an indivisible whole. It was an authentic religion that led Father Divine and his followers to see in the satisfaction of material needs the outflow of union with the Spirit of God.

The linkage between ordinary and extraordinary religion was everywhere in the cults. As another case, for instance, there was the United House of Prayer for All People, founded by Bishop Charles Emmanuel Grace (1882–1960). "Sweet Daddy Grace," as he was called by his followers, was the beginning and end of their religion. As the names Emmanuel (God with us) and Grace (the gift of God) suggested, he was God present in their midst. Worship was a time when members of the cult celebrated their joy in his person. Song and dance went together, accompanied by the rhythmic beat of drums and tambourines, with the dancers moving erotically, exclaiming "Daddy! You feel so good!" Many claimed that they had been cured, sometimes by a copy of *Grace Magazine* placed over the chest and sometimes by using Daddy Grace soap. Beyond these, Daddy Grace sold a wealth of other commodities from toothpaste and cookies to emblems and badges, and members were continually urged to contribute money to his cause. While outsiders might find this offensive, from the point of view of the religious person, it was intrinsic to the context of worship. Like an old African Trickster, Daddy Grace took from his people and profited from his taking. Yet by giving abundantly, his people experienced even more abundance. Money was a small price to pay for physical and spiritual transformation; ordinary reality was inescapably tied to the extraordinary. Using Daddy Grace products simply underlined the connection.

The Religion of Blackness

Both Father Divine (at least in part) and Daddy Grace had grown up out of the Holiness movement, and their cults were distinctive transformations of Holiness themes such as ecstasy, healing, revitalization through feeling the presence of God, and sanctification (moral perfection) in everyday life. Another side of Holiness-Pentecostal religion had been its growing regard for blackness as it reflected on the meaning of the black Jesus. It was in this vein that a different religious movement took root among Afro-Americans in the twentieth century. While their ancestors in the cotton fields of the South had witnessed to visions in which they saw the whiteness of God, now blacks began to understand that God preferred blackness. Because they were identified with blacks, Father Divine, Daddy Grace (although a mulatto), and other charismatic leaders were implicitly signaling this. Some, however, grew far more explicit, and in a new expression of the interplay between the ordinary and extraordinary, they found the outlines of a free black nation clearly visible.

Even during the time of slavery when it was common for God to be seen as white, there had been a consciousness of peoplehood among blacks. It had sometimes taken a dramatic turn, as in the slave rebellions of the early nineteenth century and, after 1846, in the formation of the Knights of Tabor, a secret society organized among the slaves to liberate themselves through the use of force. After emancipation and the turn of the century, these stirrings of black consciousness took more concrete form against a background of American racism. There was, first of all, Marcus M. Garvey (1887–1940), an immigrant from Jamaica who in 1914 established the Universal Negro Improvement Association. All through the early twenties, Garvey's star rose, as he preached the gospel of the African heritage based on the affirmation of a black God. To underline the religious character of his message, he was instrumental in the foundation of the African Orthodox Church in New York City in 1921. Anglican in background, the church fostered racial pride and fought against any semblance of white domination in black religion. At the same time, Garvey continued urging blacks to the creation of an independent state for themselves in Africa. Like the Jews in the Zionist movement, the black Israel must mount a campaign for return to the homeland. Although Garvey's dream was interrupted by his deportation in 1927 after accusations of financial fraud, his legacy of a religion of blackness lived on.

Similarly, various cults of Black Jews self-consciously promoted the Afro-American people as the true Israel, accepting the Jewish Talmud as their holy book and observing the Jewish dietary laws. Others, by contrast, turned to Islam as a vehicle for the expression of black ethnoreligious identity. Here, the Moorish Science Temple of America was an early instance. Founded by Timothy Drew (1866–1929) in the year before Garvey's Universal Negro Improvement Association, it thrived in the same atmosphere which fueled the Garvey movement and continued after the death of its prophet. Drew had been influenced by Islam and produced his own version of the Qur'an, the sacred book of the Muslims, for his followers. Interspersed with Islamic, Christian, and Garveyite messages, Drew's *Holy Koran* taught the Asiatic origins of American blacks, and demanded that they call themselves Moorish (Muslims from ancient Mauretania in Northern Africa) Americans. Noble Drew Ali, as he was renamed, urged that before a people could have a God, they must have a nationality.

After the prophet's sudden death in 1929, one of the factions of his movement in Detroit came under the spell of the mysterious Wallace D. Fard (Farrad Mohammad or Wali Farrad). He had come quite suddenly in 1930 into the city as a peddler. Thought to be of Arab extraction, he won the confidence of his listeners and gradually began to teach the true religion for black people. When there were too many to meet in a house, Fard and his followers rented a hall. They named it the Temple of Islam, and the movement known as the Black Muslims had begun. Fard continued preaching, urging the black nation to awake to the deceits of "blue-eyed devils." He taught many to read, the while explaining to them that Allah, the true God, was using the whites as instruments through whom blacks might learn their own past history and prepare themselves for their future destiny.

Fard had a gift for turning his vision into reality, and within three years, he had established an impressive organization with a temple, a University of Islam (an elementary and secondary school), a Muslim Girls Training Class, and the Fruit of Islam, a military company for the defense of the faithful. Among those who rose to positions of responsibility within the movement was a man from Georgia named Elijah Poole (1897–1975). Renamed Elijah Muhammad by Fard, he became his Minister of Islam, and when the Prophet disappeared in 1934 as mysteriously as he had come, it was Elijah Muhammad who emerged from the various factions as the leader of a reconstituted Nation of Islam. Fard, he preached to his followers, had been God in their midst, and his birthday in February came to be known as Savior's Day.

Yet the voice of Allah continued to speak through Elijah Muhammad. In the *Supreme Wisdom* and in continuing issues of *Muhammad Speaks*, he told them the will of God. After a term in jail during the Second World War because of his refusal to fight, Muhammad returned in 1946 to a movement which grew by leaps and bounds. Like the Holiness churches before him, he taught a life of self-discipline and family solidarity. The militancy of his organization was reflected in the Nation of Islam's sacred tale of origins which, as Yakub's history, taught of black superiority and the demonic plot that over centuries had produced a bleached-out white race. So, too, the Nation spoke of the formation of a separate national territory for American blacks and warned its members neither to vote, nor hold public office, nor serve in the armed forces. Drawing the boundaries tightly around the community, black pride was everywhere, and with it, black hope and a sense that blackness was a blessed condition.

Even during the lifetime of Elijah Muhammad, however, there was a variant interpretation of the Nation of Islam and the religion of blackness. Malcolm X (born Malcolm Little; 1925–1965), one of Elijah Muhammad's most trusted lieutenants, gradually came to see the message of Islam as universal human solidarity. After a pilgrimage to Mecca, he could no longer endorse the radical separatism of the Black Muslims, and he broke with the movement in 1964 to form the Muslim Mosque, Incorporated, and then the Organization of Afro-American Unity. In this second organization, especially, he had begun to explore the meaning of black nationhood without attaching it overtly to the ideology of Islam. So at the same time, Malcolm X was moving blacks closer to an orthodox and universal Islam and urging them toward a clearer sense of their own identity. The two, as he saw it, were related: people who really knew who they were could extend the hand of friendship and concern to those who were different.

Malcolm X was cut down in 1965 by members of the parent Black Muslim movement, but a decade later his ideas came home. After the death of Elijah Muhammad in 1975, his son, Wallace D. Muhammad (b. 1933), assumed control of the organization. Ironically, the son of the founder carried the movement even further in the direction Malcolm X had taken. It was the dawn of a new day, as a self-assured Wallace D. Muhammad, educated in Egypt and an Arabic speaker, broke with black separatism and moved the Nation closer to orthodox Islam. Gone was the origin myth of black priority and the inferior moral and physical status of whites. Gone, too, were the prohibitions against voting, holding political office, and joining the armed forces. To be alive was to change and keep growing, Muhammad told his people. Malcolm X was honored in death with the title of Shabazz (the ancient tribe of Abraham), and a temple in Harlem was named after him. Whites were welcome to join the organization, as a new symbolism of the Qur'an (Koran) as the universal open book was promulgated. The familiar *Muhammad Speaks* changed its name to become the *Bilalian News*, after Bilal, said to be the African convert to Islam who later became the first minister to the original prophet, Muhammad. Meanwhile, a new name—the World Community of al-Islam in the West—announced the rebirth of the movement in openness toward all people and in commitment to traditional Islam.

Like Malcolm X, Wallace D. Muhammad re-created his World Community of al-Islam in the West (in 1980 renamed the American Muslim Mission) to blend the universal religion of Islam with a keen appreciation of the meaning of blackness. Like Malcolm X, too, the World Community was recognizing that in America to be a nation meant to live alongside other peoples, establishing ties with them and communicating intentions and desires. In other words, Muhammad had loosened the boundaries of the organization, and more people were coming in. Conversely, he and his people had made a fundamental decision that, in the strength of their black center, they would join America.

It was significant that, at the other end of the spectrum of black religion in the twentieth century, the same fundamental decision had been made. In the civil-rights movement of the sixties, it was the more traditional black churches who provided the leadership and marshaled ordinary folk to a statement of the religion of blackness. In Martin Luther King, Jr. (1929–1968), the civil-rights movement had at once its clearest symbol and its most effective organizer. He came before the public eye for a brief space of twelve or thirteen years before his assassination, and it seemed that, like Wallace D. Fard, he had come from nowhere. Yet his father was a prominent preacher, and King had been nurtured on the long years of the black experience in America. He was the fruit of the black church with its history in slavery and in freedom, and when he began to employ the tactic of nonviolent resistance, his first model was inevitably that of the ancestors who had endured their lot on southern plantations. During his years at Boston University, theological reading confirmed and developed his instincts. Then, beginning with the Montgomery, Alabama, bus boycott of 1955, history provided the stage. As the minister of a local Baptist church, King found himself the leader of the boycott movement.

It was the start of a season of public witness, as King moved from place to place in the South and later the North, impelled by a sense of black dignity and peoplehood intimately bound to Christian teaching. In Birmingham, Alabama, and in Albany, Georgia, in Selma, Alabama, and in Washington, D.C., blacks were marching with King at their head. Meanwhile, a series of measures enacted by the United States Congress seemed to tread in the steps of the marchers. There were Civil Rights Acts in 1957, in 1960, and in 1964, and then in 1965 there came the Voting Rights Act.

Fired by his dream that one day the children of former slaves and former slaveholders would sit together at the table of brotherhood, King had led his people, like Moses, out of Egypt. His religion of blackness had been born in the hearts of Afro-Americans long before as they sang their spirituals, and it had been nourished in the simple, rural churches which, in cherishing a black Jesus, had taught people to cherish themselves. On a different front, as King marched, another group of blacks was beginning to articulate for the intellectual community the meaning of the religion of blackness.

There had been precedent for their efforts in the writings of W.E. Burghardt DuBois (1868–1963), the Harvard-educated professor of sociology at Atlanta University at the turn of the century. DuBois had penned long reflections on the meaning of the black Jesus and the nature of the souls of black folk. In the sixties and the seventies, a new generation of preachers and scholars took up the themes. There was, for example, Albert B. Cleage, Jr. (b. 1911), who, in a series of sermons published in 1968 as *The Black Messiah*, affirmed that Jesus was black and that his true resurrection was the awakening of the black nation. There was Joseph R. Washington, Jr. (b. 1930), who, in *The Politics of God* (1969), pondered the meaning of black suffering by seeing blacks as the true remnant of the nation of Israel, the suffering servant bearing, in the divine mystery, the sins of all people. And there was James H. Cone (b. 1938), who in a series of works self-consciously set the agenda for the construction of a black theology.

For Cone and for others attracted by his thinking, liberation was the key to theological inquiry into the black experience. The Christian gospels had revealed Jesus as a religious leader on the side of the oppressed, announcing the good news of their impending freedom. Since historically black people had been the most oppressed among the nations, Jesus must be on their side, working against the forces which beat them down. To be a Christian, in this reading, all people must become spiritually black; that is, they must identify with oppressed people and their cause. In *Black Theology and Black Power* (1969) and *A Black Theology of Liberation* (1970), Cone developed these and similar themes.

Much of the material for this theological articulation of the religion of blackness had been reinterpreted from the European Christian tradition, and much of it had little impact on ordinary black people. Yet in many ways it sprang from the same roots as they sprang. In its quest for black power and empowerment and in its mingling of religion and peoplehood, there were echoes of the African and Afro-American past. Power rained from heaven to earth, and it dissolved the separate worlds of sacred and profane, reconstituting them as one whole.

By 1970 with a black population of nearly 23 million representing about 10 percent of all Americans, freedom for the empowered black nation was not complete. But the need for it was strong and sometimes angry, and it carried blacks through the seventies. Afro-Americans had developed a clear sense of their identity as one people among the many in the United States. Indeed, with perhaps the least opportunity of any group for cultivating their heritage, they had shown the entire country what it meant to seek for roots. Like Native Americans, Jews, and Catholics, they had been pulled toward the one center, the mainstream Protestant face of American religion. Yet more than Jews and Catholics, they had explored the paths of resistance, and, like Native Americans, they had searched for ways to make their separate past more and more a present reality. Afro-Americans did have their churches of middle-class Protestant decorum. For others, the disintegrating acids of the cities, with their drugs and crime, had eaten away at the texture of black family life. Still, as people of creativity and conviction, blacks had learned to bring together things old and new in order to make their future. The African past was over; the Afro-American present was being lived at its own black center.

IN OVERVIEW

The Afro-American experience had begun in the seventeenth-century slavery which brought various West African peoples involuntarily to the New World. While these peoples were many and diverse, their religious heritage included common elements: a strong sense of community and communal responsibility, an equally strong tie with the ancestors, a sense of the nearness of various intermediary Gods, a belief in the ultimate power of the noninterfering high God, and a ritual life that expressed both extraordinary and ordinary religion.

In America, blacks preserved a number of their religious customs and practices. More important in the long run, they continued to look at the world according to the religious categories that Africa had given them. They mixed ordinary and extraordinary religion in tales of Tricksters like Brer Rabbit and in the art of conjure. And as they encountered Christianity, a few blacks became Roman Catholics, but—after a slow start—the overwhelming number became Protestants. In the "invisible institution," these black Protestants created a religion of their own. They found sacred space in public praise houses or in secret hush harbors, and they filled sacred time with sermons, spirituals, ring shouts, and various other rituals. As converts who had been "struck dead" by the power of God, blacks both affirmed and overcame the involuntary condition of slavery to experience spiritual freedom.

Meanwhile, in the early nineteenth century, free blacks were organizing in the African Methodist Episcopal Church and the African Methodist Episcopal Church Zion. Under Baptist polity, some enslaved blacks in the South also controlled their churches to some degree. After the Civil War, a series of independent black churches came into existence, and by the twentieth century a religion of blackness was growing among Afro-American people. A nation within the nation, blacks had already turned to a black Jesus in the northern cities where they embraced various Holiness and Pentecostal churches. In numerous cult movements, they honored blackness in their devotion to black cult leaders and to ideologies of chosenness such as those provided by the Black Jews and the Black Muslims. In the civil-rights movement of the sixties and the creation of a black theology, the late twentieth century contributed newer versions of the religion of blackness. With the boundaries between themselves and white America still carefully drawn, Afro-Americans continued to mingle ordinary and extraordinary religion in the black center.

Yet in America there were other centers and other hopes. Even while the slaves had been describing their visions of paradise and their children had discovered how to begin to build it on earth, other Americans had staked a claim to their piece of a heavenly landscape. Nineteenth-century new religions grew out of the visions of their founders. To imagine in America was to create and to construct.

SUGGESTIONS FOR FURTHER READING: AFRO-AMERICAN RELIGION

Fauset, Arthur H. *Black Gods of the Metropolis.* Philadelphia: University of Pennsylvania Press, 1971.

Frazier, E. Franklin. *The Negro Church in America.* New York: Schocken Books, 1964.

Genovese, Eugene D. *Roll, Jordan, Roll: The World the Slaves Made.* New York: Pantheon Books, 1974.

Hughes, Langston, and Bontemps, Arna, eds. *Book of Negro Folklore.* New York: Dodd, Mead, 1958.

Johnson, Clifton H., ed. *God Struck Me Dead.* Philadelphia: Pilgrim Press, 1969.

Levine, Lawrence W. *Black Culture and Black Consciousness: Afro-American Folk Thought from Slavery to Freedom.* New York: Oxford University Press, 1977.

Malcolm X. *The Autobiography of Malcolm X (As Told to Alex Haley).* New York: Ballantine Books, 1973.

Raboteau, Albert J. *Slave Religion: The "Invisible Institution" in the Antebellum South.* New York: Oxford University Press, 1978.

Ray, Benjamin C. *African Religions: Symbol, Ritual, and Community.* Englewood Cliffs, NJ: Prentice-Hall, 1976.

Washington, Joseph R., Jr. *Black Sects and Cults.* Garden City, NY: Doubleday, Anchor Press, 1973.

CHAPTER 6

Visions of Paradise Planted:
Nineteenth-Century New Religions

On a spring day in 1820, a teen-ager named Joseph Smith from a poor family in upstate New York knelt down to pray in the woods. He had been confused by the claims and counterclaims of mission-minded sectarians in his area, and not knowing to whom to listen, he had decided to try to listen to God. Smith was not doing anything exceptional in a district given over to religious excitement and ferment, but what followed was surely extraordinary. He watched as a pillar of light came gradually down upon him, and then he saw two "Personages" who filled him with awe and wonder. As they stood in the air above him, one pointed to the other, calling the second his beloved son and telling Smith to hear him. When Smith then asked the two persons which of the sects was right and which he should join, he was told that they were all wrong and that he should join none of them.

SECTARIANISM AND NINETEENTH-CENTURY NEW RELIGIONS

It was the inaugural vision of a prophet, and the results of Joseph Smith's experience of a world beyond live on in a people who count him the founder of their religion—the Mormons. From the first, as the vision hints, Smith and his followers thought of themselves not as a small sectarian group but instead as a church that would be all-inclusive. Still, like members of so many new religions in the nineteenth-century United States, the Mormons were considered by others to be sectarians; that is, members of a sect. This term grows out of sociological scholarship about religion, and it is in the work of Max Weber (1864–1920) and Ernst Troeltsch (1866–1923) that we find the classic descriptions of sectarianism. For Troeltsch, sects were voluntary societies of people bound to one another by mutual religious experiences of new birth. They lived in small groups separated from the rest of the world, and they emphasized a life of committed love and of law rather than one of free grace. Above all, they lived in expectation of a coming kingdom of God which would end the world as we know it.

A sect therefore was exclusive and conversional. People were not born into one, but they moved into it as the result of some decisive religious experience. This strong religious impulse often urged sectarians to intense missionary effort, but at the same time their gathered groups were the refuge for the few from every society who could give themselves totally to the religious ideal of the community. Thus, sectarians valued intense commitment and a radical lifestyle over universal availability. Theirs was a chosen society of saints instead of the huge, extended church which included saints and sinners, wheat and tares, within its membership.

Christianity, which had once itself been a tiny sect within Judaism, spawned continual sectarian movements, especially when it came to be recognized and established. While it would be interesting to trace the growth of these sects over the years from the beginning of Christianity, perhaps the most useful model for American sectarianism is that of sixteenth-century Europe, comprising what historians call the Radical Reformation. This left wing of the European religious revolution departed in major ways from the mainstream of the Protestant Reformation led by Martin Luther, John Calvin, and others. In fact, the radical ideal was so different from that of the main Protestant Reformers that they persecuted sectarians as wholeheartedly as Catholics did. Like Catholics, the Protestant Reformers were attacking those who by their teachings would murder not the bodies, but worse, the souls of human beings.

Although these Radicals were distributed among a host of different sectarian movements throughout Europe, it is possible to identify characteristics which were present in all or most of them. Different from mainstream Protestants and Catholics alike, the Radicals understood the church as a free society of people gathered out of the world. Not all of those who lived in a geographical territory should be part of the church but instead only those who chose willingly should join. Once, they thought, the Christian church had lived up to that idea; but long ago in the fourth and early fifth centuries, it had fallen. What the church needed, therefore, was not reformation, as mainstream Protestants thought, but the *restoration* of primitive Christianity.

In this context, the Radicals challenged mainstream Protestants on another front. Luther and Calvin had both preached salvation which came by the Word of God. The Word was the gospel, and the gospel was Jesus so that, although Luther and Calvin had different emphases in their understandings of the matter, salvation, or justification, came ultimately through assent to the Word of God; that is, through faith in the message which had been preached. By contrast, the Radicals saw the gospel as law, and for them the process of sanctification took the place of the Reformers' justification. Right living was the essence of true religion, and the church meant an association in which people would support one another in their quest for total personal morality. Salvation came, then, by works; by zeal for the kingdom. Jesus became a model of how to live and die more than a sacrificial victim who had gained heaven for all or for some by his atonement. Sacraments (called ordinances) were signs and memorials, teaching events which provided powerful reminders of the truths of Christian history. And since all were called to be saints, all were called to be priests both in theory and in practice.

In such societies the things of this world—politics, economics, war—were inconsequential and, indeed, distracting and dangerous in terms of the life of sanctity. More than that, the Radicals believed that they saw signs of a speedy approach of the second coming. In this atmosphere of expectation of the return of Jesus, they disdained any involvement with the state, sometimes treating it with indifference as a relic of the past and sometimes acting with hostility and open provocation toward it. Pacifism, the prohibition of oaths, and the avoidance of magistracies or other government service were all examples of the lengths to which the saints went to avoid contamination with the world.

In America the religious experience of these Radicals was repeated in movements beginning as early as the seventeenth-century Baptists of Rhode Island with Roger Williams (1603?–1683) as their head. Likewise, there were and still are movements which had descended with unbroken historical ties from the sixteenth-century Radicals, such as the Amish folk of Pennsylvania and other areas and the Hutterites of the Upper Midwest. These small groups continued to flourish in the New World, and they added to the manyness of American religions. But even more, there sprang up a host of independent sectarian movements which could not trace their lineage historically to the Radical Reformation but which, nonetheless, in religious structure and impulse resembled the Radical groups. Of course, since every historical movement has its particularities, there were also important differences between sixteenth-century Radicalism and nineteenth-century American visions of paradise planted. To cite but one example, the Mormons placed the fall of the church not in the fourth and fifth centuries but in the time of the earliest apostles. And unlike the Radicals, they emphasized the absolute necessity of a special priesthood and observation of the ordinances (sacraments), while they sought the restoration of the ten tribes of Israel as much as of the primitive church.

Nevertheless, if we remember the fact that there were differences, it is interesting to look at the early Mormons and other groups which arose in nineteenth-century America from the perspective of the Radical idea. Such an approach highlights just how different nineteenth-century new religions were from mainstream Protestantism. In other words, from a religious point of view, it is not fair to characterize these groups as "also-rans" among the Protestants. They were not simply smaller than or less popular than Baptists, Methodists, or Presbyterians. They pursued a different vision which led them to forms of ritual and common behavior distinct from these other churches. We might say that, where Protestants emphasized their sacred story by repeating the Word in sermons which had become sacraments, members of nineteenth-century new religions seized the moral instruction which the sermons contained and made deeds of righteous living the keystone of their religious way. For them, in the beginning was not the Word but the Act.

Thus, like Native Americans and like Jews and sometimes Catholics, these movements succeeded often in bringing ordinary and extraordinary religion together. The everyday was at the center of religious reality, yet religion meant at the same time the chance to pass beyond the boundaries of the ordinary to contact supernatural powers. As a matter of fact, instead of making the extraordinary ordinary as in their ways Native Americans, Jews, and Catholics tended to do because their practices were given by tradition, the sectarians reversed the process. With the zeal of their newness, they made the ordinary—each detail of daily living—an event which was fraught with the extraordinary, a window into sacred reality and a way into the other world.

This is where the time and place in which the American sectarians arose is especially important. The nineteenth century was the time of a new political and cultural reality. The Great Seal of the United States—visible still on the back of a one-dollar bill—proclaimed in the Latin phrase *novus ordo seclorum* that here was a new order of things. For Americans whose ancestors had been Europeans or who were immigrants themselves, there was a tremendous excitement about the possibilities that the new (to them) land created. It was frontier territory—a boundary place once again. It invited them to the boundaries of their own imaginations and abilities, urging them to the purity of life and commitment that could match the untainted stretches of "virgin" land.

For them, it did not matter that the land was not really "virgin" or "new" in any absolute sense but had been peopled by Indian nations for thousands of years. To eyes inherited from Europe, the land looked fresh and original—like the garden of Eden before the fall of Adam and Eve. People wanted to match the newness of the land and the newness of the democratic political experiment with a return to old beginnings or a plunge forward into completely new beginnings of their own. Either they would restore the pristine vigor of Christian origins—as the Radical Reformers had tried to do; or turning the time of beginnings inside out, they would create brand-new societies that would make flesh of the biblical prediction of the millennium. The thousand-year reign of peace and justice at the end of time would be anticipated in their efforts. Their visions would lead to the planting of paradise on American soil.

As we will see again in Part Two, this millennial fervor was quintessentially American. Although the sectarian movements never involved huge numbers of people relative to the Protestant mainstream, sectarians were acting and living out themes that were central to the culture. At the same time, sectarians in general often could not maintain the purity of their experience for more than a generation or two. So the trajectory of a sect finally led to religious transformations in which denominational respectability won the day. Like their Protestant and Catholic neighbors, with the passage of time many sectarians belonged to churches into which they were born rather than born again. Often they became almost indistinguishable from their nonsectarian associates. (After all, how could someone born in the faith be a "volunteer"?) In America, of course, that is part of the story of how manyness became oneness. For the present, however, we need to look at the early history of some major sectarian movements in order to understand their religious impulse and their contributions to pluralism.

Here it might be helpful to imagine a broad continuum along which various nineteenth-century new religions were located. At one end were those whose communities, while they maintained their exclusivity and separation from the world, still allowed, relatively speaking, for a good deal of individual initiative and activity among their membership. At the other were those who carried the sectarian principle as far as it would go, demanding a totalitarian commitment in communal living. Thus, at one end of the continuum we find groups such as Mormons, Seventh-day Adventists, and Christian Scientists, all of whom in their full vigor as movements made considerable demands of their members but stopped short of total community. At the other end we can point to groups such as the Shakers and Oneida Perfectionists, whose members lived together sharing all things in nineteenth-century communes.

THE MORMONS

We return now to the prophet Joseph Smith (1805–1844), whom we left after his first direct encounter with God. The group he founded, the Mormons, passed from an experience of more intense community living to a more individual, but still strongly bonded, form of membership. Hence, they are extremely interesting in terms of our continuum because they demonstrate the possibilities of different locations along it. At the same time, to view the Mormons solely for their place(s) on the continuum would be to look at them more sociologically than religiously. We need to find ways to get to the heart of the Mormon vision.

These ways are provided in Joseph Smith's account of the revelation which was communicated to him by the heavenly messenger Moroni. This messenger, said Smith, directed him to a place where golden plates were deposited, forming a written testimony to the spiritual history of early America. Smith also said that he found by direction two stones with silver bows attached to a breastplate, the Urim and Thummim, thus enabling him to translate what came to be known as the Book of Mormon. Moroni supplemented this founding document of the Mormon religion with other prophetic words and teachings, most significantly concerning the future destiny of American Indians and of America itself, the site of a New Jerusalem to come.

Standing beside the Bible as sacred scripture, the Book of Mormon told a sacred history of the tribe of Joseph, descendants of whom came to the American continent in ancient times before the birth of Jesus. According to the Book of Mormon, Lehi and his family left Jerusalem in 600 B.C. and were led by God to North America. But two of Lehi's sons, Laman and Lemuel, were followed by a group of people whose ways had become wicked. Hence, they were cursed by God with dark skin, and from these people, mingled apparently with others, the American Indians later came to be. These Lamanites, as they were called, turned on the white Nephites, the other branch of Lehi's family, and in A.D. 384 succeeded in destroying most of them. But Mormon, one of the Nephites who remained, buried in the Hill Cumorah of upper New York state the plates which contained the Book of Mormon. In addition, he gave a few of the plates to his son, Moroni, who finally placed them in Cumorah beside the main body. It was from the plates which Moroni had deposited that Joseph Smith translated the Book of Mormon.

The Book of Mormon, therefore, established the Hebraic origins of American Indians and supplied America with a biblical past. Its revelation was cast as history, and the nature of Smith's inspiration shaped the nature of the movement which grew up around him. When God acted in history, both in the Bible and in the Book of Mormon, he placed a certain value on the things of time. He thought they were important enough to merit his concern, and so time and history began to possess significance in their own right. Action and deed became the essence of religion, and Mormonism early expressed this religious insight in a number of ways.

First of all, for Mormons revelation was decidedly not a thing of the dead past. It lived on in the present because God continued to speak to the prophet Joseph Smith and his successors even after the Book of Mormon had been translated. Besides these extraordinary revelations, which usually occurred at times of crisis when the young church particularly needed divine guidance, revelation came in ordinary ways through the history of the Mormon community as it struggled to make its way in the world. Time after time, it was ripped apart by internal dissension and attacked by outsiders. Almost, it seemed, the Mormons in their nineteenth-century story were repeating the wanderings of Lehi and his sons of the House of Joseph, for their history was one of movement from place to place. Although the Mormons did not perceive this connection, they did see themselves as repeating the years of wandering of the first Israel recorded in the Old Testament. Indeed, they looked toward the future time of "gathering," when Zion would be established in the New World.

First, however, they moved in 1830 to Kirtland, Ohio, and then in 1837 to Independence and to Far West, Missouri. When the hostility of their neighbors drove them from Missouri, they migrated to Illinois, where they founded Nauvoo, but in 1844, hostility once more brought an armed confrontation which led to the murder of Joseph Smith while he was jailed in Carthage, Illinois. This action by an angry mob did not end the Mormon years of wandering. Under Brigham Young (1801–1877), the main body of the Mormons set out on a journey that brought them at last to the Great Salt Lake in what is now Utah. Here they founded their Zion in the mountains, the state of Deseret.

To understand the Mormons is to understand this history in which they acted out their identity. They were people of pilgrimage, people on the march, who had still to seek the final good of Zion. Hence, doing the Word was ever central. At the same time, in their conception of the nature of the church they self-consciously separated themselves from their Protestant neighbors. As we noted earlier, Joseph Smith and his followers saw their movement not simply as a restoration of the primitive church, as the Radicals had hoped, but also as a restoration of the ten tribes of Israel. Like the Radicals of the sixteenth century, the Mormons thought that reformation was not enough; but unlike them, the Mormons understood that Zion was to be gathered in the very flesh.

Even so, with this emphasis on the restoration of the gathered community and on religious action and righteous living, the Mormons did parallel the sixteenth-century Radicals. And to these common features we might add Mormon beliefs concerning the abolition of infant baptism and the coming of the millennium. However, if they resembled the Radicals of another era, the Mormons were also *American* in their religious vision and its enactment. In a curious way, their history summed up the tensions between manyness and oneness which have made America a land of many religions and one religion. Like all sectarians, they were exclusivistic and yet mission-minded. Like all sectarians, they demanded total commitment in a radical lifestyle which at some points in Mormon history involved the surrender of excess possessions to the church and the practice of polygamy for religious reasons. Yet paradoxically, their exclusivity often led them to the center of the political process. In order to preserve their separateness they had to obtain the worldly power which would enable them to form their own societies, independent of the general government around them. Thus, while in Illinois, Joseph Smith announced that he was a candidate for the presidency of the United States, and Brigham Young, at the head of Deseret, worked for years for the admission of the Utah Territory to statehood and for a time was its official governor.

Moreover, the content of Mormon revelation was, by implication, more "American" than the religions of most Americans who were part of the mainstream. We have already seen this to be the case in Mormon interest in the history and destiny of American Indians and in their millennial belief in America as the promised land where the New Jerusalem would be located. Beyond this, in their teachings about the nature of God and the nature of human beings, Mormons probed the values of American culture and exalted it to a transcendent status by giving it a theological basis. For they preached—and continue to preach—a doctrine in which the material world was sacred and ultimate. Their God was not an infinite and omnipotent creator of the universe and humanity. Rather, in a universe which had always existed, God was a finite being. He did not have the world totally under his control, but was a God of space and time, whose existence did not interfere with human freedom and could not prevent evil. He was both Father and Mother, and humans worshiped him by sealing themselves to one another in marriage. Thus, they hoped to rise one day in the spiritual realm to the celestial kingdom where they, too, should be "as Gods."

For Mormons in the nineteenth century and now, humans were not dependent on God for their existence. They accomplished their tasks through their own efforts, through merit and good work, and through achievement which brought its appropriate reward. Their souls had preexisted in a spirit realm before they entered their present bodies, but in Mormon teaching there was no pronounced dualism between spirit and matter. Things spiritual were a refined essence of the material world—all spirit was matter—so that God, as well as humanity, was testimony to the sacredness of matter. Moreover, since it was possible for Mormons themselves to become "as Gods," Mormons were moving in the direction of a polytheism in which divinity, as a principle, would be embodied in many Gods. The Gods which the Mormons became, of course, continued to possess material bodies. Because of this teaching, the human body already held a privileged status. Mormon prohibitions of alcohol, tobacco, and caffeine and their sparing use of meat were indications of the regard they felt for their human temples.

In an America which in the nineteenth century pursued material success and subscribed to the cult of worldly progress, Mormons taught their neighbors how important matter really was. While in the Protestant mainstream old Calvinist beliefs in human depravity and predestination melted away in a flood of liberal teachings about human goodness and divine compassion, Mormons went beyond this middle position to a theological stand which, though many found it bizarre, was at least consistent. If matter was good and progress was good, then Mormons knew this to be the case because revelation had shown the nature of ultimate reality to be both material and progressive. And yet, in a twist which augured the biblical literalism of twentieth-century American Fundamentalism, Mormons bound their liberalism to a literal understanding of the teachings of Smith and their later prophets. However, this, too, was consistent with their stand on the sacredness of matter. Even the revelatory Word should be respected in its material integrity, not made over into abstract, nonmaterial symbolization.

The Mormon cultus, or "temple work" as it was called, dramatized these insights in ritual activity. After a revelation in 1841, Joseph Smith told his people to build a temple in Nauvoo where the Church of Jesus Christ of Latter-day Saints (Mormonism's official title) could present to God the records of their dead. From this time, the Saints dated their practice of baptizing the living for the dead. That is, past- and present-day Mormons expressly immersed themselves in the baptismal waters in the name, usually, of individual relatives who had died without conversion. They hoped, thus, to bring all the worthy dead to salvation, and for this reason Mormon genealogical societies sprang up to assist the Saints in uncovering the names of relatives for whom they would perform the temple work.

Meanwhile, in their marriage ceremonies Mormons were encouraged to seal themselves to one another for both time and eternity. Marriage would continue in the life to come, and, in fact, full salvation could not be reached for either man or woman without marriage. Indeed, temple work included sealing ceremonies for those who had died before the time of Mormon revelation. In both cases, that of baptism and of marriage, Mormons continued once again to express their confidence in the sacredness and efficacy of matter. The dead must be subject to material rites, and the sexual as well as spiritual bond of marriage would endure in the world beyond. The millennium would not bring an end to the world and human history but would exalt and perfect them so that Zion in America, though radically different from the present era, would be *in* time and not beyond it.

Finally, the Mormons in their new faith were as American as their Puritan ancestors in New England had been. At Kirtland, at Independence and Far West, at Nauvoo, and finally in Salt Lake City, they tried to build a theocracy; that is, a religiopolitical state in which sacred and secular affairs were governed by one ultimate set of authorities. Blending the temporal and the spiritual in this way fitted Mormon teaching about the importance of matter, and the early theocracies made near-total demands on the Saints. The law of consecration and stewardship at first required each Mormon, on entering the faith, to surrender all goods to the bishop who would, in turn, give back for use what each Mormon family would need. Later, when this plan did not work for various reasons, Mormons were still required to tithe. And in Utah, although they had had no experience with dry farming, Mormons ventured to construct under their leaders an extensive irrigation system which demanded the community's full commitment to make it work.

Although theocracy officially gave way to statehood for Utah in 1896, the fusion of church and state informally lingered on. Meanwhile, the church continued to be a masterpiece of organizational efficiency, divided into stakes and wards, with stake presidents and bishops, councils, elders, and priests, and at the head of this mighty empire in the West, a president who inherited the prophetic mantle of Joseph Smith. With their combination of otherworldly experience and thisworldly acumen, the Saints of Mormon times, like the "visible saints" of the Puritan era, combined spiritual sensitivity with Yankee shrewdness and native wit. The twentieth century brought them wealth and respectability, and in many ways they had long moved away from the sectarian ideal to become a broad and inclusive church with members in other parts of the world. Yet they continued to retain so much of the heritage of their past that the historian and sociologist of religions Joachim Wach hesitated to call them a church and labeled them instead an "independent group."

THE SEVENTH-DAY ADVENTISTS

Such hesitation is in its way also appropriate for another sectarian group which emerged from the nineteenth into the twentieth century. The Seventh-day Adventists have themselves publicly raised the question of whether they are still a sect or, in fact, have become a denomination. Asking this question already indicates an awareness of change within the ranks, but at the same time it points to the continuity with their past which Adventists experience. In order to understand the sectarian characteristics of even present-day Seventh-day Adventism, we must look at that past, for the various devices which Adventists have used to maintain their boundaries against other American religions grew out of their history.

The term *Seventh-day Adventist* came into official existence in 1860, when a general conference of Adventist Christians—bound together by religious, social, and economic ties—decided to adopt it as a designation. Even before 1840, however, there was a growing body of people who awaited the second coming, or advent, of Jesus with the intense expectation that it was very near. Like others earlier in history, these people have been called millennialists. The term derives from the thousand-year period at the end of time—the millennium—when, according to the biblical book of Revelation, the just will reign with Christ and Satan will be chained up.

Millennialists existed on both sides of the Atlantic during the period of our inquiry, but in the United States by 1840 they had begun to rally around the preaching of a New England Baptist named William Miller (1782–1849) and came to be known as Millerites. A respected citizen and rather average preacher in his style and mannerisms, Miller drew large crowds as he moved from place to place because everywhere he went he spread his conviction that the second coming of Jesus would occur "about the year 1843." Miller had arrived at this conclusion after careful study of the prophetic books of the Bible and in particular of Daniel 8:14: "Unto two thousand and three hundred days; then shall the sanctuary be cleansed" (King James Version). Interpreters generally agreed that a biblical day equaled a year of ordinary time, and for Miller and others, the time of the cleansing of the sanctuary was the time also of the second coming. Beyond this, Miller taught that the 2,300 years had begun in 457 B.C. when the rebuilding of the city of Jerusalem had been inaugurated. Thus, Millerites thought the end would come between 21 March 1843 and 21 March 1844, a specific time set by William Miller after others had urged him to more and more precision.

Later, when the world continued after March 1844, Samuel S. Snow (1806–1870), a member of the Millerite movement, convinced Miller himself and others that because of differences in the old Jewish calendar the end could be calculated to arrive on 22 October 1844. While there is no evidence that the faithful donned "ascension robes" to be ready for the great day, their expectation was strong and firm and so, too, was their Great Disappointment, as the experience of October 22 was later called. Many, in fact, left the movement. Others accepted the insight of Hiram Edson (1806–1882), who explained that, although Christ had failed to appear on earth, in heaven he had entered the holiest part of the Jewish sanctuary as the preliminary to his earthly advent. Still others simply gave up time setting but retained their earlier belief that the end was very near.

It was from among the faithful remnants of the Millerites that the Seventh-day Adventists arose. Prior to the Great Disappointment, a number of Adventists had followed the practice of keeping the ancient Jewish Sabbath (Saturday) instead of Sunday as their weekly day of worship and rest. Influenced by the example of Seventh Day Baptists, some Adventists in Washington, New Hampshire, had become convinced that the Bible should be taken literally and that they should honor the seventh rather than the first day of the week as the Sabbath Day. Among those who later accepted the Sabbath teaching were a former sea captain named Joseph Bates (1792–1872) and a fragile and sickly woman, Ellen G. White (1827–1915), along with her husband, James White (1821–1881). These three provided a new leadership for the former Millerites, still Adventists, and now turned Sabbatarians. In their thinking, Adventism and seventh-day Sabbath keeping were linked by strong ties, for the restoration of the genuine Sabbath prepared Adventists for the second coming. Conversely, worship on Sunday formed an idolatrous image to the beast that represented the powers of evil in the book of Revelation (Rev. 13).

Because of the unusual character of her religious experience, Ellen White quickly came to prominence in the new movement. In December 1844, when only seventeen years of age, she had had a vision in which she saw the Adventists traveling along a path toward the New Jerusalem, all the while lighted on their journey by the message of October 22. It was divine confirmation of the rightness of the Adventist remnant, and when further visions began to come to Ellen White, she became the sure sign of heavenly favor, the charismatic mediator through whom God continued to reveal himself to his people. As the years passed, the visions as well as inspired dreams enabled White to offer pronouncements on a wide variety of concerns, ranging from child nurture and education to missions and church organization. Especially, she addressed the issue of dietary reform and health. In keeping with the thought of a number of nineteenth-century health reformers such as Sylvester Graham (from whom present-day Graham crackers descend), Larkin B. Coles, and James C. Jackson, White saw God calling the Adventist people away from not only alcohol and tobacco but also tea, coffee, and meat, with special prohibitions against pork. She also urged dress reform for women, condemning tightly fitted garments and trailing skirts in the interests of health; and she preached general rules of hygiene to maintain the vigor of the body.

Through the years, as Seventh-day Adventists adhered to their sabbatarian and dietary practices and continued in their millennial beliefs, they settled close to one another. Thus, a marked localism accompanied their movement. Towns like Battle Creek, Michigan, and Loma Linda, California, became Adventist enclaves, while an empire of Adventist medical and educational organizations sprang up in the United States and throughout the world.

We are now in a position to appreciate the sectarian character of Seventh-day Adventism. It maintained a separate and exclusive identity through its beliefs in the nearness of the millennium and the prophetic nature of Ellen G. White and through its sabbatarian and dietary practices. At the same time, its localism illustrated in physical space the boundaries which framed the inner Adventist religious world. Like so many other sectarians, Adventists were counterbalanced in their exclusivism by a missionary urge so strong that the story of twentieth-century Seventh-day Adventism is really the story of the spread of Adventist world missions. Like other sectarians, too, Adventists have been suspicious of worldly government. The earliest Adventists avoided any relationship to government when they preached their message of an imminent end, while later from the early 1850s they began to identify the political government in the United States with the beast in the book of Revelation. Even in the 1880s and later, Adventists remained at the edge of the political process, entering it only if they thought that by doing so they might be able, paradoxically, to delay the coming of the end the better to preach that it would come soon. Their logic sprang from their millennialism: if the end were soon to come, it was foolish to become involved with worldly government and dispute.

Similarly, Adventists gave wide berth to the waging of war. There was the biblical injunction not to kill as well as the practical difficulty of keeping the Sabbath in an army in which Sunday was the officially recognized day of worship. So Adventists entered military service with noncombatant status, serving generally as medics. Seeking the restoration of the primitive church rather than a reformation of the present one, thinking more of sanctification than of justification, Adventists, like Mormons, resembled the Radicals of the sixteenth century. They preached the gospel, as one Adventist scholar has put it, but they did not because of the gospel cease to preach the law. Like the Mormons, too, though not so markedly, Adventists questioned God's control over part of the universe: humans with their free will could change the course of events and so the plans of God.

Adventists, indeed, have been paradoxical in more than their desire to delay the end in order to preach the end. Today they look to the second advent when the world as we know it will cease to be. Yet with their sabbatarianism, they just as strongly affirm the material world. Unlike the Sunday celebration which honors the *resurrection* of Jesus, a symbol of spiritual triumph *over* the material world, the Saturday Sabbath commemorates God's work in creation from which, on the seventh day, he rested. Thus, it honors the natural and material, and it looks to the beginning of things as much as to the end. In reality, the first advent of the divine was in the Lord who stretched forth his hand to create. Hence, the present is a moment stretched taut between past and future, between destiny done and destiny to come. Standing in this tension as it does, the present, the time when history is made, becomes important. The implications are that Adventism must take seriously the things of time and that the natural, material world is a significant source of value. So Ellen White, like the prophet Joseph Smith, was the mouthpiece for a *progressive* divine revelation, one that took into account the transformations which time and history brought. So, too, the pronouncements which came through White's visions were seriously concerned with matters such as health reform, as ordinary matters achieved extraordinary status through the divine interference. The world which God had created, the clay of the earth, was sacred. And so finally and like the Mormons, the literal word should be taken at face value and not "spiritualized" away. Just as the Sabbath meant Saturday, creation meant the direct and immediate work of God and not new nineteenth-century teachings such as the theory of evolution and the notion that the earth was far more ancient than the Bible had taught.

However, if the Adventists in their sectarianism were paradoxical, they were mirroring a particularly American paradox. Curiously, although they worked to maintain their position of distinctiveness among the many, like the Mormons before them, they reflected the oneness of an American religion that was part of American culture. We have seen that Adventists were materialists and millennialists at once and that with their far-flung educational and medical empire they still intensely await the second advent. But the mainstream of American culture was also materialist and millennialist at once. American cultural materialism is something with which we are all familiar. More than that, Americans in general had been millennialists in the nineteenth century, believing that with the dawn of the Industrial Revolution and the rising power of the young republic, a new age in the history of the world was being inaugurated. In the American republic, they thought, the lion would lie down with the lamb, and peace, plenty, and prosperity would continue to reign. They were living in the last, best age of the world, and Americans were the most fortunate of the human species—ideas we will explore further in Part Two.

Thus, other Americans, in the general structure of their beliefs and attitudes, were very much like Seventh-day Adventists, while Seventh-day Adventists were very much like other Americans. There is an almost humorous commentary on just how much this is the case in the reference of one Adventist apologist of the twentieth century to the "scientifically proven visions" of Ellen White. (He meant that the divine advice of the visions had been corroborated by scientific evidence.)

It is perhaps in Adventist ritual that the resemblance to the Protestant and American mainstream is most striking. Adventist services, with the exception of quarterly communion and foot-washing rituals, are largely indistinguishable from general Protestant worship. For the most part, ministers are teachers more than preachers and rational more than emotional, but this is the case in many mainstream Protestant services. It is not so difficult, from the vantage point of a typical Adventist Sabbath celebration, to understand the Seventh-day dilemma with which we began: Do affluent and highly educated American Adventists belong to a sect, or are they members of a mainstream Protestant denomination? The Seventh-day dilemma is another form of the American dilemma that we notice again and again. Are Americans many, or are they one?

THE CHRISTIAN SCIENTISTS

For still another view of the dilemma, we turn to a third example, that of Mary Baker Eddy (1821–1910) and her teaching of Christian Science. Eddy had grown up in New England, an area filled with memories of the Puritan fathers who had in large part established Anglo-American civilization. She was for years a member of the Congregational church, descended from the Puritan ancestors, and she looked to the past with reverence and a spirit of piety. Thus, Mary Baker Eddy began her religious quest as part of the American mainstream, an embodiment of the kind of religion we are calling the one religion of America. In the twentieth century, her followers in Christian Science, like Mormons and Seventh-day Adventists, would in many ways be indistinguishable from their mainline Protestant neighbors. Yet in between, in the years in which the foundress's "discovery" fired her will and inspired the allegiance of her followers as a separated group of people, Christian Science stood as an example of the manyness of American religions.

Sectarians are people who maintain strong boundaries between themselves and the rest of the world, whose identity precludes much overlapping with the environment which surrounds them. Crossing the boundary, for sectarians, should occur only infrequently through ordinary and everyday encounters with others. It should come most in the extraordinary encounters that define the human relationship with God. If this is so, then the extraordinary religious experience of Mary Baker Eddy in 1866, like the earlier experiences of Joseph Smith and Ellen G. White in its results, inaugurated Christian Science as a distinct sectarian movement.

For years Mary Baker Eddy had moved from place to place, living in boardinghouses in a state of poverty, dislocation, and emotional pain, occasioned by the death of a first husband and the unfaithfulness of a second. In this situation she had suffered from the physical complaints, often called "nervous disease," which seemed so prevalent among later nineteenth-century women. In the form of chronic spinal affliction, this illness had often confined Eddy to her bed for days and weeks on end. Then in 1862, she sought out Phineas P. Quimby, a celebrated mental healer of the era, who began to help and also to teach her. But in 1866 when Quimby died, she was more bereft than ever. About a month after this traumatic event, Eddy fell on the ice and suffered what seemed a concussion and a possible dislocated spine. "On the third day," however, reading the gospel story of Jesus healing the palsied man (Matt. 9:2), she had a profoundly moving experience in which she glimpsed spiritual truth and was instantly healed. From that moment, Eddy dated the beginning of Christian Science.

During the long years of her pilgrimage to this moment of truth, she had grown more and more estranged from the ordinary rhythms of middle-class existence. Yet now her separateness assumed new form as *religious* reality, and in this form it began to attract others. The decade from 1866 to 1875, on the face of it, brought Eddy more years of wandering from one dismal New England mill town to another. But inwardly, these years were a time of quiet thinking and writing. They culminated in 1875 in the publication of the first edition of *Science and Health,* the book that ranked beside the Bible and explained it for later Christian Scientists. Four years later (1879), the Church of Christ, Scientist, was formally chartered, and the story after that, for Eddy and Christian Science, was one of growing wealth, influence, and worldly prestige, almost a direct turnabout from the fortunes of those early years.

It was true that the foundress and her movement experienced a series of defections, when former students struck out on their own as independent offshoots of the more general mind-cure movement of the period. Perhaps alienated by Mary Baker Eddy's claims to spiritual authority, perhaps inspired by it to discover the truth on their own, these former Scientists ironically only served to enhance the sectarian tendencies of those who remained with Eddy. The original group, now harassed by the accusations and even lawsuits of their former associates, turned within. So the bonds that separated Christian Scientists from the world grew stronger still.

At the core of their separate existence was the religious teaching of Mary Baker Eddy and its culminating expression in Christian Science practice. Teaching and practice together, for Eddy and her followers, were the product of a continuing divine revelation in creation. At certain privileged moments in human history, individuals caught a glimpse of this divine revelation, and when they did so, they experienced a breakthrough of light and power in their lives. In the words of the Christian gospel, they knew the truth and it established them in freedom (John 8:32). It was in such a moment that Christian Science had been discovered, and it was in such moments that Christian Scientists would find the power to heal the sick.

At the basis of these healings and the center of this discovery, Mary Baker Eddy taught, was Jesus Christ, the only person within human history who fully demonstrated what it meant to be the son of God. The revelation of Jesus was a practical ideal for others to imitate, for all people should strive, like Jesus, to realize completely their relationship to God. This meant bringing to light the perfection of their actual and God-given natures instead of accepting the limitations of their apparent natures. Christian Science was the way to break out of the illusions of the material world. It taught people to see that there were no real limits to human nature as God made it and to act on the basis of that knowledge through distinctive healing practices. Like the Mormons who aimed to live "as Gods," Christian Scientists saw a world without physical or spiritual barriers to perfection.

Hence, rooted and grounded in the revelation of Jesus, Eddy's teaching extended to include a philosophical treatment of the nature of God, human beings, and their world. In her vision God was not a person, at least in the ordinary and anthropomorphic sense in which "person" had been understood throughout the centuries of Christian thought. Rather, God was the divine Principle or Life out of which the universe emanated. God was Soul, Truth, and Love in the world. If gender designations were to be used in naming the divine Principle, then God was a Father-Mother God, for love (motherhood) was the divine Principle that had authored human beings and the universe. The Father-Mother God had engendered the world as a reflection of the infinite Mind. It followed that, as Mind, God was present in all reality, and—most significant for Christian Science practice—there was no such thing as matter. God and nature were one reality, bound by spiritual and not material laws. There was, in the world, only one true Science, the law of this divine Mind: matter was a shadow, a poor, pale correspondent to the truth of God.

It was a fact that for the material sense—the limited sense of reality that people share—matter was completely real. But from the perspective of God's Mind, human beings, as reflections of the divine Principle, were immortal. Seemingly bound by the laws of matter, they were entwined only in their own false conceptions of the nature of things. Error was at the bottom of sin and sickness, and therefore, the twin evils could be dispelled by the bright light of truth. This truth was the redemption of what Eddy called "mortal man," and it came, as in the Christian gospels, through Jesus Christ. Salvation meant *following the example of Jesus.* At-one-ment with Christ brought an end to separation from God and, consequently, redemption from both sickness and sin.

This vision of the nature of things issued concretely in healing the sick. Christian Science practitioners, many of them women, were people who devoted themselves professionally to healing others. Their methods were visiting the sick, counseling them, and, above all, praying for them. The work of Christian Science practitioners centered on this prayer, which was not a simple plea to God for help, but instead a meditation on the sick person in the presence of God. Practitioners began by going apart to gain a sense of their own personal relationship with God. Then, they quietly tried to discern and acknowledge the real (spiritual) truth of each person for whom they worked. This meant seeing through the illusion of the illness to the person as he or she actually existed in the sight of God. Practitioners held these thoughts in mind until they gained an inner sense of what a patient's problem was and broke the falsity in the truth. They worked to focus this truth on the person; and finally, the treatment completed, they firmly expected to receive word that the sick person had been healed.

Although the success of the healing process depended on the spiritual state of the Christian Science practitioner, demands were also made of patients. They might be asked to study certain passages from the writings of Mary Baker Eddy, to discipline their thoughts, or to try to realize certain truths about their lives. Meanwhile, Christian Scientists avoided alcohol and tobacco and sometimes caffeine, wishing to eliminate the presence of drugs of any kind. For a committed Scientist, no medicine could yield genuine well-being. Whether prescribed by a physician or obtained through socially accepted stimulants or depressants, drugs operated in terms of the false world of matter.

To sum up, Christian Science taught a broad understanding of Christian revelation, expounded a philosophical system to help modern people understand it, and practiced healing as the natural outcome of its beliefs about Christ and the world. Like the sectarians of the Radical Reformation, Jesus for Christian Scientists was the great exemplar of perfect humanness. Salvation came not through faith alone but, rather, through imitating the model which Jesus had provided. Moreover, like the Radical Reformers, Christian Scientists thought that they were *restoring* the teaching of the primitive church in which, to a far greater degree than in later centuries, healing had been central. While Eddy would also claim that no one before her had discovered the truth of Christian Science and that all of previous Christian history had missed the revelation, her sometime emphasis on restoration was significant. So, too, was the theology of material error which led Christian Science to adopt a position toward politics and the social order similar to that of the sixteenth-century Reformers. For if the reality of the material world was denied, it meant that participation in its business, attention to its problems, adherence to its political or social systems, could at best be only secondary concerns. Clearly, a Christian Scientist ought to keep free of its involvements.

If Christian Scientists resembled sixteenth-century Radical Reformers, however, even more did they show themselves to be citizens of nineteenth-century America. Like Mormons and Adventists, even though they tried to separate themselves from mainstream American beliefs and values, with their optimism and perfectionism they ended up affirming what they denied. They revealed themselves as authentically American in their response to religion. First of all, there was their designation of themselves as Christian *Scientists*. In a century which had witnessed startling new advances in science, such as Charles Darwin's discovery of evidence to support the theory of evolution *(The Origin of Species*, 1859), science was a word which carried considerable prestige. For Mary Baker Eddy and her followers, it meant the laws by which God governed the universe, but it also connoted the methods, or rules, used for Christian Science "demonstration" and the certainty with which these rules could be applied. In other words, Christian Science healings, like scientific experiments, were repeatable procedures. They could be counted on, so long as one had studied and practiced correctly.

Thus, Eddy cast her new teaching into a framework that had been supplied by science. Her insistence on discovery and demonstration were instances of the framework as, of course, was the name by which she chose to designate her new religious movement. So, too, was her continual reference to members of the Christian Science organization as "students," and her steadfast conception of her role as that of teacher. In 1881, just two years after the official incorporation of the church, she had received a charter for the Massachusetts Metaphysical College in which she trained future Christian Science practitioners. Moreover, for years before a church organization of any kind came into being, she had taught students her principles in rented rooms.

Secondly, there was the organizational structure which Mary Baker Eddy built—as American as the impressive business organizations that in the Gilded Age (early 1870s to late 1890s) were swiftly becoming giant corporations.

Although in the beginning Eddy had not wanted a formal institution at all, her later efforts reversed this direction. She grew dissatisfied with the rudimentary structure she had fashioned through the Church of Christ, Scientist (1879), the Massachusetts Metaphysical College (1881), and the National Christian Science Association (1886). In 1889, she gave up the charter of the college and in 1892 dissolved the association. She had been established in Boston since 1882, and now she reorganized the Boston church which, as pastor, she controlled, urging Christian Scientists throughout the country to apply for membership in the Mother Church.

Thus began a process of joint membership in which most Christian Scientists belonged to both a local organization and the Mother Church in Boston. Here, a self-perpetuating board of directors assumed a power that would live on after the death of Eddy, while meanwhile in the branch churches pastors were replaced by readers appointed for three-year terms. Worship under the guidance of the readers did not involve the traditional preaching office but, instead, the reading of assigned passages from the Bible and *Science and Health*, its sanctioned interpretation. In practice, revelation had been given to the nineteenth century only in the inspired understanding of scripture which Mary Baker Eddy opened to her followers, while other teaching was forbidden. Under these circumstances, the Christian Science organization became a masterpiece of technical efficiency. The application of bureaucratic principles betrayed a genius truly American, and in this respect, Eddy's church could compete successfully with the structures built by a John D. Rockefeller or an Andrew Carnegie.

Thirdly, the American background of Christian Science was suggested by the very character of Mary Baker Eddy's life and the lives of those who joined her. In many ways, her problems were the problems of others in the Gilded Age. For this was a time when the surface brilliance of America seemed only a gaudy tinsel to hide the spiritual malaise beneath. Recovering from the Civil War and at the same time expanding by leaps and bounds industrially, America was enlarging old cities and creating new ones. People flocked to these cities from the countryside, and people flocked there, too, from abroad, as new waves of immigrants deluged America. This was an age of genuine pluralism but also an age of Protestant predicament, as the old symbols of a supernatural order no longer rang true with everyday American experience.

Into this world, Mary Baker Eddy launched a movement and a message which provided some form of resolution for the key anxieties of the era. Herself a product of the social dislocation of the industrial age, Eddy offered her followers a bastion of security in the Mother Church. A gifted woman with strong leadership potential at a time when a woman's place was confined to marriage and family, through her church she forged a stage on which she and the others who followed her could act forcefully and effectively. Many of those who joined her were women of midlife and middle-class status, and what she had to offer them was a purposive life that could be lived *alone*. At a time when community values were breaking down under the impact of urbanization and industrialization, she taught self-reliance and self-sufficiency through correct thinking and practice. The cure of their illnesses for these women was bound up with their self-initiated action in Christian Science. Meanwhile, the denial of the social world which the new religion involved was a telling rebuttal to male-oriented America that had denied a public place to women and their concerns.

Christian Science, in other words, like Mormonism and Adventism before it, succeeded in making the ordinary extraordinary. Through the medium of the foundress's religious experience which inspired her followers, Christian Science transmuted the bleak metallic facts of Gilded Age history and sociology into spiritual—and material—gold. Christian Science had mined its situation to discover finally what all religions seek from the human situation—a transcendent meaning and purpose. But in the very act of doing so, in the process of turning the ordinary into the extraordinary, Christian Science manipulated the present order to yield material comfort. In so doing, Christian Science revealed its American spirit.

COMMUNALISM

The three religious movements that we have so far discussed in this chapter, Mormonism, Seventh-day Adventism, and Christian Science, were all examples—case studies, if you will—of sectarianism. Yet, while they involved a radical break with the surrounding world, they still maintained some relative communication with outsiders. This was apparent in the fact that none of the three movements died or disintegrated. Instead, in the twentieth century each of them moved closer to the religious center, taking the route that brought them from a more sectarian to a more denominational status. Their experience followed a pattern that held for many other American sectarians of the period.

Different from the pattern that led from sect to denomination was another in which extreme exclusivity dominated the sectarian venture until in the end it came apart. This pattern was illustrated in the histories of a variety of communal movements which flourished in the nineteenth century and thereafter all but vanished. These movements were part of the long and rich history of American communalism. Beginning in the eighteenth century and continuing with numerous examples into the present, for some Americans pursuit of the American dream meant planting a heaven on earth. They wanted to create perfect societies, communities in which all would live for the sake of each and each for all. Often they saw their planned societies as blueprints for the reforms that later would spread throughout all of America or, in a typical sectarian theme, as inaugurations of the millennium.

We will look briefly at two of these communal sects—the Shakers and the Oneida Perfectionists—to suggest the directions which many of them followed. Each of these communal groups, in the years in which it was successful, was characterized by stronger methods of maintaining its boundaries than those of more "lenient" sectarians. Each was ruled by the magnetic personality of a charismatic leader whose inspired teaching provided a mythic center for the movement. In each society, the myth (sacred story) was effectively dramatized through powerful rituals, and in each a code of living transformed the Word into flesh in ordinary, everyday existence. In objection, we might point to the charismatic leadership of a Joseph Smith, an Ellen White, or a Mary Baker Eddy. Indeed, we might notice the uniqueness of the teaching of each and the ability of their movements to provide cogent rituals and organization for daily living. What then, we might ask, distinguished the communitarians from other sectarians? The answer lies not so much in a difference of structural principles (leader, myth, ritual, everyday ethic) as in the radical extreme to which communitarians implemented these principles. Above all, the difference lay in their adoption of a communal lifestyle in which they challenged the two great principles of social independence—private property and sexual exclusivity in the family.

The Shakers

The foundress of the Shakers, Mother Ann Lee (1736–1784), had had visionary experiences from her childhood in Manchester, England. Early she had become convinced of the sinfulness of human nature, and gradually she had come to identify the root of evil in the act of sexual intercourse. When after her marriage to Abraham Standerin (Stanley) her four children died in infancy, she became even more convinced of this understanding. Already a member of an ecstatic group which had broken away from the Quakers under the leadership of Jane and James Wardley, in 1770 Ann Lee received a vision in which she saw depicted before her the original sin in Eden. Subsequently, she began to teach the importance of celibacy, and the Shaking Quakers, or Shakers, who followed her visionary directive came to call her Mother Ann or Ann the Word. When in a later vision she was urged to go to America, a small group of eight believers took ship together in 1774 and came to the land where Lee's vision foretold that the Church of Christ's Second Appearing would be established. They settled in New York state and remained there throughout the American Revolution, and although the Shakers endured persecution, they continued to preach their message until the death of Mother Ann Lee in 1784.

It was only thereafter that the United Society of Believers in Christ's Second Appearing became a communitarian body. Living together in "families" of celibates who shared all property in common, the Shakers taught, like Joseph Smith and Mary Baker Eddy, that God was a Father-Mother deity. Since human beings were made in God's image and since they were male or female, it followed that God, too, possessed the equivalent of both genders. God was a bisexual being. On earth the fullest male manifestation of God had come in Jesus Christ, and the fullest female manifestation in Ann Lee. With the familiar sectarian conviction that they were restoring the primitive church, the Shakers preached community of property and sexual abstinence. At the same time, they expounded the necessity of a separate government, the Christian duty of pacifism, and, as Mary Baker Eddy would later teach, the power of spirit over physical disease. The millennium was about to begin, they thought, because God had inaugurated his final dispensation, or era, through the second coming of Christ in Ann Lee.

It was in Shaker ritual, however, that the religious teachings of Ann Lee's followers received their strongest expression. Originating in the ecstatic and uncontrollable physical movements of the Shaking Quakers, Shaker dance became the organized enactment of the myth (sacred story) of community based on the bisexuality of God. If God was a dual person, both male and female, and if Jesus Christ and Ann Lee represented respectively the power and wisdom of God, then the formal dance of the male and female members of the community revealed that they were members all of one body, equally necessary to its existence as a reflection of the divine community. They, too, should be power and wisdom for one another as together they prayed and worked in the image of God. Similarly, if the millennium was about to begin or, indeed, had already begun in the coming of Mother Ann Lee, then the Shaker dance dramatized the myth of that millennium already begun. In it the barriers between this world and the next were dissolved, as Shakers experienced the harmonial rhythms which would govern the millennial kingdom for all. When the Shaker dancers continued their stylized movements into long hours of the night—until the movements gradually lost their stylization and the Shakers had whirled themselves into ecstasy—they experienced in their mystical union with one another in God and Mother Ann a foretaste of the bliss of paradise.

It is interesting that as the years passed and the midnineteenth century brought the Shakers years of prosperity and success, they maintained contact with their foundress by a period of ritual intensity known as "Mother Ann's Work." From 1837 to 1854, spirit mediums who could communicate with the world beyond became important "officiants" in the rituals. Shakers entertained a host of spirit visitors from American Indians to George Washington. They acted out the visions which their mediums directed, all the while convinced that in the process they were the privileged recipients of heavenly gifts.

Later, in the 1840s when the period of greatest spirit activity in the ritual had declined, the Shakers found that some among them, apparently all female, had begun to draw or paint on spiritual and mystical themes. The "spirit drawings" that resulted were gifts, they said, from heaven and often directly from Holy Mother Wisdom, recollections by inspired members of the community of visionary experiences that they had had. At their height, these spirit drawings were executed in brilliant color and careful symmetry, often emphasizing floral, leaf, and arboreal patterns. Symbols of the Father-Mother God filled them as did representations of a wealth of material goods (musical instruments, jewelry, exotic foods, and the like) which in their actual lives the Shakers denied themselves.

Spirit drawings declined after 1859. After the Civil War, so did the Shakers, until by the last quarter of the twentieth century only a few Shakers remained in two surviving New England communities. There had been a connection between the vitality of the communities and the vitality of their rituals and religious art, for symbol and rite were ways to remember, ways to re-create and make new the religious adventure that had begun with Mother Ann. In their years of greatest vigor, Shaker societies had spread from New York and New England to Kentucky, Ohio, and Indiana, numbering eighteen separate establishments and over 5,000 members. Further, they were renowned not only for the ecstatic disregard of their rituals but also for the quiet and ordered purposefulness of their lives. Indeed, the sexual equality dramatized in the ritual dance was reflected, to a great extent, in both the administration and work of the communities. Shaker furniture, with its exquisite simplicity, suggested the functional efficiency that regulated the community endeavors. Renowned for the ingeniousness of their practical inventions, for their agricultural seeds and pharmaceutical supplies, Shakers gave every evidence of being as pragmatic as they were mystical. Like Christian Scientists, whose denial of the reality of matter led to material good health and prosperity, Shakers blended otherworldliness with a thisworldly acumen that made them the envy of their neighbors.

Perhaps this is not so unusual as it seems. Religious groups that are successful seem to be able to balance many kinds of concerns at the same time, to hold in tension values that are often opposed. They are able, in the total pattern of their lives, to give expression to disparate realities which, when held together, yield a resolution in completeness. If this is so, then the key to Shaker success lay in the ability of the Shakers to combine the celibacy of their daily lives with the bisexuality of their myth, the order of their workaday world with the creative disorder of their ritual, the shrewdness of their business insights with the innocence of their mystical flights. Like the other sectarians whose lives we have examined, Shakers knew how to make the ordinary extraordinary, for no detail of life in community was insignificant. Everything in some way mirrored the great truths that the Shakers had learned from the teaching of Mother Ann. The Shakers would continue to flourish so long as through ritual and symbol they continued to remember—to see in the ordinary events of everyday reality the extraordinary spiritual gifts which, in the light of Mother Ann, the ordinary became.

The Oneida Perfectionists

As with the Shakers, optimism about the millennial age surrounded the efforts of the Oneida Perfectionists, our second case study of sectarian religious community. John Humphrey Noyes (1811–1886), the founder of the Oneida community, had as a young man become convinced that the millennium had already arrived. It had come, he thought, in A.D. 70 when the second coming had occurred, for Jesus had expected the end within a generation of his personal preaching ministry and Jesus could not have been wrong.

It followed that sinners had already, centuries ago, been separated from the saved, and those who tried to follow Jesus in the nineteenth century need not fear the snares of sin any longer. They were saints and perfect beings, since sin had been abolished in the millennial kingdom. Life on earth should be a foretaste of heavenly bliss. Further, because in heaven Christ had indicated there would be no marrying or giving in marriage, there was something wrong with the ordinary institution of marriage as the nineteenth century understood it. At the heavenly banquet, every food should be available to every guest: on earth, the restrictions of the marriage bond seemed part of a false, and even sinful, system which should not apply to the perfect.

These thoughts received a concrete and clearly articulated expression in the communities which Noyes established, first, at Putney, Vermont (1840–1847), and later and more significantly, at Oneida, New York (1848–1879). The Putney community began as a religious association composed of Noyes's own family, but in 1844, joined by others, the Putney group initiated the practice of communism. Two years later, the members of the small community were following their leader's teaching in the twin practices of male continence and complex marriage. Male continence offered a reliable system of birth control through male self-control, for men would complete their sexual activity without ejaculation. Complex marriage, made possible by this male continence, meant that every man was husband to every woman in the community and every woman was wife to every man. Only mutual agreement was needed to engage in sexual relations. At the same time, with an asceticism that belied what looked like sexual license, exclusive relationships between any two members of the community were forbidden. Sex should become the great bond of a community that mirrored the heavenly unity: it should not bring with it the divisiveness that prevented the members of one body in Christ from genuinely loving each and all.

When difficulties with outraged neighbors brought trouble to the Putney community, Noyes bought land for the group in northern New York at Oneida. Here began the most successful and best-remembered years of the Perfectionists, who readily displayed their talents not only in interpersonal relations but also in business and manufacture. After 1857, the community profited from the making of steel traps, which had begun some years earlier, and they also produced a variety of other goods for which they gained a reputation as skilled workers in the crafts. The membership grew until by 1878 it had reached over 300, and meanwhile there had been experiments in branch communities which followed the Oneida pattern. Some of the new members had joined the community, prompted often by Noyes's publications which clearly and cogently argued the rationale of Oneida Perfectionism. Others, however, were born into the community through unions that were carefully reviewed and approved by Noyes for the production of offspring.

Life in the community, from the many reports of it that have been left, was pleasurable and satisfying, with various kinds of art, literature, and amusements provided. Still, by the time the second generation of Oneida Perfectionists had grown to maturity, internal dissension became a factor in community life. These people had had no personal experience of the early struggles that had led to Oneida's foundation. They reacted against the ways of their elders, sometimes by outright agnosticism and sometimes by secret disapproval of what they regarded as the immorality of complex marriage. The misgivings of these Perfectionists, combined with the hostility of outsiders who were shocked by the community's practices, finally led Noyes to flee to Canada and to urge the dissolution of the community. Thus, community life disbanded, Oneida reconstituted itself as a joint-stock company, and ironically the strongest memory the twentieth century has of Oneida is its silverware.

At its height, however, Oneida had combined religious theory with a practical efficiency that extended to both ordinary and extraordinary concerns. The joy and ease of life in the community had been purchased by a near-monastic discipline embracing all aspects of daily existence. Both complex marriage and communism of property inculcated detachment, for complex marriage diffused the sexual passion and communism diffused intense ambition. Members of the community, moreover, in monastic fashion engaged in the regular and ritualized practice of mutual criticism. Members often requested a criticism from the group, or at times, when they seemed to be causing serious problems, they could be requested to undergo the discipline. Sometimes before all members and sometimes before a selected committee that represented the others, the person to be criticized listened quietly to what they had to say about his or her actions and the spirit in which they had been performed. The public nature of the proceeding acted as a check, and personal vindictiveness against any one person was curbed lest it lead to criticism of the critic. At the end of the meeting, the criticisms were summarized, advice offered, and encouragement given so that the member would emerge from the experience a more complete human being and a more harmonious communitarian. Mutual criticism was found so successful, in fact, that it became a form of treatment for illness. With an intuitive recognition of the connection between mind and body, Oneidans would gather at the bedside of a sick member to hasten recovery by chastening the spirit of the patient. Like Christian Scientists and the many others of the era who had come to suspect the spiritual origins of disease, the Perfectionists seemed convinced that religious means could—and did—cure.

Indeed, Oneidans saw their community as a living witness to the end of what Noyes called the "sin-system," a system to which they connected all or most of the evils that troubled Americans of the era. Apostasy, unbelief, obedience to mammon, private property, and death were links in a chain that had been destroyed at Oneida. In their place, the community was building a new chain of redemption, a system established on the restoration of true, primitive Christianity, faith and obedience to Christ, communism, and finally immortality. Christian love and responsibility would bring freedom, equality, and enduring life to all, for Christian communism meant the end of the "work-system" and the "marriage-system," replaced by a life that fit the time of the millennium.

Thus, the sectarianism of Oneida, with its carefully drawn boundaries that segregated the community from the world, provided an exemplary model of what all Christian life should be like. The Perfectionists self-consciously separated themselves in their radical life in community, and yet they saw themselves as the first wave of a future available to all who confessed Christ. Their community reached out to the America beyond the doors of Oneida, and like the other sects we have examined including the Shakers, the Perfectionists reflected the culture that they had tried to avoid in their communities. We have discussed this situation to some extent in the case of the more loosely knit sectarian bodies—the Mormons, Seventh-day Adventists, and Christian Scientists—but it is well to point to the fact that "Americanism" was the heritage of communitarians as well. The material prosperity of Shakers, Perfectionists, and others like them seemed a capsule summary of the American dream. Their millennial expectations—and realizations—complemented the general cultural millennialism of the age of progress, with its faith that a new era was dawning to end the centuries of human misery the world had previously known. Moreover, in a land of individualism and pragmatic opportunism, the communities offered a cultural balance and personal sanctuary for those uprooted by the twin facts of industrialization and urbanization. From a historical and sociological point of view, they seemed to be spin-offs of the modernization process that had reached its furthest frontier in America.

IN OVERVIEW

All of the sectarian movements that we have examined were different, yet all shared certain characteristics. Like sects in general, they were voluntary societies of committed people who guarded the boundaries between themselves and others very closely. Experiencing conversion to a life of love and law, members of the sects could be compared to the Radical Reformers of the sixteenth century in their zeal for the restoration of true Christianity, their stress on right living, their general indifference toward politics, and their millennialism. Not "also-rans" among the Protestants, they embodied a different religious vision, imbuing each detail of ordinary life with an extraordinary religious quality. At the same time, like their Protestant neighbors sectarians reflected the American experience. Their religious experiments were graphic expressions of the American experiment, emphasizing newness and human possibility with millennial themes.

In terms of the degree of their separation from the rest of society, sectarian movements ranged along a broad continuum. More accommodating movements—like Mormonism, Seventh-day Adventism, and Christian Science—did not demand total community from their members. Their respective histories led them closer and closer to mainstream denominationalism. At the other end of the continuum, movements like those of the Shakers and the Oneida Perfectionists enjoined a style of life in which members participated in total and all-embracing communities. With their concern for the boundaries which separated them from others, all of the sectarian movements were examples of the continuing concern for boundaries in pluralistic America. At the same time, whatever their Americanness, sectarians had responded to nineteenth-century situations in *religious* terms, learning to demarcate the boundaries that established their existence in this world and their future in the next, learning to observe those boundaries, and above all, learning how and when to cross them. Their blend of ordinary and extraordinary religion was not the only one that could have been made, but their blend worked for their time and maintained their continuity as part of the manyness of American religions.

Others, nevertheless, would find the sectarianism of the nineteenth-century new religions too confining or otherwise unpromising. Some would turn, instead, to the occult and metaphysical movements, which also fed the manyness. It is to these religious traditions that we now turn.

SUGGESTIONS FOR FURTHER READING: NINETEENTH-CENTURY NEW RELIGIONS

Andrews, Edward Deming. *The People Called Shakers.* New York: Dover Publications, 1963.

Arrington, Leonard J., and Bitton, Davis. *The Mormon Experience: A History of the Latter-day Saints.* New York: Alfred A. Knopf, 1979.

Carden, Maren Lockwood. *Oneida: Utopian Community to Modern Corporation.* Baltimore: Johns Hopkins Press, 1969.

Gaustad, Edwin Scott, ed. *The Rise of Adventism.* New York: Harper & Row, 1974.

Gottschalk, Stephen. *The Emergence of Christian Science in American Religious Life.* Berkeley: University of California Press, 1973.

Holloway, Mark. *Heavens on Earth: Utopian Communities in America, 1680–1880.* Rev. ed. New York: Dover Publications, 1966.

Numbers, Ronald L. *Prophetess of Health: A Study of Ellen G. White.* New York: Harper & Row, 1976.

O'Dea, Thomas F. *The Mormons.* Chicago: University of Chicago Press, 1957.

Troeltsch, Ernst. *The Social Teaching of the Christian Churches.* 1911. 2 vols. Translated by Olive Wyon. Reprint. Chicago: University of Chicago Press, 1976.

Tyler, Alice Felt. *Freedom's Ferment: Phases of American Social History from the Colonial Period to the Outbreak of the Civil War.* 1944. Reprint. New York: Harper & Row, Harper Torchbooks, 1962.

Weber, Max. *The Sociology of Religion.* 1922. Translated from the 4th ed., rev. (1956) by Ephraim Fischoff. Boston: Beacon Press, 1963.

CHAPTER 7

Homesteads of the Mind:
Occult and Metaphysical Movements

The year was 1848, and the place was an old, ramshackle house in Hydesville, New York. This home to the Fox family—John, a blacksmith; Margaret, his wife; and their two daughters, Maggie, a teen-ager, and Kate, less than twelve—in a memorable series of episodes became the site of mysterious and unexplainable knocking sounds. After a week or so of the noise in late March, the two girls or their parents grew anxious, and the girls moved their trundle bed into their parents' bedroom. The new setting made Kate and then Maggie braver; snapping their fingers and clapping their hands, they asked the knocker to make some response. It offered a series of raps in answer, and thus began a dialogue with the invisible presence. Soon the noises became the talk of the neighborhood, responding to questions as they were asked and even leading some of the neighbors to discover the identity of the rapper—a murdered peddler who claimed his remains were buried in the cellar. Such contact with the dead meant that, once again, religious excitement spread over the Burnt Over district of upstate New York, already the site of Mormon, Millerite, and Shaker preaching.

It was, for believers, the birth of modern Spiritualism, and for students of American religions, one instance of a growing trend in nineteenth-century America. Occult and metaphysical movements proliferated throughout that era and into the twentieth century. They added to the manyness of religions in America and also expressed a new oneness. Spread by the media and shared by members of the mainstream, the ideas and attitudes of those who joined these movements spilled beyond their boundaries—something we will continue to notice. Here, as we have already seen in so many instances, it is impossible to discuss every aspect of the manyness. We can select only a few major examples to suggest the development of these movements. But before we do, we need to have some idea of the meaning of occultism and metaphysics for American religion.

163

OCCULT AND METAPHYSICAL RELIGIONS

Any dictionary would explain that the word *occult* refers to something hidden and mysterious. Yet, what we often do not realize is that in the West the occult tradition is another form of *religion*, profoundly different from the Judaeo-Christian mainstream. Historically, it crystallized in a secret body of knowledge and practice, passed on by a small, select group in every age. During much of Western history, until the Enlightenment of the eighteenth century, it was still, however, in touch with major strands of the common European culture. Indeed, the science of the period shared its main insights about the nature of the universe and the place of human life within it. And while the Christian church warned against occultism, some of its clergy were familiar with it and agreed with its basic ideas.

After the Enlightenment, though, the new science brought a radical revision of the way educated people viewed the world. As the prestige of science grew and as the church stepped out of the Middle Ages, occultism became, more and more, not only secret knowledge but also rejected knowledge. It had always been an assorted mixture of elements taken from various pagan traditions blended sometimes with insights from Judaism and Christianity. Now that mixture was regarded as thoroughly suspect—the remnants of old superstition from the early ages of humanity. Thus, by the nineteenth century to hold occult beliefs meant to run counter to the main trend of culture. If an occultist was aware of the predicament, it meant, therefore, to be estranged. Alienation from the ordinary religion of culture accompanied occult beliefs and practices.

At the same time, an overview of American religious history reveals at least two kinds of occultism. There was, first of all, a natural and traditional occultism which came to the New World with the colonists. It thrived in the seventeenth century and continued strong into the eighteenth, only slowly and gradually declining. Yet even after its general decline, it flourished in rural areas and in small cultural enclaves. Blacks, immigrants from European peasant stock, and Southern Appalachians, as we will later see, all cultivated the occult beliefs and practices which their cultures had passed on to them. Secondly, there was the occultism of the nineteenth and twentieth centuries that grew, seemingly spontaneously, from new sources. Popular among middle-class people who were part of the mainstream, it was a self-conscious, educated, and deliberate movement, different from the older and inherited version.

Although the lines between the two were certainly not hard and fast, they were different from each other in further ways as well. Natural and traditional occultism supported individuals as they tried to cope with everyday tasks. It was at ease with material things and demonstrated a sense of place, of being at home in its world. People planted crops by the signs of the zodiac and doctored themselves using occult, anatomical charts, just as their grandfathers and grandmothers had. They observed rules about not spilling salt or breaking mirrors, about avoiding black cats and not walking under ladders just because this was the way things were done, the way that bad luck was avoided, and the way that a person kept in touch with a traditional framework for living. On the other hand, the more self-conscious and deliberate form of occultism sought liberation from a daily round of meaningless existence through its cultivation of higher knowledge and practice. In order to cope with life, it charted the heavens and elaborated on hidden dimensions of human nature, interested in spiritual more than material things as the sources of reality. Homeless in the world, this form of occultism sought instead homesteads in the human mind.

Metaphysical religions shared many of the basic insights of this second and more deliberate form of occultism. In its primary meaning, metaphysics refers to the kind of philosophy which studies the underlying reality of all existence. As the medievalists put it, metaphysics was the science of being as being. In American religious history, however, metaphysics became the description that many groups used to explain what they were about. Understood literally, metaphysics meant something that went beyond the physical or material. Thus, the metaphysical religions in America stressed mental or spiritual theories about life rather than historical traditions—like Judaism and Christianity—or material elements—like Roman Catholic sacramentalism. Like deliberate occultists, they sought homesteads of the mind. But different from them, they built their religious systems on more general philosophical language, simpler and more continuous with the ordinary language of culture. Thus, it was easy for metaphysical groups to relate to others among the many in America. Often, their teaching did not seem in any way unusual.

Underlying both the occult and the metaphysical movements was a fundamental world view, one with which we are already familiar from our discussion of American Indians and to some extent Roman Catholics. This world view accepted the ancient law of correspondence in which there were many levels to the universe, all of them replicating one another. The microcosm, or small world, of human life reflected the macrocosm, or great world, of the cosmos. There was, in other words, a sympathy between all things, an underlying harmony among them. Thus, the harmonial religions, as they are sometimes called, strived to bring people into harmony with the macrocosm which surrounded them. Moreover, since the macrocosm was really only a larger version of the smaller reality and since the world was really one thing, it followed that action in the microcosm had consequences for the macrocosm. Actions taken by human beings could have some effect on other aspects of the world. If everything was like everything else, then everything could act on everything else. Through manipulation of elements on a smaller scale, people could take practical action to control larger realities. Thus, magic became a valid activity, grounded in an explicit theory about how the world was put together. It contained no mystery for believers but instead expressed a harmony at work. Similarly, the human mind could act on elements of the world to bring them into harmony with the true structure of things. Mental healing, a leading example, was an ordinary fact of life from this point of view.

It should be clear from our discussion of this occult and metaphysical understanding that its followers lived in a mental world without boundaries. A universe in which microcosm and macrocosm shared the same reality and in which any action had truly cosmic repercussions was not one that could be neatly divided up into separate compartments. Religion, for the occult and metaphysical movements, as for many other groups that we have viewed, had to do with the *whole* of life. But different from the other groups, a sense of peoplehood did not locate members within well-defined boundaries, and a sense of historical tradition could not supply them either. Occult and metaphysical believers floated in universal space. They were cosmic migrants for whom everything was religious and every place was home. So they mingled Western tradition with Eastern imports at times and diffused their message throughout American culture until it became indistinguishable from that culture. Although they had begun from a position of estrangement, in the end their boundary problems led them to merge with the American mainstream.

SOURCES OF OCCULTISM IN THE WESTERN TRADITION

Before we follow the occult and metaphysical movements through American religious history, however, we need to examine their heritage. For if Jews, Catholics, and Protestants all had roots, so, too, did the occultists of America. Our search for these roots begins in the Hellenistic world during the first three centuries of the Christian era. This was the world shaped by the Mediterranean Sea and the language of ancient Greece (Hellas was another name for Greece). It was a world in which a mixture of Greek, Roman, Christian, Jewish, and other elements fused in various ways to produce a cosmopolitan religiocultural synthesis. When by the end of this period, in the fourth century, Christianity won out and became the official religion of the Roman Empire, elements of that older Hellenistic synthesis provided the ingredients for the occultism that persisted throughout the Christian centuries.

There was, first of all, Gnosticism, a religious system that had grown on the fringes of both the Jewish and Christian traditions. A Gnostic was, literally, one who knew, but the knowledge of the Gnostic was not the rational kind that could be gained by reading books and following logical arguments. Rather, it was secret knowledge, accompanied by power to save the person from the present, evil world. In fact, the Gnostic was someone within whom the saving spark of knowledge had already been planted, and once realizing the treasure hiding within the prison house of the body, the Gnostic would begin the process of liberation. By means of the spark of knowledge, a Gnostic could start the long and tedious journey leading finally to reunion with his or her divine counterpart within the Godhead. The goal was a mystical merging with the divinity that in germ the Gnostic actually held. The home of the Gnostic was not here, but in another world.

Secondly, there was Neoplatonism, a philosophical descendant of the teachings of the Greek philosopher Plato (427?–347 B.C.). Neoplatonism refashioned Platonism to make of it, once again, a Hellenistic religious system. In a variation of the theory of correspondence, Plato had taught that the real world was the world of Ideas, or Forms, on which the physical, material universe was modeled. Thus, the real tree was the abstract idea of a tree which any existing tree reflected. For Plato, too, there was a hierarchy among the Ideas, and the most ultimate among them were the Good, the True, and the Beautiful.

Neoplatonism retained Plato's theory of Ideas and the vision of a hierarchy among them. However, it saw the ultimate Idea as the One, followed by Nous, or Mind, which was in turn followed by the World Soul. From the World Soul came individual souls and, even lower in the hierarchy, the manyness of the material world. The religious task, as Neoplatonists understood it, was to reclaim oneself for the One, retracing the path of downward emanation from the One by an upward ascent of the soul. Like the Gnostic, it was clear that the Neoplatonist desired and sought mystical experience—union with the One.

A third occult religious system was provided by astrology. Already in the third millennium (B.C.) in ancient Mesopotamia, Babylonians had been observing the heavens with the understanding that the world was a whole of interdependent parts. In the Hellenistic era, astrology flourished with the mingling of Babylonians, Egyptians, Greeks, and Romans in the Mediterranean basin, and by the second century A.D., the Roman Claudius Ptolemy had written what some have called the world's greatest astrological textbook, the *Tetrabiblios.*

While some used astrological knowledge in an uncombined form and directed their lives by studying their horoscopes, many mixed astrology with other religious disciplines. In other words, astrology became a primary ingredient in a religious eclecticism in which various elements were blended to yield a new synthesis. Probably the most important example of this process, in terms of its future influence in the West, was a religious philosophy called Hermeticism. This fourth occult pathway, available at the end of the Hellenistic era, was based on a series of writings attributed to an ancient Egyptian priest called Hermes Trismegistus (the Three-Times-Great Hermes). The writings, which we know today as the *Corpus Hermeticum* and the *Asclepius,* were actually composed in the second or third century A.D., close to the time of their discovery, and Hermes Trismegistus was, no doubt, a fictional character. Yet for centuries, until critical scholarship proved otherwise, he was revered as a shadowy figure from the early ages of ancient Egyptian civilization, and thus his system possessed great authority within occult circles. Moreover, the Hermetic texts brought together Gnosticism, Platonism, Neoplatonism, astrology, and various other religious philosophies from ancient Greece. They offered a profound synthesis of mystical teaching from pagan sources, establishing a cultus to be followed in the mind, celebrating Nous (Mind) as intuition, and giving magical lessons.

Although Christian church fathers such as Lactantius (260?–340?) and Augustine (354–430) preached against the Hermetic texts, other Christians passed on their teachings. So in the Middle Ages some priests practiced magic and astrology along with their Christian sacramental duties. They also engaged in alchemy, a fifth occult discipline with religious overtones. Alchemy, the ancestor of modern chemistry, was an attempt to change less valuable metals into others regarded more highly, most significant among them, gold. In order to accomplish this, like a monk, the alchemist had to lead an ascetic life, one of self-denial, in which great purity of mind and body was necessary. For true alchemists, the process of creating gold was merely an external symbol for an internal change which the person sought. The real task of the alchemist was to discover the secret inner mystery, the divine spark which was the Self of self. Once discovered, there could be a reunification with that spark and a merging with the All, the divine power that moved the world. Once again, the alchemist pursued the same task as the other occultists. Knowledge was a secret, saving force which would bring liberation from the present world, realization of the true nature of things, and finally mystical union with Self and God.

Meanwhile, the Middle Ages, at least by the twelfth century, offered a sixth occult religious system, this time through Jewish sources. The Kabbalah, which flourished in southern France and Spain, again blended elements from many different traditions but changed them to give the material a Jewish stamp. In the *Book Bahir* (1180?) and especially the *Zohar* (1280?), Kabbalistic teachings spread. They offered a secret means of interpreting Hebrew scripture through uncovering the hidden meanings of the words that were written there. The Torah, for the Kabbalists, was the truth dressed in an earthly garment, and that garment had to be removed to behold spiritual beauty. Behind the God of Hebrew scripture lay En-Sof from whom emanated ten intelligences called Sefiroth. By means of the Sefiroth, En-Sof had created the material world. In a series of correspondences, there were connections between the Sefiroth and different parts of the human body, different names for God, and different classes of angels.

Like the Hermetic texts, the Kabbalah claimed to be a tradition handed down from the ancient past, in this case from the time of Adam. Like Neoplatonism, it taught the creation of the many (the world) by emanation from the One (here En-Sof). And like Gnosticism, it taught that liberation and the experience of God came through saving knowledge, the truth concerning the real meaning of the Torah. Eclectic as it was, therefore, the Kabbalah moved into Christian occult circles in the Middle Ages. But as we have said, occultism was a religious system different from either Judaism or Christianity. Thus, the various occult disciplines found their way into the lives of those who carried on the tradition and transmitted it, in part, to the Renaissance.

This Renaissance was a movement of cultural rebirth which began in northern Italy in the fourteenth century and spread throughout Europe over the next two centuries. It brought a revival of learning and a new spirit of confidence in human enterprise; and agreeable to both, it pioneered in a rediscovery of the occult tradition. So the *Corpus Hermeticum*, which had disappeared since antiquity, was brought in its Greek manuscript to Florence, Italy, and translated. Interest in astrology and the Kabbalah flourished, and the old routes to secret, saving knowledge, officially banned by the medieval church, now gained a new respectability despite that opposition. Learned people translated occult manuscripts and engaged in occult practices. Seemingly overnight, the Renaissance magician became a hero. In England, it was the Elizabethans who reaped the fruit of this Renaissance revival, and so Elizabethan occultism was respected and widely known. With the arrival of the sons and daughters of the Elizabethans in the New World, our sketch brings us to the English colonies.

TRADITIONAL OCCULTISM IN THE COLONIES

Keeping this background in mind, let us look first at traditional occultism as it appeared during the early period of American history. Our time span embraces the seventeenth and eighteenth centuries, from the beginning of settlement to the end of the American Revolution. At the start of this era, both learned and simple folk accepted the occult tradition as it had been handed down to them from the past. For the learned, it was the basis of the science that they read about in their few and carefully cherished books. For simpler people, it was the way things were and were done. By the end of the American Revolution, however, there was a clear divergence between the two groups. The scholarly elite had repudiated the old beliefs in favor of a new and more persuasive science. The larger body of ordinary people, especially in rural America, continued to adhere to the natural occultism they had received from their parents. Still, the times signaled the beginning of a slow decline among ordinary folk in this old occult belief and practice.

Astrology

There were various practical manifestations of occultism in the colonies. Two of the most prominent were astrology and witchcraft. Astrology came to America from the England of Queen Elizabeth I who gave her name to the time during which she ruled (1558-1603). Learned Elizabethans had based their astrological thinking on their understanding of the material composition of the universe. It was made up of various combinations of the four elements—earth, water, air, and fire—and the four qualities—hot, cold, moist, and dry. Here the elements and the qualities were correlated with each other, and so fire was hot and dry; air, hot and moist; earth, cold and dry; and water, cold and moist. Similarly, human beings were made up of four basic humors. Choler, or yellow bile, like fire, was hot and dry; blood, like air, was hot and moist; melancholy, or black bile, imitated earth in being cold and dry, while phlegm was like water in that it was cold and moist. Each of these humors had a definite part to play in the functioning of a healthy body, and when one or the other of them predominated, they stamped their imprint on the character of a person.

Within this ordered universe, astrology charted the course of the heavens and related the lives of human beings to the stars. The elements and qualities were present in the stars, some of which were fire signs and some earth signs, some identified with air and some with water. Similarly, the stars corresponded to the humors within human beings, and different stars governed each of the humors. Moreover, the stars were closely bound up with the calculation of time. In a world in which everything possessed some significance in the chain of being and in which each existing thing corresponded with many others in the universe, each moment in time also had its unique quality. The stars were like great cosmic clues to the quality of time, and through studying them, it was possible to determine good and bad days for various activities. In other words, there were signs of the times, making it possible to understand the character of a person by the time in which he or she had been born and making it possible, too, to give advice or even foretell the future.

The colonists were heir to this world of their ancestors. Like them, they continued to make a distinction between two kinds of astrology. First and most common was natural astrology, which concerned the relationship between the stars and other material things such as the rhythms of nature, the weather, and the human body. Second was judicial astrology, which probed the relationship between the stars and human choice and action. This second form of astrology implicitly challenged the Christian doctrine of freedom of the will, because it suggested to many that the stars controlled human destiny. Thus, it had traditionally been most subject to attack and least accepted. The colonists, however, readily used the insights that they gained from natural astrology. Among the learned, this material was taught in textbooks used at Harvard and Yale, while it appeared in the private libraries of prominent individuals in the late seventeenth and early eighteenth centuries. Among less educated people, it was spread by means of the almanac, which along with the Bible, was a necessary book in every colonial household.

Probably more widely read than the Bible, the almanac provided its readers with representations of the twelve signs of the zodiac as well as the names and symbols of the seven planets known to antiquity. The zodiac was a kind of sky trail created by the path of the planets as they followed the apparent orbit of the sun across the sky from sunrise to sunset and again to sunrise. Each sign was thirty degrees of the full 360-degree circle, and in many almanacs, these signs were only the most basic in a series of symbols provided by astrological charts and useful for farming, weather forecasting, and medicine.

For this last, almanacs usually printed the "anatomy," the picture of a cosmic man surrounded by the signs of the zodiac which governed each part of his body. Thus, Leo ruled his heart and would be shown next to it; Gemini controlled his arms and was appropriately positioned; Pisces was related to his feet and was printed below them on the page. Each day the moon could be found in a different sign of the zodiac, and so by locating the moon in relation to the sign, a person could decide whether it was a good or bad day to treat some part of the body medically. The presence of the moon governed favorable treatment, and by means of the moon the quality of the time was discovered. Astrology formed the basis for an ordinary religion through which people could order their existence and determine their course of action at any given moment. In short, it gave them an unfailing way to orient their lives.

Witchcraft

Witchcraft also contributed to the religious life of the colonists. Once again, it ranged from a very learned version, which was the object of scholarly inquiry, to an unscholastic type, which attracted more people. The scholarly tradition of witchcraft was carried on most notably in the Pennsylvania German community, especially in the brotherhood established under Johannes Kelpius (1673–1708) in Germantown, now part of Philadelphia. Witchcraft, as the brothers understood it, was a venerable tradition, the religion of nature that had once dominated Europe and only gradually yielded before a triumphant Christianity. The group inaugurated their settlement with the rites of summer solstice according to early German tradition. They built bonfires out of trees and bushes, raised their ritual chants, and asked the sacred powers they invoked to bless the place where they were making a home. The Woman in the Wilderness, as their community came to be called, offered its inhabitants a blend of pagan, Christian, and Jewish elements. Natural symbols and natural magic were everywhere, for the brothers wore astrological amulets, used incantations in their healing rituals, and studied long hours to learn to control nature by magical means. In their ceremonies, they expressed in rich liturgies the insights of the old heathen religions. Nature, through its fertility, was the source of sacred power, and by orienting oneself toward it and discovering its secrets, a person could change reality for the better. So the brothers were actually learned practitioners of magic, a manipulation of nature done in their case for the sake of greater good.

Among ordinary people, too, magic was practiced in the colonies. "Cunning folk," as they were called, were witches who possessed powers sometimes similar to those of American Indian shamans. They could heal the sick, find items which were lost, locate precious metal with a divining rod, or send a fair wind to a sailing ship. As in the case of the learned magicians among the Germans, these witches drew on special rituals to effect their contact with the powers of nature. In treasure hunting, for example, after the treasure was located with a divining rod, the witch might draw careful circles around it to protect it, recite words which had special power to overcome any unwilling spirits, and use nails to pin the treasure down. None of the gestures was meaningless. Rather, the circles imitated the shapes of nature and centered the object as a source of concern, hence directing human energy for its safekeeping. The ritual words were forms of speech that empowered corresponding forces in nature for the protection of the treasure. The nails were symbolic statements meant, like sacraments, to prevent the treasure from being moved.

Other witches were believed to be at work among the colonists, however, and these witches were regarded as evil. Many times they were poor, eccentric, and elderly women, unpopular in their communities because of their begging, their strange ways, or their biting tongues. In any case, these witches were thought to use the old religion of nature to practical advantage under the same principles invoked by German magicians or English cunning folk. The only difference was that they invoked their powers to the disadvantage of others. Thus, they could dry up a cow so that it would not give milk or interrupt the process by which milk became butter. They could harass their enemies and bring them illness and even, in some cases, death. These evil folk witches were joined by a fourth and still more fearful type of witch. This was the Satanic witch who had gained power by means of a pact with the devil. Here the influence of Christianity was apparent, and the witch operated as a counterforce to the power of God. Evil and Satanic witches frequently ended up in trouble with the law in the colonies, and the Salem witchcraft epidemic of 1692 is a well-remembered example. Actually, however, there had been sixty trials for witchcraft before the Salem episode, and many of the colonies had laws on their books making witchcraft a crime into the eighteenth century.

Events at Salem Village (later Danvers), in the Massachusetts Bay colony, began with Betty Parris, daughter of the town minister, and her cousin Abigail Williams. The two girls, one nine and the other eleven years old, spent many hours with Tituba, a slave from the West Indies, who taught the children something of the magical traditions she had learned. The exotic lore attracted other girls in the village, many of them teen-agers, who began to participate. When Betty Parris and then Abigail Williams fell into trances—screaming, crying, barking like dogs, and moving on all fours—the diagnosis of witchcraft was speedily pronounced. Neither doctors nor ministers could help, and so events moved to the local courthouse. In a gradual series of escalations, more and more witches were named by the afflicted girls. There was Tituba and then Sarah Good and Sarah Osborne. Before the trials had ended, nineteen witches had been hanged, and one, a man, had been pressed to death.

The clearest statement of the depth of colonial witchcraft beliefs was the admission of spectral evidence at the trials. This meant that claims by the girls that they had been attacked or harassed by a phantom in the shape of the accused individual could be used as evidence. So long as the girls saw the spectral shapes, it did not matter if they were invisible to other people. The accused person could have witnesses that she or he had been miles distant, but the defense was useless because the specter of a witch could travel anywhere. Significantly, when spectral evidence was finally banished from the courtroom, the trials came to a speedy end.

The Satanic witchcraft of Salem Village was an extreme and negative instance of occult religion in the colonies. For others, the old fertility religion of witchcraft had been more benign, and its ordering of life through nature had been a meaningful way to think and act in an agricultural society. Like astrology, it brought ordinary religion to countless numbers of people and directed their everyday lives in the ways they desired.

THE OCCULT-METAPHYSICAL REVIVAL OF THE NINETEENTH CENTURY

We have seen that, as times changed and a new science developed, by the period of the Revolution occult beliefs had been rejected among educated colonists. They were anachronisms, ideas and practices left over from another era. So the tradition, at first rejected because of the triumph of Christianity, was now rejected anew because of the triumph of science and the scientific way of looking at the world. Ordinary folk continued to carry on the remnants of the occult tradition they had absorbed, but cultural leaders took a different route. Yet occult and metaphysical religious systems were not dead. Indeed, as we have already seen, in the nineteenth century a new and deliberate occultism grew rapidly, a significant part of it once again among educated people. The new occultism was a self-conscious work of construction and reconstruction, and a groundwork for this occultism and its metaphysical counterpart was laid by a group of intellectuals, the well-known American Transcendentalists.

At the radical fringe of Unitarian liberal Christianity, the Transcendentalists were largely a group of Bostonians educated at Harvard, many of them ministers. In 1836, they began to meet in a loosely knit club for conversation about literary, philosophical, and religious issues that concerned them. Their acknowledged leader was Ralph Waldo Emerson (1803–1882); and when in 1836 he published a slim volume called *Nature*, he gave the Transcendental movement its gospel. Key to this book was a new form of the ancient theory of correspondence. Emerson and his friends looked to nature to teach them spiritual truths. They saw in the landscape of New England symbolic statements of deeper realities, and by studying nature they thought they could uncover the secrets of their inner selves and a corresponding knowledge of divine things.

All of the Transcendentalists began to speak and write in a new way, and within a decade, with Emerson, they were pondering the meaning of the Oversoul, the great World Soul of the Neoplatonists, to which individual souls were bound. They were experimenting with new ways of living, sometimes in communities formed to express the reality of the One to which all people belonged. Brook Farm and Fruitlands, both Transcendental communes, were two results. Always though, whether or not they chose community life, they followed Emerson (never a member of a commune) in the quest for self-culture. In this nineteenth-century version of the journey toward saving knowledge, each individual must turn within and there cultivate the qualities which would lead to harmony with self and universe.

In their formulation of this new teaching, Emerson and the other Transcendentalists, like many with occult and metaphysical interests, were eclectic. They mixed together elements from Oriental sources, from Neoplatonic philosophy, from European Romantic writers, and from the metaphysical system of the eighteenth-century Swedish mystic, Emanuel Swedenborg (1688–1772). From the Orient, they took especially the Hindu understanding that the world, God, and human beings all participated in one substance and that, beyond the illusion of matter, lay the reality of spirit. From Neoplatonism came the complementary teaching about the One and the Many, who were united in the Oversoul in which every soul had its being.

With the European Romantics, the Transcendentalists participated in the revolt against the intellectual movement of the Enlightenment, which had exalted reason and law. Romanticism was born in the need to break out of the boundaries imposed by the logical pattern of the mind and the ordering rule of law. Hence, among the Transcendentalists there was a desire to escape from the formality of the Unitarian church and to find religion in the unstructured freedom of nature and the inner self. (Since occult and metaphysical concerns defied any borders in their universalism, they would fit into Romantic visions of reality and, as in ages past, become sources of wisdom and truth.)

Finally, with Emanuel Swedenborg, the Transcendentalists had a model of the way that many currents of thought could be fused together in a religious system to meet the needs of a new age. The son of a Lutheran bishop and a member of the Swedish nobility, Swedenborg through his education developed a great interest in the natural sciences. In his position as a mining engineer, he traveled widely and wrote extensively on scientific subjects. But his questions concerning the deeper mysteries of life led Swedenborg to turn to anatomy and to philosophy, while his thinking brought him to conclude that only through intuition could a person truly know God or the inner nature of reality. Outward experience without such insight, he thought, was incomplete. From 1745, when he had a profound revelation from the spiritual world, Swedenborg began to use his visions and communications with angelic beings to aid him in a series of spiritual writings. Reviving Neoplatonic and Renaissance occultism, his teachings now rested on the doctrine of the correspondence between the natural and spiritual worlds. The natural world had been created in the image of the higher spiritual realm, and both worlds received the outflowing of the divine. In this vision of the nature of things, Swedenborg presented an especially detailed description of a succession of spiritual spheres which, he said, surrounded the earth. In Swedenborg's teaching, three were spheres of heaven, and three were spheres of hell. As we will see, later American occultists would build their own systems on a modified version of this notion.

POPULAR OCCULT AND METAPHYSICAL MOVEMENTS IN A NEW AMERICA

At the time that Transcendentalism flourished, weaving together themes from Hinduism to Swedenborgianism with insights drawn from life in America, the United States was undergoing a period of intense change. Emerson, in fact, had capitalized on the change and had traveled widely to many cities and towns where at public meetings he popularized the gospel of Transcendentalism. The world in which he did so was one where, with breathless rapidity, the Industrial Revolution was spreading across America. A new factory system was centralizing the production of manufactured goods, while a revolution in transportation was making it possible to travel by rail and steamboat many times faster than stagecoaches and wind-powered sails had allowed. Meanwhile, a nation of migrants was moving westward to people the frontier or cityward to produce great metropolitan centers. The old homesteads, which had housed generation after generation of families, were becoming a thing of the past, supplanted by an emerging urban middle class with some affluence, some education, and some leisure.

People praised the inventions of the age of progress and spoke of the manifest destiny of the United States to reach from one end of the continent to the other. But beneath the optimism and excitement America had become a land of geographical, social, and intellectual dislocation. Migrants and immigrants both had been uprooted from the security of their past. The middle class in the cities, neither very rich nor very poor, was searching for a sense of identity to replace the feeling of being neither here nor there. The old truths which religion had taught through the Judaeo-Christian tradition seemed less persuasive in the new situation. At the same time, science, with its growing appreciation for evolution, undermined traditional religion from another quarter, and Romanticism encouraged people to step beyond the borders of the tried and true. In this world of newness, strangeness, and confusion, the occult and metaphysical movements provided havens for those who felt homeless. They offered sanctuaries where peace and stability could reign, homesteads on a mental landscape to replace the physical ones which, seemingly everywhere, were disappearing.

We will examine some of the most important of these movements which were popular in the nineteenth century and continued into the twentieth. As we do so, our study is touching only a few significant cases. Beyond them, occult and metaphysical movements in the new America were everywhere, small and not too congenial to organization, part of the manyness that again and again we have seen in the United States.

Spiritualism

In the rappings heard by the Foxes in their old house in Hydesville, New York, we saw the event that later Spiritualists usually regarded as the beginning of their movement. But there had been forerunners of these spirits in America. The Shakers, in their ecstatic dances and religious exercises, had frequently been joined by spirit visitors ranging from George Washington and William Penn to American Indians, Chinese, Abyssinians, and even Hottentots. Meanwhile, in the larger culture popular Swedenborgianism grew. In a well-known example of the process, John Chapman (1774–1847), better remembered as Johnny Appleseed, became its missionary. As he moved through the Ohio country planting apple seeds and providing saplings to the settlers, he also distributed Swedenborgian literature—introducing to many the occult tradition that would give Spiritualists an explanation for ultimate things.

Similarly, mesmerism, or hypnotism, paved the way for Spiritualist groups. Introduced from France in 1836 and often called animal magnetism, mesmerism was believed to depend on the magnetic transference of a universal fluid from one individual to another. While mesmerism figured in the growth of other occult and metaphysical movements as well, it demonstrated trance states similar to those in which contact with the spirits was likely to happen. Andrew Jackson Davis (1826–1910), whose written work later provided a theoretical grounding for Spiritualism, in his youth came into contact with mesmerism. He discovered under hypnosis that he could see through material objects as a clairvoyant, and afterward he made contact with the spirits of Galen, a famous doctor and writer of the ancient world, and Emanuel Swedenborg. Davis began to acquire a name for himself as a healer and, more importantly, as a prolific writer. He took Swedenborg's theory of six spheres surrounding the earth and modified it so that each of them became a spiritual plane on the way toward God. When all human beings had progressed to the sixth plane beyond the physical, he taught, a new set of spheres would come into existence. The world that Davis saw was one of eternal progress, with spirits on various planes, closer or farther from the earth. Thus, contact, especially with spirits closer to the earth plane, seemed a realistic possibility.

While Davis, often called the "Seer of Poughkeepsie" (New York), was writing his huge volumes, popular Spiritualism was spreading in America. For the many who flocked to séances, Spiritualism meant a belief in and practice of communication with the spirits of the dead through the help of human mediums. Those who came were often elderly and often mourning the loss of a loved one. Many of their number were prominent individuals, and many, especially among the mediums, were women. To one and all, Spiritualism offered a reasonable approach to religion in the new age. If the ancient truths of religion were under fire in the climate of the times, Spiritualism gave empirical evidence, proof that could be seen and heard, that the dead lived on and a world beyond this one existed. Moreover, it often explained the unusual happenings, in which spirits materialized and strange objects appeared at séances, by an occult form of scientific language. It was eager to open its meetings to objective investigators who would authenticate the reality of the apparitions and communications. In other words, it sought a blending of science and religion not unlike the blending that had been part of the ancient occult tradition.

At the same time, Spiritualism brought a Romantic approach to religion. As we saw with the lectures and writings of Emerson and other Transcendentalists, Romanticism was in the air. People were often growing impatient with formal religious institutions, and they sought inner authority through the medium for their religion. In their direct experiences of contact with spirits, they understood that they were in contact with the farther reaches of the natural world, outside the boundaries that organizations had frequently set. They thought, like the Transcendentalists, that the world was one whole and that there were close ties between the spiritual and the material worlds. Spirit, for them, was higher and more perfect matter.

Throughout the time of Spiritualist development, however, most Spiritualists were far more concerned with practice than with theory. Here the medium was central, and she was the necessary agent for communication with another world. Over time, two kinds of mediumship grew up—mental and physical. Mental mediumship involved psychic happenings when the medium achieved a trance state. Her conscious mind no longer functioned, and, Spiritualists believed, a controlling spirit took its place. By the twentieth century, psychic practices had become formalized. The medium might practice billet reading by responding to questions, submitted on small pieces of paper, to a spirit. Or the medium could practice psychometry, in which she got in touch with the vibrations of a physical object and so learned all she could about people (now dead) who had touched it in the past. Again, the medium might prophesy by reading auras, bands of light of different colors which emanated from every human being. These auras recorded the life history of a person, enabling a spirit to make predictions.

In physical mediumship, the spirits took on material form at a séance so that they could be seen, heard, and sometimes felt. In the rapping at Hydesville, New York, we saw one early type of physical manifestation. But there were a wealth of others as Spiritualism grew. Sometimes the spirits tipped over tables, and sometimes they disturbed the people at a séance by sending objects flying through the air. In automatic writing, spirits used the hand of the medium to write their message, and in independent writing, they wrote, without any material guidance, on paper. On some occasions, spirits made an object disappear in one place and brought it to another where they rematerialized it. At other times, they used specially constructed trumpets to speak to people at a séance. By the twentieth century, an elaborate system had been worked out with spirit guides to aid the medium and others present. Indian Chiefs and Spirit Doctors were popular in these roles, Indian Chiefs often as Gate Keepers, who would keep unwanted spirits away, and Spirit Doctors as lecturers or advisers on spiritual subjects. Moreover, mediums sometimes developed healing gifts through a force thought to flow from their fingers.

While the Spiritualists had developed a rich liturgy in their contact with spirits, they were not so successful with organization. In the nineteenth century, they experienced a ground swell of public interest, especially in the decade after 1848 and during the time after the Civil War. Yet they resisted structure and instead splintered into small groups around different mediums or groups of mediums. After the foundation of the Theosophical Society in 1875, which we will discuss next, Spiritualists split into some groups who united Spiritualist beliefs and practices with Christianity and others who followed Theosophy. Finally, by 1893 the National Spiritualist Association of Churches came into existence, featuring a congregational government in which independent churches joined in state organizations. This became the largest and the most conservative of the Spiritualist organizations, but it was neither strong nor universal.

The inability of Spiritualists to form strong organizations was shared by most of the other occult and metaphysical groups. With their diffusive teaching about the unity of matter and spirit, with their blending of religion with an occult form of science, with their openness to believers from any ethnic or racial background, they were people without boundaries. Their mental universalism was only mirrored in the diffuseness of their organizations. As we have seen before, home was in the mind and not in the structure of society.

Theosophy

If late nineteenth- and twentieth-century Spiritualists often tended toward Theosophy, this movement had itself grown partially out of Spiritualism. The two founders had met at a farmhouse in Chittenden, Vermont, where in 1874 the frequent materialization of spirits was drawing Spiritualists and other curious people. Helena P. Blavatsky (1831–1891), world traveler and recent Russian immigrant to the United States, in her red Garibaldi shirt and short blonde hair, was as colorful that day as her life had been and would continue to be. Colonel Henry S. Olcott (1832–1907), widely respected as a corporation lawyer, agricultural expert, and sometime government official, had already written a newspaper account of the apparitions at Chittenden for the *New York Sun*, a story which was copied throughout the world. The two struck an immediate acquaintance and, drawn by their mutual interest in Spiritualism, became fast friends. A year later, with William Q. Judge (1851–1896) and a group of others, they formed the Theosophical Society in New York, an organization which aimed to carry on occult research.

Already it was clear from their statement of intentions that knowledge was the key issue for Theosophists. Indeed, theosophy, in the generic sense, was another name for the occult tradition of knowledge about the inner workings of the divine. And while Colonel Olcott provided organizational leadership for the group, it was Blavatsky, or "HPB" as her followers liked to call her, who led the way in occult knowledge. Between 1875 and 1877, she wrote *Isis Unveiled*, a lengthy book which glorified the ancient occult masters and revealed their secrets for the nineteenth century. She wanted to show the presence of a wide-ranging occultism behind the philosophies and religions of the world and especially to show that the Brahmanism of early India and, later, Buddhism were the sources for the other religions. Exhibiting an interest in Oriental thought similar to the Transcendentalists, she also taught like them the doctrine of correspondence. Matter, for HPB, was the crystallization of spirit, and magic was possible because of the grand harmony between the earthly and heavenly spheres.

In writing her vast work, Blavatsky claimed that she was aided by Mahatmas, members of a select brotherhood of individuals who, while still human beings, had evolved to degrees of perfection beyond those normally reached by people. They usually dwelled in the Himalaya Mountains, in the isolated country of Tibet, but they possessed magical abilities to materialize at will or to communicate by letters that arrived at their destination as soon as they were dispatched. Blavatsky had met them earlier in her wanderings, she said, and they had been directing her life purposively since, not simply for her own sake, but in order to help human beings attain greater spiritual growth. It was for this reason, too, that with even more assistance they helped her to write *The Secret Doctrine*, which Blavatsky published in 1888. In this, her major work, she aimed to set forth the root knowledge from which all later religion, philosophy, and science grew. She told the secrets of the origins of the world and of human life, explaining the Unmoved Mover and Rootless Root of all things, the pure impersonal Be-ness. She told, too, of the law of becoming in which each individual reaped what he or she had sowed and was periodically reincarnated to gain in spiritual maturity. Finally, she described the unity of all souls in the Oversoul, the message which before her Ralph Waldo Emerson had delivered.

Meanwhile, the Theosophical Society slowly assumed its mature form. Its purpose had become threefold. To the quest for occult knowledge, it added its intentions of forming a universal brotherhood of all people and of promoting the study of comparative religions. Thus, the research group had become a religion: it envisioned a way of life. Occult knowledge was never simply for rational understanding; it always aimed at personal transformation, at salvation through knowledge. Ideally, Theosophists lived according to a disciplined program in which, if they were ordinary members of the society, they were encouraged to perform faithfully the duties of their place in life, to live according to the ideal of brotherhood, to meditate and to regulate their diet (vegetarianism was preferred), and to make progress through study and service. In addition to the ordinary class of membership, the society offered a higher degree for an inner circle (the "Esoteric Section"). Here a person received the special teaching of the occult masters or Mahatmas and at the same time was required to live by the regimen of discipline already described. At the top of the hierarchy, the masters themselves were believed to form the third degree of membership.

After Helena Blavatsky died in 1891, Annie Besant (1847–1933) eventually became the gifted leader of the Theosophical Society. Involved in England in various social-reform movements, she had been drawn to *The Secret Doctrine* and its author. During her era at the head of the society, it grew and prospered so that by 1930 there were 50,000 Theosophists in forty countries, 10,000 of them in the

United States. Typically, they were urban middle-class people, and many among them came from the professions and had achieved prominence. Yet even before the death of Helena Blavatsky and Colonel Olcott, the society had been beset by factionalism. Thus, in 1895 William Judge led out a huge portion of the American membership to form the independent Theosophical Society in America. Other schisms followed. Once again, the boundary problem was troubling those who strived to live by the occult tradition. Their universalism made Theosophists willing to pursue the saving knowledge that was given to them wherever it would lead.

Hinduism and Buddhism had figured heavily in the society, especially in the knowledge taught by the Mahatmas to Helena Blavatsky. In fact, the movement may be read as a spiritual pilgrimage of discovery to the East, a search by "strangers" in America for their religious home abroad. Still, the Theosophical Society was truly an eclectic organization, and its eclectic blend from many traditions brought to the fore the Western masters of the occult as well as the Eastern. Moreover, in the climate of the United States, in which popular Transcendentalism, Swedenborgianism, mesmerism, and Spiritualism had all flourished, it absorbed elements from these movements and made them its own. Complex and intricate, Theosophy culled from every tradition an elaborate explanation of nature and humanity, rejecting God in any ordinary sense and supplying instead the complicated details of its great occult mythology of Absolute Reality, which ended in mysticism. If followers of occult and metaphysical teachings built homesteads of the mind, the Theosophists erected mansions.

New Thought

Even before Theosophy had attracted the attention of some Americans, foundations were already being laid for a third movement within the harmonial religion of the nineteenth and twentieth centuries. New Thought, as it came to be called, took many forms, but different from Spiritualism and Theosophy, it stressed metaphysical concerns without occult elaboration. In fact, in our discussion of Christian Science in the previous chapter, we were dealing with a close relative. But while Christian Science was a strongly authoritative sect, New Thought followed the pattern of Spiritualism and Theosophy. It, too, was diffuse and lacked boundaries—so much so that it became in its farthest outreach part of the mainstream of American culture.

The germ for New Thought was contained in the teaching and healing practice of Phineas P. Quimby (1802–1866), the mental healer who had also played a significant role in the life of Mary Baker Eddy. As a young man, Quimby had become interested in mesmerism and had begun to experiment with it when he could find a willing subject. So it was that he met Lucius Burkmar, a person who in a hypnotic trance could diagnose and heal disease. After the two had been working together, Quimby, himself in poor health, sought Burkmar's help and like the others was cured. So impressive was the experience that Quimby pondered its meaning until he was satisfied that he had discovered how Burkmar cured disease. He decided that Burkmar's healing depended on the fact that it was a person's inward belief which controlled the state of sickness or of health. Burkmar inspired belief in his patients, and so they were cured of illness. This understanding became the start of a career dedicated to healing the sick, and when in 1859 Quimby opened an office in Portland, Maine, he attracted his most famous patients, among them not only Mary Baker Eddy but also the future leaders of the New Thought movement.

Quimby was above all a practical man who wanted to cure disease. But he was also a thoughtful man, and although neither well educated nor a system builder, he pondered the basis of his healing ever more deeply. He came to reject the use of mesmerism, and his writings instead displayed a Swedenborgian influence. No doubt through his friends who were Swedenborgians, Quimby had absorbed the idea of the law of correspondence. He saw human beings as spiritual in nature, the inhabitants of a higher world above this one, and he thought of the soul as in a direct relationship with the divine mind. It followed for him that, when a person was healed, it was because of the operation of the divine spirit on the human soul. For Quimby, this came about through an awakening by which a patient became aware of his or her inner spiritual nature. Sometimes Quimby identified the means to this awakening with a wisdom or science called the Christ, and at least once he described his teaching as Christian science.

Far more the systematic theoretician for the emerging New Thought movement was Warren Felt Evans (1814–1889). Formerly a Methodist minister, in 1863 he had become a Swedenborgian, a member of the Church of the New Jerusalem, based on the teachings of the master. Around the same time, suffering from chronic illness, he had sought the help of Quimby, had been healed, and— encouraged by Quimby—had opened his own healing practice. By 1869 he had produced his first book, *The Mental Cure*, in which he explained that disease was the result of a loss of mental balance which in turn affected the body. It was the translation into flesh of a wrong idea in the mind, and the way to get well was to think rightly, bringing back the harmony between the human spirit and the divine.

In his numerous works, the God whom Evans recognized recalled the Neoplatonic Idea of the One. Yet incorporating Christianity and reshaping Quimby's teaching, Evans thought of the Christ Principle as an emanation from the One which was present within every person. Union with this Christ Principle, the divine spark within, brought wholeness and health. Evans thought that when the basic harmony was disturbed and union with the divine forces interrupted, another individual—a doctor—could help. If the patient really wanted to get better and trusted the healer, he or she could submit mentally to the doctor. This would bring a flow of thought from the healer to the patient and begin the restoration of harmony.

Above all, Evans seemed convinced of the power of suggestion in healing. His view of the relationship between patient and doctor was built on it, and even further, he could see benefits for the patient in a state of light mesmeric trance in which the sick person could be at once alert and yet submissive to healing influence. He spoke of the power of conscious affirmation, and it was his thinking that turned New Thought toward the practice. So for later New Thought, the mind cure meant that the sick person must think positively, affirming health in deliberate internal statements and banishing disease as error.

Besides the practice of Quimby and the thought of Evans, the existence of Christian Science contributed to the development of New Thought. Mary Baker Eddy's *Science and Health* from 1875 attracted readers who also read Evans. Those who were uncomfortable within the sharply drawn boundaries of Christian Science and under Eddy's authority often found themselves leaving the organization. Moreover, some of Quimby's old students felt that Mary Baker Eddy was not giving credit where credit was due. She owed the discovery of Christian Science far more to Quimby than she had acknowledged, they thought. In this atmosphere, Julius and Anetta Dresser began to practice mental healing in Boston in 1882. Many former Christian Scientists came to them, and the very strength of the Christian Science movement forced them to articulate the meaning of their work more clearly.

By 1882 or 1883, Quimby's former patients and Evans's followers were speaking of their movement as mental science. They had come to believe that thought was the greatest power in the world and that harmony with divine Thought, or Mind, was the way to all health and happiness. At the same time, their interest in the thought of Ralph Waldo Emerson was growing. The writings of Evans showed his acquaintance with Emerson, and in 1887 another writer, Charles M. Barrows, found a forerunner for mental science in the Transcendentalist leader. So began a continuing interest in Emerson until New Thought people came to regard him as the father of their movement. For unlike Christian Science, which claimed a basis in divine revelation, the teaching of Emerson supplied a foundation *in philosophy* for New Thought ideas.

By the 1890s, mental science was coming to be known as New Thought. First used in 1889, "this thought" or New Thought was distinguished from older theology, even though people in the movement for the most part did not see themselves as forming a separate church. Indeed, they had been meeting on Sunday evenings so that those who wished to attend Sunday morning services at traditional churches could do so. Still, by middecade, the Church of the Higher Life had been organized in Boston under Helen Van-Anderson. New Thought people explained that it stood for "exalted living" and had formulated no creed other than love, while among its subsidiary groups was an Emerson Study Club. Even more important to the growth of New Thought was the formation of the Metaphysical Club in Boston in 1895. It became the center for national and international development, aiming to reach the world with the gospel of New Thought.

By the turn of the century, there was an International Metaphysical League, and among other things it had announced its aim to teach the universal fatherhood and motherhood of God. New Thought was helping people not only to get well but also, by thinking correctly, to become prosperous and successful. Later, from 1915, International New Thought Congresses were held annually, bringing together the many diverse groups who all worked under the banner of New Thought. An organization called the International New Thought Alliance continued to provide leadership through the twentieth century, while the Unity

School of Christianity, with its vast publishing enterprise and ministerial training program, became probably the best known of the New Thought institutions. Specific New Thought denominations such as Divine Science, based in Denver, and Religious Science, headquartered in Los Angeles, helped to spread the message. Attempts were made to revise traditional religious liturgies so that they might express New Thought, and especially noteworthy, new words were set to older melodies to create appropriate music. Sometimes, too, poems were set to music, leading to the beginnings of an authentic New Thought hymnology.

Yet New Thought's real ambivalence about existing in separate churches proved a continuing theme. As saving knowledge, New Thought was individual more than communal in its emphasis. Like all of the occult and metaphysical movements, it led ultimately to inwardness and private religious experience. Thus, it made its biggest mark through its publishing, and many of its books became best sellers on the "self-help" market. As an example, Ralph Waldo Trine's *In Tune with the Infinite*, written in 1897, sold well over 2 million copies and continued to be reprinted regularly. Even more, New Thought influenced Liberal Protestantism so that many who were part of the mainstream absorbed its ideas and values and spread them abroad. Norman Vincent Peale (b. 1898), with his *Power of Positive Thinking* (1952), brought mental healing and the success ethic to millions of people outside the movement, while his other books and magazines continued the trend. Indeed, Peale was only the most successful of a series of writers who brought Americans a similar message. New Thought shared its fundamental assumptions with the occult tradition; and in the end, its individualism, optimism, and affirmations of health and prosperity dissolved the sense of mystery that surrounded occultism but likewise blended occultism unobtrusively with American culture in the mainstream.

Mystical and Psychic Frontiers

If the twentieth century was congenial to New Thought, it also welcomed a variety of other movements of inward exploration. Moreover, like the nineteenth century, it had its theorist to lay the groundwork for new adventures of the mind. William James (1842–1910) combined the insights of the occult-metaphysical movements, as he had received them through the thought of Emerson and through nineteenth-century American culture. He articulated them in a sophisticated scholarly context from his chair of philosophy at Harvard University, weaving together, like occultists of old, themes from religion and science. He had been fascinated by the claims of mental healing. Later, his curiosity about altered states of consciousness in religious experience grew, until he experimented with nitrous oxide and even a peyote button. His book *The Varieties of Religious Experience* (1902) stressed the inner, personal nature of religion. It consisted for James in different states of mind, and he traced these states in great psychological detail throughout the narrative, often giving examples from the private experiences of individuals. Further, from 1885 James had played a leading role in the organization and activities of the American Society for Psychical Research.

The philosophy that James came to teach was known as pragmatism, and its central conviction was that truth could be known by its consequences. Put simply, what worked in the life of an individual or a society was true. Thus, using James's ideas, there was a way to reconcile occult and metaphysical experiences with the world of modern science. If the occult-metaphysical tradition worked to create a meaningful universe for a person, its truth could not be disputed. For James, the will to believe could erase a world of doubt and uncertainty.

The legacy of William James lived on in the twentieth century, and, meanwhile, others pursued their quests for homes on a mental landscape, leading them to an involvement in mysticism and mind-expanding experiments. Most significant, perhaps, was Aldous Huxley (1894–1963), an English novelist who settled in California. During the fifties, he followed in the tradition of James by experimenting with psychedelic drugs, and in *The Doors of Perception* (1954) he broke ground in describing the experience. Yet Huxley throughout his life was conservative in his use of mescaline and LSD (lysergic acid diethylamide), and his wife afterward reminisced that he had probably used less in a lifetime than many a later youthful experimenter would use in a week. Underlying the psychedelic adventure, for Huxley, was his abiding interest in the "perennial philosophy." This was his way of identifying the major teachings of the occult and metaphysical tradition, which he said lay at the basis of all religion. Nearly a decade before his *Doors of Perception,* he had published an anthology called *The Perennial Philosophy* (1946). Here he explained that the perennial philosophy was a metaphysics which saw divine reality within both things and minds, seeking identity with the divine spark within and finding there the ground of all being.

OCCULT-METAPHYSICAL MOVEMENTS IN THE LATER TWENTIETH CENTURY

Hence, by the last third of the twentieth century there was a vital tradition from which to draw in the pursuit of occultism, mysticism, and metaphysical salvation. Moreover, many had been prepared by American culture to turn toward the self and the answering universe in their quest for religious certainty. Protestantism, in general, had supported the importance of knowledge or belief (the Word) in religion. Then Liberal Protestantism had stressed the presence of God everywhere and had underlined American optimism about human nature with its preaching of the gospel of natural goodness. With its diffusiveness and lack of strong boundaries, it had accustomed people to live comfortably without rigid organization. From its place in American culture, the Holiness tradition, too, had encouraged a perfectionism which, as we saw in the case of Father Divine, could easily be linked to metaphysical views. Meanwhile, the urban and corporate organization of society militated against strong communities. Individuals in their daily lives came to rely more and more on internal resources. So the occult and metaphysical movements blended easily with the cultural mainstream. Because they sought universality and defied institutionalization, they became impossible to count. Because they taught a message so similar to what many were already hearing, they became virtually impossible to identify. Nearly everyone, it seemed, had an occult or metaphysical skeleton somewhere in a mental closet.

The religion that occult-metaphysical movements offered people had its extraordinary aspects, but it was also a way to deal with ordinary life. Astrology gave people a sense of identity and helped them to establish relationships with others with some degree of security. Self-help literature enabled them to take steps toward greater health, prosperity, and happiness in their job and life situations. Psychics offered physical healing and spiritual advice on how to deal with whatever problems had arisen. Knowing the future gave people a way to revise it, to take the steps necessary to avoid harm and to restore balance in the business of living.

Yet by the sixties and seventies, one side of the occult and metaphysical tradition had begun to attract notice. Like the inner circle of Theosophy that surrounded Madame Blavatsky, many, especially among the young, found a way to unite the insights of saving knowledge and universal harmony with a new sense of boundary definition. The result was a series of short-lived but powerful religious movements. Often these were collectively described as counter-cultural, although it is more correct to say that they exaggerated certain tendencies within American culture so that they appeared strange and unusual. But probably, the boundaries themselves were what made these groups seem so alien. Often they encouraged members to break ties with families and friends in order to follow the new way of life more totally. They demanded everything, and new converts were willing to surrender all to demands which, they felt, were ultimately for their benefit. As explained in the introductory chapter, in the sociological and descriptive sense (and *not* negatively), we have been calling these movements cults.

In our study of black religion in the United States, we have already encountered some of the cults. Here charismatic leaders and new revelations attracted individuals in their personal quests for ecstasy, at the same time creating for them strong and important boundaries to divide them from the rest of society. Now, in a twist, occult and metaphysical movements kept their universalism but managed to act it out within the boundaries of various small and intense religious groups. These were so numerous that they are impossible to detail. Often eclectic, they perpetuated the occult-metaphysical tradition under the new circumstances of the late twentieth century. Moreover, not all of the cults that flourished at this time belonged to the religious movements we have been describing. Some were Eastern in origins and practices. Others took themes from the Judaeo-Christian tradition—especially themes concerning the end of the world—and made them the basis for their activity. But occult and metaphysical groups grew alongside of these others. Probably two of the clearest types were witchcraft covens (bands of witches) and scientific-technological cults.

In witchcraft covens, the law of harmony and correspondence operated to elevate the natural world. It was the macrocosm to which human beings should conform their lives, and witchcraft, or Neopaganism, taught reverence for nature as the great power of fertility and life. Through the use of ritual, a coven sought to create harmony for its members and others with the order of the natural world. Ritual, in this understanding, was a magical means to assure the operation of nature, and witches believed that they had discovered the key to the secrets of the powers of nature which they could turn to their advantage.

Scientific-technological cults combined science with occultism in ways that repeated the earlier blend of religion with science in ancient Western occultism. For example, UFO cults took their cue from unexplained flying objects in the space age. Members of these groups claimed to have established contact with visitors from outer space and even to have boarded their vehicles. They saw these visitors as higher and more perfect beings who wanted to teach willing human beings the mysteries of a deeper knowledge which would transform their lives. In another well-known instance, Scientology, founded by L. Ron Hubbard (b. 1911), used an electrical device called an E-meter to help a person in the spiritual quest. The E-meter, which was said to measure resistance, or tension, within a person when he or she responded to different questions, helped that individual to become "Clear" (like the "clear" button on a calculator), thus liberating consciousness so that it could control matter, energy, space, and time. The goal was total freedom, and the means—as in all the scientific-technological movements—was knowledge as a form of power.

Thus, while witchcraft cults turned people toward the natural world through the magical energies of ritual, scientific-technological cults taught that the real world lay beyond matter in secret, saving knowledge. For both, as for the long occult-metaphysical tradition, matter was controlled by the use of elite and secret techniques, part of a heritage of privileged learning. In other words, for both, the mind was the place where sacred pathways began and ended. There, where extraordinary religious experience was possible, strength was gained for the ordinary religion of living. And since the law of correspondence meant that mind equaled world, extraordinary religion could fuse with its ordinary counterpart.

In general, the occult-metaphysical movements had developed long and highly elaborate explanations of the nature of humanity and the universe. Their ethical systems and their ritual demonstrations flowed from the detailed mythology, or creed, of these movements—so much so that in a real way the knowledge became an ethic and a ritual as well. As we have seen, the ethic of these movements was one of universalism, a loosely defined charity toward all. Hence, it often expressed itself in a community life of radical and revolutionary democracy among believers, and it envisioned a world order manifested in similar terms. There had been involvement in reform activities among nineteenth-century Spiritualists and other occultists, while the healing practice of New Thought people surely was action for good in the world. Further, in the later twentieth century occultism often flourished alongside older visions of a just society of anarchic democracy.

Yet occult and metaphysical movements could also serve to legitimate a conservative social ethic. The Gnostic theories of occult and metaphysical believers supported a division of society into those who were spiritually superior and others who were not so blessed. Such spiritual elitism could easily be translated into a silent endorsement of the status quo—of social arrangements as they were. Moreover, this spiritual elitism could combine with a sense of sociopolitical chosenness. As an example, in the 1930s the "I Am" movement encouraged political reformism based on nationalistic themes. Convinced that human life had begun in America, members of the group believed that history would end here, with the nation as a vessel of light to others.

Still, in concrete ways, a social ethic was not the most important concern of the occult-metaphysical movements. In the practical workings of social and political organizations, there was no lasting significance. The new world of the occultists was one whose model lay outside human society. The real world existed in the mind or in the universe. Moreover, ritual, which was useful in mysticism and magic, especially for those who followed witchcraft traditions, was mostly a way of making concrete the deep realities of secret knowledge. It, too, led back ultimately to the mental landscape.

Above all, however, the homesteads of the mind were *American* homesteads. The picking and choosing which eclectic religion brought was congenial in a land where every religion was equal in the eyes of the law and where many peoples and many traditions encountered one another. The practicality of occult-metaphysical movements agreed with a general American practicality. Even spectacular journeys into the "other" world, for American occultists, ended by helping them to gain power in this one. In other words, extraordinary religious experience became a way to stimulate energies that would bring useful results. Talking to a dead mother could help a person resolve a present problem. Abiding by Theosophical rules could enable someone to gain confidence in self and universe. Practicing New Thought could mean renewed health and abundance of good fortune.

Finally, homesteads of the mind were good places for people whose only possibility for community must be created among strangers. In the sixties and the seventies, with a diminished sense of place and peoplehood, the children of the highway and the divorce court needed to find a secure refuge. They found it in communion with the All or divine Mind through the divine spark within. Union with universal being took the place of union with members of the human community who had shared the long years of a common history. In the end, occult and metaphysical movements appealed to many other Americans because, except for the few Native Americans and other groups who had managed to preserve their culture, every American, in a sense, was either a dislocated person or the descendant of a dislocated person.

IN OVERVIEW

Our survey of occult and metaphysical movements has shown that they had a long history in the West. Gnosticism, Neoplatonism, astrology, Hermeticism, alchemy, and the Kabbalah numbered among the forms of earlier occultism. As religions, these occult movements and their successors offered secret and, by the nineteenth century, rejected knowledge to Western peoples. During colonial times, a natural and traditional occultism thrived in America in astrology and witchcraft. Even later, traditional occultism continued to flourish among various cultural groups. Then in the nineteenth century new and self-conscious forms of occult-metaphysical movements sprang up. In this context, Transcendentalism provided an eclectic theoretical expression of concerns similar to those of the occult and metaphysical movements. Spiritualism, Theosophy, and New Thought gave popular expression to occult and metaphysical religion, while by the turn of the century William James was exploring mystical and psychic frontiers with a psychological frame of reference. In the late twentieth century, a variety of small and intense movements perpetuated the occult-metaphysical legacy, among them witchcraft covens and scientific-technological cults. In general, occult-metaphysical movements were enjoying wide popularity among middle-class people.

Both the occult and the more generally philosophical metaphysical movements based their theories on the world view of correspondence, held also by American Indians and to some extent by Roman Catholics. Like Indians and Catholics, occult-metaphysical devotees mingled ordinary and extraordinary religion. Yet more than the Indian and Catholic traditions, members of the occult and metaphysical movements used the extraordinary to achieve pragmatic and thisworldly results. Even further, without a strong sense of peoplehood, they tended to be persons without definitive social boundaries. For them, universalism was a condition of living as well as a condition of mind. Thus, occult and metaphysical disciples reflected the upheavals of traditional community in modern urban and industrial society and created mental homesteads to replace the human communities they could not find.

But even as some dislocated Americans found homesteads of the mind, others still felt estranged. For no groups was this more true than for those who found themselves in the brave new world of the West either as inheritors of a non-Western religion or as converts to one. We turn now to the religions of these strangers in a strange land. Curiously, as we will see, they were closer to home than they knew.

SUGGESTIONS FOR FURTHER READING: OCCULT AND METAPHYSICAL MOVEMENTS

Braden, Charles S. *Spirits in Rebellion: The Rise and Development of New Thought.* Dallas: Southern Methodist University Press, 1963.

Brown, Slater. *The Heyday of Spiritualism.* New York: Simon & Schuster, Pocket Books, 1972.

Campbell, Bruce F. *Ancient Wisdom Revived: A History of the Theosophical Movement.* Berkeley: University of California Press, 1980.

Ellwood, Robert S., Jr. *Alternative Altars.* Chicago History of American Religion. Chicago: University of Chicago Press, 1979.

————. *Religious and Spiritual Groups in Modern America.* Englewood Cliffs, NJ: Prentice-Hall, 1973.

Judah, J. Stillson. *The History and Philosophy of the Metaphysical Movements in America.* Philadelphia: Westminster Press, 1967.

Kuhn, Alvin B. *Theosophy: A Modern Revival of Ancient Wisdom.* New York: Henry Holt & Company, 1930.

Leventhal, Herbert. *In the Shadow of the Enlightenment: Occultism and Renaissance Science in Eighteenth-Century America.* New York: New York University Press, 1976.

MacNeice, Louis. *Astrology.* Garden City, NY: Doubleday, 1964.

Moore, R. Laurence. *In Search of White Crows: Spiritualism, Parapsychology, and American Culture.* New York: Oxford University Press, 1977.

Raschke, Carl A. *The Interruption of Eternity: Modern Gnosticism and the Origins of the New Religious Consciousness.* Chicago: Nelson-Hall, 1980.

Yates, Frances A. *Giordano Bruno and the Hermetic Tradition.* New York: Random House, Vintage Books, 1969.

CHAPTER 8

East is West:
Eastern Peoples and Eastern Religions

In 1893 an America come of age celebrated the four-hundredth anniversary of the discovery of the New World by Europeans. The Columbian Exposition, named in honor of Christopher Columbus, drew over 27 million people from at least seventy-two countries to its specially erected buildings in Chicago. It was in conjunction with this World's Fair that, during September, representatives of most major religions assembled for the World's Parliament of Religions. In a remarkable spirit of community, they took stock of the religious accomplishments of the century that was ending and planned for a new age of unity in the future.

From the perspective of mainline American denominations, the members of the group that met there were decidedly unusual. There was Annie Besant, the rising leader of Theosophy, who impressed listeners with her addresses and who, it was rumored, had a devoted Indian swami outside the door of her room to protect her. There was, besides, the persuasive Swami Vivekananda with his dramatic turban and orange and crimson garments, who also addressed the congress. There was the Buddhist Anagarika Dharmapala, later to establish Mahabodhi Societies in America; there was his fellow Buddhist, the Zen Master Soyen Shaku, from whom a Zen lineage in America would derive. And there was George A. Ford, a Presbyterian missionary, who read the paper of a fellow missionary in Syria, closing with a quotation from Baha'u'llah, the founder of a religion called Baha'i.

In the spontaneous community of the parliament, East had come West. It was the inauguration of a new era for American religious history, as more and more, Eastern religions would flourish in the United States. The World's Parliament of Religions signaled the growing American popular interest in Eastern religions, and at the same time, it signaled the beginning of a period of immigration that would bring the ethnic representatives of numbers of Eastern religions to the country.

In the twentieth century, America would be significantly affected by the new wave of pluralism. In overview, the incoming religions had originated in a vast territory scattered through much of the world. From Nearer East came Orthodoxy, the Eastern form of Christianity which had grown in a different direction from the West during the early ages of the church. Nearer geographically as well as spiritually, it was the religion of many Eastern Europeans, Russians, and nationals from the lands of the Mediterranean basin. From the Middle East came Islam, the religion of one-seventh of the world's people and a spiritual relative of Judaism and Christianity. Close behind it came Baha'i, a nineteenth-century new religion that had arisen out of the Islam of Persia.

Finally, from the Farther East came the religions of India, China, Japan, Tibet, and Korea. India sent its great traditions—collectively called Hinduism by Westerners—in philosophy, yoga, and, in the later twentieth century, intense devotionalism. China and Japan exported numerous forms of Buddhism, and Japan also contributed a number of cultic movements derived from Shinto. Tibet brought its secret and mystical forms of Buddhism, and even Korea by the late twentieth century had given America a religious movement which blended Eastern and Western themes as the Unification Church of Sun Myung Moon (b. 1920).

Besides their different points of origin, the incoming religions could be distinguished in another way. On the one hand, they were ethnic religions that for centuries had been part of the heritage of the national groups which brought them to America. Thus, they were religions of particular places and peoples, and they blended extraordinary and ordinary religion together, melting the extraordinary into the usual and everyday. Although for Americans the incoming religions seemed wholly detached from worldly concerns, for most of those who had inherited them, they provided ways to live in *this* world more than liberation into another. Their rituals expressed involvement in the here and now, even as they pointed to other realities.

On the other hand, the incoming religions became the religions of converts. Americans from Protestant, Catholic, and Jewish backgrounds began to embrace them, and in so doing, they changed the character of the imported religions. Seekers after the extraordinary, these American converts were attracted to Eastern religions because from the American perspective they were strange and even dramatic. They made it possible for nonnative converts to live an extraordinary religious life, at the boundary of worlds that suddenly opened out to them. In short, they offered mainstream Americans an avenue to transcendence and liberation that more traditional Western forms of religion had not provided for them.

These Westerners who pursued extraordinary religion were seekers after "otherness." They were drawn by the cultural strangeness of Eastern religions coming from far-off lands. With the exception of Orthodoxy, Eastern religions lay outside the Judaeo-Christian tradition. Unlike American Indian religions, they did not contain memories of presence in the land, predating the later presence of Euro-Americans. Unlike Afro-American religion, they did not have a background of close interaction with the religions of the white majority. All of this meant that the "otherness" of the East was both historical and geographical, providing an especially powerful symbol for Westerners. So Eastern religions came to stand for and express to some Americans the "other" reality of a sacred world beyond this one. Paradoxically, the ordinary religion of the immigrants, by its strangeness, became the vehicle for extraordinary religious experience for mainstream Americans.

While Eastern religions were embraced by some Westerners because the religions were considered strange, Easterners themselves felt separate from American life and culture. Decades of feeling "different" and of experiencing petty harassment and even outright discrimination were the lot of Eastern Europeans, Middle Easterners, and Chinese- and Japanese-Americans. To take a key example, Japanese-Americans quickly outstayed their welcome to the West Coast of the United States. Their first large influx into the country had come in the 1890s, and by 1907, the so-called Gentlemen's Agreement between the United States and Japan was restricting immigration to nonlaborers. Then in 1913 and 1920 the Anti-Alien Land Laws of California prevented the Japanese from controlling farmlands, making further immigration unappealing. In a Supreme Court decision of 1922, Japanese immigrants were prohibited from becoming naturalized American citizens, and in 1924 the Oriental Exclusion Act cut off the immigration of people who were ineligible for citizenship, effectively ending Japanese immigration for the time. Later events in the twentieth century were not kinder to Japanese-Americans. With the tense years of the Second World War when the United States and Japan were in conflict, Japanese-Americans were forcibly evacuated from their West Coast homes and sent to internment, or as some said, concentration camps.

To sum up, the Japanese and other Easterners felt their foreignness in the New World at the same time that numbers of mainstream Americans, alienated from *their* heritage, ironically, were becoming seekers of Eastern wisdom. Hence, the picture of the East as it came to be present in the West is, from a variety of points of view, a picture of manyness. Many nations, many religions, many ways of embracing these religions, all were part of the horizon of meaning. Once more, we cannot tell the full story here, and our approach will be by way of a few selected cases. Especially in the late twentieth century, when a flowering of Eastern cult movements spread across America, we will need to use key examples to suggest the nature of the religious landscape.

NEARER EAST: EASTERN ORTHODOXY

We begin with Orthodoxy, the Christian religious tradition embodied in the various national churches of Eastern European and Mediterranean lands. Orthodox religious contact with the North American continent had begun as early as 1743 when some Alaskans were baptized by a Russian soldier. By 1792 eight monks had made their way to Kodiak Island, off the coast of Alaska, to build an Eastern Orthodox church there. The native peoples of Alaska welcomed them, and before the end of the century several thousand had become Christian. In the nineteenth century, Orthodox religion continued to grow in Alaska, until by the start of the twentieth century about one-sixth of the population, over 10,000 people, were Russian Orthodox church members. Meanwhile, through a land sale by Russia, Alaska had become a possession of the United States. In 1872 church headquarters were moved from Alaska to San Francisco where Russians, Greeks, and Serbians from Eastern Europe turned to Russian Orthodoxy for their religious needs. And by the close of the century, the Russian Orthodox had come officially to New York, as Russian immigration to the United States increased rapidly. Within a decade, from 1906 to 1916, Orthodox church membership increased fivefold, from 20,000 to 100,000 people.

With the twentieth century, Russian Orthodox presence in America was exceeded by the Greek Orthodox church, the result of large-scale immigration beginning at the end of the nineteenth century. There were Greek churches in New York and Chicago before 1900. Throughout the century membership swelled until by 1975 it had reached a figure close to 2 million. At the same time, the Russian church was some 1 million strong, and another million or so Orthodox peoples were represented in various separate national churches—Albanian, Bulgarian, Rumanian, Serbian, Syrian, and Ukrainian. With this large numerical presence, many came to view Eastern Orthodoxy as a fourth major faith in the United States, ranking behind Protestantism, Roman Catholicism, and Judaism.

Eastern Orthodox Religion

What was the religion that these peoples brought with them to America, and how was it different from Western forms of Christianity? The answer to these questions must take us back through the centuries of Orthodox history to the beginnings of its separation from the Roman (Western) church. Here we learn that, as one student of Orthodoxy has explained, not only the religious answers were different from those of the West but even the questions. While the Roman church asked how Christianity could exist as one body, the Eastern church wondered how it could express community. While the Roman church concerned itself with questions of legal justice through a proper distribution of rights and duties to one another and to God, Easterners sought more intensely for ways to nourish contemplation and the inner life.

Later, with the birth of Protestantism, Eastern Orthodoxy seemed to Westerners even more radically "other" in its religious quest. If Protestantism tended to be a thisworldly religion, Eastern Orthodoxy—for centuries lived out under Muslim rule—was decidedly otherworldly. If Protestantism heard the Word and felt urged by it to action in the world, Orthodoxy thought of the Word as a jewel surrounded by the richness of ritual and found in it a model for interior prayer. And finally, if Protestantism tended to separate ordinary from extraordinary religion with its awareness of the gap between God and sinful human beings, Orthodoxy brought the two together. It created in its liturgical ritual a center for community that could be expressed at many levels, both spiritual and material.

For Orthodoxy, the local community *was* the church. Organized in self-governing, or autocephalous (literally, "self-headed"), churches, the Orthodox gave first rank of honor to four ancient churches which they called the patriarchates: Constantinople, Alexandria, Antioch, and Jerusalem. After these four, they recognized eleven other autocephalous churches, among them the Russian and the Greek, which would both figure so prominently in America. Below these, in later Orthodox history came churches called autonomous, self-governing in most ways but not fully independent. And finally came the provinces of Western Europe, North and South America, and Australia.

What held all of these local communities together was their witness to "right" or "correct" religion. The word *orthodoxy* means just this, and Orthodox churches understood right religion to have two sides. First of all, it was right belief, a union of Christian people in faith and doctrine through acceptance of a common tradition. Inherited through scripture, through the writings of the fathers and other authorities, and through word-of-mouth teaching, tradition established a living continuity between the generations, leading back to the time of Jesus. It accepted the authority of the seven ecumenical ("worldwide") church councils, the last in A.D. 787, as fundamental to the teaching of the church.

Secondly, right religion was right worship or communion in the sacraments. Acknowledging the same seven sacraments as the Roman church, the Orthodox saw their identity in terms of the common praise they rendered to God through the sacraments and, especially, through the Divine Liturgy in which the eucharist was celebrated. Like the Mass of Roman Catholicism, the Divine Liturgy recalled the Last Supper of Jesus and his sacrifice on the cross of Calvary. In structure it was similar to the Roman Mass and, in fact, preserved versions of that ritual older than those that had evolved in the West. For the Orthodox, however, more than for the Roman church, the worshiping community was the key to unity. Outward organization was secondary, and true unity came from the collective witness around the altar table. Those who shared the same worship were part of the same religion: there could be no clearer test.

The common Christian tradition of the earliest followers of Jesus had developed into Eastern and Western branches over centuries. In the East the cultural temper of the people and the events of their history had led to the development of a religious sensitivity different from that of the West. During the eighth and ninth centuries, a controversy over the place of images in the churches helped to crystallize Orthodox thought and practice. This controversy arose between two parties. One group, called the Iconoclasts, were literally image smashers. They were suspicious of any religious art which tried to depict the saints, Mary, Jesus, or the Godhead. For them religious art was a form of idolatry, and they demanded that icons, or religious images, be destroyed. The other group, called the Iconodules, venerated icons and wanted to preserve them. At issue in the struggle was the question of what Orthodoxy thought of the material world and, ultimately, of the human nature of Jesus. If all matter were evil and led inevitably to idolatry, then Jesus could not have taken upon himself the corruption of a human nature. On the other hand, if matter could be a way into the spiritual world, then the Incarnation, the taking of human flesh by the son of God, was possible.

In the end, the controversy was decided in favor of those who venerated images. Orthodoxy came to be a religion of icons. Behind its iconic preference lay the same sacramental sense that ran through Roman Catholicism. But the

Orthodox developed this sense even further, and, especially, they developed it to express qualities of vision and sight. An icon was something that had to be seen, and so it encouraged the quiet gaze of the contemplative person. For the Orthodox, the icon was the place where one could encounter divine things; it was a fixed meeting point where the sacred world could enter this one.

Moreover, icons came to provide a point of reference for understanding the rest of Christianity. The Bible was seen as an icon of Jesus Christ, the jewel at the heart of the liturgy that we spoke of. Human beings were seen as icons of God, and there was less emphasis on sin in Eastern Orthodoxy than in Roman Catholicism or in Protestantism. Instead, people were encouraged to look within and to seek the image of God in the human through meditation and interior prayer. Similarly, the church was viewed as the icon of the Trinity in which Father, Son, and Holy Spirit were one. Just as there was a community of diverse members in the Godhead, so there should be a community of different local churches in the larger Orthodox communion. Finally, the most important icon for Orthodoxy was Jesus Christ. He was the image of God's glory and light, the place in which the divine had entered the human world to transform it. So the Orthodox saw Jesus as a divine king and victor over the forces of evil. Even on the cross, they saw the Godhead of Jesus shining through the human icon, and their images of the Crucified One showed him crowned with gold and precious stones.

The Iconoclast controversy was one cultural event that shaped the later history of Orthodoxy. The mystical teaching of the East was a second. From the beginning, the Orthodox had leaned toward contemplation and inner spiritual transformation more than outer activism. Through the centuries, the church fathers of the East contributed to a growing body of mystical literature that became known as hesychastic. Mysticism, we remember, means a total union between the divine and the human. Hesychasm became the particularly Orthodox way of understanding mysticism. Coming from the Greek word for quiet, *hesychasm* meant a form of mysticism stressing the need for inner quiet and tranquillity to await the transforming light of God. Its goal was a vision of this divine and uncreated light, and its methods were various techniques of physical and mental control. Physically, breathing, posture, and the use of one's eyes were all directed according to specific exercises. Mentally and sometimes verbally, the use of a short prayer, repeated again and again, produced a state of inner quiet. Later in this chapter, when we encounter Hindu and Buddhist meditation practices, we will see similarities. The most "Western" part of the East, Orthodoxy was still Eastern, and its involvement in mystical prayer and mystical technique was a clear sign.

Emphasis on mystical light linked hesychasm to the iconic thought and practice of Orthodox worship. Mysticism, like the veneration of icons, was a form of seeing. The third element that shaped the history of Orthodoxy, however, was a matter of *not* seeing. For while the West, by the sixth century, had come to see and venerate the pope of Rome as the sole head of the church on earth, the East did not look at matters in this way. There was opposition to the growing Western insistence on the primacy (the firstness) of the pope. Especially troubling was a phrase that had been inserted through papal authority into the traditional creed accepted by the Eastern and Western churches. Whereas in its original form, the creed acknowledged that the Holy Spirit proceeded (came forth) from the Father, the addition to the creed affirmed that the Spirit had proceeded from the Father *and from the Son* (in Latin, *filioque*).

Since the ecumenical councils had earlier forbidden changes in the creed, there was a choice here between the authority of the pope or of the councils, of the one monarch or of the community and its representatives. The Orthodox chose the councils and the community, regarding the papal claims as a departure from the original form of Christianity. In the year 1054, the split between East and West was dramatized when a messenger from the pope left a decree of excommunication for the patriarch (bishop) of Constantinople on the high altar of his cathedral. Thus, 1054 is the traditional date given for the formal break between Eastern and Western churches. The Orthodox, however, point to the year 1204 as the real point of no return. It was in this year that the European Christian soldiers who had joined the Fourth Crusade stormed the city of Constantinople (modern Istanbul, Turkey), sacking and pillaging it. This was the final stroke of hostility between the two churches, and for the East the damage had become irreparable.

Orthodoxy in America

In every land in which it had spread, Orthodoxy blended with the cultural heritage of native peoples, survived, and grew. It was able to unite extraordinary and ordinary religious concerns, an otherworldly and mystical religion which, at the same time, expressed the common life of the people. Indeed, the church was the place where the faithful met their relatives and friends. Often, they came and left in the middle of services, talked to one another during the Divine Liturgy, or stepped outside the church for a longer conversational break. Their priests visited and blessed houses; their religious feasts became community holidays.

In America, Orthodoxy continued to be a religion of mystical contemplation and ethnic solidarity at once. The solidarity, however, was among people who had come from the old country, the national church from the land of origins. In the late twentieth century, Orthodoxy was still "other" from the vantage point of the mainstream. More than Judaism, which though a minority religion not too much larger had made a major impact on American culture, Orthodoxy remained a religion apart. Overall, in fact, there was a decline in Orthodox practice in the United States, as second- and third-generation children of the immigrants grew away from their heritage. For a number of them, Americanization meant a weakening of ties with the ancestral faith.

Yet Orthodoxy was sensitive to the needs of its adherents in the New World. Like Jews and like Catholics, many of the Orthodox reformed their liturgies to bring them closer to the Protestant and American center. English came into use in services, often alternating with various national languages spoken in the different churches. The calendar of feasts and holy days, which had followed ancient Eastern practice, was altered to bring it into conformity with the Western Christian calendar. In many churches, seats were introduced so that people would not have to stand during the Divine Liturgy as they had in the old countries. Often, instruments and mixed choirs were also used, again bringing the churches closer to other Christian churches in the United States.

Especially, Orthodoxy was affected by the manyness of America. With a multiplicity of national churches entering the country, jurisdictional claims became confused and frequently erupted into disputes. About a dozen or so Orthodox groups had overlapping claims, and disagreements sometimes became long and bitter. By the seventies, there were at least three separate branches of Russian Orthodoxy in the United States, three groups of Ukrainian Orthodox church members, and two groups of Syrian Orthodox adherents. Throughout the century, small splinter churches were formed by those who sought to make their religion more universal and more American.

Still, Orthodoxy had prospered in the New World, opening seminaries and churches, providing its people with the solace of tradition in a land where things always seemed to be changing. Its manyness could not seem unusual in a setting of pluralism. Its preference for contemplation, as we will see, was a growing choice among other Americans who thought that life in the United States was too cluttered and too fast. In the late twentieth century, Orthodoxy was in America to stay.

MIDDLE EAST: ISLAM

Close to Eastern Orthodox lands and in some cases overlapping them in the old countries were the homelands of Islamic, or Muslim, peoples. Islam was a Middle Eastern religion, both geographically and spiritually. Located between the Orient and the West, it shared many of the basic insights of Jews and Christians, but it was also very different. So in America it would be a religion of "otherness," and with the exception of their recognition of blacks who were Muslims, most Americans would hardly know that Islam existed in the United States. Yet the relationship of Islam to the New World was a long and romantic one.

Arab geographers told that their ancestors sailed the Atlantic from Spain and Portugal, landing in South America as long ago as the tenth century and on the coast of Brazil by A.D. 1150. To the north, as early as 1539 Marcos de Niza, a Franciscan friar sent to explore Arizona, had a Moor—"Istfan the Arab"—as his guide. Meanwhile, a sixteenth-century Egyptian, called by Americans "Nosereddine" (Nasr-al-Din), lived in the Catskill area of present-day New York state. As we have already seen, many West Africans, imported to the New World as slaves, were Muslims. Moreover, we know that there were Muslims in South Carolina in 1790 because of a reference to them by the state House of Representatives. Then in the 1840s, Arizona was visited again by a Muslim when Hajj 'Ali accompanied Arabian camels to the desert in conjunction with a government project. During the Civil War, descendants of the North African Ben Ali fought on the Confederate side.

However, as in the case of so many other immigrant groups, the general arrival of Muslims in the United States began toward the end of the nineteenth century. Their numbers were small, and among them the largest group were

Arabs who came from Syria and what is now Lebanon. Although mostly from an agricultural background, these Arab Muslims quickly adjusted to city life. They concentrated their settlements in industrial centers such as New York, Chicago, and Detroit, where they peddled dry goods, operated small businesses, or engaged in unskilled labor. Generally, they were economically successful. Although many had come in their youth with the intention of returning to their lands of origin, most found themselves in America when they had grown old.

In addition to the Arabs, other Muslims who immigrated to the United States were Indian, Pakistani, Palestinian, and European. Among the Europeans, over 3,000 Muslims from Poland, of Tartar origin, settled in New York. The largest number of Indian Muslims immigrated in 1906 and headed for California where they continued to be farmers. Most of them were associated with the mission-minded Ahmadiyya Movement in Islam, a reinterpretation of the Islamic tradition begun in India in 1889 by Mirza Ghulam Ahmad (1835–1908).

Hence, like Eastern Orthodoxy, Islam was an ethnic religion, reflecting the national origins of many of the immigrants. But from the beginning of its history, Islam had thought of itself as a universal religion with a message for all people, and so in America there were converts. Already in 1888 Mohammed Alexander Russel Webb had become the first mainstream American to embrace Islam. He was a former journalist who had become a diplomat, and after his contact in the Philippines with Indian Muslims, he affirmed their faith. Other converts from Protestant, Catholic, Jewish, and Mormon backgrounds came to Islam mostly through marriage. Meanwhile, black Americans were attracted by the Islamic message of universal community and equality among all races. They heard with great interest the Muslim tradition that a daughter of Muhammad, the founder of Islam, had married a black man. By the late 1970s, as we have already noted, the American Nation of Islam, reborn as the World Community of al-Islam in the West (in 1980 the American Muslim Mission), was adopting the doctrines and practices of mainstream Islam and was winning the approval of devout Arab Muslims. Other American blacks were drawn to the Indian Ahmadiyya Movement, with its message of universal peace and unity, and to other Muslim organizations. Islam, they thought, was practicing what Christianity only sometimes preached.

The Religious Meaning of Islam

The religion which all of these Muslims acknowledged had arisen in the seventh century in the Arabian desert. Its founder, Muhammad (A.D. 570?–632), had lost his father when he was young and had grown up in a humble home. But he was a member of a powerful clan, and after he entered the service of a wealthy widow, Khadijah of Mecca, as a merchant, he married her and prospered. At about the age of forty, however, Muhammad experienced a series of visions and voice revelations that changed his life and the lives of countless others. He said that, through the angel Gabriel, Allah had informed him that he was chosen as the Messenger of God. The message was at first overwhelming and even terrifying, but gradually Muhammad grew certain of its authenticity, and he began to speak as Allah had instructed him.

The message of Allah was one of radical monotheism: there was no God but Allah, and Muhammad was his Prophet. Unlike the God-man Jesus who had brought Christianity, Muhammad was only human. The worst sin possible for a Muslim would be to raise any person to the level of Allah. Yet Islam was the spiritual relative of Judaism and Christianity. Like them, it was a religion of history, enacted on the stage of public events and urging human beings to right action in the world. Like them, it gave to humanity a law by which to live, and like them, too, a sacred book, the Qur'an, in which the law was written. Like them, finally, it told of the relationship between Allah and the community that served him. Muhammad brought to Arabia and the world a new type of community in which religion and nationhood were joined under the banner of submission to Allah. Before the revelation of Muhammad, clan kinship had provided the basis for social organization. Now a new force united the people. In the community of Allah, called the *umma*, faith overcame the claims of kinship, and so Muhammad's new community was open to the entire world.

If Muhammad's teaching echoed Jewish and Christian understandings, Muhammad and his people believed that in Islam the past had been transformed. Muhammad was the last in a line of prophets that included Abraham, Moses, and Jesus. The message that Allah had given him was a purification of Judaism and Christianity, fulfilling their best ideals. Thus, while like Christianity, Islam emphasized the universality of its message, preaching a doctrine of election by grace and final judgment and resurrection, like Judaism it saw religion and politics as one reality. In every land to which it spread, it brought a government by the elect of Allah under the requirements of Islamic law. It brought ordinary and extraordinary religion together, just as ancient Israel had done.

This merging of the ordinary and the extraordinary was reflected in the Five Pillars of Islam, basic to the practice of any Muslim. First, a Muslim must affirm the central confession of the faith: there is no God but Allah, and Muhammad is his Prophet. Second, he or she must perform the ritual prayers. Five times a day, at dawn, at noon, in midafternoon, after sunset, and before sleeping, each Muslim faced the holy city of Mecca and, using prescribed gestures and vocal forms, prayed. Third, it was a Muslim's duty to give alms by means of a kind of tax and by means of other voluntary offerings. Fourth, during the Islamic month of Ramadan, a Muslim was required to fast from all food and drink from sunup to sunset, taking meals only after dark and before dawn. Fifth, at least once in a lifetime, if health and other circumstances allowed, a Muslim should make a pilgrimage to Mecca (in present-day Saudi Arabia). There, the pilgrim should perform the traditional spiritual exercises involving a ceremonial visit to the Kaaba, the holiest shrine of Islam, where the sacred black stone said to be brought to earth by the angel Gabriel was kept.

The Five Pillars, with their prescriptions for daily prayer, almsgiving, dietary regulation, and even travel, provided Muslims with a way to direct their lives with reference to both everyday and eternal claims. This fusion of the ordinary and the extraordinary was underlined in the Islamic observance of the *sunna*, or customs, which supplemented the teachings of the Qur'an. Handed on from generation to generation and acquiring written form, the *sunna* bound Muslims to the practices believed to guide the everyday behavior of the first generation in their religion. In other words, the *sunna* were a way to touch the force that came with Islam in the beginning of its history, a way to destroy the work of time and gain access to the power in the lives of the early followers of the Prophet.

The later history of Islam saw division into different religious communities. Among these, the Sunni Muslims formed the largest. They aimed to follow the *sunna* of the original Muslim community and honored the early history of Islam with its conquests by religionational leaders called caliphs. The Sunnis were countered in their claims to Islamic orthodoxy by the Shiites who quarreled with the Sunni version of early Muslim history. The Shiites were followers of the family of Ali, the son-in-law and cousin of the Prophet, who reigned as caliph from 656 until 661, when he was murdered. They considered Ali first in a line of sacred figures called imams who, for them, came to replace the caliphs of Sunni Islam. Law and authority, they thought, was voiced in every age in the person of the imam. Although long ago in the past the official line of imams had disappeared from public view, the law of the Islamic community continued to be less important than the living lawgiver, the holy leader in each era. Moreover, the Shiites awaited the reappearance of an imam from the house of Ali at the end of time. This Mahdi, as he was called, would inaugurate the final victory of justice and deliver the dead to resurrection. Intensely emotional in their religion, the Shiites became the dominant Muslims of Persia—the modern Iran—and an important element in the population of Iraq, Lebanon, and other Islamic states.

Finally, more radical in their religion than either Sunnis or Shiites were the Sufis. These were the mystics of Islam, who wandered from place to place engaging sometimes in austere practices of self-denial and at other times in the song and dance that would gain them spiritual renown. They formed themselves into religious communities, or orders, in which a group of disciples would follow the mystical teachings of a spiritual master called a *sheikh*. Of these Muslim groups, it was the Sufis who most influenced the cult movements of the late twentieth century in the United States.

Transformations of Islam in America

As the twentieth century found more and more Muslims in the United States, they became another minority among the many. It was difficult to determine how many Muslims there actually were. For the immigrants, to be Muslim in their countries of origin was a matter of birth and culture, not of religious preference. But counting by birth in the United States was misleading, as the children of the second and third generations often forgot their past. Yet despite this problem in measuring, it has been estimated that by the late seventies there were nearly half a million Muslims in the United States and Canada. Vital and important among them were the Afro-American converts whom we discussed in Chapter 5. Here we will glance briefly at the lives of the immigrants and their children.

At the beginning of the general period of immigration, the fear of losing Islam had been an important factor delaying the influx of Muslims. Significantly, Middle Eastern Christians had come to this country first, and it was only with some anxiety about their religion that Muslims later began to immigrate. Like so many other newcomers, they tended to live together in communities that were modeled on their relationships in the old countries. Often, in a city neighborhood members of almost an entire Syrian village would live within blocks of one another, renting apartments in huge buildings acquired by one wealthy villager among them.

In these Arab communities in larger cities, tensions sometimes grew between Sunni and Shiite Muslims, with Sunnis building mosques (Islamic places of worship) and Shiites preferring "national clubs." Frequently, however, the strangeness of America and the threat to their heritage led Muslims to ignore the differences of the past in their common affirmation of Islam. Moreover, since Islam had been a religion of community and of law, the mosque and its religious service had never been central. In the old countries, it had been customary for some to meet there for public prayer led by an imam (here simply a prayer leader) at noon on Fridays. So in America some mosques were built, the first at Highland Park (Detroit), Michigan, in 1919. Yet by the early seventies, there were only about twenty mosques in the country with perhaps six official imams for all of them. Islam was not a "church" religion, and the small number of mosques and imams told powerfully that ordinary and extraordinary religious needs were met in the everyday lives of Muslims by other means.

Still, in the ways in which the mosques functioned, the Americanization of Islam could be seen. No longer simply houses of prayer, in America they became multiple-purpose buildings, much like Jewish synagogues in the twentieth century. Even more, the mosques developed a "Sunday" tendency. Following the lead of their Christian neighbors, Muslims began Sunday schools for their children in order to hand on their religious heritage. Often, Sunday schools were followed by Sunday services at noon, which replaced the traditional Friday observances. With the American Islamic emphasis on the education of children, women gained a role of increased prominence. Although Islam had been a male-oriented religion in the old countries, the needs of religious education in America were met largely by women. Their positions as teachers in Muslim Sunday schools led to their greater participation in the public life of Islam and a new dependence by Muslim people on women. Meanwhile, in the fifties, a Federation of Islamic Associations and an Islamic Cultural Association in Washington, D.C., came into existence. More recently in the seventies, a Council of Imams in North America and a Coordinating Council of Muslim Organizations in America were both begun.

Even with these efforts at religious education and organization, however, there was a decline in religious practice among traditional American Muslims. Especially in the third generation, for many Arab-Americans nationalism and politics seemed to take the place that religion once had occupied. As in the case of the Eastern Orthodox, the "otherness" of the Islamic religious heritage led many of the descendants of the original immigrants to discard it. Praying five times daily was not easy in a modern, industrial society. Fasting during the month of Ramadan was an act of religious asceticism totally unsupported by the larger culture. The foreignness of Islam was painful to many of the young, who had been educated in American public schools and now looked at their religious history from the vantage point of the American mainstream. The result was a sense of estrangement from the Muslim past.

At the same time, Muslims did not run headlong to embrace American culture. The ordinary religion of Islam continued in Muslim communities. As in the old countries, family and an extended network of kin formed the basis of community. Women spent much of their leisure time in informal visiting, mostly with relatives, a pattern very similar to that in the mountain tradition of Southern Appalachia, as we will see in the next chapter. Men often gathered in coffee houses (Islam forbade alcoholic beverages) and clubs catering to different ethnic groups. The public male dominance of traditional Islam was apparent in Muslim neighborhoods in which the main street of business was frequented almost entirely by men. Although many Muslims had stopped praying five times daily, in other ways Islam kept on directing them in their ordinary lives and attitudes toward one another.

Islam and New Religions: The Example of Baha'i

As a great world religion, Islam possessed a creativity and dynamism that led to new religious movements throughout its history. In its spread, Islam came into contact with many different native cultures. Out of the mixture of the Muslim heritage with these other traditions, new religious movements arose. There are many examples of these movements that grew up in the shadow of Islam, among them the nineteenth-century new religion which originated in Persia (present-day Iran), spread from there into numerous countries, and achieved a notable following in America—the religion of Baha'i.

We have already seen that the words of Baha'u'llah, the founder of Baha'i, were used to conclude an address at the World's Parliament of Religions in 1893. The history of Baha'i, however, began with a Shiite Muslim, Siyyid Ali Muhammad (1819–1850), later called the Bab, or the *Gate*. Like other Shiites he had grown up in expectation that someday from the house of Muhammad's cousin and son-in-law, Ali, a hidden imam, the Mahdi, would return to guide Islam rightly. At the same time, his native Persia was still influenced by Zoroastrianism. This earlier Persian religion taught that after a universal war between good and evil, a prophet would come to bring in the new age of final justice. Hence, the Shiite teaching about the Mahdi drew on long roots in native Persian tradition and like Islam was influenced by Jewish and Christian messianic teachings. Thus, when Siyyid Ali Muhammad, himself a member of the house of Ali, announced in 1844 that he was the Bab, he founded a religion called Babism incorporating the ancient expectations of a new prophet to manifest God.

The Bab was martyred in 1850. Among his followers was a young man born as Husayn Ali (1817–1892), later to be known as Baha'u'llah (the Glory of God). Imprisoned after the death of the Bab, Husayn Ali came to see himself as the manifestation of God for the present age, the greatest in a long line of prophets. Thereafter, as Baha'u'llah, he spent the rest of his life, mostly in prison or in exile from Persia, proclaiming his religious vision. He taught that just as Islam had been the purification and fulfillment of Judaism and Christianity, Baha'i was the completion of Islam and of all previous religions. It was also an authentic new religion that in time would establish a new world order. Each religion had been the religious expression suited to its era, for revelation in human history had been progressive. Now the world stood at the threshold of an era of universal unity and peace, an era in which its one religion, fitted to the maturity of the age, would follow the principles of Baha'i. In this vision resembling the Christian expectation of the millennium, Baha'u'llah taught the equality of all human beings. Men and women, though different, had equal importance and equal work to do. Similarly, all races were equal in the plan of God, and Baha'i encouraged interracial marriage to smooth the way toward genuine racial harmony. Even further, it called for a reverence for all living things.

If Baha'u'llah had a vision for the Baha'i community, he also made it concrete. Through a ritual and moral program, he gave Baha'is a keen sense of their distinctiveness, so that, paradoxically, this universalist religion maintained a strong sense of boundary and identity. In a special solar calendar the year was divided into nineteen months of nineteen days each, with days added at the end of the year to keep it in time with the sun. Beginning each month, there was a feast day, while nine holy days throughout the year honored specific events in the history and revelation of Baha'i. Likewise, during the nineteenth month of the year, from March 2 to 20, Baha'is fasted, accepting the ancient Islamic Pillar and transforming it to their own purposes. In another transformation of Islamic practice, Baha'is retained the custom of prescribed daily prayers. However, they did not pray five times in a day, and they did not use the Qur'an, which had been superseded in their view by the sacred writings of the Bab and especially of Baha'u'llah. Meanwhile, at "firesides" Baha'is came together to discuss the principles of their religion with non-Baha'is.

The United States early proved important in Baha'i development. From at least 1894, when Ibrahim Khayru'llah began to offer classes in Chicago, the religion had been systematically taught. The beginning was a sign of things to come, since Chicago possessed an ideal location at the center of midwestern America, and it continued to offer a home to a thriving Baha'i movement. In the northern Chicago suburb of Wilmette along Lake Michigan, the Baha'i Mother Temple was built. Vast and impressive, it was a testimony to the significance of American Baha'i. With its optimistic message of a new era of peace and unity, Baha'i drew numbers of Americans, whose nation had been born in hopes for just such a millennium. By 1979 there were probably more than 79,000 Baha'is in the United States, and as elsewhere in the world, membership was interracial. While participation in partisan politics was forbidden as an offense against unity, efforts on behalf of the United Nations were a concrete way to advance this unity. American Baha'is continued to be active in its service.

With its strong organization, its missionary enthusiasm, and its distinctive sense of identity, Baha'i had created a time and space which changed even ordinary concerns into extraordinary religion. It thrived on the hope of becoming a world faith, and its "otherness" in America, at least from the Baha'i point of view, was only a temporary condition. Baha'i did not intend to merge with American culture but instead to bring Americans to live in accordance with its way.

FARTHER EAST: HINDUISM

As we turn to movements Farther East, we look first to India, the land that was as important spiritually to the East as Israel was to the West. India's rich and multifaceted religious system, known to the West as Hinduism, had attracted Americans as early as the era of the Transcendentalists. Ralph Waldo Emerson and his friends read the *Bhagavad Gita*, the *Laws of Manu*, and other Indian religious classics. Later, Madame Blavatsky and the Theosophical Society explored Hindu teaching as an ancient source of occult and metaphysical wisdom. Unlike other major religions, however, Hinduism was not nurtured in America through the widespread immigration of Indian people. In fact, Indian immigrants were few, and, instead, Hinduism grew in the United States through a series of missionary movements addressed by Indian spiritual leaders to American converts.

We have already seen that, in 1893 at the World's Parliament of Religions, Hinduism caught the eye of the American public in the person of Swami Vivekananda (1863–1902). For Vivekananda, success at the Parliament was the beginning of a mission that spread the ancient Indian religious philosophy of Vedanta in the United States. Vedanta Societies sprang up in various places, "churches" to bring the message of the East to Americans who were religious seekers. Then in the 1920s, a new arrival from India, Paramahansa Yogananda (1893–1952), brought to Americans the fundamental teachings of yoga. His Self-Realization Fellowship became the first in the series of yogic movements that continued and in popularized form became part of American culture. Finally, in the sixties and seventies, Hindu devotionalism appealed to some among a new generation of Americans in search of religious meaning.

Religious Themes in Hinduism

The word *Hinduism* is an all-encompassing term to sum up the religious experience and expression of most of the Indian people. It ranges from a profoundly philosophic understanding of the nature of the universe and humanity to popular devotion to one or another of the Gods in many small sects and cults. Indeed, a sensitive visitor to India might well conclude that there are hundreds of different religions in the country, some of them encouraging knowledge and enlightenment, others urging people to faithfulness in performing their allotted tasks, and still others leading them to intense devotion expressed through ritual. In other words, there was a manyness to Hinduism not unlike the manyness that we have found in American religions from Native American traditions to occultism. Yet, as in other examples of manyness that we have discussed, there were common themes to the Hindu religious movements, and it is possible to speak of Hinduism as a single religion. In this context, let us look briefly at Hindu thought and practice.

First of all, Indian speculation about the nature of the cosmos formed the backdrop for Hindu religious expression. Over the centuries, many philosophic Hindus had concluded that the world was one reality and the appearance of separation was an illusion. Behind the material world that people encountered every day was a vast, impersonal force or power. The Hindus named this power Brahman, and they thought of it as the fundamental reality in the universe. Matter, which gave rise to the sense of separation and distinctiveness, was not so real as it seemed. Beneath its masks, the person who became a realized being could trace the presence of Brahman. Most of all, within each human being lay the Atman, the spark of sacred power that linked individuals to Brahman. As a realized being, a person would come to know experientially that Atman *was* Brahman. So all beings were one being, and mystical union expressed the truest description of the cosmos.

This religious understanding, called monism, or the philosophy of oneness, was disputed by other Hindus who taught dualism. In this latter understanding, the distinctiveness of spirit and matter, of God and individual souls, formed the basis for any further religious thought or practice. Dualism—the philosophy of twoness and manyness—encouraged Hindus in their fascination with the richness of the material world. Its many shapes and colors, sounds and smells often seemed to be an intoxicating experience. Thus, the religious art of India was lavish in its use of color and detail. In like manner, the religious landscape that dualism encouraged was peopled with numbers of Gods and Goddesses, each of them intensely personal and each of them the center of a devoted religious following. Polytheism, or the worship of many Gods, spread through Indian villages and attracted Indian intellectuals as well. It brought a striking sacramentalism to Hindu religious expression, as the material world became the sacred vehicle for the journey to the divine.

Indian speculation about the nature of the cosmos was completed by a second background element in all Hinduism. As a people, Hindus were preoccupied with religious experience and especially religious discipline. Indeed, Hindu thought had been fruitful in providing maps of the various paths a person might travel in the religious journey of life. Overall, there were three broad routes to God. First of all, there was the path of devotion. Here, the God-centered culture of India expected that each family would have its statue of God—either Krishna or Vishnu or another popular deity. Religion then would center on respect and attention paid to the God through his statue. Daily, there would be the practice of *puja*, a kind of hospitality offering in which God was greeted, bathed, perfumed, clothed, and fed by the head of the household, attended at points by members of the family. Through the faithfulness of a person's devotion to God, expressed in devotion to the divine image, a Hindu could find the way to salvation. Called *bhakti*—the Indian word for devotion—this religious path stressed the importance of personal feeling expressed in the worship of at least one of India's many Gods and Goddesses. Through love of one, a person would do all that was needful, contacting the divine power of the universe as it was manifested in a single expression.

The second religious path was the way of action. Indian society had been established according to a system of classes, or castes. Each person came into the world as a member of one of these castes, and because of this inheritance, he or she was heir to a set of prescribed actions and obligations. For example, it was the duty of a (male) member of the priestly caste to teach, while it was a warrior's duty to rule and defend society. A merchant's obligation was to procure food and goods for the other members of society, while a person born into the servant caste labored at service occupations on behalf of the others. In all of the castes, a woman's normal task was to serve her husband and other members of her household. The religious way of action taught that each person must live according to the law for his or her caste, doing what needed to be done without regard to results or satisfaction gained. In other words, deeds must be performed for their own sake rather than for any fruits they might bring. Performing faithfully the actions required of one's state in life, called *karma*, would lead a person to be reborn—reincarnated—in a higher state in the next lifetime. Indeed, *karma* was the law of *all* action, leading inevitably to an equal and appropriate effect. As a person sowed, Indians thought, so that individual would reap.

The third religious path was the way of knowledge. Here, as in occult and metaphysical movements, knowledge meant more than information, argument, and rational thought. Rather, it was insight into the basic meaning of life, a total realization in mind, heart, and body of the universal being of Brahman. Called *jnana*, this knowledge came through serious cultivation of inner states of mind. Religious masters, known as gurus, gave to others various techniques for physical and mental control which were aimed to lead them into a higher state of awareness. Often there were exercises for breath and body control, calming people so that there could be the necessary interior quiet. Then there would be various methods of meditation, all of them intended to open the way toward a time of intense spiritual realization of oneness. In other words, the path of knowledge led to mystical experience. Its discipline formed a pattern for living that attempted to bring a religious seeker into an altered state of consciousness. Yet, whether that goal was reached or not, the discipline of physical and mental practice directed a person in daily life, providing a religious system that was deeply satisfying.

Hinduism in America

When Vedanta came to the United States at the end of the nineteenth century, it was bringing India's most widespread form of monistic religious philosophy to Americans. Swami Vivekananda, India's apostle to the West, had been drawn to the great mystic and religious leader Ramakrishna (1836–1886), who combined many aspects of Hindu tradition in his teaching and practice. After the death of Ramakrishna, Vivekananda shaped his movement into an international witness to Hinduism, committed to the mystical ideal of Ramakrishna but also to action in the world. Beginning in 1896 with the Vedanta Society he founded in New York, Vivekananda presented Hinduism to Americans in the form that they were most likely to understand.

The way of knowledge, or *jnana*, became largely the way of intellectual understanding, as typically, Vedanta Societies presented lectures on Vedanta philosophy and offered sessions devoted to the classics of Indian religious literature. *Jnana* gave the society its basic and overwhelming appeal in the United States. Still, the way of action, or *karma*, was important to the movement both in India and in America. In the old country, Vedanta worked as the Ramakrishna

Order to relieve the physical poverty of many of India's people. In America, where the swami had diagnosed spiritual poverty, Vedanta was the Ramakrishna Mission teaching people how to live. The way of devotion, or *bhakti*, while less important, became the "church" devotionalism that accompanied Vedanta in its temple meetings. More than any other Hindu movement in America, Vedanta conformed to Christian customs, developing a religious service that included hymn and scripture, prayer and sermonic address. *Bhakti* was also present in private shrines that members of the society kept in their homes, offering some form of *puja* on a daily basis.

Vedanta appealed to upper- and middle-class Americans who had become acquainted with the culture of India and had developed an enthusiasm for Eastern spirituality. Teaching that the real nature of people was divine and that it was each person's duty to develop the Godhead within, Vedanta offered insights which blended with Liberal Protestant teachings about the immanence of God and the goodness of human nature. Moreover, with its understanding that truth was universal, it agreed with the mood of many Americans seeking to find a common center beneath the pluralism of sects and denominations. It was significant that Aldous Huxley, the teacher of the "perennial philosophy," was a member of the Vedanta Society.

Vedanta continued into the twentieth century, but the real popularity of Hinduism lay with newer movements that stressed yoga or the way of *jnana*. In a more diffused form, the *karma* teaching also influenced Americans. Through the non-caste-oriented interpretation of Mohandas K. Gandhi (1869–1948), the political and spiritual leader of India during its struggle with Great Britain, the path of *karma* inspired the nonviolent resistance of blacks in the American civil-rights movement. Here *karma* became that form of social action demanded by justice and right and performed regardless of personal consequences. At the same time, Indian *bhakti* movements made little headway, with the exception of the Hare Krishna movement to be discussed later. Protestant evangelism, Catholic devotionalism, the late twentieth-century charismatic movement in both Protestant and Catholic circles, even Jewish forms of devotionalism based on Hasidism—all offered chances for emotional fervor in religious expression. So the needs served by *bhakti* were largely being met by Western religious forms. They were also being met—as we will see later in the chapter—by a form of Buddhism called Nichiren Shoshu and—as Part Two will discuss—by other nontraditional enthusiasms.

The man who introduced yoga to the United States was Paramahansa Yogananda. Like Vivekananda, he had come to attend a religious meeting. After taking part in the International Congress of Religious Liberals held by the Unitarians in Boston in 1920, Yogananda remained in America for the next thirty years. More than Vivekananda, he employed American techniques of gaining publicity to spread his message, beginning a practice that later Hindu gurus on mission to America would also use.

The word *yoga* means union and the discipline that brings union. Hence, yoga means teaching and practice that hopes to bring the unification of a person's inner being and the realization by that person of the basic oneness of all things in

Brahman. In the Self-Realization Fellowship which he founded, Yogananda offered Americans a religious philosophy based on the writings of the ancient Indian spiritual master Patanjali (2d cent. A.D.?). With this background, a self-realization meant an experiential union with the divine spark within and a mystical encounter in oneness with the All-Power in the universe. In a practical sense, the pursuit of self-realization led to a life of peace and tranquillity in which health and success came naturally.

The basic principles of yoga began with the body. Through a series of simple physical exercises, called *hatha yoga*, a person stretched and relaxed away the tensions that were obstacles to spiritual peace and happiness. By learning to remain for some time in various prescribed physical postures, called *asanas*, the individual shifted energy from one part of the body to another, opening spiritual centers to receive the divine energy. Through control of the breathing, called *pranayama*, again the quiet was induced that could lead to release into a state of bliss. But this bliss was a state of mind, and the point of yoga was always a mental liberation from the material world. So meditation techniques were central to yoga. A person's thoughts must be calmed, and the mind must learn to be aware without thinking anything. In order to allow this to happen, a person might fix inwardly on a sacred sound, called a *mantra*, or focus consciously on a point within the body such as the point between the eyes or below the abdomen. The aim was to reach a state of concentration that was uninterrupted. Then the body with its endless claims would fall away, and a person would realize the eternal oneness.

Yogananda spread the ancient teaching, adding to it some modifications of his own. He stressed for Americans the scientific precision of yogic philosophy and technique, and he succeeded in drawing numbers of people to his movement. By the sixties, there were some 200,000 people in the Self-Realization Fellowship, and by the early seventies, the movement had forty-four centers in the United States. Like Vedanta, a Sunday "church" service accommodated the Hindu message to the dominant Christian religious practice of this country, but more than Vedanta, the Self-Realization Fellowship pointed in the direction of the individual religious experience that would become the pattern in the later twentieth century.

In the sixties and seventies, yoga groups and teachers were a common feature of the American cultural landscape. Church organizations and community centers sponsored short courses in yoga techniques, while television programs enabled people to learn yoga in the privacy of their own homes. Drug stores and newsstands blossomed with paperback books describing various yogic postures and breaths. Yoga became a topic of conversation among groups as diverse as college students, housewives, and working people. In this atmosphere of widely diffused interest in hatha yoga, the appeal of meditation likewise grew. Again, popular books and pamphlets appeared to give instruction, while many yoga teachers explained to their students techniques for meditation and gave them opportunities to practice it. But the seed which Vivekananda and, even more, Yogananda planted was reaped during this time especially by the Transcendental Meditation Program led by the Maharishi Mahesh Yogi (b. 1911).

This popular movement of the sixties and the seventies has followed the pattern of the Self-Realization Fellowship in a number of ways. The Maharishi, who introduced his teaching to the West in 1959, capitalized on publicity even more than Yogananda had done. Like Yogananda, too, he underlined the scientific aspects of his teaching, providing data on how Transcendental Meditation (TM) lowered blood pressure, relieved stress, increased intelligence, and even reduced crime in areas in which a significant proportion of the people were meditating. And finally, like Yogananda, his teaching was a popularized form of Vedanta religious philosophy, aimed to appeal to ordinary folk and not just to an intellectual elite.

Transcendental Meditation was based squarely on the teachings of the Indian spiritual books, the Upanishads, as interpreted by the Vedanta school of Shankara (788–820). But it stressed that it was a simple and natural technique that anyone could practice with striking results. With its background of Hindu openness to many Gods, it felt at home with other religions and attracted many adherents who were also members of various other organized religious groups. In fact, in its public presentations frequently it denied that it was a religion at all. With pragmatic earnestness, the International Meditation Society—its official name—was certain that if only people would begin the *practice* of meditation, whatever theory was necessary would take care of itself. So meditators learned how to quiet themselves and meditate for fifteen or twenty minutes twice a day, using a mantra that had been given to each during a personal initiation ceremony. Those who began the practice—nearly a million by 1979—generally insisted that the Maharishi had been right. Their lives had been greatly enriched by the simple procedure they had learned.

If the sixties and seventies brought new yogic movements such as Transcendental Meditation to Americans, they also brought at least one prominent example of *bhakti*. The International Society for Krishna Consciousness became familiar at many airports where its members, sometimes dressed in colorful pink and yellow robes, offered flowers and solicited donations. Founded in 1965 by A. C. Bhaktivedanta Swami Prabhupada (1896–1977), Krishna Consciousness was based on the teachings of a dualistic sixteenth-century sect established by Chaitanya Mahaprabhu (1486–1533). At the center of the old and new devotional movements was Lord Krishna, a Hindu deity and supreme personal God for his followers. Rejecting the traditional polytheism of popular Hinduism, members of the Chaitanya sect and the Hare Krishna movement were Krishna monotheists. In an expression of great immediacy, they hailed Chaitanya Mahaprabhu as a new incarnation of Krishna, so that God was very near.

Like any intense religious movement, Krishna Consciousness emphasized the boundaries that separated its members from the rest of the world. It demanded a total surrender to Lord Krishna, a surrender made visible in the monastic style of life led by members. Rising before 4:00 A.M. and eating vegetarian food, they spent their days in work and in prayer, as they danced and repeated again and again the full "Hare Krishna" chant. The vibrations of the chant, they claimed, brought an experience of transcendental consciousness. Celibacy was the preferred lifestyle, and marriage occurred only under the direction of the spiritual master, with sexual intercourse exclusively for the production of children. While in recent years members of the society have begun to modify the strictness of some of these practices, community has continued to be intense and meaningful. The discipline of a rigorous life has increased the enthusiasm of Krishna Consciousness people. Suspected and sometimes harassed like members of nineteenth-century new religions, they have given evidence of their devotion to Lord Krishna in their dedication.

FARTHER EAST: BUDDHISM

Krishna Consciousness and some forms of meditation stressed extraordinary aspects of religion, but the general tenor of Hinduism had supported the framework of daily life as ordinary religion. While this was more true in its native India than in the United States, even in this country, the discreet Hinduism of the Vedanta Societies and the *karma* ideal of dedication to one's role in life led to involvement in the everyday world. The popularization of yoga in hatha exercise programs and in Transcendental Meditation meant that the "otherness" of Hinduism blended with considerable ease in the pluralism of American culture. In the case of Buddhism the pattern to some extent was similar. However, Buddhism, perhaps more than Hinduism, emphasized its opportunities for the practice of extraordinary religion in America.

Buddhism first came to this country with the Chinese and especially the Japanese immigrants of the late nineteenth century. Predominantly, the form of Buddhism was Jodo Shinshu, a branch of Pure Land Buddhism that flourished in the regions from which the immigrants came. In America Jodo Shinshu became the preferred Buddhism of Japanese-Americans, giving them a way of life which fused ordinary with extraordinary religion. However, the late nineteenth century saw a second introduction of Buddhism to America. This was the Buddhism that appeared at the World's Parliament of Religions and particularly the Buddhism of the Japanese Zen master, Soyen Shaku (1859–1919). There were some Japanese Zen immigrants, of course. But addressed to mainstream Americans, Zen thrived among converts, giving them a way to attain the extraordinary religious experience of enlightenment.

In general, while the first and immigrant form of Buddhism led to a "church" religion, the second, mostly convert form led to meditation. A third form, which enjoyed a spurt of growth in the sixties, was Nichiren Shoshu. This was a missionary type of Japanese Buddhism that sought to evangelize and win people to its message. Popular among both Japanese-Americans and mainstream converts, it became the most prevalent kind of Buddhism in the United States. If we compare these forms of Buddhism to the kinds of Hinduism introduced in America, there are parallels. In both a predominantly "church" form of the religion, supporting action in the world (one's *karma*), was followed by a religion stressing meditation (the way of *jnana*) and, in turn, a mostly enthusiastic and evangelical version (the way of *bhakti*). Later we will look more closely at all three.

Chapter 8

The Religion of Buddhism

Before we can understand the American paths of Buddhism more completely, however, we need to understand some basic themes in the religion of Buddhism. Its founder, Siddhartha Gautama (563?–483? B.C.), was not so much a prophet as an example of how to live. Called the Buddha, which means the "enlightened" or "awakened" one, he had left a prosperous life as a member of the warrior (ruling) caste of India to find an answer to the problem of suffering and death. Tradition has it that he sought help from various spiritual masters without success, all the while practicing great austerities and becoming physically weak. Finally, he ended this life of rigorous asceticism and began to meditate for himself. It was then that one night, sitting under a bo tree, he broke through to enlightenment. From that time, he spent his days preaching and teaching others how they, too, might come to this state.

Therefore, from the very first the religion of Buddhism stressed religious wisdom. Like the occult and metaphysical traditions in America and like some forms of Hinduism, it taught the importance of spiritual insight, an enlightenment gained not from reading books and studying arguments but through an emptying of the mind's ordinary contents so that light could enter in. The intellectual content of enlightenment was seemingly simple—yet profound. It was the Four Noble Truths taught by the Buddha. Human suffering had a cause; the cause of suffering was desire for what was not in hand; there was a way to end suffering; and the way to end it was to end desire, living in nonattachment to any people, places, or things. But the Four Noble Truths had to merge into the one moment of enlightenment when *nirvana*—or unconditioned Reality—became a religious experience of great intensity. Like Hinduism, the message that the Buddha brought was empirical.

Because the Buddhist teaching was empirical and practical, the Buddha gave his followers the Noble Eightfold Path. By walking this road, they might conduct themselves toward enlightenment. Named the Middle Path, it was a way of balance avoiding the extremes of asceticism and self-indulgence as well as all one-sided views and acts. Instead, the Eightfold Path called on Buddhists to practice right views and intentions, leading to right speech, action, livelihood, and effort, and ultimately right mindfulness and concentration. Thus, the Eightfold Path traced the pattern of a spiral: it began in the mind, at the level of ordinary knowledge, moved from mind to body through forms of speech and action, and then returned to the mind, this time at the higher level of meditation. It was the pattern of someone who wanted to break through the ordinary dimensions of life into the extraordinary. Thus, it was significant that the Buddha's closest followers from the beginning lived together in a religious order, or community. Buddhist teaching lessened the religious significance of the caste system, urging people to leave their ordinary way of life in pursuit of an extraordinary religious goal.

From the first, this radical community of monks and nuns was joined by lay followers of the Buddha, who continued to occupy their regular stations in life. And gradually Buddhism became a religion that supported the ordinary culture of India. Yet the appeal of the extraordinary world did not leave

Buddhism, and it became the great missionary religion of Asia, spreading from India to China and Japan as well as to all of Southeast Asia. Furthermore, as the Buddhist community pondered the meaning of the Buddha's message, different understandings of the teaching arose and different forms of Buddhism resulted.

By the third century B.C., two great schools of Buddhist interpretation had developed. Theravada, which became the Buddhism of Southeast Asia, stressed that it carried on the original teaching of the Buddha. Here the emphasis was on the individual, whose goal was to become a solitary spiritual hero, one who would turn within and help himself or herself to quench desire completely. In this form of Buddhism, the historical Buddha was revered as an example of what each human being might achieve, and he was reverenced because of the teaching he had brought. But in the strict teachings of the elite, Buddha was always human, never divine. Moreover, for them Theravada Buddhism was atheistic—there was no God to praise or blame an individual, no God to save or condemn a person. Everything led back to an experience of the enlightened bliss of pure nonattachment in nirvana.

The second school of Buddhism, Mahayana, became the Buddhism of China and Japan. As the larger of the two schools, Mahayana placed strong stress on the community. Instead of the solitary monk seeking personal enlightenment, its hero was the *bodhisattva*, a figure who, on the verge of experiencing nirvana, out of compassion for human beings and in order to serve them, postponed the time indefinitely. In this understanding, the compassion of Siddartha Gautama, the Buddha, was especially remembered, and his compassion was seen as an example to all. Meanwhile, his Buddhahood was a quality which others, too, could possess. Rather than emphasizing the one historical Buddha, the Mahayana school found Buddhas wherever persons had achieved the experience of enlightenment.

Gradually, a doctrine of Buddha bodies moved Mahayana toward an elaborate theology of the meaning of Buddhahood. According to the doctrine, there were three expressions of the Buddha. The first was the "body of appearance," or the physical body of the Buddha. The second was the "body of bliss" which appeared surrounded by light, the reward that the Buddha gained for his spiritual practice and the reward, too, of bodhisattvas who saw the Buddha. The third was the "body of essence," the true being of the Buddha as an absolute beyond space and time. In the body of essence and to some extent in the body of bliss, the Buddha had become in certain ways like God. Since it was theoretically possible in Mahayana for anybody to become a Buddha, instead of the atheism of Theravada, Mahayana gave the world a polytheism of many Buddha-Gods.

In time, a third school of Buddhism joined Theravada and Mahayana. From the third or fourth century A.D., Vajrayana Buddhism grew from Buddhist, Hindu, and folk religious roots to become the Buddhism, most notably, of Tibet. This form of Buddhism understood the many Buddhas of Mahayana as visualizations of the passions within each human being. In an intense process of symbolic manipulation, Vajrayana Buddhists cultivated their ability to transform these inner forces into visible and audible beings. The point of this procedure was to come to terms with each of these forces so that all would merge into a oneness at the center of the self. In other words, Vajrayana sought the mystical goal of union with the Godhead within. By dramatizing the inner process in a series of secret initiations and magical techniques, Vajrayana Buddhists were trying to make the spiritual concrete. And by making the spiritual concrete, they hoped to achieve practical control over it.

Each of the three major forms of Buddhism was expressed in many differing sects and schools of interpretation. As new spiritual leaders arose, it was inevitable that they should see aspects of Buddhist teaching that others had missed and that they should come to value one or another portion of Buddhist scripture over the rest. Thus, many Buddhist movements focused on a specific Buddhist sutra, or writing, making that the center of their devotions and lives. As we examine some of the forms of Buddhism in America, we will look at a few of the Buddhist sects in their teaching and practice.

Buddhism in America

As in the case of Hinduism, there had been a long period of preparation in American culture for the arrival of Buddhism. The Transcendentalists had turned to the East as a source of wisdom. More directly, Henry Olcott of the Theosophical Society had aided the cause of Buddhism both overseas and in this country, writing a book to discuss the religion for Westerners. His spiritual associate, Madame Blavatsky, had included Buddhist teaching in her occult works, and her Mahatmas were Tibetans familiar with the practices of Vajrayana Buddhism.

As "church," meditation, and evangelical Buddhism came to the United States, adherents ranged from ordinary ethnic followers, who accepted the religion as their religious birthright, to an elite of purists, both Japanese and mainstream Americans, who sought a Buddhism of the ancient texts. A third group, mostly Americans, became an eclectic following, blending Buddhism with other religious elements to form a religion of enthusiasm.

"Church" Buddhism came first to Hawaii in 1889 and to California a decade later. The carriers were Jodo Shinshu missionaries of the Nishi Hongwanji movement, one of the 170 or so sects of Buddhism that existed in Japan. A branch of Pure Land Buddhism, Jodo Shinshu, like all Mahayana Buddhism of the Pure Land type, taught faith in a Buddha being called Amida Buddha. At the time when he had become a Buddha, Amida had established the Western Kingdom, called the Pure Land, in fulfillment of his previous bodhisattva vows. Now it was possible for people, through trust in Amida and devotion to him, to enter the Pure Land after death and there experience enlightenment. It was not necessary to be sinless or to have developed great meditation techniques. All that one needed to do was to call on Amida with gratitude in the formula, "Hail to Amida Buddha." Thus, Pure Land Buddhism put the "other-power" of Amida in place of the "self-power" that Theravada and all the meditation forms of Buddhism taught. Of all the forms of Buddhism, it probably most resembled Christianity with its God of compassion who, through faith in his Son Jesus, brought human beings to an eternal life in paradise.

For this reason, of the various Japanese sects of Buddhism, Pure Land seemed most likely to accommodate itself to American culture. Its history in the

United States showed how much it did so. From 1899 to 1944, it was largely organized by the Nishi Hongwanji sect as the North American Buddhist Mission, and after that date it became the Buddhist Churches of America. Its membership grew until, in the seventies, probably 100,000 people were affiliated in some way, and it had become the second largest Buddhist group in the United States.

From the first, language presented a difficulty for Buddhism in America. Just as long ago Indian missionaries had struggled to translate Indian Buddhist ideas and descriptions into conversational Chinese, so Japanese Buddhist missionaries in America worked to find equivalents in the English tongue for their Buddhist terms. There were no churches of Buddhism in Japan, and community worship did not take place in a Buddhist shrine except on special occasions. Thus, to use the term *church* when speaking about Buddhism was a concession to American ears. Similarly, Buddhist churches in America began to call their overseer a "bishop," another concession to American Christianity. There were adaptations in worship as well, as Buddhist churches began Sunday services and Sunday schools. Although some worried that these changes might compromise the character of Buddhism, most accepted them as the inevitable result of Americanization. If Japanese-Americans were to retain some meaningful relationship to their religious and cultural past in the American environment, they must find a practice for themselves and their children that conformed with American customs. The Buddhist Churches of America, most felt, were the necessary compromise. They enabled Japanese-Americans to unite ordinary and extraordinary religion in a distinctive Japanese-American way of life.

The second form of Buddhism in America, stressing meditation, by the seventies was represented most notably in Japanese Zen and Tibetan varieties. Zen had originated in China as Ch'an Buddhism in the fifth and sixth centuries A.D. From there it had been imported to Japan in the late twelfth and early thirteenth centuries where, with Ch'an translated as "Zen," it flourished as a combination of Mahayana religious philosophy and Theravada meditation techniques. Thus, the goal of Zen was to bring a person to enlightenment through the practice of meditation. Furthermore, as in China, from the early history of Japanese Zen there had been two schools which advocated different methods of meditation and saw different processes at work in gaining enlightenment. One school, Rinzai Zen, taught that enlightenment was a sudden event, triggered by unusual circumstances that jolted a person into a realization of the nature of things. Hence, its practice centered on meditation using *koans*, riddles or verbal puzzles meant to baffle the ordinary working mind—as, for example, in the koan-style question, What is the sound of one hand clapping? The theory was that by pondering a koan, unanswerable by normal reasoning, the mind's hold would be broken and enlightenment would come. The other school, Soto Zen, taught that enlightenment was gradual. Its practice centered on "just sitting," meditation in which the mind was quieted and emptied of all thought so that enlightenment might grow.

Soyen Shaku had introduced Rinzai Zen at the World's Parliament of Religions. But it was his disciple, Daisetz Teitaro Suzuki (1870–1966) who, more than any other person, spread Rinzai Zen in America. From 1897 to 1909, Suzuki worked as an editor for the Open Court Publishing Company in La Salle, Illinois.

After returning to Japan, he wrote prolifically in English about Buddhism, and his many books were widely read in this country. When he came back to the United States in the fifties, he spoke frequently at universities, including one series of lectures at Columbia. Suzuki aided the communication of Zen to non-Oriental Americans by stressing themes that agreed with the contemporary Western philosophy of existentialism. At the same time, he tended to overlook the discipline and ritual attached to the Zen monastic tradition and to disregard its social setting in Japan.

In the late fifties, a group of San Francisco artists and writers that included Allen Ginsberg (b. 1926), Jack Kerouac (1922-1969), and, with qualifications, Alan Watts (1915-1973) and Gary Snyder (b. 1930) combined the interpretations of Suzuki with other elements to form an eclectic "Beat Zen." As a group, they drew on the side of Rinzai teaching in which the suddenness of enlightenment became a celebration of spontaneity and emotional freedom. So Beat Zen pursued liberation at the expense of the rigorous and ascetic meditation practices that were also part of the Rinzai Zen tradition.

However, both Alan Watts and Gary Snyder went further. Watts, with his many books, was a great popularizer of Zen, and he used Western scientific and psychological categories in order to understand it. In Romantic style, he presented Zen to the average American as a new way of life, emphasizing its "otherness," its revolution—by Western standards—in inner awareness. Snyder moved beyond the Romanticism of Watts to probe the meaning of Zen with greater rigor. With a background in anthropology and literature and an extensive knowledge of American Indian religions and ecological concerns, he wrote poetry that expressed themes of interdependence among all living creatures. But he was not content to appreciate Zen simply from the vantage point of this background. He went to Japan to study Zen, learning the language in order to do so and committing himself to a period of intensive monastic training. More than the others, Snyder brought the two sides of Zen—its meditative discipline and its spontaneity—together.

Meanwhile, the more formal and traditional practice of Zen grew with the introduction of Zen centers in California and New York by Sokatsu Shaku Roshi (1869-1954). Soto Zen also took up residence in the country when Shunryu Suzuki (1904-1971) established the San Francisco Zen Center in 1962, the largest of the American Zen centers. From here and other places, monasteries were organized where people might spend either short or extended interludes away from society. Finally, in the United States, the Rinzai and Soto lineages were united in a third form of Zen, spread especially by Philip Kapleau's book, *The Three Pillars of Zen* (1965). Kapleau (b. 1912) had visited Japan as a reporter in 1946 and over a decade later studied there. In 1966 he opened the Zen Meditation Center in Rochester, New York, where he applied the insights of his book as a teacher. Balancing the emphasis of Suzuki and Watts, Kapleau underlined the importance of the traditional practice of *zazen*, sitting meditation, as well as the relationship between master and student. Even further, at his Zen center, he worked to make Zen authentically American, using the English language, adapting rituals, and wearing Western clothes during meditation.

Most American Zen adherents were young middle-class people, well educated and white. They were converts from mainstream America, and that fact impressed itself on the character of Zen. It became in America an extraordinary religion, in which people sought to step beyond the boundaries of their time and culture in the pursuit of the transcendent. Many of the same things could be said about Tibetan Buddhism in America. Brought to the United States by Buddhist monks fleeing after the Chinese Communist take-over of Tibet, it became a felt presence here after 1965. Through Tibetans on university faculties and through the establishment of meditation centers, knowledge of Tibetan Buddhism spread. The profundity of its teachings and the heavy cloak of symbolism that surrounded them did not act as obstacles. Rather, Tibetan Buddhist masters, called *rinpoches*, found a language to express the ancient Buddhist teaching in humanistic psychology. They were able to communicate with mainstream Americans by showing the continuities between Tibetan Vajrayana thought and practice and modern American understandings. Especially under Tarthang Tulku in Berkeley, California, and Chogyam Trungpa in Boulder, Colorado, Tibetan Buddhism provided Americans with another type of Buddhism stressing meditation.

Finally, evangelical Buddhism came to America, largely in the form of Nichiren Shoshu. Its membership grew rapidly after its first appearance in America in 1960. While no separate figures are available for the United States, reports were made of at times a thousand converts a month, and by 1974 the combined membership in North and South America had risen to 230,000. Although in recent years it has begun to decline, Nichiren Shoshu is still the largest Buddhist movement in the United States.

Who were the people who turned to this form of Buddhism, and what was it that attracted so many to it? In the beginning most adherents in the United States had come from Japanese ancestry. The few mainstream Americans who joined tended to be men who had married Japanese women, and membership was overwhelmingly middle class, with many of the people involved in small businesses. Yet by 1967, almost all (95 percent) of the new converts were non-Oriental, while in the East and the Midwest, most adherents to Nichiren Shoshu had no connections with Japan. They were younger, less well established, and more diverse than the Japanese-American Buddhists. Beyond that, more than any other Buddhist group, Nichiren Shoshu drew Latins and blacks as well as whites. More than any other Buddhist group, too, it drew working-class as well as college-educated converts.

The religion which these people affirmed had roots in thirteenth-century Japan. There, a monk named Nichiren (1222–1282) was disturbed by the competing claims of the Japanese Buddhist sects, and so he began to preach the centrality of a particular Buddhist holy book, the Lotus Sutra of the Mystical Law. He told people that, instead of chanting "Hail to Amida Buddha," they should chant praise to the Lotus Sutra, which explained the fundamental laws of nature. Japan had gone astray by turning to Amida and to other forms of Buddhism. By turning to the Lotus Sutra, people would find their own Buddha-nature within and attain happiness, prosperity, and peace.

Aggressive from the first in its proclamation of this message, in twentieth-century Japan the Nichiren movement was reborn in the Soka Gakkai organization, a group of lay people who were convinced that they should use "forceful persuasion" to convert the world. Hence, Nichiren Shoshu came to the United States as a missionary movement—like many other Eastern groups but perhaps more intense. And it appealed because of its simplicity. Although there was a strong philosophical basis for its teaching, it emphasized the practice of the chant *"Nam Myoho Renge Kyo"* ("Hail to the Lotus Sutra"), reverence toward a Gohonzon altarpiece inscribed to recall the Lotus Sutra, and a pilgrimage, if possible, to the headquarters of Nichiren Shoshu in Japan. Each of these provided ways for individuals to act out their search for a center—through sound, through sight, through travel. Each of these had power to release people from a sense of confusion and to help to give them a secure identity. Indeed, as we will see in Part Two, the power behind Nichiren Shoshu had much to do with the energies released by all forms of evangelism. Here East met West in their mutual agreement that the proclamation of a sure and simple gospel would enable people, by finding a center outside themselves, ultimately to find the center within.

EAST IS WEST: SYNCRETISTIC RELIGIONS

Increasingly in the late twentieth century, syncretism—the mixture of various elements to form a new religion—became a feature of American life. With religious options as available as the food on a supermarket shelf, it seemed inevitable that people would begin to bring together religious tendencies from various cultures. The result was a proliferation of small religious movements that arose, enjoyed their day, sometimes grew stronger, and sometimes all but vanished. For many, if not most, there was a charismatic leader who combined the magical qualities of a shaman with the saving qualities of a messiah. For many, there was a sense that the activity of the particular religious group was bringing in the new age—the millennium of Christianity or the Aquarian age of astrology and occultism. Intense and enthusiastic, these groups saw a great simplicity in the nature of things. It was present in the mysticism that accompanied them when they saw all things as one thing—whether the being of a universal divine force or the total claims of their religious organization. It was present in their gospels of effective, positive action through the use of practical techniques to save themselves and the world. Again and again, it was present in the way these groups brought together East and West to form one religious universe.

A good example of religious syncretism in the seventies was the Healthy-Happy-Holy Organization (usually known as the 3HO). Founded in the United States in 1969 by the Indian Yogi Bhajan (Harbhajan Singh; b. 1929), under his charismatic leadership it combined forms of Indian yoga with the Sikh religion. This tradition arose in northern India when Nanak (1469–1539) tried to reconcile Muslim and Hindu teachings. Nanak spoke of one God in all religions, a God who could be realized through meditative practices. In America the new religion of the 3HO drew on this multiple background, blending it with a millennial expectation of the Aquarian age and an intense American patriotism. Members of the organization led a rigorous communal life, rising at 4:00 A.M., practicing demanding physical forms of yoga, and following a vegetarian diet (with dairy products but not eggs). The discipline of silence underlined the asceticism of community life, while various classes provided knowledge of subjects that harmonized with the 3HO world view. After dinner each evening a session of religious singing using guitars and a folk-rock style closed the day. The movement aimed to build a nation, to create a new society in America under God. While conceived in visionary terms rather than in plans for direct political action, the goal of building a nation combined patriotism with a leftist critique of the United States. The 3HO brought together Eastern and Western elements to respond to the present age with a new answer.

Probably the most significant religious aspect of the various syncretistic movements was the power that they captured and released to their members. In the history of religions power has always been ethically neutral—a spiritual "live wire" capable of energizing people in good or evil ways. In other words, such power has had the ability to harm as well as to help, and it has always been part of the job of religious specialists to protect people from the *dangers* of religion. Hence, it is not surprising that sometimes the power unleashed by the cults turned in the wrong direction, and people were hurt by them. Still, the same power used wisely might have led to greater good.

The presence of syncretistic religions in America, finally, must lead us back to the East and the model of religious "otherness" which it gave to the West. We have seen that both through Eastern peoples practicing their traditional religions in America and through converts who embraced them here as "new," the East had taught the West the strangeness of religion. On the other hand, because spiritually the West was seeking something "other," in some sense, the East was at home in the United States.

This relationship between East and West highlights the issue of community in America. Among those who inherited Eastern religions, there was natural community and a natural boundary separating each group from other Americans. In the cases of Greek and Russian Orthodox peoples, of Arab Muslims, and of Japanese Buddhists, we saw such communities defining reality for their people and providing for them a seamless robe of ordinary and extraordinary religion. In the case of converts, there was, instead, a cultivation of instant community with strangers. Converts made self-conscious and deliberate attempts to create a home through their association with one another. But like those who joined occult and metaphysical movements, to whom these converts were related, their homesteads were ultimately in the mind. A great part of the attraction of Hindu, Buddhist, and syncretistic forms of religion was their overall emphasis on the importance of religious knowledge and the value of practice in changing a person's mind. Enlightenment, meditation, and inner peace were all mental states. They led to a community of the parts of the person in one, holistic sense of self and, likewise, a community with the divine power of the universe. Even in American *bhakti*, the focus was on ecstatic states and internal transformations through devotion to God(s). In the process these religions tended to minimize the importance of the human community with its common traditions and history.

In the case of converts, too, the quest for religion was the quest for the

217

extraordinary. We have seen how important religious intensity was for these converts: it was essential to the experience of conversion. More than that, the quest for a separate extraordinary religion and the preference for intensity had long roots in American soil. We have only touched on the common themes that run through American religious history in Part One, but in Part Two we will pay more attention to them. Here, though, we need to observe that the bad press given to some of the cult movements has obscured the continuities between converts to Eastern and syncretistic religions and other Americans. The counter culture of the late twentieth century was not counter to culture at all but an expression of one side of American life. Our study of occult and metaphysical movements, especially, has made this apparent, and our later study of revivalism will underline the connection.

In this context, the charge that converts to Eastern and syncretistic religions have been "brainwashed" ignores the complexity of things. To be part of any culture is to be told the meaning of the world, to be a member of a particular language and value group. No child being born into a society has the choice of accepting or rejecting the language, the values, and the meanings that culture assigns to things. Hence, if any one group is brainwashed, then we all are. To think otherwise is to assume that the Gods of the converts to Eastern and syncretistic religions are not real, while our Gods are. Such a charge in the end damages the spiritual and human significance of *every* religion.

IN OVERVIEW

The end of the nineteenth century brought the growing visibility of Eastern religions in the United States. As ethnic religions that came with Eastern peoples, these religions united the ordinary and the extraordinary in traditional folkways. As the religions of American converts, they gave the extraordinary to Westerners who were seeking "otherness." Both in ethnic and conversional forms, Eastern religions strengthened the boundaries separating their adherents from mainstream America.

From Nearer East came the religion of Eastern Orthodoxy, a major branch of Christianity and the fourth major faith in the United States. Traditionally organized in self-governing local churches, the Orthodox strived for right belief and right worship, giving expression to both in their iconic theology and mystical spirituality. From the Middle East came Islam with Arab Muslims and other immigrants as well as converts from, especially, the black community. Following the austere monotheism of Muhammad, Muslims inherited a program of religious action in the Five Pillars of their faith. Meanwhile, the new religion of Baha'i, an outgrowth of Persian Islamic culture, made its presence felt in the United States.

From Farther East came Hinduism and Buddhism in both traditional and newer variants. Both religions offered followers spiritual paths through knowledge (yoga, meditation), through "churches" supporting action in the world, and through devotion. Movements related to Hinduism included Vedanta Societies, the Self-Realization Fellowship, the Transcendental Meditation

Program, the International Society for Krishna Consciousness, and many more. Buddhist presence was felt in organizations like the Buddhist Churches of America, in various forms of Japanese Zen and Tibetan Buddhism, in Nichiren Shoshu, and in other movements as well. Finally, syncretistic religions, such as the Healthy-Happy-Holy Organization, followed charismatic leaders and mystical techniques with a sense of an impending new age. Ministering to the needs of ethnic strangers in America, Eastern religions—like the occult and metaphysical movements—also provided American converts with mental homesteads to replace the homes and communities often missing in their ordinary lives.

We can learn from the religions of the Nearer, Middle, and Farther East in the late twentieth century. They enable us to see more clearly how many the many really are. When we view the religions of America in their light, the mainstream seems to dissolve into the thousands of smaller currents and streams which feed it. If Easterners, who were foreigners, were more at home in America than they knew, this was because "otherness" was a common feature of life in the United States.

This statement is only underlined by the fact that in America geography itself marked off areas that were "other." A different landscape meant, for many, a different regional culture and a different regional religion. Indeed, Easterners had many friends in their "otherness"—some of them in the mountain hollows of Southern Appalachia where, as we will see in the next chapter, there was a flourishing regional religion.

SUGGESTIONS FOR FURTHER READING: EASTERN PEOPLES AND EASTERN RELIGIONS

Bespuda, Anastasia. *Guide to Orthodox America.* Tuckahoe, NY: St. Vladimir's Seminary Press, 1965.

Bogolepov, Alexander A. *Toward an American Orthodox Church.* New York: Morehouse-Barlow, 1963.

Christopher, John B. *The Islamic Tradition.* New York: Harper & Row, 1972.

Elkholy, Abdo A. *The Arab Moslems in the United States.* New Haven: College & University Press, 1966.

Ellwood, Robert S., Jr. *The Eagle and the Rising Sun: Americans and the New Religions of Japan.* Philadelphia: Westminster Press, 1974.

———. *Religious and Spiritual Groups in Modern America.* Englewood Cliffs, NJ: Prentice-Hall, 1973.

Ferraby, John. *All Things Made New: A Comprehensive Outline of the Baha'i Faith.* Rev. ed. London: Baha'i Publishing Trust, 1975.

Hopkins, Thomas J. *The Hindu Religious Tradition.* Belmont, CA: Dickenson Publishing, 1971.

Kashima, Tetsuden. *Buddhism in America: The Social Organization of an Ethnic Religious Institution.* Westport, CT: Greenwood Press, 1977.

Layman, Emma McCloy. *Buddhism in America.* Chicago: Nelson-Hall, 1976.

Needleman, Jacob. *The New Religions.* Rev. ed. New York: Simon & Schuster, Pocket Books, 1972.

Prebish, Charles S. *American Buddhism.* North Scituate, MA: Duxbury Press, 1979.

Robinson, Richard H. *The Buddhist Religion.* Belmont, CA: Dickenson Publishing, 1970.

Ware, Timothy. *The Orthodox Church.* Rev. ed. New York: Penguin Books, 1976.

CHAPTER 9

Regional Religion: A Case Study of
Tradition in Southern Appalachia

Inland from the Atlantic Ocean a mountain range runs in a vast belt from Newfoundland to Alabama. The southern part of the chain forms a discrete area containing all of the present state of West Virginia, eastern Kentucky and Tennessee, northeastern Alabama, western Maryland, Virginia, North and South Carolina, and northern Georgia. Here geography scorns the fiction of state boundaries, and the region stands in contrast to the lowlands to either side. Southern Appalachia, as it is called, looks toward the East from its sharply rising Blue Ridge chain, its steep escarpment even now a challenge to hardy motorists on twisting mountain roads. Beyond the Blue Ridge is the central district of the Great Valley, extending from north to south with its rich and fertile farmland. Then to the west stands the more horizontal mountain area called the Cumberland Plateau.

In ages past the Indians, especially the Cherokee, had used these lands as hunting grounds, and the difficulty of entering the region from the East insured that European immigrants for many years regarded the mountains as a natural boundary to their settlements. But by 1750 whites had discovered the Cumberland Gap, a passage carved by nature into the rock near the place where Virginia, Kentucky, and Tennessee now meet. Twenty years later there were white settlers in the land to the south of the Ohio River in Kentucky, and in 1775 the future of western settlement was assured when Daniel Boone (1734–1820) cut the Wilderness Road southwest from the Shenandoah Valley, west across the Appalachians, through the gap, and into Kentucky. The Wilderness Road and after 1818 the Cumberland Turnpike brought more and more settlers to the New West beyond the mountains. Yet, even as many headed further west, others chose to remain in the highlands, casting their lot with the rugged beauty of the hills.

THE GENERAL STUDY OF REGIONAL RELIGION

As the years passed, those who remained in the mountains developed a distinctive religion and culture. It shared many ingredients from the more

221

general religiocultural synthesis of the nation, but it combined these ingredients in its own way and also added others. We call this synthesis a regional religion, just one among many such regional religions that may be found in various places throughout the United States.

Hence, as this description already hints, regional religion means a religion shaped by people who live together in a certain geographic area. It is religion born of natural geography, of past and present human history, and of the interaction of the two. In such regionalism, the common landscape becomes not just an external condition but also an internal influence, transforming the way people view both ultimate and everyday reality. In other words, religion in some measure becomes a function of the spatial location of people and the history of that spatial location *together.* By their physical closeness, humans begin to interact subtly on one another so that they create a particular and regional response to life. Often the geographic closeness is supplemented and supported by similar backgrounds in nationality and in organized religion. Such factors are important agents in strengthening the geographic bond, but regional religion becomes through the blending of all these elements just that—regional.

The boundaries of "regions," of course, are not necessarily the same as the boundaries of states or cities. Rather, they follow the natural contours of the land and the settlement patterns of people. Insofar as any region is distinct and possesses a separate identity, its ordinary religion, which directs people in everyday life, gives its character to extraordinary religion and changes it in some ways. Moreover, "regions" are not simply scarce and exotic corners of the United States or any country. They are literally everywhere. And while the number of regions is not infinite, there are far more such regions than at first we may be inclined to think. To name but a few, we can point to the Hispanic Southwest, to different Indian reservations, to various immigrant sections in large cities (Chinatowns, "Little Italys"), to the southern California coast, to the North Country around the Dakotas and Minnesota, to Amish country in Pennsylvania, Ohio, and other states, to the Ozarks, to the Deep South, to the Creole lands of Louisiana. In fact, every region of the United States on closer scrutiny bears the marks of its own identity. The sense of cultural "sameness" that we tend to have is to some extent an invention and to some extent a habit of mind that results from allowing certain sections of the country to set the pace for all the others.

THE REGION OF SOUTHERN APPALACHIA

As was the case with American Indian cultures, it would be impossible in one chapter to discuss the religion of each of the major regions in the United States. Therefore, we focus on just one of the many areas that can be studied, making that area a case study for the concept of regional religion. Our region, Southern Appalachia, is a good one for our purposes. Its separate identity is marked and striking, shaped by its physical boundaries and relative isolation from the rest of the country. Moreover, from the early nineteenth century, Americans outside the area were noticing Southern Appalachia as "other" or different from their own landscapes. When George Tucker's *Valley of the Shenandoah* was published in 1824, it spoke for an emerging awareness of the mountain people as a distinct group. The sense of "otherness" was shared by Southern Appalachians, too; and by 1834, the autobiography of David Crockett (1786–1836) was capitalizing on the frontier mystique of the mountain folk. While this sense of "otherness" may lead us to stereotype Southern Appalachians or to dismiss them as so strikingly different that they are a case apart, it may also help us to see clearly what a regional religion is and how it functions.

In addition to offering a clear regional identity, Southern Appalachia also offers a chance to study religion with a strong traditional orientation in which both ordinary and extraordinary values are blended. It provides an explicit instance of how regionalism supplies an overarching frame within which religion and culture come together. And finally, Southern Appalachia gives us a chance to study transition in regional religion. Changes and transformations affect any regional religion, not just in the present but continually. In the case of twentieth-century Southern Appalachia, the changes are striking and sometimes dramatic. By standing out so distinctly from their background, the changes help us to see more accurately how history comes to grips with the geography of a specific place.

THE ORIGINS OF THE MOUNTAIN PEOPLE

In order to understand the religion of the mountain people, we need to have some idea of where they came from and what religious roots they had. The earliest sojourners in the highlands had been Native Americans, who gradually yielded their territory before Euro-American settlers. Sometimes they remained on the edges of white settlements for many years. In the culture that came about, traces of their influence could be seen, for example, in folklore and in the healing arts. But for the most part, the regional inhabitants of Southern Appalachia had come from European stock.

First of all, some of their ancestors were English, part of the many who had left the mother country to seek their fortunes in the colonies overseas. Secondly, many of their ancestors were Ulster Scotch, or Scotch-Irish from the north of Ireland. By 1714 the Scotch-Irish were leaving northern Ireland in significant numbers, and their immigration was extensive right up to the time of the American Revolution. Even before 1750, there were probably about 100,000 Scotch-Irish in the colonies, settling especially in the Pennsylvania area. Third, others among their ancestors were German, some from the southwestern section of that country, but many from the area called the Palatinate around the upper waters of the Rhine River. Mostly farmers, these Germans had been hard pressed by religious wars in the sixteenth and seventeenth centuries. Later their farmlands were laid waste by the invading generals of King Louis XIV of France. So began a great migration to England and the English colonies in America, and after 1710 that migration had become rapid and strong.

The first pale of settlement for all of these immigrants was the eastern colonies. Some established their households in eastern and central Pennsylvania. Others moved southward to the Carolina Piedmont, extending toward the Atlantic coast from the Blue Ridge. A third group made their way to western Pennsylvania and settled in the region around what is now Pittsburgh. As these three areas of population grew denser, Southern Appalachia was still from the point of view of Euro-Americans a wilderness. Sometimes visited by hunters and traders, it was not yet a place that whites could call home.

When the picture gradually began to change after 1770, it was the valleys of the Southern Appalachian highlands that were the first areas to be settled, and it was poor but ambitious farmers from the Piedmont who began the immigration. By 1772 scattered settlements in country which later became part of eastern Tennessee formed the Watauga Association to administer local affairs and to protect against Indian attack. In the beginning many of the immigrants to the mountains were Scotch-Irish, supplemented by others who were English and some who were German. But after 1790, Scotch-Irish and German immigration began to slacken, while English settlers formed a more important element in the population. By 1850 Southern Appalachia had probably 1.6 million people within its boundaries. As we have noted, its culture possessed a sharp and distinctive regional flavor. From now on, no more migration passed through the region toward the West, for roads had become better elsewhere. Southern Appalachia had become a place apart.

Meanwhile, the religious background of the new mountain settlers could be described as left-wing Protestantism. Like many English settlers in the colonies, the English who came to Southern Appalachia were Nonconformists; that is, they were dissenters from the Church of England, part of the great Puritan movement that had resulted in Separatist and non-Separatist wings and issued in various Congregational and Presbyterian forms of church government. At the same time, the Scotch-Irish were Presbyterians, too, followers of the religious revolution which John Knox (1514?–1572) had begun in the church of Scotland. The Calvinism of both English and Scotch-Irish settlers was shared by many Germans who were members of the Reformed church. Other Germans were Lutherans and Moravians (Pietists from a Lutheran background), but many followed more radical sects such as the Dunkers and the Mennonites. The Mennonites were a group that had arisen in the sixteenth century as part of the Radical Reformation, the distinctive religious movement which, as we have already seen, thought that Lutheranism and Calvinism had not gone far enough. The Dunkers, or Brethren, were a Baptist sect which arose in 1708 out of the Pietist movement in Germany. Practicing baptism by triple immersion and foot washing, the Dunkers were to leave a strong imprint on the emerging religion of the Southern Appalachian mountain people.

THE GROWTH OF THE MOUNTAIN TRADITION

Since this religion was regional, let us take a closer look at the kind of economic and social life the Southern Appalachian region provided the settlers. From the beginning, agriculture was key. Mountain folk eked out their livings on small and "perpendicular" farms set against the steep hillsides. Those who could plant the rich bottomland prospered, but most engaged in subsistence farming on mountain slopes which developed gullies from the rain and suffered from continual erosion and soil depletion. Here corn became the chief crop and the staple of mountain life and diet. It was fed to hogs, which became the major source of animal protein, and it supplied the grain for corn bread and corn whiskey.

Later, forestry and mining became important industries. The region was invaded by a new corporate management class, representatives of "foreign" companies (from other sections of the United States), which harvested wood and extracted coal from the land. Generally, the inhabitants of Southern Appalachia did not profit from these industries. Many signed over mineral rights to their lands without realizing the immense wealth they were handing over. Others provided a pool of cheap labor for industries that found their markets elsewhere. Finally, by the middle of the twentieth century, manufacturing became an important industry in the region, once again begun largely by outsiders and employing local people as a ready labor supply to produce goods which usually ended elsewhere.

Thus, from the nineteenth century there was a class system in Southern Appalachian society. Most numerous in the early times were the rural folk, many of them inhabitants of the hollows formed by nature between the slopes of the mountains. Here, alongside the inevitable mountain creeks, they built their homesteads and farmed their land. At the head of each hollow, where the road into the nearest town passed, there would often be a more prosperous homesteader, perhaps with a small general store and, after the arrival of the automobile, a gasoline pump. At least in the twentieth century, the owner of the general store sometimes owned all or much of the land in the hollow and rented it, with its dwelling places, to people who were really tenant farmers.

In addition to these rural mountain folk, a second group of Southern Appalachians formed the commercial and professional classes in the towns. Generally located in the county seats, these townspeople fostered their own variant of Southern Appalachian regionalism and provided centers where rural people could come for necessary goods and services. Finally, as we have already noted, there was a third group who dwelled in Southern Appalachia: the "foreign" folk, who were emissaries of industries from outside the region, comprised the smallest but wealthiest and most powerful segment of the population. Yet their designation by other Appalachians as foreign suggests that they did not contribute very significantly to the rich religiocultural ethos which characterized the area. Hence, our study will take its cue from the concentration of population. We will discuss the regional religion of rural Appalachians for the most part and, when it seems important, discuss the variant culture developed by the townspeople as well.

Among these mountain people, social organization was marked by a paradoxical blend of intimacy and isolation. Kinship was the great bond that united them, and often most of the residents of any mountain hollow were related to one another. The mountains provided a huge, outdoor mansion, where the extended family could be close and yet far from their relatives. At certain times they would come together—as members of the same church or to help at barn raisings, corn huskings, or quilting bees. At other seasons they visited one another, and their visits were the cornerstone of social activity in the area.

Yet their kinship community left them a huge degree of independence and isolation. Individualism thrived in the mountain fastnesses, and so was born the mixture of pride, stubbornness, and sensitivity to criticism for which mountain people became known. Their rugged lifestyle offered few opportunities for "getting ahead" in the sense of the American middle class. Education had to fit itself around the more pressing demands of a rural household and when it was available was usually conducted in one-room church-schoolhouses, often ill equipped. A steady diet of salt pork, soup beans, and corn bread—much of it fried in heavy grease—often led to poor health. Dyspepsia (indigestion), which foreign travelers in the United States had reported as the national disease in the nineteenth century, continued into the twentieth as the regional complaint of Southern Appalachia. A system of outhouses and dug wells presented a constant danger of infection.

Mountain Character and Mountain Religion

Yet for all of the problems, the life of isolation and kinship bred a richness. Nurtured by this environment, mountain people regarded themselves and others in certain distinctive ways. They developed characteristic attitudes toward nature and, beyond it, the supernatural world their religious heritage had given them. Mountain character was formed of the intersection of traits by means of which Southern Appalachians organized reality. Although not every dweller in the hills possessed every trait, so many of them came together in the people of the region that it seems fair to call the distinct sets of traits and attitudes toward life the "mountain character." Early a part of the Southern Appalachian heritage, these traits and attitudes continued to thrive into the twentieth century and still are strong today. They are the living legacy of the mountains.

Marked by holistic and traditional understandings, mountain character formed the basis for ordinary religion in the hills. Like so many other Americans, mountain people possessed a streak of sensitivity that made them mystics and dreamers. Unlike many others, the quality of their landscape led them to foster it. Thus, ordinary religion among Southern Appalachians grew out of their temperament and their landscape, the one supporting the other in a basic way of looking at the world and the place of human beings within it.

For those whose lives were sheltered by the rugged beauty of the mountains, nature was a holy place, and spiritual power could be found amid the hills. People grew up with a sense that they belonged to the mountains, even more to their particular mountain hollow with its creek bed and its walls rising like boundaries between sacred and profane worlds. If they were forced to leave, for example, by economic necessity, they did so sadly and with great difficulty. In their new homes, usually in northern cities, they were often unhappy, finding turmoil in the process of coping with the alien character of city life. At every opportunity, they returned home to visit the hills and the kin who awaited them there. By the middle of the twentieth century, many would commute to jobs in Michigan or Ohio, only to return on weekends to the mountains. Hence, the relationship of mountain people to their landscape was one of endearment. The hills had gotten into their blood and had become necessary in a spiritual and emotional sense to their survival.

Nature became the center that directed or oriented the lives of mountain folk. Like Native Americans and like followers of various Eastern religions, they bowed before its power, knowing that they could have only the plenty nature might grant them. Life, to be livable, must conform to the patterns it set. So mountain time was slow and rhythmic, running with the organic pulse of nature. It was the time of the present in which people dwelled within the moment, not looking to the future at all and turning to the past only to support the way the present was lived. It was the time of being more than the time of doing. Like the clouds that often spread a mist over mountain valleys, a brooding quality of quiet and contemplation ran through mountain life. In the twentieth century, it was not unusual to find mountain people at midday sitting in the shade of their front porches, gently rocking and staring into the landscape, seemingly forgetful of whatever problems of poverty or illness might be there.

Similarly, mountain space was natural. It was the space of the particular, not of the abstract. It was the place in a person's own mountain valley where concrete events occurred and concrete persons or objects were cherished. Far removed from the throwaway culture of the American mainstream, the traditional mountain person held onto things with fondness and familiarity, as though to gain a new tool was to lose an old friend. As in Native American culture, mountain life fostered a regard for material places and objects, imparting to them a kind of sacramental quality so that they became vehicles for peace and contentment.

Yet unlike the Indians, the mountaineers viewed nature in the shadow of a supernatural world. If mountain people belonged to the hills, they also belonged to the God beyond nature. Their basic Calvinism taught them that they were subject to him, just as they were subject to the power of nature. In the mountain view of things, there was some space for free will, but overwhelmingly God controlled the basic lot of people. Destiny had been plotted by the divine will from eternity, and just as a person should live in harmony with nature, so he or she should also live in harmony with the designs of God. Through acceptance and resignation to God's will, a person would become the ally of the power and order that ruled the universe. In this view of things, freedom was the freedom to affirm the basic constitution of the world. Thus, prayer for mountain people was not a ceaseless plea for earthly benefits. Rather, it was an attempt to move into the right spiritual attitude, a condition of inner contentment in which a person yielded freely to let God have his way. God's way was the right way. By living in harmony with it, salvation in the next life could be assured, and peace in this one could be obtained as well.

Running as a counterpoint to this theme of acceptance and inner peace, the mountain relationship with the supernatural world was one of passion and drama. The avenue to God led through crisis and trouble which confronted the mountaineer with the primary choice of human life. Mountain people were here on earth to make a decision—for this world or for the next one, for sin and personal ease or for their immortal souls and God. So the center of the mountain bond with the supernatural was the crisis moment of conversion when, for believers, an intimate and enduring attachment to the person of Jesus Christ was begun. Here there was little interest in a day-by-day development of religious knowledge through a program of education. Instead, the power of God entered a person's life all at once, generating an excitement that made the extraordinary quality stand out sharply against the background of everyday existence. The "thisworldliness" of nature was balanced for mountain folk by an otherworldliness that brought home to them the conviction that their real life was lived in another landscape. Much as they loved the hills, they were only a foretaste of the world to come.

Mountain character had established a way to relate to both the natural and supernatural worlds, but finally, it also charted relationships within the human world. Once again, a sense of belonging and being "at home" with people was primary. So mountain folk turned to others as blood kin or personal friends. Independent though they proclaimed themselves, in an emotional sense they depended on one another, and their attachments ran deep. Indeed, just as mountaineers were subject to nature and to God, they were also subject to one another. There was little group leadership and community organization in the mountain hollows because to stand out of the crowd in a position of leadership would threaten the basic structure of dependence within each person. No one could lead because to lead meant to break away and set the pace for others. Similarly, a rupture in the bond of relationship could bring sudden violence, and in earlier times the hills were known for their blood feuds and personal vigilante style of justice. As in the relationship with the supernatural world, the quiet, stolid face of a mountain person often hid a world of passion beneath the surface.

In the mountains, a stranger was someone from the next county, and a foreigner was a person from outside the region. Every exchange, whether business or pleasure, depended on the quality of relationship between persons within the fixed boundaries of mountain space. In traditional mountain culture, it was more important to establish the right relationship between persons than to attend to things. Moreover, that right relationship involved a history of other relationships. It was important to know the family of a new friend, and it was important to have had dealings with one or another of the kin. It was necessary to know where a person lived and to be able to say something about the neighbors. The world made sense only if it was familiarized and humanized: to be a stranger in the mountains was to be invisible.

Among the kin and neighbors who inhabited this close-knit world, there was a definite sense of place and role. People were divided by sex and by age. Men and women lived in socially separate worlds in which deep feelings were not often shared with each other. Traditional churches, in fact, were a graphic reminder of the structure of society in Southern Appalachia. It was customary for the men to sit on one side and the women on the other. And except for unusual circumstances, such as the felt inspiration of the Holy Ghost, it was customary for women to remain silent, allowing their men to run affairs and make basic decisions in the congregation.

Likewise, in the running of a family farm, men and women had their separate cultural assignments. If women had been silent in church, in the home they ruled and ordered things. Meanwhile, their menfolk conducted the practical affairs of the farm, responsible for animals and crops except in times of special need, when the women might be recruited to help. In young manhood, husbands spoke with the voice of authority, especially as they managed the family's dealings with the world beyond the homestead. Yet old age turned the tables, and if a woman lived to be a grandmother, she became mistress of all. In a world in which childbearing frequently made women old at twenty, those who reached their sixties were venerated for their wisdom and honored as old prophetesses. Often their healing abilities with herbs or with more occult medicine were sought by their neighbors, and they freely gave advice to younger folk who asked it.

Underlying the network of interpersonal relationships that formed society in the mountains was a basic suspicion of human nature which the mountain people shared. Humans were powerless and, worse still, evil without God. Human life was cracked and flawed; only the grace of God could heal and redeem it. If a person could trust only kin and close neighbors, then to be saved meant to become part of the family of God, touched by his hand and living in vital, inner relationship with him. The lifeline of grace changed nature, but there could be weakness and backsliding still. So, in a culture of paradox mountaineers belonged to the hills, to God, and to kin, all the while knowing that each of these relationships was precarious. However deep the peace, there was always the possibility of violent change, of an alteration in the course of intimate relationship whether with nature, with God, or with people.

Organized Religion in the Mountains

The rich and paradoxical structure of mountain character provided the base from which more specific religious belief and action sprang. The mountain character, forged in the loose community of the hills, expressed its insights in a distinct religious system which was Protestant Christianity. We look now at the history of Protestantism in Southern Appalachia.

As the first settlers, many of them Scotch-Irish, trickled into the mountains, they brought with them a Presbyterian era in mountain religion. Like the rest of the country in the era of the American Revolution, fewer than 10 percent of the people were actually church members, but what religion there was for the most part was Presbyterian Calvinism. The Germans did have their own churches, but they formed a minority in the vast territory of the hills, and, as we have seen, organized religion itself was a minority experience. To some extent, this would continue to be true as the years passed. Church membership in Southern Appalachia grew, but in the nineteenth century it grew more slowly than in the rest of the country. By the twentieth century, as we will see, this intensely religious people would have the least need for official church structures of perhaps any people in the United States.

At the beginning of the nineteenth century, Southern Appalachia, like the East Coast and the New West, entered a period of religious fervor. The frontier version of the Second Great Awakening—the Great Revival—while it began further to the west in the bluegrass region of Kentucky, came across the mountain passes with its message of repentance and faith. Preachers rose up, filled with the Holy Ghost, to warn and inspire people to seek salvation. At long sessions called "protracted meetings" and held out of doors in hastily constructed camp sites, people were alternately threatened by "spiritual" preachers with the fires of hell and consoled by hymn-singing congregations with the joys of heaven. Stretched taut in the tension between the two, they found themselves turning, in moments of intense emotional excitement, to Jesus. From now on, the episodic conversion experience became the mainstay of Southern Appalachian religion. "Getting religion" became the test of faith, a test that could only be passed by a depth of feeling which broke the monotony of everyday life with a leap across the boundaries of the human into the extraordinary world.

In this world in which religious passion meant so much, the older Presbyterian ideal of an educated ministry was supplanted by the presence of the new, "spiritual" preacher. He had felt the call in the depths of his being by the power of the Holy Ghost, and the measure of his authenticity was his ability to preach without learning or preparation from what God put into his heart and on his tongue. His great text was the Bible, the Word of God, which he spoke from memory. Many a preacher, like many of the other descendants of the first generation, had little ability to read. And in another of the mountain paradoxes, the Bible that mountaineers kept and quoted with such delight was often known only at second hand. Still, second hand seemed sufficient as far as the mountain people were concerned. The Bible formed their intellectual food and drink, and they quoted it frequently, disputing vigorously over the meaning of the text.

Hence, with the Great Revival came a sectarian spirit. Many new and Nonconformist churches arose in the mountains, combining their traditional heritage with the environment of the mountains and the character of the mountaineers. First among them, Baptists took the position of importance formerly occupied by the Presbyterians. After the Revolution there had been a great exodus of Baptists to the West as more and more English people entered the mountains, but Baptists had had a long history in the colonies, beginning with Roger Williams and his foundation of Rhode Island. On the East Coast as early as 1707 General Baptists, who taught that salvation was open to all people, had combined in the Philadelphia Association. As time passed, however, their churches, now known as Regular Baptist groups, again were teaching the Calvinist belief in the predestination of the elect and the damned. Baptist ranks were swelled after 1734 when the Great Awakening inspired some groups to split off as Separate Baptists from New England Congregationalism. The Separate Baptists took up the older Baptist belief that salvation was possible for all and, preaching this gospel, moved to North Carolina and Virginia. When they met with scorn and persecution, many fled to the highlands.

Thus, both General and Separate Baptists were preaching in Southern Appalachia. Later, when some members of both churches joined together, there was a further blurring of boundaries. Like Presbyterians, Baptists seemed to teach the old Calvinist doctrine of predestination, but they brought to the teaching a vaguely defined sense of freedom of the will which suited the mountain spirit. Moreover, without a tradition of an educated ministry, Baptist farmer-preachers spoke as they said the Holy Ghost compelled, spreading their religion in a way that the Presbyterians were unable to imitate. With their complete sense of religious liberty and their simple gospel, they spoke straight to the needs of their mountain neighbors.

Besides the modified Calvinism of Baptist preaching and the availability of lay preachers, what drew people to the Baptists was the biblical ordinances they practiced. Following the Anabaptists of the Radical Reformation, they brought two profoundly moving rituals to the people of Southern Appalachia. The first was baptism, which they sought to perform usually in a running stream and by the process of triple immersion, once for each of the persons of the Trinity. The second was foot washing, in which the actions which Jesus performed at the Last Supper (John 13:3–14) were imitated by the people of a congregation.

With the coming of the German Dunkers, both of these practices had been in the mountains from the first decade of settlement. But now, under the gospel of the new Baptist farmer-preachers, they spread throughout the region. While Southern Appalachians feared and opposed Roman Catholicism, they had unconsciously absorbed a sacramental sense not unlike that of Catholicism. Their lives in the mountains had led them to have regard for nature and the material world. Now they began to find the essence of religion in the practice of those material actions which would provide access to God. Protestant in their attachment to a religion of the biblical Word and the felt experience of the heart, they wove their Protestantism with a new sacramentalism which spoke to their condition. Sometimes, too, they turned to other ordinances such as the celebration of the Lord's Supper, performed usually with crackers and wine or grape juice in humble country churches. Yet, perhaps because it smacked too clearly of Roman Catholicism, the communion service was not nearly so powerful a religious ritual among the mountain people as baptism or foot washing.

Baptist success indicated the direction in which the mountain tradition was developing. Even within Presbyterian ranks, the new spirit spread, bringing a sectarian movement that resulted in the formation of the Cumberland Presbytery in 1810. Later the Cumberland Presbytery split completely from the parent Presbyterian church as an independent movement. Its leaders had been persuaded by English and German traditions of lay preaching in the Baptist churches. Likewise Cumberland Presbyterians embraced modified Calvinism and held to the emotional intensity that had inspired the Baptist preaching. In other words, while still maintaining an institutional affiliation with Presbyterianism, the Cumberland church had become an expression of the religion that was sweeping the mountains.

Larger than the Cumberland Presbyterian movement was the Methodist presence in Southern Appalachia. Francis Asbury (1745–1816), the first bishop of the Methodist church in America, was an untiring missionary to the western frontier. He and other Methodist circuit riders came to the mountains, and with the Great Revival, their gospel spread. Even more than the Baptists and the Cumberland Presbyterians, the Methodists, as we have already seen, preached that salvation was available to all. Their preaching of this basic equality in spiritual condition appealed to the democratic instincts of the mountaineers who so valued individual autonomy. Moreover, the Methodists exalted the importance of the uneducated preacher in their circuit rider. Like his Baptist and Presbyterian brothers, the circuit rider spoke as the Holy Ghost bid him, stirring the emotions of the people who listened. Indeed, it was not unusual for Baptist, Presbyterian, and Methodist preachers to cooperate in a camp meeting, each of them taking over one corner of a field to share in the task of waking sinners to repentance.

Finally, as we have already discussed in the chapter on mainstream Protestantism, the "Christian" churches emerged from the context of the Great Revival on the frontier. Coming out of the Presbyterian and Baptist traditions, they preached a more radical doctrine of free grace and called people to unite in the creation of an authentic New Testament church. As in the primitive church, each religious society should be autonomous, conducting its own affairs as the Bible and the Holy Ghost inspired. Thus, with their emphasis on the authority of the Bible, their democratic preference for the local congregation, and their involvement in the problem of predestination versus freedom of the will, the Christians (Disciples of Christ) again conformed in general outline to the religion of the mountains.

By means of the Great Revival, the Southern Appalachian churches increased their membership, and it grew throughout the nineteenth century, with Baptists and Methodists taking the lead and far surpassing the original Presbyterians. By the first decade of the twentieth century, there were over 600,000 Baptists in the region and nearly 475,000 Methodists. Presbyterians numbered fewer than 95,000, while the Disciples of Christ counted almost 70,000 adherents. About 90 percent of all church members were Protestant, but in keeping with the mountain tradition, the number of church members out of the total population was roughly one-third.

Meanwhile, the nineteenth-century history of Protestantism in Southern Appalachia was a continued saga of sectarianism. Among the Baptists after 1820, an antimission movement attacked the interest in missions and missionary churches that characterized mainline Baptists along with other Protestant denominations. The Antimission Baptists looked to the New Testament in which, they said, there was no mention of missionary societies. They thought that such societies strengthened central control within a denomination, violating the free and democratic spirit of the New Testament and the mountains. God had his own means to save those whom he had chosen, and so human efforts to preach missions were useless and even an expression of lack of faith. The education of preachers was wrong for the same reasons, and so, too, was the formation of Sunday schools.

By 1846, Antimission Baptists had become a formidable movement, almost a third as large as the Missionary Baptists and mostly concentrated in the mountains of Southern Appalachia. More than 68,000 strong, they did not form themselves into a denomination, but, instead, they belonged to various associations, each with a confession of faith printed with the minutes of the annual meeting of the association. Among themselves, the associations exchanged programs, and fellowship was established among those whose principles were in agreement. They called themselves by various names,

Primitive Baptist being the most popular, although it was common to hear, too, of Old School, Regular, Antimission, and even Hard Shell Baptists. Still others, with an explicit doctrine of the seeds of good and evil, one of them planted in each human being from the beginning, formed the Two-Seed-in-the-Spirit Predestinarian Baptists. Although this movement had begun in the late eighteenth century, it flourished in the climate of the mountains in the middle of the nineteenth century. At the same time, many of the United Baptists came to share in antimission sentiments.

With the slavery question and the Civil War came an additional source of division for the churches, and agitation over these issues caused many denominations to split. In the midst of southern territory, mountain people, with their intense love of freedom, often found themselves supporting the northern cause. Sometimes, too, the highlands were the scene of bitter clashes between the two armies. But the legacy of the Civil War, in general, affected the structure of mountain religion less than a new force that was rising. In the last third of the nineteenth century, the classic churches of the mountaineers were joined by the Holiness movement, as we have already seen, an outgrowth of Methodism. As a protest against formalism in religion, Holiness after 1870 gave the mountain people a further way to express the intense emotionalism of their religion.

Holiness taught that it was important to *feel* God, and it viewed the outward and ecstatic actions that characterized its worship as manifestations of the divine presence. It offered to mountain people a religious holism that fitted Southern Appalachian temperament. In other words, as a religion in which head, heart, and body were all involved, it appealed to the Southern Appalachian sense of the wholeness of things. With his rhythmic and singsong style of preaching, the Holiness preacher, much like the black preacher, worked his people toward emotional religious expression, stirring them with the force of his personality and the Holy Ghost. His message turned on the scripture and on the purity of life that must be followed in the strict Holiness way. Sabbath breaking, alcohol, gambling, cardplaying, and dancing were all works of the devil, and sexual temptation was the chief of Satan's wiles.

Independent and autonomous like all of mountain religion, Holiness flourished in the hills. After the turn of the century the Pentecostal movement spread along with it, and scores of affiliated or independent Pentecostal churches encouraged the ecstatic experience of speaking in tongues. In the mountains as elsewhere, in small organizations like the Assemblies of God and various Churches of God, Pentecostal Christians essentially accepted the Holiness way but added to it the new element of their special gift from the Holy Ghost. Furthermore, at about the same time that Holiness had begun to spread, Fundamentalism was gathering strength as a religious force. As it moved throughout the country, it found a congenial home in the mountains, where love for the Bible and commitment to the discovery and practice of its literal meaning had always been intense. Thus, Fundamentalism as a movement gave official sanction to what mountaineers had always known, at a time when the world beyond the mountains began to look more and more threatening.

Finally, sectarianism in the mountains was enhanced by the growth of nondenominational churches. These groups carried the tendencies within mountain religion to their logical conclusion, as one individual or another (usually male) among the people became convinced that God was calling him to preach and exhort. So he would set about establishing a church of his own, often on his property, either in his house or a separate building he might construct. Like a patron to his neighbors in a lonely mountain hollow, he invited them to join with him in seeking the Word and will of God. Here all the characteristics of mountain religion came together at their fullest expression: the uneducated preacher, the independent church, the primacy of the Bible, and the strong emotionalism of religious worship. The nondenominational church was the fruit of the mountain spirit and the mountain religious tradition.

TRADITION AND CHANGE IN THE TWENTIETH CENTURY

As the twentieth century dawned, the mountain tradition was alive and strong. In the rural sections of the highlands, it thrived within the isolated communities of a freedom-loving people. As the century progressed, the mountain tradition slowly began to decline, but still it endured stubbornly and sometimes showed signs of revival and greater strength. Even today for many the mountain tradition is unforgotten, as its values continue to shape their lives. In the towns of Southern Appalachia, however, change is evident, as more and more Appalachian churches resemble those of mainstream religion anywhere in the nation. We will look first at traditional rural religion in the mountains and then, briefly, at the changes that have eroded the past and brought the people, especially in the towns, into the mainstream of American religion and culture.

The Rural Tradition

Let us begin by recalling that the rural tradition was one of both ordinary and extraordinary religion, often fused together in the holistic identity of the mountain folk but also separate to some extent in their experience. Ordinary religion was the property of every person in the hill country, but especially it was the property of the unchurched. At the beginning of the century, about two-thirds of all mountaineers fell into this category, and as late as the second half of the century, over half of the population still did not belong to any religious organization. It was true that during the interim church membership had grown faster in Southern Appalachia than anywhere else in the nation. Still, the general pattern remained the same as in the past. Here was an intensely religious people, seeking after not only ordinary expressions of religion, but also the supernatural world. Yet this people did not think that baptism necessarily led into the church. In many a mountain household in eastern Kentucky and elsewhere, people would patiently explain to "foreign" visitors that they cherished the Bible but did not regularly attend a church. On the wall would be a picture of Jesus of Nazareth; on the table, a worn copy of the family Bible. The silent witness was eloquent.

Ordinary Religion in Rural Appalachia

In this setting in which religion did not always mean the church, the family was the most important religious and social institution, and the church came second. While by the last third of the twentieth century, this picture had sometimes been reversed, the strength of family religion was still apparent. Religious beliefs and practices were an ordinary part of living. The Bible was regularly quoted in everyday conversation and in time of trouble. If special help were needed in a crisis, it might be opened at random after a short prayer. By means of this divinatory technique, mountaineers expected to receive a specific message from God as their eyes lit on a particular passage. Like members of the American counter culture who in the 1960s had appropriated the ancient Chinese classic, the *I Ching,* mountain folk found that God's Word was expressly tailored to their need and their situation. They could close the Bible and know how they should act in the midst of their trials.

Similarly, particular verses of the Bible were often used by healers who practiced for their neighbors in the mountain hollows. The knowledge of herbs and of medicine had been handed down in many families, sometimes as far back as the first generation in the mountains when contact with Cherokee healing had been more frequent. Beyond the herbal "root work" of both Indians and mountaineers, however, there was the faith healing that came through the power of one individual over the evil that had invaded another. The laying on of hands for healing was part of the Holiness tradition. But outside the churches, like Indian shamans, old "grannies" and menfolk exercised their mysterious ability by blowing away the heat of a burn, stopping blood caused by an accident or another unnatural cause, or getting rid of "thrash," a disease that afflicted mountain children with yellow blisters, even inside their mouths.

Often at the center of this shamanistic healing was the recitation of a particular verse from the Bible in a ritualistic manner. For the treatment of serious bleeding, a healer might recite Ezekiel 16:6, "And when I passed by you, and saw you weltering in your blood, I said to you in your blood, 'Live,'" substituting the name of the person for the "you" of the biblical verse. Among many of the old healers, there were special rules for the transmission of their sacred knowledge, and it could only be passed down to certain individuals, perhaps two in a given healer's lifetime. Thus, the healing lore was kept secret, and at the same time it was perpetuated.

Ordinary religion thrived, too, in a series of practices connected with planting. Many sowed their crops by an intricate method based on the signs of the zodiac, justifying their efforts by reference to the biblical account of creation: "And God said, 'Let there be lights in the firmament of the heavens to separate the day from the night; and let them be for signs and for seasons and for days and years'" (Gen. 1:14). Yet the appointed days and years of Genesis were expressing not so much biblical religion but the harmonial religion of nature. For mountain people followed the ancient horoscopes which correlated the stars with the twelve signs and with corresponding parts of the human body. From this basic source, planting calendars plotted out each month according to the zodiacal signs. First of all, each sign appeared at least once in a month, and then it reappeared for a two- or three-day sequence. Some of the signs were moist and fruitful, and these were best for planting. Seeds sown during barren times would result in a poor crop, and all these signs were good for was trimming or destroying (weeds). Moreover, there were special rules for each and every crop. Beans should be planted when signs were in the arms (of the human body), and potatoes in the feet. The new moon was a bad day for planting anything, and crops planted under the signs of Taurus and Cancer would have a great ability to withstand drought.

Ordinary religion appeared again in the tales of various sorts that mountaineers delighted to tell. There were ghost tales and hunting tales, animal stories and snake lore. Sometimes the stories told of an almost Indian sense of kinship with the animals, as in the tale of a little girl who daily fed a snake behind the barn with some of her own milk and bread. When a man followed her and discovered what she was doing, he killed the snake—and the girl died, too. In some mysterious fashion, she had been identified with the snake, and the death of the reptile meant the death of the human person. Indeed, omens, dreams, and visions were everywhere in the world of the mountains. They were avenues to knowledge which supplemented the commonsense view of reality. They deepened the sense of meaningfulness in mountain life by relating people to the secrets of the natural and supernatural worlds.

Mountain people saw signs and heard voices when other folk experienced nothing. A person had to curse in order to raise gourds, and he or she had to be bad tempered in order to raise healthy peppers. If someone made a feather bed over into pillows, that person would have bad luck until the pillows wore out, and if a bird included a hair from someone's head in the nest it was building, that individual's head would ache until the nest crumbled to pieces. There were cradle signs both to bring good fortune to the newborn child and to foresee the future for others. A necklace of corn beads would help the baby to have an easy time teething, and a bullet or coin might prevent nosebleed. The number of creases in the baby's legs, if the same in both, would guarantee that the next child born would be a girl. The first wood tick found on the baby's body had to be killed with an axe if the child were to become a good worker. And if the child were to have a good voice for singing, the wood tick had to be killed on a bell or banjo.

Similarly, there were weather signs to guide every human activity. Forecasters predicted the weather by counting fogs in August, by noting the color of woolly caterpillars, and by observing how close to the ground hornets made their nests. The moon also controlled human enterprise. Potatoes planted or pork killed in its light both came to grief. Soap had to be made at just the right time of the moon, and roofs had to be nailed down at the appropriate interval.

Thus, mountain people surrounded themselves with a symbolic system based, for the most part, on nature. They used the system to orient themselves in everyday life, seeking to live in peace and harmony by performing each action at the time when nature decreed it should be done. For them, as for Native Americans, Easterners, and Western occultists, there was a correspondence between themselves and nature. A great law of resemblance directed all things, and to live well meant to live in tune with cosmic rhythms as the signs and omens revealed them. If this religion was not Christian, it still ran deep, and it gave the mountain people a way to guide behavior within the ordinary world.

Extraordinary Religion in Rural Appalachia

As we have already seen to some extent in our discussion of the rise of the churches of Southern Appalachia, extraordinary religion was not eclipsed by the ordinary religion of the hills. Rather, extraordinary religion flourished, and despite the multiplicity of churches, there was a basic unity in mountain religion. Like any religion, it possessed a creed, or body of belief, a code, or moral system for everyday behavior, and a cultus, or ritual expression of its creed and code. Finally, creed, code, and cultus were the property of a community, a group of people who, whatever their differences, identified closely with one another.

The creed of extraordinary religion in the mountains taught that life was a drama of estrangement from God. Divine predestination and redemption controlled a person's destiny, although to some extent human free will entered into the script. In the Bible, a person could find all that was necessary for salvation, and following the Word of the Bible literally was fundamental. At the same time, religion was feeling deeply felt, and the human experience of conversion was at once the beginning and the end of the religious life. Thus, while ordinary religion offered mountain folk rules for guidance in everyday situations, the Christianity of the mountains preached extraordinary and intense feeling as a way to contact the divine power that lay behind and beyond this world. Ordinary religion kept people moving effortlessly through the monotonous round of daily tasks and oriented them within the boundaries of their hills. Extraordinary religion jolted them out of their usual track with sudden emotion and salvation.

Likewise, the moral code of Christianity provided a new set of rules for everyday behavior. Epitomized by the Holiness churches, the code was taught with more or less emphasis by every church of the mountains. It was also put into practice by many who chose not to belong to any church but lived out their religion in a family setting. This code forbade swearing and Sabbath breaking by engaging in labor on the day of rest. It exhorted against drinking, gambling, cardplaying, and dancing. It regarded sexual expression outside of marriage as wicked and sinful.

Yet alongside the code, there was a different, more permissive ethic in the mountains—its legacy from ordinary religion. Purity of life might be the ideal, but in practice there was tolerance for a variety of actions that violated the Christian standard. A relative degree of sexual freedom did exist, and illegitimate offspring were accepted into mountain families without rebuke. "Moonshine," or corn whiskey, provided a ready cash "crop" for a hard-pressed mountain farmer. As we have already mentioned, there was an undercurrent of violence running through mountain society, and ordinary life produced its dramas as intense as the experience of conversion. In earlier times, the kin of a victim of murder or violent crime meted out justice to the criminal, and no court system stood in the way of a person and this vindication through feuding. By the twentieth century, when feuding days were almost a thing of the past, there was a new form of sensation seeking provided by the automobile. Racing their cars along twisting mountain roads, young men would often chalk up a car wreck to their credit before they were twenty, bragging that they had "totaled" the automobile. Mountain preaching was curiously silent on these forms of abuse. Rarely did a social ethic enter the usual sermon. Moral injunctions were delivered generally only against private or traditionally identified forms of vice.

But in the mountains as elsewhere, the heart of extraordinary religion lay in its cultus, or ritual practice. People felt their religion in terms of what they did, especially when they were at worship. Here sacred space was provided, sometimes at meetings in the brush, in cemeteries, or at baptismal streams—but especially by the thousands of small churches on country roads or up hidden mountain hollows. The congregations in the old churches might be less than twenty, with a high proportion of women and girls. Many of the churches were simple, one-room frame or log buildings, and they were usually bare, devoid even of the wild country flowers that were everywhere. There was an unspoken love of simplicity, a fear that ornament of any kind might lead to distraction from the religious business at hand. Simplicity, however, did not mean formality. A typical congregation wandered into the church gradually, the members exchanging greetings with relatives and friends even though the service might have started. Often there was kissing all around, regardless of age or sex. On hot summer days, a water dipper was freely passed, and an atmosphere of spontaneity filled the church so that prayer and feeling could rise effortlessly. In the center of the building, there would be a simple stand as pulpit, while to the front on one side was the amen corner. Leading from here, a group of men lined out the verses of the hymns, while the rest of the men and the women, in the old congregations sitting separately, took up the melody.

Sacred time occurred at intervals throughout the year. The old churches held a preaching once a month, and many mountain people divided their Sundays between various churches so that, nearly every week, they could hear a rousing sermon. But there were other sacred times as well as the Sunday service. The annual baptism ceremony was a very special occasion, as was the service of foot washing. In addition, there were protracted meetings (usually annually, when a revival was preached), funeral preachings (often, as among blacks, long after death and burial), and decoration services (to lay flowers on the graves of the dead). Like many traditional peoples, mountain folk remembered the time of their ancestors.

Although there was continuing sectarianism among mountaineers and many an argument about the meaning of the scripture, in practice, preaching was very similar in the mountain churches. With the Protestant heritage of the hills, the Word was central, and preaching accompanied every ritual from a decoration to a foot washing. Called by the Holy Ghost, the preacher was not a highly educated man, and he gloried in his lack of formal learning. Moreover, he did not command a salary from a traditional mountain congregation, for to do so would have meant working on Sunday—Sabbath breaking. Instead, like the old Baptist farmer-preachers, he supported himself at a regular job and preached out of his sense of the inspiration of God. Sometimes his congregation would collect a few coins to help defray expenses, but a person preached because he felt a divine gift, and even beyond Sabbath breaking, how could one put a price on a gift of God?

Sermon subjects might be a combination of themes, including Old Testament stories, autobiographical anecdotes by the preacher, and exhortations to personal holiness. Above all, though, the preacher brought home the message of sin and salvation, of death and judgment and the eternal mercy of God. Sermon style, as we have already indicated, resembled the style of black folk preaching. The preacher worked himself up to a rhythmic chant, pacing back and forth as he did so, and then rocking forward and backward to do his "driving." The listening congregation began to sway forward and backward with him to the rhythm of his chant, and as they did so, they started to moan, wail, then shriek and shout. There was an intricate liturgy to the process, a complex ritual exchange in which preacher and people each knew their part and performed it in concert to make their worship to God. If the preacher failed to get into stride or if his people failed to respond, the liturgy had failed, and religion had not come out of the preaching.

The singing of hymns complemented the preacher's efforts, as the voices from the amen corner gave the cue and the congregation picked up the tune. Many of the hymns which Southern Appalachian churches sang had descended from the eighteenth century, some of them composed by such great English hymn writers as Isaac Watts (1674–1748) and John Newton (1725–1807). There was a strange, haunting quality to these old songs. Their Anglo-Saxon chant lines, based on modal scales from British oral tradition, were reminiscent of Roman Catholic Gregorian chant. They told by their texture of another world, and their words reinforced the message. Often the theme was heaven or divine grace, the fear of damnation or humility before the all-powerful God. Sometimes, too, there were newer gospel hymns which carried the sound of the later country music of the mountains. These were livelier in tempo, and their words were often highly sentimental in the late nineteenth-century style. Both kinds of hymns were sung in unison. Both were integral to the worship service, loosening people to express religious feeling just as the words of the preacher did.

A typical service included hymns and prayers offered spontaneously by the preacher or members of the congregation and, whatever the sequence, was climaxed by the sermon. At the end of the sermon came an altar call, when troubled people would arise and usually come forward. With the prayerful support of the congregation, they would try to pray through to decision (conversion). Many churches, too, interspersed their services with times when people could witness—either to the trouble they had endured, the healing they were seeking, or the manifestations of God's grace that had come into their lives. Then at the end of the service, in a ritual expression of community, the right hand of fellowship was extended. People clasped hands in a simple ceremony that renewed their bonds with one another, ready now to bring the gospel message to their everyday lives.

Among Holiness churches, emotional expression was even more intense and the liturgy more elaborate. Holiness services were held several times a week, with the length of a typical meeting about two and one-half to three hours. In these settings, self-disclosure by members of the congregation was carried still further than in the other churches. People spoke and witnessed; they prayed together and laid hands on one another for healing; they walked to the altar where, when the preacher stretched out his hand to touch them, they were "slain" by the power of the Holy Ghost and fell in a trance-like state at his feet. Some Holiness people who were Pentecostal, as we have already seen, felt God's power by speaking in tongues. Others, in Holiness fire-handling churches, felt the power and placed their hands in flame without being scorched or blistered. Still others, in snake-handling churches, at the height of their ecstasy danced with serpents and swallowed strychnine or lye and water without harm.

The origins of fire handling are unknown, but snake handling had begun in 1909 in Tennessee. It spread to six states in the mountain area, although it was illegal in all but West Virginia. Based on a literal reading of Mark 16:18, "They will pick up serpents, and if they drink any deadly thing, it will not hurt them," snake handlers acted in the power of their faith and saw their ritual as a gospel sign. They were a tiny minority among the mountain congregations—in the present perhaps some thirty-six churches—but their ritual had deep religious meaning in their lives. It was a way of demonstrating the power over death that Christian faith gave, and it was at the same time a celebration of life and resurrection. Mountain folk who handled serpents expressed how deep their yearning for extraordinary religious experience was: they were willing to endure pain and suffer even death in order to gain a sense of God in their lives.

Like baptism and foot washing, fire and snake handling were ordinances performed because, as these mountaineers read the Bible, God had so commanded. But like baptism and foot washing, they were also sacraments, sacred actions which signified the power of God and by means of the sign brought the reality into being. Surrounded as they were by nature, in fire and in serpents mountaineers had natural elements which led them to supernatural faith. In the ritual setting, the grace of God *empowered* them, so that they experienced a measure of control over nature and the hidden forces which seemed to dictate the course of their lives.

There was probably a connection between the poverty of numerous twentieth-century Southern Appalachians and the experience of these Holiness zealots. Many of the mountain people had felt control of their lives slip away, the prey of foreign corporations and economic depression. Yet what was important here was that ordinary problems had been transformed to become the raw material of spiritual experience. For mountain people, extraordinary religion should be truly extraordinary. If a person were to make contact with a divine world beyond the borders of this one, that contact should express itself in a manner at once awesome and faith inspiring. So some of the Southern Appalachian people handled fire, and others handled serpents—not unlike other spiritual devotees from different religions in the world. Whatever the path that mountain people chose, the bottom line was very simple: Appalachians wanted to feel the presence of God.

To sum up, religious ritual among the mountain people disclosed a keen sacramental sense, which had grown up in the midst of the Nonconformist tradition. It provided for members of the community the inward consolation that they sought when faced with the difficulties life brought them. And finally, it provided people with one of their few opportunities for social contact, when the bonds of friendship and unity could be reaffirmed and reinforced.

Changing Conditions and Religion in the Towns

We have been describing the rural Southern Appalachian tradition as a distinct religious system with an identity separate from that of the rest of America. In this context, it is important to realize that some of what has been described as mountain religion was going on outside the highlands, too. We have alluded at various points to blacks and to Western occultists, to Native Americans, Catholics, mainline Protestants, and followers of Eastern religions. What made Southern Appalachian religion regional was not so much the presence of unique elements as the way the elements were combined to form a religious system and the way that the system expressed the experience of life within the boundaries of the hills and with one another.

But even within the area in which the regional religion of Southern Appalachia flourished, there were other expressions of religion and, as the twentieth century progressed, increasing signs of change. Hence, Roman Catholicism had maintained a small but growing presence in the mountains from the time that it arrived in the nineteenth century, mostly with the "foreign" element who controlled the economic order. By the second half of the twentieth century, Roman Catholicism was the fourth largest organized religious body in the mountains, ranking after the Baptists, Methodists, and Presbyterians. Its presence was still small, especially when compared with the overwhelming Baptist population, but in the sixties and seventies Catholicism became vocal and visible. Moving away from its position as the church of a managerial elite, it began to take seriously the social teaching of modern popes and worked for social justice and the alleviation of poverty in the mountains.

Meanwhile, as cities multiplied and towns enlarged in the region, more and more urban Protestant churches were similar to those in other parts of the nation. They tended to be conservative, but they also tended toward decorum and emotional control. Their affiliations were with denominations of major importance, so that Southern Baptists, United Methodists, and congregations of the Presbyterian Church, U.S.A., built substantial edifices, different from the one-room frame structures of the open country. In percentage, there tended to be more church members in the towns than in rural areas, again coming closer to national trends. Social scientists who conducted studies of religious beliefs and attitudes found Fundamentalist and otherworldly views declining, general community participation increasing, and the level of education among ministers rising. Churches were becoming more prosperous, and people—while they sometimes expressed the old adherence to a simple way of living—were becoming more interested in gaining material success.

For twenty years, from about 1940 to 1960, the quest for economic prosperity had led to a huge out-migration from the area. But in the late sixties and continuing into the seventies, the developing energy crisis brought new employment, as coal grew in demand to supplement dwindling oil supplies. Out-migration became in-migration, and at the present more people are moving into the mountains than leaving. In this setting, the traditional churches still flourish. Although there are signs of confusion in values, the old order provides a

241

framework for the lives of many. Rural religious practices survive and prosper, while there are pockets of tradition even in the larger cities. Rich in its ability to express paradoxical and often contradictory religious insights, the inherited mountain religion can still offer Southern Appalachians a holistic blend of ordinary and extraordinary belief and practice. In the traditional sense, it is probably the most American religion in the nation, maintaining its ties with ancestral understandings from the time when America was young and the nation as a whole an agricultural society.

Indeed, with its stress on the Bible, on preaching the Word, and on experiencing it in a free and democratic congregational setting, throughout its history mountain religion mirrored the insights of historical mainstream Protestantism. Beyond that, its need for crisis and drama leading to the moment of decision betrayed a mind-set that, as we will see, continued to be part of the dominant center of American religion. Its accommodation of paradox likewise was a familiar American cultural trait, present from the time of the Puritans who combined Yankee business shrewdness with a deep strain of religious vision. In other words, the public face, the dominant center, of religion in America was present in the mountains from at least the beginning of the nineteenth century. And when, even among Appalachian traditionalists, change came in the twentieth century, the direction of that change made it more and more like the religion of the American mainstream. In the new churches of mountain towns and cities were the signs of the one religion of all Americans. Even in many a mountain hollow, there were also signs.

IN OVERVIEW

Our study has focused on religion in Southern Appalachia as just one example—a case study—of regional religion in the United States. Looking at one instance of how geographical closeness and common histories create a distinctive religious response can give us some idea of how the process works in other areas. In the mountains and in various regions in the United States, we see how spatial boundaries emphasize religious distinctiveness. In the case of Southern Appalachia, Native Americans were supplanted by Euro-American settlers, mostly English, Scotch-Irish, and German. Living a rugged life together in the mountains, they developed a distinctive "mountain character." Respect for nature was key, but mountaineers always saw beyond nature the controlling power of the supernatural world. Meanwhile, they cherished the ties of kinship and friendship they had developed over the years.

With this background, organized and extraordinary religion was mostly Protestant and, in large measure, Calvinistic. Fed by the revivals, a sectarian spirit grew among the mountaineers, yet there was much that the different sects held in common even as they disputed. The mountain creed taught predestination as well as the importance of the Bible and of intense feeling in religion. The mountain code stressed personal holiness and yet, influenced by ordinary religion in the mountains, could be permissive regarding human weaknesses. The mountain cultus expressed the centrality of preaching and the significance of ordinances such as baptism and foot washing.

Ordinary religion was pervasive in the hills, where many of the people were unchurched. The Bible was quoted and used for divination; healers were thought to possess occult powers; planting took place according to the astrological signs; and natural coincidences were viewed as predictions of human destiny. But as changes began to come to Appalachia, its religion—already a reflection of historical American Protestantism—became more and more like the contemporary "one religion" of Protestant America.

We have mentioned this "one religion" a number of times in our extended discussion of the manyness of religions in America. We have looked at length at that manyness, trying to bring sharply into focus the reality of these different centers of meaning and value that flourished in the pluralism of the United States. Now it is the problem of the public oneness that must engage us. In Part Two, we will ask a question fundamental to the study of American religious history: If American religions are so many, how in any way can they be one?

SUGGESTIONS FOR FURTHER READING:
SOUTHERN APPALACHIAN RELIGION

Campbell, John C. *The Southern Highlander and His Homeland.* 1921. Reprint. Lexington: University Press of Kentucky, 1969.

Dickinson, Eleanor, and Benziger, Barbara. *Revival!* New York: Harper & Row, 1974.

Ford, Thomas R., ed. *The Southern Appalachian Region: A Survey.* Lexington: University of Kentucky Press, 1962.

Hooker, Elizabeth R. *Religion in the Highlands.* New York: The Home Missions Council, 1933.

Miles, Emma Bell. *The Spirit of the Mountains.* 1905. Reprint. Knoxville: University of Tennessee Press, 1975.

Photiadis, John D., ed. *Religion in Appalachia: Theological, Social, and Psychological Dimensions and Correlates.* Morgantown: West Virginia University, Center for Extension and Continuing Education, 1978.

Stephenson, John B. *Shiloh: A Mountain Community.* Lexington: University of Kentucky Press, 1968.

Weller, Jack E. *Yesterday's People: Life in Contemporary Appalachia.* Lexington: University of Kentucky Press, 1965.

Wigginton, Eliot, ed. *The Foxfire Book.* Garden City, NY: Doubleday, Anchor Books, 1972.

———. *Foxfire 2.* Garden City, NY: Doubleday, Anchor Books, 1973.

———. *Foxfire 3.* Garden City, NY: Doubleday, Anchor Books, 1975.

———. *Foxfire 4.* Garden City, NY: Doubleday, Anchor Books, 1977.

PART TWO

The Oneness of Religion in America

CHAPTER 10

Public Protestantism: Historical Dominance and the One Religion of the United States

In 1739 Benjamin Franklin found himself in a crowd of Philadelphians absorbed in the message of George Whitefield, the famous Methodist preacher spreading a religious revival from one end of the colonies to the other. Whitefield was also raising money for an orphanage in Georgia, and Franklin, who had previously disapproved of certain details of the plan, had refused to contribute. Now, though, he was so moved by the speaking gifts of Whitefield in the sermon that, despite his best efforts to stop himself, he emptied his pocket—copper, silver, and gold—into the collector's plate. Religiously, Franklin was a deist and rationalist, and he stood at the other end of the world from the pious Whitefield. Yet, melted by his oratorical powers, Franklin had yielded and contributed to the collection. Later, he heard Whitefield speak again out of doors and estimated that the preacher's voice could easily carry to 30,000 people. The quality of the sound must have been as impressive as the strength, for David Garrick, the great English actor of the period, thought that if Whitefield said the word "Mesopotamia" from the stage, he would move his audience to tears.

Franklin, despite a highly self-conscious religious identity, had been persuaded by the golden-tongued Whitefield to join in a mass religious episode. The persuasion was temporary and minimal in Franklin's case: Whitefield got Franklin's money but not his mind and heart. Yet in the case of thousands of others, the persuasion was more lasting. These Americans were responding to a ritual that, as the years passed, would continue as a highly visible feature of religion in America. Not only individuals but sometimes entire religious traditions would embrace it. Revivalism would be a major element among the common themes that made up the one religion of Americans.

Benjamin Franklin's experience with the revival brings to mind the story of the elephant and the blind men in the Introduction. The elephant, we suggested, was like religion in America—a gigantic creature to be examined piece by piece. Like the blind men of the parable, we have been acquiring knowledge of different parts of the animal. We have been reviewing the separate and distinct religious movements that were and are key examples of the manyness of religions

247

in America. In fact, so separate and distinct have been the various movements we have examined that, as we said in the Introduction, it seemed as if we were describing different animals and even different species. Not only were there many religious traditions within the geographical boundaries of the United States, but there was manyness *within* traditions. American Indians belonged to separate nations, each with their own religion. Protestants showed as much manyness with their numerous denominations. Catholics displayed ethnic identities that made for considerable tensions within a supposedly unified Roman Catholic church, while occult and metaphysical movements seemed almost as numerous as the people who turned to them.

By the same token, even as we immersed ourselves in this religious pluralism, from time to time we could not fail to notice the way different movements and traditions seemed to take on some of the characteristics of the Protestant mainstream. Reform Jews of the late nineteenth century moved their Sabbath services to Sunday morning and imitated the style of Protestant worship. Catholics after Vatican II moved to a leaner and simpler version of the Mass, closer to the demands of the Protestant Reformation. Mormons and Adventists in their affirmations of the good life in this world resembled Liberal Protestants in their optimism, while Japanese Buddhists in the new land spoke of churches, acknowledged bishops, and initiated Sunday services. Meanwhile, blacks who became middle class often gravitated toward congregations that were integrated or that resembled in their decorum the churches of white mainline Protestantism. In these and other instances, manyness was still thriving, but there were numerous ways that the boundaries of the separate traditions were overlapping the boundaries of Protestantism.

Even further, in the chapter on Protestantism, we spoke of denominationalism, revivalism, and related questions, noticing the ways in which Protestants, though many, often looked very much alike. We promised to address this issue of oneness in Part Two, and it is time now to make good on the promise. For the similarity *among* Protestants also became a similarity *with* other Americans. The majority tradition acted in subtle and not-so-subtle ways to wear away the sharp edges of separateness and bring people toward itself. Hence, in this chapter we will discuss more directly a theme that we have observed all along—how Protestantism acted as the dominant and public religion of the United States. We will see that the dominant and public religion included the inheritors of the Reformation but also millions of "cultural" Protestants who had through the American experience absorbed aspects of the dominant tradition. Then, in later chapters, we will look at related elements of the oneness of religion in America.

By saying that Protestantism acted as the dominant and public religion of the United States, we are saying that Protestantism became the one religion of the country. Whatever it meant in the personal lives of millions of individuals, publicly Protestantism meant acknowledged ways of thinking and acting supported by most institutions in society—by the government (though unofficially), the schools, the media, and countless Protestant churches and families. If in Part One we saw the many in their manyness by examining different religious communities and their histories, here we face the situation of social, political, and economic power.

Before we go further, we need to make some distinctions. First of all, religion, we have said, is both extraordinary—beyond the boundaries of our everyday world—and ordinary—within its limits. In these terms, Protestantism formed the basis for both extraordinary and ordinary religion in the United States. The chief extraordinary religion in America was and is Protestantism, and similarly, the ordinary religion of mainstream American culture displays characteristics which derive historically from the Protestant experience in the New World. Although it is not possible to draw a sharp line between these two forms of Protestantism, we can at least see different instances in which one or the other has predominated.

Secondly, the oneness of religion in America was historically present from the time the English colonies were established. But it also grew with the years, so that various parts of the common witness acquired new features and became more prominent or—like the Calvinist belief in predestination to heaven and hell—gradually faded. Thirdly, the oneness of religion was related to the continuance of a certain community, the early settlers and their offspring, who were of Anglo-Saxon and Northern European stock. But it was also related to the widespread adoption by others of the creed, code, and cultus that the original community handed on. Although many times they were unaware of it, Catholics and Jews, Buddhists and Eastern Orthodox Christians could and did share in public Protestantism. So did countless others from among the many. Hence, as we try to understand the one religion of Americans, we will have to be aware of the complexity involved in its existence.

AMERICAN RELIGIOUS HISTORY
AND PUBLIC PROTESTANTISM

To locate the dominant Protestant community and understand its religion, later shared by others, is to encounter a group of related characteristics. Some were elements of a code of everyday behavior; some were aspects of a cultus, or system of ritual expression; and some were parts of a creed, or set of beliefs. Together they formed a complete religious system in which the various elements interrelated with each other to form a coherent religious whole. That is to say, one characteristic led logically and psychologically to the next one, and the last characteristic led back to the first. This religious system—which we call public Protestantism—did grow and change with the years; but in order to simplify, we will sketch only continuing elements and major moments in the life of the public Protestant religious system.

Public Protestantism originated in the Calvinist Christianity of the early Puritan settlers. As we discussed in Chapter 4, Puritanism, in one form or another, was widespread in the colonies. Puritan attitudes and folkways characterized the public life from Massachusetts Bay to the southern settlements. To put this into statistical terms, out of 154 congregations in the colonies in 1660, nearly 90 percent (138) could be described in the broad sense as Calvinist in inclination. Of these, seventy-five were Congregational, forty-one Anglican, five Presbyterian, four Baptist, and thirteen Dutch Reformed. Eliminating these last leaves over 80 percent who had, generally speaking, not only Calvinist but also Puritan roots. That kind of numerical predominance would continue to be a feature of organized Protestantism in the United States. By the time of the first great revival (the Great Awakening from about 1726 to 1745), roughly three-fourths of the colonists still leaned toward Calvinism. By the time of the census of 1790, 83.5 percent of enumerated Americans were counted as English, and they were overwhelmingly Protestant. Even today, as we saw earlier, almost two-thirds of all Americans consider themselves Protestant (61 percent in 1975), and again the churches of Calvinist heritage form the largest block by far in the listing.

If these massive numbers of religious adherents helped to shape the public Protestantism, so did the educational earnestness of Puritan Christians. With its opening lines, "In Adam's Fall/We sinned all," *The New England Primer* (1683?) was printed in an estimated 7 million copies by 1840. Together the opening lines and the publishing data suggest the enormous religious influence that this single Puritan reader was to have in the early education of other Americans. As we saw in both the Introduction and Chapter 4, New England settlers stressed education from the first. The Massachusetts Bay colonists founded Harvard College in 1636, and shortly it was bequeathed a library of 400 books by the young minister John Harvard (1607–1638). By 1639 the first printing press in the colonies was operating from the Harvard College Yard, and the *Primer* as well as the famous *Bay Psalm Book* was printed there.

On the elementary level efforts were as strenuous. A legislative act of 1642 made it the responsibility of parents in Massachusetts Bay to educate their children in the "three Rs." Later, towns that had reached the size of fifty families were legally bound to obtain a schoolmaster to teach their children. The Connecticut and New Haven colonies shortly enacted similar laws. Puritans wanted their children to be able to read in order that they might understand the Bible for themselves. People of the Word needed to be literate, and people called by the Word to a vocation in the world also needed to be able to communicate in writing and to use numbers in order to do business. Thus, Puritan education began and ended in religion, so that the textbooks written for the schools, like *The New England Primer*, spread the message of Calvinist Christianity among the young. As education became more common in the colonies and then in the nineteenth century was mandated by law in state after state, it was not surprising that the early New England textbooks provided models for the teaching material that came into use. Clearly, New England had established a corner on the material that appeared in educational texts. Into the twentieth century, it was the Puritan vision of American life that predominated in the textbooks used by school children from coast to coast.

Similarly, the politics of leadership in the colonies helped to create public Protestantism. From the first, many of the people who governed were representatives of a committed elite of Calvinist Christians. In Massachusetts Bay, for example, only males who were church members were considered freemen who could vote and hold civil office. In Pennsylvania leadership remained in the hands of the founding Quakers and their descendants into the eighteenth century. The Dutch colony of New Amsterdam (later New York) had Dutch Reformed lay leadership until it fell to the English, while lay members of the

Anglican church governed in colonial Virginia. Especially in New England and in Pennsylvania, a self-conscious moral and religious intent pervaded government. Political leaders shaped the civil life of their colonies to reflect their religion. The prestige of their positions lent to Protestantism added public importance.

Besides this prestige through political association, Protestantism enjoyed legal privilege through an official and established Anglicanism in the southern colonies and through a Puritan establishment in New England. Such establishments fell away in the late eighteenth and early nineteenth centuries, but the religious imprint left by early colonial history was not easily erased. As newcomers arrived in the United States, it was natural that they should absorb an esteem for Protestantism along with their regard for the institutions of American government and life. Hence, the religious stamp of the colonies lingered on in the public life of the nation, something we will have more to say about in our discussion of civil religion in Chapter 11.

Finally, the usefulness of Calvinist Christianity in helping people to meet the demands of their New World environment also enhanced its stature. Protestantism assumed historical dominance in part because there was a good fit between the thisworldly ethic of Protestantism and the needs of settling a new country. Indeed, Protestantism seemed an ideal religion for those who wanted to "tame" a landscape and lead it from its "wilderness" condition into a fair replica of the best in Old World civilization. If New England were to resemble a reformed old England, and if Virginia were to prove a tribute to the Virgin Queen, Elizabeth I, then hard work, commitment, and frugality must exist in plenty. At the same time, worship must be simple and streamlined, capable of thriving no less in a bare, log chapel than in a mighty and elaborate church. Later, as the United States grew and prospered, Calvinist Christianity offered a good fit for a culture bent on material progress and industrial efficiency. With its Word that led into the world and its understanding of the religious significance of success, it nurtured the energies of a developing nation. It was only a very recent awareness that led to major questioning of the goals of the age of progress. Well into the twentieth century, Calvinist Christianity supported the public aims and intentions of the United States as well as the private ends of millions of its citizens.

THE PROTESTANT CODE

Earlier in the text, we treated religious systems by looking first at their creeds, or systems of belief, and then moving to a discussion of their ritual and ethical expressions in cultus and code. However, as we investigate the dominant and public Protestantism of America, it will be easier to reverse the order, discussing first the everyday attitudes and behavioral styles that form the Protestant code. This code is a large part of the body of connecting religious characteristics of which we have spoken. Present nearly everywhere in Protestant America, it has expressed itself as clear conditions, institutions, and patterns of existence within the mainstream. In fact, this code has been the most readily identifiable feature of American Protestant religion and culture—although, as we will see, ritual and creedal expressions are easy to identify as well.

The Conditions: Religious Liberty, Democratic
Equality, Separation of Church and State

The code begins with *religious liberty* and *democratic equality*, the social conditions that became a pattern of life, at first unevenly in the colonies and later with more consistency in the young republic. Religious liberty and democratic equality were important ideals for social life even in many colonies with religious establishments. New England Puritans, although they tried to keep Quakers and other dissenters away, had come to the New World in order to enjoy religious liberty for themselves. Meanwhile, in colonies like Pennsylvania and Maryland, pluralism was a fact and religious liberty much of the time a reality. There *were* distinct political inequalities in the English settlements. Full citizenship with voting rights was never the possession of everyone. Religious, racial, sexual, and property qualifications existed, and only a certain class of men were truly "equal." Still, the ideal was often read into existing conditions by these men of property and proper religious preference, while the history of the United States later became one of increasing movement toward full realization of the idea.

Moreover, the heritage of the Radical Reformation partially influenced many of the colonists. The English Puritans had absorbed a strain of Calvinism which was mingled in their minds with Radical ideas. In New England the congregational form of church government was based on the Radical concept of the gathered or free church, a community of commitment entered without force. The corollary of such a gathered congregational church was religious liberty, for how could a church be truly free if people entered it by birth or by provision of a ruler? Thus, religious liberty was a necessity, at least in theory, for the operation of Puritan principles. The fruit of these principles was reaped when Roger Williams was banished from Massachusetts Bay. After his extreme Separatist convictions had led him into trouble with the authorities, he founded the Rhode Island colony as a refuge for religious seekers (1635). As leader of the Baptists there, he proved the sincerity of his commitment to religious liberty when he provided a haven for Quakers even though he heartily disapproved of their teachings. And as Baptist churches grew in number and influence in the eighteenth century, their message played an important role in laying the groundwork for religious liberty in the new nation.

When the Constitution was adopted in 1789, religious liberty was legally specified in the *separation of church and state*, or religious disestablishment. Congress could make no law either establishing a religion or prohibiting its "free exercise." Nor could the government require any religious affiliation for officeholding. This disestablishment referred only to the new federal government, but by 1833 the last state, Massachusetts, had fallen into line and abolished its religious establishment. The reasons for the arrangement were both practical and ideological. With the diversity of religious settlements in the various colonies, it would have proved impossible to unite them except on terms which recognized the religious rights of all. Beyond that, after the adoption of the Declaration of Independence in 1776, Enlightenment teachings about equal and unalienable rights given by nature had become part of the public rhetoric. Even earlier in the century, British soldiers had brought the Enlightenment to ordinary folk during the course of the French and Indian War. So notions concerning natural liberty blended in the climate of the times with other ideas about religious liberty derived from Baptist and free-church sources.

Separation of church and state was a new and, indeed, revolutionary settlement of the religious question. Until the Reformation of the sixteenth century, Europe had understood itself as Christendom—one great and theoretically unified kingdom of Christ in which spiritual and worldly power were separate aspects of the whole. Even after the Reformation, leading Reformers, such as Martin Luther and John Calvin, and Roman Catholics had agreed that spiritual and worldly government went hand in hand. As we saw earlier, both persecuted the Radical Reformers who with their sectarian principle were viewed as dangerous to the church-state unity of Christendom. Official state churches, whether Protestant or Catholic, were the rule in Europe. Holland, the most liberal nation in its tolerance for dissent in the seventeenth and eighteenth centuries, still had a state Reformed church until 1795. England during the same period continued to maintain a religious establishment. Hence, when Americans instituted a clear separation of church and state in their new federal government, even though they understood themselves still as Christian and predominantly Protestant, they had created a radically new condition for religion.

The Institutions: Denominationalism and Voluntaryism

This new condition became part of the Protestant code and in turn led to the next characteristics of the dominant and public religion. These were the institutions of *denominationalism* and *voluntaryism*. We have already had occasion to discuss denominationalism in earlier chapters. The key point here is that the conditions of religious liberty, democratic equality, and church-state separation determined the ways in which religious communities could organize most effectively. Since religious associations could not count on state support, they could not hope to include all the inhabitants of a territory, for the country was being settled by members of many different religious bodies. By the same token, because religious associations did not need to worry about state interference, they were being invited subtly to loosen their boundaries and to mingle freely in society. Thus, one of the factors that in Europe had made for the creation of separate and exclusive sects was missing. Under circumstances of official governmental neutrality, an unofficial "establishment" grew up in the United States. The dominant and public religion, recognized and approved by society, was denominational. Denominations thought their specific teachings were important, and they did not consider one religious group just the same as any other. Yet they saw themselves as part of the larger spiritual organization of the Christian church, even as they were willing to embrace the idea of separate jurisdictions. Moreover, since religious liberty was a matter of law, nobody could be forced to join a denomination, and no outside assistance could be expected in running its internal affairs or in bringing its Christian witness to others outside the denomination.

The response of the denominations to this situation was voluntaryism. Remember that denominations already consisted entirely of groups of volunteers: they were from the first *voluntary* societies. Soon, however, voluntaryism became a principle of their activity. Financially, they depended on voluntary support by their members instead of a public tax. Managerially, even during the days of state establishment, Protestantism had fostered lay control of many aspects of each organization, and if anything, the new arrangements only increased this tendency. But by the nineteenth century, the denominations were looking outward in their voluntaryism. More and more, members of different denominations began to cooperate in the formation of voluntary societies beyond their official jurisdictions. Their aims in each case were to spread the fundamentals of the Christian message in America and the world. Despite their doctrinal differences, there were many points on which most could agree—the basic importance of the Bible, the use of Sunday schools to spread Christian teaching, the distribution of pamphlet literature about shared Christian understandings, even common missionary efforts.

So in the space of a few years, national voluntary societies came into existence. Organizations like the American Board of Commissioners for Foreign Missions (1810), the American Education Society (1815), the American Bible Society (1816), the American Sunday School Union (1824), and the American Tract Society (1825), all were agents of the dominant and public Protestantism of the nation. Run by wealthy and influential lay Protestant citizens, these societies often shared many of the same individuals in leadership roles. Directors of one organization frequently appeared on the board of directors in another. By the 1830s, they were controlling what many historians have described as a "benevolent empire."

The Patterns: Activism and the Search to Simplify

Later we will see how voluntaryism fanned out to take up issues of moral and social reform. Now, however, we need to notice a further interlocking element in the Protestant code. Recall that religious liberty, democratic equality, and separation of church and state were background conditions in which religion must live and that denominationalism and voluntaryism were institutions. With the next item, we encounter a pattern to which everyday behavior conformed. That pattern was *activism*. There were deep historical roots for the activism that flourished within the Protestant churches, and our discussion in Chapter 4 stressed how the Word led outward into the world. But in America, there were new reasons for religious people to be active. Denominationalism and voluntaryism meant that individuals had to take part in energetic efforts to advance the case for their religion among their fellow citizens. In a young nation which had to build and to plant to insure the future, religious organizations had to do the same. The result was increased religious busyness, a spiritual style that put its premium on public and expressive behavior.

Missionary efforts were only part of this story of activism. Despite their cooperation on many counts, without state support the denominations engaged in strenuous competition. To survive meant to dispute the wrongheaded teachings of other churches and to strive to bring more and more people into one's own. Furthermore, the situation demanded the construction of churches, seminaries, and colleges. Especially on the frontier, where institutions arrived after the pioneers, Protestants saw their task as the advancement of Christian civilization. They thought that unless they provided the necessary structures to generate Christian influence, chaos and barbarism would thrive. In the larger sense, it is possible to consider the establishment of these institutions part of a home missionary campaign, as they surely were. Still, the point is that it was not enough simply to speak out for Protestantism. Material efforts had to be made so that buildings could rise. Active people, living an active Christianity, were required.

The energies of this Protestant activism blended indistinguishably with the energetic style of a growing America. In other words, both the extraordinary religion of Protestantism and the ordinary religion of American culture reflected the activist impulse. Americans, as people, were doers more than thinkers. They loved to speed, and in the nineteenth century they marveled at the invention of rail transportation that carried people at seven times the speed of stage coaches. When steam engines hastened travel on western rivers, they delighted to run races with the boats—sometimes to the point of disastrous explosions and accidents. Over a century later, it was much the same. Fast food had become a symbol of American culture with the golden arches of McDonald's hamburgers; the imposition of a fifty-five-mile-an-hour speed limit was a national tragedy; and jogging had become a national religion. To be active was to be oriented rightly in this world. To be fast was to be happy and whole.

Religious liberty, democratic equality, and church-state separation had been ordinary conditions for the existence of extraordinary religion. Denominationalism and voluntaryism had been ordinary institutions, sociologically speaking, that housed the extraordinary commitments of many people. Here though, we are faced with a behavioral pattern that had both extraordinary and ordinary aspects. Protestant activism in the end melted into the larger activism of American culture, for Protestantism was indeed *public*. To ask which activism caused the other would be very much like asking the old chicken-and-egg question. The relationship between ordinary and extraordinary activism was circular and mutually reinforcing. There were roots in the history of Protestantism. There were other roots in the needs generated by the American environment. Protestantism strongly influenced American culture, but American culture kept changing Protestantism.

The activist impulse within the churches had further implications for the code of continuity. *Reductionism* affected the way people dealt with religion in general, while *antiintellectualism* affected the way they treated ideas, and *ahistoricism* influenced their attitudes toward the past. Let us look in turn at each of these characteristics of public Protestantism.

Reductionism meant reducing things to their lowest common denominator—to their simplest terms. Such reductionism was related to activism, because activism encouraged a paring away of religion to the bare essentials. If people were to busy themselves in the enormous task of building a Protestant civilization, they did not have much time for niceties and elaborations, whether of religion or of anything else. They had to be content with laying out the basic structure. Attention to details would come later, if at all. The enormity of the Protestant task was compounded by the realities, in many cases, of frontier life, far away from big cities with their intellectual excitement and material goods and services. In America there was, it seemed, limitless space and limited time. So a "bare-bones" approach characterized the spread of Protestantism. As we will see later in the chapter, both creed and code came to be very simple—a few clear-cut and easily grasped ideas; an equally simple and effective ritual life. Meanwhile, reductionism itself became part of the behavioral code. People were uncomfortable with ambiguities, and they wanted precise rules for their deeds. Either an action was right, or it was wrong. People could live with "Yes," or "No," but they could not be comfortable with "It depends."

The results of this pattern of reductionism were evident in both extraordinary and ordinary religion. Within the Protestant churches, crusades like temperance, to be discussed in more detail later, developed in an all-or-nothing direction. Either people did not drink at all, or they would become disreputable and depraved individuals. Either Christians were "saved" and wholly in the camp of Jesus, or they were hell-bound sinners. At the same time, within American culture a related preference for simple rules of everyday behavior was encouraged. The old code of honor between men, for example, required that an insult be righted by a dual. Social shame was a matter of life or death with little in between. Similarly, nineteenth-century Americans frequently reacted to the poor quality of medical care in their society by turning to patent drugs that promised to be miracle cures for every ailment. And, as another instance, writers were fond of describing their period as a time of "ultraisms," their term for extremisms of many types.

Twentieth-century religion and culture continued to reflect these basic attitudes concerning sharp divisions between different courses of action. After midcentury, conservative and Fundamentalist Protestant churches grew rapidly while the Liberals marked time. Among the reasons for the statistics was the clear and simple ethic that the conservatives taught. Sex outside of marriage was wrong, and Christian witness was right. Gambling and alcohol led to trouble, but love for country and loyalty in war were right and good. General American culture taught a related message about the clear division between good and evil. Television Westerns had their heroes and villains, the "good guys" and the "bad guys," while one widely promoted advertisement for automobiles capitalized on the pattern by telling Americans that the "good guys" always wore white hats.

In the area of ideas, reductionism became a more specific antiintellectualism. Active Americans tended to have limited intellectual opportunities and time for thought. Moreover, they were impatient with purely theoretical distinctions that could not be put to practical use. In a widely read nineteenth-century biography, George Washington was praised because he did not study the impractical dead languages of Latin and Greek. In like fashion, the full title of the American Philosophical Society, founded in the eighteenth century, announced that it promoted "useful knowledge." This meant everything from preserving wine to cultivating silkworms, but it did *not* mean abstract metaphysics. Later Americans followed in the path of their ancestors. The nineteenth and twentieth centuries saw them develop astounding practical technologies for home, industrial, and wartime use. Yet thoughtful Americans continued to complain that we did not have a national literature or philosophical tradition that rivaled the European contribution. Meanwhile, in the late twentieth century the school systems in many states were in trouble because adequate taxes had not been collected to finance them.

If antiintellectualism was a feature of ordinary American culture, it was also a part of the dominant and public Protestantism of the country. Although European Protestantism had flourished in a strongly theological atmosphere and New England Puritanism had encouraged the development of religious thought, the nineteenth century saw an increasing unwillingness among many Protestants to engage in hard theological thinking. With the background of democratic equality and the institution of voluntaryism to stimulate them, ordinary folk felt that theology, as much of it as was necessary, was their province. They did not require an elite to do their thinking for them.

Beyond that, as the tradition of a learned ministry fell away because of the demands of preaching a simple gospel on the frontier, theology lost its subtlety. Like intellectual activity in general, American theology needed to be useful. Significantly, the greatest Protestant theologian that America produced— Jonathan Edwards—was an eighteenth-century representative of the Puritan and Calvinist traditions who lived well before the age of the largest frontier expansion. In the later twentieth century, the new theologies that Americans expounded were directed toward practical issues—the problems of blacks and women, the need for economic liberation in Third World countries, the relationship between Christianity and religious nationalism (civil religion).

What antiintellectualism did for the mental "space" of ideas, ahistoricism did for time. Ahistoricism was the refusal to dwell in the past or feel bound by the events of European history. And like antiintellectualism, it was an example of the reductionist tendency to simplify. Yet in America, this ahistoricism was a complex reality, one that was part of Protestantism and also part of mainstream culture.

The Reformation of the sixteenth century had urged Christians to forget the centuries of tradition that had intervened between the time of Jesus and its own age. It had proclaimed the authority of the Bible alone, and it had tried to clear away what it regarded as corruption and superstition. By skipping over the medieval centuries in its quest for meaningful time, the Reformation had started Protestantism down a path on which it became easier to disregard history. In Europe, with its history written into the landscape of ancient shrines and churches, tradition still played an important part in Protestant life. In America, though, where no European memorials from the past were located, it was easier to forget the ancestors. Moreover, the ordinary images and metaphors that were used to describe America suggested the absence of links with the past. It was a New World; it had been "discovered" by Europeans; the national government of the United States was founded on a "revolution." With this background, Americans were far more interested in making history than in reading or honoring it.

Protestant life in the new country both reflected and helped to create the general situation. Churches were forced in one way or another to cut their ties with the past. After the Revolution, Anglicanism, as the established Church of England, was unwelcome in the new United States. So members of that religious

257

community reconstituted themselves as Episcopalians. Likewise, the Methodists, supplied with new American bishops, went their own way, separate from the mother country. Neither congregational nor presbyterian forms of church government favored close ties with European religious communities, while in the nineteenth century the religious needs of the frontier meant intense preoccupation with the present. For Protestants as for other Americans, the past seemed dead and unreal in comparison with the demands and opportunities of the moment. New denominations sprang up, and the fact that they did not have a past was an asset rather than a liability. If there was a direction in which Protestants and others looked, it was certainly not the past but the future.

Significantly, many of the new religious movements that arose emphasized their roots in a sacred, biblical time outside the ordinary run of history. Seventh-day Adventism had sprung up during the time of Enoch before the coming of Jesus. The Churches of Christ dated back to the time of Jesus. Christian Science restored the healing practices of the primitive church. In each of these examples and many others like them, the appeal was to a mythic era that leaped over the centuries of ordinary time. By the twentieth century, Fundamental and conservative churches were illustrating the pattern in their involvement in millennialism, a subject that we will take up later in the chapter. General American culture repeated the story as well. The original Henry Ford was reputed to have said that history was bunk. The flower children of the sixties wanted to burn the past as they looked to the dawning of a new age of harmony and love. Other young people, who were more conservative, withdrew in massive numbers from university history courses as soon as they were no longer required to take them.

The Patterns: Moralism

So far we have seen that certain conditions (religious liberty, democratic equality, the separation of church and state) and institutions (denominationalism and voluntaryism) favored the growth of various behavioral patterns—the code of Protestant America. Activism, reductionism, antiintellectualism, and ahistoricism were all among these patterns. Probably the most important, though, is the one we will discuss now. If any one characteristic gave its overall shape to the Protestant code, that characteristic was *moralism*. The activism of Protestant Americans and their wish to simplify life led to a concern for the rules of action. Morality became the uppermost test of Christian witness and the key reality in Christian life.

Interest in morality had long roots in the Judaeo-Christian tradition. In our discussion of the Hebrew prophets, we could not fail to notice their intense ethical impulse. Similarly, when we examined the birth of the mainstream of the Reformation, we saw clearly that the Word of scripture led to moral action in the world, while we saw, too, the quest for moral purity in the sectarianism of the Radical Reformers. Developments in seventeenth- and eighteenth-century Europe further encouraged a moralistic attitude among Protestants. We have seen that Calvinism came gradually to regard good works and righteousness as central. At the same time, other Protestants began to feel that the descendants of the Reformation had grown stale. They were too involved in preserving correct doctrine and did not inspire people to an enthusiastic attachment to Christianity. Many of these Pietists, among them Lutherans, Separatists, and Moravians, later immigrated to America.

In this country, the concern for morality combined with Puritan and Enlightenment influences as well as other currents in the culture to produce an ordinary and extraordinary religion of moralism and reform. Even before the arrival of the continental Pietists, the New England Puritans had fostered their own form of pietism in their demand for an experience of conversion and upright moral witness for full church members. Moreover, Puritan sermons early came to reflect a classic style, so that historians call them jeremiads. Like the Old Testament Lamentations of the prophet Jeremiah, jeremiads were sermons filled with woe. They bewailed the sins of individuals and the whole community and warned that these sins would force the hand of God in punishment. These Puritan sermons, often printed and distributed after they were given, set the tone of guilt and a consequent need for repentance and action that became characteristic of the public language of America. As we will see in Chapter 11, the same tone was reflected in political speeches and in civil religion. Here it is important to note that the style of the jeremiad led to a felt need for moral purification in society— something that bore fruit in crusades like the temperance and antislavery campaigns of the nineteenth century.

Meanwhile, another strand in Protestantism came to influence the dominant and public religion toward moralism. Gradually, the character of Puritan preaching began to change, and especially in and near Boston, ministers of the eighteenth century were spreading liberal Christianity. Important to this change was their acceptance of the so-called Arminian teachings. A product of seventeenth-century Holland, Arminianism countered the stern Calvinism of an earlier era with the message that Jesus had died for all people. Conversely, no one's salvation was assured, and each person must strive earnestly to persevere in the Christian life. Morality became the key to authentic Christianity, and the Boston ministers echoed the message by preaching sermons filled with directions concerning how to live.

From another quarter, the moral teachings of Arminianism were receiving encouragement. As we saw in Part One, Enlightenment deism taught a simple creed of belief in God and an afterlife of future reward or punishment. But most important to deistic or "natural" religion was a good and moral life. In effect, what a person believed was not so significant as what that person did or did not do. The real test of religion was moral effort. When the liberal Christians of New England became Unitarians after 1825, their teaching was in many ways close to Enlightenment deism. Until the time of the Civil War, their "moral philosophy" remained the same, providing the background for New Englanders who took action in various moral crusades of the period. Likewise, evangelical Protestants who had been stirred by the great revivals (to be discussed) were treading their own moral ground. Like the Puritans of an earlier time, they needed to purify themselves and remain free from sin. Alcohol, gambling, sexual promiscuity, even dancing could corrupt people and separate them from Jesus. Besides, zeal for the gospel meant that evangelicals needed to labor for moral reform in society.

Hence, by the nineteenth century Protestant America had a history that urged it toward moralism. One strand, descended from the evangelical side of Puritanism, led toward various Protestant movements for immediate purification, either from private vices like alcoholism or from public sins such as slavery. The other strand, brought together from the liberal side of Puritanism, Enlightenment deism, and as we will discuss later, general Protestant perfectionism and millennialism, committed itself to efforts to achieve social justice. This could mean work for antislavery, for women's rights, for peace, or for other reform causes. At the same time, a third strand, derived from general American culture, joined forces with Protestantism in the various reform movements. The reconstruction of society was a task that stirred many nineteenth-century Americans. Whether as part of an extraordinary commitment to the God beyond this world or as an ordinary venture for common decency, the moral reforms for which Americans labored were the same or nearly so.

To take one example of a campaign largely for moral purity, we glance briefly at the antebellum (pre–Civil-War) nineteenth-century temperance movement. Historical evidence concerning early Americans suggests that they drank hard liquor quite a bit. In fact, estimates of how much alcohol they used range from two and one-half gallons annually for each person in 1792 to seven and one-half gallons in 1823. Benjamin Rush, the famous physician of the revolutionary and postrevolutionary years, had warned in a publication of the dangers of alcohol to body and mind, and members of the American Tract Society, who reprinted the work, agreed. At first, efforts were directed toward moderating the use of alcohol rather than banishing it, although Methodists and Quakers disapproved of liquor entirely. By the early-to-middle years of the nineteenth century, however, the spread of the right to vote to men without property encouraged social leaders to push to insure a sober electorate. Moreover, the existence of social problems such as poverty and crime also caught the attention of social leaders, who associated these evils with drunkenness.

In this general atmosphere, the clergy launched a vigorous campaign for the temperance cause. Congregations were bombarded with sermons on the evils of drink, and by 1813, the Massachusetts Society for the Suppression of Intemperance had come into existence. Then after 1825 the focus of the movement shifted, and total abstinence from alcohol became the cry. Temperance became an absolute proposition, in line with the characteristic American demand for simplicity. Drinking must end *now* as the code of moral purity required. The well-known Lyman Beecher—whom we met in Chapter 4— began preaching sermons calling for complete renunciation of drink. The American Society for the Promotion of Temperance was born in 1826, immediately waging a highly successful campaign to get people to sign a teetotaler's pledge not to drink. And after 1833, the American Temperance Society became the national focus of the abstinence crusade.

There was a brief period of decline at the end of the decade, but the movement found new allies in a society of reformed drunkards and in the work of novelists such as Timothy Shay Arthur, whose *Ten Nights in a Bar Room* (1854) became a best seller. Meanwhile, women had moved to the side of the clergy as their staunch supporters, and in states like Maine (1846), Vermont (1852), and New York (1854), prohibition of alcoholic beverages became the law of the land. Prohibition legislation spread until a total of fourteen states and one territory had laws on their books. Only the tensions over slavery and the shadow of the coming Civil War distracted the reformers and diffused the energies of the temperance fighters, so that the heyday of the antebellum nineteenth-century temperance movement was over.

Temperance, abstinence, and prohibition all derived from a desire for purification. By renouncing strong drink, a person would cleanse the body of physical and, more important, moral evil—evil that could weaken an individual's self-control and lead to further sinful deeds. By banishing drinking as a social habit, the body of society would also be purged—of crime, poverty, and an ignorant and irresponsible citizenry. Both for extraordinary and ordinary reasons, people rallied to the cause of purity, together giving testimony to a dominant and public religion that was both Protestantism and culture. In the antislavery crusade, however, the urge to purity was joined more clearly by the yearning of some for social justice. Hence, we need to take a quick look at this movement in nineteenth-century American history.

From colonial times, there had been opposition to slavery, and in fact one version of the Declaration of Independence had expressed antislavery sentiments. The logic of the doctrine of natural rights, affirming that all were equal, demanded the recognition of the natural freedom of black people. It was only political expediency that led the framers of the Constitution to accept by their silence the working principle of state jurisdiction in matters of slavery. By 1817 the American Colonization Society was seeking to relocate emancipated slaves and free blacks in a territory reserved for them in Africa. But others even at that time thought that the colonization movement was wrong or too timid. Abolition societies already were springing up. Then in 1831 William Lloyd Garrison (1805–1879) began to publish *The Liberator*, a weekly newspaper with militant abolitionist views. His gospel was freedom *now* for black people, and the antislavery movement had entered a new phase.

In the New West, converts from the great revival preached by Charles Grandison Finney took up the antislavery cause, among them Theodore Dwight Weld (1803–1895), who led a group of radical students from Lane Theological Seminary in Cincinnati to Oberlin College in northern Ohio in a dispute over slavery and attitudes toward blacks in general. This linkage between antislavery and revivalism was to yield great success, for Weld had connections with wealthy evangelical Protestants in the East. At the same time, the American Anti-Slavery Society, founded in 1833, took up the cause. In New England, an antislavery society had already been active, and liberal ministers gradually began to give public support to abolition. Thus, a coalition of northern evangelicals and liberals joined with other Americans in the crusade against slavery. The blend of Protestantism and politics gave birth eventually to the Republican party and the election in 1860 of Abraham Lincoln who emancipated the slaves. Ordinary and extraordinary religion mingled freely in the movement, and so did energies inspired by the need for immediate moral purity and others generated by the demands of social justice. The antislavery movement was a classic case of moral reform in America.

By the end of the century, social justice became the concern of the Liberal Protestant Social Gospel movement, as we saw in Part One. Beyond that, Jewish involvement in socialist causes as well as Jewish and Roman Catholic efforts in the early labor movement signaled that major non-Protestant groups could embrace on their own terms a similar dedication to justice. In Judaism, as we have seen, the ethical heritage of the classical Hebrew prophets supported the new endeavors. In Catholicism, the social teachings of Pope Leo XIII (1810–1903), as well as historic elements in the Catholic tradition, provided theoretical encouragement. Yet, from a practical point of view, the urge to the reform of society was in the air, for it was the backbone of the dominant and public religion. So it was not surprising that some Jews and Catholics found the best way to be American was to work for social justice.

In the more recent history of the twentieth century, we may see a mixture of elements at work in various movements for the reform of society. Earlier in the century, the enactment of the Prohibition (Eighteenth) Amendment to the Constitution (1919) signaled the opening, a year later, of an era of public abstinence. It was an expression of the dominant Protestant character of America, and themes of public moralism continued long after the death of the amendment in 1933. By the seventies, as we noted in Chapter 3, the Protestant style had spread to Catholics who, with the cooperation of Orthodox Jews and conservative Protestants, led a crusade for the "right to life," a national protest against legalized abortion. Here both the need for moral purification and the demands of extraordinary religion were uppermost.

A decade earlier, the side of the dominant moralism that demanded social justice for its own sake had been more in evidence. President Lyndon B. Johnson (1908–1973) had launched the Great Society, and civil-rights legislation was carried through the Congress. Various programs emerged to fight poverty in urban slums and to upgrade nutritional and educational opportunities for the disadvantaged. Then the war in Vietnam became the focus for a national protest that embraced widely different elements in American society. Ministers and priests joined with flower children and the mothers of soldiers to argue their case against the war. Television news programs and newspapers were filled with accounts of protests, from the ritual burning of draft cards and of the American flag to mass rallies in front of the White House. It was obvious that both people with extraordinary religious commitments and others with more ordinary concerns had joined in these activities. But not to be overlooked in the presence of the cry for justice was the fact that the old urge to immediate moral purity was also involved in the antiwar movement. Many Americans feared they would bear the guilt of a terrible national sin if they continued to destroy the lives and landscapes of innocent Vietnamese. The war was "dirty," and people who would remain clean must be free of it at once.

When on the heels of the end of the war, the Watergate scandal began to occupy Americans, the same double thread of moralism was in evidence. The venerable doctrines of the Enlightenment, memorialized in the Constitution, were being threatened by President Richard M. Nixon (b. 1913), who was violating the demands of justice and natural right. At the same time, as Nixon's lawyer John Dean had warned, a cancer was growing on the presidency. There was moral corruption and a consequent need for moral purification. The body of society needed to expel the evil and cleanse itself so that it might function once more in good health. Again, the needs for justice and purity were felt by people with a range of commitments, from Protestant evangelist William F. (Billy) Graham (b. 1918) to many an agnostic humanist. Hence, moralism knitted together Americans of many persuasions, whether ordinary or extraordinary, and whether Protestant or non-Protestant. The point was that moralism was no longer simply a feature of Protestantism: it had become a general characteristic of American culture.

THE PROTESTANT CULTUS

Patterns of behavior are expressed in symbolic statements of the meaning of things, acted out in rituals and thought through in creeds. Our examination of the public Protestant religious system leads us to the ritual actions that were logically and psychologically related to moralism, activism, and the search for simplicity. We call these ritual actions by the general term *revivalism*, and we understand revivalism as a community cultus to stimulate an immediate emotional experience of conversion or religious devotion.

In our general discussion of Protestantism in Part One, we saw that the Reformers of the sixteenth century wanted to emphasize the separation between the divine and the human worlds, clearing away much of the Catholic sacramental system that partially closed the gap. As a religious ritual, revivalism was built on this Reformation sense of the distance between God and human beings, and it made the sense of human estrangement from God an intense emotional experience. Likewise, the Reformers had stressed the free grace and mercy of God that brought sinners close to him, and revivalism was based on the belief that grace and mercy came through personal experience. Indeed, early American revivalism increased the awareness of a gap between the divine and the human, thriving on a world view in which an all-powerful God, like a lightning bolt in his suddenness and force, overwhelmed a powerless sinner. During the time of conversion or intense devotion, a person was, literally, out of control, with feelings and even physical movements under the power of the Spirit. Paradoxically, the effects of this loss of control were felt in a greater degree of order and control in the later conduct of daily life.

As a ritual, though, revivalism offered a formal and repeated set of practices that might help to bring conversion or strong devotion. Sacred space was marked off, either in a church, a public building, or an open field at a camp meeting. Then during the sacred time of the service, hymns, prayers, testimonies, and especially revival sermons worked to create in an individual a sense of the heavy burden of personal sin and, in earlier forms, of the torments of hell that would result. Alternately, hymns and personal testimonies pointed to the present joy of conversion and the future bliss of heaven. Being a Christian was not a

263

matter of belief but of experience, so that salvation hung on the sense of emotional liberation and inner peace that the grace of God was thought to give. Therefore, the older revival practices had strived to produce an unbearable tension between sin and possible grace, between the terrors of hell and the anticipated joys of heaven. When the tension had become great enough, the conviction of sin sufficiently painful, the sinner might, so to speak, be exploded into paradise.

The connections between both the earlier and later, non-Calvinist ritual of the revival and the behavioral patterns of the Protestant code are not hard to find. The activism of the Protestant style was satisfied in active congregations who sang, prayed, witnessed, and more important, felt the burden of sin and the compassion of God in a direct and personal manner. Individuals *worked through* or prayed through to conversion and the attainment of strong feelings toward God. Especially after the beginning of the nineteenth century, when Calvinism fell away, more and more emphasis was placed on the active role a person played in the entire process.

Further, the Protestant desire for simplification was met by the ritual expression of the revivals. Religion had been boiled down to its essentials: sin and grace, or hell and heaven. There was no need for an elaborate and sophisticated theology in this way of doing things. Similarly, the practice of the revivals led away from any concern for tradition and into a vivid concentration on the present—or a future outside the time of history. Finally, Protestant moralism was served by the revivals. The pattern of overwhelming guilt and the immediate need for moral purification fit the experience of sinners at the revivals, while the authenticity of conversion and devotion was expressed in the reformed character of the lives of Christians. Thus, the private vices that moralism sought to cleanse—radically, instantly, and all at once—were the signs of the need for revival, while their eradication was the signal of revival success. Thus, too, the zeal of converts and devoted Christians often led to their involvement in humanitarian reforms, as we saw in the case of antislavery.

Behind the behavioral patterns of Protestantism were the conditions and institutions that had made them possible. Here also there was a goodness of fit with revivalism. In a situation of religious liberty, the revivals gave people a democratic God who might come to rich or poor, model citizen or town derelict, with his help. There was no elite class to benefit from salvation, except the elite of everybody's people, any one of whom might feel the grace of God. In the legal setting of separation of church and state, the revivals provided a mission field to be mined by denominations in search of new church members. The voluntaryism of the revival experience helped to fill congregations with volunteers who would work in and out of official organizations for the Christianization of America.

The Protestant History of Revivalism

In order to gain a sense of just how significant revivalism was in the dominant and public religion, let us roughly sketch its story in this country. In Part One, we saw the importance of the Great Awakening in introducing the pattern of the revivals, and in our episode at the beginning of this chapter, we met again the commanding figure of George Whitefield. Recall that he made acceptable to many throughout the colonies the innovations of an itinerant ministry and open-air preaching. Whitefield also employed in his sermons a vivid rhetoric aimed to arouse the emotions of his listeners. But it was Jonathan Edwards who provided the theological grounding for the new preaching. Bringing together a basic Calvinism and the philosophical writings of the Englishman John Locke (1632–1704), Edwards thought, like Locke, that understanding came to human beings when their senses were directly affected. The logic of this theory, called "sensationalism," was that the more strongly a person's senses were affected, the more clearly he or she would attain knowledge. Furthermore, Edwards added to the five traditional senses the sense of the heart. In the sermons that he preached in his church at Northampton, Massachusetts, Edwards painted striking pictures of, for example, the sinner hanging like a spider by a thread over the abyss of hell. In this way, he believed, God could use him (Edwards) as an instrument to excite in the hearts of members of the congregation an awareness of their true spiritual condition. Then, if God had so chosen, the sinner would be brought to conversion.

Edwards told how members of his congregation groaned, shrieked, and fell as they were overwhelmed by a keen sense of their sinfulness and God's power. Throughout the colonies, from all reports, the results were similar. Probably 30,000 to 40,000 out of a total population of 1 million fell under the hand of God and were raised to the new life of grace. As these events happened, it seemed that the estrangement people felt from God, now overcome in the revival, was paralleled by estrangement in their general social situation.

There was something very American about the revival experience. This was a land in which the distance of an ocean cut off the sons and daughters of Europeans from their roots, so that the separation between themselves and England was continually being felt by the colonists. Likewise, by the eighteenth century the gap between ordinary folk and their religious and political leaders had grown greater, and so had economic differences between people. Hence, if the revival was about anything, it was about estrangement; and estrangement was both a spiritual and a social condition. As we saw in Part One, millions among the many in America carried within themselves the feeling of being separated from their deepest roots. As we see now, their estrangement was at the very center of the dominant and public religion of the land.

When the eighteenth century drew to a close and became the nineteenth, a Second Great Awakening spread across the United States. In the East, by 1802 Yale College was the site for a remarkable outpouring of the Spirit under the preaching of Timothy Dwight (1752–1817), the grandson of Jonathan Edwards. As president of Yale, Dwight conducted services in the college chapel that resulted in the conversion of over a third of the students. Lyman Beecher, later at the center of the awakening, was one of his students, and so was Nathaniel W. Taylor (1786–1858), who became the leading theologian of this revival. Furthermore, ministers from Yale and other schools to which the revival spread carried the flame to their congregations in town or countryside.

In the West, the Great Revival provoked excitement among thousands at huge camp meetings. Frequently, people came from fifty miles or farther and set up tents where they could camp for several days. Often there were several preachers from different denominations—Methodist, Baptist, and Presbyterian the most frequent. At evening meetings, the campground became a sacred space with a raised platform for the preacher in the front, a sinner's "pen" where those overcome with a sense of their sinfulness could pray, and behind them space for the rest of the crowd. Here renowned men like James McGready (1758-1817), Peter Cartwright (1785-1872), and Barton W. Stone held forth. At these meetings and elsewhere in the new revivals, sin was no longer a secret gnawing at an individual's heart. Rather, it was publicly acknowledged by presence in the pen and by other physical signs. Like Roman Catholics with their sacrament of penance, Protestants had found a way to turn private into public property. They felt relieved when they no longer had to bear the burden of their guilt alone.

At excited meetings such as the one at Cane Ridge, Kentucky, in 1801, people shrieked, cried, and fell into trance under the weight of their sins. Some of them could not control the motor functions of their bodies, and they jerked or danced or even "barked." If all the revivals fed on a human sense of estrangement, here the reasons for estrangement were multiplied. Away from eastern cities and from the comforts and conveniences of more settled territory, the people who staked their claims on the frontier felt themselves to be on the edge of civilization. They were surrounded by Indians and "wilderness" country and isolated by distance from those they had left behind. So it was not surprising that their sense of separation from God was also magnified and that they expressed it with a "wildness" and lack of control that paralleled the wildness they imagined to be around them.

Moreover, theologically speaking, the western and eastern versions of the Second Great Awakening taught the same message. The stern Calvinism of Edwards's day was giving way before Arminian views. The old doctrine of predestination was all but forgotten, and optimistic understandings of the role that people could play in their own redemption came to the fore. Jesus had died for all, not some. If humans truly desired salvation, then the grace of God would find a way to break through.

This sense of human responsibility in the process of conversion was carried still further in the revivals preached by Charles Grandison Finney. Beginning in the mid-1820s, this charismatic leader electrified his congregations in upstate New York, the area known as the Burnt Over district, swept clean as it was by the fires of revival. Later Finney widened his field to preach in eastern cities like Philadelphia and New York. More than any other individual, he set the pace for revivalism in the later nineteenth century and in the twentieth century as well. He thought carefully and self-consciously about the role of the preacher in bringing on a revival, and he concluded that revivals were not miracles but the natural products of deliberate means.

Thus, Finney introduced a series of "new measures" that were widely imitated by other revival preachers. His preaching was far more direct than that of previous generations of revivalists, using the second-person singular "you," staring boldly, and pointing his index finger into the crowd. He spoke spontaneously, without prepared notes, and was often theatrical in his delivery of the gospel, using body language to effect. He instituted inquiry meetings and

266

prolonged services late into the night. At these "protracted meetings," he set up an "anxious bench" in the front where, as in the sinners' pens of the camp meetings, people could benefit by the special attention. Sometimes when he preached and prayed out loud, he called sinners by name, and he encouraged spontaneous prayer from members of the congregation, both male and female. The practice of public prayer by females, as well as other Finney innovations, shocked the eastern establishment during this period, but Finney's new measures were destined to become standard techniques for professional revivalists thereafter.

Finney might be seen as the transitional leader between the older revivalism and what was to come within organized Protestantism. Some of his new measures, such as the anxious bench and the encouragement of public prayer, had been approximated in the frontier revivals, but Finney packaged them as part of a professional repertoire of techniques to be used by revival preachers. Although he had begun in the traditional way in rural districts and small towns, he moved to the cities to spread his gospel. Thus, he pointed the way to the future of professionally managed, urban revivalism.

As revivalism moved to the cities and became more carefully staged and controlled, unrestrained expression of feelings and undirected body movements became largely a thing of the past. This kind of emotional and physical abandon continued within Protestantism in the Holiness and Pentecostal movements. But revivalism itself came to favor sentimentality over strong, uncontrolled feeling. Response to an altar call by moving to the front of the congregation or signing one's name to a "decision card" became more normal expressions of inner feeling. The change did not come all at once, but in the "businessmen's revival" of 1857–1858, the new style of revival was evident. Here business people in the cities held noon prayer meetings. Prayer, testimony, and hymn singing took the place of a sermon, while religious passion had been socialized in such a way that it was expressed within well-contained bounds. As Calvinism disappeared, so did hell. Instead, the joys of heaven were stressed in revival hymns.

In Dwight L. Moody (1837–1899), urban revivalism had its most successful innovator, and the late nineteenth century its most important revivalist. Unlike earlier leaders of the revivals, Moody was a lay person and not an ordained minister. In the 1870s and thereafter, he promoted his revivals with shrewd business judgment. An advance team would precede his arrival in a city, publicizing the revival and generating interest and excitement. At the revivals themselves, the famous gospel singer Ira D. Sankey (1840–1908) accompanied him, and the two worked closely to insure the outcome of their meetings. Moody preached sermons that were a testimony to the simple style, filled with Bible stories, anecdotes of home and family, and a continuing emphasis on salvation. Antiintellectual, sentimental, and nostalgic, he urged his hearers to a conversion as easy as accepting Christ and filling out a decision card. Moody wanted his converts to join a church, but which one did not concern him so long as the denomination was evangelical. Salvation for him was joyful, not tortuous; the Christian life, a surrender to a loving Jesus, not an initiation into theological abstractions.

It was a persuasive, if conservative, message. Bankrolled by wealthy members of the business community, it created a world of down-home religious comfort that helped to keep urban dwellers content and attached them more firmly to the middle-class values they already held. For the new converts, the content of both the hymns and the sermons suggested their yearning for a sanctuary, a safe place where they could feel secure in the midst of urban confusion. In the large and faceless crowd of strangers at a revival, hymns and sermons brought decision for Christ, moral purification, and an immediate community based on shared feeling. Once more, the revival helped to ease estrangement, the feeling of rootlessness that the converts, many of them newcomers to northern cities, must have faced. Rubbing shoulders with immigrants with strange languages, habits, and religions, far away from the farms and small towns of their memories, these converts retreated into the pietism of Moody's evangelical message. In finding heaven, they were finding home.

Moody's revivals were a part of the response of the dominant and public religion to the presence of the many, a topic that we will discuss in more detail in the Conclusion. For now, though, it is important to point out that twentieth-century revivalism generally followed the path that Moody had charted. Early in the century, the revival hero was William A. (Billy) Sunday (1862–1935), a former baseball player who captivated his audiences with dramatic gestures and antics mimicking the sport, along with slang and colloquial speech. From 1912 to 1918 his popularity was at its peak, as he preached sermons weaving together themes of Fundamentalism and Prohibition with hostility toward "modernists" and the enemies of America. God, home, and motherhood became a new trinity, while Sunday enthusiastically affirmed the virtue of patriotism by waving the American flag from his pulpit. His revivals continued and intensified the quest for a moral community, a pure America that could counter the forces of evil with its commitment to right feeling. Sunday's brand of revivalism, preached in the shadow of the First World War, illustrated the mingling of the gospel with civil religion, which we will examine in the next chapter. Once more, his revivalism brought to legions of somewhat bewildered and confused middle-class Americans a safe haven where they did not need to feel threatened by the alien world around them.

With the revivalism of Billy Graham in the second half of the century, preaching became more dignified and media oriented, but revivalism remained in many ways the same. Through the fifties and into the sixties and seventies, Graham used the media to bring people to their "hour of decision." His huge rallies, held in major cities, were often videotaped for television viewing. A film center was established to distribute special Billy Graham evangelical showings. Graham became the friend of presidents, his evangelical conservatism interwoven with a political conservatism as thoroughgoing. (He was deeply embarrassed by his loyalty to President Richard M. Nixon after Nixon's guilt in the Watergate scandal became clear.) Curiously, Graham had begun by preaching that the end of the world was coming very soon—a recurring theme within the American millennial tradition, as we will see. But he ended by supporting a political establishment based on the belief in the continuance of a strong and thisworldly America. For Graham, the two were, and are, related because the sure defense of America is Jesus. In his simple, uncomplicated biblical message, Billy Graham appealed to millions who sought rescue from modern ills.

For every Billy Sunday and Billy Graham, there were thousands of other revival preachers in the history of Protestantism in the United States. We have seen that the cultivation of right feeling was central to the revival ritual throughout its development, and we have seen continually that the ritual worked to ease the sense of estrangement from God and from human society that many Americans experienced. As theological beliefs changed, we noticed that the human role in bringing about the good feelings of revival was more and more acknowledged. And in the twentieth century, we found that patriotism and the meaning of America were woven into the revival message.

Revivalism in American Culture

But if revivalism was part of the history of Protestantism in this country, it was also part of the history of American culture. Like a magnet, public Protestantism drew the many toward its center. We have already noticed in Part One how Roman Catholicism had its parish mission movement which paralleled Protestant revivalism and must have been reinforced by it. Similarly, we have mentioned the recent upsurge of Jewish interest in Hasidism, a Jewish mystical and devotional movement that encouraged pietism. Blacks for their own reasons had also adopted the religion of feeling, and similarly we may note that many, if not all, of the nineteenth-century new religions were born in revivalistic fervor. Mormons and Millerites, Shakers and Christian Scientists, all grew out of deeply shared common experience. Whether with the charisma of a prophet, the keen expectation of the millennium, the ecstasy of the dance, or the power of spiritual healing, these groups encouraged pietism and knit strangers into communities. Although they had surely struck out on new paths, there was a oneness to their witness, shaped as it was by the dominant and public religion.

In more recent times, a series of Eastern and occult religious movements have become for some Americans new and transformed versions of the old ritual of revival. The message of these religions, of course, is no longer the Christian gospel, but there has been great continuity in the themes that gave the revival its power. Indeed, in Chapter 8 we saw that one reason why *bhakti* groups did not grow larger and more numerous was the presence already within American culture of ways to express devotional needs. In movements like the International Society for Krishna Consciousness and Nichiren Buddhism, people became a community not because of shared backgrounds or work but out of the experience of their ritual. In other words, it was *feeling* that made them one and feeling that overcame the estrangement that modern lifestyles had created. Likewise, the intertwining of political with religious factors was evident in these movements during the era of the Vietnam War. While Billy Sunday and Billy Graham waved the flag to support American efforts in foreign wars, these people cared as deeply but saw the meaning of America in the context of a vision of peace and world community. Though many Eastern, occult, and political enthusiasts would have been shocked by the relationship, a bond of pietism linked them to the sons and daughters of the Protestant revivals.

All of these movements were attempts to reach beyond the boundaries of ordinary life in quest of extraordinary religious meaning. While as in every extraordinary religion, elements of the ordinary were intermingled, these groups shared the extraordinary religious commitment of Protestantism. But ordinary religion—American culture—took on the revival-bred characteristics of the dominant and public religion as well. During times of conflict like the American Revolution and the Civil War, as we will see in Chapter 11, popular behavior frequently resembled a mass revival. Other vast collective spectacles, such as national elections every four years, often evoked the enthusiastic spirit of the revivals.

Outside of war and organized politics, we may see in recent times how general American culture still bears the imprint of the revival. To cite one example of a mass ritual in the revival tradition, there is the Woodstock Rock Festival that gave a generation its name as the Woodstock Nation. During three days in August 1969, 400,000 young people gathered at a farm in New York to hear rock groups perform, to smoke marijuana, to absorb stronger drugs, and to experience a oneness with one another in an atmosphere of good feelings that has become legendary. Indeed, during the decade of the sixties it seemed that millions had been swept into a thisworldly revival. The Broadway musical *Hair* gave Americans the age of Aquarius, a time when there would be harmony, understanding, sympathy, and trust. In its music and its words, the echo of revival gospel hymns lurked in the background. For the generation that wanted to make love and not war, it was clear that feeling and experience were primary values, and immediate community was keenly sought. We will pursue these themes further in Chapter 12, but it should be evident here that they are strongly related to some of the major values engendered by the revivals.

More conservatively, other aspects of American popular culture expressed the relationship. Sentimentality and nostalgia were not only features of the revival but common aspects of the everyday world. Messages on greeting cards and Mother's Day celebrations, television movies and popular love ballads proclaimed a world of sentiment that bound people together into a safe community, leaving problems and pain behind. Here feelings were refined to their proper degree, socialized and civilized like the revivals, ordering the world and bringing it under control. In short, revivalism provided the pattern for some of the major themes in American popular culture, although the themes were expressed in ways having to do with the present world and not the world beyond. Ritual life in general American culture has learned much from the patterns of meaning stressed in the revivals.

THE PROTESTANT CREED

Rituals, in general, are related to myths or creeds, sacred stories or statements that express basic beliefs. Protestant revivalism is no exception, and the ritual of the revival was connected, again logically and psychologically, to further elements in public Protestantism. These elements formed its religious world view. In overview, we can isolate three major understandings that were present. First of all, there was belief in the *importance of the individual,* an idea that assumed significance during the Reformation and was intensified by the American experience of Protestantism. Secondly, there was regard for a *higher law* that transcended human legislation and institutions. Thirdly and most prominently, there was the affirmation of different forms of *millennialism* and a related perfectionism. We will look at each of these in turn.

Individualism

Revivalism did work to help create community, as we have seen. But let us not forget that, as religious experience, revivalism focused on individuals. In the older form of revivalism, the individual was at the mercy of higher forces, as God and Satan wrestled for the soul. In the later development of the ritual, an individual decided by an act of personal will to accept Christ. In both cases, religious belief centered on what each individual experienced in the solitary space of mind and heart. In fact, American Protestant revivalism lived with a tension in which it at once *believed* in individualism and then immediately sought to change it. Revivalism tried to make community out of many private experiences by establishing a common place and language in which these experiences could become public. Yet through it all, revivalism spoke out of the creed of individualism.

So there is a strong, if problematic, bond between revivalism and the American estimate of the importance of the individual. Earlier, the Reformation of the sixteenth century had departed from medieval Catholicism by seeing the individual at the heart of religion. As we saw in Chapter 4, the shift from a sacramental church to one grounded on the Bible meant a new definition of the directness of the relationship between human beings and God. For the rising middle class as they embraced Protestantism, the shift was a happy parallel to growing involvement in individual decision and responsibility.

Circumstances in the New World only encouraged the drift toward greater individualism. The presence of vast stretches of land, the clear business opportunities created by the absence of an economic establishment, and the necessity of self-reliance for people uprooted from traditional community ties combined to emphasize individual worth. Patterns of ever-greater mobility developed to increase the trend. The Industrial Revolution shifted huge portions of the population from rural to urban settings. The lure of the frontier attracted others further and further westward. The multiplication of cheaper and more rapid means of transportation promised new opportunities that could be easily reached and also the hope that loved ones could be visited from time to time. By the late twentieth century, the cloverleaf at highway interchanges and the long-distance telephone line had become major symbols of American life.

The political shape of the nation resembled the socioeconomic pattern of individualism. It was significant that the union formed between the colonies was a federal union—one in which thirteen sovereign states yielded some small part of their independence for the benefits of common defense and welfare. Under the loose Articles of Confederation and later the Constitution, the states were like so many separate and individual planets revolving around the federal sun. Or to use another figure of speech, they were like individual atoms existing as wholes within a larger body. In the nineteenth century, the doctrine of states' rights complicated the moral issues raised by slavery. The Civil War not only spoke to the issue of slavery but also the other issue of how far the rights of individual states could extend. However, the twentieth century did not end the issue of political individualism. In national debates concerning the role of the federal government, in questions like the propriety of a national welfare system for the poor or national health insurance for everybody, the question resurfaced.

Meanwhile, the glorification of the common people became part of the political myth of America. Although in practice democratic equality was a long way from being realized in the eighteenth and early nineteenth centuries, the belief persisted that in America all were equal. Indeed, by the late twentieth century, the power of the myth was being felt as different minority groups—blacks, Hispanics, American Indians—and a majority group—women—demanded that the words of the founders be made good. Individuals were significant in America, and equality was only the dues paid by society to that fact.

The public school system also played its part in this emphasis on the individual. In texts like the *McGuffey Eclectic Readers* of the nineteenth century, the individual virtues that would help a person to succeed were stressed. These schoolbooks promoted such qualities as independence, thrift, industry, and perseverance. Still further, an extensive national literature reflected the significance of each person. Ralph Waldo Emerson's famous essay "Self-Reliance" (1841) became a classic, while by the late nineteenth century Horatio Alger (1832–1899) had written over 100 novels, many of them based on the formula of a rise to success through luck and persistent effort. Alger's boy heroes, a number of them orphaned or at least without a father, were enterprising adventurers who won out over obstacles. They caught the fancy of millions of young Americans, as the sale of some 20 million copies of the Alger stories attests.

Hence, as part of their ordinary and everyday orientation, Americans valued individuals. But it was organized Protestantism that had provided a theological home for individualism, and the Protestant influence on developing American individualism was crucial. Denominationalism and voluntaryism had supplied an institutional framework in which individual efforts were the bulwark of church organizations. The activist style relied for its success on the individual involvement of thousands of responsible church members, while the simplifications Protestantism fostered were precisely because, in a world in which every individual counted equally, material and intellectual subtleties had to be reduced to a minimum. Through the various programs for moral reforms—many of them directed toward private vices—it was only as individuals that people could achieve purity, for morality could never be simply a group affair. Ultimately, a moral act or a moral failure rested at the door of a single individual.

It was, finally, the ritual of revivalism that, despite the tensions, helped to shape American Protestantism as a religion of individualism. We have already seen the connecting links. Here it is important to note that the content of the preaching in sermon after sermon on the revival circuits had much to do with the spread of the individualistic world view. The preacher who wished to stimulate his congregation toward conversion or devotional experience was required to deal with individual themes. It was the relationship between the sinner and God that was uppermost in the sermons—not the Christian community, the communion of saints, or the general plan of God for the world. Moreover, the substance and style of revival sermons became the substance and style of much ordinary Sunday preaching as well. Week after week, year after year, church folk were hearing a description of the divine-human relationship in which the individual figured at stage center. It was not surprising that they should conclude that this pattern was in the very nature of things. The pattern of Protestant revivalism both shaped and reflected the larger pattern of ordinary American culture. For the dominant and public religion in both its ordinary and extraordinary forms, in the beginning was God—and the individual.

The Higher Law

If individualism was basic to the American creed, the sources of public order became a logical next question. In a nation of self-reliant and self-directed individuals, what law or authority could be the final court of appeal? Could equal individuals in the nation be finally submissive to a king, a president, or a written law? Could equal individuals in the churches be forced to obey the dictates of a pope, a bishop, a synod, or elders of a denomination? The answers to these questions were complex, and we cannot discuss them fully here. Yet there was a common theme that emerged from the questions, a theme that became a tenet of the American creed.

While a respect for the written law was a continuing aspect of American life in both church and state, Americans believed that the authority of any written law rested on its agreement with a higher, unwritten law. If written law and unwritten law were in conformity, then the written law should be respected and obeyed. But if there was a discrepancy, if the written law violated the higher law, then free individuals owed allegiance to the higher order. There was always the possibility that disobedience to human law was the greatest of the virtues.

Sources for this notion in the American creed were various. The heritage of the Reformation—especially in its Radical form—had given the early colonists a sense of the significance of individual conscience. Puritanism, which adopted the free-church tradition of the Radicals, could not fail to recognize, at least theoretically, the rights of conscience. How could churches be genuinely free if people were forced to join them? And how could people freely join or refuse to do so, unless they listened to the still, small voice of conscience?

The Quakers, with their teaching concerning the "Inner Light," especially stressed the importance of turning within. Their assumption—and the assumption of all Protestants who recognized the rights of conscience—was that if people listened with sincerity, the voice that spoke to them from conscience would be the voice of God. The Baptists, in turn, argued for separate churches in New England and protested the Congregational church establishment. For them conscience became the bar of justice. Moreover, the entire pattern of religious dissent supported this understanding. In order to justify a departure from the established order, an individual needed to find a law beyond private whim. Since the colonists in the large sense were mostly religious dissenters, the rights of conscience were basic to their religious position.

From the heritage of the Enlightenment came another source for American belief in the higher law. The idea of a law of nature to which human life must conform had received active support among the Puritans. The rationalism of their intellectual tradition turned easily toward it, and this was an important reason for the ready acceptance of Enlightenment beliefs in the colonies. Framed in the political rhetoric of the nation's foundation, the higher law became the law under which a God of nature had given unalienable rights to individuals. This law was absolute and fundamental. It could justify the separation of the colonies from the government of King George III of England, as the Declaration of Independence made clear. Political states and their laws must exist as reflections in specific human situations of the higher law of nature. Otherwise, it might become necessary in the course of events to resist them.

Practically speaking, Americans sometimes made use of popular versions of the idea of the higher law in order to justify their acquisition of territory from the Indians. For the Puritans, the myth of conquest was based on the distinction between "civilized" and "savage" peoples. "Savages," by definition, could not be fully human and therefore could not be civilized. Hence, God required that the wilderness be snatched from their hands and given to people who would turn it into a Christian garden. By the nineteenth century, President Andrew Jackson (1767–1845) could justify the removal of the southeastern Indians to lands further west by a modified version of the myth. White Americans, as farmers, would bring a higher state of civilization to Indian lands. Native Americans retarded progress. Removed west of the Mississippi River, perhaps they could be brought to share in civilization.

Although today we condemn the logic of both the Puritans and President Jackson, it is important to see that they were appealing their actions to a law of nature or, more and more in the nineteenth century, a law of progress beyond themselves. By midcentury, as we will see in Chapter 11, that law had taken new form as manifest destiny, and in this form it had become a part of the civil religion. In all of these cases, the point of the appeal was that it gave to individuals a weighty and transcendent justification for any actions they might take. In a nation in which moralism was the fundamental behavioral pattern, such justification was necessary. It could be and often was self-serving, as in the examples involving the Indians, but it could also be an act of moral courage.

In one memorable instance from the nineteenth century, the American writer and Transcendentalist Henry David Thoreau (1817–1862) spent a night in jail because he refused to pay his poll tax during the Mexican War. The tax would aid the southern slave power, and Thoreau would have no part of it. This act of civil disobedience bore fruit in the twentieth century when Martin Luther King, Jr., learning of it indirectly through Mohandas Gandhi, willingly went to jail many times to advance the black struggle for civil rights. In these and other instances of civil disobedience, individuals appealed against the written law to the higher law which, they argued, justified their actions. For many during the era of the Vietnam War, the belief in the higher law supported their efforts to resist the draft in various ways and to engage in active protest against the war. Although large numbers of their fellow citizens disapproved of their actions and regarded them as disloyal, we should see that they were part of a long tradition of

Americans who thought that no human law could be final and that the rights of conscience preceded any government.

As we have examined it, the belief in the higher law is an instance of the ways in which ordinary and extraordinary religious values have mingled almost indistinguishably in the American creed. It is difficult to say where the Protestant heritage ended and ordinary American culture began in the affirmation of the unwritten law. But because the belief is so clearly tied to the idea of God or transcendence, there is an extraordinary quality about it in every situation. Indeed, the justification of Indian removal is so repugnant because, by appealing to a higher law, it brought the idea of God to the service of the ugliest of human motives. The higher law, if it really was higher, justified the ordinary by reference to the extraordinary. The measure of its power in American life was the measure of the power of Protestantism as the dominant and public religion.

Millennialism

We have noted that the higher law had been conceived in various ways in the course of American religious history. For some, it meant the voice of the biblical God speaking to conscience. For others, it meant the God of nature at work through his law in governing the world. And for others still, it meant the law itself as an absolute—an almighty nature or an unfailing law of progress. This movement from the biblical God to nature to an abstract law of progress is tied to the third and most significant belief in the American creed, the belief in the coming of the millennium. As we will see, this belief—and action generated by it—formed what was probably the strongest theme in the one religion of the United States. Significant in public Protestantism, it proved to be more powerful still in civil religion and general cultural religion. In the millennial vision of things, the higher law was the decree of the God of the future and the unraveling of the inevitable events that would bring about that future. We have already met millennial beliefs in abundance in our survey of nineteenth-century new religions and elsewhere, but now let us review and expand the discussion.

In the strict sense, millennialism is related to a specific book in the Christian New Testament, the book of Revelation. Since a millennium means a period of a thousand years, millennialism refers to beliefs regarding the thousand-year period at the end of time closely connected to the second coming of Jesus. According to the book of Revelation, in the great battle of the final age the Word of God will ride forth with his army to fight the beast who is the embodiment of evil. After the beast is overcome, Satan will be chained up for a thousand years, and those who have witnessed to Jesus will rule with him. Then at the close of the thousand-year era will come the great war between God and Satan when Satan will be finally defeated (Rev. 19:11–20:10).

In a looser sense, however, millennialism can mean religious beliefs in any tradition in which there is intense expectation that the end of the present world order is near. Millennialists see radical change in the future. They draw strength and religious excitement in the present from their anticipation of the approaching end—or beginning. For common to all millennial beliefs is the faith that with the future a new age will dawn, an age of peace and prosperity and

275

the fulfillment of all hopes. In the ghost dance religion among American Indians in the late nineteenth century, we have already encountered one example of non-Christian millennialism.

Finally, millennialism can refer to beliefs outside of any extraordinary religion. The intense expectation of a new era of peace and plenty can take place in terms of ordinary culture. Elation over an age of progress and wonder at the miracles of modern times can give rise to popular beliefs that a totally new period in world history is beginning. So millennialism can be a way to make sense of life within the boundaries of the everyday world. Mainstream American culture, especially in the late eighteenth and nineteenth centuries, would reflect this kind of millennialism.

As we glance quickly through American religious and cultural history, we find millennial beliefs in abundance. The New England Puritans frequently discussed millennial themes, and many of them seemed convinced that the end of the world was coming soon. Thus, Cotton Mather (1663–1728) firmly expected the end to come in 1697. When it did not arrive then, he recalculated and predicted 1736 and later, 1716. By the eighteenth century, we know that some Puritans, like Jonathan Edwards, had begun to believe that the thousand-year period could begin without the physical coming of Christ but instead was a time of intense preparation for it. For Edwards, this understanding was closely tied to the marvelous outpouring of God's grace that he had seen in the Great Awakening. The revival had convinced him that a new era was about to dawn in America and that the era would be the beginning of God's millennial kingdom for the entire world.

Since there was general agreement that the prophecies of Revelation were cast in symbolic language, it was possible to interpret them in various ways. By the nineteenth century, two schools of millennial thought arose, which came to be known as premillennialism and postmillennialism. Briefly, the premillennalists believed that Jesus would come *before* the millennium to bring it on by his power. Postmillennialists thought that Jesus would return *after* the millennium had come through the Spirit working in the church. Along with premillennialism went the expectation of a reign of evil through a figure called the Antichrist. Many trials and tribulations would occur before Christ would come again, and premillennialists regarded any signs that the world was growing worse as evidence that the end was near. Conversely, postmillennialists found signs of gradual human betterment to be evidence that perhaps the millennium was beginning. At the same time, they thought that by working to spread the gospel and improve the human condition, they could hasten the coming of the millennium.

We have already met nineteenth-century premillennialists in the early Mormons, the Millerites, and later the Seventh-day Adventists. At the same time, liberal Protestants, such as the Unitarians, and also moderate evangelicals, like Lyman Beecher, held postmillennialist views. The Methodist teaching of perfection as a second work of grace after conversion was postmillennial in its thrust, and this perfectionism was spread by the revivals until it became a widespread popular belief. Charles G. Finney brought the message wherever he preached, while groups as diverse as the Oneida Perfectionists and even the

Spiritualists held their own versions of the perfectionist creed. These people saw a new world open within themselves, with the dream of human perfection either realized or in process of being realized. Likewise, they were filled with optimism by the spiritual and material progress they saw around them in a growing America. They read the signs of the times positively. They were convinced that a new age was dawning and that it would dawn for the whole world in the United States. Yet for both premillennialists and postmillennialists, the Civil War was a time of crisis, and we will have more to say about this topic in the next chapter.

After the Civil War, however, came a resurgence of premillennialism. By 1875 premillennialists were attracting new adherents and preaching their message especially in the form called dispensationalism, which had been preached in America by the visiting Englishman John Nelson Darby. The dispensationalists were convinced that none of the biblical prophecies regarding the end had yet been fulfilled. They thought that the world was growing steadily more evil, that Antichrist would soon control it, and that after this period of tribulation, Jesus would return, conquer the Antichrist, and establish his kingdom for a thousand years. Meanwhile, the members of the church would, according to scripture, finally meet Jesus in the air (I Thess. 4:15-17), and dispensationalists believed that this "rapture" would happen *before* the Antichrist came to rule the world. Perhaps more significant than the exact details was the emphasis of premillennialists on the literal nature of their beliefs. As we saw in the chapter on Protestantism, it was the combination of millennial and rationalistic beliefs that gave birth to Fundamentalism. The millennialists in question were dispensationalists. Wherever Fundamentalism thrived, so did premillennialism.

In the later twentieth century, when after a period of decline Fundamentalism again became widespread, so did premillennialism. In fact, it attracted considerable attention for Fundamentalism in American popular culture, as the popularity of Hal Lindsey's best-selling book, *The Late Great Planet Earth*, attested. With over 12 million copies sold between 1970 and 1978 alone, Lindsey's work tried to show that the biblical signs and prophecies of the approaching end were being realized in the present time. The sense of impending doom, reflected in this book and in the general premillennial message, led many believers to a kind of activism. With so short a time before the blast of the final trumpet, they wanted to rescue as many people as they could. For some, revival and foreign-mission activity became a way to hasten the second coming of Jesus, while for others such activity was a pious expression of love and compassion for others. For whatever reasons they worked, premillennialists tried to save as many souls as possible before the end.

Premillennial efforts were directed mostly toward the salvation of individuals on otherworldly terms. In general, the premillennialists had little interest in social reform, and the postmillennial logic of the gradual dawning of the millennium as humans created a better society was not theirs. Still, there were people who spread the postmillennial gospel in America after the Civil War. These Americans used new language to express their ideas, and in the Social Gospel movement they spoke of the future event as the coming of the kingdom of God. For them, the kingdom was not merely a spiritual reality but a material transformation of human society in which poverty, ignorance, and disease would be banished. Often with a belief in the basic goodness of America, those who preached and practiced the Social Gospel saw their task as making America better still. Their work was to realize the long dream of humanity since the Christian gospel had appeared—to build the kingdom of God on earth.

Like Fundamentalism, the postmillennial dream of the Social Gospel went through a period of decline in the early-to-mid years of the twentieth century. Still, it never died. In the sixties, Liberal Protestantism again threw itself more completely into the task of building the kingdom. Stimulated by the civil-rights movement and the war against poverty, Liberal ministers were numbered in the forefront of the various social movements that emerged. For them the message of the Christian gospel was one of social change. Jesus had said that God's kingdom must rise within the human *community*, not simply individual human hearts. So the Liberals found themselves working to create the millennium alongside other Americans who were inspired not by the kingdom at all but by the non-Christian humanistic desire to create a more perfect society.

Theirs was millennialism in the loosest sense of all—the optimistic expectation that the best of all possible ages was about to dawn. Indeed, understood in terms of ordinary culture, this best of ages had been dawning in America since the late eighteenth century. Revolutionary and postrevolutionary ferment had included golden visions of America as the place where the noblest society in human history would flourish, where there would be peace and abundance, technical progress and the abolition of life's ills. As the industrial and transportation revolutions ushered in a series of modern miracles, the enthusiasm of the age of progress became an ordinary religion of millennialism. Building on the Puritan understanding of America as a new Israel, ordinary millennialists did not use the language of Israel any longer, but they still thought of the nation as a promised land. The presence of seemingly endless territory in the early national period fed the enthusiasm of many, while by midcentury the various expansionist adventures of the United States in Texas, in Mexico, and in California were partially inspired by millennialist dreams.

For other Americans, however, the millennium of ordinary religion came in the new age of convenience and comfort that seemed to be beginning. With the telegraph of the 1840s and the electric light of the late 1870s as symbols of an age of technical progress, Americans marveled at the changes they were witnessing. By the end of the century, advances in the knowledge of disease microorganisms were leading to the development of new ways to prevent sickness.

Meanwhile, the abolition of slavery signaled to many that the goal of perfection in human society was near at hand. Knowledge of Charles Darwin's theory of evolution was spreading, and the biological theory (that humans had evolved from other animals) stimulated a social or cultural version. Known as Social Darwinism, it taught that just as human bodies had evolved, so had human cultures. On the basis of this belief, numbers of Americans came to see themselves as the most highly evolved people on earth. Truly, they thought, in their society the age-old vision of the millennium was becoming reality.

The twentieth-century—with its two world wars and painful smaller conflicts—put an end to much of this postmillennial optimism. Tensions long quiet between the races came to new life; poverty was discovered to be a national problem of greater seriousness than had been thought; and despite the new medicine, disease seemed as weighty a problem as ever. By the seventies, there were clear signals that the nation's energy expectations could not be fully met, and long lines at gasoline stations threatened an end to the American romance with the automobile. Yet if the millennium had not exactly dawned, millennialism was still a continuing feature of much popular American life. The social protests of the sixties had thrived on millennial anticipation. In the seventies the popularity of science fiction novels and films of the *Star Wars* variety indicated that millennialism was very much alive in the mainstream American imagination—a theme we will explore more fully in Chapter 12.

We have seen millennialism to be part of extraordinary and ordinary religious life in America. Its extraordinary witness has been both premillennial and postmillennial. Sometimes millennialism has prompted pessimism about the world and urged Christians to rescue as many individuals as they can for Jesus. At other times, millennialism has led to a thoroughgoing optimism about human beings and human society, inspiring a host of reform efforts to hasten the dawning of the new era. In both cases, millennialism began in Protestantism, but the millennial fever was shared by other, non-Protestant religious movements. Finally, the postmillennial version of the message was reflected in an ordinary American religion of progress with America—as a perfect society—at its center.

In all of these forms, millennialism was closely tied to the behavioral code, the cultus, and the other elements of the creed of the dominant and public religion. In both premillennial and postmillennial forms, it was surely activistic—either saving and rescuing souls or bringing about the social reform of the nation. In both its forms, also, it expressed the strength of the American Protestant urge to simplify. Millennial dreams were cast in terms of clear alternatives of good and evil, of war between the opposite factions, of final triumph for good without the intrusion of any evil. Similarly, both forms of millennialism embraced the demands of moralism. Premillennialists sought to purify themselves and other persons by their adherence to the simple truth of the Christian gospel without Liberal corruptions. At the same time, they sought to purify themselves by leading lives of virtue. Postmillennialists sought the radical reconstruction of society that the new age demanded.

For the two schools of millennial thought, the evangelical model of the relationship between God and the individual provided a ritual foundation. For postmillennialists, the fervor of a religious awakening was a sign of the nearness of the millennial kingdom. For both, with its pull toward the future, millennialism echoed the message of the revival—that humans were estranged and uprooted from God and from one another. The millennial society was always *being* made, never made. It was planted in a paradise of future time, in a community not based on a common past and history but on a radical vision of newness. Once again, like the revivals, the millennial creed was built on a community of strangers. Such a community, of course, was consistent with the individualism that was part of the Protestant and American creed, and as we saw earlier, it was connected to the belief in a higher law.

The movement from code to cultus to creed has provided a survey of the characteristics which, linked together, form public Protestantism. Interestingly, if we go forward one more step, we will find ourselves back at the beginning—with the social conditions tied to the development of the Protestant code. It is easy to take the step. Postmillennialists reveled in America as the land of religious liberty and democratic equality, guaranteed by separation of church and state, and institutionalized in denominationalism and voluntaryism. Premillennialists could not exactly revel in any worldly government, but in practice they found in the American arrangement the freedom that God intended for them to preach the gospel. So millennialism led finally back to liberty and equality.

IN OVERVIEW

To sum up, public Protestantism was and is the dominant religion of the United States. Present from colonial times in Calvinistic Christianity, sheer numbers, political and social prestige, economic power, and an early educational monopoly all contributed to the ascendancy of public Protestantism in the "one religion." The many who were not Protestant also contributed to its ascendancy by their acceptance of its influence and their imitation of its ways. Hence, as both extraordinary and ordinary religion, public Protestantism shaped America.

As a religious system, this public Protestantism offered a code, a cultus, and a creed to Americans, the three elements closely interlinked to form a whole. The code began in the conditions of democratic equality and religious liberty, later expressed legally in separation of church and state. These conditions for the existence of religion encouraged the growth of denominationalism and voluntaryism as organizational characteristics of the one religion. Against this backdrop, patterns of activism, a search for simplicity (reductionism, antiintellectualism, ahistoricism), and—most prominently—moralism flourished in the Protestant behavioral code.

Related to the code, the public Protestant cultus of revivalism stressed activism in working through to conversion, simplicity in its religion of bare essentials, and moralism in its emphasis on sin and the need for purification. Historically, the revivals helped to deal with estrangement by creating a place and time in which private feelings could legitimately be expressed in public. In this way people could have a sense of community without confronting the hard facts of their lack of knowledge of one another or their absence of intellectual agreement.

Code and cultus were connected to the creed of public Protestantism in which beliefs about the importance of the individual, the higher law, and millennialism were key. While individualism was often more an ideal than a reality and while the higher law could be manipulated to practical advantage, in millennialism public Protestantism shaped and was shaped by a central affirmation in American culture.

Moralistic in code, revivalistic in cultus, and millennial in creed, the dominant and public religion of America acted as a solvent for the separate centers of the many religions. The dominant and public tradition worked to break down barriers and to confuse boundaries so that a religious culture of oneness could be formed. As a key element in that oneness, millennialism inevitably led toward the political state on which the postmillennialists heaped their expectations and the premillennialists their suspicions. Civil religion—the religion of nationalism—existed in American religious history as a further way to weaken boundaries between peoples and to bind the many into one. We need to look again at the American flag that Billy Sunday chose to wave.

SUGGESTIONS FOR FURTHER READING: PUBLIC PROTESTANTISM

Brauer, Jerald C. *Images of Religion in America.* Philadelphia: Fortress Press, 1967.

Bruce, Dickson D., Jr. *And They All Sang Hallelujah: Plain-Folk Camp-Meeting Religion, 1800–1845.* Knoxville: University of Tennessee Press, 1974.

Davidson, James West. *The Logic of Millennial Thought: Eighteenth-Century New England.* New Haven: Yale University Press, 1977.

Handy, Robert T. *A Christian America: Protestant Hopes and Historical Realities.* New York: Oxford University Press, 1971.

McLoughlin, William G. *Revivals, Awakenings, and Reform.* Chicago History of American Religion. Chicago: University of Chicago Press, 1978.

Mead, Sidney E. *The Lively Experiment: The Shaping of Christianity in America.* New York: Harper & Row, 1963.

Niebuhr, H. Richard. *The Kingdom of God in America.* 1937. Reprint. New York: Harper & Row, Harper Torchbooks, 1959.

Richey, Russell E., ed. *Denominationalism.* Nashville: Abingdon Press, 1977.

Sizer, Sandra S. *Gospel Hymns and Social Religion: The Rhetoric of Nineteenth-Century Revivalism.* American Civilization Series. Philadelphia: Temple University Press, 1978.

Tuveson, Ernest Lee. *Redeemer Nation: The Idea of America's Millennial Role.* Chicago: University of Chicago Press, 1968.

Tyler, Alice Felt. *Freedom's Ferment: Phases of American Social History from the Colonial Period to the Outbreak of the Civil War.* 1944. Reprint. New York: Harper & Row, Harper Torchbooks, 1962.

Weber, Timothy P. *Living in the Shadow of the Second Coming: American Premillennialism, 1875–1925.* New York: Oxford University Press, 1979.

Weisberger, Bernard A. *They Gathered at the River: The Story of the Great Revivalists and Their Impact upon Religion in America.* Boston: Little, Brown, 1958.

CHAPTER 11

Civil Religion: Millennial Politics and History

Many an American has visited the National Archives Building in Washington, D.C., to see the original copies of the Declaration of Independence and the Constitution. There the documents rest in a special case filled with helium and covered with protective glass to preserve them. Each night they descend into a steel vault where tons of metal prevent any accident or sabotage. Then the next day they rise to be viewed by tourists in the nation's capital. Still more Americans have probably attended a ball game and stood in the bleachers with the crowd, singing a rousing version of "The Star-Spangled Banner" to the accompaniment of the local band. And practically everybody remembers the ceremony that began the class day in primary and secondary school. Teacher and pupils rose and facing the American flag—each person with hand on heart—recited a pledge of allegiance to the flag and "the Republic for which it stands." Practically everybody remembers doing it, that is, except the Jehovah's Witnesses.

Members of this large millennial religious movement, which originated as a nineteenth-century new religion, refused to salute the American flag. Arguing before the Supreme Court in 1940, the Witnesses claimed that the pledge of allegiance was an act of idolatry, homage to an earthly government by people who had made a covenant with God to do his will. In other words, the Witnesses were saying that the pledge of allegiance was a religious act and that, as a religious act, it conflicted with the demands of their own millennial faith. This argument by the Witnesses should prompt us to look again at the ceremonies just described. The solemn preservation and veneration of the Declaration and the Constitution, the singing of the national anthem, and the pledge of allegiance are acts that suggest, by their seriousness and deliberateness, the rituals of organized religion. They are surely attached to ideas about the meaning of America, and they are encouragements to loyal and patriotic behavior. As rituals, they help people to center and orient themselves by reference to the nation.

For well over a decade the religion against which the Jehovah's Witnesses were protesting has been called by scholars *civil religion*. While there are various

283

definitions of it, generally, civil religion refers to a religious system that has existed alongside the churches, with a theology or mythology (creed), an ethic (code), and a set of symbols and rituals (cultus) related to the political state. As a shorthand, we might say that civil religion has meant religious nationalism. Historically, we know that the term *civil religion* was used by Jean-Jacques Rousseau (1712–1778) in Enlightenment France. And although the term did not come into repeated use in this country until 1967, the reality to which it refers is as old as the roots of Western civilization.

Thus, ancient Israel understood its government as a theocracy, literally a government by God—through his representatives. In this view of the state, religious and political institutions were united, and one person—the inspired leader or later, the king—was responsible for both. Even more, God was the true king of Israel, ruling by his law and under a covenant that he had made with his chosen people. Before God had made the covenant with Israel, other covenants had been made in the land between warring kings to establish the relationship between them. So a covenant was a *political* agreement, and a king, of course, was a political figure, ruling by establishing control over territory. Hence, the empire of God was the Hebrew state, and as the Hebrew conception of God grew larger, his empire became the universe.

The roots of the majority religion in the United States are, like the roots of all Christianity, bound up with the history of Israel. But the second major source for Western European civilization was Graeco-Roman culture. By the time Rome was ruling over the Mediterranean world in the first centuries of the Christian era, the empire was linked by a common ideal for living—the Roman Way of Life—and by a ritual centered around the emperor. This head of all the Romans and of the conquered nations possessed a spiritual double called his *genius*. Romans considered the genius of the emperor divine, so that throughout the empire people were required to take part in an annual ceremony rendering homage to the genius. In this way, the state composed of many different ethnic and religious groups maintained a degree of unity. The Roman Way of Life, summed up in ritual homage to the emperor, acted as a social cement to bind the many into one.

With only the Jews and, on the Mediterranean coast, a few Muslims as dissenters, medieval Europe also held to a religiopolitical unity. As we noted in Chapter 10, Christianity united Europeans into Christendom, and religion was a political as well as a pious act. Similarly, the New World had its native civil religions in the traditional ways of the many Indian nations that populated the land. Here chiefs and holy men were "civic" authorities in tribal cultures, while both interpreted the meaning of the tribe to ordinary members. Later the European immigrants were not too different. As we saw briefly in Chapter 4, the Puritans readily mixed religion and government. As early as 1749, Benjamin Franklin in Pennsylvania was speaking about the need for "publick religion." A quarter century afterward, the deliberations of the Continental Congress that gave birth to the United States were filled with attention to religious details.

From the past of Western society, two models for a civil faith had grown up. The first was the Hebrew model in which one nation, bound by ties of blood, history, and language, expressed these bonds in combined religious and political language and actions. The second was the Roman model in which different peoples, with different ethnic heritages, were brought together from the top down, so to speak, through formal ceremonies and ideals. In the United States, civil religion took something from each of these models. For this reason, its nature and its specific history have proved difficult to chart. Briefly, some of the major symbols of the American civil religion rose out of Puritan experience, the expression of a people united by ethnic ties and traditions. But the history of civil religion made it increasingly a bond designed to unite *many* peoples from *many* different nations into one state.

The distinction is important. A political state such as the United States means a civil government which contains within its jurisdiction distinct ethnic and religious groups. A nation, in the true sense, means a group of people bound by language, past history, and real or alleged kinship, like each of the American Indian tribal cultures. A nation-state means a nation which had taken on a formal and political expression so that government is identified with one nation. The modern state of Japan is a nation-state.

In previous chapters, we have followed common usage in speaking loosely of the United States as a "nation." But here we need to be careful in our choice of words. Civil religion in this country was an attempt to create a nation and a nation-state, partially on the basis of the English Puritan national heritage, partially on the basis of more universal symbols derived from the Enlightenment, and partially through symbols that grew out of American political history. Yet as the years passed, more and more Americans did not share either the English Puritan national tradition or an ancestry in America during past eras of its history. At the same time, the Enlightenment, as a cultural event, receded into the past. Thus, civil religion grew less meaningful. At best, civil religion was never more than the expression of many of the American people some of the time. Still, with its overtones of extraordinary religion, it is an important example of the religion of oneness in this country. It well bears scrutiny if we are to understand religious America.

THE FOUNDATIONS OF THE CIVIL RELIGION

Civil religion grew and changed throughout American history, and its presence was particularly visible in millennial fervor during wartime. Yet its essentials came from the seventeenth and the eighteenth centuries. By the time George Washington took his oath of office as first president of the United States, the fundamentals of the civil religion were in place. They had arisen out of New England Puritanism, but especially out of the fusion of Puritanism with the engagement of Americans in the Revolutionary War. In this setting, the Puritan past was reinterpreted, linked more strongly to the Enlightenment (it had already been so linked), and joined finally to the legend that Americans were creating by their own deeds in the war — deeds that were widely understood as the beginning of a millennial era. We will look first at Puritanism from the perspective of the civil religion and then at the era of the Revolutionary War. After that, we will be able to examine the civil faith as a religious system and to tell its story in later American religious history.

Puritanism and Civil Religion

Centuries after the area we call New England was peopled by the Algonkians, it was colonized by English Puritan nationals, who brought with them a distinct culture and way of life. We have already encountered these New England Puritans in our discussion of Protestantism, but we need to look again at their relationship to the civil religion. They had come to the New World from England simmering with religious dissent and millennial hopes. They had grown up on tales of the Protestant martyrs who had suffered and died for their convictions during the Catholic reign of Bloody Mary (1553–1558). They had read these tales as evidence of the unending war between God and Satan, and they thought of England as the particular place where that war was being waged.

When they immigrated from England to their colonies along the Atlantic coast of America, the Puritans came to see themselves as the true chosen people from an almost-chosen England. They understood themselves and their projects in terms of the millennial vision inspired by the Protestant martyrs. Their covenant with God was a bond that expressed their elect status before him. They were predestined for paradise, and as "visible saints," they should be busy in doing God's work on earth. The Puritans conceived of this work that they must accomplish in two ways. First of all, they were to be an *example* for all the world to see—a society of God's elect in which righteousness had triumphed and sin would reign no more. Secondly, they had a *mission* to spread the message and the meaning of their gospel to others. Since Puritan society embodied that gospel, the mission meant convincing others to live as they (the Puritans) were doing.

Puritan sermons expressed the sense of being an example for others by speaking of New England society as a light to the world and a city upon a hill. The sermons described the mission of Puritanism in the language of destiny and an errand into the wilderness. Being an example and performing a mission, both tasks that were Puritan obligations under their covenant with God, were also tasks that needed to be done with millennial fervor. The Puritans thought that the days of the world were numbered. Their witness was perhaps the last chance for a sinful world to overcome the deceits of Antichrist and to seize the truth of the gospel. In short, the Puritans were people who did not have time to lose. God's business demanded total dedication in light of the millennial future.

What made these themes especially important for American civil religion was that all of them were understood in political terms. Practically speaking, as we have seen, Puritan New England was a theocracy—a church-state synthesis in which government was in the hands of the saints (although not in the hands of the clergy). These fully converted members of the church ruled the New England colonies in the name of those who were drawn together in the civil or political covenant. While not all members of the political covenant were members of the covenant of grace (the church covenant), the ideal of the society was that the two should be one. More than that, the Puritans with their Calvinistic heritage had formed the political covenant using the covenant of grace as a model. They came to interpret their government in terms of destined tasks and millennial visions. Government was really the arm of God reaching into the world through the visible saints to create a society that was publicly committed to the Word. Although there might be—and were—sinners in New England, the colonies—as public and political communities—should be holy. Indeed, when preachers urged the Puritans to be as a city upon a hill, they were expressing the civil character of religion in Puritan culture, for a city is a *political* unit. In the way the Puritans saw the world, the civil and the religious were fused, and—here at least—ordinary and extraordinary religion were united.

We can see from this description that there was much in Puritan society that resembled Old Testament understandings. The Puritans were aware of the similarities and, as we noted in Chapter 4, envisioned themselves as a New Israel. They had linked their millennial yearnings to an older religious model, and so the experience of the ancient Hebrews had parallels in their own mythology. In other words, if every people has a sacred story about who they are and where they have come from, then the stories of the ancient Hebrews and the seventeenth-century American Puritans were in some respects alike. When we spoke about the history of Jewish religion, we noted that the Jews early thought of themselves both as a chosen people and as a suffering people. Among the Puritans, there was the same double message. The Puritans were saying that they were a chosen people, but they were also saying that they were a suffering people. We have already glanced at their chosenness, but now let us take a closer look at their suffering.

We need to realize at the start that all suffering arises from subjective experience. We can finally only imagine the depths of other people's suffering, for none of us is able to crawl into another person's skin. Moreover, language in some sense creates suffering. If people say that they are suffering and believe that they are, then they are. These warnings are necessary because it may be difficult for us to recapture the Puritan sense of their own suffering. From the point of view of outsiders, it may not seem nearly so intense, for example, as the suffering of the Jews.

Puritans saw themselves as suffering in two ways. First of all, they thought of themselves as suffering through outside forces. Like their ancestors during the reign of Bloody Mary, they were now being persecuted by the Church of England. The unkindness of the church and its corruption had forced them to make the journey over an ocean. Here they were compelled to live, to use one of their favorite phrases, in a "howling wilderness." They were surrounded by "savages" (the Indians), who were in league with the devil. So both their fellow Christians in England and their harsh environment in the New World were external sources of discomfort.

Secondly, the Puritans were suffering from conditions within their own souls. Especially after the first generation in New England, public sermons began to portray the Puritans as guilty sinners. They were not living up to their side of the covenant with God, and therefore all kinds of afflictions were coming to them. God was forced to punish them through disease and harsh weather, through Indian wars and the failure of many of their children to be converted. We have already encountered these sermons of affliction: they are the jeremiads that we spoke of in the preceding chapter. In fact, these jeremiads were rituals that relieved some of the guilt the Puritans felt. By enumerating their sins and calling loudly for repentance, they were paying back the first penny on the debt they owed to God. If the rest of the debt went unpaid, that was a matter for later concern. The present, at least, had been taken care of.

It is hard to put a finger on the reasons for Puritan guilt, and we would need to turn to psychological study in order to do so fully. It is possible that the Puritan break with people in England helped to bring it on. It is also possible that, after the first generation in New England, people looked back on the era of the pioneers with a certain awe. Nothing in the lives of settled farmers and tradespeople could quite match the daring stories of the heroism of those who had crossed the sea. But there was another reason for Puritan guilt—the sense of millennial chosenness itself. The Puritans had carved a lofty niche for themselves in the divine plan. They were the elect nation who in the last ages of the world were giving an example and were possessed of a mission to all the nations. As visible saints, they walked with God, and they were emissaries of his Word. But the visible saints must have noticed that sometimes they and their friends were walking in unsaintly ways. Like all people, they had their feet of clay; like all people, they blundered and made mistakes.

Hence, the gap between the Puritan vision of their role and their experience of themselves must have produced a sense of guilt. The theocratic myth of the Puritans possessed a dynamic in which being chosen and being sufferers were two aspects of the same story. The connection between these themes is important because, as we will see, much of the Puritan story became the public and official story of later American civil religion. When America became a chosen nation, there would be a good deal of anxiety attached. Americans would simultaneously proclaim their innocence and feel guilty.

The Civil Religion of the American Revolution

By the time we reach the late eighteenth century, the New England Puritans had thrown in their lot with the other colonists in a growing rupture with the mother country. In the era of the American Revolution, from the first acts leading up to the war to the final adoption of the Constitution in 1789, a civil religion was born. Much from that civil religion was a new version of the old Puritan story. Other parts of it had been gleaned from the Enlightenment, and still other aspects from the revolutionary experience of Americans. Let us look at each in turn.

The Puritans had been a melodramatic people. Some of the later Protestant search to simplify was already theirs, for their millennialism divided the world into a battlefield between two forces. On one side were God and his saints; on the other, the devil and his agents. In this dualistic world, reality was made up of sharp contrasts—good and evil, heaven and hell, truth and falsehood. Even more, significant divine and human actions were perceived by their sharp contrast with the humdrum routine of everyday life. God acted through "remarkable providences" by which he saved the saints from Indian attack, brought them an exceptionally bountiful harvest, or softened the heart of a hardened sinner for conversion. Humans acted in a way to be remembered when they, too, performed unusual or heroic deeds.

By the eighteenth century, the Puritan way of seeing things by means of dramatic contrasts was intensified by the Great Awakening. Jonathan Edwards, we recall, had worked to make his revival sermons "sensational." The more vivid and striking their language, the more the sinner might realize the terrors of hell and turn earnestly to God to seek salvation. Similarly, the behavior of sinners was also sensational. Accounts of the revivals were filled with references to the moans of anguish, the tears of repentance, the fits of fainting experienced by those struck by the power of God. And as the revivals spread throughout the colonies, they brought interaction between people from different parts of the country and a growing sense of community that, some scholars believe, was essential for the occurrence of the American Revolution.

When the Revolution and the events preceding it did come, much of the rhetoric that inflamed people, whether from church pulpits, political songs and rallies, or public newspapers, had a Puritan millennial and revivalistic ring. As late as the close of the French and Indian War in 1763, Americans had regarded English soldiers with gratitude and had been proud to be part of the British overseas empire. Now, however, they saw the British as Satan's troops in a clear battle between the forces of good and evil. The Americans were "our Israel," and the British were the Egyptians at the time of the exodus. Oppressed and persecuted, the Americans had been enslaved by the mother country. They were engaged in a righteous attempt to gain their freedom. It seems curious to find colonists who owned black slaves using this kind of language. But from the perspective of the Puritan heritage of millennialism, it made considerable sense. The colonists were living out of a powerful myth that explained the meaning of reality to them. In the strength of that myth, they could exert their fullest efforts to win the war. If they felt guilty for speaking of slavery in the presence of slaves, they probably felt greater guilt for breaking with the land of their ancestors and sometimes for having very human motives—like economic considerations—in the midst of their sacred war. But the guilt did not become part of the public rhetoric, and the cries of righteous battle grew all the louder.

Likewise, descriptions of the war by people involved in events often sounded like descriptions of the revivals. Enthusiasm was everywhere. Its spirit gripped the public so that they were carried along by it. People spoke about zeal, the work of Providence, and the need to be awakened. Chaplains left their churches to march off to war, and many in their congregations followed. The American force that tried to conquer Quebec stopped first at George Whitefield's tomb. Meanwhile, newspaper accounts of various battles reported God's "remarkable providences." The British had been overwhelmed, the accounts ran, but the Americans lost hardly a person.

Out of the sensational accounts and the sensational rhetoric, Americans were molding a civil religion in which the only way to see was to see vividly and strikingly. Events must be spectacular to be significant; in some way they had to outstrip every other happening and to outweigh every other event. Making history meant performing these spectacular deeds on the public stage in the presence of witnesses who would record events for future generations. Like the Judaeo-Christian God who acted in history and like the millennial Word who would lead his troops at the final battle, patriotic Americans had to do remarkable deeds in order to make their actions meaningful. Like the Puritans, later Americans were a melodramatic people.

In their melodrama, they had absorbed a large share of the Puritan world view (its myth, or creed) and the Puritan behavioral code (the ethic of the battle with evil). They also perpetuated Puritan rituals (the cultuses) in the days of fast and thanksgiving that were observed. Ordered by the Continental Congress, these special times were modeled on older Puritan days of public prayer. They were occasions to call patriotic Americans to repentance for their sins, which could damage the Revolutionary-War effort, and to thank God for successes obtained in battle. They were kept throughout the colonies with great seriousness, for Americans engaged in the battle with evil thought they should keep themselves pure and righteous. The God of the covenant and of battles demanded it of them.

If Puritanism contributed to the civil religion, so did the American Enlightenment. With the growing Arminianism of Puritan liberals, morality and human effort had become uppermost. Thus, Puritans were prepared for the moral emphasis of Enlightenment deism—and its God who, as we will see, worked by letting human beings work. Further, the Puritans had always had an appreciation of God's hand in nature, and by the early eighteenth century that appreciation had begun to assume political form. The Puritans grew familiar with the language of reason and nature that had arisen in the European Enlightenment. John Wise (1652–1725) thought in 1717 that civil power came from the people who were by nature free and equal. Others, especially colonial leaders, became acquainted with nature's laws and nature's God through Freemasonry.

Organized in lodges in the towns of the colonies, Freemasonry had arrived in 1731 when St. John's Lodge was formally recognized in Philadelphia by the Grand Lodge of London. By 1776 there were over forty lodges, and they offered fellowship to members of other lodges who might be traveling in their area. In fact, the Masonic lodges—as secret societies linked to the occult heritage of the colonies—were like a network of churches of the same denomination: they were one more way that bonds were formed between the various colonies before the war. The Masons neither approved nor condemned Christianity, but they saw it as one form of religion that had grown strong and would eventually decay. At the same time, the Masonic lodges thought of Christianity as part of a larger whole. That whole included the religion of nature, and it was expressed by the ceremonies of the Masonic brotherhood.

So Freemasonry became a way to spread deism. Fifty-two of the fifty-six signers of the Declaration of Independence were Masons, and so were a majority of the members of the Continental Congress. With such numbers on his side, it was no wonder that the God of nature provided a new source of unity for Americans in the war. Moreover, the God of nature was familiar also to ordinary folk. As we have seen, British soldiers had spread Enlightenment views in this country. With the French alliance during the war, a popular grasp of the

Enlightenment was only encouraged. At the same time, newspapers, songs, and speeches helped to acquaint Americans with the God of nature.

In the Freemasonic and Enlightenment view, far from being a God of battles, the supreme power in the universe was identified with natural law. In other words, God worked through the system he had designed without altering it or interfering. The Masons liked to think of him as a Grand Architect. The symbolism of Masonic ceremonies was based on implements from the building trade that were reinterpreted in a spiritual way. And the God who was a Grand Architect was especially appealing because, like the God of nature, the Grand Architect did not interfere with his creation once he had fashioned it.

Again, God was often regarded as the Great Governor of the universe. In this title, the God of nature had entered political life, since a governor suggested affairs of state. However, for the colonists the ideal governor was one who interfered as little as possible and instead allowed Americans to run things for themselves. So the greatest governor was one who governed least. In this understanding, patriotic Americans had a political God who acted like a God of nature, not altering the machinery of state once it had been set in motion. Just as the ancient Hebrews had thought of God in the political terms of their monarchy and made of him a king, now patriotic Americans were thinking of God in the terms of their colonial governments and making him a governor. In both cases, religion and politics had been united. God had become a fit sponsor for civil religion.

Behind all of these ways of speaking of God—the God of nature, the Grand Architect, the Great Governor—there was the sense that God was an absolute power that called into question every human authority. Thus, Americans could appeal their disobedience of British legislation to this God, who had become the higher law that we discussed in the last chapter. Identified with natural law, he had *become* natural law and natural right. Not many Americans in 1776 would have accepted this radical way of speaking, but the path was open for a later America to make a different use of the heritage of the Enlightenment if it chose.

Moreover, just as this heritage gave revolutionary Americans a system of beliefs, it also told them how to act and provided necessary rituals. The Enlightenment code of behavior appealed to reason. This ability that all humans possessed within themselves was thought to be an inner law of nature and an inner governor. It prompted people to act according to its dictates, and therefore, they became reasonable people. In this understanding, reasonable behavior was moderate behavior, a golden mean between too much and too little. Above all, it was moral behavior. Reason taught people how to act according to nature, and behaving naturally in the eighteenth century meant behaving morally.

Finally, Enlightenment rituals flourished in the rich liturgies available in the Freemasonic brotherhood. In the secret ceremonies of the lodges, Masonry used an architectural mythology to initiate men (no women were allowed) into Enlightenment religion. The square and compass, tools of building, became symbolic of the task of building a perfect human character. Here the square stood for earth, while the compass suggested the sky. The message was clear: out of nature, humans fashioned their character, and by using nature well, they could become perfect human beings. They must be "square" in their dealings with others. They must use the compass to set the boundaries of their aspirations. The square was placed within the compass, and together the two expressed ordinary religion (the square in the center) and extraordinary religion (the compass at the outer limits).

In other ways, the Masonic brothers also dramatized the religion of nature and Enlightenment. The sun was a familiar symbol within the lodges, and during initiation ceremonies, the brothers faced east. Like reason, the internal light, the sun was the external light of the world, the center around which all nature revolved. In keeping with this importance of the sun, the two great feasts of the Masonic calendar were June 24 and December 27. These were the Christian feasts of Saint John the Baptist and Saint John the Evangelist, so that Christian Masons could observe them fully. But these feasts were also commemorations of summer and winter solstice, the longest and shortest days of the year. They celebrated the sun that had reached its farthest limit in the heaven and the sun that hung lowest in the winter sky, just before its long climb back to summer.

The Enlightenment had provided for Americans a set of universal symbols around which they could build a civil religion. Since the God of nature and the Grand Architect was also the Great Governor, they could understand the evolution of the United States as a "natural" result that had come through the workings of natural law. They could see it also as a great building that had been completed by the Architect; and, indeed, when the new Constitution was adopted in 1789, Americans liked to call it the "new roof." Finally, they could see the civil government as the authentic expression of the Great Governor. They could think of their republic as a place where reason and morality would teach all people to govern themselves, even as they dwelled together in harmony under the law.

On the face of it, there should have been considerable tension between the Enlightenment version of civil religion and the older Puritan millennial vision. How could a God of battles leading his hosts in an out-and-out fight with evil be reconciled with a morality of the golden mean, the moderate and reasonable way of life? How could rituals built on the Christian call for repentance through the grace of God be harmonized with rituals that celebrated human perfectibility through nature? One answer was that, like all people, Americans did not always live by logic. Even more than most, they were practical and took what they could use from both Puritanism and the Enlightenment as they needed it. Moreover, the idea of human perfectibility through nature had its own muted millennial ring. It looked ahead to the dawning of the age of progress when a postmillennial vision would capture much of American culture. Still further, in the nineteenth century Masonry fell into disrepute, and civil religion drew far more on the old Puritan symbols. As time passed, aided by the public school system and by the Protestant character of the dominant and public religion, Puritanism continued to enjoy a privileged position within the civil religion.

But in the era of the American Revolution, there was a third and final factor involved in civil religion. That factor was the self-creation of Americans out of the history of their struggle with Great Britain. Its presence is easiest to chart through its symbolism, so we will begin there. Even before the war broke out, in the midst of protests against the Stamp Act (1765), the practice spread in

New England and elsewhere of holding ceremonies around a tree called the Liberty Tree. In Boston this was a huge elm tree in a central location. In other towns and villages, the pattern was similar. Sometimes figures to represent unpopular British or American leaders were hung in effigy from the tree. Sometimes there were liberty processions and speeches under its branches. On at least one occasion, in Rhode Island, a tree received a conscious religious dedication. And whenever they could, British soldiers set upon a town's Liberty Tree to destroy it, as the colonists told the tale, with "diabolical" malice.

In each place where a Liberty Tree stood, it provided a center for community orientation around the values of the Revolution. The sacred stories of many nations had included reference to a tree of the world, or cosmic tree, thought to exist at the center of the earth and to connect it with the sky. In these mythic tales, the tree was a way to climb from earth to heaven. In its American setting, however, the Liberty Tree symbolized the way the colonists were climbing on the limbs of their own aspirations. It stood for their desire to make a mark for themselves, to stand taller, fight harder, and be remembered longer than any other people on earth. In short, it stood for an ordinary religion of trying to become extraordinary, of human beings trying to become "as Gods."

But the greatest symbol of the godlike quality of true Americans was George Washington (1732–1799). In the revolutionary era, people revered him as a divine man, and in doing so, they were venerating the divine abilities present in all. Like later Americans, the colonists were already many. In the figure of Washington, they found a person, larger than life, who could help to make them one. So while he lived, Washington became the center of a cultus. Locks of his hair were treasured, babies were baptized in honor of him, and legends were circulated about his miraculous abilities as a war leader. Actors read speeches in his honor from the stage, and birthday celebrations for him were elaborate even during his lifetime. By 1779 a German-language almanac had already called him the father of his country, while oratory everywhere was praising him in the most dramatic terms. When Washington traveled to New York for his first inauguration, his route became the scene for elaborate rituals that expressed his greatness. In Philadelphia a new bridge was constructed to float across the river like a triumphal arch, and a little child crowned him. At Trenton several hundred little girls dressed in white serenaded him. At New York accounts spoke of tens of thousands there to greet him.

Interestingly, Washington was compared by his contemporaries to both Jewish and Roman heroes. He was the Moses of his people, freeing them from slavery in Egypt, or he was Joshua, one of the inspired war leaders that God had chosen to save Israel. Alternately, he was Cincinnatus, the great Roman general who had left his plough to fight for his country and then, when the task was done, dropped the sword to return to his farm. This double identification with themes both Jewish and Roman expressed the complex nature of American civil religion that we spoke of earlier. Like the civil religion of Israel, it grew out of the dominant national culture of Protestantism. Like the civil religion of Rome, it summed up the pluralism of many different peoples dwelling in one state.

By the nineteenth century, the Liberty Tree had all but disappeared as a ritual center for the civil religion, but the cultus of George Washington grew and flourished, perpetuated especially by the public school system. The same was true for two other major symbols of the civil religion of the Revolution—the Declaration of Independence and the Constitution. During the revolutionary era, it was the *act* of declaring liberty and not the document that was celebrated. Similarly, it was the *act* of constitution making, not the original pen, ink, or paper, that was hailed. In fact, John Adams thought that July 2—the day that Congress declared independence—would be celebrated by future generations, not July 4— the date that the document was formally approved. And the original document of the Constitution was never publicly exhibited until the twentieth century.

After the Congress proclaimed independence, its declaration was solemnly read throughout the colonies. Cannons were fired, cheers raised, toasts made, and liquor consumed. A year later, there were unofficial celebrations with bells and fireworks along with the cannons, cheers, and toasts. In 1778 Congress gave official orders to honor the Fourth of July and a year afterward told its chaplains to prepare sermons suitable for the event. By the following decade, Americans were giving similar praise to the Constitution. Huge constitutional parades were staged in most of the new state capitals to pay tribute.

The one in Philadelphia, held on the Fourth of July, 1788, after enough states had ratified the Constitution to make it the law of the land, was particularly spectacular. It seemed as if the whole city was either participating or standing in the ranks to watch the eighty-eight divisions that extended for a mile and a half. Exhibits included the "new roof" of the Constitution, erected in a carriage pulled by ten white horses, and the federal ship of state on another float. Meanwhile, tradespeople walked to express their enthusiasm as workers in the new union. There were sacks of federal flour and signs for a federal cabinet shop and a federal printing press. Most significant was the division of the clergy. Here members of different Christian denominations and the Jewish rabbi walked together linking arms—eloquent testimony to the sermon that the parade was preaching. The real ground of unity in the United States was not any of the sects or denominations but the civil religion of the American Revolution that the Constitution summed up.

This attempt to make a new religious statement through the Revolution and to create a religion around it was nowhere better expressed than in the search for a design for the Great Seal of the United States. Three committees worked on the problem over six years before, in 1782, a seal was finally adopted. Among the early suggestions were Benjamin Franklin's of Moses dividing the Red Sea in two, Thomas Jefferson's of the children of Israel marching in the wilderness, and John Adams's of Hercules framed by Virtue pointing him up a rugged mountain and Sloth enticing him down paths of pleasure.

The final design rejected both Jewish and classical themes for a symbolic statement that the real religion of the American Revolution was a religion of newness. An eagle with an olive branch and thirteen arrows to represent the states announced, in Latin, *e pluribus unum;* that is, one from many. On the back of the seal, an uncompleted pyramid was capped by a symbolic eye. Beneath the pyramid was printed *novus ordo seclorum,* the new order of the ages. There were Masonic overtones to the Great Seal, but the message went beyond Freemasonry and the Enlightenment. Americans were saying that they had brought something new into the world. They had inaugurated the golden age of the millennium for which all history had waited. The American Revolution itself became the sacred tale of origins, the center and the source for an American civil religion. In the power of their revolution, Americans hoped, they would be able to create one millennial nation from many different peoples.

The Structure of the Civil Religion

By 1790 elements of creed, code, and cultus had come together to form a loose religious system. This system continued into the nineteenth and twentieth centuries, absorbing new elements and discarding old ones but keeping the same basic structure. Let us look briefly at this structure of the civil religion.

Its creed rested on fundamental assumptions that the United States was a chosen and millennial nation. Both qualities could be understood either in Christian or in more general terms. Chosenness might come from God, from nature, or from historical events. Millennialism could mean the coming of the kingdom of God or a golden age of peace and prosperity that Americans created for themselves without requiring God. In any case, chosenness separated Americans from members of other societies in the world. It burdened them with the twin tasks of being an example of democratic equality and fulfilling a mission to bring that democracy to others. Millennialism split the world into simple alternatives of good and evil and at the same time encouraged both optimism and anxiety regarding America's future. Both chosenness and millennialism were attempts to create a nation out of a political state. They were religious concepts that, it was hoped, could forge one people out of many peoples, giving them a history and identity in the American Revolution, interpreted according to Puritan, Enlightenment, and new American themes.

The code of the civil religion was already contained in its creed. Being an example and fulfilling a mission meant that citizens in the chosen nation must engage in public activity. Loyalty and patriotism as inner qualities were not enough. Rather, as in the majority religion of Protestantism, citizens must *work* for the republic. Voting in official elections became a symbolic action to sum up the duty of the citizen. But in the ideal formula of the code, civil religion required far more. Citizens must read and be informed so that they might vote intelligently. They must be willing to enter public life themselves. And if they were male, the ultimate action that might be required of them was service in their country's armed forces and even death in its defense. Here human sacrifice for religious reasons had not ended but instead was demanded in a new form. On the domestic side, the code urged Americans to succeed economically and to blossom technologically so that the millennium would come fully.

However, the code went beyond statements about how individuals should act in the United States. It was a statement about the political community and how it should behave toward the world. Being an example and having a mission were directives for foreign policy, and America would make good on them in a series of encounters with other states. Although it would not be until the twentieth century that the United States became a world power, the rhetoric of the American Revolution had already predicted as much. From this perspective, world leadership was a self-fulfilling prophecy. Similarly, the wars in which the United States engaged were always fought under the mythology of the moral crusade. As we will see in our discussion later, missionary labors did not end when the Constitution guaranteed separation of church and state.

At the same time, the code of the civil religion had another side. Just as the millennial mission of the Puritans had been linked to themes of guilt and repentance, in the United States the civil religion perpetuated the political jeremiad. In days of fast and thanksgiving and later in oratory and debate bewailing their country's failings, Americans continued to experience the tensions of being chosen. Sometimes the guilt led to stronger statements about being chosen and stronger protests of innocence, as America refused to face its problems. This was the case, for example, in the many conflicts created in the nineteenth and twentieth centuries by racism and nativism. Sometimes, too, the guilt became a great political upheaval in an attempt at moral purification. This was true in the crisis over slavery which led to the Civil War; and as we noted earlier, this was also the case in the Watergate scandal of the 1970s.

Finally, the cultus of the civil religion was already rich in 1790 and kept on growing in the next two centuries. First of all, the necessary conditions for ritual had been provided: there were sacred space and sacred time. Sacred space included shrines and holy places like George Washington's home in Mt. Vernon, Virginia, and Independence Hall in Philadelphia. With the planned development of the new capital in the District of Columbia, the city of Washington, with its classical buildings and memorials on the grand scale, furnished an ideal ritual setting. As time went on, historical sites—such as battlefields that had figured prominently in America's wars—offered other holy places. In the revolutionary era, the Fourth of July and Washington's birthday were already coming to be sacred time. In later years, new commemorations joined them, such as Memorial Day after the Civil War and Armistice Day after the First World War.

Secondly, there was a catalogue of national saints, individuals to be honored because they embodied the ideals of the civil religion. George Washington was only the first among a community of founders who came to be venerated in the public life of the country—men like Thomas Jefferson, Benjamin Franklin, and John Adams. The nineteenth century brought new heroes and saints, like Andrew Jackson and Abraham Lincoln, while the twentieth century contributed its own figures in men like Franklin Delano Roosevelt and John F. Kennedy.

Thirdly, there were sacred objects as well as sacred figures to be venerated by rituals. The original copies of the Declaration of Independence and the Constitution were the most well remembered by the twentieth century, but from the beginning there were other relics of the Revolution. One Liberty Tree destroyed by the British in South Carolina, for example, had its stump preserved by being carved into cane heads.

Last, formal ritual practices were associated with the sacred space and time, commemorating the founders of the republic and venerating the objects that also helped people to remember. Fourth of July fireworks and more solemn sermons were early examples. Later, each special time developed its own liturgy of public addresses, processions, or other events. What all of these rituals had in common was their desire to unify people so that they would be truly a political community and a nation. Like all rituals, the rituals of the civil religion were trying to change the many into one.

The Meaning of the Civil Religion

Creed, code, and cultus together formed the visible structure of the civil religion. But at a deeper level, its meaning was more than the sum of its parts. At the same time, that meaning was ambiguous. Civil religion pulled in different directions at once, and contradiction was basic to its makeup. Rooted in the Puritan and revolutionary past, it urged Americans toward a millennial future. At first glance, an ordinary religion based on life within the human political community of one country, it had extraordinary aspirations. Because it was firmly based in the Judaeo-Christian tradition and, indeed, in Protestant evangelism, it saw America in a transcendent light as an ideal beyond the boundary of the everyday. Civil religion, therefore, contained a good deal of the power of extraordinary religion.

Beyond that, the civil religion was a self-conscious and deliberate faith contrived by the leaders of the revolutionary era to meet their need for a political ideology. Yet there was genuine enthusiasm and spontaneity in the people's response to the new symbols. Millennial excitement could not be produced at will: it had to exist first in the minds and hearts of the people. So the leaders who were trying to make a religion found it already made, the product of a Puritan past and a revolutionary present. All they did was to tap the power that was there and manipulate it for their purposes.

In another contradiction, the civil religion perpetuated the problem that chosenness had created for the Puritans. Chosenness led to guilt and anxiety. Belief in the millennium brought fear of corruption and decline in the earthly paradise. Thus, the combination of millennial chosenness and accompanying guilt encouraged people to disguise serious problems that the country faced. To admit that too much was wrong could jeopardize America's status as a chosen and millennial nation. The acceptable lamentations were often, like the Puritan jeremiads, somewhat hypocritical. In the later history of the republic, problems like racism, nativism, and inequities in the economic system tended to be swept under the carpet, confronted only, if at all, under carefully controlled conditions. They violated the basic identity that the civil religion gave to Americans. Chosen people, living in the millennium, must be innocent and righteous. Americans could not admit the deepest sources of their guilt without destroying their sense of who they were.

Despite this hypocrisy built into the civil religion, it *was* an attempt to find some basis for public unity in the vulnerable federal republic. In the beginning, the vulnerability had more to do with the newness of the governmental apparatus than the character of the peoples it represented. But as time passed, the pluralism, which was already present, grew more and more to be a feature of American life. By the late twentieth century, government was vulnerable because of the diversity of peoples and interest groups it encompassed. In a political state beset with boundary questions between social groups, civil religion proposed a common and, it argued, natural boundary based on the fundamental truths of its natural-rights philosophy. Civil religion was trying to merge the separate boundaries of the many into a single nation-state.

If there was a central meaning to the civil religion in the midst of these ambiguities, that center was millennial politics and history. Whether looking to past or to future, under God or under America, deliberate or spontaneous, hypocritical or sincere, the civil religion revolved around memorable deeds that Americans had performed on the public stage to initiate an age unknown ever before in history. Actions had to be striking to be seen; events had to make history to be meaningful. For people who did not like to dwell in the past, Americans were very anxious to achieve a past on a grand scale. The sensationalist philosophy of Jonathan Edwards sounded and resounded in later American life, and all paths in the civil religion led to the triumph of millennial politics and history.

CIVIL RELIGION IN THE NINETEENTH AND TWENTIETH CENTURIES

So far we have examined the origins of civil religion in Puritanism and in the era of the American Revolution. We have found that the New Israel of the Puritans continued into the revolutionary generation. We have also found that the religion of the Enlightenment, as well as a new religion built around the deeds of patriotic Americans, merged with the New Israel. We noticed a distinct creed, code, and cultus in the civil religion that evolved, and despite its ambiguities, we discovered a core of meaning centering on the values of millennial politics and history. In our discussion, we made occasional references to the nineteenth and twentieth centuries. Now we will pay more attention to civil religion during these two centuries.

The Nineteenth Century

In overview, nineteenth-century civil religion was rooted in the Puritan and revolutionary heritage we have examined. The legacy of the Enlightenment, in the nineteenth century and thereafter, became less clear. Its ethic of the golden mean was cast aside by Americans who were striving for the stars. At least in the nineteenth century, its Freemasonic rituals came under challenge for their undemocratic secrecy, the clannish political tactics they fostered, and, said many ministers, their godlessness. Yet elements of the creed of the Enlightenment did continue. The proclamations of the Declaration of Independence—that all were equal in the sight of God and that all were endowed with natural rights—were, at least theoretically, sacred truths. Still further, the world view of the Enlightenment continued in a new form by blending with a territorial version of millennialism in the age of manifest destiny.

Generally, themes of millennial chosenness, outstanding example as an innocent and righteous nation, and historic deeds and destiny shaped the civil religion. Carried especially in growing numbers of public schools, the civil religion was expressed in history books and readers that told the story of the Revolution and its heroes, inspiring young Americans to patriotic virtue. It was ritualized in regular annual observances as well as in a series of anniversary commemorations of revolutionary events. Since it will not be possible to discuss the nineteenth-century history of civil religion fully, we will look first at the presence of (extraordinary) biblical millennial themes, especially in the Civil War, and then at the more ordinary millennialism that combined Puritan with Enlightenment ideas. Finally, we will glance at how the living memory of the Revolution relieved anxieties and continued to shape the civil religion.

With the War of 1812 (1812–1814), fresh blood from the new conflict with Britain flowed to quicken the civil religion. Congress had declared war because of the British impressment of American sailors into maritime service (in the context of a British struggle with France in which the rights of neutral governments were forgotten) and because of quarrels with Britain over land in the American West. While a considerable number of Americans opposed the war, once it had begun, many viewed it as a Christian crusade. Public fasts multiplied — some of them observed locally and others throughout the country. Because for political reasons the British had supported Pope Pius VII (1740–1823) against France, in American eyes this identified Britain with the Antichrist. Thus, the war was read as a millennial confrontation. The last days were at hand, and when the fortunes of the pope sank, this was a sure sign of fulfillment of the prophecies. For these Americans the War of 1812, like the Revolution, was a holy war.

If the War of 1812 was fought with strong millennial overtones, a half century later it was the Civil War (1861–1865) that played out these themes as *the* millennial war of the century. The Civil War swept up legions of Americans in the final battle between good and evil, as Northerners and Southerners alike drew on the biblical heritage. In the South, the Confederacy became the authentic New Israel facing the armies of Egypt. Southerners believed that slavery was in the plan of God, for blacks had descended from the biblical Ham, the son of Noah who had shamed his father by entering his tent when Noah lay there naked and drunk (Gen. 9:20–25). Noah had awakened to curse Ham and predict for him a life of slavery. Hence, the present enslavement of blacks was right and just. By contrast, the northern abolitionists were atheists and unbelievers. War with such people was an obvious defense of the cause of God and religion. For Southerners, in the millennial vein, this war was the most important struggle through which the country had passed.

In the North, millennial dating convinced people that the end was at hand. According to one theory, the Antichrist had come to power in the year A.D. 606. A symbolic reading of the book of Revelation (Rev. 11:3) indicated that his reign would extend 1,260 years; and therefore, Antichrist must fall in the year 1866. Even in the liberal religious circles of Boston, far from the millennial and evangelical Protestantism of much of America, the vision of Revelation marshaled people to the cause. There Julia Ward Howe (1819–1910), who did not believe in miracles or a special revelation in the Bible, wrote "The Battle Hymn of the Republic." She had visited an army camp, and after the experience the poem came to her, filled with images that must have arisen from long-forgotten childhood memories. Published in 1862, the hymn stirringly described the coming of the Lord for the final battle. It was written in the vivid and dramatic language of the millennium, with the sounds of the march of God interwoven in the sounds of the march of the Union army. The moral of the story was clear: scratch the surface of liberal culture in America, and beneath it, the millennial themes lived on, ready to shape the interpretation of events and give them powerful meaning.

So the war was fought in millennial terms. Then, five days after it ended, Abraham Lincoln (1809–1865) was assassinated. He had just begun his second term of office, telling Americans that they should bear malice toward no one and have charity for all. As it happened, the president had been shot on Good Friday, and that fact was not lost on others. He had been sacrificed, they said, as Jesus had been on the cross—one victim to redeem all the people. While the sacrifice of Jesus had pointed the way for men and women to enter heaven, the sacrifice of Lincoln brought them together in unity for a better earth. Blood had paid the price of liberty. Lincoln's blood, shed for his country, mingled in the ground with the blood of the nameless soldiers who had made the ultimate gift of their lives for their country. Popular oratory echoed with these ideas, as a new divine man and event entered the mythology of the civil religion.

While biblical interpretations—and especially biblical millennialism—dominated during times of greatest crisis for the country, at other moments millennial chosenness wore the garments of ordinary religion. The clearest example was during the era of "manifest destiny" in midcentury. Recall that the Enlightenment God of nature had guaranteed natural law and also natural rights. That guarantee had, in effect, allowed Americans to follow the dictates of their own self-interest, breaking the ties with Britain to achieve political and economic independence. The philosophy of natural rights took many turns in the nineteenth century, as it blended with a sense of national chosenness and a belief in the dawning of a new age that had become part of mainstream American culture. The result was the doctrine of manifest destiny that justified the expansionist ventures of Americans in the West.

Natural rights were rights given by nature to the political community. In the nineteenth-century understanding of them, nature grew less philosophical and more geographical. People began to think that the physical terrain, in its very contours, *contained* the law. In other words, there were natural boundaries to a country—rivers, oceans, sometimes mountains. The existence of these boundaries was a law written into the landscape which Americans should learn to obey, extending their state from one end of the continent to the other. By doing so, they would be spreading the area of freedom and democracy at the same time that they improved the earth for farming, its predestined and highest use. In this way of seeing things, true ownership of land came, not from written documents, but from the higher law of destiny that matched the land with the people most fit to cultivate it. Clear necessity demanded that Americans should have new territory, for like a biological organism, the United States ought to stretch to the limits nature had intended for it. Besides, the task of Americans was to regenerate conquered peoples, raising them up by educating them in democracy. Indeed,

Providence demanded that the United States absorb surrounding land to fulfill this great and moral mission.

The journalist John L. O'Sullivan used the term *manifest destiny* in 1845. In that year, an article in his *Democratic Review* argued regarding the question of Texas that it was America's manifest destiny to expand across the continent. After that, the phrase became a catchword to sum up a spirit and a time, but the ideas it expressed had been present in outline early in the century. Here we cannot trace the growth and changes in the country's commitment to manifest destiny throughout the century, but it is important to point out the continuance of the past in this new era and, later, into the period of the Spanish-American War of 1898. Mainstream Americans still believed that they were a chosen people, whether they expressed that chosenness in the language of the Bible, of the Enlightenment, or of nineteenth-century ordinary culture. Likewise, they still believed that they must be an example to the nations and, even more, that they had a mission to perform. Whether Providence, destiny, or the land itself commanded them, the mission of America was to establish a millennial age of empire. The natural right and providential plan for Americans was to hold more land.

It is clear from the hindsight of well over a century that Americans had manipulated language and ideals for their own self-interest. But as we pointed out earlier, this was a problem built into the very structure of the civil religion. Even without the use of the specific biblical language of the millennium, the problem would not disappear. Meanwhile, even as Americans ventured forward aggressively to create their future, they were deeply anxious, and they clung to signs of divine favor tied to their heritage in the Revolution.

Thus, when the Marquis de Lafayette (1757–1834) visited this country as an old man in 1824, Americans staged what amounted to a revival in the civil religion. Lafayette had been the "adopted" son of George Washington. The presence in the flesh of the son intensified the memory of the Father, now dead for a quarter of a century. Like a sacrament, Lafayette made the Father live again through the closeness of past ties with him. And with the presence of the Father came the presence of the Revolution—and the power of the Revolution made available anew. Heaven was surely speaking to them in the visit of Lafayette, Americans thought, for a rainbow had hung over his ship both when it arrived and when it departed from port. Moreover, an eagle, the symbolic bird of America, had been spotted flying over Washington's tomb as Lafayette walked into it to pay his respects. As Americans shared the news of Lafayette's descent into the tomb, it seemed as if they, too, followed him—not to death but to a rebirth in the spirit of the Revolution.

Then, some two years later, the deaths of both John Adams and Thomas Jefferson on the Fourth of July, 1826, awed and impressed Americans. The two had died hours apart on the fiftieth anniversary of the signing of the Declaration of Independence. Once more, Americans believed they had a sign from God as to the lofty significance of their experiment in democracy. Again in the following decade, when the physical remains of George Washington were placed in a new marble coffin, Americans learned that his body was physically nearly intact. No odor offended those present; the broad temples and chest were there; and one member of the party quickly laid his hand on Washington's head. In these physical remains, Americans had a relic of unusual power. The wholeness of Washington's body seemed a sign of the wholeness of America grounded on its past. Moreover, keeping in touch with the body of Washington was a sacramental way to keep in touch with the Revolution.

Less dramatically, keeping in touch came not through the deaths of the men of the Revolution but through the ceremonial recollection of the events through which they had lived. The fiftieth anniversary of the Declaration (1826), the hundredth anniversary of the birth of Washington (1832), the fiftieth jubilee of the Constitution (1839), the seventy-fifth anniversary of the Declaration (1851), the centennial of the Revolution (1876), and the centennial of the Constitution (1889) were all such occasions. Americans could draw strength from their past as they faced the tensions that their millennial dreams of progress brought them. The liturgies of the civil religion reassured them that their cause was high and their motives under the direction of the Almighty.

The Twentieth Century

With the twentieth century, civil religion continued to interpret for Americans the meaning of their existence as a political community. With the First and Second World Wars the old millennial themes were visible. In more peaceful times, the regular liturgies of the Fourth of July, Memorial Day, the birthdays of Washington and Lincoln, and Thanksgiving recalled the heritage of the past. After the First World War, Armistice Day, later called Veterans Day (1954), joined them. But as time passed and the events of the Revolution became old chapters in the history books, the power of the civil religion to inspire Americans began to fail. Even more, the second half of the century brought wars in Korea and Vietnam that did not lend themselves easily to the familiar millennial interpretations. Moral ambiguity clouded the domestic scene as well, so that civil religion grew to be the faith of fewer Americans less of the time.

The period preceding the American entry into the First World War (1914–1918) was a time of political isolation from foreign involvements—traditional during much of the country's history before the United States became a world power. Here the mythology of chosenness was expressed through the example America gave to a "corrupt" world. In its innocent righteousness America was a new Eden, the garden in which progress blossomed and peace shone. In fact, when Woodrow Wilson (1856–1924) was reelected to the presidency in 1916, his campaign was built around the slogan, "He kept us out of war." The First World War had begun over two years earlier, and Americans had tried to remain neutral. But by 1917 the loss of American lives through German submarine warfare made that impossible, and the country mobilized for war. Wilson, with a strict Presbyterian upbringing, brought moral earnestness and zeal born of sincerity to the task. Under a committee on public information, the government began a propaganda effort to convince Americans of the righteousness of this new crusade.

Once again, the millennial myth of the final battle between the forces of good and evil was tapped. The success of the campaign showed how deeply the myth was rooted in the American spirit. Motion pictures portrayed the wicked and barbarian Huns, so that people might realize they were fighting the agents of Satan. Some states passed laws to forbid the teaching of the German language in schools and colleges; people threw German books out of the libraries; German and Austrian artists and their music were banned from public performances. Speakers appeared at public meetings and at film theaters to deliver brief addresses in support of the war effort. Newspaper editorials and pamphlets hammered home the corruption of the Germans, as the clergy from their pulpits took up the cry of the New Israel engaged in a holy war against evil.

Billy Sunday—whom we have already met waving the American flag as he preached—thought that if hell were turned upside down, the phrase "made in Germany" would be seen stamped across the bottom. Meanwhile, Roman Catholic and Jewish leaders supported the Protestant interpretation of the war. Catholics were told of the parallel between the sufferings of Israel in the desert on the way to the promised land and the sufferings of America in the massive war effort. Jews were reminded that they were once again fighting against the forces of oppression, as they had done so many times before in their history. From the side of ordinary American culture, the war whipped patriotism to new religious zeal. By 1918 at least one book—William Norman Guthrie's *The Religion of Old Glory*—was telling Americans of the greatness of their flag, suggesting a ritual for its worship.

According to the phrase that rallied millions of Americans, the war had been fought to "make the world safe for democracy." America had committed itself one more time in a mission to the world, combining extraordinary and ordinary versions of the myth of millennial chosenness to do so. As the "world's policeman," America had entered a new era in international affairs, but it read the new era through the pages of the old story of the civil religion. Then, after another period of isolation, the Second World War (1939-1945) meant a return to the familiar themes, although less intensely than during the Wilson years.

Still, the dualism of good and evil rode the public airwaves. The totalitarian form of government in the Axis states (Germany, Italy, and Japan) lent itself easily to the millennial interpretation. After Americans entered the war in 1941, convinced of the importance of bombing (some would say, despite evidence to the contrary), they used air power in dramatic displays of force. Making history had become more awesome and spectacular than at any time in previous wars, as the night skies were lit by the flaming missiles of death and destruction. When the United States finally dropped atomic bombs on Hiroshima and Nagasaki, Japan, in 1945, totalitarianism had been countered with total force. If the final battle of Armageddon had not come, Americans had done all in their power to bring it.

In the midst of these years, Franklin Delano Roosevelt (1882-1945) presided over the country, determined from the first to make America an "arsenal of democracy." Elected to an unprecedented third term in office, he told Congress in January 1941 that America should support the countries which were fighting to defend the Four Freedoms—freedom of speech, freedom of religion, freedom from want, and freedom from fear. In the ringing phrases of his oratory, he was calling all Americans to respond to their mission. It was not sufficient to be an example to the nations, as isolationist policy allowed. The Israel of the Puritans must march again though it spoke in thisworldly fashion and wore the uniforms of a government theoretically separate from religion.

Less spectacularly, civil religion continued through the annual calendar of public observances in which great moments or men from America's past were remembered. Like any ritual of remembrance, these liturgies were sacramental in nature. They were ways to make the past present again, attempts to destroy the work of time in order to live in the power of the nation's greatest moments. Living mythically in this way would bring the spiritual energies of the past to bear on present problems. Yet by the fifties, a long and gradual period of decline began to affect the observances and the spirit of the civil religion. While we cannot tell the whole story here, as an example let us look at what happened to the annual Memorial Day commemorations.

Memorial Day had begun in the millennial aftermath of the Civil War, in an America haunted by the sacrifice of Lincoln and deeply aware of the sacrifices of all the dead. In fact, there were both northern and southern theories of its origins. Northerners recounted that General John A. Logan, commander-in-chief of the Grand Army of the Republic, in 1868 established the observance by his orders. Southerners said the remembrance had started in 1866 in Columbus, Mississippi, when women of the town paid homage to the war dead by decorating the graves of both Confederate and Union soldiers. The separate accounts suggest how deep the rupture had been between the two sides. They also suggest the intensity of feeling that marked these early Memorial Day commemorations. As time passed, the presence of veterans who had fought in the war continued to give intensity to the annual Memorial Day liturgies, but when the veterans began to die, a bond with the past was broken. Try as they might, later generations could not recapture the spirit that came with the presence of living witnesses to the war.

Then, in the fifties and afterward, time eroded the strength and significance of Memorial Day ceremonies even further. Remember that in both the North and the South, the day had paid tribute to the sacrifices of countless soldiers who had given their lives in the cause of their country. By doing so, it had given expression to the unity of the community that remained. By honoring those who had died, people renewed their own sense of sacrifice for the good of the whole American community. But the simple formula did not work when applied to the Korean War (1950–1953) and later the Vietnam War (1954–1973), with growing American involvement in the sixties. Many were less sure of the significance of sacrifices in foreign adventures that were clouded with ambiguity. The community was no longer united in its support of war, and Memorial Day, therefore, could not express the themes it was meant to.

In the fifties, newspaper editorials complained about the lack of enthusiasm for Memorial Day, while by the sixties, apathy was evident in accounts of poorly attended Memorial Day parades and gaudy souvenirs that cluttered and cheapened the observances. Journalists asked where the spirit of American patriotism had gone, and by the era of the Vietnam War, the answer was that it had become identified with right-wing causes. To be patriotic during the late sixties and early seventies was to make a cultural statement that identified a person with complaint against hippies, draft dodgers, and other long-haired heroes. To be patriotic meant to be a self-declared enemy of the Woodstock generation. Hence, far from being a solemn celebration of national unity, Memorial Day had become a sad reminder of division. The civil religion in some respects was failing, for the many were not being knitted together into one.

If regular observances of the civil religion like Memorial Day reflected the decline of the tradition, so did the anniversary celebration of America's two-hundredth year. January to December 1976 had been planned as a long remembrance of the events that established the United States. The Fourth of July was to be the peak of the yearlong celebration, a fitting tribute to the deeds of the ancestors and the values on which America was built. But coming on the heels of the demoralizing finish of the Vietnam War and the resignation of President Richard M. Nixon because of the Watergate scandal, the bicentennial caught many Americans not in the mood for celebration. The American Revolution Bicentennial Administration (ARBA), in charge of official government planning, was plagued with disagreements about how the bicentennial could best be commemorated. When early plans were floated to select one bicentennial city, prime candidates like Boston and Philadelphia thought approvingly of the financial gain for their cities from the influx of tourists. But when, for example in the case of Philadelphia, plans grew more concrete with a specific city neighborhood designated as the focus for the celebration, the city government responded to pressures from neighborhood residents. The bicentennial would bring strange people, and especially black people, to their doorsteps. People in the Eastwick section of the city did not approve.

Finally, the ARBA settled on a decentralized plan for the bicentennial. No one city would be *the* center of solemnities. Throughout the country, small cities and towns began to erect signs which proclaimed that each of them was a duly authorized bicentennial city. In truth, the many proclamations mirrored the pluralism of the country at its two-hundredth anniversary. The ARBA had stumbled into a version of America that fittingly summed up the realities of national life. In 1976 no one center could speak for all Americans, for there were too many languages to speak and too many stories to be told.

As if to emphasize the existence of different visions of America, the official ARBA had competition in its planning. The People's Bicentennial Commission (PBC), with its newsletter titled *Common Sense,* challenged the ARBA from a leftist perspective. For Americans of the PBC, the myth of the American Revolution still had power to inspire, but a new enemy of America replaced King George III. In the late twentieth century, the real enemy of America was the giant corporation, and the power of the revolutionary myth should be harnessed to fight the entrenched business establishment. So on the celebration of the two-hundredth anniversary of the Boston Tea Party in 1973, 25,000 supporters of the PBC enacted their own interpretation of events. On the deck of their ship were oil drums prominently displaying the names of the largest oil companies in the United States. The new Boston patriots threw the drums into the water, using the power of the past to register their protest of the present.

Against this background of conflicting ideas of what America meant, the observances of the civil religion on the occasion of the bicentennial were sometimes lavish but mostly quiet and contained. There were gaudy mementos of every description, as commercial interests hurried to profit from events. But cities expecting large numbers of tourists did not get nearly so many as they expected. Police waiting for fights and accidental deaths in the huge crowds at commemorations found far less happened than they had anticipated. Generally, Americans celebrated the Fourth of July soberly more than enthusiastically. There were huge spectacles in big cities, like an impressive procession of tall ships bearing masts that sailed through New York harbor. But in the atmosphere of the late twentieth century, the civil millennial dream had been interrupted, if not ended. A new national consensus about the meaning of America had not been formed.

The slow decline did not go unheeded by thoughtful people. In fact, since at least the sixties, a number of scholars had begun to ponder the meaning of America as they examined the civil religion. It was one of these scholars, the sociologist Robert N. Bellah, who by 1967 employed the term *civil religion* to describe the religious system we have been discussing throughout the chapter. For some sociologists, like Bellah, and for some historians, like Sidney E. Mead, scholarship about civil religion became an earnest attempt to revitalize the tradition. Bellah's article "Civil Religion in America" spoke of the growing (at that time) conflict in Vietnam as America's third time of trial, a new crisis on the order of the American Revolution and the Civil War. Sidney E. Mead's many essays on the "religion of the Republic"—and later its theology—identified sectarianism as the cause of national disunity and praised the universal religion of the Enlightenment, born in the Revolution. This religion, he thought, offered Americans real hope of unity. In the year before the bicentennial, Bellah published a book-length essay, *The Broken Covenant*. Subtitled *American Civil Religion in Time of Trial*, it began with the power of the American myth of origins and, in contrast, found the civil religion of the present empty and broken. Bellah called for a return to the true and original meaning of the covenant, to a millennium brought by God and not by human beings, and to the continuance of the old dreams and visions.

So in their awareness of the lessening hold of the civil religion, descriptive scholars had become theologians and preachers. Their reflection and writing was really an attempt to make the civil religion strong again. While we cannot predict if they will succeed, we need to step back from their problems and ideals in order to sum up what we have learned. In his article in 1967, Bellah had identified the existence of civil religion by studying presidential inaugural addresses to find in them references to God. It is interesting that in the excerpts he included from the 1961 inaugural address of President John F. Kennedy (1917–1963), there were as many references to history or our "forebears" as to God. Later, at the height of the Watergate scandal, President Richard M. Nixon continually referred to history as the judge of his deeds. He had wanted to make history, and so he had taped presidential conversations in the Oval Office to preserve them. His unwillingness to destroy the tapes—his bond with history—in the end brought him down.

In America from the beginning, making history had been identified most closely with politics. The public space of government—and the conversations and acts that took place there—gave many Americans a sense of clear direction in the ordinary world. In a key example, in 1823 as an old man Thomas Jefferson wrote to John Adams, including in his letter the wish that the two would meet again in heaven with their colleagues in the Congress. Happiness, for Thomas Jefferson, John Adams, and many others, meant politics.

Indeed, in the late twentieth century the statement was as true. News accounts revolved around the (often crisis-ridden) doings of the president and the Congress, while every four years, the country passed through a season of millennial revival as the presidential election campaign was waged. As the now-retired Walter Cronkite ended his presentation of the news each evening on CBS television, he told millions of Americans, "That's the way it is." Meant to be a catchphrase to close the broadcast, the statement was profoundly philosophical—and religious. The real world, as proclaimed by Walter Cronkite and CBS, was the world of public events and striking deeds. It was the world of political and sometimes military action, the account of old records surpassed, new goals achieved, and public acclaim captured. Americans were still melodramatic people, and they were still sensationalists. That is how they made sense of their world, lived their daily lives, and solemnized their actions in rituals.

Yet as we have already seen, in their involvement in history and politics, Americans showed little interest in the chronological account of the unfolding of the past. If they looked to America's time of origins in the Revolution, they looked more to their achievements in the present and to their plans for the future. Civil religion was the triumph of politics and history, but the history involved was, in reality, ahistorical. It was the history that Americans performed with an eye to the millennial new day that counted, not the weight of tradition. In effect, as we noticed earlier, the civil religion was caught in a double bind: it needed the past to be meaningful—to give the present a solid foundation. Yet the values it encouraged were values that rejected the past for the future.

As the past became older and the revolutionary events more distant, it was no wonder that many Americans had trouble relating to the myth. At the same time, for old Americans who were red or black and for immigrants who were newer and more diverse, the ties with the past that did remain in the civil religion proved not especially meaningful. Civil religion could give Americans a creed, a code, and a cultus, but it could not transform them into one community. Ambiguous in its relationship to tradition, civil religion, with its dream of millennial chosenness, could not awake to the manyness of the present. It was caught between the past and the future. It had no formula for the community that needed to be created in the present from what *all* the people in the United States shared in common.

Still, there was another side to this complex issue. From the first, civil religion was a religious system that had sprung up in addition to the churches. It had brought ordinary American history into touch with extraordinary religion. Yet unlike being Methodist or Jewish or Presbyterian, being a believer in the national faith did not mean belonging to an organization or breaking ties with a previous church to which a person belonged. Despite the contrary evidence of the Jehovah's Witnesses, a believer in the civil religion might also be a Baptist, a

Catholic, or a Mormon. Indeed, a believer in the civil religion might conceivably be an atheist, since a good part of the symbolism of the civil religion could be used without reference to God. Thus, despite its limitations, to some extent civil religion *was* an answer to the problem of manyness—an overarching religious system under which most of the denominations and sects might thrive. Civil religion was a "one story" created, whatever its problems, to forge the many into one.

IN OVERVIEW

We have seen that civil religion is a recent name for religious nationalism as institutionalized in a loose religious system. Its foundations were laid by the New England Puritans and, later, by the patriots of the American Revolution, who linked Puritan millennial themes to Enlightenment religion and the experience and remembrance of their own deeds in the war. By the time of George Washington's first inauguration, the creed, code, and cultus of the civil religion were firmly in place, and through them the ordinary history of the country was linked to extraordinary religion.

The creed proclaimed the United States as a chosen and millennial nation, saddled with the twin charge of providing an example and fulfilling a mission to raise up others to democracy. The code emphasized right and patriotic behavior by citizens and government, thus setting example and accomplishing the American mission. At the same time, the code institutionalized the jeremiad, the public lament about the guilt of America that took the place of real action to correct problems. Interlinked with creed and code, the cultus of the civil faith designated sacred space and time in national shrines and patriotic holy days. It offered a series of national saints, holy objects, and ritual practices to help people keep touch with creed and code. Although there were many ambiguities in the meaning of creed, code, and cultus, their central affirmation was the millennial politics of making history by deeds of greatness.

In the nineteenth century, the War of 1812 and the Civil War carried forward the millennial theme, while the doctrine of manifest destiny applied the theme to the acquisition of land. Then in the twentieth century, the First and Second World Wars heightened millennial fervor, but beginning in the fifties a long period of decline beset the civil religion. Celebration of the cultus grew even less enthusiastic as, for example, at Memorial Day observances and during the bicentennial. Against this background, a scholarly revitalization movement explored the meaning of the civil faith and tried to revivify and strengthen it. Beleaguered by its problems, civil religion could not create authentic community: it was the religion of, at best, many of the people some of the time. Yet it did offer a framework within which the many could come together as Americans and still pursue their separate religions.

However, civil religion was only the tip of the continent, so to speak. Although they were many, Americans in their public space had created a dominant culture that, as one, told them who they were, advised them how to act, and provided them with rituals to express these meanings. George Washington was not the only American divine man. Arguing politics and celebrating the

Fourth of July were not the only American rituals. Beyond the civil religion there was general American culture. We need to examine further its religious dimensions, for we need to gain a clearer sense of what ordinary religion means in the American setting. As we will see, George Washington shared his power with Elvis Presley, and arguing politics yielded before the great public spectacle of the American baseball game.

SUGGESTIONS FOR FURTHER READING: CIVIL RELIGION

Albanese, Catherine L. *Sons of the Fathers: The Civil Religion of the American Revolution.* Philadelphia: Temple University Press, 1976.

Bellah, Robert N. *The Broken Covenant: American Civil Religion in Time of Trial.* New York: Seabury Press, 1975.

Cherry, Conrad, ed. *God's New Israel: Religious Interpretations of American Destiny.* Englewood Cliffs, NJ: Prentice-Hall, 1971.

Gribbin, William. *The Churches Militant: The War of 1812 and American Religion.* New Haven: Yale University Press, 1973.

Herberg, Will. *Protestant—Catholic—Jew.* Rev. ed. Garden City, NY: Doubleday, Anchor Books, 1960.

Hudson, Winthrop S. *Nationalism and Religion in America: Concepts of American Identity and Mission.* New York: Harper & Row, 1970.

Jewett, Robert. *The Captain America Complex: The Dilemma of Zealous Nationalism.* Philadelphia: Westminster Press, 1973.

Mead, Sidney E. *The Nation with the Soul of a Church.* New York: Harper & Row, 1975.

Moorhead, James H. *American Apocalypse: Yankee Protestants and the Civil War, 1860–1869.* New Haven: Yale University Press, 1978.

Richey, Russell E., and Jones, Donald G., eds. *American Civil Religion.* New York: Harper & Row, 1974.

Strout, Cushing. *The New Heavens and New Earth: Political Religion in America.* New York: Harper & Row, 1974.

Tuveson, Ernest Lee. *Redeemer Nation: The Idea of America's Millennial Role.* Chicago: University of Chicago Press, 1968.

Weinberg, Albert K. *Manifest Destiny: A Study of Nationalist Expansionism in American History.* 1935. Reprint. Chicago: Quadrangle Books, 1963.

Wilson, John F. *Public Religion in American Culture.* Philadelphia: Temple University Press, 1979.

CHAPTER 12

Cultural Religion: Explorations in Millennial Dominance and Innocence

In 1968 the *Whole Earth Catalog* came into existence as a counter-cultural Sears and Roebuck catalog. One of the regulars who contributed to its pages was Gurney Norman. As a strong advocate of composting, Norman in one issue described his composting class for readers. The group began its session with tea, drunk quietly and ceremonially while sitting on cushions. Then the class moved on to actual discussion in which practical techniques and questions were aired. Finally, at the end of the meeting each person reverently sprinkled used tea leaves on the compost pile and took away a cup of the half-finished compost and two worms. These items were seed for the compost pile that class members would later begin at home.

It was a small and humble liturgy that Norman and his class had followed, but nevertheless it was a definable ritual. Sacred space was created by the cushions on which members of the group sat during the tea ceremony and by the common compost pile at the end. Sacred time had been separated from the rest of time by the deliberate acts of drinking tea, sprinkling tea leaves, and taking away the compost. These acts were performed formally and self-consciously with a sense of their symbolic meaning. And clearly, they were related to belief and behavior systems held by class members. Here were people interested in the natural cycle of growth, destruction, and renewal. Here were people about to take up backyard composting on their own.

Gurney Norman and his friends thought themselves different from mainstream Americans, and in some ways they were. But their ritual in the midst of ordinary life was only one instance of various kinds of symbolic action that Americans—and all people—perform regularly. Human beings, whether they hold to organized religions or not, find ways to express in ritual the deep meanings and values they place on the world. Everyday life is punctuated with these symbolic actions, often even humbler and less deliberate than those in Norman's class. The rituals of ordinary culture are frequently vague and highly diffused. To the untrained eye they may be invisible, but with the background of our continuing discussion of ordinary religion, it is time to think about them.

RELIGION AND ORDINARY AMERICAN CULTURE

In the terms of our text, we would call the composting session of Gurney Norman and the others a series of religious actions. These were ritual gestures related to a creed and a code that in its complete form included all of life. To be sure, the gestures were not a part of any traditional religion, and Norman and his friends would have been the first to protest if we had said that they were. It is clear, for example, that no institution stood behind the composting class, and if the composters thought themselves part of a larger movement, that movement gave out no membership cards, possessed no group statistics, and claimed no constitution. Norman, in the ritual setting, did act as a priestly leader, but his priesthood was temporary and self-appointed. Furthermore, the boundaries of his group were loose and fluid. Members of the class, aside from their composting practices, did not necessarily separate themselves from the rest of society. And while they did have a set of beliefs and actions that marked them, they could also be members of other religious groups. Finally, in Norman's ceremonies, no language of the supernatural, no mention of God, entered the format of the ritual. The message of tea and compost was related to this world without reference to any other.

In our discussion of civil religion, we have already encountered a religious system without formal institutionalization. Custom demanded certain kinds of activities, such as Fourth of July ceremonies, but no Church of the Civil Religion distributed membership cards or conducted initiation ceremonies. Except for naturalized citizens, membership came with birth—as general a commitment as being part of American culture. Similarly, while God was acknowledged in much of civil religion, we saw that it was not necessary to affirm him in order to practice it. In the final analysis, the civil faith centered on the political community, with the hope of creating out of the many an American nation-state. Thus, civil religion demonstrated for us that changing the language—from God to history—did not completely change the religious system. Words are symbols, and as symbols they stand for realities beyond themselves. In the case of civil religion, we saw that even when the words changed, what they symbolized remained. The values of the civil religion were the same or very nearly so, although language might no longer be openly religious. Hence, civil religion is our first example of a diffuse and part-time religion that is still a religion. Without institutionalization and without an absolute need for the language of the supernatural, civil religion lives on in recognizable form.

With this background, it should not surprise us that in ordinary culture people often find additional symbolic centers. Besides civil religion, there are other means by which people order their lives and search for meaning within the everyday world. Beyond civil religion, too, there are other ways that people reach moments of transcendence, using ordinary culture as a window into an "other" world. As we said in the last chapter, civil religion is only the tip of the continent. That means that there is a whole landscape of religion still to explore. In this chapter, we cannot hope to cover this vast continent, but at least we can take a few steps. We can try to understand tentatively what the religion of culture is about. In the pages that follow, first, we will take a brief survey of major expressions of cultural religion. Secondly, as a specific case study, we will examine in more depth the ways in which the natural world has provided the center for some kinds of cultural religion, as in the composting class. Thirdly, we will try to sift through the complexities of what we have learned to arrive at some general conclusions.

CULTURAL RELIGION: A BRIEF SURVEY

Cultural religion, as we know it today, roughly began to assume its shape in late nineteenth-century America. In this era, the crisis of the Civil War had passed; industrialization was changing the face of the United States; cities were multiplying in number and in size; and the most massive waves of immigration to date were flooding them. At the same time, such familiar features of American life as organized sports, expanding technologies, and in literature, Western novels were becoming commonplace. While it would be instructive to study earlier cultural religion in America, here we will mostly limit ourselves to this later and, especially, our contemporary period. More than looking at the changes in cultural religion through the years, now we need to identify what cultural religion in the United States looks like in the present. As we will see, there are lines connecting our cultural religion to the dominant and public religion of Protestantism and to the American civil religion. Themes of millennialism—as both a form of dominance and a form of innocence—figure prominently in cultural religion. Linked to the millennialism, quests for ecstasy and the creation of a community of feeling run through many forms of everyday behavior, while voluntaryism is the great given that provides the background. Cultural religion simply carries these themes into a less openly "religious" setting.

The American Ritual Calendar

Probably the most observable aspect of cultural religion in this country is the American ritual calendar. We have already seen parts of it in the Fourth of July, the birthdays of Washington and Lincoln, Memorial Day, Veterans Day, and Thanksgiving. But there are other special days as well. Encircling the year are a series of holidays (holy days) that bring people together as part of American culture. Thus, the early winter cycle of feasts begins with Halloween, includes Veterans Day and Thanksgiving, and then culminates in the Christmas and New Year's celebrations.

At least three of these occasions have historic roots associated with extraordinary religion. Halloween was once All Hallows' Eve, the night before the Catholic feast of All Saints' Day, when all hallowed, or holy, people in heaven were remembered. Thanksgiving, we recall, was a harvest festival originating with the Pilgrims to thank God for his blessing on the crops after a successful planting in the New World. Christmas was the Christian commemoration of the birth of Jesus Christ. In their twentieth-century American setting, however, these three feasts have grown away from their origins. A Jew or a Muslim can—in some ways and in many cases—celebrate any one of them, for the symbols of these feasts no longer require Christian interpretation. Halloween has become a beggars' night for neighborhood children; Thanksgiving, a family feast of abundance centering on the overstuffed turkey and its trimmings on the festival table; Christmas, a winter feast of evergreens and the ever-jolly department-store Santa.

On the other hand, without distinct Christian roots, New Year's Eve is a feast that resembles classical pagan festivals. In social gatherings, people are able to behave spontaneously, letting out all the stops, so to speak, in a night of fun and revelry. Alcohol and food flow freely to oil the social process, and as the clock strikes twelve, people join together in a rousing toast to the new year. Letting out all the stops, in America and in many other societies, has been a way to imitate what is happening to time. The old year—the old forms—are running down and being destroyed; a new order is rising. Hence, people traditionally break up their old patterns of behavior by their revelry. They share the creation of a new order later as they make their annual New Year's resolutions.

In the first half of the new year, another series of holidays makes symbolic statements about the meaning of life in America. First, there are the remembrances of the civil faith in the February commemoration of the birthdays of Washington and Lincoln, now celebrated together as Presidents' Day; in Memorial Day at the end of May; in Flag Day on June 14. Then there is the trinity of Valentine's Day, Mother's Day, and Father's Day, which tell of the importance of feeling and sentiment in the private sphere. In a highly industrialized society with its impersonality in work and business, these occasions pay tribute to home, family, and personal affection.

The great midsummer feast of Americans is the Fourth of July, when picnic, fireworks, and patriotic displays bring family, friends, and community together. After this the summer weeks pass in some two months of unmarked time—the traditional vacation period. Then, as summer unofficially closes in time for school, comes Labor Day. On this first Monday in September, Americans honor their own work in the foundation and continuance of their society. And in honoring work and working people, they also show their regard for the Puritan and Calvinist virtues of industry, hard work, and efficiency, through which Americans believe their society became great.

It is worth pausing for a moment to reflect on the cumulative meaning of this annual cycle. Six holidays belong to the calendar of the civil religion, and of these, four—the Fourth of July, Memorial Day, Veterans Day, and Presidents' Day—are associated with apocalyptic millennial themes that recall catastrophic wars and sacrificial deeds on behalf of country. A fifth holiday of the civil religion, Thanksgiving, is millennial as well, but here the golden age of peace and plenty rather than the final battle is celebrated. The sixth holiday, Flag Day, honors the flag as symbolic of America. Themes of millennialism and sacrifice are implicit, for a flag is a war standard. But Flag Day is a minor occasion, observed legally only in the state of Pennsylvania.

At the other end of the spectrum, there are at least five holidays in which family or domestic themes are highlighted. Halloween and Christmas belong to children who, on both occasions, receive the gifts and goodwill of neighbors, family, or Santa Claus. Adults, when they participate in these feasts, renew personal bonds with one another through parties, or at Christmas, through family reunions. Similarly, Valentine's Day, Mother's Day, and Father's Day show regard for a special person within the context of a close relationship. What all of these occasions have in common is that they pay respect to innocence. There is the natural innocence of children on Halloween and Christmas and the virtuous innocence of family and friendship on all of the feasts. Coming as they do to interrupt the economic cycle of the marketplace, the sanctity of their domestic themes is only underlined.

Labor Day strikes a middle position between the public and private spheres, for it honors each American's personal contribution to the whole society through the public activity of productive work. Begun in 1882 by the Knights of Labor, this holiday with its union roots suggests the golden age of equality, when the common folk create a new America with the work of their hands. In the same way as Thanksgiving, it has the ring of the millennium of peace and plenty. Moreover, like Thanksgiving, it weaves private and domestic themes into the millennial cloth, subtly introducing American innocence once again.

Finally, New Year's Eve combines millennialism with innocence in its anticipation of the dawning of a new era when the mistakes and misfortunes of the past will be erased. With its destruction of old forms, New Year's Eve envisions the world born anew. The symbolism associated with the celebration appropriately summarizes these themes. Old Father Time hobbles along on his cane, his white beard reaching almost to his ankles. Then, at midnight, the diapered infant of the new year appears, fresh and innocent to encounter what the future may bring.

We may note, too, that in at least three of the celebrations—Memorial Day, the Fourth of July, and Labor Day—picnics are traditional. These summer feasts provide an occasion for people to leave the cares and congestion of urban life to return to the peace of a natural setting. Such a return to nature is a mythic journey into the innocence of the garden of Eden and, at the same time, the innocence of the millennial era. It bypasses history—the world of everyday work—to give people a chance for rest and renewal.

In sum, the liturgical cycle of ordinary American culture tells us that millennialism—as both dominance and innocence—is as important there as it is in public Protestantism and, as the cycle partially reflects, in civil religion. Furthermore, the cycle shows us that millennial dominance and innocence are closely related. Apocalyptic conquest and destruction are not so far as we may think from the innocence of babies and of family reunions. The soldiers of the millennium are righteous and pure, persons who do not know evil. The literal meaning of innocence is the same: not knowing evil. Neither the millennial soldier nor the innocent American can be comfortable with the ambiguities of a world not black or white, but muddled shades of gray.

American Mythologies

Mythologies, we recall, are sacred stories (or sets of stories). As such, they tell people who they are, where they have come from, what their tasks ought to be, and what their world means. In other words, mythologies tell people the deepest truths they hold about their human condition. American mythologies unite the many in the country by providing them with a common fund of meaning for all to share. In short, American mythologies give people a creed, or system of beliefs, regarding their place as part of one people. The creed is carried by television and film, spread by popular literature and magazines, and embodied in popular heroes and entertainment stars. It surrounds Americans in public places and, through television and the print media, enters the privacy of their homes. More strongly than the gospel of any church, which is heard perhaps once or twice in a week, it shapes Americans from cradle to grave. While its message is complex and many sided, we can single out a few major themes for discussion.

We know from the study of drama and literature that the thousands of plots enacted on the stage or developed in novels and short stories can actually be reduced to very few. The names, personalities, and events on the surface change, but the underlying patterns remain the same. We all can name a number of the basic plots: boy meets girl, boy wins girl, eternal triangle complicates the romance, trusted friend betrays the family, and other familiar tales. Thus, when the plots of television serials and Hollywood films are examined, it should not be surprising to find a limited number of basic plots being repeated time after time. As we watch a dramatized story, frequently we know how things will end. The good side will win; the captive girl will be rescued; the criminals will be caught and taken to jail. With this near certainty before the story unfolds, the question is, Why do we bother to watch? Some may argue that the answer is "just entertainment," but others would say that powerful mythic truths about life are being expressed and reinforced in the television and film dramas. We watch and listen because, through the medium of the story, we are being told *what* the world means and *how* it means. With our basic understandings of the nature of things confirmed by the electronic media, we can go about our lives refreshed and reinvigorated.

In other words, the fictional tales presented on television and film work much as the sacred stories fundamental to the different religious traditions. Like these sacred stories, they establish a world that makes sense and give people a feeling for their place in the scheme of things. These fictional tales come in many artistic styles. Some are Westerns; some, detective or crime stories; some present us with science fiction; and some are old-fashioned soap operas. Yet despite the differences in style, considerable evidence shows that one favorite plot, with variations, dominates in a number of these dramas. This plot organizes a great many stories, and further, it is the skeleton of many of the all-time successes in living room and at box office. Not surprisingly, this preferred plot is related to the millennial Puritan and revolutionary background of American culture and, in fact, is a modified version of it.

The plot might be summarized as trouble in paradise with eventual redemption for the hard-pressed community. Typically, the story turns on a wholesome and innocent society invaded from outside by some overwhelming evil. Members of the society are caught off guard and unable to defend themselves because of circumstances. But just in the nick of time, a powerful stranger, also from outside, comes to save them. His past and his background are noble but unclear; and he seems to want nothing, not even sexual favors, from members of the community. Once he has conquered the forces of evil through acts of sudden and righteous violence, he leaves the people in the redeemed society to continue their peaceful lives as before. Superman, the Lone Ranger, and—with a change of gender—Wonder Woman, all conform to this basic plot outline. So, too, do such science fiction successes as the former television series *Star Trek* and the film *Star Wars.* With some variations, the well-remembered *Jaws* fits the pattern. So also do the adventures of heroines like Little Orphan Annie and heroes like Dr. Marcus Welby, if subtle forms of manipulation are substituted for righteous violence.

One reason for the massive popular appeal of these dramas and many like them is that they tap the fundamental understanding of themselves and their world held by mainstream Americans. To the extent that the many, with their different backgrounds, find themselves caught by the power of the television and film tales, they have joined the mainstream and, in a loose and diffused way, the one religion of Americans. For in the dramas there are visible still the themes of millennial dominance and righteous innocence of the old Puritan and revolutionary visions. The saving stranger, though disguised by the trappings of role and character, is the messiah of the final battle, the Word riding forth at the head of his troops for Armageddon. Hence, the violent destruction of evil in the plot is religious and right. As the stranger fades into the distance, a millennium of peace and justice can reign in the redeemed community.

Popular literature, especially science fiction and Western novels, repeats many of these themes. Gangster and detective stories bring the lonely hero of the Western or science fiction tale into the city, and they also confuse the clear dualism of good and evil as they unfold. We admire the gangster's skill at survival even though we know that he represents evil and in the end must die. We realize that even the detective is guilty in some ways in the corrupt atmosphere of urban life. Still, figures like Columbo—with his name hinting of Christopher Columbus and Columbia, an alternative name for America—evoke millennial themes, if more subtly. In their successes and failures, even more in their traits of character, we see idealized versions of the values that our culture promotes. Here the millennial promise of the New World is realized in the self-made people, the doers, and the go-getters who shine in their quickness and coolness. The individualism celebrated by the American imagination is celebrated again in these fictions. We come away from reading them with our belief in the strength of individual action confirmed and restored.

We do not have space here to treat such criticisms of the prevailing style as anti-Westerns and satiric humor. But, generally, these forms of drama and literature succeed precisely because of the strength of the myths they are criticizing. Thoughtful people applaud the antiliterature because in some ways they are aware of their cultural dependence on the dominant mythologies of the land. In the antiliterature, they find a space that gives them a measure of cultural freedom.

Meanwhile, tales of love and romance give us a more intimate world than the one we have been describing, and popular magazines, written especially for men or for women, provide mythic models for personal identity. Generally, millennial themes are even more subdued in this literature, but the perfectionism of the millennial dream lives on as problems of sexual role and relationship are explored. It is worth noticing how much the American *ideal* of individualism provides a background for these books and magazines, even though in reality they foster conformity to media models of living.

As an example, magazines for men include, first of all, *Playboy* and its rivals, and secondly, *Argosy, Field and Stream,* and other periodicals that promote the "masculine" ideal of strength and skill. Both types tell men how to be men, offering them models of sexual success or masculine achievement. They appeal to men as free and independent individuals able to develop all their powers to perfection and to embody the ideals the magazines present. Similarly, women's magazines such as *Women's Day* or *Good Housekeeping* hold out to women the ideal of the homemaker. Others, like *Cosmopolitan,* cater to women who aim to be free of attachments, successful at career and sex but not encumbered by home and family. Still others, like *Ms.*, appeal to women with feminist leanings, promoting the message that fulfillment may come with or without men. Each type of magazine gives women a model for imitation. At the same time, each appeals to individualist and perfectionist sentiments with its subtle version of the gospel of success—whether as homemaker, career woman, or feminist.

If television, film, and print provide a web of fundamental beliefs for Americans, so does music, and so do the popular singers who embody the themes they sing. Indeed, the entertainment industry provides America with men and women who become ideal types for their fans. All of us have seen or read accounts of film idols mobbed by their admirers and spending hours to sign autographs for them. All of us know about fan mail and fan clubs, fan magazines and the paraphernalia that go with being a "star." In fact, entertainment idols are one kind of American hero. Like political leaders, Western roughriders, and self-made men and women who rose from rags to riches, the stars of the entertainment empire demonstrate the qualities that Americans most admire. They are living myths who give people an example in the flesh of the power of the story. We might say that, for those who believe, the heroes are "as Gods." That is why they are called idols. That is why the attention paid to them is similar to the religious worship offered, for instance in India, to avatars, or persons believed to be living deities.

It would be fascinating to pursue this theme by studying the many heroes who have inspired Americans at different points in our country's history. But since we do not have space, let us instead briefly consider the career of one such recent hero, an idol of popular music acclaimed by millions as the "king" of rock and roll. For over twenty years, Elvis Presley (1935–1977) reigned in his musical kingdom, and even after his death, people continued to pay him homage in what became a cult of devoted followers. What power did Elvis Presley have over so many people? What was the source of a popularity that began when he was a teenager, thrived when he was middle-aged and overweight, and continued even after death?

Presley came from humble, working-class origins, and he attracted the attention of the recording industry by a stroke of good fortune. But his success, like the success of so many of the symbols of the civil religion, came not from the managers but from the people. When RCA Victor released Presley's recording of

"Heartbreak Hotel" in 1956, it became an immediate hit and led all competitors for eight weeks. In the same year, Presley gave the public in quick succession "Don't Be Cruel," "Hound Dog," "Blue Suede Shoes," and "Love Me Tender." Wiggling his hips as he sang, he sent his fans into enthusiastic shouts and shrieks. Teen-age girls became nearly hysterical when they saw him, and when Presley finally appeared on national television on the *Ed Sullivan Show*, cameras recorded his movements only from the waist up. The saga of his swift climb to riches and fame thereafter was astounding. "Heartbreak Hotel" sold 2 million copies, while a worldwide Presley fan club at one time boasted of 400,000 members. A series of films were produced with Presley cast in the leading role, and in the first two years of national acclaim, some said he had earned 100 million dollars.

After two years in the army beginning in 1958, Presley returned to private life in the sixties. He continued to be popular, although not nearly in the style of the midfifties. Still, with neither personal nor television appearances in the early sixties, he was taking in 5 million dollars a year simply by making a few recordings and films. Then, in the seventies, a public nostalgic for the innocence of the fifties rediscovered him. Middle-aged men and women, perhaps the same people who were his teen-age fans in the past, joined a new generation of young people who loved him. By 1977, he had earned forty-five gold records, each for a song that had sold more than 1 million copies.

When Presley died suddenly in 1977, 25,000 people stood for hours to view his body. They cried as if a family member had passed away, and their cars began to display bumper stickers proclaiming "Elvis lives." T-shirts were sold in front of Graceland, the Presley mansion, printed with the message "Elvis Presley, In Memory, 1935–1977." Jewelry and dinner plates commemorated him; needle-point could be worked in a pattern to produce his image; an original Presley recording came to cost as much as $500. From one point of view, all of this was gaudy and tasteless commercialism. Yet as in so many other displays of popular religion, people were rendering homage and carrying away relics of an avatar or saint. For the millions who loved him, Presley spoke to the inner spirit, assuring them that the values they cared about still were real. In short, there were spiritual reasons for Presley's success.

In the first place, he had grown out of the Pentecostal evangelical tradition. During his childhood in Tupelo, Mississippi, he had sung with his parents in a trio at church conventions, revivals, and camp meetings. Gospel was in his blood, for gospel music had been his earliest love. Later some would say that his singing style was simply an exaggeration of gospel music. Whether or not that was the case, he took from his evangelical background the strong sentimentality that ran through his music and his personality. People loved Presley because of the tenderness of his songs and also because they thrived on stories like those of how he gave away numerous Cadillacs in compassion for others less fortunate than himself. For many who had never heard the gospel preacher, Presley created the cherished community of feeling that the revivals brought—the millennial moment of a common enthusiasm and joy.

In the second place, Presley's power came from the way he combined black rhythm and blues with white rock and roll. In the poor neighborhood in which he was raised, he had rubbed shoulders with blacks and absorbed something of their musical style. When he came to RCA Victor, he was a white singer with "soul," a youth who looked like many mainstream Americans but who sang with the abandonment and spontaneity of black musicians. At the height of the Eisenhower era of controlled respectability, Elvis Presley, overnight dubbed "the Pelvis," sang America's freedom. A teen-age rebel, he took the old ecstasy of the revival into a new setting. He made of it a sensual and sexual passion, giving people a freedom that was at once the liberty of the "natural man" and the condition of a paradisal age when all people would be brothers and sisters.

In the third place, Presley became a legend because, by the seventies, he was a symbolic reminder to Americans of the innocence of the fifties. In a wave of nostalgia, people looked back twenty years to a time when the old truths were still true, when good and evil were lined out clearly in black and white, when the harmless swivel of a singer's hips and the sultry glance of his eye had been thought risqué. Presley stood for America's innocence—a shy teen-ager made good to his own astonishment. And he stood for the golden age of the millennium that Americans recalled in the Eisenhower years, a time when they saw peace and plenty, without energy crises, or severe inflation, or world affairs that could not be settled by simple formulas of right and wrong.

Finally, Presley's attraction lingered on after his death perhaps because, as the many stories told, he was a victim of his own success. The symbol of spontaneity could not appear freely as he chose. One anecdote recounted how he tried to attend a church service by slipping unobtrusively into a back pew with his bodyguards. When people in the congregation began to turn around to stare, he and his friends were forced to leave. The public for which Presley lived had become his torture. According to reports, he turned to drugs as stimulants and depressants so that he could sing or sleep as the occasion demanded. When he died because of a heart problem, despite official denials rumors floated that the drugs had in the end destroyed him. (By 1980, Presley's personal physician would be found guilty of malpractice.) The apostle of innocence, Presley had become an innocent victim, with a heart of gold and a fate to be lamented. Presley's fans had come a long way from the jeremiads of the Puritans, but in identifying with their musical hero they voiced the collective anxieties that were part of the American heritage. To borrow the words of Richard Nixon about the United States, like a confused America, Presley was a "pitiful giant." There were echoes of the Puritan and revolutionary past here, for suffering in America was the role of the innocent and the companion of millennialism.

Presley was only one among the heroes and saints; his songs, only a small number among the ballads and tunes that told people who they were and what their lives meant. Together, heroes and songs, literature and magazines, films and television serials surrounded Americans with mythologies that reassured and reinforced their system of beliefs. Although the language was disguised and not often openly religious, the gospel that popular culture brought through the media was a powerful persuader because it built on what people already knew. Far more than any organized religious denomination, it was able to capture the public eye and ear. Created by society, it was also creating a society in its image.

American Codes of Living

The ritualization of American life takes place, in part, during an annual calendar of holidays. The mythologies that the rituals express are communicated, too, through the media. However, a religious community expresses its beliefs, not just in myth and ritual, but also in everyday behavior. We need to examine the codes for living that ordinary culture gives Americans and to discover what patterns of behavior govern their usual interactions with one another. As in the cases of myth and ritual, the codes are many and they are complex. In order to suggest the scope that they present, let us look at a few of the most prominent. As we will see, sports, technology, and popular psychology all provide behavioral codes for many Americans. Later, in our study of nature religion, we will discuss the code of living that nature provides.

Organized sports in America are less than a century old. It is true that a few sports had become popular in the earlier part of the nineteenth century and that baseball had been played as long ago as 1845. But it was in the 1870s and 1880s that organized sports activities became prominent, growing rapidly with the railroads and improved communication. The first professional baseball team came into existence in 1869; a major league followed in 1876; and by the turn of the century, baseball had become a favorite American sport. Meanwhile, football, at first an upper-class activity, had become a popular game by 1900. What distinguished baseball and football from other activities such as fishing and solitary running was that they were contests; that is, they were games of competition in which there was a winner and a loser. This characteristic of baseball, football, and other games like them would be important in furthering an American code.

Before we can turn to the code, however, we must notice the religious overtones that have surrounded public games. Historically, games of sport originated in deliberate religious rituals. Structurally, sports activities still resemble rituals in their form. We have already met one example of religious play in the sacred ball game that was one of the seven rites of the Oglala Sioux. Religious games of various kinds were part of many of the Native American traditions in this country. They were also part of the European heritage of other Americans. In ancient Greece, funeral games were held in honor of slain heroes, and various Greek city-states held sacred games to offer reverence to one of the Gods. Thus, the Olympic games, held at Olympia, honored Zeus, while the Pythian games at Delphi paid homage to Apollo and the Isthmian games at Corinth celebrated Poseidon.

Moreover, there are many ways in which even the sports of modern America are like deliberate (extraordinary) religious rituals. Both mark out a separate area for their activities—a "playground" or sacred space. Both also divide the time of their performance from the ordinary passage of minutes and hours. Furthermore, both are examples of dramatic actions in which people take on assigned roles, often wearing special symbolic clothing to distinguish them from nonparticipants. Sports and deliberate religious rituals, through their performances, create an "other" world of meaning, complete with its own rules and

321

boundaries, dangers and successes. Finally, in sports and deliberate religious rituals, the goal of the activity *is* the activity. While there may be good results from the game or rite, there is a reason implicit in the action for performing it. Play or ritual is satisfying for its own sake, for each is an activity in which people may engage because of the pleasure it gives in itself.

From this perspective, with their ordinariness in our society, sports have provided a ritual-like setting for millions of Americans. By setting up boundaries and defining the space of the game, sports have helped Americans fit a grid to their own experience in order to define it and give it structure. Hence, it is not surprising that our public games have given people a code of conduct for everyday living. If the ball field is a miniature rehearsal for the game of life, it tells us that life is a struggle between contesting forces in which there is a winning and a losing side. It tells us, too, that success depends on teamwork in which members of the winning side conquer the opposing team by pulling together. And in this contest to the end, competition becomes a value in itself and generates a set of accompanying virtues that identify a good team player. Loyalty, fair play, and being a "good sport" in losing are all examples of these virtues. So, too, are self-denial and hard work to achieve the winning play.

We may note that the division into two teams who battle each other in the game resembles the dualistic scheme of the final millennial battle. Like that ultimate war, in the game it is clear that there is a team that is good (our side) and another that is bad (the opposing team). Coaches urge the members of their team to pour all their efforts into winning—as if this were the last game they would play on earth. Each team, in its own understanding, is on the side of righteousness, and so each team stands on its innocence. Preparatory exercises in self-denial and self-purification by team members—diet, calisthenics, sleep requirements—are evidence. To underscore the point, many players, when they are in the midst of a winning streak, indulge in various private rituals to insure that the winning will continue.

While sports are surely an important feature of most human societies, here we need to look at how they function in an American context. To be understood fully, they cannot be separated from other aspects of this country's life. It is the web of interrelated cultural forms, rather than any one element in isolation, that is persuasive. Hence, the code that the games offer to Americans is one that subtly agrees with the themes of millennial dominance and innocence that we have seen before. It is a code that can guarantee success in business, industry, or government, for in it individualism bows before the unity of the community of the chosen. Corporate executives may have risen on their merits from rags to riches, but in the executive suite they must be good team players. The same is true for government officials and Cabinet members, as both Presidents Richard Nixon and Jimmy Carter liked to remind their assistants. Finally, within the field with its opposing teams, competition becomes the ethic of success. Life is a game of winners and losers, and only those who compete are the brave and the true. Rigorously prepared for the fight by their previous exercises in self-denial, those who compete to the end should win the day—or at the very least, lose with the grace and dignity demanded by the code.

A second code for everyday living comes to Americans from their experiences with technology. Since the Industrial Revolution of the nineteenth century, Americans saw their agricultural way of life transformed dramatically by mechanization. New forms of transportation—the railroad, the steam engine, and in the twentieth century, the automobile and the airplane—brought parts of the country closer together. With their ability to provide food and manufactured goods for vast numbers of people, they encouraged the growth of cities. The development of the factory system gathered people together under one roof, attracting them away from their farms and leading again to the growth of centers of population. New labor-saving devices cut the amount of time needed to complete many tasks. At the same time, many of these devices lessened the need for human workers and often, therefore, sharply reduced the cost of manufactured goods.

For all intents and purposes, it looked as if the machine was bringing the golden age of the millennium to the United States. Many early observers of the Industrial Revolution held this view of the miracle they were witnessing, and accounts of the new machines were often filled with wonder. The Centennial Exhibition held in Philadelphia in 1876 displayed the new ideas and inventions proudly, for they were sure evidence of the horn of plenty brought by the age of progress. But in places where the machine entered the garden of rural America, a number of people saw in it a symbol of the other, apocalyptic millennium. Early descriptions of locomotives sometimes used the language of hellfire and demons to express impressions of the train as it plunged through the countryside, its coal-fed fires flaming up and its whistle screeching fiercely. For some of America's writers, like Nathaniel Hawthorne and Ralph Waldo Emerson, the roaring engines violated the innocence of an older way of life. Significantly, mechanization had arisen to supply the needs of war. Eli Whitney (1765–1825) had created the first system of interchangeable parts in this country in order that firearms could be mass-produced, and after 1798 his factory was turning out muskets for the United States government. (In our own day, after a nuclear accident at Three Mile Island in Pennsylvania [1979], the potential for catastrophe brought by technology has received new attention.)

Thus, whether the new machines were interpreted according to premillennial or postmillennial models, Americans had associated them with their futuristic myth. And despite the fears of some, for the most part Americans admired their machines and gadgets, while their culture came to reflect the admiration in numerous ways. As early as the eighteenth century, the Enlightenment with its interest in science had fostered the idea that human beings were like machines. By our own era, promoted by a huge advertising industry, technology became a central symbol in American life. People unconsciously adopted the machine as a model for their humanness. They saw their bodies as complex machines; and hence, in many aspects of their lives, they patterned their behavior accordingly. Although technology has not been acknowledged nearly so much as sports as a guide for action, the machine provides many Americans with a code for living.

Stated simply, the technological code demands of Americans that, with the perfection required of a millennial people, they act like their machines. This means, first of all, that they be as efficient as the technological process. Corporate life is built on the image of the machine with well-oiled parts, each properly performing its function. Bureaucracies are huge machines in which people are expected to do their jobs efficiently, without attracting undue attention to themselves or creating undue stress by forming time-consuming relationships with their coworkers. Similarly, trade and commerce are streamlined so that people interact with one another in quick, automatic exchanges with no more than the necessary information and action. Unlike small-town America of a century ago, where a shopkeeper was a friend and a person who had time to share, the contemporary salesperson is generally impersonal. In government the operating model is again that of a vast bureaucratic machine, with each person expected to attend to the assigned job as quickly and impersonally as possible. Meanwhile, the family has shrunk from the extended clan of several generations in one household to the nuclear family of parents and children. Unlike the extended family with its roots in the soil over many years, the nuclear family is mobile. Like the automobile and the train, it can move speedily from place to place, ready to pull up stakes and start again somewhere else, if economic interests so demand.

Secondly, the technological code prompts Americans to be as cool and passionless in public as their machines. The media promote the image of the unflappable individualist—the low-keyed detective or cowboy hero, the rigidly controlled pilot who unleashes weapons of destruction as duty requires, the unexcited business executive who discusses his company's failures with an expressionless face and tone of voice. According to the ethic of the machine, people should always be in control, without strong displays of feeling, either positive or negative. To do otherwise is to risk impropriety. It is to be marked as not quite acceptable—someone, so to speak, with loose ends trailing. In this model of human behavior, the evangelical search for a community of feeling seems inappropriate. Still, there need not be a contradiction. The ethic puts its premium on the man or woman who is cool *in public*. On the other hand, the religion of the heart belongs to the private sphere. Figures like the Playboy and Cosmo Girl, both supremely cool, do remind us that here is a behavioral code that in some respects runs counter to the sentimental leanings of the mainstream. Yet both the ethic of the machine and the ethic of evangelicalism demand refinement of emotion—the cultivation of "polite" feelings that can be shared without embarrassment.

In a third and related demand, the technological code requires that people be uniform and standard. Like the interchangeable parts produced by the factories, they must be able to replace one another. Here the aim is to be like everybody else so that no one stands out by being different. In this effort, clothing becomes a badge of commonality, and manners provide a way for people to be as indistinguishable from one another as they can. Americans eat the same fast food at thousands of chain restaurants; they watch the same television shows and shop at the same national discount, drug, and supermarket concerns. Many live in subdivisions in houses that closely resemble their neighbors'. Still more, the code defines no person as absolutely necessary. Because they can replace one another, people—like cogs in a machine—are expendable.

The technological code has also altered the way that Americans think of time. The day on a farm extended from sunup to sunset with the hours measured by their natural rhythms—by the location of the sun in the sky, the feeling of weariness in the bones or of hunger. With the introduction of the machine came factory time, measured by the precise movements of the clock. In the nine-to-five day of our era, each moment is exactly like every other moment, qualitatively no different. Like people, time has been divided into interchangeable parts. A job demands exactly the eight hours of the working day, no more and no less.

Finally, the technological code urges people to be consumers. In the paradise of plenty, the products of the machine must be purchased so that the economic wheels of society will turn. Often they are deliberately planned to wear out quickly in order to be replaced, thus providing jobs and employment for workers. Advertising creates new needs, people keep buying, and the consumer society spends itself to own more and more. So the technological code gives Americans standards of efficiency, coolness, uniformity, mechanical time, and consumption. Ironically, it also gives them a return to another kind of innocence. There is no ambiguity in the world that the machine controls, for it is as precise and measured as interchangeable parts. Seen historically by Americans in millennial terms, technology reinforces a view of the world in which it is complex on the surface but ultimately very simple.

Much different from the behavioral code derived from the machine is the code that modern psychology provides Americans. Psychology as an organized body of knowledge was born in the nineteenth century at the end of the Romantic revolt against the Enlightenment. While it has developed along more rigidly scientific lines in the behavioral school of psychology, in forms like the human potential movement of the 1960s and the 1970s, psychology was linked to organic and Romantic themes. Like the Enlightenment, the Romantic movement centered on nature. But while the Enlightenment saw nature as an intricate machine moving according to regular and unchanging laws, Romanticists thought of nature as freedom and spontaneity. They linked it to feeling and emotion, and so, one continual theme of the Romantic movement was inwardness.

As we will see in our discussion of nature religion, by the 1960s a new wave of Romanticism had spread across America. With it came an emphasis on exploring inner frontiers. Turning within became a way to "turn on" to worlds that transcended the humdrum daily routine. Revolutionary new ways to inner knowledge and peace blossomed, and many people sought direction from the gurus of popular psychology. As they did so, themes of perfection and paradisal innocence thrived. The inner world was good and even divine: nothing ultimately evil could come from confronting its depths. Esalen Institute, along the California coast at Big Sur, and its founder, Michael Murphy (b. 1930), became symbols for the movement. In 1967 alone, Esalen conducted seminars for 4,000 people, among them 700 psychologists who received instruction in such techniques as sensory awareness and encounter therapies. In the initial seven months of the Esalen Institute's San Francisco branch, 12,000 people came for lectures and seminars.

The new psychologies that inspired these people were distinguished in several ways from the therapies of the past. First of all, they did not so much seek to heal the mentally disturbed as to bring ordinary people with ordinary problems to the perfection of their capacity for happiness and creativity. Second, while the old psychologies had been built on the authoritarian model of the relationship between doctor and patient, in many cases the new therapies stressed community and peer relationships in a new democracy of the "saints." At other times, they became essentially self-help techniques that closely paralleled the practices, like meditation, of some contemporary religious movements. Third, while the more traditional psychologies had developed a technical language that was scientific, the new forms used a vocabulary that was, sometimes openly and sometimes more subtly, religious. Significantly, the openly religious language was borrowed from Eastern traditions, especially Buddhism, Hinduism, and Taoism (a Chinese religion of nature). Fourth, unlike the therapies of the past which were seen as lengthy but still temporary processes, the new psychologies gave people instruction in a way of life. Lectures, seminars, and workshops were intensive sessions devoted to the cultivation of techniques that should be used for a lifetime.

What were—and are—these new therapies? They are too numerous to be detailed fully here, but prominent among them is the Gestalt psychology of Frederick S. (Fritz) Perls (1894–1970), in which, aided by members of a working group, a person dramatizes inner conflicts by playing the parts of the different voices within. Other encounter groups focus completely on the relationships within the group itself so that members learn to express positive feelings and air grievances without fear. For some people, the new psychologies harness technology to the needs of inner awareness, as in the biofeedback machines used to teach how to distinguish between calm and excited brain-wave patterns and even how to control blood pressure, heartbeat, and other automatic processes. Still others, like the followers of Carl G. Jung (1875–1961), keep dream diaries and try to understand themselves through the symbolism of their personal myths. For many, Timothy Leary (b. 1920), a former Harvard professor of psychology, became the leader of a movement for increased self-awareness through drugs and especially LSD.

Along with Fritz Perls, perhaps the most respected theorist of the human potential movement is Abraham Maslow (1908–1970), a former president of the American Psychological Association. For Maslow, self-actualization was the goal of life and of therapy. This meant the fullest use of all the talents and capacities a person had (perfection once again). It meant spontaneity, initiative, and self-directed action. Closely related to self-actualization for Maslow and his followers was a personal state that he named the "peak experience." Similar to the mystical experiences described in the literature of different religious traditions, a peak experience wiped out the sense of separateness so that a person felt at one with the universe and at the same time intensely aware of life all around. "Peakers" were people in touch with themselves and their world. They were the doers and the achievers, the ones who realized and actualized themselves. "Nonpeakers" were individuals who were too organized and too tightly controlled.

For Maslow and the human potential movement in general, control and organization, the key virtues of the technological ethic, were the enemy. Thus, the behavioral code of the movement was and is opposed to the code of the machine. Just as the first Romanticism arose as a revolt against the Enlightenment, the new Romanticism is a revolt against the order of a technological society. While the code of the machine draws tight and rigid boundaries around behavioral expectations, the code of the human potential movement turns people loose in an emotional world in which the boundaries are, theoretically, their own limits. It stresses the free expression of feeling, the formation of communities of openness, the achievement of health and happiness through mental wholeness. At the same time, it turns people toward themselves rather than the public world, seeing meaning in inner states more than in outer, societal problems.

Some think this ethic alien to American culture, an exotic import, perhaps fed by the Eastern religious movements of the sixties and seventies. Yet the human potential movement is as American as motherhood, apple pie—and the innocence of the millennium. It is part of the mainstream and an expression of the one religion of Americans. This is true in two ways. First of all, from the point of view of numbers, the movement is far more widespread than a simple catalogue of those who have participated in an encounter weekend. The millions who read *Psychology Today* magazine and various self-help manuals purchased at the newsstand are being shaped by the psychological code. So are those who attend sessions at their local church on Parent Effectiveness training, Transactional Analysis, making marriage work, or subjects of a similar nature. Professional educators have adopted many of the awareness and encounter techniques as their own, using them regularly in the classroom to facilitate group experience. Radio and television talk shows feature guests who give popular psychological advice, while soap operas daily probe the inner workings of their characters' psyches in the language and style of the human potential movement.

Secondly, the new psychologies are an expression of mainstream American culture because the code of inwardness is really a version of the code of millennial innocence. While the ethics of sports and technology draw on the millennial dominance of the final battle to make history, the ethic of the human potential movement reverses the coin. It seeks the ideal society of perfect—fully developed, totally good—human beings. It seeks, too, the community of free and spontaneous feeling which means the planting of paradise among creative, self-actualizing individuals. In our study of civil religion, we saw how innocence was expressed from time to time in American history in political isolationism. Shortly, we will see how it has been expressed historically in American attitudes toward nature. Here it is important to note that turning within has also had long roots in American culture, dating back to the Puritans who kept careful spiritual diaries and autobiographies in order to be sure of their righteousness. Although the Puritans did not stress emotional spontaneity, they did pay great attention to their feelings, and they cultivated themselves as so many gardens to prepare for the Lord of the millennium.

Throughout American religious history, as we have seen, revivalism taught the importance of right feeling. In the nineteenth century, "self-culture" became a watchword of the Transcendentalists and of the developing occult and metaphysical movements in their own ways as well. People were turning to an inner world in order to create utopia. The perfectionism that ran through these attempts was a general cultural property of the times, stimulated by everything from Methodist theology to the successes of the age of progress. The innocence that these movements displayed was both their belief that they really could achieve perfection and their certainty that the inner world was a land of virtue.

Hence, the ethic of inwardness in the later twentieth century is based on major interpretive themes that have been part of American culture. The same is true for the religion of nature, a flourishing expression of mainstream America both in the past and at present. In order to deepen our understanding of the dynamics of cultural religion, we will use nature religion as a case study. By focusing on how Americans thought, acted, and built community around the symbol of nature, we may gain a better sense of how people use other symbols as well to orient themselves in the ordinary world—and sometimes to go beyond its boundaries in moments of transcendence.

A CASE STUDY IN NATURE RELIGION

Studying nature religion is particularly appropriate because theologies have traditionally dealt with three general topics—God, human beings, and the natural world. In looking at the relationship between Americans and nature, we will be following the guidance of major religious systems of the past. Furthermore, because of the overwhelming physical fact of open space in the New World, we will be dealing with an aspect of their environment that deeply impressed Americans. Generally, mainstream Americans saw nature in millennial terms, sometimes by linking it to their plans for final dominance and conquest and other times by seeing it from the perspective of utopian innocence. In a brief survey of nature religion in the past, we will see both of these tendencies at work. Then we will look at the presence of nature religion in our own era, when rituals like those in Gurney Norman's composting class take place.

Early America

Our study of Native American traditions has already shown us the importance of nature in these religions. What the supernatural God was to the Judaeo-Christian tradition, nature was to the Indians. While it surrounded them and was the source of all their sustenance, it was also a Friend or many Friends to whom they could speak and from whom they could receive answers. Their human societies should correspond to the natural world as closely as possible, and spiritual wholeness and health came from being in harmony with nature.

For the Puritans, coming from a European and Judaeo-Christian civilization, the nature of the New World greeted them in a far different way. Their traditions had often understood nature in negative terms. It was mostly a wilderness, and only occasionally with a great deal of human cultivation it became a garden. In this way of seeing things, the wilderness was a place inhabited by wild beasts and nameless terrors. It was a place to which civilization had not penetrated, out of control, like the teeming forests and the dense vegetation. For the Romans, the wilderness had been inhabited by Gods and demons, often half-human, half-animal in shape. For the people of Central and Northern Europe, the woods were the haunt of trolls, man-eating ogres, and werewolves.

Yet Judaism and Christianity had brought another meaning to the wilderness. While God did not reveal himself *in nature* as the sacred powers did in Native American traditions, he did use nature as the background against which he came. Thus, he manifested himself to the Hebrews after they had left the fleshpots of Egypt and wandered in the desert of Sinai. He came to Christian monks after they had fled from the centers of Roman civilization to the Egyptian desert. The wilderness was a barren place, empty of the corruptions of worldly life that had kept people from God. The wilderness meant the end of distraction, a silence and openness that could leave people ready for the coming of God.

At the same time, Judaism and Christianity had taught that nature was subservient to human beings. Just as there was a great gap separating human beings from God, there was another separating them from nature. The Bible told people that they were made in the image of God, not in the image of nature (Gen. 1:27). It told them that they should "have dominion over the fish of the sea, and over the birds of the air, and over the cattle, and over all the earth" (Gen. 1:26). According to God's command, they were to multiply, fill the earth, and subdue it (Gen. 1:28). This order assured Jews and Christians alike that their task was to dominate the wilderness, taming it to the human plan.

Thus, when the Puritans set foot in the New World, their attitudes toward their surroundings were deeply ambivalent. In the first place, they feared the land as wild territory, filled with dangerous beasts and demonic Indians. Because they were an ocean away from European civilization, the wildness they saw in the forests presented a new threat: it might tempt them to forget the centuries of control their ancestors had learned and revert to the "savagery" of the Indians and wild beasts. In spite of the rhetoric of righteousness, the Puritans were suspicious of the depths of their own hearts, afraid that civilization was only a veneer that would melt away in a "savage" environment. Yet even with the fear the Puritans had of the wilderness, they held a second attitude toward it. The Bible told them that their task was to subdue it. Their errand into the wilderness meant carving farms out of the hillsides and plotting towns and settlements. It also meant bringing the Indians to Christianity, thus "taming" and "civilizing" them. In these ways, the Puritans hoped to build their millennial city on the hill, the light to the nations that it was their mission to let shine.

And finally, the Puritans looked at their surroundings with qualified approval. If they obeyed the God of the covenant, they could turn the land into a sanctuary enclosed by the "hedge" of his grace. The wilderness had always been the proving ground for God's saints, and now, away from the corruption of England, they could be tested by God and show forth the power of his righteousness. At the same time, promotional literature stressed that the New World was "good land," land that could eventually become a paradise.

Hence, while the Puritans saw good wilderness as wilderness transformed into farms and towns, they also saw the opportunities the land gave them. They associated the openness of the country with moral purity and regeneration—with their abiding desire for a return to innocence. With the passage of time, they felt less need for sanctuaries and more desire to expand their presence further into the wilderness. The land at once became a source of vigor and life—a paradise of innocence—and a vast territory to be mastered by the representatives of European civilization. If the Puritans were awaiting the final battle of Armageddon, their efforts could insure that at least some of the wilderness had already been taken from the red agents of Satan before the coming of the Word.

Further, the grandeur of the mountains and forests was not lost on sensitive Puritans. There was a strain of nature mysticism in their response to its awesome beauty. Thus, by the eighteenth century Cotton Mather in the *Christian Philosopher* could see the harmony and order in nature as a second revelation of God. And Jonathan Edwards could ponder his religious experiences in the woods and later create a theology of beauty.

At the time of the Revolution and its aftermath, several strands of Puritan response to the land had become general throughout the colonies. The freshness and purity of the New World in contrast to the tired corruption of Europe became an important ideological theme in the growing nationalism. A popular play of the period, *The Contrast* by Royall Tyler (1787), celebrated the virtues of the roughshod Colonel Manly and the simple Maria Van Rough as opposed to the perfumed decadence of Maria's Europeanized suitor, Dimple. Earlier, during the war American soldiers had worn hunting shirts on the western frontier, terrifying the British, who saw in them a symbolic wildness, and at the same time proclaiming the wilderness as a source of American strength. Further, Americans wore homespun made from their crops, partly because of the economic blockade of British goods but partly, too, as a ritual expression of their identification with the land. So meaningful was the symbol that George Washington took his oath of office to the presidency wearing a suit of homespun.

If nature meant energy and power in contrast to the weariness of Europe, it was also a landscape to be tamed. For revolutionary Americans, good land was farmland. Many, like Thomas Jefferson, thought of the future of America as tied to agriculture and simple manufactures in wholesome innocence of European corruption. When Hector St. John Crèvecoeur's *Letters from an American Farmer* appeared in 1782, it sang the praises of the "new" person in the new land. In the free and open expanses of the countryside, agriculture would yield a bounty, while Europe, on the other hand, was weighted down with its past. By 1803 Thomas Jefferson had negotiated the Louisiana Purchase to add a vast new tract of land to the territory of the United States. He did so in part for political reasons but also to provide land for the nation of farmers that he envisioned. Hence, in these understandings nature was a place to be dominated and subdued—gently and wisely so that the land would give its fruit.

Beyond this, some Americans did look at their surroundings with feelings of awe and wonder. In his *Notes on the State of Virginia* (1785), Jefferson spoke of the intensity of his feelings on seeing Natural Bridge, and he marveled at the size of mammoth bones that had been discovered. The botanist William Bartram (1739–1823) thrilled at the magnificence of the view from a mountain that he climbed in Georgia, and there were others who expressed similar sentiments.

To sum up, in the revolutionary era the land was a millennial symbol of New World purity, a place to be farmed wisely in order to maintain this innocence, and a sublime masterpiece to be regarded for its own sake. In all of these ways of looking at nature, Euro-Americans thought of it as "virgin land" or open space. They overlooked the evidence that the land had been inhabited for centuries by many Indian peoples, and they did not recognize in the tribal societies the presence of civilizations as meaningful as their own. If Indians did figure in the way that nature was seen, they were signs of the wildness that lurked in the woods, of the danger that lay in the absence of civilizing influences. The nineteenth century would pick up on all of these themes.

Nature in the Nineteenth Century

Romanticism flowered in nineteenth-century America and with it a greater sensitivity to the beauties of the natural world. In the 1830s the Transcendentalists, ambivalent about the machinery of the Industrial Revolution, turned to the land for spiritual refreshment. With Ralph Waldo Emerson, their leader, many of them found God more clearly in nature than in the church. In our study of occult and metaphysical movements, we have already mentioned the general direction of Transcendentalist thought. It is worth reviewing the contents of Emerson's little book *Nature*, however, because Emerson's ideas became the foundation for an increasing religious appreciation of nature among mainstream Americans. Like the Indians, Emerson had discovered the correspondence between human beings, the natural world, and spiritual reality. He pondered the meaning of human language, seeing words as "signs," or symbols, of natural facts, of the world around him. Likewise, for Emerson the natural world was a sign—of the world of spirit that went beyond it. In this way of looking at things, humans could understand spiritual truth by looking at nature, where the truth was written in a material form. Nature pointed the way to God. To use the traditional term, it was the sacrament of God.

With his experience as a practical American, as Emerson looked at nature, he was concerned to explain its uses. First of all, nature was the source for the satisfaction of all physical needs. This was true in agriculture, but it was also true in the developing technologies in which people looked to nature for clues as to how best to construct their machines. Second, the beauty in nature was useful, too, because it acted like a tonic for tired minds and bodies, and, further, it gave people moral, artistic, and intellectual inspiration. Third, nature was useful because it shaped language and metaphor. Without the world, there would be nothing to name and no way to measure what any inner experience was like. Finally, nature was useful because it acted as a discipline for people. It was just *there*, so that there was no quarreling with its objectivity and the laws that it followed. More than that, it was a moral teacher which instructed people in the laws of right and wrong.

Emerson's statement of the uses of nature was surely broad, including many that others would have considered idealistic and impractical. Yet the fact that Emerson and the other Transcendentalists thought and spoke in terms of nature's uses was important. While, in general, the Transcendentalists saw themselves sitting at nature's feet as humble pupils, other Americans thought that using nature meant, as the biblical book of Genesis had said, in some fashion dominating and controlling it. In their way of seeing things, reverence for nature meant a wise use of natural resources. In the conservation movement near the end of the nineteenth century, wise use would be a strong argument.

Meanwhile, the Transcendentalists celebrated their religion of nature, sometimes through solitary walks in the woods and sometimes through the gathering of like spirits in Transcendental communes. At Brook Farm and at Fruitlands, they tried their social experiments in organic community, where harmony and cooperation—as in nature—could replace the competitive way of life. Appropriately, like the many other communes in nineteenth-century America, they had selected a natural setting, away from the distractions of city life. Like these other communes, their societies were expressions of American innocence. At Fruitlands, Bronson Alcott (1799–1888) would not wear wool because to do so exploited sheep. Even further, he would not eat carrots because they did not grow toward the sun. At Brook Farm, people pitched in to perform the hard work of running farm and household. Years later they remembered this period (1841–1847) as the happiest time of their lives. Both of these idealistic experiments in utopian socialism failed, but the fact that they existed and survived, even for a time, bore witness to the dreams of Americans. Creating a perfect society and living in total harmony with nature were twin hopes. In their realization, Americans thought, a new era would dawn. It was the nineteenth-century age of Aquarius; it was, once again, the millennium.

Transcendentalism was linked in spirit to a web of occult, metaphysical, and other experimental movements in the nineteenth century, movements which made an impact far beyond the actual numbers who directly participated in them. Instead of movie theaters, nineteenth-century American towns often had a lyceum, a public building where lectures, concerts, and other entertainments were held. Traveling the lyceum circuit became a favorite way to spread the gospel of nature religion, as various speakers went from town to town to tell their good news to others. One area in which they did so was that of health. Meanwhile, other Americans expressed related attitudes regarding their physical well-being, and nature religion became popular religion in nineteenth-century America through the spread of alternative healing methods. Let us look briefly at what happened.

A favorite on the lyceum circuit at midcentury was the animal magnetizer. This person was a hypnotist who could perform demonstrations in which a subject, even from the audience, obeyed the magnetist's instructions after being cast into a light sleep and then awakened. But magnetists were often healers, and there were dramatic accounts of their abilities to relieve people of serious illnesses. According to the magnetic theory, as we have seen, a universal energy or fluid flowed through the natural world. The planets and the other stars produced tides or movements in this fluid, so that as it passed through people, it produced the state of health. But if any blockage interfered with the free flow of energy, sickness resulted. Somehow the magnetic doctor was able to control the flow of energy, for the presence of the doctor acted on the tides and the blocked situation to redirect magnetic fluid and so restore health.

In his early work, Phineas P. Quimby, whom we met in connection with both Christian Science and New Thought, was one such magnetic doctor. So mind cure had roots in natural magnetic healing. But other late nineteenth-century healing methods did, too. Techniques of physical manipulation, like osteopathy and chiropractic, were based on theoretical foundations akin to animal magnetism. In chiropractic, for example, health was the result of the free movement of an energy called "Innate," which traveled down the spinal column. When the chiropractor manipulated a person's spine, the doctor was simply freeing the patient from an obstruction so that Innate could continue to give health. Innate was identified with nature, God, or intelligence, both within and outside of a person. When healing came, it came from within—and from nature. While in the twentieth century, osteopathy became closely aligned with orthodox medicine, chiropractic continued to function as a separate healing art. Like a ripple in the water, magnetic healing had made many waves, some of them far removed from the occult background of its origins.

But nineteenth-century natural healing went beyond even the loose boundaries of animal magnetism. The old sense of the land as source of vigor and refreshment reappeared in a number of systems of herbal medicine. The Indians, symbols of the regenerative power of the wilderness, were seen as natural healers of great ability. As early as 1813 Peter Smith had published *The Indian Doctor's Dispensatory* to give Americans a chance to use the herbal remedies of the Indians. By the 1820s the Thomsonian system of natural herbs used, among others, American Indian natural herbs, while many Americans visited "Indian medicine shows" at state fairs throughout the century.

Then in the 1830s homeopathy, a new system from Germany, began to spread in the United States. In its own version of the law of correspondence, it taught that like healed like. In other words, the proper herbal remedy to use for a sickness was one which, in a healthy person, produced the same symptoms as the disease. Combining this rule, called the law of similars, with a second rule, called the law of infinitesimals, homeopathy gave to sick people minute—almost microscopically small—quantities of specific natural herbs in order to heal them. With the "infinitesimal" doses hardly more than a taste of the medicine, healing really was coming naturally. Significantly, for part of the century homeopathy rivaled traditional medicine as a healing method. Millions of Americans, alienated by the bleeding, purging, and violent drugs of the medical doctors, had turned to nature.

Indeed, the nineteenth century was a century of natural health, as from many different quarters people supported the idea that nature had energies to cure people and keep them strong. After 1840 the water cure, or hydropathy, became popular. Sick people submitted to a variety of healing baths, showers, and compresses, hot and cold, in the belief that water could work the cure they sought. Meanwhile, vegetarianism thrived as a way to gain greater health and preserve the energies a person already had. Nineteenth-century new religions encouraged the general interest in health. As we saw, Ellen G. White, the prophetess of Seventh-day Adventism, advocated a variety of health reforms, including vegetarianism, and her influence was responsible for a continued Adventist interest in healing. Likewise, Mormons forbade the use of alcohol, tobacco, or caffeine, and Christian Scientists banished alcohol and tobacco. In these and other cases, the reasoning was that such substances were poisons or drugs that interfered with nature's workings in the body. What interfered with the beneficent processes of nature was wrong. People should reverence their bodies as the gifts of God and nature and learn never to abuse them.

In these healing methods, we see rituals and a behavioral code built on a creed about the ultimacy of nature. Themes of millennial innocence are expressed in beliefs about the powers of American nature and its products to heal. But the other side of millennialism—millennial dominance—also found expression in the symbolism of nature. As an example, let us look at the fictional career of Davy Crockett during the age of manifest destiny. The real David Crockett had been three times a United States Congressman from the state of Tennessee and had died in violent circumstances at the Alamo in the Texan war for independence from Mexico. In 1834 he had published an extremely successful autobiography, *A Narrative of the Life of David Crockett*, which traded on the popular image of the rough-and-ready frontiersman in order to make its author a hero.

In the same year as the autobiography, the first number of an annual almanac about Crockett appeared in Nashville. Building on some of the exploits of the Tennessean in his autobiography, the almanac embroidered them to such a degree that the exaggerations, already present in the supposedly factual autobiography, became outlandish. This thin volume and several series of others in eastern cities used the device of the almanac, with its calendar information, as a way to delight the public with anecdote after anecdote about the heroism of Crockett. Filled with lively graphics, the almanacs were in fact nineteenth-century comic books, and the figure of Crockett that they presented told a great deal about the mainstream American myth of nature. The fact that Crockett almanacs sold extremely well indicated that they had struck the right chord somewhere in the national spirit.

In many respects, Crockett was the embodiment of American innocence, strong with the strength of nature, outwitting slick Easterners who did not have the advantage of life in the woods. Yet, in his relationship to nature and its forces, Crockett was above all the master of the wilderness. Typically, the anecdotes told of conquests of wild animals, blacks, and Indians, in which he fought with his bare hands instead of a rifle and frequently used his teeth. This fictional Crockett bragged that he had thumbnails at least two inches long, which he dug into eyes or veins with equal delight. He especially liked to kill Indians and, in one gruesome episode, hungry and without a supper, ate two of his red victims. In the descriptions of Crockett in these violent encounters, it was clear that he achieved a sense of ecstasy in the experience of blood. He bragged continually about his identification with wilderness forces: he was half-horse and half-alligator and even part snapping turtle. Savage like nature, he wanted to out-savage it. As a hunter, he won his game by becoming like the thing he hunted. In calmer moments, he contented himself with making pets of the bears and alligators that he conquered. When the spirit of wildness came over him, he preferred to drink blood.

From the point of view of religion, Crockett experienced mystical moments of total oneness with nature through his violence. These peaks of ecstasy renewed the vigor of the man of the woods—and equally important, renewed his success in politics. For the fictional Crockett, like the real one, was a Congressman. The almanacs were filled with political and patriotic references— to the Congress, to the flag, and to the practical expression of manifest destiny. Crockett continually talked of Mexico, Texas, Oregon, and California. He boasted about the times he had outlicked or outsmarted the Mexican general, Antonio de Santa Anna, spoke of flogging Mexico and annexing Texas, and wanted to extend Uncle Sam's "plantation" throughout the continent. So there was a fusion of civil religion and nature religion in the character of Crockett. And nature religion meant no longer the peaceful millennium of the horn of plenty but instead a cult of violence in which power came from battling the wilderness in order to dominate it. Indeed, Crockett had even proved himself master of the sun. When it froze, he took bear's grease, worked it loose, and walked away with some of the sunrise in his pocket.

Taming the wilderness and taming the nations were similar acts for the fictional Crockett and many historical Americans like him. Millennial dominance, present in the Revolution in the symbols of hunting shirt and homespun, grew stronger in the nineteenth century. Toward the end of the century, though, a renewed appreciation for the beauty of nature was expressed in the conservation movement. The spirit of mastery grew more refined, as the old sense of millennial innocence asserted itself. By this time the Industrial Revolution had changed the face of America. The frontier had all but disappeared, and the cities were growing ever larger. A wave of Romantic nostalgia swept over Americans. They feared that, without the presence of true wilderness, they might lose their youth and purity and become old and corrupt like Europe.

In 1872, preservation of the wilderness was insured legally when President Ulysses S. Grant (1822–1885) put his signature to the bill that created Yellowstone National Park. A little more than a decade later, the state of New York set aside a huge region in the Adirondack Mountains as a forest preserve. Various arguments had moved the legislatures toward their acts, and it was not until the passage of the Yosemite Act in 1890 that Congress acted with the express intention of preserving the wilderness for its own sake. The apostle of the new movement was John Muir (1838–1914), a Scotch-born naturalist who fell in love with the landscapes of his adopted country, hiking for miles through its forests and climbing its mountains. A friend of Emerson and an admirer of Henry David Thoreau, he made the Transcendental teachings a way of life. He became the first president of the Sierra Club, formed in 1892 to foster exploration of the Pacific coastal mountains and to press the government for legislation to preserve the Sierra Nevada Mountains. Muir's books and magazine articles did much to sway the public toward his concern for wilderness preservation. His efforts pointed the way for the ecology movement of the later twentieth century.

With Muir and his followers, the wilderness as the true source of America's innocence and strength was safeguarded. Under Gifford Pinchot (1865–1946), the second segment of the conservation movement found its leader. A Yale graduate, Pinchot worked as the first professional forester in this country and by 1898 had become head of the Bureau of Forestry in the United States Department of Agriculture. For Pinchot, forests should be used wisely by being managed well. This meant that only a certain proportion of the lumber should be

Chapter 12

harvested each year, while at the same time new trees were planted. In this way, people could enjoy the forests, but they could reap their benefits, too. Here the biblical command to master nature was realized in a carefully controlled process. Unlike the wild excesses reflected in the Crockett almanacs, humans were acting as prudent stewards of nature's gifts. But by the turn of the century, celebration of wilderness had become a national movement. Pinchot's work for wise use of resources was overtaken by waves of popular enthusiasm for unspoiled nature.

Nature in the Twentieth Century

The first decades of the twentieth century brought greater intensity to the pleas for the preservation of wild land. Especially, the fear of national degeneration surfaced in people's awareness. Without the fountain of nature to drink from, Americans would become just like the rest of the world. They would lose their innocence and strength, like people out of touch with the saving power of sacred myth and ritual. Democracy, Americans thought, had grown up in the wilderness; without its presence, they stood in danger of losing their most precious possession. In this mood of anxiety, the Boy Scout movement was born in 1910, to give the boys of the country a chance to live close to nature and so to develop the moral and spiritual qualities that the wilderness fostered. As people of the time saw it, there was a connection between the forests where the Boy Scouts camped and the Boy Scout Code by which the young people were taught to live.

Meanwhile, "primitivists" began a new celebration of savagery as a source of strength, and hunting, camping, and mountain climbing became popular sports. As early as 1888, Theodore Roosevelt (1858–1919), later president of the United States, had organized the Boone and Crockett Club to foster big-game hunting and to build character. By 1914, Edgar Rice Burroughs had published *Tarzan of the Apes*, giving expression to the image of the Romantic savage in a figure who became a continuing national fictional hero. And after midcentury, Americans were again hearing the call of the wild when in 1955 a Davy Crockett revival reached millions, many of them young, with its Walt Disney television series and film, *Davy Crockett, King of the Wild Frontier*, and its song success, "The Ballad of Davy Crockett."

Throughout the twentieth century, the religion of nature continued to be an impulse in the national life. Sierra Club, Boy Scouts—joined by Girl Scouts and Campfire Girls—Tarzan, Crockett, and other nature heroes were solidly established on the national scene. Then in the decades of the sixties and the seventies, under the banner of ecology the movement gained renewed strength and support. Years of concern and efforts to preserve the wilderness culminated in 1963 when the National Wilderness Preservation System was created. The Congress had been convinced that the wilderness would lead to greater physical and mental health for Americans and that it would promote their freedom and self-sufficiency. At the same time, ecologists spoke of the delicate balance of nature in any environment and cautioned that humans could upset the harmony by their interference. Humans were part of nature, meant to coexist with other species, not to destroy them. By altering the natural balance of forces, people

336

could bring overpopulation by one species and the extinction of another. More important, they could begin to destroy the water that they drank, the air that they breathed, and the very cells of their own bodies which would sicken and die from the poisons they were unleashing in the atmosphere.

Mainstream Americans worried about what they were doing to their environment, and as the Vietnam War became a memory, they turned to the ecology movement as a new cause. As more and more cancer-causing chemicals were found in their air and food, the movement gained strength. In the seventies, increased awareness of the dangers of nuclear power brought still more converts. Nature had become a central symbol by which Americans oriented themselves, expressed in everything from natural cereals to the use of earth tones for room decoration and yoga and jogging for health. By the late sixties and early seventies, periodicals sprang up to express and reinforce the sentiments of nature lovers, among them the *Mother Earth News* from 1970 and the *Whole Earth Catalog* from 1968 to 1971, with the *Whole Earth Epilog* in 1974. Within their pages, the American involvement with nature became an identifiable religious system.

In order to understand more precisely what nature religion involves, let us look quickly at its expression in these magazines. There we find elements of a creed, a code, and a cultus directed toward the central symbol of nature. There, too, the innocence of paradise planted offers a new version of the old millennial dream. Expressing their natural creed, both periodicals reject permanence and see the world as a process in which they participate. Both prefer to avoid making distinctions and to picture reality as a harmonious merging of elements in one whole. Like the Transcendentalists of the nineteenth century, the periodicals teach correspondence—between self and world, between earth and the rest of the universe. For them, the microcosm reflects the macrocosm, and the two follow the same laws and display the same patterns. So it is possible, according to the creed, to see the whole in the part and to find parts repeated in other parts, all together forming the harmony of the world.

Significantly, the *Whole Earth Catalog* declares in its statement of purpose that people are "as gods" and urges them to get good at the role. They are particles in the divine whole, and that whole is symbolized by the image of planet Earth on the cover. The *Mother Earth News*, more concerned with small-scale organic farming, has made it clear that it is committed to the preservation of the ecosystem. By 1975 the title page was telling its readers that it was not simply a magazine but a way of life. Thus, the creed of harmony between human beings and the planet was turned into a code for living.

When we examine that code in both periodicals, it is evident that this is where their practical interest lies. Each sees ecological living as an act of religion, and each provides knowledge and support for doing so in everyday settings. In their vision, as part of the greater whole, a person should not seek to dominate the natural world. Rather, he or she should develop a rhythm of relationship with the world in which nature is friend and fellow creation. Like Native American traditions, the periodicals teach a practical reverence for nature in which it is used but not violated and imitated rather than conquered. In the *Catalog*, for example, books on healing herbs and organic foods are reviewed regularly. There is great interest in natural shelter in sacred circles and squares—domes, zomes, tipis, yurts, and related structures. Within these dwellings, the preferred lifestyle is communal, and the communities seek country locations where their work will lead them back to nature. At the same time, crafts associated with a preindustrial and rural past are highlighted. Pottery and quilt making, embroidery, weaving, woodcarving, and blacksmithing are cultivated, and, as we have already seen, natural waste disposal through composting is urged. In one issue the *Catalog* advertises its plans for a section on "Death, Old Friend" and asks readers to send photographs and accounts for publication. Like compost, the human body is organic waste and must return to the earth to nourish it.

The *Mother Earth News* pursues a similar course in showing people how to live naturally. Countless articles give explicit directions on planting, canning, or building. The magazine features long correspondence sections in which readers can express their views or advertise their needs to fellow readers. Many write seeking others who will farm organically with them or who want to form a rural commune. Skills such as dowsing (searching for water through the divinatory powers of a branch or twig) are respected. Natural medicine and homeopathic healing are favored. Indeed, the kind of natural occultism that we discussed in Chapter 7 in early America and the continued occultism of Southern Appalachian mountaineers is quite in keeping with the spirit and advice of the *Mother Earth News.* These are ways of living that grow out of the harmonial view of the world. They are spontaneous expressions of nature religion in daily routine.

If both periodicals share a common creed and offer similar advice for a behavioral code, both also support the cultus of nature religion. The cultus is expressed in a series of rituals, coming from many sources, but all reinforcing beliefs and behavior related to the correspondence between human beings and nature. In general, the rituals rise out of Eastern and Western (mostly occult) traditions, out of combinations of either or both, and out of the experience of people in the human potential and ecology movements. All are powerful rites for both periodicals, because all can express, communicate, and reinforce the central myth of nature religion. Thus, all the rituals give energy to participants for ordinary life according to the tenets of their faith.

In the *Whole Earth Catalog,* advertisements regarding Buddhist or Hindu religious texts are welcome. Yoga and Transcendental Meditation are good friends, and the Chinese classic, the *I Ching,* becomes almost the Bible of *Catalog* readers. The *Catalog* also expresses enthusiasm concerning the peyote rituals of Carlos Castaneda, described in *The Teachings of Don Juan* (1968). From the West, astrology is favored, palmistry is encouraged, and tarot cards are thought useful. Books from the human potential movement are regularly advertised, and ecological rituals receive considerable attention. Earth flags and the picture of the whole earth become fixed points on which people can concentrate for meditation. We have already seen Gurney Norman's rituals for his composting class, and there are other new rituals from various people in the movement as well.

The *Mother Earth News,* likewise, welcomes practitioners of Eastern religious rituals in its pages. Correspondents whose letters appear link themselves with Zen monasticism, yoga, or Krishna Consciousness. A favorite way for readers to identify themselves is by giving their astrological sign, and when they seek companions of the opposite sex, they also indicate which signs are acceptable. Many correspondents exhibit interests which range over various ritual expressions of nature religion. They mingle, for example, yoga and meditation with astrology. In humanistic psychology, they speak of the various groups that they have been part of, while the *Mother Earth News* prints advertisements concerning Gestalt, bioenergetics, and psychic healing. There are advertisements, too, for ecology flags and earth flags, so that, like the *Whole Earth Catalog*, ecological ritual is in evidence.

Hence, the two periodicals provide a focus for like-minded and like-hearted people who share in the religion of nature. They support believers in a creed, urge them to live the creed in a daily behavioral code, and show them how they may find ritual expression for their beliefs and behavior in various cultuses. In all of these expressions of nature religion, they seek a return in some ways to an older, rural America. Their spirit is the familiar one of millennial innocence that we have seen so many times before. They show us that the occult side of American life has spread to touch the lives of many not closely identified with one specific movement, and with their often forlorn letters of correspondence, they remind us that creating community in America can be difficult. Finally, the pluralism of their ritual life sums up in its manyness the social history of the country. The Romantic pluralism of nature religion mirrors the pluralism of American society. The merging of cultuses together so freely suggests the tendency of cultural religion to make the many into one.

There is much more that might be said about the penetration of nature religion into all segments of our society. Campers, backpackers, and hikers threaten to overrun our wilderness areas more thoroughly than any bulldozers could, and the advertising industry, in an age of chemical pollution, has found that the surest way to sell something is to say that it is natural. Nature has meant many things to Americans—a new birth to millennial innocence, a place to be wild (and, as in the millennial age, without a history), an obstacle to master (with the dominance of the millennial history-maker), a resource to be used. In all of these ways, nature has given Americans meaning and direction, while more often than not, that meaning and direction have been millennial. With this abiding vision of things, nature has taught mainstream Americans how to live in the ordinary world. On the peaks of mountains and in the calm of an evening's sunset, it has also provided times of reaching beyond the boundary.

AFTERTHOUGHTS ON CULTURAL RELIGION

Our survey has given us an introduction to cultural religion and provided a historical and contemporary discussion of the religious meaning of nature. It is important here that we try to sort out some of the things that we have learned. We have been speaking in very broad terms—with a few specific case studies—and we have covered the ground very rapidly.

First of all, the complexity of the cultural processes we are describing should not escape us. We spoke at the outset of taking a few steps on the continent, and we need to underscore the point. Although it may seem as if we have traveled far, there are vast areas that we have not touched on and rich materials for constructing a religious history of culture from different perspectives. Second, we should not lose sight of the fact that the religious expressions we have explored are diffused and scattered. The religions that we studied in Part One, organized in specific traditions, were strongly articulated and easily identifiable. The religion we associate with general American culture, on the other hand, is vague, partial, and ever shading off into indistinctness. It would not be fair to think of the two as the same, but it is fair to see the two as, in some ways, similar. Identifying the religious dimension of culture can help us to understand the power of culture to knit many people together. It can also show us why some stories, persons, and songs have such persuasiveness.

In the third place, the distinction between ordinary and extraordinary religion needs to be redrawn to take account of cultural religion. In the Introduction and elsewhere, we spoke of ordinary religion as more or less synonymous with culture, while specific religious organizations gave people the fundamentals of extraordinary religion. That distinction is, for the most part, useful. As people who were part of a culture, members of religious organizations easily blended ordinary and extraordinary concerns, or seeking a sharper definition of their religious identity, they tried in various ways to separate the two. On the other hand, the general culture went its own way, giving people the means to make sense of the world in its everyday reality. Yet, as we have seen in our discussion of cultural religion, sometimes the mythologies, behavioral codes, and rituals of culture push *beyond* the boundaries of daily routines. Fictional dramas *can* be windows into a transcendent world. Sports, either alone or with others, can yield moments of ecstasy, while trying to develop human potential can bring peak experiences. Drugs induce chemical mysticism, and the fictional Davy Crockett drank the blood of wildlife to reach a mysticism of violence. Listening to the voice of Elvis Presley stretched the limits of the ordinary world for millions of his fans.

Thus, just as people who practiced extraordinary religion in one way or another expressed the ordinary religion of culture, so culture, too, has its moments when it becomes extraordinary. In the twentieth century, since the role of organized religion has shrunk to carefully defined and set limits and since it cannot unify all Americans, it is not surprising to find culture expressing its share of transcendence. Legal declarations and technological revolutions cannot banish the quest for extraordinary experience from public life. Like an air bubble flattened out of one place, it will only crop up in another.

Fourth, at the same time we need to be cautious about determining how much cultural religion unites Americans. Like civil religion, we can surely say that it is the (mostly) ordinary religion of many Americans some of the time. In fact, as we see now, civil religion is one expression of the larger reality of cultural religion; and to locate civil religion in this way gives us a clue about how we need to look at the many other aspects of cultural religion we have examined. They are all many smaller circles within the greater circle of culture. People who live by the ethic of sports may never become involved in the human potential movement. Corporate executives who embody the technological ethic may look askance at young couples who build a cabin in the wilderness of the Pacific

Northwest. Science fiction fans may find country music not to their taste, and readers of *Ms.* magazine may scorn the readers of *Women's Day.*

On the other hand, there *are* ways that these smaller circles overlap. Business executives are often avid sports fans, and people in farming communes sometimes practice encounter-group techniques. Science fiction fans may read *Ms.*, and lovers of country music may like to try the recipes in *Women's Day.* Beyond the overlap, we have seen major themes that bind many of these cultural expressions together. Indeed, we have identified the single theme that runs through much of our culture as millennialism. With a long history among us, millennialism has repeatedly appeared in one of two forms. Sometimes it has been the dominating millennialism which takes its cue from visions of the final battle when good will triumph over evil. Other times it has been the innocent millennialism which seeks to make utopia in the uncorrupted landscape. Both kinds of millennialism provide Americans with an ordinary religion that yet contains extraordinary moments. Both direct them in the course of their lives, interpreting the meaning of things and offering occasions for ritual. With millennialism as the unifying center, dominance and innocence have been two sides of the same cultural coin. Those who dominate and win need to find ways to prove their righteousness and innocence. Those who dwell in innocence find that the world will not run away and that the same struggles for power beset utopia as trouble any human venture.

Furthermore, dominance and innocence share the dualistic way of looking at things that millennialism brings. Good *or* evil, right *or* wrong, this *or* that provide a framework for thinking and acting. The instincts of the dominant and public center—of public Protestantism—are at home here. Moralism, the search for simplicity, and the activism of doers and achievers are part of the millennial theme. Significantly, though, in many of the expressions of cultural religion especially in the nineteenth and twentieth centuries, American individualism is countered by expressions of community. Mythologies of teamwork and cooperation are as frequent as those of solitary success. While American cultural religion pays lip service to the historic individualism of the mythology, it also preaches the need to live and act together. And in its cultivation of togetherness among the many, once again cultural religion has learned from the values taught by public Protestantism. Voluntaryism is to be encouraged, but in a land of different peoples and different traditions, the only possible way to be alike is to feel alike. So the community that cultural religion seeks to create is, finally, a community of feeling.

IN OVERVIEW

As a religious system, cultural religion—although diffuse and loose—provides a mostly ordinary expression of the one American religion. A brief survey of its manifestations, especially in our contemporary era, has shown familiar elements of cultus, creed, and code. But whether these three shaped or were shaped by a mainstream American community is problematic.

The cultus of cultural religion was present in the annual ritual calendar that celebrated themes of millennial dominance in patriotic holidays and millennial innocence in familial and sentimental feasts. The creed of cultural religion unfolded in popular mythologies spread, for example, by television, film, literature, and entertainment stars. Millennial dominance appeared in recurring plot structures of violent redemption for a besieged community, while perfectionism was embodied in men's and women's magazines and the ideal of millennial innocence lived on in the legacy of Elvis Presley. Finally, the code of cultural religion expressed norms of behavior guided by millennial dominance and perfectionistic innocence in the ethics of sports, technology, the human potential movement, and nature. In a case study of nature religion as one form of cultural religion, we explored its presence in early America and then in the nineteenth century. In our own era, we noted its continuing power, and its expression in the *Whole Earth Catalog* and the *Mother Earth News.*

This study of cultural religion has tried to suggest its complexity while only scratching the surface. At the same time, thinking about cultural religion has hinted at new ways of conceiving the boundaries between ordinary and extraordinary religion. In the end, with its problems in creating community, in order to assess the impact of cultural religion we need to place it beside the other expressions of the one religion. As public Protestantism, civil religion, and general cultural religion, the one religion seeks to dissolve the differences in American life in a final unity. The power of the one religion is evident in the facts that most of the time it really does work in public, and part of the time it also works in private. Hence, we are left on one side with many religions, each trying to maintain its separate identity, and on the other, with one religion trying to unite them. But to say this does not really tell us much about the relationships between the two. For if culture is complex, so are these relationships. And there are many questions still to answer.

What was it like to be white, Anglo-Saxon, and Protestant in the land of the many? What did it mean to be among the many in the land of white, Anglo-Saxon Protestants? And finally, what did the presence of other minorities do to the experience of separate groups among the many? These are important boundary questions. They are also important questions about the interactions of ordinary and extraordinary religion. We need to address these questions, at least briefly, and we will do so now in the Conclusion.

SUGGESTIONS FOR FURTHER READING: CULTURAL RELIGION

Albanese, Catherine L. *Corresponding Motion: Transcendental Religion and the New America.* Philadelphia: Temple University Press, 1977.

Carroll, Peter N. *Puritanism and the Wilderness: The Intellectual Significance of the New England Frontier, 1629–1700.* New York: Columbia University Press, 1969.

Cawelti, John G. *The Six-Gun Mystique.* Bowling Green, OH: Bowling Green University Popular Press, 1970.

Gustaitis, Rasa. *Turning On.* New York: Macmillan, 1968.

Huizinga, Johan. *Homo Ludens: A Study of the Play Element in Culture.* 1938. Reprint. Boston: Beacon Press, 1955.

Jewett, Robert, and Lawrence, John Shelton. *The American Monomyth.* Garden City, NY: Doubleday, 1977.

Lewis, R.W.B. *The American Adam: Innocence, Tragedy, and Tradition in the Nineteenth Century.* Chicago: University of Chicago Press, 1955.

Marx, Leo. *The Machine in the Garden: Technology and the Pastoral Ideal in America.* New York: Oxford University Press, 1964.

McLuhan, Marshall. *The Mechanical Bride: Folklore of Industrial Man.* 1951. Reprint. Boston: Beacon Press, 1967.

Nash, Roderick. *Wilderness and the American Mind.* New Haven: Yale University Press, 1967.

Nelson, John Wiley. *Your God is Alive and Well and Appearing in Popular Culture.* Philadelphia: Westminster Press, 1976.

Novak, Michael. *The Joy of Sports: End Zones, Bases, Baskets, Balls, and the Consecration of the American Spirit.* New York: Basic Books, 1976.

Nye, Russel. *The Unembarrassed Muse: The Popular Arts in America.* Two Centuries of American Life Bicentennial Series. New York: Dial Press, 1970.

Reich, Charles A. *The Greening of America.* New York: Random House, 1970.

CONCLUSION

Many Centers Meeting

In 1834 a group of Roman Catholic nuns, the Ursulines, were conducting a convent school in Charlestown on the outskirts of Boston. The institution had attracted the daughters of some of Boston's first families as well as those of wealthy families in the vicinity. These pupils were Protestant and, specifically, Unitarian. As liberals, their parents were drawn to the educational advantages that contact with Catholicism might provide. They felt little sympathy for what they regarded as the narrowness of Congregationalism in the public schools. On the other hand, the citizens who lived and worked in the vicinity of the Charlestown convent were poorer people, suspicious of "papist" superstition, and resentful of upper-class Unitarians who seemed to prefer the mysteries of Catholicism to the heritage of the Reformation.

Writers of the period had been warning of the dangers of Catholicism. They said the Catholic church was trying to convert Protestant children, especially females, so that gradually it could gain control. In other words, there was a papist plot afoot, and the plot was a conspiracy. Supported by official Congregational institutions and orthodox ministers, the fears of Catholicism and of education at the Charlestown convent spread. Lyman Beecher, whom we have already met several times, turned his revivalistic preaching to the cause of anti-Catholicism and warned of the connection between the pope and despotism. In this emotionally charged atmosphere, a series of circumstances provided the final sparks. Then in August, a mob of working-class citizens lit a torch and burned the convent and a nearby farmhouse down. They were well organized, and there were hints that some of Boston's prominent citizens may have been involved. They had shown the Catholics of Massachusetts and the world what the true heirs of the Reformation thought of the papist church and its plot. They had also let Protestant liberals know what some other Protestants thought of their betrayal.

With the dynamics of social class and ideology added to the question of religious preference, the affair at the Charlestown convent was a symbol of the complexity and ambivalence of Protestant attitudes toward the many. On the one

345

side, there was suspicion, hatred, and fear, as exemplified by the working people who came, many of them, from the brickyards at Charlestown. Fed by class jealousy and outrage at liberal ideology, nourishment for these feelings came, too, from the extraordinary religious commitment of the Reformation, as interpreted in the Puritan tradition. On the other side, there was a fascination with the many and a pragmatic willingness to use their resources to community advantage, as illustrated by the Unitarians in their movement toward Catholicism. An expression of their cosmopolitan breadth and upper-class "freedom" from old prejudices, the Unitarian attraction for things Catholic marked these liberal Christians as "worldly-wise." It also marked their disapproval of the rigorous legacy of Puritanism that still thrived and of the classes that were its carriers.

From the point of view of our discussion, the issue of the Ursuline convent underlined, once again, the boundary question. This time it was the boundary question of the one religion, of the dominant and public mainstream, as it tried to determine its own borders in the presence of outsiders. For some, like the strict Congregationalists, it was important to maintain strong boundaries, preserving integrity in a situation seen as threatening. Here foreign religious ideas were a source of disorder; they might lead to a rearrangement or reconstruction of the Protestant heritage. For others, like the liberal Unitarians, it was preferable to be open for exchanges. Liberals felt comfortable with more gates in the fence. They were willing to go out farther and to absorb more inside. We might say that their sense of religious identity was more diffused than that of their stricter fellow Protestants.

If the burning of the Charlestown convent was a symbol, we need to look more closely at what it symbolized. In this chapter, we will examine in more detail the ways the one religion of Protestantism responded to the many religions of other Americans. Then we will review what we have already seen to some extent in Part One—the ways these many religious traditions responded in America to Protestantism. Finally, we will need to sketch briefly the ways the many responded to one another. All of these movements were a series of cultural exchanges that involved boundaries. By the late twentieth century, all of them had led to some restructuring in the relationships among the various religious centers.

In general, there were visible patterns in the history of these relationships. Each religious center, Protestant or part of the many, moved toward others in exchanges that loosened boundaries. But each center also retreated in fear or out of a desire to maintain the purity of its past identity. Sometimes this defensiveness took the form of an offensive against other religious centers, either in missionary efforts or in warnings against the dangers of outside influences. Sometimes the movements of one center toward another or away from it were extremely ambivalent, resulting in a complicated series of interchanges.

At least in the first three centuries in America, the response of the dominant and public tradition was more negative than positive toward the religions of the many. And because the one center *was* dominant—in power—this meant various kinds of discrimination and disability for religions among the many. In contrast, the response of the many religious traditions toward the public Protestantism was much more evenly divided between those who wanted to maintain a separate identity and those who wanted to "Americanize" by becoming more like the Protestants. Lastly, the response of the many religions toward one another was more often negative than positive. Let us look at each of these series of responses in turn.

DEFENSIVE DEITIES: THE ONE CONFRONTS THE MANY

Protestantism was the religious giant in the land. Yet Protestants generally displayed anxiety toward the cultural invaders who were adopting America as their home. So the main thrust of Protestant response to different religious orientations was a retreat into purity. Convinced of Anglo-Saxon chosenness and superiority, Protestants barred the gates more than they opened them. In a sense, the "others" were social "dirt," which polluted the body politic and religious. Thus, in the interests of both ordinary and extraordinary religion, it was necessary to purge the Protestant community of any contamination. Foreign religions and their representatives, in the midst of the New Israel, were matter out of place. To rid the public space of these sources of social disorder, ritual purification was necessary.

We saw in the Introduction how charged with danger the boundaries of the human body were. People in many societies often had to be careful about the food that they ate and even about what happened to their hair and nail parings lest they fall into the wrong hands. In similar vein, the Protestant quest for public cleanliness was an attempt to preserve the social body—to keep the wrong substances from entering and corrupting it and to prevent its energies from being drained away by alien forces. Hence, while this impulse toward social purity led Protestants to engage in some ugly border wars, we need to recognize that the impulse itself is a powerful element in all religions. Defending the Gods, historically, has aroused the passions of millions of religious men and women.

In the instance of American Protestantism, the result was discrimination against different religious and ethnic groups. Generally, both the ordinary and extraordinary religions of these groups proved threatening to the mainstream. The reaction of Protestants was, as in the example of the Ursulines, a mingling of social, economic, political, and more openly religious elements. From the beginning, the Indians felt the brunt of Protestant fears. As we saw in our discussion of nature religion, beneath the Puritan attitude toward Indians was the fear that, away from the centers of European civilization, Euro-American Christians would forget what the centuries had taught them and revert to the savagery they imagined in the Indians. Symbolic of this "savagery" was the heathen worship that the tribal cultures practiced and the moral code that it inspired. Puritans thought that the Indians were cannibalistic and sexually promiscuous. They feared captivity by the Indians, especially for their women. They aimed as much as possible to avoid cultural contact between the two peoples.

Similarly, Protestants feared any genuine human encounter with their black slaves. When the slaves were freed, the dominant culture continued to uphold, as much as it could, the tradition of separate societies with as little contact as possible. At the same time, the nineteenth-century influx of immigrants challenged Protestants with new religiocultural contacts that they preferred to keep at a minimum. From the Protestant point of view, it seemed that foreign peoples on all sides were ready to overwhelm them, and so Protestants must fight hard to maintain their moral superiority as the chosen nation. Indeed, the various reform movements that Protestants led in the nineteenth century appear in a new light, if we remember this general background of contact with different cultures. And in the twentieth century, the movement in the dominant culture to rid the body politic of various forms of corruption takes on new meaning. The Red Scare of the twenties and the McCarthy congressional hearings of the fifties, both directed against Communists, were the public expressions of an old religious fear. Even the Watergate purge of the seventies, with its references to the Germanic dominance of the White House by Nixon's aides, H. R. Haldeman and John Ehrlichman, had echoes of the same theme.

In spite of the attempt to maintain its boundaries against the onslaught of alien cultures, Protestantism showed real ambivalence, as we will see. The long era of unrestricted immigration is a strong statement to that effect; and as we discuss Protestant bigotry, we need to remember this second side to the story. In order to understand the dominant response to the "others" more thoroughly, let us look at two case studies of Protestant resistance to different religiocultural groups. We will look first at Protestant attitudes toward Roman Catholicism, and secondly, toward Judaism. In both cases, Protestant fears became general cultural fears of the outsider.

The Roman Catholic Plot

Extraordinary religion played strong in Protestant fears of Roman Catholicism. True to the heritage of the Reformation, American Protestants thought of the pope as the Antichrist in a millennial drama. In familiar pattern, they stood on the side of the Lamb in the war between good and evil, while the pope and the church he headed were the emissaries of the devil. For colonial and nineteenth-century Protestants, in fact, Catholics were not even Christians. Their leaders were engaged in a secret and powerful plot to take over the world. They were imperialists of the first order, and, worse still, the immorality of these priests and their female counterparts, the nuns, would wreck the moral order of America. Usually this meant that, like blacks and Indians, Catholics engaged in wild sexual promiscuity and also, like blacks and Indians, they were deceitful and cunning beyond measure.

When they looked at Catholics and when they looked at each group among the "others," Protestants, in their desire to defend their boundaries, displaced their own forbidden fantasies by attributing them to others. The urge to moral purity, increased by the presence of alien forces, led them to expel the side of themselves they did not wish to see. The hidden sources of Protestant guilt could be acknowledged when they became the open sins of Catholics and Jews, Indians and blacks. In emotional terms, the dynamics of projection were at work in the Protestant image of Catholics and the rest of the "others." By regarding these "others" as they did, Protestants were looking safely at the shadow side of themselves.

By the revolutionary era, a second element helped to form the Protestant attitude toward Roman Catholics. The Enlightenment view of Catholicism mingled with older Protestant ideas. The thinkers who shaped the Enlightenment had themselves been shaped by protest against the medieval superstition of the Catholic church. Its priestcraft had kept people in intellectual darkness, they thought, preventing them from seeing the light of true knowledge. Its papal and authoritarian system had deterred them from acknowledging the sovereignty of reason, the inner governor and source of light.

Finally, in the nineteenth century, when massive waves of immigration began to flood America, social and economic reasons joined the other sources of Protestant prejudice. Roman Catholic immigrants were mostly Irish and very poor. As Protestant Americans saw it, they strained the social services that government and private agencies could provide, often arriving penniless and blighting the cities with their slums, their diseases, their lack of cleanliness, and their foreign ways. According to Protestants, they brought unwelcome competition for jobs and so reduced the wages the market would pay to all.

Already in the seventeenth century, although there were few Catholics in the English colonies, there had been clear anti-Catholicism, especially in Maryland and Massachusetts Bay. In Maryland, Protestants felt threatened by the Catholicism of the proprietor of the colony, Lord Baltimore. In Massachusetts Bay, the strong Puritan atmosphere led to a vigorous anti-Catholicism, too. When in 1690 war broke out with France and Spain, the other European landlords on the continent, there was new cause for anti-Catholic sentiment, so that by 1700 Rhode Island was the only colony to grant Catholics complete civil and religious rights. The eighteenth century continued this story of legal disabilities for Catholics, now justified by new wars with Catholic France.

During the Revolution the alliance with France against Britain in 1778 brought an era of relative toleration. Still, despite the spirit of the Declaration of Independence, state constitutions after the war continued to limit the role that Catholics could play in government. It was in the nineteenth century, however, that old fears of Catholic power revived, as the immigrants began to come. The trusteeship controversy within Roman Catholicism—over the question of lay control of church property—generated unfavorable publicity. The new Protestant converts, born out of the zeal of the Finney revivals, spread anti-Catholicism in the various voluntary societies they joined. Religious newspapers by 1827 began to warn their readers of the tyrannies of the pope and the dangers of the Catholic church. By 1832 the New York Protestant Association had been founded to promote the Reformation by public discussions that would bring the true character of Catholicism to light.

In this climate of opinion, the burning of the Ursuline convent in 1834 was the first act in a continued Protestant war against nunneries. Two years later, after several books were published claiming to reveal the horrors of convent life, Maria Monk's *Awful Disclosures of the Hotel Dieu Nunnery of Montreal* appeared. An example of nineteenth-century pornography, Monk's book professed to be the work of an escaped nun. Among her "awful disclosures" were the secret sexual unions between priests and nuns. The children born of these relationships, according to Monk, were strangled in infancy after being duly baptized. Their bodies were hidden in a secret passage that linked the convent to the home of the priests.

Actually written in New York at the urging of a group that included several ministers, the book, needless to say, created a sensation. Although the Hotel Dieu was finally searched by trustworthy investigators who found no evidence to support even the floor plan of the convent as described by Maria Monk, many still believed the allegations of her book and subsequent publications. The Reformation had brought Protestants a new religious spirit, and they regarded celibacy as an unnatural state. Moreover, mysteries that took place behind the cloistered walls of the convent, so different from the openness honored in a democratic republic, also disturbed Protestant Americans. Together celibacy and secrecy could add up to no good. So the rumors flew, and the convents were subject to harassment.

At the same time, Protestants had new cause for worry as additional rumors spread of a papal plot to take control of the Mississippi Valley with the aid of European despots. Lyman Beecher wrote his *Plea for the West* (1835), warning of Catholic plans to use schools as a way to win converts and so win the country. For this reason, Protestant schools and colleges had to be established in the new territories. In the East, Catholicism became embroiled in other scholastic controversies as church leaders protested against the reading of the King James (Protestant) Version of the Bible in the public schools. Further, Catholics were upset by many of the textbooks that their children were required to use because they thought that the books presented an unfair and untrue picture of Catholicism. In Philadelphia, these and similar issues provoked a confrontation between Protestants and Irish Catholics that led in 1844 to the burning of two Catholic churches in the Kensington suburb of the city. Spurred on the Protestant side by the publicity given to the issue by the American Protestant Association, the discontent between the two factions brought a state of civil riot and mob action to Philadelphia.

There had been arrogance and political insensitivity on the part of the Catholic bishops in these and other instances, but the roots of the problem, as we have seen, ran deep. Protestants continued to form organizations to counter the Catholic threat. Through many of the best-known voluntary societies—the American Tract Society, the American Home Missionary Society, and others—anti-Catholic attitudes were spread. Then in the mid-1840s Protestant nativism assumed political form as the Native American party, which demanded that the naturalization law be changed to require a twenty-one year wait before an immigrant could become a citizen. A five-year wait had been the law of the land since the presidency of Thomas Jefferson, but the nativists reasoned that it took twenty-one years for a native-born American to receive full rights as a citizen. Foreigners, though adults, should expect a similar waiting period. More important, nativists thought that the lengthy prohibition would cut down on the number of Catholic immigrants who became citizens, thus lessening their political power to control public policy through the ballot box.

By the early 1850s, the secret Order of the Star Spangled Banner, known in its public maneuvers as the Know-Nothing party, had come into existence as the enemy of Roman Catholicism. With local, county, state, and national councils, the order was a masterpiece of tight and effective organization. Its members, bound by the elaborate ritual of their secret society, "knew nothing" when publicly questioned. But they staged write-in campaigns during the elections and succeeded in bringing their slate of candidates to office in local contests. Later, the Know-Nothing party began to carry states—Massachusetts, Delaware, and Pennsylvania among them. In 1854 it sent a delegation of about seventy-five Congressmen to Washington, D.C., all united in their commitment to anti-Catholic principles. So confident was the party that it looked ahead to capturing the White House in 1856. However, without a majority in the Congress, the party could not translate its programs into law, and, in the end, the movement failed.

Political nativism was swept away by the slavery controversy that erupted shortly later in the Civil War. The country did not experience another strong resurgence of anti-Catholic sentiment until the 1870s and especially the 1880s, when the heaviest immigration in American history began to sweep into the land. When in 1886 a bomb exploded in the midst of the police force called to Chicago's Haymarket Square during an anarchist meeting, the incident triggered a renewal of nativism, directed now against Jews as well as Catholics. By 1887 the American Protective Association had formed to defend Protestant boundaries by never voting for a Catholic and, if members were able, by never hiring one. Anti-Catholic feeling continued for roughly the next fifty years and lingered in subdued form even later. Thus, by 1915, the revived Ku Klux Klan had made Catholicism one of its targets. Meanwhile, theories of scientific racism alleged that the Teutonic, or Northern European, race was superior, and so the Protestant peoples, the Germans and the English, were the lifeblood of the nation. On the other hand, the Mediterranean race, represented by hordes of Southern European Catholic immigrants, would weaken the strength of America.

When in 1928 New York's Governor Alfred (Al) Smith (1873–1944) ran for the presidency on the Democratic ticket, his Catholicism became a central issue in his campaign defeat. America was not ready to elect a Roman Catholic president until 1960, when, not without questions concerning his religion, John F. Kennedy (1917–1963) won the office. The second half of the century had brought a new era for Catholicism. Now anti-Catholic sentiment was more discreet, and when it surfaced, it was educated, sophisticated, and "polite." The best example was the Protestants and Other Americans United for the Separation of Church and State (POAU), which after 1948 warned of the growing authority of the Catholic church in the United States. The POAU found the possibility of federal aid to parochial schools particularly disturbing. A good deal of Protestant anxiety was expressed through the public controversy stimulated by the organization.

The Jewish Conspiracy

Unlike anti-Catholicism, anti-Semitism did not become a real factor in American life until the later nineteenth century. There were several reasons for this. First of all, the old Puritan myth of the covenant had fostered a strong identification with the biblical Israel. As chosen people and visible saints, Puritans inherited the mantle of divine election that had formerly protected the Jews. As descendants of the people who once had played such an honored role in God's plan, seventeenth-century Jews did not inspire the hatred and alarm that Catholics did. Secondly, outside of the heritage of extraordinary religion, there were social, political, and economic reasons why Jews appeared less threatening. From the beginning, their presence in the colonies was minimal—less by far than the presence of Roman Catholics. Moreover, no Jewish power, such as the Catholic powers of Spain and France, opposed English presence in the New World. Finally, early Jewish immigrants did not tax public welfare programs. They were largely tradespeople able to earn their own livings. When problems did arise, individual Jews turned to the Jewish community for help and support.

Still, there *were* reasons for Protestants to erect barriers against the Jews. As a religious organization, the Christian church had been born out of conflict with the Jewish synagogue. The gospels, written during the period of struggle, reflected the attempts of the Christian movement to assert its own identity not only positively but also negatively. In other words, Christians had to show how and why the Jews were wrong. So the gospels, and especially the gospel of John, portrayed the Jews as disobeying God and rejecting his prophets. The ultimate rejection had come, according to Christian accounts, when they refused to recognize the messiah in their midst and even persecuted and crucified him. By the third century, condemnation of the Jews had escalated, and the learned Christian scholar Origen (185?–254?) was saying that all the Jews had killed Christ. A tradition had been formed. Throughout the Middle Ages and into the era of the Reformation, the charge that the Jews were Christ-killers stuck, often combining with other factors to lead to ugly episodes of persecution.

Meanwhile, because the medieval church prohibited usury (lending money with an interest charge), European Jews became identified with moneylending and banking to accommodate Christian needs. Thus began a continuing Jewish association with business and financial interests, an association in which prominent members of the Jewish community lent money to their Christian neighbors, grew wealthy, and frequently attracted their resentment. From the Christian point of view, there was something suspicious— and even wrong—with wealth that was obtained not by the productive work of one's hands but from unproductive money. Seeds planted in the ground would grow and reproduce their kind. Hands skilled at their work would create the arts and crafts needed by society. But money could not be planted and, in its own form, could not be used. It must be an agent of the devil.

These attitudes, the common possession of all Christians before the Reformation, continued among both Protestants and Roman Catholics after the sixteenth century. So despite their identification as the New Israel, American Protestants had ordinary and extraordinary reasons to suspect the Jews. Even in colonial times, therefore, prohibitions against atheists and non-Christians slowed Jewish immigration, while the Jews also suffered legal disabilities. Yet in comparison with the kinds of restrictions the Jews had endured in Europe, America was the promised land, and the Jewish community prospered. It was not until the era of the Civil War that anti-Semitism became noticeable, as Jews in both the North and the South were blamed with profiteering from the war and with treason. In a notorious order later reversed by President Abraham Lincoln, General Ulysses S. Grant commanded all Jews to leave the Tennessee military district. The citizens of one Georgia town agreed to banish them, too; and meanwhile, in an act of open discrimination, Congress legislated that only Christians could serve as chaplains to the Union army.

After 1880 the huge immigration of Eastern European Jews, poor and distinctively foreign, brought Jewish people increasingly to public attention. At the same time, the success of the older Jewish Americans, sometimes greater than that of Protestant Christians, aroused hostility. Jews found themselves barred from prestigious social clubs and summer resorts. College fraternities began to exclude Jewish students at eastern schools, while, increasingly, Jews faced difficulties in obtaining the housing they desired. By the 1890s anti-Semitic feeling had crystallized around the suspicion that the Jews were responsible for an international conspiracy to base the economy on the single gold standard. The prominence of European Jewish banking families, such as the Rothschilds, fueled these fears, for the Rothschilds and other Jews were thought to have a corner on the world gold market. This was the era when ordinary Americans were organizing politically to protect the silver standard. People believed that the "free" coinage of this second metal, while it produced inflation, would ease conditions, especially for farmers and working folk.

The People's or Populist party had begun in 1889, backed by southern and western agricultural organizations, and through the regular Democratic party as well as through its own political machinery, it was making its presence felt. Beginning with legislation in 1878, the government had subsidized silver producers and farmers by requiring the purchase of silver bullion for coinage. Then in 1890 the Sherman Silver Purchase Act raised the amount of silver to be purchased by the treasury to twice the former amount. When a financial panic swept the country in 1893, the steady drain of gold from the treasury to purchase silver became a matter of serious concern. At a special session of Congress, the Silver Purchase Act was repealed.

Farmers and working people felt betrayed, and after President Grover Cleveland (1837–1908) obtained a gold loan from the Rothschilds, anti-Semitism flared. Many thought that America had sold out to an international banking conspiracy headed by the Jews. The Populists, through their own party and within Democratic ranks, expressed the sentiments that these Americans shared. At the Democratic convention in 1896, William Jennings Bryan (1860–1925) gave the famous "Cross of Gold" speech that won him the presidential nomination. "You shall not crucify mankind upon a cross of gold," he declared in a ringing oratorical statement.

Whether or not he was consciously aware of it, Bryan's rhetoric was a masterstroke in defense of conservative Protestant cultural boundaries. He had deftly combined the old charges—that the Jews were Christ-killers and that they were banking conspirators—with the Populist cry for free silver. And he had done it with innuendo and suggestion, so that Jews had not directly been named but everybody understood. Others were more direct. During these years anti-Semitic rhetoric and literature became an open part of American life. Indeed, the pattern continued until after the Second World War, and the first half of the twentieth century brought the Jews little relief from anti-Semitism.

An often-cited example is the Leo Frank case in Atlanta in 1913. New city dwellers with a rural background were tense and uncomfortable in the urban setting, for the city had long been a symbol for evil in American mythology. In addition, the physical and emotional problems of adjustment increased tension, and there were periodic eruptions of violence, such as a race riot in Atlanta in 1906. In this atmosphere of conflict and fear, the Southern Baptists, who played a large role in the religious life of the city, thought of immigrants as one of the greatest contemporary threats to America. The Jew, historically identified with cities rather than farms, stood as a strong symbol of all that these Americans hated and feared.

So when thirteen-year-old Mary Phagan was assaulted and murdered one night at the National Pencil Factory, her employer, Leo M. Frank, was immediately suspected. Although Frank had witnesses to his whereabouts during the fatal day and evening, he was placed on trial for the crime. He had admitted to seeing the Phagan girl alive on the day before the night of the crime (nobody would admit to having seen her later), and strands of her hair as well as blood stains had been found in a workroom opposite his office. Furthermore, he possessed something of a reputation for making advances toward his female employees. The Jewish superintendent and part owner of the factory was railroaded through a trial in the midst of a great public outcry, so that it was no surprise when the jury found him guilty. Public oratory and newspaper editorials made the identification between the northern Jew, the evils of the city, and the death of the "little factory girl." Stories circulated that Frank's Jewish friends had tried to bribe the jury, while his lawyers received anonymous threats. After fruitless appeals all the way to the United States Supreme Court, Frank's sentence to death by hanging was commuted by the governor of Georgia to life imprisonment. But shortly after the decision, in 1915 the prison was stormed, and Frank was kidnapped and lynched. Vigilante justice had insured that the will of the people was done.

The same year as Frank's murder, the revived Ku Klux Klan began directing its attacks against Catholics and Jews, as well as blacks, as we have already seen. The new Klan was an identifiably Protestant organization with its own chaplains and hymns that it had adapted specially to express its creed and code. By 1923 it had grown to nearly 3 million members, a militant reminder of the threat felt by many Protestants in a mixed society. During this decade, too, Henry Ford in 1920 championed the American publication of the *Protocols of the Elders of Zion*, the fraudulent account of a conference of nineteenth-century Jews planning to overthrow Christianity and gain control of the world. Significantly, the gold standard would be the Jewish weapon in the attempted subversion. Once again, religious and economic prejudices were linked in a work that became a continuing justification for anti-Semitism.

In the cases of Frank, the Klan, and the *Protocols*, hatred of the Jews was crude and blatant. But now a "polite" form of anti-Semitism began to spread, as Harvard and other universities questioned their admissions policies and introduced quota systems to prevent too many Jews from altering the traditional Anglo-Saxon character of their institutions. A decade later in the thirties, public sentiment against the Jews only grew stronger, as the Great Depression and the growth of European Fascism stimulated American prejudices. As we will see, many Catholics as well as Protestants had become openly anti-Semitic; and in speaking of the boundaries of Protestant identity, we are speaking about the cultural Protestantism that was the dominant and public religion of the land. In this blend of ordinary and extraordinary religion, Jews had come to stand for many of the ills that troubled the republic. Their unbelief challenged Christianity; their wealth outstripped that of the leaders of the New Israel; their cosmopolitan identification with the city corrupted the wholesome rural flavor of America. Within the boundaries of the one religion, Jews had come to represent the monster at the gates.

Overtures toward the Many

Yet the dominant and public religion, in spite of its defensiveness, did initiate exchanges with the "others." The record was far from being all negative, however insecure the mainstream had been. Perhaps the single most important sign was the fact that only with the twentieth century did the era of unlimited immigration end. It was a fact, too, that there were strong economic reasons for the open immigration policy of the United States. But the millennial dream of Americans that they stood at the dawn of a golden age, that they were an example and possessed a mission to all less fortunate peoples, was also involved. Thus, immigration continued throughout the nineteenth and into the twentieth century until a series of congressional measures in 1917, in 1921, and then in 1924 reduced it drastically. The laws of 1921 and 1924 introduced a quota system, which clearly favored Northern Europeans in its restrictions. Then in 1965 the law of 1924 gave place to one which restricted immigration but not on the basis of national origins. In a further legislative testimony to a new mood in America, Congress in 1973 passed the Ethnic Heritage Act, providing funds for programs that would improve public understanding of different cultural groups within the United States.

From the beginning of the mainstream encounter with the many, however, there were a series of exchanges, each of them a different way of meeting the "others." In general, we may single out three. The first move, sometimes tied to the fear of being swept away in foreign religions and cultures, was the traditional attempt to do missionary work among them. Here extraordinary religion led the way, but in various projects for the social welfare and cultural integration of blacks, American Indians, and immigrants, ordinary religion was involved as well. The second move, in a different mood, went outward toward the "others" with a sense of interest and openness. Again, extraordinary religion was prominent, since Protestant liberalism and, in the twentieth century, the ecumenical movement were carriers for this kind of exchange. Finally, the third move was an imaginative preoccupation with the "others" that drew the mainstream into an enchantment with those who were different. Played out mostly within ordinary religion and culture, it found expression in literature and the arts. We will glance briefly at each of these moves toward the many.

Protestant commitment to missionary effort was as old as official English colonization of the New World. The charter of the Virginia Company, like nearly every colonial charter, had recognized the conversion of the Indians as one of the reasons for the settlement. Later the House of Burgesses in 1619 legislated that Virginia towns should each undertake to educate a number of Indians so that they might attend college. Even more, plans were afoot to found a missionary university on 10,000 acres to be set aside for the purpose.

Among the Puritans of New England, the Mayhew family maintained a mission to the Indians at Martha's Vineyard for a century, while Roger Williams in 1643 published a treatise on Indian language. During the same era, John Eliot (1604-1690) devoted his life to work among the Indians, learning to preach to them in their own language. With assistance from the Society for the Propagation of the Gospel in New England, he established about fourteen villages for "praying" Indians. His Bible, translated into the Algonkian tongue, was the first to be published in America (1661-1663). Yet by the end of the seventeenth century, Puritan missions to the Indians had declined in a general atmosphere of war with the Indians and lessening fervor.

With the Great Awakening, however, came a new wave of missionary zeal. Eleazar Wheelock (1711-1779) founded an Indian school at Lebanon, Connecticut, in 1755, and one of the students there was later ordained. David Brainerd (1718-1747) preached among the Indians in New York and New Jersey, inspiring the efforts of others after the end of his short life. In the nineteenth century, Protestants continued to found missions, sometimes also receiving government funds to be used in their schools. Congress had appropriated money to assist the tribes, but it had no machinery for its distribution, and so the missionary schools became agencies for the federal outreach. Earlier, in 1787 the Society for Propagating the Gospel among the Indians had been founded an an interdenominational society. By 1810 another interdenominational organization, the American Board of Commissioners for Foreign Missions provided assistance, and in 1881 the National Indian Association came on the scene. Various denominations meanwhile extended their work so that, in the end, they contributed the bulk of the effort. Different denominations had their heroes in these missions, such as Isaac McCoy (1784-1846) among the Baptists and Jason Lee (1803-1845) among the Methodists.

Protestant missionary presence became a continuing feature of the white relationship with the Indians—a presence which remains into our own day. Churches of various denominations dot the reservations, and Protestant missionaries have helped to bring white ways as well as Christianity to tribal cultures. Among blacks, as we have already seen, the Protestant missionary presence was a similar story. Although Anglican missionaries did not meet with great success among the slaves, their Methodist and Baptist fellow Protestants did. In the post-Civil-War era, the American Missionary Association, as well as individual denominations, worked to establish schools where black leaders could be trained. Baptists and Methodists were at the forefront of these efforts, while the American Missionary Association, supported mostly by Congregationalists, founded as many as twenty schools, among them Fisk University in Nashville and Hampton Institute in Virginia, both in 1866.

Protestants had worked to bring about emancipation. Now they continued their evangelical efforts among blacks out of the nineteenth century and into the twentieth. At the same time, Protestant attitudes toward both Indians and blacks had been marked by ambivalence. Racism was an ongoing characteristic of American culture, and the religion of Protestant chosenness bore its share of the responsibility. Thus, missionary effort was the other side of the Protestant retreat from cultural contact. By the same token, the anti-Catholicism and anti-Semitism that we have already examined were sometimes intertwined with missionary efforts.

In the case of Jewish people, as early as 1667, well before any Jews settled in Boston, Increase Mather (1639–1723) had published a set of sermons directed to Jewish conversion. Because of the small number of Jews in the country, however, it was only in the nineteenth century that missionary efforts became significant. By 1823 the activities of the interdenominational American Society for Meliorating the Condition of the Jews prompted the publication of a Jewish periodical as a rebuttal. Jews did not look kindly on the work of Christian missionaries, as succeeding issues of *The Jew* made clear. Later in the century, a number of denominations—among them Episcopalians and Baptists as well as Old School and United Presbyterians—sponsored official or semiofficial efforts to convert the Jews.

In similar vein Protestants worked to convert Catholics, and by 1842 the American Tract Society established plans to send missionary agents to them. Two years later, the American Protestant Society was holding monthly prayer sessions for the conversion of Catholics and fielding missionaries as its active agents. Subsequently incorporated into the American and Foreign Christian Union, its labors became more extensive, spreading especially to areas where Protestants could encounter Catholic immigrants. Likewise, the American Home Missionary Society worked to spread Protestant truth in the New West, where Catholic influence was likely to be met.

By the 1890s, when immigration had become the largest in American history, Protestants worked in settlement houses among Jewish and Catholic immigrant groups. Here and in the many labors of the Social Gospel movement, they brought economic assistance and American cultural influence to the newcomers. Just as the government throughout the nineteenth century had tried to acculturate and "civilize" the Indians, and just as the Freedmen's Bureau after the Civil War had tried to do the same for blacks, the organizations to assist the immigrants brought the ordinary religion of Americanism to their doorstep.

Yet if missionary outreach was one move toward the "others," the second move was one of attraction and interest without missionary aspirations. The liberal, upper-class Unitarians who sent their daughters to the Ursuline convent at Charlestown in 1834 were examples of this second move. Here there was a recognition that a different cultural tradition could enrich the heritage of the mainstream. There was, as the image of the school so clearly expresses, a willingness to be taught. In fact, part of this willingness came from practical considerations, a situation, we recall, that repeated itself in the West in these decades. In the new land, there were few opportunities for a solid education. Catholicism, which had long experience through its teaching orders of nuns and priests, sometimes supplied the community's needs.

However, it remained for the twentieth century to bring Protestantism to a new degree of openness toward the many. The changes that resulted in the ecumenical movement were complex, involving developments on the world religious scene and within religious organizations outside of Protestantism. As early as 1928, the National Conference of Christians and Jews had been formed for the mutual educational benefit of both groups. The conference was publicly active in a number of ways, among them the inauguration of Brotherhood Day and later, National Brotherhood Week. Then, two years after the establishment of the World Council of Churches, the National Council of Churches in America came into existence in 1950. As an expression of the ecumenical movement, the council aimed to study the faith and life of the churches in relationship to one another. It wanted also to understand the meaning of the unity and universality that Christians had traditionally associated with the church and to find ways to make the unity and universality more than an ideal. Organizationally, it included among its members the representatives of various Eastern Orthodox churches, and so dialogue beyond Protestant boundaries had become possible within its ranks.

After 1960 the ecumenical movement began to gain rapid ground in a world religious climate considerably changed by the election of Pope John XXIII (1881-1963) and his plans for Vatican Council II. An example of the new mood was the suggestion by the Jewish scholar Will Herberg for a book exploring interfaith questions written by the Protestant theologian Robert McAfee Brown and the Catholic priest and scholar Gustave Weigel. In the resulting work, *An American Dialogue: A Protestant Looks at Catholicism and a Catholic Looks at Protestantism* (1960), Protestantism was viewing Catholicism in a new way— without either a desire to convert or to be converted. Protestant identity remained. Yet meaningful exchanges were being conducted across the boundary of another religious world.

The third Protestant move toward the many was an enchantment with "otherness." Outside of the mainstream, this "otherness" combined with a haunting familiarity, so that when Protestants looked to the many, in some ways they recognized the human possibilities that they had denied in themselves. The "others" showed passion and spontaneity, creativity and strength. "Reverse" acculturation was almost inevitable, as the dominant and public religion found that strange religions and cultures were often very close to home. Thus, the nineteenth-century Unitarians who sent their children to the Catholic convent school had been at least aware of the trappings of medieval culture that came with Catholicism. Later the Transcendentalists were drawn by the richness of this Catholic heritage. Ralph Waldo Emerson, after he traveled in Europe, had come away with a strong sense of the power of Roman Catholic sacramentalism in its ritual splendor. Indeed, at least two of the Transcendentalists became prominent Catholic converts, and both Isaac Hecker (1819-1888) and Orestes Brownson (1803-1876) contributed much to their new church.

Yet it was within ordinary religion and culture that the mainstream made its closest contacts with the "others," often through literary and artistic means. The Euro-American relationship with Indian Americans was a case in point. Although a long heritage had taught whites to shrink from association with the "savage" and "uncivilized" tribal cultures, the same history told them that the Indian was a noble creature of the forests. As the Romantic relationship with the wilderness grew in the nineteenth century, the Indian came to stand for the purity and regeneration that uncorrupted nature gave to America.

For example, in the famous *Leatherstocking Tales* of James Fenimore Cooper (1789–1851), the frontier life of Natty Bumppo, or Leatherstocking, embodied the qualities of the "noble savage." A guide for other whites, often extricating them from dangerous situations, Leatherstocking maintained close ties with Indian peoples. He had learned their ways and could survive in the forest. He could respect their code of honor and sympathize with their plight under the pressures created by the coming of more and more whites. Yet Natty Bumppo often boasted that he was a man "without a cross" (of blood), and he continued to stand on the boundary—never quite an Indian, but never an ordinary white man either.

Even more than Leatherstocking, David Crockett in his autobiography spoke proudly of his Indian skills. He could use his tomahawk to chop a tree, to obtain some honey, or to break ice when the river was frozen. He explained that he scalped squirrels, and in one incident during an Indian war, he imitated the behavior of some friendly Choctaw warriors by striking the severed heads of his victims. Just as the Indians, Crockett became like the animals he stalked and killed. As in the case of the fictional Crockett of the almanacs (discussed in Chapter 12), in the pages of the autobiography, Crockett demonstrated many times his readiness for wild and "savage" actions. Once he came close to Indian "cannibalism" when, hungry and without food, he and other soldiers during an Indian war ate potatoes from a cellar, although the oil from Indians they had killed had dripped onto them. If Indians ran naked in the woods, Crockett had his tale of how, in an accident during a trip to float some logs down the Mississippi, he had lost his clothes. If Indians could not read or write, Crockett bragged of his own difficulties with book learning. Crockett was a hero and a great Congressman, as the autobiography told it, because of his closeness to wilderness forces. Crockett had become an ideal American, a character to be admired and imitated, because he had become like an Indian.

In our own era, the fascination with Indian cultures, if anything, has grown stronger. Children play "Indian," wearing Plains Indian war bonnets to express their identification with the first Americans. College students avidly read accounts of Indian culture as told from the Indian point of view, while films such as *Little Big Man* and *A Man Called Horse* have given them insights into tribal cultures. At the same time, a flowering of Indian crafts, especially in the Southwest, has brought Navajo jewelry and blankets and Pueblo pottery and baskets into demand. Indian designs appear on towels and bed linens, adding a Native American flavor to the art of interior decorating.

We do not have space to explore all of the ways that the mainstream has reached out to the many and taken elements to itself. German Christmas tree customs, Italian spaghetti and pizza, and Chinese food are all instances. Even more, black music and entertainment have enriched twentieth-century art forms. Indeed, what is most distinctive about American music has been what blacks have brought to it. Gospel, jazz, and blues owe their genesis to Afro-American musical genius. Elvis Presley, we recall, took part of his success from the "soul" quality he gave to white rock and roll.

Finally, the presence of "otherness" had led to *discontinuity* within the dominant religion. Mainstream religion has become partial to meditation and contemplation as well as to activity. It has absorbed elements of the occult, has found its children living in communes, and has listened to the messages of new and foreign cults. Even among the middle class, casual clothes and lifestyle and the use of marijuana have symbolized a departure from the moral rigor of the past. The public face of American religion has begun to look different in the strong and compelling presence of the "others."

ACCULTURATIVE RELIGION: THE MANY ENCOUNTER THE ONE

Throughout Part One, we noticed the ways in which religious people among the many tried to come to terms with the dominant and public religion of the mainstream. Generally, they either turned to the resources within their own communities, attempting to preserve their original identity in the new situation. Or they decided to turn outward, becoming as American as they could, even as they preserved some of the heritage of the past. Or lastly, they employed missionary efforts—either in traditional churches like Roman Catholicism, or among the members of intense religious groups who maintained strong boundaries against the world and at the same time worked zealously to win converts to their cause. Since we have examined these moves in some detail, let us simply summarize them here.

First of all, the many used their distinctive rituals and ways of life to preserve their religiocultural identity intact. In the case of black Americans, during their long years in slavery, preservation of remnants of the African past became a survival technique. More than that, when blacks began to use a Christian religious language, they evolved their own Afro-American form of Christianity that sought not to imitate the mainstream but to be true to inner voices and needs. In the style of their preaching, in spirituals, in marriage and funeral customs, and in the blend of idea and emotion that characterized their worship, blacks spoke and acted their ordinary and extraordinary religion within the circle of Afro-American identity. In root work and voodoo and later in religious movements that made blackness central, they had drawn the line between themselves and white society.

For Indians, the story was similar, although in their case the boundaries were not so much encouraged by mainstream culture as maintained in spite of it. Christian missions and government agencies alike tried to break down the old tribal ways and replace tradition with Christianity and modernity. The results were often destructive to tradition, leaving tribal peoples in a confused and demoralized state. Still, many fought back and in spite of the odds preserved their religious and ethnic identity. In the later twentieth century, the return to tradition became a movement that penetrated reservation cultures. The peoples who had separated themselves most effectively from outsiders, usually because of historical accident, found themselves often in more satisfying condition than other, more "Americanized" Indians.

In the examples of the Hopi and the Oglala Sioux, we saw how ordinary and extraordinary religion worked together to create a meaningful world of belief, behavior, and ritual drama. In other cases, Christian elements were reinterpreted to maintain the boundaries between Indian and white society. Thus, the Rio Grande Pueblos of New Mexico accepted Roman Catholic ritual as a new source of power that could be added to their already rich liturgical life. More radically, the Paiutes who created the ghost dance transformed Christian millennialism into an expression of Indian renewal in which the remnants of white culture would be swept away and a new earth restored to Native Americans.

Among whites, the non-Protestant religions also used boundary markers to tell themselves and their Protestant neighbors that they were different. The Jewish dietary laws expressed a commitment to the religion of Israel and likewise distinguished Jews in a public way from the Gentiles. After 1880 the emergence of Conservatism and the self-conscious preservation of Orthodoxy underlined the Jewish desire to keep alive past traditions. Similarly, the growth of the parochial school system among Catholics indicated the strength of the Roman refusal to be assimilated to mainstream Protestantism through the cultural persuasion of the public schools.

In a related move, within Roman Catholicism different ethnic groups strived to maintain their religious traditions in the face of the dominant Irish power—closer, for them, to the Protestant mainstream. Germans and Poles fought to keep their native languages in religious services. Italians steadfastly continued their devotions to their favorite saints, lavishing attention on traditional statues and lighting candles in the saints' honor. Different ethnic groups blended extraordinary religion with distinctive folk customs for the celebration of various church feasts. They kept to marriage and funeral customs that they had brought from the old countries, using their separate practices as badges of identity for themselves and for others.

Meanwhile, the new religious movements that arose in America also adopted badges of identity. Seventh-day Adventists adhered to rigorous dietary laws, and Christian Scientists distinguished themselves with their characteristic ritual of healing. Mormons created a separate society in Utah with temple ceremonies forbidden to outsiders and, again, distinctive dietary practices. Shakers lived apart in celibacy, and Spiritualists drew a boundary between themselves and other Americans through their practice of communication with the dead in séances. Twentieth-century followers of Lord Krishna wore saffron robes and sandals and chanted publicly in honor of their God.

In all of these instances—and in the cases of the many Eastern religions whose ethnic representatives settled in the United States—people worked to separate themselves from the mainstream, finding a source of comfort and strength in the traditions they had inherited or the new religions they had embraced. Far from wanting to be like the followers of the dominant and public religion, they chose instead to be different. To be different, they thought, was to be themselves.

Yet, secondly, there was a countermove among the many to draw closer to the mainstream. In America to be different most of the time was to be inferior. The dominance of the one religion insured that its particular view of the world would affect the others. The sense of chosenness that characterized mainstream Protestantism was bound to make its mark on American culture. Even as the public religion tried to maintain its boundaries against the outsiders, it made it clear where power and authority lay. So acculturation to Protestant America changed the religions of the many. Instead of excluding American culture, they went out to meet it and brought it into their world.

Hence, the Reform movement that spread through nineteenth-century Judaism brought changes that made it more "American." Decorum became a feature of worship, and for a period, Sunday services and Protestant-style hymns came into use. Theological liberals reinterpreted the meaning of Israel, so that the ethics of the biblical prophets provided support for the voluntaryism and activism of the American religious style. Jewish scholarship, traditionally focused on the Torah and the Talmud, both in America and abroad came to mean achievement at the university and in Gentile society. Meanwhile, Reform, Conservatism, and Orthodoxy took shape as Jewish denominations in a larger Jewish "church."

Catholics early identified with the host culture as, in the nineteenth century, they struggled with their bishops to control church property through the system of democratic lay trustees. Later, with a series of liberal bishops, they sought to "Americanize" the church until a message from Rome put a stop to the most open attempts. At the same time, Irish clerical leadership was showing in its activism, moralism, and search for simple, "nonintellectual" answers how close to the mainstream it really was.

In the twentieth century, a new generation of Catholic scholars, both in this country and abroad, looked at the era of the Reformation more honestly and more kindly, fostering ecumenical dialogue with Protestants. When Vatican Council II opened the gates of world Catholicism to change, American Catholics quickly showed signs of their movement toward Protestant America. The English Mass became an appeal to the Word of God with a corresponding deemphasis on the more elaborate aspects of sacramentalism. Many of the symbolic badges of Catholicism, such as Friday abstinence from meat and old-style paraliturgical devotions in the churches, began to disappear. The Catholic mission movement of the nineteenth century had its successor in the charismatic movement which brought Pentecostal tongues and revivalistic fervor to many members of the church. Prophets, such as the radical Berrigan brothers and the conservative Right-to-Lifers, engaged in "Protestant" moral crusades. Democracy reinforced the rights of private conscience as many priests and nuns left their religious orders and many lay people made decisions about moral issues like birth control that often flew in the face of traditional Catholic teaching.

For blacks, emancipation brought a social revolution with accompanying religious changes. The class divisions, often disguised during the years in slavery, came out into the open, and religious preferences came to reflect the new situation. Holiness and Pentecostal churches became havens in the cities to which many blacks moved, providing emotional religious experiences and a perfectionist behavioral code shared by many Protestants in the mainstream. Likewise, Baptist and Methodist churches, affiliated with white denominations, introduced middle-class blacks to the controlled and more formal worship preferred by most other Protestants. Black religious leadership in the civil-rights era of the 1960s and afterward did draw on its own traditional resources. But it also drew on the mainstream of the Protestant theological tradition, as reflected in the seminary education of church and social leaders like Martin Luther King, Jr. Blacks were gaining political power and socioeconomic success in white society in proportion as they learned to speak the cultural language. Black Protestantism had been a key factor in the process.

Among Native Americans, some followed the strong suggestion of church and government, leaving the reservation and adopting white clothes, white ways, and white society. Others, while they remained at home, became Christian Indians. They substituted beliefs in the universal God of Christianity and his son, Jesus, for the old tribal sacred powers and expressed their religious sentiments in Christian worship instead of traditional ritual. Acceptance of Christianity frequently went along with willingness to be educated in government programs and to live in new housing, even on the reservation. By the later twentieth century, tribal councils, elected according to mainstream democratic rules, governed the reservations. Indian traditionalists often found themselves in conflict with many aspects of reservation life.

Sects followed a typical pattern in which, more and more, they became denominations. By the same token, in their attempts to create separate and exclusive religious societies, they ended by reflecting the dominant religion and culture they had sought to escape. So America became a central symbol for the Mormons, who, in their millennialism, shared the dream of Zion that bound together the members of the mainstream. Likewise, Mormon theology affirmed material abundance. It carried Arminian doctrines of free will to their logical conclusion, seeing unlimited possibilities for human beings to become "as Gods." And like mainstream Protestants, Mormons made theology second to the moralism and activism of their lives, preferring to act their religion more than to think it.

The pattern was similar in other new religious movements. They reflected the general cultural millennialism of America, sometimes in specific teachings about the end of the world, as in the cases of the Shakers and the Seventh-day Adventists. They displayed, as well, the pragmatic American quality that made of religion a means to the practical manipulation of the world for personal advantage. Thus, like the Mormons, the Seventh-day Adventists affirmed the material world of abundance they found in American culture. The Christian Science and New Thought movements fulfilled mainstream culture more than they departed from it, while Spiritualism and Theosophy were also built on respect for modern science. The mental homesteads provided by occult and metaphysical movements were only prominent examples of the general tendency in postindustrial America to create private havens where personal relationships and interests would take the place of community. The evangelical cultivation of a private relationship with Jesus, the revivalistic quest for right personal feeling, and the conservative tendency to overlook the socioeconomic problems of public life were not too different in style from these occult and metaphysical worlds.

Even further, estrangement was the common bond that linked members of the sects and cults with the mainstream. In the twentieth century, the new religious movements which turned to Eastern and Western occult and mystical ideas often tried to leave American society. Yet time and again, they came to imitate it. Their innocence as they embraced nature was one example of the larger innocence of American culture, part of its religion of chosenness. Their use of various techniques, such as meditation, yogic exercises, or rhythmic chanting, reflected the general American search for tools that worked. More deliberately, ethnic peoples who had inherited Eastern traditions sought to "Americanize" their religious expression. Japanese Buddhists spoke of their churches and bishops. Muslims attended their mosques on Sunday, instead of the prescribed Friday. Eastern Orthodox Christians introduced the English language into the Divine Liturgy and placed Western-style pews in their churches for the comfort of their worshipers.

In short, the many were ambivalent about their manyness. While they did not wish to throw away their distinctive religious worlds, they did want to make them acceptable in light of the dominant and public religion. The process was complex, for it did not mean simply imitating Protestants in order to win approval. Rather, it involved internal changes within the separate communities so that creeds, codes, and cultuses became authentic expressions of new meanings and values. Americans were new people. Every American faith, in a sense, became a new religion.

Even the revival of ethnicity in the later twentieth century did not alter this ambivalence. The mood of separatism was built at least partially on nostalgia and sentimentality, both, as we know, strong characteristics of the dominant culture. Hence, the mood of separatism is only one move in a complex dialectic in which the many try to find a public space to be acceptable and to be themselves. In the midst of the faceless crowd, they seek their roots in old identities. Yet the search for the old is really a search to make sense of the new. The "others" in the twentieth century belong to *American* religions, and for them the boundaries have been redrawn.

Finally, there was a third move among some but not all of the many. Like representatives of the mainstream, they labored as missionaries of extraordinary religion, trying to bring members of the one religion into their separate communities. For traditional churches, missionary work was an old and familiar activity, not to be neglected in the new situation. The chief example was Roman Catholicism. With its self-understanding as a universal church and its long history of missionary involvement, Catholicism countered Protestant efforts with its own.

Many Catholic parishes held inquiry classes for the members of other denominations. And the Catholic mission movement of the nineteenth century had as its secondary goal the aim of making Protestants better acquainted with the Roman church. Catholic schools, which in the nineteenth century sometimes catered to Protestants, hoped to influence their charges in the direction of the faith. Meanwhile, bishops who debated Protestant preachers, either in person or through the press, wanted ultimately to bring Catholic truth home to them. Likewise, when the Transcendentalist Isaac Hecker became a Roman Catholic convert and priest, he founded the Paulist order (1858), dedicated to missionary work in Protestant America. In the twentieth century, radio and television have helped Catholicism to make its message known; and in a well-remembered example, Bishop Fulton J. Sheen (1895–1979) carried on a media ministry from 1930 to 1957. The millions who watched his *Life Is Worth Living* series after 1951 were learning how Roman Catholics saw the world.

However, it was the intense religious groups, the sects and cults, that expended the most efforts in missionary work. Paradoxically, the strength of their boundaries, based on a conviction of exclusive possession of valuable religious truth, led them to go out toward others. Like evangelical Protestants, they must witness to the truth and rescue as many individuals as they could from the confusion of the world. Hence, missionary work, both theoretically and practically, was part of the very substance of these movements. So it became customary for young Mormon men to spend two years in missionary work, while earlier, in the nineteenth century, Shaker preachers followed the revivals to gain converts. In the twentieth century, in a more subdued example, Christian Scientists have established reading rooms in the business districts of cities and towns across America to attract downtown shoppers. At the other end of the spectrum, Jehovah's Witnesses publish *Awake!* and *The Watchtower* twice a month in twenty-seven languages, with a circulation of over 6.5 million copies. At the same time, individual Witnesses, called "publishers," spend on the average almost three hours a week in door-to-door visitation.

Among the newer movements, members of the International Society for Krishna Consciousness sell flowers in airport terminals to finance their ventures and also to find a way to speak to mainstream Americans. Members of Sun Myung Moon's Unification Church sometimes go from door to door for similar purposes. Followers of Eckankar, a group that teaches soul travel, or astral projection, distribute literature on college campuses, while members of the International Meditation Society lecture on campuses, in public libraries, and elsewhere in order to introduce people to Transcendental Meditation. In these and many other cases like them, aggressive missionary work is a way to maintain the religious identity of the group and at the same time to argue for the truth of the new religion in mainstream society. Members of these groups are saying, in effect, that the gates lead in as well as out.

COLLIDING ATOMS: THE MANY FACE THE MANY

So far we have looked at the responses of the one religion to the many and, in parallel ways, of individual groups among the many to the one. But the many also had to come to terms with one another, and it is to a consideration of this process that we now turn. Studies from both the social sciences and humanities are necessary to fill out the picture, but at least we can glance at the major lines of interaction among the "others" to complete our discussion. In what follows, we will sketch briefly the main directions of these multiple and intricate relationships.

In general, members of the various groups frequently responded negatively to one another. Members of intense religious groups, who thought themselves in possession of unique and privileged truth, could at best work to evangelize other religious peoples. At worst, they could denounce them as wrong and confused or accuse them of deliberate falsification. On the other hand, members of ethnic religious communities had their own reasons to experience friction with the many.

Each of the groups shared a common outsider status and a common realization of the dominance of the one religion. Hence, on the level of ordinary religion, each of the groups competed with others for the attention and resources of the mainstream. To a certain extent, because the one religion was public and dominant, it had succeeded in convincing all Americans of its importance. Hostility toward one group among the many by another of these "outgroups" allowed the first group to feel closer to the mainstream. By expressing such hostility, a group could also express its identification with the one religion and so take on meaning and stature from the relationship. By the same token, hostility by one group toward the others could underline its own sense of distinctiveness. By drawing a sharp line between itself and the many, a group could articulate its separate identity and its uniqueness.

Still, on occasion members of the various groups did respond positively to one another. From the perspective of extraordinary religion, missionary efforts were genuine attempts to communicate with others, while within the boundaries of ordinary religion, support and encouragement could be shared between various groups. While their common status as outsiders could lead them apart, it could also bring them closer together. Many groups found that there was strength in unity. Banding together gave them leverage in their relationship with the mainstream, and so they learned to be friends.

One example of a negative response by one group among the many toward another is Roman Catholic anti-Semitism. Like all Christians, Roman Catholics had inherited the twin images of the Jew as Christ-killer and conspiratorial moneylender. Indeed, it was the medieval church that had underlined these ideas in Christian awareness, and until the aftermath of Vatican Council II, the Roman Catholic liturgy for Good Friday spoke of the "perfidious Jews."

In a prime American instance of Catholic anti-Semitism, during the 1930s Father Charles E. Coughlin (1891–1979) influenced millions of Americans through his radio sermons from Royal Oak, Michigan. A commentator on many of the political and economic issues of the time, by the latter part of the decade he was telling his listeners that the greatest dangers facing America were Communism and the wealthy financial interest. Linking the two together were the Jews. They had been key leaders in the Communist movement in Russia, and during the Spanish Civil War, they had spread Communist propaganda, opposing the Catholic General Francisco Franco. For Coughlin, Nazism, like Fascism, was a defense against Communism, and European Jews were persecuted because they were in alliance with Communism and frequently unpatriotic. Likewise, in an old argument, most of those who controlled the world's wealth were Jewish, and with their money they dominated the press and shaped public opinion to their purposes. Coughlin added insult to injury by calling on Jews to accept Christ as a way to banish the "Jewish problem." He reprinted the *Protocols of the Elders of Zion* in his weekly newspaper and, in general, continued to spread anti-Semitism until he was ordered to be silent by his religious superiors.

A second example of the tensions that could arise between groups among the many occurs in the relationship between blacks and Jews. Often blacks followed Jews into older inner-city neighborhoods. Thus, the landlords and storekeepers with whom they dealt were often Jewish. When rent and prices were high, money scarce, and buildings overcrowded and run-down, blacks expressed their anger toward the Jews. Blacks found, too, that, just as other whites, Jews discriminated against them in hiring and employment practices. And Jews lived in wealthy suburban neighborhoods where blacks could not obtain housing, even if they had the money. From the Jewish perspective, there was also a good deal of antiblack feeling. Stereotyped attitudes toward blacks were common. Like other whites, Jews often thought of Afro-Americans as lazy, intemperate, and not too intelligent. They saw them as rowdy and culturally strange. When blacks supported quota systems in the university and on the job, Jews, remembering their own experiences with quotas, fought their efforts. So the two communities, both outsiders, found themselves at odds with each other. Like countless groups among the many, estrangement from the mainstream was accompanied by estrangement from each other.

While we could point to numerous other instances of suspicion, tension, and even hatred among the many, there *were* positive moves by members of different groups. Some took the risk of establishing honest communications across the boundary, and some joined forces to achieve mutually desirable goals. For example, let us look at the cases of Catholic-Jewish and Jewish-black relations once again. In both instances, there were ongoing efforts to achieve openness and community, and real alliances were forged.

Vatican Council II set the stage for a new era in Roman Catholic-Jewish communication. In a formal document, the Declaration on the Relationship of the Church to Non-Christian Religions (1965), the council addressed the ancient charge that the Jews were Christ-killers. It explicitly rejected the notions that all Jews or the Jews of today were responsible for the death of Christ. Further, it warned that the Jews ought not to be characterized as "cursed by God," and it acknowledged the common heritage shared by Catholics and Jews. Some Jews thought that the language of the document did not go far enough, since the specific accusation that the Jews were guilty of deicide (the murder of God) was not condemned and since no contrition was expressed for the church's long history of anti-Semitism. Moreover, some were disappointed because the document did not flatly reject attempts to convert the Jews. Still, the council had taken a major step forward for Catholic-Jewish relations.

In recent years, Jews and Roman Catholics (like other Christians) have engaged in a Jewish-Christian dialogue, as new understandings of their extraordinary religious commitments have arisen between the partners.

Sometimes, at the grass-roots level, interested Catholics have shared the Passover *seder* with Jews in household settings, and Jews have attended Roman Catholic services to learn about them. Ordinary Catholics have discovered the importance of the Law in Jewish life, and, conversely, Jews have become familiar with Christian theological concepts.

While Jewish-Catholic relations have explored the meaning of extraordinary religion for both groups, Jewish-black relations have dealt with the needs of ordinary life. Jews and blacks had much in common, for both had endured years of suffering and persecution at the hands of white Christians. Both thought of themselves as separate nations, and both blended ordinary and extraordinary religion with their nationhood in distinctive religioethnic identities. During the civil-rights struggle of the sixties, Jews were prominent among the whites who supported the black effort. They contributed substantial funds, and they marched beside blacks in demonstrations and protests. On the whole, they have expressed more concern than other whites about racism and have been more willing to hire blacks when they were employers. Jews have been active in the foundation of the National Association for the Advancement of Colored People (NAACP), an organization to win black equality through legal contests in the courts. They have also made efforts on behalf of black education. Although blacks have had neither the wealth nor the occasion to return the gestures in kind, they have formed social and political alliances with Jews for mutual goals. And the dialogue between the two groups has been characterized by a frankness and honesty that indicate the willingness of both to be open to the exchange.

Indeed, alliance has been the key to positive relationships in ordinary life among the many. Just by sharing the status of "otherness," the many in the long run have made it more acceptable to be different. Moreover, the example of one group has sometimes provided a model for others. Thus, in the twentieth century the black power movement of the sixties spurred the expression of a more militant ethnic and religious awareness among American Indians, Mexican-Americans, and even the descendants of various Catholic immigrant groups—the "white ethnics." Here there was imitation more than alliance on the practical level, but on the psychological plane, the relationship between the rise of the different ethnic movements was clear.

In more concrete terms, regional religion often provides an example of alliance among the "others." As we saw in our study of Southern Appalachian religion, many small and unconventional churches in the mountains shared a world view and a way of life different from that of the contemporary Protestant mainstream. These churches often disagreed on doctrinal points and specific ritual practices, but in many ways they resembled one another. More than that, the mountain folk who did not belong to any church generally were linked to church members in more religious ways than they were separated from them. The overwhelming majority of the people of Southern Appalachia agreed on fundamentals of belief and behavior that involved both ordinary and extraordinary religion. Though many in their church allegiances or lack of any, they were one in their dealings with the world outside the mountains.

Similarly, party politics has offered a vehicle for alliance. The Democrats, historically, have been the party of the poor and the immigrant, the black and the

Jew. Through a coalition of these groups, the party has successfully challenged the wealth and power of a dominant elite, obtaining social programs and policies that benefit the many. While banding together politically, in fact, has been a step in becoming like the established culture by learning to "make history," so to speak, it is also an exercise in learning to get along among the many. It is a commitment to engage in the rites of exchange across the boundaries.

Finally, missionary work went forward among the many. It thrived not only in attempts to convert members of the mainstream but also in efforts to acquaint the many with the truth of one particular group. We have already seen these efforts in the relationship of the many to the one, and the pattern of their outreach toward one another was similar, if not the same. Pluralism meant that each could witness to all, and each had the freedom to listen to the message of meaning presented by all. Against a backdrop of religious liberty and organizational voluntaryism, missionary activism was often a way to survive and grow. So in ordinary and extraordinary terms, the many learned to speak to one another.

SUMMING UP THE PRESENT

We have moved rapidly to sketch the main directions in the relationship between the religions and religion of the United States. There has been a continual danger of oversimplification, for movements of exchange between peoples are usually subtle, ambiguous, and complicated. Still, the idea of boundaries—between the ordinary and extraordinary and between the one and each of the many—has been helpful. In the situation of intense pluralism, the question of boundaries is a highly meaningful one, for it is on the boundaries that most of the issues lie. In our own day, some of the sharp edges have softened for the mainstream and the "old" immigrant religions, but as new intense religious groups arise, the boundaries are strong and tightly drawn.

Meanwhile, as the many centers meet, all the old moves are still there. The one religion is anxious about its dominance, while the many seek to challenge it in the preservation of their separate identities. Patterns of housing, job, and educational discrimination still exist for blacks, Indians, and other groups. Christian Scientists come off slightly worse than others in some books, while the term *cult* has become a signal for condemnation. Southern Appalachians who migrate to northern cities are sometimes derided as "hillbillies." At the same time, in their desire to remain apart, members of the International Society for Krishna Consciousness erect a lavish Indian temple on their land in West Virginia, suggesting by the character of the architecture their wish to separate themselves from the mainstream. Arab Muslims live in ethnic neighborhoods and rent apartments in the same buildings. Pueblo Indians prefer to live in their own adobe villages, laid out with central plazas for the performance of sacred dances.

Although some ethnic peoples retreat from the mainstream, others seek greater assimilation. Some Poles and Jews still change their last names to blend into the "melting pot," even as other ethnics proclaim themselves unmeltable. Seventh-day Adventists discuss whether or not they have become a denomination, even while members of the Unification Church maintain their separateness. Blacks move to the suburbs, and Catholics, with their own colleges, attend great public universities. Jews, to the disappointment of rabbis, frequently intermarry and drift away from affiliation with a synagogue.

When the many meet the many, they often find reason to be hostile to each other. Vietnamese boat people engage in fights with Mexican-Americans at a housing project, while blacks protest loudly at the subsidized housing that the Vietnamese obtain. Native Americans and Hispanics in Santa Fe, New Mexico, resent and live in mutual suspicion of each other as well as of the Anglo-American inhabitants of the city. Blacks and Jews face tensions as the (black) Southern Christian Leadership Conference takes a public stand on the issue of self-determination for Palestinians in the Middle East.

To sum up, throughout American religious history Protestant attitudes toward the many have been complex and ambivalent, ranging from a predominant fearful hostility to conversion attempts, struggling openness, and even fascination. The attitudes of the many toward public Protestantism have divided mainly between those who wished to preserve their old ways in the new land and those others who wanted to become more American and—it followed—more Protestant. At the same time, representatives of some groups have tried to win converts from the one (mainstream) religion. Finally, as the many have encountered one another, frequently they have exchanged insecurities by mutual suspicions and accusations. Still, some have found common worlds to share and made alliances with one another, while others have expressed their social and religious commitments in missionary zeal directed toward the different groups and persons among the many.

What does this all mean, and to what does it all add up? The United States of America is probably the most pluralistic religious and social experiment in human history. Its people live in a social situation complicated by a diversity unknown in even the most cosmopolitan societies elsewhere. Religions abound, and so do peoples, their beliefs, styles of worship, and moral codes. Community is fragile and temporary, and estrangement probably the one thing many have in common. While the vast machinery of government goes on and the equally vast machinery of the corporate industrial complex continues as well, the frictions that face Americans are a recurring feature of life. The manyness of groups and movements heightens the need for everyone to mark the boundaries very carefully. At the same time, the one religion of millennial chosenness, innocence, and hidden guilt intensifies the need for boundaries in the cultural mainstream.

Thus, living with so many boundaries has proved a difficult task for the American people. There is, indeed, a tremendous gap between the millennial dream of community and the realities of estrangement only thinly veiled. Faced with the problems of impersonality that accompany the corporate organization of any modern urban and industrial society, America has been beset with the serious *religious* problem of crossing the human boundaries that hinder community. That problem has had a long history: it began with the first collision between Native American ways of seeing and European interpretations of Native American life. And it began with the political realities of a power situation in which, though insecure and fearful, Puritans could dissolve their fright in millennial fervor with the guns of dominance and the righteousness of innocence to back them up. The balance of political power has always complicated the picture of religious America.

Still, to live without a public center—a one religion—seems in the human realm of things an impossibility. Shared meanings and values, however loosely expressed, must provide some kind of bonding, or society would lose all cohesion and fall apart. To live without the many who form so significant a part of religious America seems an equal impossibility. Although sometimes less fully organized and less visible, the many have deeply affected American life—which would not be American without them.

American religious reality is a dialectic between the one and the many. The one religion suits active and energetic people who need clear and simple directives for their work. Its evangelical warmth provides solace for Americans uprooted by a society ever on the move. Huge numbers, strong institutionalization, wealth, and political prestige have given it a clear role of leadership in shaping America. So in Part Two we paid careful attention to the one religion in its various forms. At the same time, the many possess religious insights of both ordinary and extraordinary keenness. Their ways of living within boundaries and learning how to cross them tell us many things about human possibility and realization that the story of the one religion cannot tell. In a word, both America and American religious history would be impoverished without the many. Their stories need to be told with a sense of texture and a feel for detail that hints of who they are and what material and spiritual wisdom they have acquired. This we tried to do in Part One.

The coexistence through several centuries of one religion and many religions is, of course, a fact of American life. But it is also a significant ordinary and extraordinary religious achievement, an achievement that suggests the vast potential capital to be tapped and the basic fund of regard and respect to be counted. Still more, the tension between the one and the many is not simply a burdensome condition with which American religious history has been saddled and with which it has dealt in a successful way. Rather, the strength of religious America lies in the dynamic tension created by point and counterpoint. The tension has meant a more complex, more ambiguous, and finally more "live" religious situation for all Americans. To say this, however, is not to say all. In the end, we need to return to the problem of making community in the New World.

Over the years, as pluralism grew stronger, the problem of making community became more acute. People spoke but often did not speak; they heard sermons and gave speeches but frequently did not communicate. Instead, they bypassed their differences and their fears of one another. Sometimes they did so through pragmatic and functional interactions, cooperating when a set of circumstances could be manipulated politically for mutual advantage. They jockeyed their concerns to create a "new" order of things in which the old ways of thinking remained largely unexamined and unchanged. Interfaith and multidenominational efforts were accepted styles of relating among some religious groups, but they were styles in which people mostly did not face the hard facts of their differences.

Other times Americans chose a community of feeling—private emotion that through a complex religious etiquette could legitimately be expressed in public. Shared feeling could make the "others" no longer other and knit the many into one. Significantly, the shared feeling that could evoke community most effectively, again and again, was the violent feeling that generated millennial dominance and, as its underside, righteous innocence. Americans were never more a community than when, under the banner of their civil religion, they marched to war. Inflated with the rhetoric and passion of the millennial dream, Americans saw grandeur and glory in their historic venture more than the humbler, more modest reality of human beings and groups who needed in all honesty to speak to one another.

Under the terms of the millennial covenant, in all honesty they could *not* speak. The chosen, like an army in a colonial fortress, could not let down the bridge to the "others." To do so might lessen the monopoly of the dominant center and lead to a situation of *decenteredness* or, in other terms, to a loss of purism and the creation of a new religious center. The many, beleaguered and precarious, could not begin the conversation either. They were too involved in the task of defining and maintaining their boundaries—their side of the territory. So behind the problem of community in America is another one. The ordinary and extraordinary religious problem of America is finally the content of the one religion and the many religions insofar as they share the millennial dream.

Dreams, we know, are not reality. Although they can be the source of creativity and vital energy, they can also weave illusions that leave people ill prepared to cope with daytime problems. In the case of millennialism, the irony of the dream is large. Bound to the vision of a new heaven and a new earth, millennialism is an *old* dream from an *Old* World. Although it thrived in the context of the discovery of a continent and an encounter with its meaning, millennialism is largely a product of the European heritage and the European imagination. Up until this time in our study, we have stressed the Americanness of American religions and religion, but now at the core of the new creation, we must confront the presence of the old. Millennialism represents what Europeans have thought and conjured over centuries more than a fresh and open response to situations. Its continuing versions, evoking either Armageddon or paradise, prevent the realities of New World existence from being adequately seen and met.

In short, millennial time is not *lived-through* time; and it cannot help Americans to know and care for one another. It is true that in the midst of the millennial dream the sleeping giant of American religious history has tossed fitfully at times—as if half awake or just about to awaken. Yet a completely American religion has not yet come to be. People in the New World are still learning to do something really new.

SUGGESTIONS FOR FURTHER READING: MANY CENTERS MEETING

Ahlstrom, Sydney E. *A Religious History of the American People.* New Haven: Yale University Press, 1972.

Bedell, George C., Sandon, Leo, and Wellborn, Charles T. *Religion in America.* New York: Macmillan, 1975.

Billington, Ray Allen. *The Protestant Crusade, 1800–1860: A Study of the Origins of American Nativism.* 1938. Reprint. Chicago: Quadrangle Books, 1964.

Carroll, Jackson W., Johnson, Douglas W., and Marty, Martin E. *Religion in America: 1950 to the Present.* New York: Harper & Row, 1979.

Dinnerstein, Leonard, ed. *Antisemitism in the United States.* New York: Holt, Rinehart & Winston, 1971.

———, **Nichols, Roger L., and Reimers, David M.** *Natives and Strangers: Ethnic Groups and the Building of America.* New York: Oxford University Press, 1979.

Douglas, Mary. *Purity and Danger: An Analysis of Concepts of Pollution and Taboo.* London: Routledge & Kegan Paul, 1966.

Gaustad, Edwin Scott. *A Religious History of America.* 2d ed. New York: Harper & Row, 1974.

———. *Historical Atlas of Religion in America.* Rev. ed. New York: Harper & Row, 1976.

Handlin, Oscar. *The Uprooted.* New York: Grosset & Dunlap, 1951.

Higham, John. *Strangers in the Land: Patterns of American Nativism, 1860–1925.* New Brunswick, NJ: Rutgers University Press, 1955.

Hudson, Winthrop S. *Religion in America.* Rev. ed. New York: Charles Scribner's Sons, 1973.

Marty, Martin E. *A Nation of Behavers.* Chicago: University of Chicago Press, 1976.

Williams, Peter W. *Popular Religion in America: Symbolic Change and the Modernization Process in Historical Perspective.* Englewood Cliffs, NJ: Prentice-Hall, 1980.

INDEX

Abenaki Indians, 63
Abraham, 46, 198
Acadians, 63
Acculturative religion, 360–65
Activism, 254–58, 263, 264, 280, 341, 362, 369
  and millennialism, 279
  and Mormonism, 363
Act of Toleration, 63
Adams, John, 294, 296, 301, 307
Advent, 67
African Methodist Episcopal Church, 105, 124, 134
African Methodist Episcopal Church Zion, 124, 134
African Orthodox Church, 130
African Union First Colored Methodist Protestant Church, 124
Afro-American religion. *See* Black American religion
Ahistoricism, 255, 257, 258, 280
Ahmadiyya Movement, 197
Alacoque, Margaret Mary, Saint, 69
Alchemy, 167–68, 186
Alcott, Bronson, 332
Alger, Horatio, 272
Ali, 199, 201
Ali, Ben, 196
Ali, Hajj, 196
Ali, Husayn, 201
Ali Muhammad, Siyyid, 201
Ali, Noble Drew, 130
Allen, Richard, 124
All Saints' Day, 313
All Souls' Day, 36
American and Foreign Christian Union, 357
American Anti-Slavery Society, 261
American Bible Society, 254
American Board of Commissioners for Foreign Missions, 254, 356

American Colonization Society, 261
American Dialogue, An, 358
American Education Society, 254
American Home Missionary Society, 350, 357
American Indians. *See* Native Americans
American Missionary Association, 356
American Muslim Mission, 132, 197
American Philosophical Society, 256
American Protective Association, 351
American Protestant Association, 76, 350
American Protestant Society, 357
American Revolution, 14, 64, 96, 97, 110, 155, 169, 172, 223, 228, 229, 230, 257, 270, 285, 295, 301–02, 305, 330
American Revolution Bicentennial Administration, 305
American Society for Meliorating the Condition of the Jews, 357
American Society for Psychical Research, 182
American Society for the Promotion of Temperance, 260
American Sunday School Union, 254
American Temperance Society, 260
American Tract Society, 254, 260, 350, 357
Amida Buddha, 212, 215
Amish, 11, 139
Anabaptists, 231
Anagarika Dharmapala, 189
Andover, 100
Anglicanism, 64, 90–92, 94, 97–98, 249, 257
  and Catholicism, 90
  and politics, 250–51
  and Protestantism, 90
  in Virginia, 93–94
Animal magnetism, 332–33
Anti-Alien Land Laws, 191
Anti-Catholicism, 76, 345, 349–51, 357

Index

Jews (continued)
Sephardic (Spanish), 39, 40–41, 55, 61, 62
Jnana, 205, 206, 209
Jodo Shinshu, 209, 212
John XXIII, Pope, 358
Johnny Appleseed, 175
Johnson, Lyndon B., 262
Joliet, Louis, 63
Jones, Absalom, 124
Judaeo-Christian tradition, 45, 47, 116, 164, 168, 174, 184, 190, 258, 328
Judaism, 35–59, 180, 192, 329. *See also* Booths; Day of Atonement; Feast of Lights; *Hanukkah*; Jews; Jewishness; Kabbalah; Passover; *Purim*; *Rosh Hashanah*; Torah; Weeks; *Yizkor* days; *Yom Kippur*
Americanization of, 56
Conservative, 43, 47, 54–58, 361–62
and denominationalism, 54–58
and liturgy, 45, 49–52
and morality. *See* Code and Judaism
Orthodox, 42, 47–48, 53–58, 361–62
Reform, 40–42, 47, 53–58, 362
Judaism as a Civilization, 55
Judge, William Q., 177, 179
Jung, Carl G., 326

Kaaba, 198
Kabbalah, 168, 186
Kachina
dancers, 24, 33–34
dolls, 33
rituals, 32–34
Kaddish, 51
Kaplan, Mordecai, 55
Kapleau, Philip, 214
Karma, 205, 206, 209
Kelpius, Johannes, 170
Kennedy, John F., 296, 306, 351
Keresans, 30
Kerouac, Jack, 214
Khadijah, 197
Khayru'llah, Ibrahim, 202
Kiddush, 48
King, Martin Luther, Jr., 132–33, 274, 363
Kino, Eusebio Francisco, 62
Kiowa, 22
Knights of Labor, 77, 315
Knights of Liberty, 125
Knights of Tabor, 130
Know-Nothing party, 76, 351
Knox, John, 224
Koans, 213
Kohler, Kaufmann, 53
Korean War, 302, 304
Krishna, 204
Ku Klux Klan, 76, 351, 354

Labor Day, 15, 314–15
Lactantius, 167
Lafayette, Marquis de, 301
Laman, 141
Lane Theological Seminary, 101
Last Supper, 65, 68
Late Great Planet Earth, The, 277
Latin Catholics, 75, 82
Latter House of the Lord for All People and the Church on the Mountain, Apostolic Faith, 127
Law
higher, 271, 273–75, 300
natural, 14, 71, 82, 291–92, 300
religion of, 89
Laws of Manu, 203
Leary, Timothy, 326
Leatherstocking Tales, 359
Lee, Ann, 155–57
Lee, Jason, 356
Lehi, 141–42
Lemuel, 141
Lent, 67, 69
Leo XIII, Pope, 77, 78, 262
Letters from an American Farmer, 330
Liberal Protestantism, 102, 103–04, 106, 110, 248, 256, 278
Liberator, The, 261
Liberty Tree, 293, 296
Lincoln, Abraham, 123, 261, 353
birthday celebration, 302, 313–14
as divine man, 300
Lindsey, Hal, 277
Literature, popular, 317–18
Little, Malcolm. *See* Malcolm X
Locke, John, 265
Logan, John A., General, 304
London Company, 94
Lord Baltimore, 63, 349
Lord Krishna, 208–09, 361
Lotus Sutra, 215–16
Louis XIV, King, 223
Louisiana Purchase, 73, 330
Lutheranism, 88, 96, 101, 107–08, 224, 259
Luther, Martin, 86, 88–89, 91, 138, 253

McCoy, Isaac, 356
McGready, James, 266
McGuffey Eclectic Readers, 272
McQuaid, Bernard, Bishop, 76–77
Mahabodhi Societies, 189
Mahayana Buddhism, 211–13
Mahdi, 199, 201
Mahesh Yogi, Maharishi, 207–08
Mainstream Protestantism, 14, 42, 73, 82, 86, 92, 94, 107, 232, 234, 242, 362. *See also* Protestantism; Public Protestantism
and black American religion, 124, 126, 133, 248

382

Index

Westminister Confession, 97
Wheelock, Eleazar, 356
White Buffalo Calf Woman, 27, 29
White, Ellen G., 146-48, 149, 155, 333
White, James, 146
Whitefield, George, 97, 247, 265, 289
Whitney, Eli, 323
Whole Earth Catalog, 311, 337-39, 342
Whole Earth Epilog, 337
Williams, Abigail, 171-72
Williams, Peter, Sr., 124
Williams, Roger, 139, 230, 252, 356
Wilson, Jack, 36
Wilson, Woodrow, 302
Wise, Isaac M., 42, 53
Wise, John, 290
Witchcraft, 169, 170-72. *See also* Cults, witchcraft
Woman in the Wilderness, The, 170
Women's Day, 318, 341
World Community of al-Islam in the West, 132, 197
World Council of Churches, 108, 358
World's Parliament of Religions, 189, 201, 203, 213
World War I, 101, 268, 302
World War II, 303, 354

World Zionist Congress, 55
Wounded Knee Massacre, 25, 36
Wovoka, 36
Wuwuchim, 34

Yale College, 100, 170, 265
Yellowstone National Park, 335
Yizkor days, 51
Yoga, 190, 203, 206-09, 218, 338-39, 364
Yogananda, Paramahansa, 203, 206-08
Yom Kippur, 49-50
Yosemite Act, 335
Young, Brigham, 142-43

Zazen, 214
Zen Buddhism, 189, 209, 213-15, 219, 338
Zion, 43, 58, 144
Zion Church, 124
Zionism, 55
Zohar, 168
Zoroastrianism, 201
Zuni, 30